THE COMPLETE POEMS
OF GEORGE BARKER

THE
COMPLETE MEMOIRS OF
GEORGE SHERSTON

by

SIEGFRIED SASSOON

FABER AND FABER
London & Boston

First published 1937
by Faber and Faber Limited
3 Queen Square, London W.C.1
First published in this edition 1972
Reprinted 1980
Printed in Great Britain by
Whitstable Litho Ltd Whitstable Kent

ISBN 0 571 06146 X (hard-bound edition)
ISBN 0 571 09913 0 (Faber Paperbacks)

CONTENTS

MEMOIRS OF A FOX-HUNTING MAN

MEMOIRS OF AN INFANTRY OFFICER

SHERSTON'S PROGRESS

MEMOIRS OF
A FOX-HUNTING MAN

" This happy breed of men, this little world."

PART ONE: EARLY DAYS

I

My childhood was a queer and not altogether happy one. Circumstances conspired to make me shy and solitary. My father and mother died before I was capable of remembering them. I was an only child, entrusted to the care of an unmarried aunt who lived quietly in the country. My aunt was no longer young when I began to live in her comfortable, old-fashioned house with its large, untidy garden. She had settled down to her local interests, seldom had anyone to stay with her, and rarely left home. She was fond of her two Persian cats, busied herself sensibly with her garden, and was charitably interested in the old and rheumatic inhabitants of the village. Beyond this, the radius of her activities extended no further than the eight or ten miles which she could cover in a four-wheeled dogcart driven by Tom Dixon, the groom. The rest of the world was what she described as "beyond calling distance".

Dixon was a smart young man who would have preferred a livelier situation. It was he who persuaded my aunt to buy me my first pony. I was then nine years old.

My aunt had an unexplained prejudice against sending me to school. So I remained at home until I was twelve— inefficiently tutored by a retired elementary schoolmaster, a gentle, semi-clerical old person who arrived every morning, taught me a limited supply of Latin, and bowled lobs to me on the lawn. His name (which I have not thought of for I don't know how many years) was Mr. Star.

Apart from my aunt's efforts to bring me up nicely, my early education was exclusively controlled by Mr. Star and Dixon, who supplemented Mr. Star's lobs with his more intimidating overarm bowling, and never lost sight of his intention to make a sportsman of me. For the vaguely apo-

logetic old tutor in his black tail-coat I felt a tolerant affection. But it was Dixon who taught me to ride, and my admiration for him was unqualified. And since he was what I
afterwards learnt to call "a perfect gentleman's servant", he
never allowed me to forget my position as "a little gentleman": he always knew exactly when to become discreetly
respectful. In fact, he "knew his place".

I have said that my childhood was not altogether a happy
one. This must have been caused by the absence of companions of my own age. My Aunt Evelyn—who was full of
common sense and liked people (children included) to be
practical in their habits and behaviour—used to complain
to Mr. Star that I was too fond of mooning aimlessly about
by myself. On my eighth birthday she gave me a butterfly-
net and a fretwork saw, but these suggestions were unfruit-
ful. Now and again she took me to a children's party given
by one of the local gentry: at such functions I was awkward
and uncomfortable, and something usually happened which
increased my sense of inferiority to the other children, who
were better at everything than I was and made no attempt
to assist me out of my shyness. I had no friends of my own
age. I was strictly forbidden to "associate" with the village
boys. And even the sons of the neighbouring farmers were
considered "unsuitable"—though I was too shy and nervous to speak to them.

I do not blame my aunt for this. She was merely con-
forming to her social code which divided the world into
people whom one could "call on" and people who were
"socially impossible". She was mistaken, perhaps, in applying this code to a small, solitary boy like myself. But the
world was less democratic in those days, and it must not be
thought that I received any active unkindness from Aunt
Evelyn, who was tender-hearted and easy-going.

As a consequence of my loneliness I created in my childish
day-dreams an ideal companion who became much more
of a reality than such unfriendly boys as I encountered at
Christmas parties. (I remember a party given by my aunt,
in the course of which one of my "little friends" contrived
to lock me in a cupboard during a game of hide-and-seek.

And, to tell the truth, I was so glad to escape from the horrors of my own hospitality that I kept as quiet as a mouse for the best part of an hour, crouching on the floor of that camphor-smelling cupboard.) The "ideal companion" probably originated in my desire for an elder brother. When I began these reminiscences I did not anticipate that I should be describing such an apparently trivial episode—and I doubt whether such a thing can be called an episode at all —but among a multitude of blurred memories, my "dream friend" has cropped up with an odd effect of importance which makes me feel that he must be worth a passing mention. The fact is that, as soon as I began to picture in my mind the house and garden where I spent so much of my early life, I caught sight of my small, long-vanished self with this other non-existent boy standing beside him. And, though it sounds silly enough, I felt queerly touched by the recollection of that forgotten companionship. For some reason which I cannot explain, the presence of that "other boy" made my childhood unexpectedly clear, and brought me close to a number of things which, I should have thought, would have faded for ever. For instance, I have only just remembered the tarnished mirror which used to hang in the sunless passage which led to my schoolroom, and how, when I secretly stared at my small, white face in this mirror, I could hear the sparrows chirping in the ivy which grew thickly outside the windows. Somehow the sight of my own reflection increased my loneliness, till the voice of my aunt speaking to one of the servants on the stairs made me start guiltily away. . . .

And now, as I look up from my writing, these memories also seem like reflections in a glass, reflections which are becoming more and more easy to distinguish. Sitting here, alone with my slowly moving thoughts, I rediscover many little details, known only to myself, details otherwise dead and forgotten with all who shared that time; and I am inclined to loiter among them as long as possible.

II

Now that I come to think about it, it seems to me to be quite on the cards that, had my Aunt Evelyn employed an unpretentious groom-gardener (who would really have suited her original requirements far better than jaunty young Dixon) I should never have earned the right to call myself a fox-hunting man. Dixon's predecessor was a stolid old coachman who disliked riding. One of my earliest recollections is the advent of Dixon, who lost no time in persuading my aunt to pension off her pair of worn-out carriage horses, which he replaced by two comparatively juvenile animals "warranted quiet to ride or drive". Dixon dearly loved to do a deal, and my aunt was amenable to his influence. She even went so far as to sanction the purchase of a side-saddle, and although a timid and incompetent horsewoman, she came to the conclusion that riding was good for her health.

Two or three times a week, then, on fine days, shepherded by the dignified and respectful groom, she was to be seen ambling along the lanes in a badly cut brown habit. She never attended a meet of the hounds however, for we lived in an unhunted part of the country, and the nearest meet was more than eight miles away.

So far as I was concerned, for several years "the hounds" remained a remote and mysteriously important rumour, continually talked about by Dixon, who never ceased to regret the remoteness of their activities. Foxes were few in our part of the country, and the farmers made no secret of shooting them. In fact ours was a thoroughly unsporting neighbourhood. There wasn't so much as a pack of beagles in the district. But Dixon was deeply imbued with sporting instincts. From the age of fourteen he had worked in stables, and had even shared, for a few months, the early rising rigours of a racing stable. He had been "odd man" to a sporting farmer in the Vale of Aylesbury, and had spent three years as under-groom to a hard-riding squire who subscribed handsomely to Lord Dumborough's Hounds.

Dumborough Park was twelve miles from where my aunt lived, and in those days twelve miles meant a lot, from a social point of view. My aunt was fully two miles beyond the radius of Lady Dumborough's "round of calls". Those two miles made all the difference, and the aristocratic yellow-wheeled barouche never entered our unassuming white gate. I never heard my aunt express any regret for her topographical exclusion from the centre of county society. But for Dixon it was one of the lesser tragedies of life; he would have given anything to be able to drive "the mistress" over to Dumborough Park now and again, for the Kennels were there, and to him the Kennels were the centre of the local universe. As it was, he had to be content with a few garden-parties, where he could hob-nob with a crowd of garrulous grooms, and perhaps get a few words with that great man, Lord Dumborough's head coachman.

Nevertheless, as the slow seasons of my childhood succeeded one another, he rattled my aunt along the roads in her four-wheeled dogcart at an increasingly lively pace. He must have been very adroit in his management of my gentle relative and guardian, since he perpetually found some plausible excuse for getting rid of one of the horses. Invariably, and by gentle gradations toward his ideal "stamp of hunter", he replaced each criticizable quadruped with one that looked more like galloping and jumping. The scope of these manœuvrings was, of course, restricted by my aunt's refusal to pay more than a certain price for a horse, but Dixon always had his eyes open for a possible purchase from any sporting farmer or country gentleman within riding distance; he also assiduously studied the advertisements of the London horse sales, and when he had finally established his supremacy "the mistress" unprotestingly gave him permission to "go up to Tattersalls", whence he would return, sedately triumphant, accompanied by the kindly countenance of what he called "a perfect picture of an old-fashioned sort". (A "sort", as I afterwards learned, was a significant word in the vocabulary of hunting men.)

How vividly I remember Dixon's keen featured face, as he proudly paraded his latest purchase on the gravel in front of the house, or cantered it round the big paddock at the back of the stables, while my aunt and I watched, from a safe distance, the not infrequent symptoms of a sprightliness not altogether to her taste.

"Yes, 'm," he would say, in his respectful voice, as he pulled up and leant forward to clap the neck of the loudly snorting animal, "I think this mare'll suit you down to the ground."

"Fling you to the ground" would, in one or two cases, have been a more accurate prophecy, as Aunt Evelyn may have secretly surmised while she nervously patted the "new carriage-horse" which was waltzing around its owner and her small nephew! And there was, indeed, one regrettable occasion, when a good-looking but suspiciously cheap newcomer (bought at Tattersalls without a warrant) decided to do his best to demolish the dogcart; from this expedition my aunt returned somewhat shaken, and without having left any of the cards which she had set out to distribute on "old Mrs. Caploss, and those new people over at Amblehurst Priory". So far as I remember, though, the unblenching Dixon soon managed to reassure her, and the "funny tempered horse" was astutely exchanged for something with better manners.

"He looked a regular timber-topper, all the same," remarked Dixon, shaking his head with affectionate regret for the departed transgressor. He had a warm heart for any horse in the world, and, like every good groom, would sit up all night with a hunter rather than risk leaving a thorn in one of its legs after a day's hunting.

So far as I know, Dixon never made any attempt to get a better place. Probably he was shrewd enough to realize that he was very well off where he was. And I am certain that my aunt would have been much upset if he had given notice. The great thing about Dixon was that he knew exactly where to draw the line. Beyond that line, I have no doubt, lay his secret longing to have an occasional day with the Dumborough Hounds on one of his employer's horses. Obviously there was no hope that "the mistress" could ever be manipulated into a middle-aged enthusiasm for the hazards of the chase. Failing that, his only possible passport into the distant Dumborough Elysium existed in the mistress's nephew. He would make a sportsman of him, at any rate!

*   *   *

My first appearance in the hunting-field was preceded by more than three years of unobtrusive preparation. Strictly speaking, I suppose that my sporting career started even earlier than that. Beginning then with the moment when Dixon inwardly decided to increase my aunt's establishment by the acquisition of a confidential child's pony, I pass to his first recorded utterance on this, to me, important subject.

I must have been less than nine years old at the time, but I distinctly remember how, one bright spring morning when I was watching him assist my aunt into the saddle at her front door, he bent down to adjust a strap, and having done this to his final satisfaction made the following remark: "We'll soon have to be looking out for a pony for Master George, 'm."

His tone of voice was cheerful but conclusive. My aunt, who had, as usual, got her reins in a tangle, probably showed symptoms of demurring. She was at all times liable to be fussy about everything I did or wanted to do. As a child I was nervous and unenterprising, but in this case her opposition may have prejudiced me in favour of the pony. Had she insisted on my learning to ride I should most likely have felt scared and resentful.

As it was, I was full of tremulous elation when, one afternoon a few weeks later, Dixon appeared proudly parading a very small black pony with a flowing mane and tail. My aunt, realizing that it was about to become her property, admired the pony very much and wondered whether it went well in harness. But since it was already wearing a saddle, I soon found myself on its back, my aunt's agitated objections were rapidly overruled, and my equestrianism became an established fact. Grasping the pommel of the saddle with both hands, I was carried down the drive as far as the gate; the pony's movements were cautious and demure: on the return journey Dixon asked me whether I didn't think him a little beauty, but I was speechless with excitement and could only nod my assent. Even my aunt began to feel quite proud of me when I relinquished my apprehensive hold on the saddle and, for the first time in my life, gathered up the reins. Dixon greeted this gesture with a glance of approval, at the same time placing a supporting hand on my shoulder.

"Stick your knees in, sir," he said, adding, "I can see you'll make a rider all right."

He had never called me "sir" before, and my heart warmed toward him as I straightened my back and inwardly resolved to do him credit.

III

Although, in my mind's eye, that first pony is clearly visible to me, I am not going to delay my already slow progress toward fox-hunting by describing him in detail. It will be sufficient if I quote Dixon, who called him "a perfect picture of a miniature hunter". His name was Rob Roy, and I thought him the most wonderful pony in the world. Nimble and lightly built, his courageous character never caused him to behave with more than an attractive friskiness. My devotion to him was therefore well justified. But as I sit here reconstructing my life from those remote beginnings, which are so difficult to recover in their authentic aliveness, I cannot help suspecting that I was, by nature, only half a sportsman. Dixon did his best for me as he patiently coaxed me toward my first fence (the idea of "jumping" made me horribly nervous for fully twelve months after I became a proud owner of horseflesh), but there must have been moments when he had grave doubts about my future as a horseman.

When I began my rides on Rob Roy, Dixon used to walk beside me. Our longest expedition led to a place about three miles from home. Down in the Weald were some large hop-farms, and the hop-kilns were interesting objects. It was unusual to find more than two hop-kilns on a farm; but there was one which had twenty, and its company of white cowls was clearly visible from our house on the hill. As a special treat Dixon used to take me down there. Sitting on Rob Roy at the side of the road I would count them over and over again, and Dixon would agree that it was a wonderful sight. I felt that almost anything might happen in a world which could show me twenty hop-kilns neatly arranged in one field.

It is no use pretending that I was anything else than a dreaming and unpractical boy. Perhaps my environment made me sensitive, but there was an "unmanly" element in my nature which betrayed me into many blunders and secret humiliations. Somehow I could never acquire the knack of doing and saying the right thing: and my troubles were multiplied by an easily excited and emotional temperament. Was it this flaw in my character which led me to console my sense of unhappiness and failure by turning to that ideal companion whose existence I have already disclosed? The fantasies of childhood cannot be analysed or explained in the rational afterthoughts of experienced maturity. I am not attempting to explain that invisible but unforgotten playmate of mine. I can only say that he was a consolation which grew to spontaneous existence in my thoughts, and remained with me unfalteringly until gradually merged in the human presences which superseded him. When I say that he was superseded I mean that he faded out of my inward life when I went to school and came in crude contact with other boys. Among them he was obliterated but not replaced. In my memory I see him now as the only friend to whom I could confess my failures without a sense of shame. And what absurd little failures they were!

At this moment I can only recall a single instance, which happened about eighteen months after the arrival of Rob Roy. By that time I was going for rides of six or seven miles with Dixon, and the "leading-rein" was a thing of the past. I was also having jumping lessons, over a small brush-

fence which he had put up in the paddock. One day, inflated with pride, I petitioned, rather shyly, to be allowed
to go for a ride by myself. Without consulting my aunt,
Dixon gave his permission; he seemed pleased, and entrusted me with the supreme responsibility of saddling and
bridling the pony without his help. I managed to do this,
in my bungling way, and I have no doubt that I felt extremely important when I tit-tupped down to the village
in that sleepy afternoon sunshine of thirty years ago. Rob
Roy probably shared my feeling of independence as he
shook his little black head and whisked his long tail at the
flies. I was far too big a man to look back as we turned out
of my aunt's white gate into the dusty high road; but I can
imagine now the keen sensitive face of Dixon, and his reticent air of amusement as he watched us go out into the
world by ourselves. My legs were then long enough to give
me a pleasant feeling of security and mastery over my
mount.

"Here we are, Rob," I remarked aloud, "off for a jolly
good day with the Dumborough."

And, in spite of the fact that it was a hot August afternoon, I allowed my imagination to carry me on into fox-
hunting adventures, during which I distinguished myself
supremely, and received the brush from the Master after a
tremendous gallop over hill and vale. I must mention that
my knowledge of the chase was derived from two sources:
firstly, the things I had heard in my conversations with
Dixon; and secondly, a vague but diligent perusal of the
novels of Surtees, whose humorous touches were almost
entirely lost on me, since I accepted every word he wrote as
a literal and serious transcription from life.

Anyhow, I had returned home with the brush and received the congratulations of Dixon when my attention
was attracted by an extra green patch of clover-grass by
the roadside: I was now about a mile beyond the village
and nearly double that distance from home. It seemed to
me that Rob must be in need of refreshment. So I dismounted airily and intimated to him that he ought to eat
some grass. This he began to do without a moment's delay.

But there was mischief in Rob Roy that afternoon. With one knee bent he grabbed and munched at the grass with his diminutive muzzle as though he hadn't had a meal for a month. Nevertheless, he must have been watching my movements with one of his large and intelligent eyes. With characteristic idiocy I left the reins dangling on his neck and stepped back a little way to admire him. The next moment he had kicked up his heels and was cantering down the road in the direction of his stable. It seemed to me the worst thing that could possibly have happened. It would take me years to live down the disgrace. Panic seized me as I imagined the disasters which must have overtaken Rob Roy on his way home—if he *had* gone home, which I scarcely dared to hope. Probably his knees were broken and I should never be able to look Dixon in the face again. In the meantime I must hurry as fast as my dismounted legs could carry me. If only I could catch sight of that wretched Rob Roy eating some more grass by the roadside! If only I hadn't let him go! If only I could begin my ride all over again! How careful I would be!

Hot and flustered, I was running miserably toward the village when I turned a corner and saw, to my consternation, the narrow, stooping figure of Mr. Star. His eyes were on the ground, so I had time to slow down to a dignified walk. I advanced to meet him with all the nonchalance that I could muster at the moment. The silver-haired schoolmaster greeted me with his usual courtesy, as though he had forgotten that he had been attempting to teach me arithmetic and geography all the morning. But I was aware of the mild inquiry in his glance. If only I'd been carrying my green butterfly-net instead of the rather clumsy old hunting-crop of which I was usually so proud! I have never been a clever dissembler, so I have no doubt that my whole demeanour expressed the concealment of delinquency. Mr. Star removed his black wideawake hat, wiped his forehead with a red handkerchief, and genially ejaculated, "Well, well; what a gloriously fine afternoon we are having!"

As I was unable to say anything at all in reply, he continued, with gentle jocularity (running his eyes over the brown corduroy riding-suit which I was just beginning to grow out of), "And what have you done with your pony? You look almost as if you'd lost him."

At this appallingly intuitive comment I gazed guiltily down at my gaiters and muttered abruptly, "Oh, I'm going to take him out after tea; I was just out for a walk."

My voice died unhappily away into the dusty sunshine. . . . After tea! For all I knew, darling Rob Roy might be *dead* by then. . . . For two pins I could have burst into tears at that moment, but I managed to control my feelings: Mr. Star tactfully informed me that he must be getting on his way, and our constrained interview ended. Half an hour afterwards I slunk into the stable-yard with a sinking heart. Dixon's black retriever was dozing with his head out of his kennel under the walnut tree. No one seemed to be about. I could hear the usual intermittent snorts and stampings from inside the stable. There were two stalls and a loose-box. My pony occupied the stall in the middle. My heart thumped as I peeped over the door, the upper half of which was open. Rob Roy was facing me; he was attached to the "pillar-reins", still saddled and bridled. I am certain that his face wore a look of amusement. A sense of profound relief stole over me. . . . A moment later the stable-boy came whistling out of the barn with a bucket. On seeing me he grinned derisively and I retreated toward the house in dignified silence. As I passed the kitchen window Mrs. Sosburn, the fat, red-faced cook, dropped the cucumber which she was peeling and greeted me with a startled squeal.

"Lawks, Master Georgie, whatever 'ave you bin up to? The mistress 'as been in an awful state about you, and Dixon's gone down to the village to look for you. We thought you must 'ave broke your neck when the pony came trotting back without you."

And the well-meaning woman bustled officiously out to make sure I hadn't any bones broken, followed by the gaping kitchen-maid; a moment later the parlour-maid came helter-skelter out of the pantry, and I was inundated by exasperating female curiosity and concern.

"Gracious goodness! To think of him going off by himself like that, and no wonder he got thrown off, and the wonder was he wasn't killed, and the pony too," they chorused; whereupon my aunt's head popped out of an upper window, and they clucked like hens as they reassured her about my undamaged return.

Infuriated by all this feminine fussiness I pushed past them and scurried up the back stairs to the schoolroom, whither Aunt Evelyn immediately followed me with additional exclamations and expostulations. I was now not only humiliated but sulky, and had I been a few years younger my rudeness would have ended in my being smacked and sent to bed. As it was I was merely informed that unless I learnt to behave better I should never grow up into a nice man, and was left alone with my tragic thoughts. . . .

Next morning I paid my customary visit to the stable with a few lumps of sugar in my pocket. Dixon was polishing up a stirrup-iron at the door of the little harness room; he stopped in the middle of a jaunty snatch of song to give me his usual greeting. All my embarrassment faded out of me. His impassive face made not the slightest reference to yesterday's calamity and this tactful silence more than ever assured me of his infinite superiority to those chattering females in the kitchen.

IV

Since the continuity of these memoirs is to depend solely on my experiences as a sportsman, I need not waste many words on the winter, spring, summer and autumn that chronologically followed the last episode which I narrated. Outwardly monotonous, my life was made up of that series of small inward happenings which belong to the development of any intelligent little boy who spends a fair amount of time with no companion but himself. In this way I continued to fabricate for myself an intensely local and limited world. How faintly the vibrations of the outer world reached us on that rural atmosphere it is not easy to imagine in this later and louder age. When I was twelve years old I hadn't been to London half a dozen times in my life, and the ten sleepy miles to the county town, whither the village carrier's van went three times a week, were a road to romance. Ten miles was a long way when I was a child. Over the hills and far away, I used to think to myself, as I stared across the orchards and meadows of the Weald, along which ran the proverbially slow railway line to London.

There were a few events which created in my mind an impression out of proportion to the architecture of my earthly ideas. Among them was Queen Victoria's Diamond Jubilee (though I cannot pretend to remember exactly how it struck me at the time, except that I counted fifty bonfires from the hill near our house). This was balanced by Canterbury Cricket Week. (I went there by train with Dixon and spent a long hot day watching Prince Ranjitsinhji make about 175 not out. My aunt's black Persian cat was called Ranji, which made the celebrated Indian cricketer quite a comfortable idea for me to digest.)

Almost my favourite books were *The Palace in the Garden* and *Four Winds Farm*, both by Mrs. Molesworth. Naturally there were other more impressive phenomena which cropped up in my mental existence, such as Scott's *Ivanhoe* and Longfellow's poem *Excelsior*, and Beethoven's piano sonatas. But all these things clothed themselves in local associations. Sir Walter Scott had no existence outside of my aunt's voice as she read him aloud in the evening, Longfellow was associated with Mr. Star in the schoolroom, Beethoven lived somewhere behind the faded silk on the back of the upright piano, and I never imagined any of them as in any other edition than those in which I knew them by sight. The large photograph of Watt's picture, "Love and Death", which hung in the drawingroom, gave me the same feeling as the "Moonlight" sonata (my aunt could only play the first two movements).

In this brightly visualized world of simplicities and misapprehensions and mispronounced names everything was accepted without question. I find it difficult to believe that young people see the world in that way nowadays, though it is probable that a good many of them do. Looking back across the years I listen to the summer afternoon cooing of my aunt's white pigeons, and the soft clatter of their wings as they flutter upward from the lawn at the approach of one of the well-nourished cats. I remember, too, the smell of strawberry jam being made; and Aunt Evelyn with a green bee-veil over her head. . . . The large rambling garden, with its Irish yews and sloping paths and wind-buffeted rose arches, remains to haunt my sleep. The quince tree which grew beside the little pond was the only quince tree in the world. With a sense of abiding strangeness I see myself looking down from an upper window on a confusion of green branches shaken by the summer breeze. In an endless variety of dream-distorted versions the garden persists as the background of my unconscious existence.

*   *   *

I had always been given to understand that I had a delicate constitution. This was one of the reasons which my aunt urged against my being sent to school when Mr. Pennett, the pink-faced solicitor who had charge of our affairs, paid us one of his periodic visits and the problem of my education was referred to in my presence. The solicitor used to come down from London for the day. In acknowledgment of his masculinity my aunt always conceded him the head of the table at lunch. I can remember him carving a duck with evident relish, and saying in somewhat unctuous tones, "Have you reconsidered, my dear Miss Evelyn, the well-worn subject of a school for our young friend on my left?"

And I can hear my aunt replying in a fluttering voice that she had always been nervous about me since I had pneumonia (though she knew quite well that it was only slight inflammation of the lungs, and more than two years ago at that). Fixing my gaze on his fat pearl tie-pin, I wondered whether I really should ever go to school, and what it would feel like when I got there. Nothing was said about Mr. Star, but Mr. Pennett usually had a private conversation with him on the subject of my progress.

"Your guardian seems an extremely well-informed gentleman," Mr. Star would say to me after one of these interviews. For Mr. Pennett had been to Harrow, and when Mr. Star spoke of him I was vaguely aware that he had made the modest old man feel even more humble than usual. My aunt was perfectly satisfied with Mr. Star, and so was I. But the solicitor knew that I was growing out of my tutor; and so, perhaps, did Mr. Star himself. . . . Indeed, I was getting to be quite a big boy for my age. People in the village were saying that I was "filling out a fair treat", and "shooting up no end". . . .

To one little incident I can give an exact date—not always an easy thing to do when one is looking back such a long way. It was in 1896, on the last Wednesday in May, and I had just returned from my afternoon ride. My aunt was out in the garden, wearing her leather gauntlets to cut some lilac, when I dashed excitedly across the lawn shouting, "Isn't it splendid, Auntie—the Prince of Wales has won the Derby!"

"Oh, how splendid—has he really?" she exclaimed, dropping the branch of white lilac which she had just snipped off the bush with her huge pair of scissors.

"Yes", I continued, bursting with the important news, "we stopped at the station on our way home, and the station-master showed Dixon the telegram."

"What was it called?" she queried.

"Persimmon, of course; I should have thought you'd have known that!"

"Really, Georgie dear, you shouldn't speak so rudely to your aunt."

I was silent for a moment, feeling crestfallen. Then I remarked, in a subdued voice: "Earwig was third."

"Earwig! What an odd name for a horse!" And then, as I bent down to pick up a spray of lilac, she added, "Good gracious, darling, how you've grown out of your riding-breeks! I really must get you another corduroy suit". . . .

But my increasing size had another and far more important effect. I was growing out of Rob Roy. My aunt showed her inevitable lack of initiative in the matter: she said that a small pony was safer for me. During the summer, however, Dixon persistently drew her attention to the obvious fact that my legs were getting nearer and nearer to the ground, although he had the highest respect for gallant little Rob Roy, who was beloved by all who knew him. The end of it was that a "perfect home" was found for him, and he trotted out of my life as gaily as he had trotted into it. After his departure I had a good cry by myself in the kitchen garden.

"I shall never be so fond of anyone again as I was of Rob Roy," I thought, mopping my eyes with a grubby handkerchief. Subsequent events proved my prophecy incorrect. And anyhow it was a fine day, early in September; a few minutes afterwards I was clambering up into a plum tree. The plums were particularly good that year.

*　　　　　*　　　　　*

As might be expected, Dixon lost no time in discovering an adequate substitute for my vanished favourite. For several weeks he remained reticent on the subject, except that once or twice he mentioned mysteriously that he thought he had heard of something. Conscientious enquiries among coachmen, innkeepers, and the local vet, and the insertion of an advertisement in the county paper, culminated in the arrival of a fourteen-hand, mouse-coloured Welsh cob called Sheila. The sight of Sheila struck awe into my heart. She looked as much too big for me as Rob Roy had looked too small. I also divined that she was enormously expensive.

"Do you really think Master George'll be able to manage her, Dixon?" asked my aunt, regarding Sheila with deprecatory approbation. Dixon reiterated his belief that the mare was thoroughly handy and as quiet as an old sheep: he added that we'd never get such a bargain again for thirty pounds.

"Jump on her back, Master George, and see if she doesn't give you a good feel," suggested that inexorably encouraging voice which was to make a sportsman of me. Whereupon he quickly circumvented the obvious fact that this was no jumping matter by giving me a leg-up into the saddle (a nearly full-sized one). There was no doubt at all that I was a long way from the ground. Rather timidly I surveyed the stable-yard from my new altitude. Then Dixon led the cob carefully through the gate into the paddock and she broke into a springy trot.

V

November, with its darkening afternoons and smell of burning weeds, found me gradually becoming acclimatized to "the new mare", as I importantly called her (using Dixonian phraseology). The groom was able to give me all his attention, since my aunt never rode in the winter. We now went longer distances; sometimes he would tell me that we were "on the edge of the Dumborough country", and he would pull up and point out to me, a few miles away, some looming covert where they often went to draw.

The Dumborough, as I afterwards discovered, was a scrambling sort of country to hunt in—heavily wooded and hilly. But as we turned away from its evening-lighted landscape I would listen eagerly to Dixon's anecdotes of the sport he had seen there. He spoke often of Mr. Macdoggart, Lord Dumborough's hard-riding agent, and how one year he had seen him win the Hunt Steeplechase by a short head from a famous "gentleman rider": and how, another year, Mr. Macdoggart had got concussion of the brain while riding in the same race.

Our afternoon expeditions usually took us in the Dumborough direction, and I suspect that Dixon always had a faint hope that we might "chip in with the hounds", though he knew too well that the foxes rarely ran our way. He also showed an increasing antipathy to the high road, and was continually taking short cuts across the country.

"It'll do them good to have a pipe-opener," he would say, turning in at a gate and setting his horse going up a long stretch of meadow, and my confidence in Sheila increased as I scuttled after him.

Sometimes we would pretend to be "riding a finish", and I would say, "Tom, show me how Mr. Macdoggart won the Hunt Cup on Nobleman."

I had never seen a race in my life; nor had I ever been to a meet of the hounds. But I assiduously studied the novels of Surtees, of which my aunt had a complete set. She dipped into them herself now and again, and we often used to talk about Mr. Jorrocks.

As Christmas approached Dixon drew her attention to my rapid improvement as a rider. Finally he took the bull by the horns and intimated that it would do me no harm to go and have a look at the hounds. She seemed taken aback by this, but he assured her that he would only take me as far as the meet. When she suggested that he could drive me there in the dogcart Dixon's face assumed such an air of disapproval that she gave way at once, and it became only a matter of waiting for the next "near meet".

"I think, 'm, you can rely on me to take proper care of Master George," he remarked rather stiffly; the next moment he looked at me with a grin of delight followed by a solemn wink with the eye furthest away from my aunt.

A few days later I found him studying the local paper in the leather-smelling little harness room. "They're meeting at Finchurst Green on Saturday," he announced with appropriate seriousness. It was an important moment in my life. Finchurst Green was not quite nine miles away.

*   *   *

It was a grey and chilly world that I went out into when I started for my first day's fox-hunting. The winter-smelling air met me as though with a hint that serious events were afoot. Silently I stood in the stable-yard while Dixon led Sheila out of her stall. His demeanour was business-like and reticent. The horses and their accoutrements were polished up to perfection, and he himself, in his dark-grey clothes and hard black hat, looked a model of discretion and neatness. The only one who lacked confidence was myself.

Stuffing a packet of sandwiches into my pocket and pull-

ing on my uncomfortably new gloves, I felt half aware of
certain shortcomings in my outward appearance. Ought
one really to go out hunting in a brown corduroy suit with
a corduroy jockey-cap made to match the suit? Did other
boys wear that sort of thing? . . . I was conscious, too, that
Dixon was regarding me with an unusually critical eye.
Mute and flustered, I mounted. Sheila seemed very fresh,
and the saddle felt cold and slippery. As we trotted briskly
through the village everything had an austerely unfamiliar
look about it, and my replies to Dixon were clumsy and
constrained.

Yet the village was its ordinary village self. The geese
were going single file across the green, and Sibson, the
lame shoeing-smith, was clinking his hammer on the forge
as usual. He peered out at us as we passed, and I saluted
him with a slightly forlorn wave of the hand. He grinned
and ducked his head. Sheila had had her shoes looked to
the day before, so he knew all about where we were going.

As we jogged out of the village, Dixon gazed sagaciously
at the sky and said with a grim smile, "I'll bet they run
like blazes to-day; there's just the right nip in the air," and
he made the horses cock their ears by imitating the sound
of a hunting-horn—a favourite little trick of his. Secretly I
wondered what I should do if they "ran like blazes". It
was all very well for *him*—he'd been out hunting dozens of
times!

As we neared the meet I became more and more nervous. Not many of the hunting people came from our side
of the country, and we saw no other horsemen to distract
my attention until we rounded a bend of the road, and
there at last was Finchurst Green, with the hounds clustering in a corner and men in red coats and black coats moving to and fro to keep their horses from getting chilled. But
this is not the last meet that I shall describe, so I will not
invent details which I cannot remember, since I was too
awed and excited and self-conscious to be capable of observing anything clearly.

Once we had arrived, Dixon seemed to become a different Dixon, so dignified and aloof that I scarcely dared to

speak to him. Of course I knew what it meant: I was now his "young gentleman" and he was only the groom who had brought me to "have a look at the hounds". But there was no one at the meet who knew me, so I sat there, shy and silent—aware of being a newcomer in a strange world which I did not understand. Also I was quite sure that I should make a fool of myself. Other people have felt the same, but this fact would have been no consolation to me at the time, even if I could have realized it.

* * *

My first period of suspense ended when with much bobbing up and down of hats the cavalcade moved off along the road. I looked round for Dixon, but he allowed me to be carried on with the procession; he kept close behind me, however. He had been sensible enough to refrain from confusing me with advice before we started, and I can see now that his demeanour continued to be full of intuitive tactfulness. But he was talking to another groom, and I felt that I was being scrutinized and discussed. I was riding alongside of a large, lolloping lady in a blue habit; she did not speak to me; she confined herself to a series of expostulatory remarks to her horse which seemed too lively and went bouncing along sideways with its ears back, several times bumping into Sheila, whose behaviour was sedately alert.

Soon we turned in at some lodge gates, crossed the corner of an undulating park, and then everyone pulled up outside a belt of brown woodland. The hounds had disappeared, but I could hear the huntsman's voice a little way off. He was making noises which I identified as not altogether unlike those I had read about in Surtees. After a time the chattering crowd of riders moved slowly into the wood which appeared to be a large one.

My first reaction to the "field" was one of mute astonishment. I had taken it for granted that there would be people "in pink", but these enormous confident strangers overwhelmed my mind with the visible authenticity of their brick-red coats. It all felt quite different to reading Surtees by the schoolroom fire.

But I was too shy to stare about me, and every moment
I was expecting an outburst of mad excitement in which I
should find myself galloping wildly out of the wood. When
the outbreak of activity came I had no time to think about
it. For no apparent reason the people around me (we were
moving slowly along a narrow path in the wood) suddenly
set off at a gallop and for several minutes I was aware of
nothing but the breathless flurry of being carried along,
plentifully spattered with mud by the sportsman in front of
me. Suddenly, without any warning, he pulled up. Sheila
automatically followed suit, shooting me well up her neck.
The next moment everyone turned round and we all went
tearing back by the way we had come. I found Dixon in
front of me now, and he turned his head with a grin of
encouragement.

Soon afterwards the hunt came to a standstill in an open
space in the middle of the wood: the excitement seemed to
be abating, and I felt that fox-hunting wasn't so difficult as
I'd expected it to be. A little way below I could hear a confused baying of the hounds among the trees. Then, quite
close to where I had halted, a tall man in a blue velvet
cap and vermilion coat came riding out from among the
undergrowth with one arm up to shield his face from the
branches. His face was very red and he seemed upset about
something. Turning in my direction he bawled out in an
angry voice, "What the bloody hell do you think you're
here for?"

For a moment I sat petrified with terror and amaze-
ment. He was riding straight at me, and I had no time to
wonder what I had done to incur his displeasure. So I
stared helplessly until I was aware that he had passed me
and was addressing someone immediately behind my
horse's heels. . . . Looking round I saw a surly-featured
elderly man with side-whiskers: he was on foot and wore
the weathered garments of a gamekeeper.

"What the hell do you mean by leaving the main-earth
unstopped?" the infuriated voice continued.

"Very sorry, m'lord," the man mumbled, "but I never
heard you was coming till this morning, and——"

"Don't answer me back. I'll get you sacked for this when Major Gamble comes down from Scotland. I tell you I'm sick of you and your god-damned pheasants," and before the man could say any more the outraged nobleman was pushing his way into the undergrowth again and was bawling "Go on to Hoath Wood, Jack," to the invisible huntsman.

I looked at Dixon, whose horse was nibbling Sheila's neck. "That's the Master", he said in a low voice, adding, "his lordship's a rough one with his tongue when anyone gets the wrong side of him." Silently I decided that Lord Dumborough was the most terrifying man I had ever encountered. . . .

Dixon was explaining that our fox had gone to ground and I heard another man near me saying: "That blighter Gamble thinks of nothing but shooting. The place is crawling with birds, and the wonder is that we ever found a fox. Last time we were here we drew the whole place blank, and old D. cursed the keeper's head off and accused him of poisoning the foxes, so I suppose he did it to get a bit of his own back!" Such was my introduction to the mysteries of "earth-stopping". . . .

The comparatively mild activities of the morning had occupied a couple of hours. We now trotted away from Major Gamble's preserves. It was about three miles to Hoath Wood; on the way several small spinneys were drawn blank, but Hoath Wood was a sure find, so Dixon said, and a rare place to get a gallop from. This caused a perceptible evaporation of the courage which I had been accumulating, and when there was a halt for the hunt-servants to change on to their second horses I made an attempt to dispel my qualms by pulling out my packet of sandwiches.

While I was munching away at these I noticed for the first time another boy of about my own age. Dixon was watching him approvingly. Evidently this was a boy to be imitated, and my own unsophisticated eyes already told me that. He was near enough to us for me to be able to observe him minutely. A little aloof from the large riders round him, he sat easily, but very upright, on a corky

chestnut pony with a trimmed stump of a tail and a neatly
"hogged" neck.

Reconstructing that far-off moment, my memory fixes
him in a characteristic attitude. Leaning slightly forward
from the waist, he straightens his left leg and scrutinizes it
with an air of critical abstraction. He seems to be satisfied
with his smart buff breeches and natty brown gaiters.
Everything he has on is neat and compact. He carries a
small crop with a dark leather thong, which he flicks at a
tuft of dead grass in a masterly manner. An air of self-
possessed efficiency begins with his black bowler hat, continues in his neatly-tied white stock, and gets its finishing
touch in the short, blunt, shining spurs on his black walking
boots. (I was greatly impressed by the fact that he wore
spurs.) All his movements were controlled and modest, but
there was a suggestion of arrogance in the steady, unrecog-
nizing stare which he gave me when he became conscious
that I was looking at him so intently. Our eyes met, and
his calm scrutiny reminded me of my own deficiencies in
dress. I shifted uneasily in my saddle, and the clumsy un-
presentable old hunting-crop fell out of my hand. Dis-
mounting awkwardly to pick it up, I wished that it, also,
had a thong, (though this would make the double reins
more difficult to manage) and I hated my silly jockey-cap
and the badly-fitting gaiters which pinched my legs and
always refused to remain in the correct position (indicated
by Dixon). When I had scrambled up on to Sheila again—
a feat which I could only just accomplish without assistance—I felt what a poor figure I must be cutting in Dixon's
eyes while he compared me with that other boy, who had
himself turned away with a slight smile and was now
soberly following the dappled clustering pack and its attendant red-coats as they disappeared over the green, rising
ground on their way to Hoath Wood.

*   *   *

By all the laws of aunthood we should by now have been
well on our way home. But Dixon was making a real day of
it. The afternoon hunt was going to be a serious affair.

There never appeared to be any doubt about that. The field was reduced to about forty riders, and the chattersome contingent seemed to have gone home. We all went into the covert and remained close together at one end. Dixon got off and tightened my girths, which had got very loose (as I ought to have noticed). A resolute-looking lady in a tall hat drew her veil down after taking a good pull at the flask which she handed back to her groom. Hard-faced men rammed their hats on to their heads and sat silently in the saddle as though, for the first time in the day, they really meant business. My heart was in my mouth and it had good reason to be there. Lord Dumborough was keeping an intent eye on the ride which ran through the middle of the covert.

"Cut along up to the top end, Charlie," he remarked without turning his head; and a gaunt, ginger-haired man in a weather-stained scarlet coat went off up the covert in a squelchy canter.

"That's Mr. Macdoggart," said Dixon in a low voice, and my solemnity increased as the legendary figure vanished on its mysterious errand.

Meanwhile the huntsman was continuing his intermittent yaups as he moved along the other side of the wood. Suddenly his cheers of encouragement changed to a series of excited shoutings. "Hoick-holler, hoick-holler, hoick-holler!" he yelled, and then blew his horn loudly; this was followed by an outbreak of vociferation from the hounds, and soon they were in full cry across the covert. I sat there petrified by my private feelings; Sheila showed no symptoms of agitation; she merely cocked her ears well forward and listened.

And then, for the first time, I heard a sound which has thrilled generations of fox-hunters to their marrow. From the far side of the wood came the long shrill screech (for which it is impossible to find an adequate word) which signifies that one of the whips has viewed the fox quitting the covert. "Gone Away" it meant. But before I had formulated the haziest notion about it Lord Dumborough was galloping up the ride and the rest of them were pelting after him as though nothing could stop them. As I happened to be standing well inside the wood and Sheila took the affair into her own control, I was swept along with them, and we emerged on the other side among the leaders.

I cannot claim that I felt either excitement or resolution as we bundled down a long slope of meadowland and dashed helter-skelter through an open gate at the bottom. I knew nothing at all except that I was out of breath and that the air was rushing to meet me, but as I hung on to the reins I was aware that Mr. Macdoggart was immediately in front of me. My attitude was an acquiescent one. I have always been inclined to accept life in the form in which it has imposed itself upon me, and on that particular occasion, no doubt, I just felt that I was "in for it". It did not so much as occur to me that in following Mr. Macdoggart I was setting myself rather a high standard, and when he disappeared over a hedge I took it for granted that I must do the same. For a moment Sheila hesitated in her stride. (Dixon told me afterwards that I actually hit her as we approached the fence, but I couldn't remember having done so.) Then she collected herself and jumped the fence with a peculiar arching of her back. There was a considerable drop on the other side. Sheila had made no mistake, but as she landed I left the saddle and flew over her head. I had let go of the reins, but she stood stock-still while I sat on the wet ground. A few moments later Dixon popped over a gap lower down the fence and came to my assistance, and I saw the boy on the chestnut pony come after him and gallop on in a resolute but unhurrying way. I scrambled to my feet, feeling utterly ashamed.

"What ever made you go for it like that?" asked Dixon, who was quite disconcerted.

"I saw Mr. Macdoggart going over it, and I didn't like to stop," I stammered. By now the whole hunt had disappeared and there wasn't a sound to be heard.

"Well, I suppose we may as well go on." He laughed as he gave me a leg up. "Fancy you following Mr. Macdoggart over the biggest place in the fence. Good thing Miss Sherston couldn't see you."

The idea of my aunt seemed to amuse him, and he slapped his knee and chuckled as he led me onward at a deliberate pace. Secretly mortified by my failure I did my best to simulate cheerfulness. But I couldn't forget the other boy and how ridiculous he must have thought me when he saw me rolling about on the ground. I felt as if I must be covered with mud. About half an hour later we found the hunt again, but I can remember nothing more except that it was beginning to get dark and the huntsman, a middle-aged, mulberry-faced man named Jack Pitt, was blowing his horn as he sat in the middle of his hounds. The other boy was actually talking to him—a privilege I couldn't imagine myself promoted to. At that moment I almost hated him for his cocksuredness.

Then, to my surprise, the Master himself actually came up and asked me how far I was from home. In my embarrassment I could only mutter that I didn't know, and Dixon interposed with "About twelve miles, m'lord," in his best manner.

"I hear he's quite a young thruster." . . . The great man glanced at me for a moment with curiosity before he turned away. Not knowing what he meant I went red in the face and thought he was making fun of me.

*   *   *

Now that I have come to the end of my first day's hunting I am tempted to moralize about it. But I have already described it at greater length than I had intended, so I will only remind myself of the tea I had at an inn on the way home. The inn was kept by a friend of Dixon's—an ex-butler who "had been with Lord Dumborough for years". I well remember the snug fire-lit parlour where I ate my two boiled eggs, and how the innkeeper and his wife made a fuss over me. Dixon, of course, transferred me to them in my full status of "one of the quality", and then disappeared to give the horses their gruel and get his own tea in the kitchen. I set off on the ten dark miles home in a glow of satisfied achievement, and we discussed every detail of the day except my disaster. Dixon had made enquiries about "the other young gentleman", and had learnt that his name was Milden and that he was staying at Dumborough Park for Christmas. He described him as a proper little sportsman; but I was reticent on the subject. Nor did I refer to the question of our going out with the hounds again. By the time we were home I was too tired to care what anybody in the world thought about me.

VI

It was nearly seven o'clock when we got home; as Aunt Evelyn had begun to expect me quite early in the afternoon, she was so intensely relieved to see me safe and sound that she almost forgot to make a fuss about my prolonged absence. Dixon, with his persuasive manner next morning, soon hoodwinked her into taking it all as a matter of course. He made our day sound so safe and confidential. Not a word was said about my having tumbled off (and he had carefully brushed every speck of mud off my back when we stopped at the inn for tea).

As for myself, I began to believe that I hadn't done so badly after all. I talked quite big about it when I was alone with my aunt at lunch on Sunday, and she was delighted to listen to everything I could tell her about my exploits. Probably it was the first time in my life that I was conscious of having got the upper hand of my grown-up relative. When she asked whether there were "any other little boys out on their ponies" I was nonplussed for a moment; I couldn't connect young Milden with such a disrespectful way of speaking. Little boys out on their ponies indeed! I had more than half a mind to tell her how I'd followed the great Mr. Macdoggart over that fence, but I managed to remind myself that the less said about that incident the better for my future as a fox-hunter.

"Yes," I replied, "there was a very nice boy on a splendid little chestnut. He's staying at Dumborough Park." When I told her his name she remembered having met some of his people years ago when she was staying in

Northamptonshire. They had a big place near Daventry, she said, and were a well-known sporting family. I packed these details away in my mind with avidity. Already I was weaving Master Milden into my day dreams, and soon he had become my inseparable companion in all my imagined adventures, although I was hampered by the fact that I only knew him by his surname. It was the first time that I experienced a feeling of wistfulness for someone I wanted to be with.

*   *   *

As a rule I was inclined to be stand-offish about children's parties, though there weren't many in our part of the world. There was to be a dance at Mrs. Shotney's the next Friday, and I wasn't looking forward to it much until my aunt told me that she had heard from Mrs. Cofferdam that Lady Dumborough was going to be there with a large party of jolly young people. "So perhaps you'll see your little hunting friend again," she added.

"He's not little; he looks about two years older than me," I retorted huffily, and at once regretted my stupidity. "My hunting friend!" I had been allowing her to assume that we had "made friends" out hunting. And when we were at the party she would be sure to find out that he didn't know me. But perhaps he wouldn't be there after all. Whereupon I realized that I should be bitterly disappointed if he wasn't.

At seven o'clock on Friday we set off in the village fly. While we jolted along in that musty-smelling vehicle with its incessantly rattling windows I was anxious and excited. These feelings were augmented by shyness and gawkiness by the time I had entered the ballroom, which was full of antlers and old armour. Standing by myself in a corner I fidgeted with my gloves. Now and again I glanced nervously round the room. Sleek-haired little boys in Eton jackets were engaging themselves for future dances with pert little girls in short frocks. Shyness was being artificially dispelled by solicitous ladies, one of whom now swooped down on me and led me away to be introduced to equally

unenterprising partners. The room was filling up, and I
was soon jostling and bumping round with a demure little
girl in a pink dress, while the local schoolmaster, a solemn
man with a walrus moustache, thrummed out "The Blue
Danube" on an elderly upright piano, reinforced by a
squeaky violinist who could also play the cornet; he often
did it at village concerts, so my partner informed me, biting her lips as someone trod on her foot. Steering my
clumsy course round the room, I wondered whether Lady
Dumborough had arrived yet.

There was Aunt Evelyn, talking to Mrs. Shotney. She
certainly didn't look half bad when you compared her with
other people. And old Squire Maundle, nodding and smiling by the door, as he watched his little granddaughter
twirling round and round with a yellow ribbon in her hair.
And General FitzAlan with his eyeglass—he looked a jolly
decent old chap. . . . He'd been in the Indian Mutiny. . . .
The music stopped and the dancers disappeared in quest of
claret-cup and lemonade. "I wonder what sort of ices
there are," speculated my partner. There was a note of
intensity in her voice which was new to me.

*   *   *

"Oh, *do* come on, Denis, the music's begun," cried a
dark attractive girl with a scarlet sash—tugging at the arm
of a boy who was occupied with an ice. When he turned to
follow her I recognized the rider of the chestnut pony.
From time to time as the evening went on I watched him
enjoying himself with the conspicuous Dumborough Park
contingent, which was dominating the proceedings with a
mixture of rowdiness and hauteur. Those outside their
circle regarded them with envious and admiring antagonism. By a miracle I found myself sitting opposite Denis
Milden at supper, which was at one long table. He looked
across at me with a reserved air of recognition.

"Weren't you out last Saturday?" he asked. I said yes.

"Rotten day, wasn't it?" I said yes it was rather.

"That's a nice cob you were on. Jumped a bit too big for
you at that fence outside Hoath Wood, didn't she?" He

grinned good-humouredly. I went red in the face, but managed to blurt out a confused inquiry after the health of his chestnut pony. But before he could reply the Dumborough boy had shouted something at him and I was obliged to pay attention to the little girl alongside of me.

"Do you hunt much?" she inquired, evidently impressed by what she had overheard. Rather loftily I replied that I hunted whenever I got the chance, inwardly excusing myself with the thought that it wasn't my own fault that I'd only had one chance so far. . . .

I was now positively enjoying the party, but shortly afterwards Aunt Evelyn came gliding across the dark polished floor at the end of a polka and adroitly extricated me from the festivities. . . . "Really, darling, don't you think it's almost time we went home?"

I wished she wouldn't call me darling in public, but I fetched my overcoat and followed obediently down to the draughty entrance hall. Denis happened to be sitting on the stairs with his partner. He jumped up politely to allow my aunt to pass. I shot a shy glance at his face.

"Coming to Heron's Gate on Tuesday?" he asked. Deeply gratified, I said I was afraid it was too far for me.

"You ought to try and get there. They say it's one of the best meets." He sat down again with a nod and a smile.

"Wasn't that young Milden—the nice-mannered boy you spoke to as we went out?" asked Aunt Evelyn when our rattle-trap conveyance was grinding briskly down the gravel road to the lodge gates.

"Yes," I replied; and the monosyllable meant much.

VII

Next morning I was a rather inattentive pupil, but Mr. Star rightly attributed this to the previous night's gaieties and was lenient with me, though my eyes often wandered through the window when they ought to have been occupied with sums, and I made a bad mess of my dictation. Mr. Star was still great on dictation, though I ought to have been beyond such elementary exercises at the age of twelve. "Parsing" was another favourite performance of his.

The word parse always struck me as sounding slightly ridiculous: even now it makes me smile when I look at it; but it conjures up for me a very clear picture of that quiet schoolroom: myself in a brown woollen jersey with my elbows on the table, and my tutor in his shabby tail-coat, chalking up on the blackboard, for my exclusive benefit, the first proposition of Euclid. Above the bookcase (which contained an odd assortment of primers, poetry, and volumes of adventure) hung a map of the world—a shiny one, which rolled up. But the map of the world was too large for me that morning, and I was longing to look at the local one and find out how far it was to Heron's Gate (and where it was).

As soon as Mr. Star had gone home to his little house in the village I slyly abstracted the ordnance map from the shelf where my aunt kept it (she was rather fond of consulting the map), and carried it back to the schoolroom with a sensation of gloating uncertainty. Heron's Gate was hard to find, but I arrived at it in the end, marked in very small print with *Windmill* right up against it and a big green patch called *Park Wood* quite near. I wondered what it would look like, and at once visualized a large, dim bird sitting on a white gate. . . . I had never seen a heron, but it sounded nice. . . . But when I began measuring the distance with a bit of string both bird and gate were obliterated by the melancholy number of miles which meandered across the map. The string told its tale too plainly. Heron's Gate was a good twelve miles to go. . . .

The situation now seemed desperate, but Dixon might be able to do something about it. Without saying a word to Aunt Evelyn I waited until we were well away on our afternoon ride, and then asked, quite casually, "Have you ever been to Heron's Gate, Tom?" (I had been telling him about the dance, but had not mentioned Denis Milden.) Dixon gravely admitted that he knew Heron's Gate quite well. There was a short silence, during which he pulled his

horse back into a walk. "Is it far from us?" I remarked
innocently. He pondered for a moment. "Let's see—it's
some way the other side of Hugget's Hill. . . . About twelve
miles from us, I should think." I fingered Sheila's mane
and tried another tack. "How far were we from home
when we finished up the other night?"

"About twelve miles."

Unable to restrain myself any longer, I blurted out my
eagerness to go to the meet next Tuesday. I never suspected
that Dixon had known this all the time, though I might
have guessed that he had looked up the list of meets in the
local paper. But he was evidently pleased that my sporting
instinct was developing so rapidly, and he refrained from
asking why I specially wanted to go to Heron's Gate. It
was enough for him that I wanted to go out at all. We
duped Aunt Evelyn by a system of mutual falsification of
distances (I couldn't find the map anywhere when she
wanted to look it up), and at half-past eight on the Tuesday morning, in glittering sunshine, with a melting hoar-
frost on the hedgerows, we left home for Heron's Gate.

*   *   *

Emboldened by the fact that I was going out hunting
with an inward purpose of my own, I clip-clopped alongside of Dixon with my head well in the air. The cold morning had made my fingers numb, but my thoughts moved
freely in a warmer climate of their own. I was being mag-
netized to a distant meet of the hounds, not so much
through my sporting instinct as by the appeal which Denis
Milden had made to my imagination. That he would be
there was the idea uppermost in my mind. My fears lest I
should again make a fool of myself were, for the moment,
as far below me as my feet. Humdrum home life was behind
me; in the freshness of the morning I was setting out for an
undiscovered country. . . .

My reverie ended when Sheila slithered on a frozen
puddle and Dixon told me to pay attention to what I was
doing and not slouch about in the saddle. Having brought
me back to reality he inspected his watch and said we were

well up to time. A mile or two before we got to the meet he stopped at an inn, where he put our horses into the stable for twenty minutes, "to give them a chance to stale". Then, seeing that I was looking rather pinched with the cold, he took me indoors and ordered a large glass of hot milk, which I should be jolly glad of, he said, before the day was out. The inn-parlour smelt of stale liquor, but I enjoyed my glass of milk.

The meet itself was an intensified rendering of my initiatory one. I was awed by my consciousness of having come twelve miles from home. And the scene was made significant by the phrase "one of their best meets". In the light of that phrase everything appeared a little larger than life: voices seemed louder, coats a more raucous red, and the entire atmosphere more acute with imminent jeopardy than at Finchurst Green. Hard-bitten hunting men rattled up in gigs, peeled off their outer coverings, and came straddling along the crowded lane to look for their nags. Having found them, they spoke in low tones to the groom and swung themselves importantly into the saddle as though there were indeed some desperate business on hand. . . .

Heron's Gate was a featureless wayside inn at the foot of a green knoll. I had not yet caught a glimpse of Denis when the procession moved away toward Park Wood, but I looked upward and identified the bulky black Windmill, which seemed to greet me with a friendly wave of its sails, as much as to say, "Here I am, you see—a lot bigger than they marked me on the map!" The Windmill consoled me; it seemed less inhuman, in its own way, than the brusque and bristling riders around me. When we turned off the road and got on to a sodden tussocked field, they all began to be in a hurry; their horses bucked and snorted and shook their heads as they shot past me—the riders calling out to one another with uncouth matutinal jocularities.

I was frightened, and I might have wondered why I was there at all if I had been old enough to analyse my emotions. As it was I felt less forlorn and insecure when we pulled up outside Park Wood and I caught sight of Denis on his chestnut pony. For the time being, however, he was unapproachable. With a gesture of characteristic independence he had turned his back on the jostling riders, who were going one by one into the wood through a narrow hunting-gate. I envied the unhesitating self-reliance with which he cantered along the field, turned his pony to put it at the low fence, and landed unobtrusively in the wood. It was all accomplished with what I should to-day describe as an unbroken rhythm. Thirty years ago I simply thought "Why can't I ride like that?" as I tugged nervously at Sheila's sensitive mouth and only just avoided bumping my knee against the gate-post as I went blundering into the covert. Dixon conducted me along one of the by-paths which branched from the main ride down the middle.

"We'll have to keep our ears open or they'll slip away without us," he remarked sagely. "It's an awkward old place to get a fox away from, though, and we may be here most of the morning." Secretly I hoped we should be.

Where we rode the winter sunshine was falling warmly into the wood, though the long grass in the shadows was still flaked with frost. A blackbird went scolding away among the undergrowth, and a jay was setting up a clatter in an ivied oak. Some distance off Jack Pitt was shouting "Yoi-over" and tooting his horn in a leisurely sort of style. Then we turned a corner and came upon Denis. He had pulled his pony across the path, and his face wore a glum look which, as I afterwards learnt to know, merely signified that, for the moment, he had found nothing worth thinking about. The heavy look lifted as I approached him with a faltering smile, but he nodded at me with blunt solemnity, as if what thoughts he had were elsewhere.

"Morning. So you managed to get here." That was all I got by way of greeting. Somewhat discouraged, I could think of no conversational continuance. But Dixon gave him the respectful touch of the hat due to a "proper little sportsman" and, more enterprising than I, supplemented the salute with "Bit slow in finding this morning, sir?"

"Won't be much smell to him when they do. Sun's too bright for that." He had the voice of a boy, but his manner was severely grown-up.

There was a brief silence, and then his whole body seemed to stiffen as he stared fixedly at the undergrowth. Something rustled the dead leaves; not more than ten yards from where we stood, a small russet animal stole out on to the path and stopped for a photographic instant to take a look at us. It was the first time I had ever seen a fox, though I have seen a great many since—both alive and dead. By the time he had slipped out of sight again I had just begun to realize what it was that had looked at me with such human alertness. Why I should have behaved as I did I will not attempt to explain, but when Denis stood up in his stirrups and emitted a shrill "Huick-holler," I felt spontaneously alarmed for the future of the fox.

"Don't do that; they'll catch him!" I exclaimed.

The words were no sooner out of my mouth than I knew I had made another fool of myself. Denis gave me one blank look and galloped off to meet the huntsman, who could already be heard horn-blowing in our direction in a maximum outburst of energy.

"Where'd ye see 'im cross, sir?" he exclaimed, grinning at Denis with his great purple face, as he came hustling along with a few of his hounds at his horse's heels.

Denis indicated the exact spot; a moment later the hounds had hit off the line, and for the next ten or fifteen minutes I was so actively preoccupied with my exertions in following Dixon up and down Park Wood that my indiscretion was temporarily obliterated. I was, in fact, so busy and flurried that I knew nothing of what was happening except that "our fox" was still running about inside the wood. When he did take to the open he must have slipped away unnoticed, for after we had emerged the hounds feathered dubiously over a few fields and very soon I found myself at a standstill.

Dixon was beside me, and he watched intently the mysterious operations of Jack Pitt, who was trotting across a ploughed field with the pack behind him. Dixon explained that he was "making a cast". "He must be a long way ahead of us; they could scarcely speak to him after they took the line out of covert," he commented.

All this was incomprehensible to me, but I was warned by my previous blunder and confined myself to a discreet nod. Dixon then advised me not to wear my cap on the back of my head: I pulled the wretched thing well down over my eyes and made a supreme effort to look like a "hard man to hounds". . . . I watched the riders who were chatting to one another in sunlit groups: they seemed to be regarding the proceedings of Jack Pitt with leisurely indifference.

Denis, as usual, had detached himself from his immediate surroundings, and was keeping an alert eye on the huntsman's head as it bobbed up and down along the far side of the fence. Dixon then made his only reference to my recent misconception of the relationship between foxes and hounds. "Young Mr. Milden won't think much of you if you talk like that. He must have thought you a regular booby!" Flushed and mortified, I promised to be more careful in future. But I knew only too well what a mollycoddle I had made myself in the estimation of the proper little sportsman on whom I had hoped to model myself. . . . "*Don't do that; they'll catch him!*" . . . It was too awful to dwell on. Lord Dumborough would be certain to hear about it, and would think worse of me than ever he did of a keeper who left the earths unstopped. . . . And even now some very sporting-looking people were glancing at me and laughing to one another about something. What else could they be laughing about except my mollycoddle remark? Denis must have told them, of course. My heart was full of misery. . . . Soon afterwards I said, in a very small voice, "I think I want to go home now, Tom." . . . On the way home I remembered that Denis didn't even know my name.

PART TWO: THE FLOWER SHOW MATCH

I

Ten minutes late, in the hot evening sunshine, my train bustled contentedly along between orchards and hop gardens, jolted past the signal-box, puffed importantly under the bridge, and slowed up at Baldock Wood. The station was exactly the same as usual and I was very pleased to see it again. I was back from Ballboro' for the summer holidays. As I was going forward to the guard's van to identify my trunk and my wooden play-box, the station-master (who, in those days, wore a top-hat and a baggy black frock-coat) saluted me respectfully. Aunt Evelyn always sent him a turkey at Christmas.

Having claimed my luggage I crossed the bridge, surrendered my ticket to a red-nosed and bearded collector, who greeted me good-naturedly, and emerged from the station with my cricket bat (which was wrapped in my cricket pads) under my arm. Dixon was waiting outside with a smart pony and trap. Grinning at me with restrained delight, he instructed my luggage-trundling porter to put it on the village omnibus and I gave the man the last sixpence of my journey-money. As we rattled up the road the unpunctual train with a series of snorts and a streamer of smoke sauntered sedately away into the calm agricultural valley of its vocation.

How jolly to be home for the holidays, I thought to myself. So far neither of us had said a word; but as soon as we were out of the village street (it wasn't our own village) he gave the pony a playful flick of the whip and made the following remark: "I've got a place for you in to-morrow's team." Subdued triumph was in his voice and his face.

"What, for the Flower Show Match!" I exclaimed, scarcely able to believe my ears. He nodded.

Now the Flower Show Match was the match of the year, and to play in it for the first time in my life was an outstanding event: words were inadeqate. We mutually decided not to gush about it.

"Of course, you're playing too?" I inquired. He nodded again. Dixon was one of the mainstays of the village team —a dashing left-hand bat and a steady right-arm bowler. I drew a deep breath of our local air. I was indeed home for the holidays! Expert discussion of to-morrow's prospects occupied the remaining mile and a half to the house.

"Miss Sherston won't half be pleased to see you," he said as we turned briskly in at the white gate. "She misses you no end, sir."

Aunt Evelyn had heard us coming up the drive, and she hurried across the lawn in her white dress. Her exuberant welcome ended with: "But you're looking rather thin in the face, dear. . . . Don't *you* think Master George is looking rather thin, Dixon? . . . We must feed him up well before he goes back." Dixon smiled and led the pony and cart round to the stable yard.

"And now, dear, whatever do you think has happened? I've been asked to help judge the vegetables at the Flower Show to-morrow. Really, I feel quite nervous! I've never judged anything except the sweet peas before. Of course, I'm doing them as well." With great restraint I said that I was sure the vegetables would be very interesting and difficult.

"I'm playing in the match," I added, with casual intensity. Aunt Evelyn was overjoyed at the news, and she pretended to be astonished. No doubt she had known about it all the time. The roast chicken at dinner tasted delicious and my bed felt ever so much more comfortable than the one at school.

*   *   *

My window was wide open when I went to bed, and I had left the curtains half-drawn. I woke out of my deep and dreamless sleep to a gradual recognition that I was at home and not in the cubicled dormitory at Ballboro'. Drowsily grateful for this, I lay and listened. A cock was crowing from a neighbouring farm; his shrill challenge was faintly echoed by another cock a long way off.

I loved the early morning; it was luxurious to lie there, half-awake, and half-aware that there was a pleasantly eventful day in front of me. . . . Presently I would get up and lean on the window-ledge to see what was happening in the world outside. . . . There was a starling's nest under the window where the jasmine grew thickest, and all of a sudden I heard one of the birds dart away with a soft flurry of wings. Hearing it go, I imagined how it would fly boldly across the garden: soon I was up and staring at the tree-tops which loomed motionless against a flushed and bright-ening sky. Slipping into some clothes I opened my door very quietly and tiptoed along the passage and down the stairs. There was no sound except the first chirping of the sparrows in the ivy. I felt as if I had changed since the Easter holidays. The drawing-room door creaked as I went softly in and crept across the beeswaxed parquet floor. Last night's half-consumed candles and the cat's half-empty bowl of milk under the gate-legged table seemed to belong neither here nor there, and my own silent face looked queerly at me out of the mirror. And there was the familiar photograph of "Love and Death", by Watts, with its secret meaning which I could never quite formulate in a thought, though it often touched me with a vague emotion of pathos. When I unlocked the door into the garden the early morning air met me with its cold purity; on the stone step were the bowls of roses and delphiniums and sweet peas which Aunt Evelyn had carried out there before she went to bed; the scarlet disc of the sun had climbed an inch above the hills. Thrushes and blackbirds hopped and pecked busily on the dew-soaked lawn, and a pigeon was cooing monotonously from the belt of woodland which sloped from the garden toward the Weald. Down there in the belt of river-mist a goods train whistled as it puffed steadily away from the station with a distinctly heard clanking of buffers. How little I knew of the enormous world beyond that valley and those low green hills.

*   *   *

From over the fields and orchards Butley Church struck five in mellow tones. Then the clock indoors whizzed and confirmed it with a less resonant tongue. The Flower Show Match was hours away yet—more than six hours in fact. Suppose I'd better go back to bed again, I thought, or I'll be feeling tired out before the match begins. Soon the maids would be stirring overhead, padding about the floor and talking in muffled voices. Meanwhile I stole down to the pantry to cut myself a piece of cake. What a stuffy smelling place it was, with the taps dripping into the sink and a bluebottle fly buzzing sleepily on the ceiling. I inspected the village grocer's calendar which was hanging from a nail. On it there was a picture of "The Relief of Ladysmith". . . . Old Kruger and the Boers. I never could make up my mind what it was all about, that Boer War, and it seemed such a long way off. . . . Yawning and munching I went creaking up to my room. It was broad daylight out of doors, but I was soon asleep again.

II

After breakfast there was no time to be wasted. First of all I had to rummage about for the tin of "Blanco", which was nowhere to be found. Probably the parlour-maid had bagged it; why on earth couldn't they leave things alone? I knew exactly where I'd left the tin at the end of last holidays—on the shelf in the schoolroom, standing on an old case of beetles (of which, for a short time, I had been a collector). And now, unless I could find the tin quickly, there'd never be time for me to "Blanco" my pads, for they took ever so long to dry in the sun, even on a blazing hot day like this one. . . .

"Really, it's a bit thick, Aunt Evelyn; someone's taken my tin of 'Blanco'," I grumbled. But she was already rather fussed, and was at that moment preoccupied in a serious discussion with Mabb, the gardener, about the transportation of the crockery which she was lending for the Cricket Tea.

In a hasty parenthesis she confessed that she had given the tin to Dixon only a week or two ago, so I transferred myself and my grimy pads to the harness room, where I discovered Dixon putting the finishing touches to his white cricket boots; he had already cleaned mine, and he apologized for not having done my pads, as he had been unable to find them. While I busied myself with dabbing and smearing the pads we had a nice chat about county cricket; he also told me how he had taken a "highly commended" at the Crystal Palace Dog Show with one of the smooth-haired collies which he had recently begun breeding. There had been a lull in his horse-buying activities after I went to school; since then I had given up my riding, as my aunt could not afford to keep a cob specially for me to ride in the holidays. So Dixon had consoled himself with his collies and village cricket: and the saddles were only used when he was exercising the sedate horse which now shared the carriage work with the smart little pony Rocket.

Leaving my pads to dry in the sun, I sauntered contentedly back to the house to have a squint at the morning paper, which never arrived until after breakfast. I had a private reason for wanting to look at the *Morning Post*. I was a firm believer in predestination, and I used to improvise superstitions of my own in connection with the cricket matches I played in. Aunt Evelyn was rustling the newspaper in the drawing-room, where she was having a short spell of inactivity before setting forth to judge the vegetables and sweet peas. Evidently she was reading about politics (she was a staunch Tory).

"I can't understand what that miserable Campbell-Bannerman is up to: but thank heaven the Radicals will never get in again," she exclaimed, handing me the sheet with the cricket news on it.

Carrying this into the garden I set about consulting the omens for my success in the match. I searched assiduously through the first-class scores, picking out the amateurs whose names, like my own, began with S, and whose initial was G. There were only two that day: the result was most unsatisfactory. *G. Shaw run out*, 1: *G. Smith, c. Lilley, b.*

Field, o. According to that I should score half a run. So I called in professional assistance, and was rewarded with: *Shrewsbury, not out*, 127. This left me in a very awkward position. The average now worked out at 64. The highest score I had ever made was 51, and that was only in a practice game at Ballboro'. Besides, 51 from 64 left 13, an unlucky number. It was absurd even to dally with the idea of my making sixty-four in the Butley Flower Show Match. Anything between twenty and thirty would have been encouraging. But Aunt Evelyn's voice from the drawing-room window informed me that she would be starting in less than ten minutes, so I ran upstairs to change into my flannels. And, anyhow, the weather couldn't have been better. . . . While we were walking across the fields Aunt Evelyn paused on the top of a stile to remark that she felt sure Mr. Balfour would be a splendid Prime Minister. But I was meditating about Shrewsbury's innings. How I wished I could bat like him, if only for one day!

* * *

The village of Butley contained, as one of its chief characters, a portly and prosperous saddler named William Dodd. It was Dodd who now greeted us at the field-gate and ushered Aunt Evelyn into the large, tropical-temperatured tent where the judges had already begun their expert scrutiny of the competing vegetables.

In the minds of most of the inhabitants of Butley William Dodd was an immemorial institution, and no village affairs could properly be transacted without his sanction and assistance. As a churchwarden on Sundays his impressive demeanour led us to suppose that, if he was not yet on hat-raising terms with the Almighty, he at any moment expected to be. During a Parliamentary Election he was equally indispensable, as he supervised the balloting in the village schoolroom; and the sanguine solemnity with which he welcomed the Conservative candidate left no doubt at all as to his own political opinions. He was a man much respected by the local gentry, and was on free and easy terms with the farmers of the neighbourhood. In fact, he was a sort of unofficial mayor of the village, and would have worn his robes, had they existed, with dignity and decorum. Though nearer fifty than forty, he was still one of the most vigorous run-getters in the Butley eleven, and his crafty underarm bowling worked havoc with the tail-end of many an opposing team. On Flower Show day he was in all his glory as captain of the cricket team and secretary and treasurer of the Horticultural Society, and his manner of receiving my aunt and myself was an epitome of his urbane and appreciative attitude toward the universe with which the parish of Butley was discreetly associated. Waggish persons in the village had given him the nickname "Did-I-say-Myself". Anyone who wanted to discover the origin of this witticism could do so by stopping outside the saddler's shop on a summer morning for a few minutes of gentle gossip. Laying aside whatever implement of his craft he happened to be using, he would get up and come to the door in his protuberant apron, and when interrogated about "the team for to-morrow", "Let me see," he would reply in a gravely complacent voice, "Let me see, there's Mr. Richard Puttridge; and Myself; my brother Alfred; Tom Dixon; Mr. Jack Barchard; young Bob Ellis—and did I say Myself?"—and so on, counting the names on his stubby fingers, and sometimes inserting "and I think I said Myself" again toward the end of the recital. But his sense of his own importance was justified when he had a bat in his hand. No one could gainsay that.

Having, so to speak, received the freedom of the Flower Show from this worthy man, there was nothing more for me to do until the rest of the players had arrived. At present there wasn't a cricketer to be seen on the small but well-kept ground, and it seemed unlikely that the match would start before noon. It was now a little after eleven and a cloudless day. Sitting in the shadow of a chestnut tree I watched the exertions of a muscular man with a mallet. He was putting up a "coconut shy" in the adjoining meadow, where a steam roundabout, some boat-swings, a shooting gallery, and other recreative facilities were in readiness for the afternoon. On the opposite side of the cricket field had been erected a Tea Tent, which would contain such spectators as were prevented, by their social status, from shying at coconuts or turning almost upside-down in a boat-swing. The ground sloped from the Tea Tent to the side where I was sitting (twenty-five summers ago), so that the genteel onlookers were enabled to feel themselves perceptibly above the rest of the proceedings.

Behind the Tent was a thick thorn hedge; beyond the hedge ran the dusty high road to the village. In the later afternoon of a cricket match there would be several dila-tory vehicles drawn up on the other side of the hedge, and the drivers would watch the game in Olympian detachment. There would be the carrier's van, and the brewer's dray, and the baker's cart, and the doctor's gig, and sometimes even a wagon-load of hay. None of them ever seemed to be pressed for time, and once they were there they were likely to stay till the end of the innings. Rooks would be cawing in the vicarage elms, and Butley, with its huddle of red roofs and square church tower, was a contented-looking place.

In my retrospect the players are now beginning to appear in ones and twos. Some skim easily across the greensward on bicycles; others arrive philosophically on foot, pausing to inspect the wicket, which has a nasty habit of causing fast bowling to "bump" after a spell of dry weather.

Dixon and I were having a little practice up against the fence when Aunt Evelyn emerged from the Flower Show Tent with a bevy of head-gardeners. She signalled to me, so I clambered over the palings and went up to her. She only wanted to tell me that she would be back again after lunch and did so hope she wouldn't miss my innings.

"I'm feeling quite proud that Master George is playing in the match," she exclaimed, turning to a short, clean-shaven, small-eyed man in a square bowler hat and his dark Sunday suit, who was standing near her. And then, to me, she added, "I was just congratulating Mr. Bathwick on his wonderful vegetables. We've given him the first prize, and he thoroughly deserves it. You never *saw* such tomatoes and cucumbers! I've been telling Mr. Bathwick that he's a positive *example* to us all!" . . .

Sam Bathwick, who had a very large mouth, grinned bashfully, though his heavy, sallow face had an irrepressibly artful look about it. He farmed a little bit of land in an out-of-the-way corner of the parish, and was reputed to have put by more money than he admitted to.

Climbing over the fence again I became aware of the arrival of the Rotherden eleven in a two-horse brake. It was close on twelve o'clock, but they'd had a fourteen-mile drive and the road was up and down hill all the way. How enormous they looked as they sauntered across the ground—several of them carrying cricket bags. I should be lucky if I made any runs at all against such men as they were!

*　　　　*　　　　*

Butley Church clock was tolling twelve while our opponents were bearing down on us from the other side of the field, with William Dodd already half-way across to meet them. But the Rotherden men appeared to be in no great hurry to begin the game as they stopped to have a look at the wicket. Meanwhile Butley bells chimed sedately to the close of the mellow extra celebration which Providence allowed them every three hours without fail. . . .

"I suppose they've got their best team?" I faltered to Dixon, whose keen gaze was identifying the still distant stalwarts.

"You bet they have!" he replied with a grim smile.

Two of the tallest men had detached themselves from the others and were now pacing importantly down the pitch with Dodd between them. Dixon indicated this group. "They've got Crump and Bishop, anyhow," he remarked. . . . Crump and Bishop! The names had a profound significance for me. For many years I had heard Dixon speak of them, and I had even watched them playing in a few Flower Show Matches. Heavily built men in dark blue caps, with large drooping moustaches, one of them bowling vindictively at each end and Butley wickets falling fast; or else one of them batting at each end and Butley bowling being scored off with masterful severity.

But they had also produced a less localized effect on me.

Rotherden was on the "unhunted" side of our district; it was in a part of the county which I somehow associated with cherry-blossom and black-and-white timbered cottages. Also it had the charm of remoteness, and whenever I thought of Crump and Bishop, I comprehensively visualized the whole fourteen miles of more or less unfamiliar landscape which lay between Butley and Rotherden. For me the names meant certain lovely glimpses of the Weald, and the smell of mown hayfields, and the noise of a shallow river flowing under a bridge. Yet Crump was an ordinary auctioneer who sold sheep and cattle on market days, and Bishop kept the "Rose and Crown" at Rotherden.

III

Butley had lost the toss. As we went on to the field I tightened the black and yellow scarf which I wore round my waist; the scarf proved that I had won a place in my House Eleven at school, and it was my sole credential as a cricketer. But to-day was more exciting and important than any House Match, and my sense of my own inferiority did not prevent me from observing every detail of the proceedings which I am now able to visualize so clearly across the intervening years.

The umpires in their long white coats have placed the bails on the stumps, each at his own end, and they are still satisfying themselves that the stumps are in the requisite state of exact uprightness. Tom Seamark, the Rotherden umpire, is a red-faced sporting publican who bulks as large as a lighthouse. As an umpire he has certain emphatic mannerisms. When appealed to he expresses a negative decision with a severe and stentorian "Not Oout": but when adjudicating that the batsman is out, he silently shoots his right arm toward the sky—an impressive and irrevocable gesture which effectively quells all adverse criticism. He is, of course, a tremendous judge of the game, and when not absorbed by his grave responsibilities he is one of the most jovial men you could meet with.

Bill Sutler, our umpire, is totally different. To begin with, he has a wooden leg. Nobody knows how he lost his leg; he does not deny the local tradition that he was once a soldier, but even in his cups he has never been heard to claim that he gave the limb for Queen and Country. It is, however, quite certain that he is now a cobbler (with a heavily waxed moustache) and Butley has ceased to deny that he is a grossly partisan umpire. In direct contrast to Tom Seamark he invariably signifies "not out" by a sour shake of the head: when the answer is an affirmative one he bawls "Hout" as if he'd been stung by a wasp. It is reputed that (after giving the enemy's last man out legbefore in a closely-fought finish) he was once heard to add, in an exultant undertone: "and I've won my five bob." He has also been accused of making holes in the pitch with his wooden leg in order to facilitate the efforts of the Butley bowlers.

The umpires are in their places. But it is in the sunshine of my own clarified retrospection that they are wearing their white coats. While I was describing them I had forgotten that they have both of them been dead for many years. Nevertheless, their voices are distinctly audible to me. "Same boundaries as usual, Bill?" shouts Seamark, as loudly as if he were talking to a deaf customer in his taproom. "Same *as* usual, Muster Seamark; three all round and four over the fence. Draw at six-thirty, and seven if there's anything in it," says Sutler. And so, with an intensified detachment, I look around me at the Butley players, who are now safely distributed in the positions which an omniscient Dodd has decreed for them.

I see myself, an awkward overgrown boy, fielding anxiously at mid-on. And there's Ned Noakes, the whiskered and one-eyed wicketkeeper, alert and active, though he's forty-five if he's a day. With his one eye (and a glass one) he sees more than most of us do, and his enthusiasm for the game is apparent in every attitude. Alongside of him lounges big Will Picksett, a taciturn good-natured young yokel; though over-deliberate in his movements, Will is a tower of strength in the team, and he sweeps half-volleys to the boundary with his enormous brown arms as though he were scything a hayfield. But there is no more time to describe the fielders, for Dodd has thrown a bright red ball to Frank Peckham, who is to begin the bowling from the top end. While Crump and Bishop are still on their way to the wickets I cannot help wondering whether, to modern eyes, the Butley team would not seem just a little unorthodox. William Dodd, for example, comfortably dressed in a pale pink shirt and grey trousers; and Peter Baitup, the ground-man (whose face is framed in a "Newgate fringe") wearing dingy white trousers with thin green stripes, and carrying his cap in his belt while he bowls his tempting left-hand slows. But things were different in those days.

In the meantime Bill Crump has taken his guard and is waiting with watchful ease to subjugate the first ball of the match, while Peckham, a stalwart fierce-browed farmer, takes a final look round the field. Peckham is a fast bowler with an eccentric style. Like most fast bowlers, he starts about fifteen paces from the wicket, but instead of *running* he *walks* the whole way to the crease, very much on his heels, breaking his aggressive stride with a couple of systematic hops when about half-way to his destination. Now he is ready. Seamark pronounces the word "Play!" And off he goes, walking for all he is worth, gripping the ball ferociously, and eyeing the batsman as if he intended to murder him if he can't bowl him neck and crop. On the ultimate stride his arm swings over, and a short-pitched ball pops up and whizzes alarmingly near Crump's magnificent moustache. Ned Noakes receives it rapturously with an adroit snap of his gauntlets. Unperturbed, and with immense deliberation, Crump strolls up the pitch and prods with his bat the spot where he has made up his mind that the ball hit the ground on its way toward his head. The ground-man scratches his nose apologetically. "Don't drop 'em too short, Frank," says Dodd mildly, with an expostulatory shake of his bristly grey cranium. Thus the match proceeds until, twenty-five years ago, it is lunch time, and Rotherden has made seventy runs with three

wickets down. And since both Crump and Bishop have
been got rid of, Butley thinks it hasn't done badly.

*   *   *

The Luncheon Tent stood on that part of the field where
the Flower Show ended and the swings and roundabouts
began. Although the meal was an informal affair, there
was shy solemnity in the faces of most of the players as they
filtered out of the bright sunshine into the sultry, half-lit
interior, where the perspiring landlord of the "Chequers"
and his buxom wife were bustling about at the climax of
their preparations. While the cricketers were shuffling
themselves awkwardly into their places, the brawny barman (who seemed to take catering less seriously than his
employers) sharpened the carving-knife on a steel prong
with a rasping sound that set one's teeth on edge while
predicting satisfactory slices of lamb and beef, to say nothing of veal and ham pie and a nice bit of gammon of
bacon.

As soon as all were seated Dodd created silence by rapping the table; he then put on his churchwarden face and
looked toward Parson Yalden, who was in readiness to
take his cue. He enunciated the grace in slightly unpar-
sonic tones, which implied that he was not only Rector of
Rotherden, but also a full member of the M.C.C. and first
cousin once removed to Lord Chatwynd. Parson Yalden's
parishioners occasionally complained that he paid more
attention to cricket and pheasant shooting than was fit and
proper. But as long as he could afford to keep a hard-
working curate he rightly considered it his own affair if he
chose to spend three days a week playing in club and
country-house matches all over the county. His demeanour
when keeping wicket for his own parish was both jaunty
and magisterial, and he was renowned for the strident and
obstreperous bellow to which he gave vent when he was
trying to bluff a village umpire into giving a batsman out
"caught behind". He was also known for his habit of genially engaging the batsman in conversation while the bowler
was intent on getting him out, and I have heard of at least

one occasion when he tried this little trick on the wrong man. The pestered batsman rounded on the rather foxy-faced clergyman with, "I bin playing cricket nigh on thirty years, and parson or no parson, I take the liberty of telling you to hold your blasted gab."

But I hurriedly dismissed this almost unthinkable anecdote when he turned his greenish eyes in my direction and hoped, in hearty and ingratiating tones, that I was "going to show them a little crisp Ballboro' batting".

The brisk clatter of knives and forks is now well started, and the barman is busy at his barrel. Conversation, however, is scanty, until Tom Seamark, who is always glad of a chance to favour the company with a sentiment, clears his throat impressively, elevates his tankard, fixes Jack Barchard with his gregarious regard, and remarks, "I should like to say, sir, how very pleased and proud we all are to see you safe 'ome again in our midst." Jack Barchard has recently returned from the Boer War where he served with the Yeomanry. The "sentiment" is echoed from all parts of the table, and glasses are raised to him with a gruff "Good 'ealth, sir," or "Right glad to see you back, Mr. Barchard." The returned warrior receives their congratulations with the utmost embarrassment. Taking a shy sip at my ginger-beer, I think how extraordinary it is to be sitting next to a man who has really been "out in South Africa". Barchard is a fair-haired young gentleman farmer. When the parson suggests that "it must have been pretty tough work out there", he replies that he is thundering glad to be back among his fruit trees again, and this, apparently, is about all he has to say about the Boer War.

But when the meal was drawing to an end and I had finished my helping of cold cherry-tart, and the barman began to circulate with a wooden platter for collecting the half-crowns, I became agonizingly aware that I had come to the match without any money. I was getting into a panic while the plate came clinking along the table, but quiet Jack Barchard unconsciously saved the situation by putting down five shillings and saying, "All right, old chap, I'll stump up for both." Mumbling, "Oh, that's jolly decent of you," I wished I could have followed him up a hill in a "forlorn hope". . . . He told me, later on, that he never set eyes on a Boer the whole time he was in South Africa.

*   *   *

The clock struck three, and the Reverend Yalden's leg-stump had just been knocked out of the ground by a vicious yorker from Frank Peckham. "Hundred and seventeen. Five. Nought," shouted the Butley scorer, popping his head out of the little flat-roofed shanty which was known as "the pavilion". The battered tin number-plates were rattled on to their nails on the scoring-board by a zealous young hobbledehoy who had undertaken the job for the day.

"*Wodger* say last man made?" he bawled, though the scorer was only a few feet away from him.

"Last man, *Blob*."

The parson was unbuckling his pads on a bench near by, and I was close enough to observe the unevangelical expression on his face as he looked up from under the brim of his panama hat with the M.C.C. ribbon round it. Mr. Yalden was not a popular character on the Butley ground, and the hobbledehoy had made the most of a heaven-sent opportunity.

From an undersized platform in front of the Horticultural Tent the Butley brass band now struck up "The Soldiers of the Queen". It's quite like playing in a county match, I thought, as I scanned the spectators, who were lining the fence on two sides of the field. Several easily recognizable figures from among the local gentry were already sauntering toward the Tea Tent, after a gossiping inspection of the Flower Show. I could see slow-moving Major Carmine, the best dressed man in Butley, with his white spats and a carnation in his buttonhole; and the enthusiastic curate, known as "Hard Luck" on account of his habit of exclaiming, "Oh, hard luck!" when watching or taking part in games of cricket, lawn tennis, or hockey. He was escorting the Miss Pattons, two elderly sisters who always dressed alike. And there was Aunt Evelyn, with her red sunshade up, walking between rosy-faced old Captain Huxtable and his clucking, oddly dressed wife. It was quite a brilliant scene which the Butley Band was doing its utmost to sustain with experimental and unconvincing tootles and drum-beatings.

Soon afterwards, however, the Soldiers of the Queen were overwhelmed by the steam-organ which, after a warning hoot, began to accompany the revolving wooden horses of the gilded roundabout with a strident and blaring fanfaronade. For a minute or two the contest of cacophonies continued. But in spite of a tempestuous effort the band was completely outplayed by its automatic and unexhaustible adversary. The discord becoming intolerable, it seemed possible that the batsmen would "appeal against the music" in the same way that they sometimes "appeal against the light" when they consider it inadequate. But William Dodd was equal to the emergency; with an ample gesture he conveyed himself across the ground and prohibited the activity of the steam-organ until the match was finished. The flitting steeds now revolved and undulated noiselessly beneath their gilded canopy, while the Butley Band palavered peacefully onward into the unclouded jollity of the afternoon.

*   *   *

The clock struck four. Rotherden were all out for 183 and Tom Dixon had finished the innings with a confident catch on the boundary off one of Dodd's artfully innocent lobs. No catches had come my way, so my part in the game had been an unobtrusive one. When Dodd and Picksett went out to open our innings it was a matter of general opinion in the Beer Tent that the home team had a sporting chance to make the runs by seven o'clock, although there were some misgivings about the wicket and it was anticipated that Crump and Bishop would make the ball fly about a bit when they got to work.

Having ascertained that I was last but one on the list in the score-book, I made my way slowly round the field to have a look at the Flower Show. As I went along the boundary in front of the spectators who were leaning their elbows on the fence I felt quite an important public character. And as I shouldn't have to go in for a long while yet, there was no need to feel nervous. The batsmen, too, were shaping confidently, and there was a shout of "Good ole Bill! That's the way to keep 'em on the carpet!" when Dodd brought off one of his celebrated square-cuts to the hedge off Bishop's easy-actioned fast bowling. Picksett followed this up with an audacious pull which sent a straight one from Crump skimming first bounce into the Tea Tent, where it missed the short-sighted doctor's new straw hat by half an inch and caused quite a flutter among the tea-sipping ladies.

"Twenty up," announced the scorer, and the attendant hobbledehoy nearly fell over himself in his eagerness to get the numbers up on the board. A stupendous appeal for a catch at the wicket by the Reverend Yalden was countered by Sutler with his surliest shake of the head, and the peg-supported umpire was the most popular man on the field as he ferried himself to his square-leg location at the end of the over. Forty went up; then Dodd was clean bowled by Crump.

"'Ow's *that*?" bawled a ribald Rotherden partisan from a cart in the road, as the rotund batsman retreated; warm but majestic, he acknowledged the applause of the onlookers by a slight lifting of his close-fitting little cap. Everybody was delighted that he had done so well, and it was agreed that he was (in the Beer Tent) "a regular chronic old sport" and (in the Tea Tent) "a wonderful man for his age". Modest Jack Barchard then made his appearance and received a Boer War ovation.

Leaving the game in this prosperous condition, I plunged into the odoriferous twilight of the Horticultural Tent. I had no intention of staying there long, but I felt that I owed it to Aunt Evelyn to have a look at the sweet peas and vegetables at any rate. In the warm muffled air the delicate aroma of the elegant sweet peas was getting much the worst of it in an encounter with the more aggressive smell of highly polished onions. Except for a couple of bearded gardeners who were conferring in professional undertones,

I had the tent to myself. Once I was inside I felt glad to be loitering in there, alone and away from the optical delirium of the cricket. The brass band had paused to take breath: now and again the brittle thud of a batsman's stroke seemed to intensify the quiescence of the floralized interior.

As I sniffed my way round I paid little attention to the card-inscribed names of the competitors (though I observed that the Miss Pattons had got second prize for a tasteful table decoration): I found many of the flowers tedious and unpleasing—more especially the bulbous and freckled varieties with the unpronounceable names—the kind of flowers which my aunt always referred to as "gardeners' greenhouseries". On the whole the fruit and vegetables gave me most enjoyment. The black cherries looked delicious and some of the green gooseberries were as large as small hen's eggs. The two gardeners were concentrating on Sam Bathwick's first-prize vegetables and as they seemed to grudge making way for me I contented myself with a glimpse of an immense marrow and some very pretty pink potatoes. As I passed, one of the gardeners was saying something about "copped 'im a fair treat this time", and I absent-mindedly wondered who had been copped. When I emerged the home team had lost two more wickets and the condition of the game was causing grave anxiety. Reluctantly I drifted toward the Tea Tent for a period of social victimization.

* * *

The Tea Tent was overcrowded and I found Aunt Evelyn sitting a little way outside it in comparative seclusion. She was in earnest communication with Miss Clara Maskall, a remarkable old lady who had been born in the year of the Battle of Waterloo and had been stone-deaf for more than sixty years.

My aunt was one of the few people in the neighbourhood who enjoyed meeting Miss Maskall. For the old lady had a way of forgetting that the rest of the world could hear better than she could, and her quavering comments on some of the local gentlefolk, made in their presence, were often too caustic to be easily forgotten. She was reputed to have been kissed by King George the Fourth. She was wearing a bunched-up black silk dress, and her delicately withered face was framed in a black poke-bonnet, tied under the chin with a white lace scarf. With her piercingly alert eyes and beaky nose she looked like some ancient and intelligent bird. Altogether she was an old person of great distinction, and I approached her with an awful timidity. She had old-fashioned ideas about education, and she usually inquired of me, in creaking tones, whether I had recently been flogged by my schoolmaster.

But the menace of Roman Catholicism was her most substantial and engrossing theme; and up to the age of ninety she continued to paste on the walls of her bedroom every article on the subject which she could find in the *Times* and the *Morning Post*. Aunt Evelyn told me that the walls were almost entirely papered with printed matter, and that she had more than once found Miss Maskall sitting on the top step of a library ladder reading some altitudinous article on this momentous question of "the Scarlet Woman". To the day of her death she never so much as trifled with a pair of spectacles. But she was still very much alive when I saw her at the Flower Show Match. Sitting bolt upright in a wicker-chair, she scrutinized me keenly and then favoured me with a friendly little nod without losing touch with what my aunt was engaged in telling her by "finger-talk".

"*What* is it the man has been doing, Evelyn?" she asked, her queer, uncontrolled voice quavering up to a bird-like shrillness. There was something rather frightening about her defective intonation.

"Write it down; write it down," she screeched, clawing a tablet and pencil out of her lap and consigning them to Aunt Evelyn, who hurriedly scribbled two or three lines and returned the tablet for her to read aloud; "such a dreadful thing, the judges have found out that Bathwick has been cheating with his prize vegetables". She passed it back with a tremulous cackle.

"How did he do it?" More scribbling, and then she

read out, "He bought all the vegetables at Ashbridge. The judges suspected him, so they went to his garden in a pony trap and found that he has *no glass*—not even a cucumber frame." Miss Maskall chuckled delightedly at this, and said that he ought to be given a special prize.

"I call it downright dishonest. Almost as bad as embezzlement," wrote Aunt Evelyn who, as one of the judges, could scarcely be expected to treat the offence in a spirit of levity.

Miss Clara now insisted that she must herself inspect the fraudulent vegetables. Rising energetically from her chair, she grasped her ebony stick with an ivory knuckled hand and shaped an uncompromising course for the Horticultural Tent with Aunt Evelyn and myself in tow. The villagers at the gate made way for her with alacrity, as though it had dawned on them that she was not only the most ancient, but by far the most interesting object to be seen at the Flower Show Match.

*   *   *

Miss Maskall had made the game seem rather remote. She cared nothing for cricket, and had only come there for an afternoon spree. But she was taciturn during her tour of the Flower Show: when we tucked her into her shabby old victoria she leant back and closed her eyes. Years ago she must have had a lovely face. While we watched her carriage turn the corner I wondered what it felt like to be eighty-seven; but I did not connect such antiquity with my own future. Long before I was born she had seen gentlemen playing cricket in queer whiskers and tall hats.

Next moment I was safely back in the present, and craning my neck for a glimpse of the score-board as I hustled Aunt Evelyn along to the Tea Tent. There had been a Tea Interval during our absence, so we hadn't missed so very much. Five wickets were down for ninety and the shadows of the cricketers were growing longer in the warm glare which slanted down the field. A sense of my own share in the game invaded me and it was uncomfortable to imagine that I might soon be walking out into the middle to be bowled at by Crump and Bishop, who now seemed gigantic and forbidding. And then impetuous Ned Noakes must needs call Frank Peckham for an impossibly short run, and his partner retreated with a wrathful shake of his head. Everything now depended on Dixon who was always as cool as a cucumber in a crisis.

"Give 'em a bit of the long handle, Tom!" bawled someone in the Beer Tent, while he marched serenely toward the wicket, pausing for a confidential word with Noakes who was still looking a bit crestfallen after the recent catastrophe. Dixon was a stylish left-hander and never worried much about playing himself in. Bishop was well aware of this, and he at once arranged an extra man in the outfield for him. Sure enough, the second ball he received was lifted straight into the long-off's hands. But the sun was in the fielder's eyes and he misjudged the flight of the catch. The Beer Tent exulted vociferously. Dixon then set about the bowling and the score mounted merrily. He was energetically supported by Ned Noakes. But when their partnership had added over fifty, and they looked like knocking off the runs, Noakes was caught in the slips off a bumping ball and the situation instantly became serious again.

Realizing that I was next in but one, I went off in a fluster to put my pads on, disregarding Aunt Evelyn's tremulous "I do so hope you'll do well, dear". By the time I had arrived on the other side of the ground, Amos Hickmott, the wheelwright's son, had already caused acute anxiety. After surviving a tigerish appeal for "leg-before", he had as near as a toucher run Dixon out in a half-witted endeavour to escape from the bowling. My palsied fingers were still busy with straps and buckles when what sounded to me like a deafening crash warned me that it was all over with Hickmott. We still wanted seven runs to win when I wandered weakly in the direction of the wicket. But it was the end of an over, and Dixon had the bowling. When I arrived the Reverend Yalden was dawdling up the pitch in his usual duck-footed progress when crossing from one wicket to the other.

"Well, young man, you've got to look lively this time," he observed with intimidating jocosity. But there seemed to be a twinkle of encouragement in Seamark's light blue eye as I established myself in his shadow.

Dixon played the first three balls carefully. The fourth he smote clean out of the ground. The hit was worth six, but "three all round and four over" was an immemorial rule at Butley. Unfortunately, he tried to repeat the stroke, and the fifth ball shattered his stumps. In those days there were only five balls to an over.

Peter Baitup now rolled up with a wide grin on his fringed face, but it was no grinning moment for me at the bottom end when Sutler gave me "middle-and-leg" and I confronted impending disaster from Crump with the sun in my eyes. The first ball (which I lost sight of) missed my wicket by "a coat of varnish" and travelled swiftly to the boundary for two byes, leaving Mr. Yalden with his huge gauntlets above his head in an attitude of aggrieved astonishment. The game was now a tie. Through some obscure psychological process my whole being now became clarified. I remembered Shrewsbury's century and became as bold as brass. There was the enormous auctioneer with the ball in his hand. And there I, calmly resolved to look lively and defeat his destructive aim. The ball hit my bat and trickled slowly up the pitch. "Come on!" I shouted, and Peter came gallantly on. Crump was so taken by surprise that we were safe home before he'd picked up the ball. And that was the end of the Flower Show Match.

PART THREE: A FRESH START

I

Except for the letters written to me by Mr. Pennett I have no documentary evidence concerning the young man who was existing under my name in the summer after I left Cambridge. The fact that I have preserved them is a proof that I was aware of their significance, although it is now nearly twenty years since I last read them through. In these days they would be typewritten; but in those days they were fair-copied by a clerk, and the slanting calligraphy helps me to recapture my faded self as I was when I apprehensively extracted them from their envelopes. Even now they make rather uncomfortable reading, and I find myself wondering how their simple-minded recipient managed to repel such an onslaught of worldly wisdom.

But Tom Dixon was still about the place to pitchfork me into the village cricket team; and it happened that it was on a showery June morning, when I was setting out for one of the Butley matches, that I received the first really uncomfortable letter from Mr. Pennett. We were playing over at Rotherden, which meant an early start, as it was fourteen miles away. So I slipped the letter into my pocket unopened and perused it at intervals later on in the day. My Aunt Evelyn, I may say, never made any attempt to influence me in my choice of a career. Like me, she preferred to procrastinate, and her intuition probably warned her that my mind was unlikely to habituate itself to the quibbling technicalities of the legal profession. But whatever she thought she kept to herself. She was still addicted to saying that I was "none too strong", and this delicacy of constitution which she ascribed to me was in itself a more than adequate argument against my overtaxing my health with tedious text-books in the unwholesome air of a London office.

"George is a boy who ought not to be interfered with too much," she would say. And I agreed with her opinion unreservedly.

Mr. Pennett, however, had conscientiously dictated to his clerk a couple of pages of expostulation and advice with the unmistakable object of interfering with me as much as possible. But the letter remained in my pocket until after we had arrived at Rotherden.

The air was Elysian with early summer and the shadows of steep white clouds were chasing over the orchards and meadows; sunlight sparkled on green hedgerows that had been drenched by early morning showers. As I was carried past it all I was lazily aware through my dreaming and un-observant eyes that this was the sort of world I wanted. For it was my own countryside, and I loved it with an intimate feeling, though all its associations were crude and incoher-ent. I cannot think of it now without a sense of heartache, as if it contained something which I have never quite been able to discover.

Thus we jogged and jingled along in the rumbling two-horse brake with the Butley team talking their parish talk, and every house and hamlet animating William Dodd to some local-flavoured anecdote. Dodd was in a holiday humour, and there wasn't much that he didn't know about the living-memoried local history which lay between But-ley and Rotherden. The doings of the county cricket team were also discussed; Dodd had watched them at Dum-bridge last week and had spoken to Blythe, who was, in his opinion, the best slow left-hand bowler in England. The road went up and down hill by orchards and hop-gardens and parks crowded with ancient oaks. Nearly all the way we were looking, on our left-hand side, across the hop-kiln-dotted Weald. And along the Weald went the railway line from London to the coast, and this gave me a soberly romantic sense of distances and the outside world of un-familiar and momentous happenings. I knew very little about London, and I had never been across the Channel, but as I watched a train hurrying between the level or-chards with its consequential streamer of smoke, I meditated on the coast-line of France and all the unvisualized singularity of that foreign land. And then Rotherden Church hove in sight with its square battlemented tower, and we turned into the stableyard of the "Rose and Crown", where Bert Bishop, the landlord, was waiting to welcome us—a stouter man than he used to be, but still as likely as not to hit up a hundred.

*   *   *

Butley batted first. I was in eighth. Mr. Pennett's letter was still in my pocket. Sitting on a gate in a remote corner of the ground I opened the envelope with a sinking heart. Mr. Pennett wrote as follows:

"My dear George, I have learned from your College Tutor, much to my regret, that you have gone down from Cambridge, at any rate for this term. I think that you have made a mistake in so doing and that this arises from perhaps a lack of appreciation on your part of the value of an University education. One of the objects of an University career is to equip the student for the battle of life, and as you grow older you will find that people are estimated in the world by the results which they have obtained at the Varsity. It is a kind of stamp upon a man and is supposed to indicate the stuff of which he is made. With a degree you start with so much capital to the good, but if on the other hand having once commenced an University career you abandon it, the fact will militate against you in almost everything you undertake hereafter. Although you are nearly twenty-two you cannot be expected yet to look at things in precisely the same light as those who have had more experience, but knowing as I do the great importance of the whole matter I do most earnestly beg you to reconsider the decision at which you have arrived. G. Sherston, M.A., will rank higher than plain G. Sherston, and the mere fact of your being able to attach the magic letters to your name will show that whatever may be your capabilities you have at any rate grit and perseverance. I hope, therefore, that you will see that the step you have taken is one of unwisdom and that before it is too late you will carefully reconsider it. Forgive this homily, but I am sure that whether it is to your taste or not you will at least acknowledge that it proceeds from a strong desire to be of use to you from—your sincere friend, Percival G. Pennett.''

It amuses me now when I think of the well-meaning lawyer dictating that letter in his Lincoln's Inn office, and of myself with my gaze recoiling from the wiseacre phraseology to follow a rook which was travelling overhead with querulous cawings. Everything the letter said was so true; and yet, I wondered, was it really possible for P.G.P. to tell me what was best for my future? His letter had one effect which would have astonished him. Worried and put out of temper by it, I slouched to the wicket after lunch without caring a hoot whether I stayed there or not. The result was that, favoured by a fair amount of luck, I "carted" the bowling all over the field; at the end of our innings I was not out forty-three. This was the highest score I had ever made for the village; and, although we lost the match by five wickets, I finished the day in a glow of self-satisfaction which was undamped by a tremendous thunderstorm which overtook us on our way home.

*   *   *

Mr. Pennett's procedure for bringing me to my senses about "an University degree" was an excellent example of preaching to the winds. Good advice seldom sinks into the wayward mind of a young man, and in this case the carefully composed phrases meant nothing to me. The utmost I could do was to transmute his prudent precepts into some such sentiment as this: "The silly old blighter is trying to make me stay up at Cambridge when I'm absolutely fed up with the whole concern." Not that I made any serious attempt to "carefully reconsider" my decision. I had not yet begun to train myself to think rationally about anything. No one was ever less capable of putting two and two together than I was. And he made a strategic mistake when he adjured me to "look ahead".

I very much doubt whether anybody wants to look ahead unless he is anxious to escape from one condition

into another more desirable one. Children hanker to be
grown-up because they want liberty. But why should a
young man who has inherited a net income of about six
hundred a year find it easy or necessary to imagine himself
as ten or twenty years older? If I ever thought of myself as
a man of thirty-five it was a visualization of dreary decrepitude. The word maturity had no meaning for me. I did not
anticipate that I should become *different*; I should only become *older*. I cannot pretend that I aspired to growing
wiser. I merely *lived*, and in that condition I drifted from
day to day. Ignorantly unqualified to regulate the human
mechanism which I was in charge of, my self-protective
instincts were continually being contradicted by my spontaneously capricious behaviour. When Mr. Pennett referred me to what he called "after-life", he was unaware
that for me the future was a matter of the four seasons of
the year. There was next autumn, and next winter, and
after that next spring. But this summer was the only thing
that I cared about. The phrase "after-life" was also vaguely confused with going to church and not wanting to be
dead—a perplexity which can be omitted from a narrative
in which I am doing my best to confine myself to actual
happenings. At the age of twenty-two I believed myself to
be unextinguishable.

II

It was a wet and windy afternoon toward the end of September. We were on our way home from a seaside place in
Devonshire, where we had been staying for a change of air.
Aunt Evelyn was going through a period of bad health,
and her headaches were probably much worse than she
admitted. Anyhow, she had been content to do very little,
and I caused her no anxiety, for I had "taken up golf" and
most of my time and energy had evaporated on the links.
The people I played with at Bidmouth were equally engrossed by the game, and if they had any ideas about things
other than golf they showed no inclination to share them

with me. Aunt Evelyn wasn't sorry to be going home again; there was plenty to be done in the garden, and how the cats had got on without her she couldn't imagine.

Of my own sensations about our return I have no recollection: I may have felt vaguely dissatisfied, but I did not consciously allow myself to criticize the purposeless existence I was leading. At Waterloo Station we changed from one train to another for the final stage of our "through" journey. On account of her feeling unwell, Aunt Evelyn had taken first-class tickets, and this made me conscious that we had a social position to keep up. Gratified by the obsequious attentions of the green-flagged guard, I couldn't help wishing that my aunt had tipped him more than a shilling. As she remarked, he was such a very nice-mannered man, and I assumed that he was expecting half a crown.

At any rate, it was a relief to settle down in a corner of the dark blue cushioned compartment after my aunt's unnecessary fussification about the luggage. Raindrops trickled down the windows as we steamed out of the station, and I was glad to avert my gaze from the dingy and dilapidated tenements and warehouses which we were passing. Poverty was a thing I hated to look in the face; it was like the thought of illness and bad smells, and I resented the notion of all those squalid slums spreading out into the uninfected green country. While I perused a magazine called *Golf Illustrated* I stole an occasional glance at the two very first-class looking passengers who occupied the other corners of the compartment. One of them was a grey-haired lady with a crocodile-skin dressing-case and a fur cloak. She was reading a book with an air of refined hauteur. The other was a middle-aged man with a neatly trimmed grey beard and a glossy top-hat which he had ceremoniously arranged on the rack above him. He was glancing at *Blackwood's Magazine*, and he had a bunch of violets in the buttonhole of his opulent dark blue overcoat. From the tone of voice in which he inquired whether she would prefer the window down a little I inferred that the lady was a stranger to him. Compared with these influential-looking people,

Aunt Evelyn in her countrified tweed coat and skirt and her dowdy little hat seemed only just presentable. I had yet to make the significant discovery that the most distinguished personages are sometimes the most untidy.

Fortunately for her peace of mind, my aunt was much too tired to worry about the impression which her exterior might be creating on two complete strangers who were surveying her for the first and probably the last time on earth. What she really cared about was a cup of hot tea. But we should be in the train another hour, and we couldn't possibly get home before six o'clock. Aunt Evelyn, however, though she seldom travelled, was not without resourcefulness in the matter of railway journeys, and what she didn't know about picnics wasn't worth knowing. Now among the numerous light articles which she had brought into the carriage there was a certain plebeian-looking basket which contained every facility for making tea. Most essential among the facilities was a patent spirit-lamp for boiling the water; and this lamp was apt to misbehave itself and produce an unpleasing smell. Had we been alone I should have been willing enough to set it alight, and the whole business would have been quite companionable and cosy. But now, with those impeccably dressed people in their corners, I felt nothing except discomfort and disapproval when my aunt became busy with her basket. I totally dissociated myself from her preparations, while she muddled about with the lamp, which for some time refused to function and then flared up with sudden explosive ardour.

"I was quite afraid it was going to be tiresome," she remarked, screening it with the *Pall Mall Gazette* and looking across at me with a smile. But the expected response was absent. I glowered contemptuously at the apparatus which she had placed on the floor. She then began measuring out the tea. In the meantime I was conscious that our fellow-travellers were exchanging scandalized glances, and their haughtiness intensified itself with every phase of the capricious conduct of the lamp.

"There now! It's gone out again!" exclaimed Aunt Evelyn, who had become slightly flustered, since she had observed that she was getting herself into bad odour with the other passengers.

By dint of striking several more matches and much twiddling of the wick she got the conflagration well under way again, although she had some difficulty in shielding it against a dangerous draught caused by the gentleman, who had let down his window with expostulating asperity.

As for me, I considered that Aunt Evelyn was making a regular exhibition of herself, and when her persistence had been rewarded by a cloud of steam and she held out a cup of moderately hot China tea, I felt so annoyed that I could almost have chucked it out of the window. However, I expressed my feelings adequately by muttering, "No, *I* don't want any," and putting my paper up as a barrier between myself and the objectionable sight of Aunt Evelyn sipping her tea with mechanical enjoyment. As there was a spare cup in the basket she politely said to the lorgnette-raising lady, "May I offer you a cup of tea, madam?" But the amenity was declined with an air of social remoteness.

For the remainder of the journey I couldn't bring myself to say another word, and Aunt Evelyn endured my sulky silence—wearily apologetic. By the time we were home I knew quite clearly that my attitude toward the tea-making had been odious; and the more I realized it the more impossible it seemed for me to make amends by behaving gently to her. It was one of those outwardly trivial episodes which one does not forget.

III

It was now an accepted fact that I had quitted Cambridge University. During that autumn I was limply incorporating myself with Aunt Evelyn's localized existence. Nothing was being said on the subject of what I was going to do, and I cannot remember that the problem was perplexing my thoughts, or that I felt any hankerings for more eventful departments of human experience. I was content to take it easy until something happened. But since I had no responsibilities and no near relatives except my aunt, whose connection with the world beyond her own "round of calls" was confined to a few old friends who seldom wrote to her, the things which could happen were humdrum and few.

"What are you doing to-day, George?" asks Aunt Evelyn, as she gets up from the breakfast table to go down to the kitchen to interview the cook.

"Oh, I shall probably bike over to Amblehurst after lunch for a round of golf," I reply.

Over at Amblehurst, about four miles away, there is a hazardless nine-hole course round Squire Maundle's sheep-nibbled park. The park faces south-west, sloping to a friendly little river—the Neaze—which at that point, so I have been told, though I never troubled to verify it—divides the counties of Kent and Sussex. On the other side of the river is the village. Squire Maundle's clanging stable clock shares with the belfry of the village school the privilege of indicating the Amblehurst hours. My progress up and down the park from one undersized green to another is accompanied by the temperate clamour of sheep-bells (and in springtime by the loud litanies of baa-ing lambs and anxious ewes). The windows of Squire Maundle's eighteenth-century mansion overlook my zigzag saunterings with the air of a county family dowager who has not yet made up her mind to leave cards on those new people at the Priory. As a rule I have the links to myself, but once in a while "young" Squire Maundle (so-called because his eighty-seven-year-old father is still above ground) appears on the skyline in his deer-stalker hat, with a surly black retriever at his heels and we play an amicable round.

Without wishing to ridicule him, for he was always kind and courteous, I may say that both his features and his tone of voice have something in common with the sheep who lift their mild munching faces to regard him while he plays an approach shot in his cautious, angular, and automatic style. He is one of those shrewdly timorous men who are usually made a butt of by their more confident associates. Falstaff would have borrowed fifty pounds off him, though he has the reputation of being close with his money. His vocabulary is as limited as his habit of mind, and he speaks with an old-fashioned word-clipping conciseness. His lips are pursed up as if in a perpetual whistle. The links —on which he knows every tussock and ant-hill intimately —are always "in awful good condition"; and "That's a hot'un!" he exclaims when I make a long drive, or "That's for Sussex!" (a reference to the remote possibility that my ball may have gone over the river). But the best instance I can give of his characteristic mode of expressing himself is one which occurred when I once questioned him about a group of little grey stones among the laurel bushes outside his stable-yard. After whistling to his retriever he replied, "House-dogs bury in the shrubbery: shooting-dogs bury in the park". . . .

Aunt Evelyn always enjoyed a game of croquet with him at a garden party.

But in my spontaneous memories of Amblehurst I am always playing by myself. The sun is in my eyes as I drive off at the "long hole" down to the river, and I usually slice my ball into a clump of may trees. I am "trying to do a good score"—a purpose which seldom survives the first nine holes—but only half my attention is concentrated on the game. I am wondering, perhaps, whether that parcel from the second-hand bookshop at Reading will have arrived by the afternoon post; or I am vaguely musing about my money affairs; or thinking what a relief it is to have escaped from the tyranny of my Tripos at Cambridge. Outside the park the village children are making a shrill hubbub as they come out of school. But the sun is reddening beyond the straight-rising smoke of the village chimneys, and I must sling my clubs across my shoulder and mount my bicycle to pedal my way along the narrow autumn-smelling lanes. And when I get home Aunt Evelyn will be there to pour out my tea and tell me all about the Jumble Sale this afternoon; it was such a success, they made more than six pounds for the Mission to Deep-sea Fishermen.

*　　　　*　　　　*

The days were drawing in, though it was only the second week in October.

"There's a nice fire up in the schoolroom, Mr. George; and a parcel of books come by the carrier's van," said Miriam, when she was taking away the tea things.

Miriam (and I might well have mentioned her before, since she had already been with Aunt Evelyn for nearly seven years) was a gaunt woman who had looked more than middle-aged ever since I first saw her. Miriam's hair had perhaps begun by being golden, but it was now a faded yellow remnant, drawn tightly back from her broad forehead and crowned by a skimpy lace cap. Her wide-set eyes had a strained and patient expression, as though expecting to be rather sharply ordered to lug a heavy scuttle of coals up four flights of steep stairs. She was unobtrusively humpbacked and round shouldered, which suggested that when not carrying scuttles upstairs she had been burdened with heavy trays or had been stooping over a scullery sink to wash and wipe a lifetime of crockery. Her voice, too, had a long-suffering note in it—most noticeable when she was doing her best to be gay. These outward characteristics were the only legacy which she had received from her late mistress who had for a long period of years exploited Miriam's abnormal willingness for work. In such drudgery she had used up her youth and maturity, thereby acquiring an habitual capacity for taking on her own shoulders a load of domestic duties which never seemed to have struck her as being excessive. She was what is known as "a treasure". The difficulty, as Aunt Evelyn often said, was to persuade her to sit down and shut her eyes for a few minutes and allow the other maids to do their fair share of the housework. But Aunt Evelyn's kindness only stimulated Miriam to renewed activity, and her response to ordinary civility and consideration reflected no credit at all on her former employer. In those days I used to look upon her as a bit of a joke, and I took for granted the innumerable little jobs she did for me. She was no more than an odd-looking factotum, whose homely methods and manners occasionally incurred my disapproval, for I had a well-developed

bump of snobbishness as regards flunkeydom and carriage-
and-pair ostentation as a whole. Now and again, however,
I was remotely affected by the smile which used to light up
her sallow humble face when I said something which
pleased her. It is the memory of that smile which has
helped me to describe her. For there was a loveliness of
spirit in her which I did not recognize until it was too late
for her to know it.

*   *   *

On my way up to the schoolroom, which had formerly
been known as "the day-nursery", I decided that the
name needed further promotion. "Study" was inappropriate and sounded elderly. "Smoking-room" wouldn't do
either, because I hadn't begun smoking yet, although puffing my pipe by the fireside on winter evenings was a comfortable idea. "Library", I thought (pausing in the dark
passage with a hand on the brass door-knob) was too big a
jump from "schoolroom". Besides, there wasn't any library. "Library" meant glass-fronted bookcases with yellow busts of Julius Cæsar and Cicero on the top. Entering
the fire-lit room, I pounced on the bulky package which
Miriam had deposited on the table. "Book-room", I
thought, as I tugged impetuously at the thick string. And
"book-room" it rather tentatively became.

There was no doubt that I had a fondness for books—
especially old ones. But my reading was desultory and un-
assimilative. Words made a muddled effect on my mind
while I was busy among them, and they seldom caused any
afterthoughts. I esteemed my books mostly for their out-
sides. I admired old leather bindings, and my fancy was
tickled by the thought of firelight flickering on dim gilt,
autumn-coloured backs—rows and rows of them, and myself in an armchair musing on the pleasant names of Addison and Steele, Gibbon and Goldsmith. And what wonderful bargains were to be discovered in the catalogues of
second-hand booksellers at Birmingham! Only last week I
had acquired (for seven and sixpence) *Dr. Burnet's Rights of
Princes in the Disposing of Ecclesiastical Benefices*, 1685. FIRST

EDITION. *Original sheep*, scarce. And there were Tillotson's
Sermons, ten imposing volumes in sage green morocco. I
had bought them along with a twelve-volume edition of
Doctor Johnson's Works (in contemporary sprinkled calf),
and had even read a few of the shorter *Lives of the Poets*
(such as Garth, Broome, Mallet, and Sprat). I had also
made a short-winded effort to read *Rasselas*. . . .

And now (disentangling the cord and rending the brown
paper wrappings) Pope's *Homer* had actually arrived. Six
folio volumes, first edition, and they had only cost fifteen
bob plus the postage. When I wrote for them (to a philan-
thropist named Cowler, at Reading) I made sure that
someone else would have snapped them up. But no; here
they were; in quite good condition, too. And how splendid,
to be able to read both Pope and Homer at once! Homer
had been impossible to enjoy in the fifth form at Ballboro',
but he would seem ever so much easier now. I resolved to
read exactly a hundred lines every day until I waded
through the whole six volumes. And when I'd marshalled
them on the top shelf—for they were too tall to fit into any
other—between the quarto sets of Smollett's *History of
England* and Tickell's *Addison*, I solemnly abstracted the
first volume of the Iliad and made a start.

> *The wrath of Peleus' son and that dire spring*
> *Of woes unnumbered, heavenly goddess, sing*. . . .

IV

To those who are expecting to see me in the saddle again
it may seem that I have delayed over-long in acquiring my
first hunter. But I take this opportunity of reminding my
invisible audience that there was no imperative reason why
I should ever have bought a horse at all; in fact candour
compels me to confess that if I had been left to my own
devices I should probably have spent the forty-five guineas
on something else. For though I was living so quietly and
paying Aunt Evelyn nothing for my keep, I never seemed

to have much of a balance at the bank. And Mr. Pennett, who appeared to consider me utterly irresponsible in matters of money, had so far refused to disgorge more than £450 a year out of my estimated income of £600. So, what with buying books and a new bicycle, and various other apparently indispensable odds and ends, I found myself "going in for economy" when early in January Dixon began his campaign to revive my interest in the stable.

During the winter I had been taking a walk every afternoon. I usually went five or six miles, but they soon became apathetic ones, and I was conscious of having no genuine connection with the countryside. Other people owned estates, or rented farms, or did something countrified; but I only walked along the roads or took furtive short cuts across the fields of persons who might easily have bawled at me if they had caught sight of me. And I felt shy and "out of it" among the local landowners—most of whose conversation was about shooting. So I went mooning, more and more moodily, about the looming landscape, with its creaking-cowled hop-kilns and whirring flocks of starlings and hop-poles piled in pyramids like soldiers' tents. Often when I came home for five o'clock tea I felt a vague desire to be living somewhere else—in 1850, for instance, when everything must have been so comfortable and old-fashioned, like the Cathedral Close in Trollope's novels. The weather was too bad for golf, and even "young" Squire Maundle was obliged to admit that the Amblehurst course was in far from first-rate condition. And there never seemed to be any reason for going to London, although, of course, there were interesting things to see there. (Aunt Evelyn was always intending to run up for the day and go to a matinee of Beerbohm Tree's new Shakespearean production.)

I seldom spoke to anyone while I was out for my walks, but now and again I would meet John Homeward, the carrier, on his way back from the county town where he went three days a week. Homeward was a friendly man: I always "passed the time of day" with him. He was a keen cricketer and one of Dixon's chief cronies. The weather and next year's cricket were the staple topics of our conversation. Homeward had been making his foot-pace journeys with his hooded van and nodding horse ever since I could remember, and he seemed an essential feature of the ten miles across the Weald to Ashbridge (a somnolent town which I associated with the smell of a brewery and the grim fact of people being hung in the gaol there). All the year round, whether there was snow on the ground or blossom on the fruit trees, the carrier's van crawled across the valley with its cargo of utilities, but Homeward was always alone with his horse, for he never took passengers. In my mind's eye he is invariably walking beside his van, for he always got out at the steep hill which winds down to the Weald. His burly figure and kindly bearded face must have gone up and down that hill about five thousand times before he retired to prosper with a small public-house. I used to wonder what he thought about while on the road, for he had the look of a man who was cogitant rather than vegetative. Dixon told me that he spent his whole time weighing the pros and cons of the half-crown bets which he made on races. In matters connected with the Turf he was a compendium of exact knowledge, and his profession allowed him ample leisure to make up his mind about likely outsiders and nicely handicapped horses at short odds.

Another feature of the local landscape was Joey, who worked on the roads, mostly at flint-breaking. I never knew his real name, though I'd known him by sight ever since I could remember. He was a lizard-faced man and the skin of his throat hung loose and shrivelled. I had named him Joey—in my mind—after a tortoise which I had owned when I was a child. Sitting on a heap of stones on the main road, alone with the humming telegraph poles and the clack of his hammer, he always saluted me as I passed, but I never conversed with him and he never seemed to get any older. He might have been any age between forty and seventy. . . .

But I must hurry myself along a bit, for it is high time that I was on the back of my new hunter.

*   *   *

On New Year's Day I was half-pedestrian and half-bicyclist, with no idea of being anything else. Within a week I found myself a full-blown horse-owner, and was watching Dixon exerting himself with a hammer and chisel as he opened the neat wooden case which contained a new saddle from that old-established West End firm, Campion & Webble. The responsibility for these stimulating occurrences rested with Dixon.

One morning after breakfast Miriam announced that Dixon had something he particularly wished to speak to me about and was waiting in the servants' hall. Wondering what on earth it would be, I asked her to send him up to the book-room. I was there before him; a minute or two later the sound of his deliberate tread was audible in the passage; he knocked portentously and entered respectfully, introducing a faint odour of the stables. He had an air of discreetly subdued excitement and there was a slight flush about the cheekbones of his keen face. Without delay he produced a copy of *Horse and Hound* from his pocket, unfolded it carefully, and handed it to me, merely saying, "I want you to have a look at *that*, sir." *That*, as indicated by his thumb, was the following item in Tattersall's weekly sale list.

"The Property of Cosmo Gaffikin, Esq., Harkaway III. Chestnut gelding; aged; sixteen hands; a good hunter; an exceptionally brilliant performer; well known with the Dumborough Hounds, with whom he has been regularly hunted to date. Can be seen and ridden by appointment with Stud Groom, Mistley House, Wellbrook."

I read the advertisement in a stupefied way, but Dixon allowed me no time for hesitation or demur.

"It struck me, sir, that you might do worse than go over and have a look at him," he remarked, adding, "I saw him run in the Hunt Cup two years ago; he's a very fine stamp of hunter."

"Did he win?" I asked.

"No, sir. But he ran well, and I think Mr. Gaffikin made too much use of him in the first mile or two." For lack of anything to say I re-read the advertisement.

"Well, sir, if you'll excuse me saying so, you don't get a chance like that every day."

An hour later Dixon had got me into the dogcart and was driving me over to Wellbrook—a distance of ten miles. It was a mild, grey morning, and as I felt that I had lost control over what was happening, there was no need to feel nervous about the impending interview. In response to my tentative inquiries Dixon displayed a surprisingly intimate knowledge of everything connected with Harkaway and his present owner, and when I suggested that the price expected would be too high for me he went so far as to say that he had very good reason to believe that he could be bought for fifty pounds.

When we arrived at Mistley House it soon became clear even to my unsuspicious mind that the stud groom had been expecting us. When Harkaway was led out of his stable my first impression was of a noticeably narrow animal with a white blaze on his well-bred and intelligent face. But I felt more impelled to admire than to criticize, and a few minutes later Mr. Gaffikin himself came clattering into the stable-yard on a jaunty black mare with a plaited mane. The stud groom explained me as "Mr. Sherston, sir; come over from Butley to have a look at Harkaway, sir". Mr. Gaffikin was about thirty-five and had a rather puffy face and full-sized brown moustache. He was good-humoured and voluble and slangy and easy going, and very much the sportsman. He had nothing but praise for Harkaway, and seemed to feel the keenest regret at parting with him.

"But the fact is", he explained confidentially, "the old horse isn't quite up to my weight and I want to make room for a young 'chaser. But you're a stone lighter than I am, and he'd carry you like a bird—like a bird, wouldn't you, old chap?"—and he pulled Harkaway's neat little ears affectionately. "Yes," he went on, "I don't mind telling you he's the boldest performer I've ever been on. Nailing good hunter. I've never known him to turn his head. Absolute patent-safety; I can guarantee you that much, Mr. Sherston."

Whereupon he urged me to jump on the old horse's back and see how I liked the feel of him. (He used the adjective "old" as if in the case of Harkaway age was an immensely valuable quality.) Conscious of the disparity between my untidy grey flannel trousers and Mr. Gaffikin's miraculously condensed white gaiters and perfectly cut brown breeches, I clambered uncouthly into the saddle. As I jogged out of the yard I felt myself unworthy of my illustrious conveyance. Conscious of the scrutiny of the experts whose eyes were upon me, I also felt that Mr. Gaffikin was conferring a privilege on me in affording me this facility for making up my mind about "the old horse". When I had been down to the gate and back again everyone agreed that Harkaway and myself were admirably suited to one another.

"I'm asking fifty for him—and he'd probably make a bit more than that at Tatts. But I'm awful keen to find the old chap a really good home, and I'd be glad to let you have him for forty-five," Mr. Gaffikin assured me, adding, "Forty-five *guineas*: it's very little for a horse of his class, and he's got many a hard season in him yet." I agreed that the price was extremely moderate. "Well, you must come in and have a bit of lunch, and then we can talk it over." But it was obvious that the transaction was as good as concluded, and Dixon had already made up his mind to put a bit more flesh on the old horse before he was much older.

That evening I composed a mildly defiant letter to Mr. Pennett, explaining that I had found it necessary to buy a horse, and asking him to provide me with an extra fifty pounds.

*   *   *

The arrival of Harkaway was a red-letter day for our uneventful household. Dixon and I had agreed to say nothing about it to Aunt Evelyn, so there was a genuine surprise when we were finishing our lunch two days later and Miriam almost fell through the dining-room door with a startled expression on her face and exclaimed, "Oh, sir, your horse has come, and he don't half look a beauty!"

"Good gracious, George, you don't mean to tell me you've bought a horse?" said Aunt Evelyn, fluttering up out of her chair and hastening to the window.

Sure enough, there was Harkaway with Dixon on his back, and we all three went outside to admire him. Aunt Evelyn accepted his advent with unqualified approval, and remarked that he had "such a benevolent eye". Dixon, of course, was beaming with satisfaction. Miriam hovered on the doorstep in a state of agitated enthusiasm. And altogether it seemed as if I had accomplished something creditable. Self-satisfied and proprietary, I stroked the old horse's neck, and felt as though in him, at least, I had an ally against the arrogance of the world which so often oppressed me with a sense of my inferiority. But the red-letter day was also a lawyer's letter day. My complacency was modified by Mr. Pennett's reply, which arrived in the evening. When I had carried it upstairs and digested it I had an uncomfortable feeling that the schoolroom was still the schoolroom in spite of its new and more impressive name. In fairness to the writer I must again quote his letter *in toto*, as he would have phrased it.

"Dear George, I confess I am disappointed with your letter. £450 a year is a big sum and should be more than ample for *all* your requirements. I do not propose to comment on the fact that you have found it necessary to buy a horse, although I am not surprised that you find that time hangs heavy on your hands. When I last saw you I told you that in my view the best thing you could do would be to qualify to be called to the Bar, that you should go into a barrister's chambers and work there steadily until you were called. The training is excellent, it gives you an insight into business matters, and enables you to acquire the power of steady concentration. I have also intimated to you as strongly as I could that you are wasting your time and energies in pursuing a course of desultory reading. I consider it a shame that a young fellow with your health and strength and more than average amount of brains should be content to potter around and not take up some serious calling and occupation. I venture to prophesy that this will one day be brought home to you and perhaps too late. My view is, 'Don't ride the high horse.' He won't carry you across country and the chances are you will come a cropper at your fences. Yours sincerely, Percival G. Pennett, P.S.—£50 is a large sum to spend for the object you propose. I am therefore paying into your account £35, which sum will be deducted from the next instalment of your income."

Dismissing the idea of working steadily in a barrister's chambers, which was too unpalatable to be dwelt on, however briefly, I wondered whether the truth of Mr. Pennett's prophecy would ever be "brought home to me". It was a nuisance about the money, though; but Harkaway had been brought home to me, anyhow. So I consolidated my position by writing out a cheque to Cosmo Gaffikin, Esq., there and then. After that I erected an additional barrier against the lawyer's attack on my liberties by settling down to a steady perusal of *Mr. Sponge's Sporting Tour*, which I had brought up from the drawing-room. And while I relished Mr. Sponge's desultory adventures I made up my mind to go out with the Dumborough Hounds as soon as I felt myself qualified to appear in public on my exceptionally brilliant performer.

*   *   *

If Mr. Pennett could have prevented me from purchasing Harkaway (or any other quadruped) he would have done so. It was his mundane duty as my ex-guardian and acting trustee. Nor can it be denied that Dixon's loyalty to his profession required him to involve me as inextricably as possible in all that concerned the equine race. Dixon had emerged victorious. A raw youth who refuses to read for the Bar is persuaded by the family groom to buy a horse. How tame it sounds! But there was a lot more in it than that—a statement which can be applied to many outwardly trivial events in life when one takes the trouble to investigate them. And while I am still at the outset of my career as a fox-hunting man, I may as well explain Dixon's method of collaborating with me in my progress toward proficiency. When I made my fresh start and began to ride the gallant old chestnut about the wintry lanes I was inwardly awake to the fact that I knew next to nothing about horses and hunting and was an indifferent rider. And Dixon knew it as well as I did. But his policy was to watch me learn to find my way about the fox-hunting world, supplementing my ignorance from his own experience in an unobtrusive manner. He invariably allowed me to pretend that I knew much more than I really did. It was a delicately adjusted, mutual understanding. I seldom asked him a straight question or admitted any ignorance, and he taught me by referring to things as though I already knew them. I can remember no instance when he failed in this tactful behaviour and his silences were beyond praise.

Meanwhile I am still reading *Mr. Sponge* in the schoolroom. But it must not be supposed that I launched myself in the hunting-field with unpremeditative temerity. Far from it. It was all very well to be reading about how Mr. Sponge bought a new pair of top-boots in Oxford Street sixty years ago. But the notion of my inexpert self acquiring such unfamiliar accoutrements seemed problematic and audacious. My trepidation blinded me to the obvious fact that bootmakers were willing, and even eager, to do their best for me. Nevertheless, I enjoyed dressing up as a sportsman, and the box-cloth gaiters which I had bought in Ashbridge were a source of considerable satisfaction when they encased my calves, and Miriam's long-suffering face looked in at the book-room door with "Your horse, sir"—for Dixon liked to bring the horse round to the front door when I was going out for a ride.

I always went out alone, for the driving horse was a nonentity and seldom appeared without the dogcart. Also, as I have already explained, I was making my equestrian experiment without active interference or supervision. When I got home again Dixon would ask, "Did he go all right?" and I would hang about the loose-box while Harkaway was being rubbed down. I always had a few things to tell Dixon about my two hours' exercise—how I'd been through the Hookham woods and had given him a nice gallop, and how I'd jumped the hedge by Dunk's Windmill on the way home (it was a very small hedge, and I lost a stirrup and very nearly fell off, but there was no need to mention that). And then we would agree that the old horse was looking grand and improving every day. It was also agreed that Mr. Gaffikin must have given him a pretty thick time out hunting and that a spell of easy work would do him all the good in the world.

Until the middle of February his reappearance with the hounds was not referred to. But one afternoon (when I had modestly admitted that we had jumped a small stile when taking the short cut between Clay Hill and Marl Place) Dixon interrupted his hissing to look up at me, and said in his most non-committal tone, "I see they're meeting at Finchurst Green on Tuesday." The significance of this remark was unmistakable. The next day I bicycled to Ashbridge and bought a pair of ready-made "butcher-boots".

*   *   *

Of all the pairs of hunting boots which I have ever owned, the Ashbridge pair remain vividly in my mind as a long way the worst. Judged by the critical standard which I have since acquired, their appearance was despicable. This was equalled by the difficulty of struggling into them, and the discomfort they caused while I wore them. Any long-legged "thruster" will tell you that a smart pair of boots is bound to cause trouble for the first few days. It is the penalty of smartness. (And I have heard of a young man with a broken ankle who, though almost fainting with the pain of his boot being pulled off, was able to gasp out: "Don't cut it; they're the best pair Craxwell's ever made for me.") But the Ashbridge boots, when I started for Finchurst Green, hung spurless on each side of Harkaway, stiff, ill-shaped, and palpably provincial in origin. And for some reason known only to their anonymous maker, they persistently refused to "take a polish". Their complexion was lustreless and clammy, although Aunt Evelyn's odd man had given them all the energy of his elbow. But it wasn't until I had surreptitiously compared them with other boots that I realized their shortcomings (one of the worst of which was their lack of length in the leg). A boot can look just as silly as a human being.

However, I had other anxieties as I rode to the meet, for I was no less shy and apprehensive than I had been on my way to the same place ten years earlier. At the meet I knew no one except Mr. Gaffikin, who came oscillating up to me, resplendent in his pink coat and wearing a low-crowned "coachy" hat cocked jauntily over his right ear. After greeting me with the utmost geniality and good-fellowship, he fell into a portentous silence; bunching up his moustache under his fleshy nose with an air of profound cogitation and knowingness, he cast his eye over Harkaway. When he had concluded this scrutiny he looked up and unforeseeably ejaculated, "Is that a Sowter?" This incomprehensible question left me mute. He leant forward and lifted the flap of my saddle which enabled me to blurt out, "I got it from Campion and Webble." (Sowter, as I afterwards discovered, is a saddle-maker long established and highly esteemed.) Mr. Gaffikin then gratified me greatly by his approval of Harkaway's appearance. In fact, he'd "never seen the old horse looking fitter". During the day I found that the old horse was acting as my passport into the Dumborough Hunt, and quite a number of people eyed him with pleased recognition, and reiterated his late owner's encomiums about his condition.

But as it was a poor day's sport and we were in the woods nearly all the time, my abilities were not severely tested, and I returned home satisfied with the first experiment. Harkaway was not a difficult horse to manage, but I did wish he would walk properly. He was a most jogglesome animal to ride on the roads, especially when his head was toward his stable.

*   *   *

Three nondescript days with the Dumborough were all the hunting I did on Harkaway during the remainder of that season. But the importance which I attached to the proceedings made me feel quite an accredited fox-hunter by the time Dixon had blistered Harkaway's legs and roughed him off in readiness for turning him out in the orchard for the summer. The back tendon of his near fore-leg was causing a certain anxiety. February ended with some sharp frosts, sharp enough to make hunting impossible; and then there was a deluge of rain which caused the country to be almost unrideable. The floods were out along the Weald, and the pollard willows by the river were up to their waists in water.

On one of my expeditions, after a stormy night, at the end of March, the hounds drew all day without finding a fox. This was my first experience of a "blank day". But I wasn't as much upset about it as I ought to have been, for the sun was shining and the primrose bunches were brightening in the woods. Not many people spoke to me, so I was able to enjoy hacking from one covert to another and acquiring an appetite for my tea at the "Blue Anchor". And after that it was pleasant to be riding home in the latening twilight; to hear the "chink-chink" of thrushes against the looming leafless woods and the afterglow of sunset; and to know that winter was at an end. Perhaps the old horse felt it, too, for he had settled into the rhythm of an easy striding walk instead of his customary joggle.

I can see the pair of us clearly enough; myself, with my brow-pinching bowler hat tilted on to the back of my head, staring, with the ignorant face of a callow young man, at the dusky landscape and its glimmering wet fields. And Harkaway with his three white socks caked with mud, his "goose-rump", and his little ears cocked well forward. I can hear the creak of the saddle and the clop and clink of hoofs as we cross the bridge over the brook by Dundell Farm; there is a light burning in the farmhouse window, and the evening star glitters above a broken drift of half-luminous cloud. "Only three miles more, old man," I say, slipping to the ground to walk alongside him for a while.

It is with a sigh that I remember simple moments such as those, when I understood so little of the deepening sadness of life, and only the strangeness of the spring was knocking at my heart.

V

I was now eager to find out all I could about riding and hunting, and it was with this object in view that I made up my mind to go to the Ringwell Hunt Point-to-Point Races. I had already been to the Dumborough Hunt Steeplechases on Easter Monday and had seen Mr. Gaffikin ride a whirlwind finish on his black mare. He was beaten by half a length, and I lost ten shillings. Even to my inexperienced eyes it seemed as if he was far too busy with his arms and legs as he came up the straight. He appeared to be trying to go much faster than his mount, and the general effect differed from what I had seen described in sporting novels, where the hero never moved in his saddle until a few strides from the post, when he hit his thoroughbred once and shot home a winner.

What with the crowds jostling in front of the bellowing bookmakers, the riders in their coloured jackets thrashing their horses over the fences and the dress and demeanour of the sporting gentlefolk, there was a ferocity in the atmosphere of Dumborough Races which made me unable to imagine myself taking an active part in such proceedings, although it was obviously the thing to do, and to win such a race as the Hunt Cup would be a triumph to which I could not even aspire.

So I went home feeling more warned than edified, and it was a relief to be reading Tennyson in my room while the birds warbled outside in the clear April evening, and the voice of Aunt Evelyn called to one of her cats across the lawn. But I still wanted to go to the Ringwell Point-to-Points, for Dixon had said that it was "a real old-fashioned affair", and from the little I had seen and heard of the Ringwell country I had got an idea that it was a jolly, Surtees-like sort of Hunt, and preferable to the Dumborough.

The Ringwell Hunt was on the other side of the Dumborough; its territory was almost double as large, and it was a four-day-a-week country, whereas the Dumborough only went out on Tuesdays and Saturdays. The races were being held about three miles from Downfield, the county town, which was in the middle of the Ringwell country. So in order to get there I had to bicycle nearly seven miles and then make the twenty-five mile train journey from Dumbridge to Downfield. It was a journey which subsequently became tediously familiar, but it felt almost adventurous on the fine mid-April day which I am describing.

In deference to the horsey events which I was intent on witnessing, I was wearing my box-cloth gaiters, and as I bicycled out of the unhunted Butley district I felt that I was indeed on my way to a region where things really happened. In fact, I might have been off to Melton Mowbray, so intense were my expectations. As the train puffed slowly into Sussex I eyed the densely wooded Dumborough country disparagingly. At the point where, so far as I could judge, there should have been a noticeable improvement, the landscape failed to adapt itself to my anticipations. The train had entered Ringwell territory, but there was still a great deal of woodland and little open country.

As we got nearer Downfield the country became more attractive-looking, and I estimated every fence we passed as if it had been put there for no other purpose than to be jumped by Harkaway. I had yet to become aware of the farmer's point of view. A large crowd of people riding over someone else's land and making holes in the hedges is likely to create all sorts of trouble for the Master of Hounds, but I had not thought of it in that way. The country was there to be ridden over. That was all. I knew that I ought to shut the gates behind me (and some of them were an awful nuisance to open, when Harkaway was excited), but it had not occurred to me that a hole in a fence through which fifty horses have blundered is much the same as an open gate, so far as the exodus of a farmer's cattle is concerned. However, this problem of trespassing by courtesy has existed as long as fox-hunting, and it is not likely to be solved until both the red-coated fraternity and the red-furred carnivorous mammal which they pursue have disappeared from England's green and pleasant land. But I was occupied with my speculations about the point-to-point course, and at Harcombe Mill, the last little station before Down-field, I got out of the train, lonely but light-hearted.

The direction of the course was indicated by a few gigs and other vehicles on the road, and by a thin stream of pedestrians who were crossing some upland fields by a foot-path. When I came to the crest of the hill I caught sight of some tents on a tree-clustered knoll about a mile away, and the course evidently made a big ring round this central point. A red flag stuck on the top of an oak tree was the only indication of a racecourse, though here and there a hairy-looking hedge had been trimmed for a space of a few yards.

An elderly labourer was sitting in a ditch eating his bread and cheese and I asked him which way they went.

"Ay, it's a tricky old course, and no mistake," he re-marked, "and the ground be terrible heavy down along the brook, as some of 'em'll find afore they're much older."

Following his directions I made my way from one ob-stacle to another, inspecting each one carefully. Most of them looked alarming, and though the brook was not quite so wide as I had expected, it had boggy banks. As there was still plenty of time before the first race I was able to go about half-way round the course before I joined the throng of people and carriages on the hillside.

The course, though I was not aware of it at the time, was one of the old-fashioned "sporting" type, and these races had a strong similarity to the original point-to-point which was run over a "natural" line of country, where the riders were told to make their way to some conspicuous point and back again as best they could. The Harcombe course was "natural" in so far as there were no flags stuck in the fences, a fair proportion of which had been left in that state which the farmer had allowed them to assume. This type of course has now been almost universally superseded by a much tamer arrangement where the riders usually go twice round a few fields, jumping about a dozen carefully made-up fences which can be galloped over like hurdles.

On the cramped Harcombe course there were nearly fifty obstacles to be surmounted, and most of them were more suited to a clever hunter than to an impetuous and "sketchy" jumper. Consequently these races were slower and more eventful than the scurrying performances which in most provincial hunts are still called point-to-point races. A course of the Harcombe type, though almost too interesting for many of the riders, had grave disadvantages for the spectators, who saw little except the start and the finish. But the meeting had a distinctive character of its own—the genuinely countrified flavour of a gathering of local people.

When I arrived at the centre of operations the farmers and puppy-walkers were emerging from the marquee where they had been entertained by the Hunt, and their flushed, convivial faces contributed to the appropriate atmosphere of the day. They had drunk the Master's health and were on the best of terms with the world in general. Had I been inside the tent as representative of the *Southern Daily News*, I should probably have reported the conclusion of his speech in something very like the following paragraph:

"He was glad to say that they had had a highly successful season. A plentiful supply of foxes had been forthcoming and they had accounted for fifty-eight and a half brace. They had also killed three badgers. He would like to repeat what he had said at the commencement of his speech, namely, that it must never be forgotten that the best friend of the fox-hunter was the farmer. (Loud applause.) And he took the liberty of saying that no hunt was more fortunate in its farmers than the Ringwell Hunt. Their staunch support of the hunt was something for which he had found it impossible to express his appreciation in adequate terms. An almost equal debt of gratitude was due to the Puppy Walkers, without whose invaluable aid the huntsman's task would be impossible. Finally he asked them to do everything in their power to eliminate the most dangerous enemy of the hunting-man—he meant barbed wire. But he must not detain them any longer from what promised to be a most interesting afternoon's sport; and amidst general satisfaction he resumed his seat."

*   *   *

I bought a race-card and went in the direction of "the paddock", which was a hurdled enclosure outside some farm buildings. Several people nodded to me in a friendly manner, which made me feel more confident, although it puzzled me, for I couldn't remember that I had seen any of them before. The first race was almost due to start, and the bookmakers were creating a background of excitement with their crescendo shoutings of "Even money the Field" and "Two to one bar one".

"I'll lay five to one Monkey Tricks; five to one Monkey Tricks," announced a villainous-looking man under a vast red umbrella—his hoarse and strident voice taking advantage of a momentary lull in the lung-bursting efforts of the ornaments of his profession on either side of him. "Don't forget the Old Firm!" he added.

Looking down from above the heads and shoulders of their indecisive clients, the Old Firms appeared to be urging the public to witness some spectacle which was hidden by the boards on which their names were gaudily displayed. The public, however, seemed vaguely mistrustful and the amount of business being done was not equivalent to the hullaballoo which was inciting them to bet their money.

There was a press of people outside the paddock; a bell jangled, and already the upper halves of two or three red- or black-coated riders could be seen settling themselves in their saddles; soon there was a cleavage in the crowd and the eight or ten competitors filed out; their faces, as they swayed past me, varied in expression, from lofty and elaborate unconcern to acute and unconcealed anxiety. But even the least impressive among the cavalcade had an Olympian significance for my gaze, and my heart beat faster in concurrence with their mettlesome emergency, as they disappeared through a gate in the wake of the starter, a burly, jovial-faced man on a stumpy grey cob.

"Having a ride to-day, sir?" asked a cadaverous blue-chinned individual, who might have been either a groom or a horse-dealer. Rather taken aback by this complimentary inquiry, I replied with a modest negation.

"I see your brother's riding Colonel Hesmon's old 'oss in the 'Eavy Weights. He might run well in this deep going," he continued.

I did not disclaim the enigmatic relationship, and he lowered his voice secretively. "I'm putting a bit on Captain Reynard's roan for this race! I've heard that he's very hot stuff." And with a cunning and confidential nod he elbowed his way toward the line of bookmakers, who were now doing a last brisk little turn of business before the destination of the Light Weight Cup was decided over "Three and a half miles of fair hunting country".

The card informed me that Lieut.-Col. C. M. F. Hesmon's Jerry was to be ridden by Mr. S. Colwood. "It can't be Stephen Colwood, can it?" I thought, visualizing a quiet, slender boy with very large hands and feet, who had come to my House at Ballboro' about two years after I went there. Now I came to think of it his father had been a parson somewhere in Sussex, but this did not seem to make it any likelier that he should be riding in a race.

At any rate, I wanted to see this Colwood, for whose brother I had been mistaken, and after the next race I walked boldly into the paddock to see the horses being saddled for the Heavy Weights. There were only five of them, and none of the five looked like going very fast, though all were obviously capable of carrying fourteen stone on their backs. But since one of them had got to come in first, their appearance was creating an amount of interest quite disproportionate to their credentials as racehorses, and their grooms and owners were fussing around them as if they were running in the Grand National.

"I've told the boy that if he wins I'll *give him the horse*," exclaimed an active little old gentleman with a straggling grey moustache and a fawn-coloured covert coat with large pearl buttons: his hands were full of flat lead weights, which he kept doling out to an elderly groom, who was inserting them in the leather pouches of a cloth which was to go under the saddle.

"Yes, the old fellow's looking well, isn't he?" he went on, dropping another lump of lead into the groom's outstretched hand. "I don't think I've ever seen him look fitter than he does to-day." He gazed affectionately at the horse, a dark bay with unclipped legs and a short, untidily trimmed tail.

People kept on coming up and greeting the affable and excited owner with cordial civility and he made the same remarks to each of them in turn. "Yes, I've told the boy that if he wins I'll *give him the horse*—are you quite sure those girths are all right, Dumbrell?" (to the groom, who was continuing his preparations with stoical deliberation) "and 'pon my word I'm not at all sure he won't win—the old fellow's fit to run for his life—never saw him look better —and I know the boy'll ride him nicely—most promising boy—capital eye for a country already—one of the keenest young chaps I've ever known."

"Well, Colonel, and how's the old horse?" ejaculated an exuberant person in a staring check suit and a protuberant canary-coloured waistcoat, extending an immense red hand toward the little man—who dropped the lead weights in a fluster with "Ah, my dear chap, how are you —how are you—delighted to see you"—followed by a reiteration of his repertoire about "the boy" and "the old horse".

The fact that this was Lieut.-Col. C. M. F. Hesmon was conveyed to me by the arrival of my former schoolfellow, Stephen Colwood. "Ah, there you are, my boy—that's capital," said the Colonel, moderating his agitation in order to adopt the important demeanour of an owner giving his final admonitions to a gallant young gentleman rider.

Stephen, who was wearing a pink silk cap and a long-skirted black hunting-coat, silently received from the groom the saddle and weight-cloth and disappeared into the weighing tent, accompanied by the Colonel, who was carrying a cargo of surplus lead. When they reappeared Stephen looked even more pale and serious than before. At the best of times he had a somewhat meditative countenance, but his face usually had a touch of whimsicality about it, and this had been banished by the tremendous events in which he was at present involved.

The combined efforts of Colonel and groom were now solemnly adjusting the saddle and weight-cloth (though it is possible that the assistance of the Colonel might have been dispensed with). Meanwhile the old hunter was standing as quiet as a carriage horse.

Stephen was holding the bridle, and in the picture which my memory retains of him at that moment he is looking downward at the horse's lowered head with that sensitive and gentle expression which was characteristic of him. It was nearly three years since I had last set eyes on him, but I had known him fairly well at school. As I watched him now I felt almost as nervous as if I were about to ride the Colonel's horse myself. I assumed that it was the first race he had ever ridden in, and I knew that he was feeling that if anything went wrong it would be entirely his own fault and that he would never be able to look the Colonel in the face again if he were to make a fool of himself. And he had probably been suffering from such apprehensions for several days beforehand. It was not surprising that he patted Jerry's philosophic profile with a visibly shaking hand. Then he looked up, and encountering my sympathetic gaze his face lit up with recognition. It was a time when he badly needed some such distraction, and he at once made me feel that I was an opportune intruder.

"Why, it's old Sherston!" he exclaimed. "Fancy you turning up like this!" And he gave me a wry grin which privately conveyed his qualms.

He told me afterwards that there were two things which he wished at that moment: either that the race was all over, or that something would happen to prevent it taking place at all. It is sometimes forgotten that without such feelings heroism could not exist.

He then made me known to the Colonel, who greeted me with a mixture of formality and heartiness and insisted that I must come round to his brake and have a glass of port and a sandwich after the race.

It seemed as though my diffident arrival on the scene had somehow relieved their anxieties, but a moment later the stentorian voice of the starter was heard saying, "Now, gentlemen, I'm going down to the post," and I stood back while Stephen was given a leg up by the groom. Then he bent his head to hear the Colonel's final injunctions about "not making too much of the running" and "letting him go at his own pace at the fences", ending with a heartfelt valediction. Stephen was then turned adrift with all his troubles in front of him. No one could help him any more.

Colonel Hesmon looked almost forlorn when the horse and his long-legged rider had vanished through the crowd. He had the appearance of a man who has been left behind. And as I see it now, in the light of my knowledge of after-events, there was a premonition in his momentarily forsaken air. Elderly people used to look like that during the War, when they had said good-bye to someone and the train had left them alone on the station platform. But the Colonel at once regained his spryness: he turned to me to say what a pity it was that the course was such a bad one for the spectators. Then he got out his field-glasses and lost consciousness of everything but the race.

*   *   *

The horses appeared to be galloping very slowly when they came in sight for the last time. I was standing up on the hill and couldn't see them distinctly. They had undoubtedly taken a long time to get round the course. Three of them jumped the last fence in a bunch, and Jerry was one of the three. For years afterwards that last fence was a recurrent subject of conversation in the Colwood family, but there was always a good deal of uncertainty about what actually happened. Stephen admitted that it was "a bit of a mix-up". Anyhow, one of them fell, another one pecked badly, and Jerry disengaged himself from the group to scuttle up the short strip of meadow to win by a length.

The Colonel, of course, was the proudest man in Sussex, and I myself could scarcely believe that Stephen had really won. The only regrettable element was provided by the dismal face of the man who was second. This was a Mr. Green, a lean and lanky gentleman farmer in a swallow-tailed scarlet coat—not a cheerful-looking man at the best of times. He made no secret of the fact that, in his opinion, Stephen had crossed him at the last fence, but as he never got beyond looking aggrieved about it no one really minded whether Mr. Green had been interfered with or not, and Jerry's victory appeared to be an extremely popular one. The Colonel was bombarded with cordialities from all and sundry, and kept on exclaiming, "I said I'd give the boy the horse if he won and I'm dashed glad to do it!"

Stephen, who now emerged after weighing in, wore an expression of dreamy enthusiasm and restricted himself to a repetition of one remark, which was, "By Gosh, the old horse jumped like a stag"; now and again he supplemented this with an assertion that he'd never had such a ride in his life. He gazed at the old horse as if he never wanted to look at anything else again, but the Colonel very soon piloted him away to the port and sandwiches. As they were going Stephen pulled me by the arm with, "Come on, you queer old cuss; you aren't looking half as bright as you ought to be." As a matter of fact I was thinking what a stagnant locality I lived in compared with this sporting Elysium where everything seemed a heyday of happiness and good fortune.

When we had regaled ourselves with the Colonel's provisions, Stephen led me off into the fields to watch the Farmers' Race, which was usually a very amusing show, he said. As we strolled along by ourselves I told him how I'd been mistaken for one of his brothers, and I asked what had happened to his family that day. He told me that both his brothers were abroad. Jack, the elder one, had gone to India with his regiment a month ago. The younger one was in the navy, and was with the Mediterranean Fleet.

"They're both of them as keen as mustard on the chase. It'll be pretty mouldy at the Rectory without them when hunting starts again," he remarked.

I asked why his father wasn't there to see him ride. His face clouded. "The Guv'nor'll be as sick as muck at missing it. Poor old devil, he had to take a ruddy funeral.

Fancy choosing the day of the point-to-points to be buried on!" . . .

*   *   *

It was after eight o'clock when I got home and Aunt Evelyn was beginning to wonder what had happened to me. I had enjoyed my day far more than I could possibly have anticipated, but my gentle and single-minded relative came in for nothing but my moody and reticent after-thoughts and I was rather ungracious to poor Miriam when she urged me to have a second helping of asparagus. Her face expressed mild consternation.

"What, no more asparagus, sir? Why it's the first we've had this year!" she exclaimed.

But I scowled at the asparagus as if it had done me an injury. What was asparagus to me when my head was full of the Colonel and his Cup, and the exhilarating atmosphere of the Ringwell Hunt? Why on earth had Aunt Evelyn chosen such a rotten hole as Butley to live in? Anyhow, Stephen had asked me to go and stay at Hoadley Rectory for the Polesham Races next week, so there was that to look forward to. And Aunt Evelyn, who had relapsed into a tactful silence (after trying me with the latest news from her bee-hives) was probably fully aware that I was suffering from the effects of an over-successful outing.

PART FOUR: A DAY WITH THE POTFORD

I

The summer was over and the green months were discarded like garments for which I had no further use. Twiddling a pink second-class return ticket to London in my yellow-gloved fingers (old Miriam certainly had washed them jolly well) I stared through the carriage window at the early October landscape and ruminated on the opening meet in November. My excursions to London were infrequent, but I had an important reason for this one. I was going to try on my new hunting clothes and my new hunting boots. I had also got a seat for Kreisler's concert in the afternoon, but classical violin music was at present crowded out of my mind by the more urgent business of the day.

I felt as though I had an awful lot to do before lunch. Which had I better go to first, I wondered, (jerking the window up as the train screeched into a tunnel) Craxwell or Kipward? To tell the truth I was a bit nervous about both of them; for when I had made my inaugural visits the individuals who patrolled the interiors of those eminent establishments had received me with such lofty condescension that I had begun by feeling an intruder. My clothes, I feared, had not quite the cut and style that was expected of them by firms which had the names of reigning sovereigns on their books, and I was abashed by my ignorance of the specialized articles which I was ordering. Equilibrium of behaviour had perhaps been more difficult at the boot-maker's; so I decided to go to Kipward's first.

Emerging from Charing Cross I felt my personality somehow diluted. At Baldock Wood Station there had been no doubt that I was going up to town in my best dark blue suit, and London had been respectfully arranged at the other end of the line. But in Trafalgar Square my gentlemanly uniqueness had diminished to something almost nonentitive.

Had I been able to analyse my psychological condition I could have traced this sensation to the fact that my only obvious connections with the metropolis were as follows: Mr. Pennett in Lincoln's Inn Fields (he was beginning to give me up as a bad job) and the few shops where I owed money for books and clothes. No one else in London was aware of my existence. I felt half-inclined to go into the National Gallery, but there wasn't enough time for that. I had been to the British Museum once and the mere thought of it now made me feel bored and exhausted. Yet I vaguely knew that I ought to go to such places, in the same way that I knew I ought to read *Paradise Lost* and *The Pilgrim's Progress*. But there never seemed to be time for such edifications, and the Kreisler concert was quite enough for one day.

So I asserted my independence by taking a hansom to the tailor's, which was some distance along Oxford Street. I wasn't very keen on taxicabs, though the streets were full of them now.

The lower half of Kipward & Son's shop window was fitted with a fine wire screening, on which the crowns and vultures of several still undethroned European Majesties were painted. In spite of this hauteur the exterior now seemed quite companionable, and I felt less of a nobody as I entered. A person who might well have been Mr. Kipward himself advanced to receive me; in his eyes there was the bland half-disdainful interrogation of a ducal butler; for the moment he still seemed uncertain as to my credentials. On the walls were some antlered heads and the whole place seemed to know much more about sport than I did. His suavely enunciated "what name?" made the butler resemblance more apparent, but with his, "Ah, yes, Mr. Sherston, of course; your coat and breeches are quite ready for you to try, sir", and the way he wafted me up a spacious flight of stairs, he became an old-fashioned innkeeper who had been in first-rate service, and there seemed nothing in the world with which he was not prepared to

accommodate me. To have asked the price of so much as a
waistcoat would have been an indecency. But I couldn't
help wondering, as I was being ushered into one of the fitting compartments, just how many guineas my black hunting-coat was going to cost.

A few minutes later I was sitting on a hard, shiny saddle
and being ciphered all over with a lump of chalk. The sallow little man who fitted my breeches remarked that the
buff Bedford cord which I had selected was "a very popular one". As he put the finishing touch with his chalk he
asked me to stand up in the stirrups. Whereupon he gazed
upon his handiwork and found it good. "Yes, that's a beautiful seat," he remarked serenely. I wondered whether he
would say the same if he could see me landing over a post-
and-rails on Harkaway. The artist responsible for my coat
was a taciturn and deferential Scotchman, stout, bald, and
blond. He, too, seemed satisfied that the garment would do
him credit. My sole regret was that I hadn't yet been asked
to wear the Hunt button. Downstairs in the dignified and
reposeful reception room the presiding presence was warming himself in front of a bright fire. As he conducted me to
the door I observed with secret awe some racing colours in
a glass case on the wall. In after years I recognized them as
being Lord Rosebery's.

Craxwell & Co. was a less leisurely interior. As might
have been expected, there was an all-pervading odour of
leather, and one was made to feel that only by a miracle
could they finish up to time the innumerable pairs of top-
boots for which they had received orders. The shop bristled
and shone with spurs; and whips and crops of all varieties
were stacked and slung and suspended about the walls.
Pace was indicated everywhere and no one but a hard-
bitten thruster could have entered without humility. A
prejudiced mind might have imagined that all Craxwell's
customers belonged to some ultra-insolent, socially snobbish, and libertine breed of military Mohocks. But the per-
centage, I am sure, was quite a small one, and my boots,
though awkward to get into at first, were close-fitting and
high in the leg and altogether calculated to make me feel

that there were very few fences I would not cram my horse at. In outward appearance, at least, I was now a very presentable fox-hunter.

Stephen Colwood had advised me to patronize those particular places, and it was no fault of his that I was still a comparative greenhorn. Anyhow, young Mr. Craxwell (who looked quite as much a gentleman as the self-satisfied sportsmen I saw in his shop) was kind enough to tell me that I had "a very good leg for a boot".

*　　　*　　　*

By the time I had put my bowler hat under my seat in the grand circle at Queen's Hall I was in a state of unsporting excitement about Kreisler. The name itself was suggestive of eminence, and I was aware that he was a great violinist, though I did not know that he would afterwards become the most famous one in the world. I was also unconscious that I was incapable of discriminating between a good violinist and a second-rate one. My capacity for admiration was automatic and unlimited, and his photograph on the programme made me feel that he must be a splendid man. I was influenced, too, by the audience, which showed its intensity of expectation by a subdued hubbub of talk which suddenly ceased altogether and was swept away by the storm of clapping which greeted the appearance of Kreisler.

That he was an eminent violinist was obvious, even to me, before he had played a single note of the Handel Sonata with which the concert began. There was something in the quiet and confident little swing of his shoulders as he walked on to the platform; something about the way he bowed with his heels together; something about his erect and dignified attitude while the accompanist flattened the pages of the music on the piano; this "something" impressed me very much. Then with a compact and self-possessed nod he was ready, and his lofty gaze was again on the audience.

During the serenely opening bars of the accompaniment both the bow and the violin were hanging from his left hand, and the inevitable gesture with which he raised the instrument to his chin seemed to sustain the rhythm of my excitement which reached its climax as I heard the first calm and eloquent phrase. The evergreen loveliness of the sonata unfolded itself, and Kreisler was interpreting it with tenderness and majesty. For him the concert was only one in that procession of recitals which carried him along on his triumphant career. But I knew then, as I had never known before, that such music was more satisfying than the huntsman's horn. On my way home in the train my thoughts were equally divided between the Kreisler concert and my new hunting things. Probably my new boots got the best of it.

II

Sitting by the schoolroom fire after tea on the last Saturday in November, I cleaned my almost new pipe (for I had taken to smoking, though I hadn't enjoyed it much so far) with a white pigeon's feather from the lawn.

I had got home early after a rotten half-day with the Dumborough. I'd had four days with them since the opening meet, and it was no use pretending that I'd enjoyed myself. Apart from the pleasure of wearing my self-consciously new clothes I had returned home each day feeling dissatisfied. It wasn't so much that the Hunt seemed to spend most of its time pottering round impenetrable woodlands as that the other subscribers appeared to be unwilling to acknowledge my existence except by staring me into a state of acute awareness of my ignorance of what was being done and how to do it. There was also the problem of Harkaway, who demonstrated more clearly every time I took him out that his stamina was insufficient for a hard day's hunting. It was only his courage which kept him going at all; in spite of Dixon's efforts in the stable the old horse was already, as he ruefully remarked, looking "properly tucked-up", and the long distances to the meets were an additional hardship for him.

As I lit my pipe I felt that I ought to be blissfully reconstructing the day's sport. But there seemed to be no blissful details to reconstruct. The hounds had run fairly well for about half an hour, but very little of it had been in the open. And I had been so busy hanging on to my excitable horse that I had only a hazy recollection of what had happened, except that Bill Jaggett had damned my eyes for following him too closely over the only jumpable place in a fence. Bill Jaggett was, to my mind, one of the horrors of the Hunt. He was a hulking, coarse-featured, would-be thruster; newly rich, ill-conditioned, and foul-mouthed. "Keep that bloody horse well out of my way," was a specimen of his usual method of verbal intercourse in the hunting-field. What with the vulgarly horsey cut and colour of his clothes and the bumptious and bullying manners which matched them, he was no ornament to the Dumborough Hunt; to me he was a positive incubus, for he typified everything that had alarmed and repelled me in my brief experience of fox-hunting. Except for the violent impression he made on my mind I should have said nothing about him; but even now I cannot remember his behaviour without astonishment. He was without exception the clumsiest and most mutton-fisted horseman I have ever observed. No horse ever went well for him, and when he wasn't bellowing at his groom he was cursing and cropping the frothing five-year-old which was carrying his fifteen stone carcass. (He usually rode young horses, since he flattered himself that he was "making" them to sell at a profit; but as he was short-sighted he frequently fell on his head and gave me the satisfaction of watching him emerge from a ditch, mud-stained and imprecating.) He took no interest in anything except horses and hunting, and it was difficult to believe that he had ever learnt to read or write.

He was one of a small contingent who fancied themselves as hard riders. Owing to the character of the country they always had to be looking for something to jump, whether the hounds were running or not, and they were often in trouble with Lord Dumborough for "larking" over unnecessary fences. In this they were conspicuous, for the other followers of the Hunt were a pusillanimous lot of riders, and there was always a queue of them at the gaps, over which they bobbed and bounced like a flock of sheep. Musing on my disappointing experiences, I decided that next week I would go and have a day with the Potford Hounds who were no further off than the Dumborough. They were said to be short of foxes, but Dixon had heard that their new Master had been showing good sport.

*   *   *

Elaborate arrangements had to be made for my day with the Potford. The distance to the meet was nearly fourteen miles, and Dixon decided that the best plan was for him to ride Harkaway over the night before. This outing was very much to his taste, and it was easy to imagine him clattering importantly into the yard at the Bull Inn with Harkaway's rug rolled on the saddle in front of him, and doing everything that was humanly possible to make the old horse comfortable in the strange stable. It is equally certain that, over his glass of beer, in the evening, he would leave no doubt in the minds of the gossips in the bar-parlour that his young gentleman was a very dashing and high-class sportsman. All this he would do with the sobriety and reticence of an old family servant; before going to bed he would take a last look at Harkaway to see whether he had finished up his feed.

Driving myself to the meet in the soft, cloudy morning, I enjoyed feeling like Mr. Sponge on his way to look at a strange pack. The only difference was that Sponge was a bold and accomplished rider and I was still an experimental one.

But my appearance, I hoped, would do Dixon no discredit, and on the seat beside me was my newest acquisition, a short leather hunting-crop with a very long lash to it. The length of the lash, though extremely correct, was an embarrassment. The crop had only arrived the previous day, and I had taken it out on to the lawn and attempted to crack it. But I was unable to create the echoing reports which hunt servants seemed to produce so effortlessly, and

my feeble snappings ended with a painful flick on my own
neck. So I resolved to watch very carefully and see exactly
how they did it. Big swells like Bill Jaggett never lost an
opportunity of cracking their whips when they caught sight
of a stray hound. I couldn't imagine myself daring to do
that or shout "Get along forrid" in such tremendous tones;
but it would be nice to feel that I could make the welkin
ring with my new crop if I wanted to. I had yet to learn
that the quiet and unobtrusive rider is better liked by a
huntsman and his assistants than the noisy and officious
one.

I wondered whether I should know any of the people out
with the Potford, and wished I had made a better job of
tying my white stock that morning. Tying a stock was very
difficult, especially as I didn't know how to do it. Mr.
Gaffikin's was wonderful, and I wished I knew him well
enough to ask him how the effect was produced.

I was keen to see what the new Master of the Potford
was like. Dixon had heard quite a lot about him. His name
was Guy Warder, and he was a middle-aged man who
hunted the hounds himself and did everything as cheaply
as possible. He bought the most awful old screws for next
to nothing at Tattersalls, made his stablemen ride them all
the way down from London to save the expense of a horse-
box, and brought them out hunting next day. It seemed
that the Hunt was already divided into factions for and
against him, and it was doubtful whether he would be
allowed to hunt the country another season. It was said
that he was a bad rider and always held on to the pommel
of his saddle when jumping his fences. It was also rumoured that he sometimes got very drunk. People complained that he was slow, and often drew the coverts on
foot. But he was popular with the farmers, and had been
killing an abnormal number of foxes.

There he was, anyhow, sitting low down in the saddle
among his hounds on a patch of grass in front of the Bull
Inn. He was a dumpy little man with a surly red face, and
he wore a coat that had once been scarlet and was now
plum-coloured. He was on a good-looking horse, but the

whips were mounted on under-bred and raw-boned animals which might well have been sent to the kennels for the hounds to eat. The hounds were dull-coated and hungry-looking. Evidently Mr. Guy Warder cared nothing for smartness.

Dixon saw me into the saddle with a quietly satisfied air and I rode out of the stable-yard. The first person I recognized was Bill Jaggett, who was hoisting himself on to the back of a slim, skittish, and startled-looking roan mare. He greeted me with a scowl and then remarked with a grunt, "You've brought your old skin over here, have you? Don't give him much rest, do you?" The sneer in his voice made me hate him more than ever, but I was too diffident and confused to reply.

With him was his boon companion, Roger Pomfret, a ginger-haired, good-for-nothing nephew of Lord Dumborough who blundered about the country on a piebald cob and vied with Jaggett in coarseness of language and general uncouthness. But Pomfret, who was impecunious and spent his spare time in dubious transactions connected with the Turf, had a touch of bumpkin geniality about him, and was an amiable and polished gentleman when closely compared with his unprepossessing associate, who, at that moment, was adjuring him (with the usual epithets) not to knock the guts out of that horse or he'd never lend him another (at the same time jogging his own mare unmercifully in the mouth and kicking her with one of his long spurs). "*Will* you stand still, you ——" but before the last word was out of his mouth the huntsman had shaken up his hounds with a defiant toot of the horn and was trotting down the road.

"The old rat-catcher doesn't allow much law, does he? It's only six minutes past eleven now!" remarked Pomfret, consulting his ticker with an oafish grin.

I dropped behind them, and was at once joined by Mr. Gaffikin, effusively cheerful, elbows well out, and a bunch of violets in his buttonhole. His friendliness revived my spirits, and he seemed to regard Jaggett and Pomfret as an excellent joke. "It's as good as a play when they start slanging one another," he said, eyeing their clumsy backs as they tip-tupped along.

He then told me, in an undertone, to keep pretty wide-awake to-day, as he'd heard that old Warder'd got something up his sleeve. He winked expressively. "I hear they've had one or two *very queer* foxes lately," he added. I wasn't sure what he meant, but I nodded sagaciously.

Nothing exciting happened, however, at the first covert. In accordance with his usual habit, the huntsman got off his horse and plunged into the undergrowth on foot.

"They say the old boy's got a better nose than any of his hounds," someone remarked.

In spite of my anxiety to avoid him, I found myself standing close behind Jaggett, who was bragging about a wonderful day he'd had "up at Melton" the week before. But I was feeling more at my ease now, and I was expressing this by swinging the lash of my crop lightly to and fro. The result was appalling. Somehow the end of it arrived at the rump of Jaggett's roan mare; with nervous adroitness she tucked in her tail with my lash under it. She then began kicking, and in my efforts to dislodge the lash I found myself "playing" Jaggett and his horse like a huge fish. The language which followed may be imagined, and I was flabbergasted with confusion at my clumsiness. When I had extricated my thong and the uproar had subsided to a series of muttered imprecations, I retreated.

To my surprise Mr. Gaffikin came up and congratulated me admiringly on the way I had "pulled Bill Jaggett's leg". He said it was the neatest thing he'd ever seen and he wouldn't have missed it for worlds. He slapped his leg in a paroxysm of amusement, and I modestly accepted the implication that I had done it on purpose. Guy Warder then emerged from his investigations of the undergrowth and blew his hounds out of covert.

"Where are you going now, Master?" shouted a sharp-faced man with a green collar on his cut-away coat.

"You'll find out when I get there," growled Warder, hunching his shoulders and trotting briskly down the lane.

Mr. Gaffikin explained that the green-collared man was

a notoriously tardy and niggardly subscriber. Nevertheless, we were apparently making an unexpected excursion, and people were audibly wondering what the old beggar was up to now. Anyhow, I gathered that we were heading for the best bit of the vale country, though it had been expected that we would draw some big woods in the other direction. After a couple of miles he turned in at a gate and made for a small spinney. Word now came back from the first whip that "an old dog-fox had been viewed there this morning". Half-way across the field to the spinney the Master pulled up, faced round, and exclaimed gruffly, "I'd be obliged if you'd keep close together on this side of the covert, gentlemen." He then cantered off with his hounds and disappeared among the trees.

"Stick close to me," said Mr. Gaffikin in a low voice. "The old devil's got a drag laid, as sure as mutton."

He was right. A minute afterwards there was a shrill halloa; when we got round to the far side of the spinney there was the huntsman going hell for leather down the slope with his hounds running mute on one side of him. With my heart in my mouth I followed Mr. Gaffikin over one fence after another. Harkaway was a bold jumper and he took complete control of me. I can remember very little of what happened, but I was told afterwards that we went about four miles across the only good bit of vale in the Potford country. The gallop ended with the huntsman blowing his horn under a park wall while the hounds scrabbled and bayed rather dubiously over a rabbit-hole. There were only eight or ten riders up at the finish, and the credit of my being among them belonged to Harkaway. Jaggett, thank heaven, was nowhere to be seen.

Warder took off his cap and mopped his brow. Then he looked with grudging good humour at the remnant of his field and their heaving horses. "Now let the bastards say I don't go well enough!" he remarked, as he slipped his horn back in its case on his saddle.

III

My successful scramble across the Potford Vale obliterated all the dreariness and disappointment of my days with the Dumborough. My faith in fox-hunting had been reinforced in the nick of time, and I joggled home feeling a hero. Highly strung old Harkaway seemed to share my elation. His constitution was equal to a fast hunt, but he needed to be taken home early in the afternoon. The long dragging days in the Dumborough woodlands wore him out. Even now he had a dozen miles to go to his stable, but they seemed short ones to me for I was thinking all the way how pleased Dixon would be. For the first time in my career as an independent sportsman I had a big story to tell him.

In the light of my mature experience I should say that I had very little to tell Dixon, unless I had told him the truth. The truth (which I couldn't have admitted, even to my inmost self) was that my performance had consisted not so much in riding to hounds as in acting as a hindrance to Harkaway's freedom of movement while he followed Mr. Gaffikin's mare over several miles of closely-fenced country —almost pulling my arms out of their sockets in the process. Had I told the truth I'd have said that during that gallop I was flustered, uncomfortable, and out of breath; that at every fence we jumped I was all over the saddle; and that, for all I had known, there might have been no hounds at all, since they were always a couple of fields ahead of us, and we were, most of us, merely following the Master, who already knew exactly which way they would go.

I lay stress on these facts because it is my firm belief that the majority of fox-hunting riders never enjoy a really "quick thing" while it is in progress. Their enjoyment, therefore, mainly consists in talking about it afterwards and congratulating themselves on their rashness or their discretion, according to their temperaments. One man remembers how he followed the first whip over an awk-

ward stile, while another thinks how cleverly he made use
of a lucky lane or a line of gates. Neither of them was able
to watch the hounds while they were running. And so it
was with me. Had I been alone I should have lost the
hounds within three fields of the covert where they started.

But my complacency had been unperturbed by any
such self-scrutinies when I clattered into the stable-yard
in the twilight, just as Dixon emerged from the barn with
a sieve of oats and a stable-lantern. His quick eyes were all
over the horse before I was out of the saddle.

"Going a bit short in front, isn't he?" was his first
remark.

I agreed that he *was* going a bit queer. Dixon had seen in
a moment what I had failed to notice in twelve miles. My
feeling of importance diminished. I followed the two of
them into the loose-box. Dixon's lantern at once discovered
an over-reach on the heel of one of Harkaway's front feet.
No reference was made to my having failed to notice it;
and as we said, it was a clean cut, which was much better
than a bruise. When asked whether it had been a good day,
I replied "Topping," but Dixon seemed in no hurry to
hear about it, and he went out to get the gruel. I stood
silent while the old horse drank it eagerly—Dixon remarking with satisfaction that he'd "suck the bottom out of the
bucket if he wasn't careful".

Unable to restrain myself any longer, I blurted out my
news: "They ran slap across the vale for about twenty-five
minutes; a five-mile point without a check. It must have
been seven or eight miles as they ran!"

Dixon, who was already busy brushing the dried mud
off Harkaway's legs, straightened himself with a whistle.
"Did you see it all right?"

"The whole way; there were only ten up at the finish."

"Did they kill him?"

"No, he got into a rabbit-hole just outside Cranfield
Park. The Master said it was no good trying to get him out
as it was such a big place." Dixon looked puzzled.

"That's funny," he remarked. "They told me at the
'Bull' last night that he's a great one for terriers and dig-

ging out foxes. A lot of the subscribers complain about it. They say he's never happy unless he's got his head down a rabbit-hole!"

With a knowing air I told him that Mr. Gaffikin had said it was a drag.

"By Jingo! If it was a drag they must have gone like blazes!" I asserted that they *did* go like blazes.

"You must have jumped some big places."

There was a note of surprise in his voice which made me feel that I had been doing more than was expected of me. Could it be possible, I wondered, that Dixon was actually proud of his pupil? And, indeed, there must have been a note of jubilation in his voice when, as he bent down to brush the mud off Harkaway's hocks, he asked: "Did Mr. Gaffikin see him jumping?"

"Yes. I foll——I was close to him all the way."

Perhaps it was just as well that Harkaway, munching away at his feed, was unable to lift his long-suffering face and say what *he* thought about my horsemanship! Looking back at that half-lit stable from the detachment of to-day, I can almost believe that, after I had gone indoors to my boiled eggs, Dixon and the old horse had a confidential chat, like the old friends that they were. Anyhow, the horse and his groom understood one another quite as well as the groom understood his master.

*   *   *

Aunt Evelyn did her best to come up to the scratch while I was talking big at the dinner-table. But the wonderful performances of Harkaway and myself during our exciting half-hour in the Potford Vale were beyond her powers of response, and her well-meant but inadequate interjections caused my narrative to lose a lot of its sporting significance. Anxiety for my safety overshadowed her enthusiasm, and when I was telling her how we jumped a brook (it was only a flooded ditch, really) she uttered an ill-timed warning against getting wet when I was hot, which nearly caused my narrative to dry up altogether.

Faithful Miriam made things no better by exclaiming,

as she handed me a plate with two banana fritters on it, "You'll break your neck, sir, if you go out with them hounds much oftener!"

What was the good of trying to make them understand about a hunt like that, I thought, as I blundered up the dark stairs to the schoolroom to dash off a highly coloured account of my day for Stephen Colwood. He, at any rate, was an audience after my own heart, and the only one I had, except Dixon, whose appreciation of my exploits was less fanciful and high-flown. Writing to Stephen I was at once away in a world of make-believe; and the letter, no doubt, was a good example of what he used to call my "well-known sprightly insouciance".

Poor Stephen was living in lodgings in London, and could only get home for a hunt on Saturdays. A wealthy neighbour had promised Parson Colwood an opening for his son if he could qualify as a chartered accountant, and this nauseating task occupied him five days a week. So my visualization of Stephen, exiled in a foggy street in Pimlico, made it doubly easy for me to scribble my lively account of a day which now seemed so delightfully adventurous.

Stephen's reply was a telegram asking me to stay at the Rectory for as long as I liked, and this was followed by a letter in which he announced that he'd got a month's holiday. "If your old nag's still lame I can get you some top-hole hirelings from Downfield for thirty-five bob a day, and I've ordered the Guv'nor to offer up prayers next Sunday forbidding the Almighty to send any frost to Sussex."

Aunt Evelyn considered this almost blasphemous; but she thought my visit to Hoadley Rectory an excellent idea, for Stephen was quite one of her favourites, and of the Rev. Colwood (whom she had met at a diocesan garden-party) she had the highest possible opinion. "Such a fine face! And Mrs. Colwood seemed a real fellow creature—quite one of one's own sort," she exclaimed, adding, "D'you mind holding his hind-legs, dear?" for she was preoccupied at the moment in combing the matted hair out of one of her Persian cats.

PART FIVE: AT THE RECTORY

I

Stopping at every station, a local train conveyed me sedately into Sussex. Local and sedate, likewise, were the workings of my brain, as I sat in an empty compartment with the *Southern Daily News* on my knees. I had bought that unpretentious paper in order to read about the Ringwell Hounds, whose doings were regularly reported therein. And sure enough the previous day's sport was described in detail, and "Among the large field out" was the name, with many others, of "Mr. Colwood, junr.". Although I had yet to become acquainted with the parishes through which Reynard had made his way, I read with serious attention how he had "crossed the Downfield and Boffham road, borne right-handed into Hooksworth Wood, turned sharply back, and worked his way over the country to Icklesfield," etc., etc., until "hounds ran into him after a woodland hunt of nearly three hours". The account ended with the following words: "If ever hounds deserved blood they did this time, as they had to work out nearly every yard of their fox's line."

Having read this through twice I allowed my thoughts to dally with the delightful prospect of my being a participator in similar proceedings next day. Occasionally I glanced affectionately at the bulging kit-bag containing those masterpieces by Craxwell and Kipward which had cost me more than one anxious journey to London. Would Stephen approve of my boots, I wondered, staring out of the window at the reflective monochrome of flooded meadows and the brown gloom of woodlands in the lowering dusk of a heavily clouded December afternoon.

Whatever he might think of my boots, there was no doubt that he approved of my arrival when the fussy little train stopped for the last time and I found him waiting for me on the platform. I allowed him to lug my bag out of the station, and soon he had got it stowed away in the old yellow-wheeled buggy, had flicked his father's favourite hunter into a trot ("a nailing good jumper, but as slow as a hearse"), and was telling me all about the clinking hunt they'd had the day before, and how he'd enjoyed my account of the Potford gallop. "You've got a regular gift for writing, you funny old cock! You might make a mint of money if you wrote for *Horse and Hound* or *The Field*!" he exclaimed, and we agreed that I couldn't write worse than the man in the *Southern Daily*, whose "Reynard then worked his way across the country" etc. afterwards became one of our stock jokes.

In describing my friendship with Stephen I am faced by a difficulty which usually arises when one attempts to reproduce the conversational oddities of people who are on easy terms. We adopted and matured a specialized jargon drawn almost exclusively from the characters in the novels of Surtees; since we knew these almost by heart, they provided us with something like a dialect of our own, and in our care-free moments we exchanged remarks in the mid-Victorian language of such character-parts as Mr. Romford, Major Yammerton, and Sir Moses Mainchance, while Mr. Jorrocks was an all-pervading influence. In our Surtees obsession we went so far that we almost identified ourselves with certain characters on appropriate occasions. One favourite role which Stephen facetiously imposed on me was that of a young gentleman named Billy Pringle who, in the novel which he adorns, is reputed to be very rich. My £600 a year was thus magnified to an imaginary £10,000, and he never wearied of referring to me as "the richest commoner in England". The stress was laid on my great wealth and we never troubled to remember that the Mr. Pringle of the novel was a dandified muff and "only half a gentleman". I cannot remember that I ever succeeded in finding a consistent role for Stephen, but I took the Surtees game for granted from the beginning, and our adaptation of the Ringwell Hunt to the world created by that observant novelist was simplified by the fact that a large proportion of the Ringwell subscribers might have stepped straight out of his pages. To their idiosyncrasies I shall return in due course: in the meantime I am still on my way to Hoadley Rectory, and Stephen is pointing out such fox-hunting features of the landscape as are observable from the high road while we sway companionably along in the old-fashioned vehicle.

*　　　*　　　*

"That's Basset Wood—one of our werry best Wednesday coverts," he remarked, indicating with the carriage-whip a dark belt of trees a couple of miles away under the level cloud-bars of a sallow sunset. He eyed the dimly undulating pastures which intervened, riding over them in his mind's eye as he had so often ridden over them in reality.

"We'll be there on Monday," he went on, his long, serious face lighting up as his gaze returned to the road before him. "Yes, we'll be drawing there on Monday," he chuckled, "and if we can but find a straight-necked old dog-fox, then I'll be the death of a fi'-pun'-note—dash my wig if I won't!"

I said that it looked quite a nice bit of country and asked whether they often ran this way. Stephen became less cheerful as he informed me that there was precious little reason for them to run this way.

"There's not a strand of wire till you get to the road," he exclaimed, "but over there"—(pointing to the left) "there's a double-distilled blighter who's wired up all his fences. And what's more, his keeper shoots every fox who shows his nose in the coverts. And will you believe me when I tell you, George my lad, that the man who owns those coverts is the same ugly-mugged old sweep who persuaded the Guv'nor to get me trained as a chartered accountant! And how much longer I'm going to stick it I don't know! Seven months I've been worriting my guts out in London, and all on the off-chance of getting a seat in the office of that sanctimonious old vulpicide."

I consoled him with a reminder that he'd spent most of August and September shooting and fishing in Scotland. (His father rented a place in Skye every summer.) And during the remainder of the drive we debated the deeply desirable and not impossible eventuality of Stephen's escape from chartered accountancy. His one idea was "to get into the Army by the back door". If only he could get into the Gunners he'd be happy. His elder brother Jack was in the Gunners, and was expecting to be moved from India to Ireland. And Ireland, apparently, was a fox-hunting Elysium.

"I really must have a chat with Colonel Hesmon about it. By the way, the dear old boy's asked us both to lunch to-morrow."

This led to a rhapsody about that absolutely top-hole performer Jerry, who had been given him by the Colonel after he'd won the Heavy Weight Race. My Harkaway on the other hand, was more a subject for solicitude, and I reluctantly confessed that he didn't seem up to my weight. It was a thousand pities, said Stephen, that I couldn't have bought that six-year-old of young Lewison's. "Given him for his twenty-first birthday by his uncle, who'd forked out £170 for him. But young Lewison couldn't ride a hair of the horse, though he was a nailing fine 'lepper' and a rare good sort at that. They sent him up to Tatts last week, and he went for £90, according to the paper. Gosh, what a bit of luck for the cove who got him so cheap!"

My appetite for horseflesh was stimulated by this anecdote, but I wondered what Mr. Pennett would say if I wrote and told him that I'd bought another ninety pounds' worth! For Mr. Pennett still refused to allow me more than £450 of my £600. The balance, he said, must be "invested for a rainy day".

*　　　　*　　　　*

Stephen's visionary contemplations of "being stationed at the Curragh and riding at Punchestown Races" were interrupted by our arrival at the Rectory. I had stayed there more than once in the summer, so I received a surly but not unfriendly salute from Abel, the grim little old groom with iron-grey whiskers who led our conveyance soberly away to the stable-yard. This groom was an old-fashioned coachman, and he had never been heard to utter a sentence of more than six words. His usual reply, when asked about the health of one of the horses, was either, "Well enough" or "Not over-bright". Stephen now re-minded him (quite unnecessarily, and probably not for the first time) that two of the horses would be going out hunt-ing on Monday. Abel grunted, "Got 'em both shod this afternoon," and disappeared round the corner of the shrub-bery with the buggy.

There was only one thing against him, said Stephen, and that was that he hadn't a ghost of an idea how to trim their tails, which were always an absolute disgrace. "I've told him again and again to *pull* the hair out," he remarked, "but he goes on just the same, cutting them with scissors, and the result is that they come out at the opening meet with tails like chrysanthemums!"

From this it may be inferred that there were many things in the Rectory stable which fell short of Stephen's ideal. He and his brothers were always trying to bring "the old guv'nor" into line with what they believed to be the Mel-ton Mowbray standard of smartness. There was also the question of persuading him to buy a motor car. But Parson Colwood was a Sussex man by birth and he valued his native provincialism more than the distant splendours of the Shires toward which his offspring turned their unso-phisticated eyes. The Rectory, as I knew it then, had the charm of something untouched by modernity.

The Rev. Harry Colwood, as I remember him, was a composite portrait of Charles Kingsley and Matthew Arnold. This fanciful resemblance has no connection with literature, toward which Mr. Colwood's disposition was respectful but tepid. My mental semi-association of him with Arnold is probably due to the fact that he had been in the Rugby eleven somewhere in the 'sixties. And I have, indeed, heard him speak of Arnold's poem, *Rugby Chapel*. But the Kingsley affinity was more clearly recognizable.

Like Kingsley, Mr. Colwood loved riding, shooting and fishing, and believed that such sports were congruous with the Christian creed which he unobtrusively accepted and lived up to. It is questionable, however, whether he would have agreed with Kingsley's Christian Socialism. One of his maxims was "Don't marry for money but marry where money is", and he had carried this into effect by marrying, when he was over forty, a sensible Scotch lady with a fortune of £1,500 a year, thereby enabling his three sons to be brought up as keen fox-hunters, game-shooters, and salmon-fishers. And however strongly the Author of his religion might have condemned these sports, no one could deny him the Christian adjectives gentle, patient, and just.

At first I had been intimidated by him, for the scrutinizing look that he gave me was both earnest and stern. His were eyes that looked straight at the world from under level brows, and there was strictness in the lines of his mouth. But the kindliness of his nature emerged in the tone of his voice, which was pitched moderately low. In his voice a desire for gaiety seemed to be striving to overmaster an inherent sadness. This undertone of sadness may have been accentuated as the result of his ripened understanding of a world which was not all skylarking and sport, but Stephen (who was a lankier and less regular-featured edition of his father) had inherited the same quality of voice. Mr. Colwood was a naturally nervous man with strong emotions, which he rigidly repressed.

When I arrived that afternoon both the Rector and his wife were attending some parochial function in the village. So Stephen took me up to the schoolroom, where we had our tea and he jawed to me about horses and hunting to his heart's content. He ended by asserting that he'd "sooner cheer a pack of Pomeranians after a weasel from a bath-chair than waste his life making money in a blinking office".

II

A tenor bell in Hoadley Church tower was making its ultimate appeal to those who were still on their way to morning service. While Stephen and I hurried hatless across the sloping cricket-field which divided the Rectory garden from the churchyard I sniffed the quiet wintry-smelling air and wondered how long Mr. Colwood's sermon would last. I had never been to his church before; there was a suggestion of embarrassment in the idea of seeing him in a long white surplice—almost as if one were taking an unfair advantage of him. Also, since I hadn't been to church with Aunt Evelyn for Heaven knew how long, I felt a bit of an outsider as I followed Stephen up the aisle to the Rectory pew where his matronly mother was awaiting us with the solemnly cheerful face of one who never mumbled the responses but made them as though she meant every word. Stephen, too, had the serene sobriety of an habitual public-worshipper. No likelihood of his standing up at one of those awkward places when everyone kneels down when you don't expect them to.

As the service proceeded I glanced furtively around me at the prudent Sunday-like faces of the congregation. I thought of the world outside, and the comparison made life out there seem queer and unreal. I felt as if we were all on our way to next week in a ship. But who was I, and what on earth had I been doing? My very name suddenly seemed as though it scarcely belonged to me. Stephen was sitting there beside me, anyhow; there was no doubt about his identity, and I thought what a nice face he had, gentle and humorous and alight with natural intelligence. I looked from him to his father who had been in the background, so far, since the curate had been reading the service (in an unemphatic businesslike voice). But the Rector's eye met mine, which shied guiltily away, and my wool-gathering was interrupted. Even so might his gaze have alighted on one of the coughing village children at the back of the church.

My sense of unfamiliarity with what was going on was renewed when Colonel Hesmon's wizened face and bushy grey eyebrows appeared above the shiny brass eagle to read the First Lesson. This was not quite the same Colonel who had been in such a frenzy of excitement over the point-to-point race eight months ago, when he had exclaimed, over and over again, "I've told the boy that if he wins *I'll give him the horse!*"

The Colonel's voice was on church parade now, and he was every inch a churchwarden as well. He went through the lesson with dispassionate distinctness and extreme rapidity. Since it was a long passage from Isaiah, he went, as he would have said, "a rattling good gallop". But the words, I thought, were incongruous ones when uttered by the Colonel. "And he will lift up an ensign to the nations from afar, and will hiss unto them from the end of the earth: and, behold, they shall come with speed swiftly: none shall be weary nor stumble among them; none shall slumber nor sleep; neither shall the girdle of their loins be loosed, nor the latchet of their shoes be broken: whose arrows are sharp, and all their bows bent, their horses' hoofs shall be counted like flint, and their wheels like a whirlwind: their roaring shall be like a lion, they shall roar like young lions: yea, they shall roar, and lay hold of the prey, and shall carry it away safe, and none shall deliver it. And in that day they shall war against them like the roaring of the sea: and if one look unto the land, behold darkness and sorrow, and the light is darkened in the heavens thereof. Here endeth the First Lesson." And the brisk little man turned over the leaves to a passage from Peter, arranged the gold-embroidered marker, and returned to his pew with erect and decorous demeanour.

Twenty minutes later Mr. Colwood climbed the pulpit steps to the strains of "O God our help in ages past". My own vocal contribution was inconspicuous, but I had a stealthy look at my watch, which caused Stephen, who was giving a creditable performance of the hymn, to nudge me with his elbow. The sermon lasted a laborious twelve minutes. The Rector had a nervous mannerism which consisted in his continually gathering up his surplice with his left hand, as if he were testing the quality of the linen with his fingers. The offertory was for a missionary society, and he took as his text: "*He that hath two coats, let him impart to him that hath none; and he that hath meat, let him do likewise.*" The results of the collection were handed to him on a wooden plate by the Colonel, who remarked afterwards at lunch that he "didn't mind saying that with the best will in the world he'd have preferred to give his half-sovereign to someone nearer home"—Stephen having already made his rather obvious joke—"Whatever the Guv'nor may say in his sermon about 'imparting', if I ever get a new hunting-coat I'm going to ruddy well keep my old one for wet days!"

The sun was shining when we emerged from the musty smelling interior. The Colonel, with his nattily rolled umbrella, perfectly brushed bowler hat, and nervously blinking eyes, paid his respects to Mrs. Colwood with punctilious affability; then he shepherded Stephen and myself away to have a look round his stables before lunch. We were there in less than five minutes, the Colonel chatting so gaily all the way that I could scarcely have got a word in edgeways even if I had felt sufficient confidence in myself to try.

The Colonel had been a widower for many years, and like most lonely living people he easily became talkative. Everything in his establishment was arranged and conducted with elaborate nicety and routine, and he took an intense pride in his stable, which contained half a dozen hunters who stood in well-aired and roomy loose-boxes, surrounded by every luxury which the Colonel's care could contrive: the name of each horse was on a tablet suspended above the manger. Elegant green stable-buckets (with the Colonel's numerous initials painted on them in white) were arranged at regular intervals along the walls, and the harness-room was hung with enough bits and bridles to stock a saddler's shop. It was, as Stephen pointed out to me afterwards, "a regular museum of mouth-gear". For the Colonel was one of those fussy riders with indifferent hands who are always trying their horses with a new bit.

"I haven't found the key to this mare's mouth yet," he would say, as the irritated animal shook its head and showered everyone within range with flecks of froth. And when he got home from hunting he would say to his confidential old head-groom: "I think this mare's still a bit under-bitted, Dumbrell," and they would debate over half the bits in the harness room before he rode the mare again.

"Sunday morning stables" being one of his favourite ceremonies, the Colonel now led us from one loose-box to another, commenting affectionately on each inmate, and stimulated by the fact that one of his audience was a stranger. Each of them, apparently, was a compendium of unique equine qualities, on which I gazed with unaffected admiration, while Stephen chimed in with "Never seen the old chestnut look so fit, Colonel", or "Looking an absolute picture", while Dumbrell was deferentially at hand all the time to share the encomiums offered to his charges. The Colonel, of course, had a stock repertory of remarks about each one of them, including how they had won a certain point-to-point or (more frequently) why they hadn't. The last one we looked at was a big well-bred brown horse who stood very much "over at the knees". The Colonel had hunted him twelve seasons and he had an equivalently long rigmarole to recite about him, beginning with "I remember Sam Hames saying to me (I bought him off old Hames of Leicester, you know)—that horse is the most natural jumper I've ever had in my stable. And he was right, for the old horse has only given me one bad toss in twelve years, and that was no fault of his own, for he landed on the stump of a willow tree; it was at that rough fence just outside Clout's Wood—nasty place, too—you remember I showed it you the other day, Steve"; all of which Stephen had probably heard fifty times before, and had been shown the "nasty place" half a dozen times into the bargain. It was only when he heard the distant booming of the luncheon-gong that the Colonel was able to tear himself away from the brown horse's loose-box.

While going into the house we passed through what he

called "the cleaning room", which was a sort of wide corridor with a skylight to it. Along the wall stood an astonishing array of hunting boots. These struck me as being so numerous that I had the presence of mind to count them. There were twenty-seven pairs. Now a good pair of top-boots, if properly looked after and repaired, will last the owner a good many years; and a new pair once in three years might be considered a liberal allowance for a man who has started with two or three pairs. But the Colonel was nothing if not regular in his habits; every autumn he visited, with the utmost solemnity, an illustrious bootmaker in Oxford Street; and each impeccable little pair of boots had signalized the advent of yet another opening meet. And, since they had been impeccably cared for and the Colonel seldom hunted more than three days a week, they had consequently accumulated. As we walked past them it was as though Lord Roberts were inspecting the local Territorials, and the Colonel would have been gratified by the comparison to the gallant Field-Marshal.

It did not strike me at the time that there was something dumbly pathetic about those chronological boots with their mahogany, nut-brown, and salmon-coloured tops. But I can see now that they symbolized much that was automatic and sterile in the Colonel's career. He had retired from the Army twenty years before, and was now sixty-six, though active and well preserved. And each of those twenty years had been as stereotyped as his ideas. The notions on which he had patterned himself were part regimental and part sporting. As a military man he was saturated with the Balaclava spirit, and one could also imagine him saying, "Women and children first" on a foundering troopship (was it the *Warren Hastings* which went down in the early 'nineties?). But the Boer War had arrived seven years too late for him, and the gist of the matter was that he'd never seen any active service. And somehow, when one came to know him well, one couldn't *quite* imagine him in the Charge of the Light Brigade: but this may have been because, in spite of the dashing light-cavalry tone of his talk, he had served in a line regiment, and not at all a smart one either. (His affluence dated from the day when he had married where money was.)

As a sportsman he had modelled himself on what I may call the Whyte-Melville standard. His conversational behaviour echoed the sentiments and skylarking vivacities of mid-Victorian sporting novels and the coloured prints of a slightly earlier period. And yet one could no more imagine him participating in a moonlight steeplechase than one could visualize him being shot through the Bible in his breast pocket in a death or glory attack. Like many chivalrous spirits, he could never quite live up to the ideal he aimed at. He was always talking about "Brooksby", a hard-riding journalist who, in the Colonel's heyday, had written regularly for *The Field*. He had several volumes of these lively scribblings and he had read and re-read them in his solitary evenings until he knew the name of every gorse-covert and woodland in the Shires.

But, as Stephen might have said (if he'd been capable of relaxing his admirable loyalty to his god-father) "The dear old Colonel's always bucking about Leicestershire, but I don't suppose he's had half a dozen days there since he was foaled!" And when the Colonel asked one to dine at "the Club" ("You'll always find me in town in Ascot week, my dear boy") "the Club" (he had two) wasn't quite up to the standard he set himself, since instead of being that full-blown fogeydom "The Naval and Military", it had to face things out as merely ("Capital Club! Lot of nice young chaps there!") "the Junior".

On this special Sunday, however, I could still estimate the Colonel's importance as being equivalent to twenty-seven pairs of top-boots. In fact, I thought him a terrific swell, and it wouldn't have surprised me to hear that he'd won the Grand National when he was a gallant young sub-altern. At luncheon (roast beef and apple tart) he was the most attentive of hosts, and by the time we had finished our port—("I think you'll find this a nice light-bodied wine. I get it through the Club")—he had given most of his favourite anecdotes an airing. While the decanter was on its way round Stephen tackled him about the miseries of learning to be a chartered accountant. The lament was well received, and when he said, "I've been wondering, Colonel, whether I couldn't possibly get into the Gunners through the Special Reserve," the idea was considered a capital one.

The Colonel's face lit up: "I tell you what, my boy, I'll write at once to an old friend of mine at the War Office. Excellent officer—used to be in the 'Twenty-Third'. Very useful man on a horse, too."

Warmed up by the thought of Stephen getting a commission, he asked me whether I was in the Yeomanry. Reluctantly confessing that I wasn't, I added that I'd been thinking about it; which was true, and the thought had filled me with unutterable alarm. When we rose from our chairs the Colonel drew my attention to the oil-paintings which adorned the walls. These were portraits of his past and present hunters—none of whom, apparently, "knew what it was to put a foot wrong". Among many other relics and associative objects which he showed us was a large green parrot which he "had bought from a sailor five-and-twenty years ago". He had taught the bird to ejaculate "Tear 'im and eat 'im", and other hunting noises. Finally, with a certain access of grand seigneur dignity, he waved to us from his front doorstep and vanished into the house, probably to write a letter to his old friend at the War Office.

III

At nine o'clock next morning my cold fingers were making their usual bungling efforts to tie a white stock neatly; but as I had never been shown how to do it, my repeated failures didn't surprise me, though I was naturally anxious not to disgrace the Rectory on my first appearance at a meet of the Ringwell Hounds. The breakfast bell was supplemented by Stephen's incitements to me to hurry up; these consisted in cries of "Get-along-forrid" and similar hunt-servant noises, which accentuated my general feeling that I was in for a big day. While I was putting the final touches to my toilet I could hear him shouting to the two Scotch terriers who were scuttling about the lawn: (he was out there having a look at that important thing, the weather.)

Fully dressed and a bit flurried, I stumped downstairs and made for the low buzz of conversation in the dining-room. Purposing to make the moderately boisterous entry appropriate to a hunting morning, I opened the door. After a moment of stupefaction I recoiled into the passage, having beheld the entire household on its knees, with backs of varying sizes turned toward me: I had entered in the middle of the Lord's Prayer. After a temporizing stroll on the lawn I re-entered the room unobtrusively; Stephen handed me a plate of porridge with a grin and no other reference was made to my breach of decorum.

After breakfast he told me that I'd no more idea of tying a stock than an ironmonger; when he had re-tied it for me he surveyed the result with satisfaction and announced that I now "looked ready to compete against all the cutting and thrusting soldier-officers in creation".

By a quarter past ten the Rector was driving me to the meet in the buggy—the groom having ridden his horse on with Stephen, who was jogging sedately along on Jerry. The Rector, whose overcoat had an astrakhan collar, was rather reticent, and we did the five miles to the meet without exchanging many remarks. But it was a comfort, after my solitary sporting experiments, to feel that I had a couple of friendly chaperons, and Stephen had assured me that my hireling knew his way over every fence in the country and had never been known to turn his head. My only doubt was whether his rider would do him credit. We got to the meet in good time, and Mr. Whatman, a very large man who kept a very large livery-stable and drove a coach in the summer, was loquacious about the merits of my hireling, while he supervised my settlement in the saddle, which felt a hard and slippery one.

As I gathered up the thin and unflexible reins I felt that he was conferring a privilege on me by allowing me to ride the horse—a privilege for which the sum of thirty-five shillings seemed inadequate repayment. My mount was a wiry, nondescript-coloured animal, sober and unexcitable. It was evident from the first that he knew much more about the game than I did. He was what is known as a "safe conveyance" or "patent safety"; this more than atoned for his dry-coated and ill-groomed exterior. By the time I had been on his back an hour I felt more at home than I had ever done when out with the Dumborough.

The meet was at "The Five Bells", a wayside inn close to Basset Wood, which was the chief stronghold of fox-preservation in that part of the Ringwell country. There was never any doubt about finding a fox at Basset. Almost a mile square, it was well-rided and easy to get about in, though none too easy to get a fox away from. It was also, as Stephen remarked when we entered it, an easy place to get left in unless one kept one's eyes and ears skinned. And his face kindled at the delightful notion of getting well away with the hounds, leaving three parts of the field coffee-housing at the wrong end of the covert. It was a grey morning, with a nip in the air which made him hopeful that "hounds would fairly scream along" if they got out in the open and, perhaps for the first time in my life, I felt a keen pleasure in the idea of sitting down and cramming my horse at every obstacle that might come in our way.

In the meantime I had got no more than a rough idea of the seventy or eighty taciturn or chattering riders who were now making their way slowly along the main-ride while the huntsman could be heard cheering his hounds a little way off among the oaks and undergrowth. I had already noticed several sporting farmers in blue velvet caps and long-skirted black coats of country cut. And scarlet-coated Colonel Hesmon had proffered me a couple of brown-gloved fingers with the jaunty airified manner of a well-dressed absent-minded swell. He was on his corky little grey cob, and seemed to be having rather a rough ride. In fact the impetuous behaviour of the cob suggested that the Colonel had yet to find the key to his mouth.

An open space toward the top end of the wood formed a

junction of the numerous smaller paths which were tributaries of that main channel—the middle-ride. At this point of vantage a few of the more prominent characters from among the field had pulled up, and since the hounds had yet to find a fox I was able to take a few observations of people who afterwards became increasingly familiar to me in my mental conspectus of the Ringwell Hunt. Among them was the Master, of whom there is little to be said except that he was a rich man whose resignation was already rumoured. His only qualification was his wealth, and he had had the bad luck (or bad judgment) to engage a bad huntsman. Needless to say the Master's perplexities had been aggravated by the criticisms and cavillings of subscribers who had neither the wealth, knowledge, nor initiative necessary for the office which this gentleman had found so ungrateful. Much of this I had already learned at the Rectory, where he was given his due for having done his best to hunt the country in handsome style. Sitting there that morning on a too-good-looking, well-bred horse, he seemed glum and abstracted, as though he suspected that most of his field would poke fun at him when his back was turned. One of his troubles was that he'd never learnt how to blow his horn properly, and his inexpert tootlings afforded an adequate excuse for those who enjoyed ridiculing him.

Chief among these was Nigel Croplady. When I first observed him he was sitting sideways on his compact short-tailed brown horse; a glossy top-hat was tilted over his nose. His supercilious, clean-shaven face was preoccupied with a loose-lipped inspection of his own left leg; his boot-tops were a delicate shell-pink, and his well-cleaned white "leathers" certainly justified his self-satisfied scrutiny of them.

"That blighter's always talking about getting a flying-start," remarked Stephen in an undertone, "but when hounds run he's the most chicken-hearted skirter in Sussex." I was able to verify this later in the day when I saw him go irresolutely at a small fence on a bank, pull his horse across it with a shout of "'Ware wire!" and hustle away in search of a gate, leaving a hard-riding farmer to take it in his stride—the wire having been an improvisation of Croplady's over-prudent mind.

The group which I was watching also included two undemonstrative elderly men (both of whom, said Stephen, were fifty pound subscribers and important covert owners) and several weather-beaten ladies, none of whom looked afraid of a liberal allowance of mud and water.

The Rev. Colwood (who was on a one-eyed screw which his soldier-son had picked up for seventeen pounds at a sale of Army remounts) now joined the group. He was sitting well forward in the saddle with the constrained look of a man who rather expects his horse to cross its front legs and pitch him over its head. Beside him, on a plump white weight-carrier, was a spare-built middle-aged man in a faded pink coat who scattered boisterous vociferations on everybody within hail. "Morning, Master. Morning Mrs. Moffat. Morning, Nigel!" His beaming recognitions appeared to include the whole world in a sort of New Year's Day greeting. And, "Hallo, Stephen ole man," he shouted, turning in our direction so suddenly that his animal's rotund hind quarters bumped the Rector's horse on his blind side and nearly knocked him over. The collision culminated when he grabbed my hand and wrung it heartily with the words, "Why, Jack, my lad, I thought you were still out in India!" I stared at him astonished, while his exuberance became puzzled and apologetic.

"*Is* it Jack?" he asked, adding, with a loud laugh, "No, it's some other young bloke after all. But you're the living split of Steve's elder brother—say what you like!"

In this way I became acquainted with one of the most popular characters in the Hunt. Arthur Brandwick was a doctor who had given up his small country practice some years before. "Always merry and bright" was his motto, and he now devoted his bachelor energies to the pursuit of the fox and the conversion of the human race to optimism.

A solemn purple-faced man, who had been eyeing me as if he also had his doubts about my identity, now came up and asked me for a sovereign. This was Mr. McCosh, the

Hunt secretary, and it was my first experience of being "capped" as a stranger. I produced the gold coin, but he very civilly returned it when Stephen informed him that I was staying at the Rectory.

Just as these negotiations concluded, a chorus of excited hallooings on the outskirts of the wood proclaimed that Reynard had been viewed by some pedestrians.

"Those damned foot people again! I'll bet a tenner they've headed him back!" sneered Croplady, whose contempt for the lower classes was only equalled by his infatuation for a title. (His family were old-established solicitors in Downfield, but Nigel was too great a swell to do much work in his father's office, except to irritate the clients, many of whom were farmers, with his drawling talk and dandified manners.)

"Come on, Snowball!" exclaimed Brandwick, shaking his corpulent white steed into a canter, and away he went along the main-ride, ramming his hat down on his head with the hand that held his whip and scattering mud in every direction.

"Chuckle-headed old devil! Mad as a hatter but as kind-hearted as they make 'em," said Stephen, watching him as he dipped in and out of the hollows with his coat-tails flapping over his horse's wide rump. And without any undue haste he started off along one of the smaller rides with myself and my hireling at his heels.

Everybody hustled away into the wood except the stolid secretary and two other knowledgeable veterans. Having made up their minds that the fox would stick to the covert, they remained stock-still like equestrian statues, watching for him to cross the middle-ride. They were right. Fox-hunting wiseacres usually are (though it was my wilful habit in those days to regard everyone who preferred going through a gate to floundering over a fence as unworthy of the name of sportsman).

Later on, while Stephen and I were touring the covert with our ears open, we overtook a moody faced youth on a handsome bay horse. "Hullo, Tony! I thought you'd parted with that conspicuous quad of yours at Tatts last week," exclaimed Stephen, riding robustly up alongside of him and giving the bay horse a friendly slap on his hind quarters.

Young Lewison (I remembered what Stephen had said about him and the expensive hunter which he "couldn't ride a hair of") informed us that the horse had been bought by a Warwickshire dealer and then returned as a slight whistler. "I'm sick of the sight of him," he remarked, letting the reins hang listlessly on the horse's neck.

Gazing at the nice-looking animal, I inwardly compared him with dear old Harkaway. The comparison was all in favour of the returned whistler, whose good points were obvious even to my inexperienced eyes. In fact, he was almost suspiciously good-looking, though there was nothing flashy about his fine limbs, sloping shoulders, and deep chest.

"His wind can't be very bad if you'd never noticed it," remarked Stephen, eyeing him thoughtfully, "and he certainly does look a perfect gentleman."

Meanwhile the horse stood there as quiet as if he were having his picture painted. "I wish to goodness someone would give me fifty pounds for him," exclaimed Lewison petulantly, and I had that queer sensation when an episode seems to have happened before. The whole scene was strangely lit up for me; I could have sworn that I knew what he was going to say before a single word was out of his mouth. And when, without a second's hesitation, I replied, "*I'll* give you fifty pounds for him," I was merely overhearing a remark which I had already made.

Young Lewison looked incredulous; but Stephen intervened, with no sign of surprise, "Damn it, George, you might do worse than buy him, at that price. Hop off your hireling and see what he feels like."

I had scarcely settled myself in the new saddle when there was a shrill halloa from a remote side of the covert. We galloped away, leaving Lewison still whoaing on one leg round the hireling, who was eager to be after us.

"Well, I'm jiggered! What an enterprising old card you are!" ejaculated Stephen, delightedly slapping his leg with his crop and then leaning forward to listen for the defect in the bay horse's wind. "Push him along, George," he added; but we were already galloping freely, and I felt much more like holding him back. "Dashed if *I* can hear a ghost of a whistle!" muttered Stephen, as we pulled up at a hunting-gate out of Basset Wood.

"We're properly left this time, old son." He trotted down the lane and popped over a low heave-gate into a grass field. My horse followed him without demur. There wasn't a trace of the hunt in sight, but we went on, jumping a few easy fences, and my heart leapt with elation at the way my horse took them, shortening and then quickening his stride and slipping over them with an ease and neatness which were a revelation to me.

"This horse is an absolute dream!" I gasped as Stephen stopped to unlatch a gate.

But Stephen's face now looked fit for a funeral. "They must have run like stink and we've probably missed the hunt of the season," he grumbled.

A moment later his face lit up again. "There's the horn —right-handed—over by the Binsted covers!" And away he went across a rushy field as fast as old Jerry could lay legs to the ground.

A lot of hoof-marks and a gap in a big boundary fence soon showed us where the hunt had gone. We were now on some low-lying meadows, and he said it looked as if we'd have to jump the Harcombe brook. As we approached it there was a shout from downstream and we caught sight of someone in distress. A jolly faced young farmer was up to his arm-pits in the water with his horse plunging about beside him.

"Hullo, it's Bob Millet and his tubed mare!" Stephen jumped off Jerry and hurried to the rescue.

"I'm having the devil's own job to keep the water out of my mare," shouted Millet, who didn't seem to be worrying much about getting soaked to the skin.

"Haven't you got a cork?" inquired Stephen.

"No, Mr. Colwood, but I'm keeping my finger on the hole in her neck. She'll be drowned if I don't."

This peculiar situation was solved by Stephen, who held the mare by her bridle and skilfully extricated her after several tremendous heaves and struggles.

We then crossed the brook by a wooden bridge a few hundred yards away—young Millet remarking that he'd never come out again without his cork. Soon afterwards we came up with the hounds, who had lost their fox and were drawing the Binsted covers without much enthusiasm. Colonel Hesmon commiserated with us for having missed "quite a pretty little dart in the open". If he'd been on his brown mare, he said, he'd have had a cut at the Harcombe brook. "But this cob of mine won't face water", he remarked, adding that he'd once seen half the Quorn field held up by a brook you could have jumped in your boots.

*　　　*　　　*

The huntsman now enlivened the deflated proceedings by taking his hounds to a distant holloa on the other side of the brook. A man on a bicycle had viewed our fox returning to Basset Wood. The bicyclist (Stephen told me as we passed him in the lane where he'd been providing the flustered huntsman with exact information) was none other than the genius who reported the doings of the Hunt for the *Southern Daily News*. In the summer he umpired in county cricket matches, which caused me to regard him as quite a romantic personality.

While they were hunting slowly back to the big wood on a very stale line, young Lewison reappeared on my hireling. Looking more doleful than ever, he asked how I liked Cockbird. Before I had time to answer Stephen interposed with "He makes a distinct noise, Tony, and his wind's bound to get worse. But my friend Sherston likes the feel of him and he'll give you fifty."

I concealed my surprise. Stephen had already assured me that the whistle was so slight as to be almost undetectable. He had also examined Cockbird's legs and pronounced them perfect. Almost imperceptible, too, was the wink with which Stephen put me wise about his strategic

utterance, and I met Lewison's lack-lustre eyes with contrived indifference as I reiterated my willingness to give
him fifty. Internally, however, I was in a tumult of eagerness to call Cockbird my own at any price, and when my
offer had been definitely accepted nothing would induce
me to get off his back. We soon arranged that Mr. Whatman's second horseman should call for the hireling at
Lewison's house on his way back to Downfield.

"We'll send you your saddle and bridle to-morrow,"
shouted Stephen, as Cockbird's ex-owner disappeared
along the lane outside Basset Wood. "Tony never thinks
of anything except getting home to his tea," he added.

We then exchanged horses, and though the hounds did
very little more that afternoon, our enthusiasm about my
unexpected purchase kept our tongues busy; we marvelled
more and more that anyone could be such a mug as to part
with him for fifty pounds. As we rode happily home to the
Rectory, Cockbird jogged smoothly along with his ears
well forward. Demure and unexcited, he appeared neither
to know nor to care about his change of ownership.

* * *

"Mr. Pennett can go to blazes!" I said to myself, while
I was blissfully ruminating in my bath before dinner.
Stephen then banged on the door and asked if I intended
to stay in there all night, so I pulled the plug out, whereupon the water began to run away with a screeching sound
peculiar to that particular bathroom. (Why is it that up-
to-date bathrooms have so much less individuality than
their Victorian ancestors? The Rectory one, with its rough-
textured paint and dark wooden casing, had the atmosphere of a narrow converted lumber-room, and its hot-
water pipes were a subdued orchestra of enigmatic noises.)

While the water was making its raucous retreat my flip-
pant ultimatum to the family solicitor was merged in a
definite anxiety about paying for Cockbird. And then there
was (an additional fifteen guineas) the question of my subscription to the Ringwell.

"Of course you'll enter him for our point-to-point,"

Stephen had said while we were on our way home. "He's a lot faster than Jerry, and he'll simply walk away with the Heavy Weights. Send in your sub. and start qualifying him at once. You've only got to bring him out eight times. He's done nothing to-day, so you can have him out again on Wednesday."

The idea of my carrying off the Colonel's Cup had caused me delicious trepidations. But now, in the draughty bathroom and by the light of a bedroom candle, I was attacked by doubts and misgivings. It was easy enough for Stephen to talk about "qualifying" Cockbird; but how about my own qualifications as a race-rider? The candle flickered as if in ominous agreement with my scruples. There was a drop of water on the wick and the flame seemed to be fizzling toward extinction. Making it my fortune-teller, I decided that if it went out I should fall off at the first fence. After a succession of splutters it made a splendid recovery and spired into a confident survival.

*   *   *

At the dinner-table the Rector glowed with austere geniality while he carved the brace of pheasants which represented a day's covert-shooting he'd had with Lord Dumborough—"a long-standing annual fixture of mine", he called it. During our day's hunting we had only caught occasional glimpses of him. But he had got away from Basset Wood with the hounds, and had evidently enjoyed himself in his reticent way. We discussed every small detail of our various experiences. Kind Mrs. Colwood kept up with the conversation as well as could be expected from an absentee who hadn't ridden since she was quite a girl. She was interested and amused by hearing all about who had been out and what they had said, but she obviously found some difficulty in sharing her husband's satisfaction about the clever way in which "Lord Nelson" (the one-eyed horse) had popped over a stile with an awkward take-off and a drop on the landing-side. She must have endured many anxious hours while her family were out hunting, but her pinnacle of perturbation had been reached when

Stephen rode in the Hunt Races—an ordeal which (unless Jerry went lame) was re-awaiting her the next April. She could never be induced to attend "those horrible point-to-points" which, as she often said, would be the death of her.

On this particular evening my new horse was naturally the main topic, and his health was drunk in some port which had been "laid down" in the year of Stephen's birth. After this ceremony the Rector announced that he'd heard for certain that the Master was sending in his resignation.

"Here's to our next one", he added, raising his glass again, "and I hope he'll engage a first-rate huntsman."

I assumed a sagacious air while they deplored the imperfections of Ben Trotter, and the way he was for ever lifting his hounds and losing his head. Stephen remarked that whatever those humanitarian cranks might say, there was precious little cruelty to foxes when they were being hunted by a chap like Ben, who was always trying to chase his fox himself and never gave his hounds a chance to use their noses. The Rector sighed and feared that it was no use pretending that the Ringwell was anything but a cold-scenting country. We then adjourned to the study, where we soon had our own noses close to the ordnance map. At this moment I can see Mr. Colwood quite clearly. With a slight frown he is filling his pipe from a tin of "Three Nuns" mixture; on the wall behind him hangs a large engraving of "Christ leaving the Praetorium".

IV

Early in the afternoon of the following Thursday I journeyed homeward in the jolting annex of a horse-box. Although it was a sort of fifth-class compartment I felt serenely contented as I occasionally put my hand through the aperture to stroke Cockbird's velvet nose. He appeared to be a docile and experienced railway traveller, and when he stepped out of the box at Dumbridge Station he had an air of knowing that he'd saved himself a twenty-mile walk.

The porters eyed him with the respect due to such a well-bred animal. Having arranged for my kit-bag to be conveyed to Butley on the carrier's van, I swung myself into the saddle which I had borrowed from the Colwoods. It was a mellow afternoon for mid-winter, and our appearance, as reflected in the Dumbridge shop-windows, made me feel what, in those days, I should have called "a frightful nut". Cockbird's impeccable behaviour out hunting on the previous day had increased my complacency, and it was now an established fact that I had got hold of a top-hole performer with perfect manners.

Nobody at home was aware of what I'd been up to down in Sussex, and Dixon got the surprise of his life when we clattered into the stable-yard. So far as he was concerned it was the first really independent action of my career. When I arrived he was having his tea in his cottage above the coach-house; I could hear him clumping down the steep wooden stairs, and I sat like a statue until he emerged from the door by the harness room with his mouth full of bread and butter. The afternoon was latening, but there was, I think, a quietly commemorative glow from the west. He stood with the sunset on his face and his final swallowing of the mouthful appeared to epitomize his astonishment. Taken aback he undoubtedly was, but his voice kept its ordinary composure. "Why, what's this?" he asked. I told him.

*   *   *

Aunt Evelyn behaved like a brick about Cockbird. (How was it that bricks became identified with generous behaviour?) Of course she admired him immensely and considered it very clever of me to have bought him so cheap. But when it came to writing out the cheque for him I was obliged, for the first time in my life, to ask her to lend me some money. She promised to let me have it in a few days.

Next morning she went to London, "just to do a little Christmas shopping at the Army and Navy Stores." I was in the drawing-room when she returned. I heard the dogcart drive up to the front door, and then Aunt Evelyn's voice telling Miriam how tired she felt and asking her to make some tea. I didn't bother to get up when she came into the room, and after replying to my perfunctory inquiry whether she'd had a good day she went to her bureau and fussed about with some papers. Somewhat irritably I wondered what she was in such a stew about as soon as she'd got home. Her quill-pen squeaked for a short time and then she came across to the arm-chair where I was sitting with Edmund Gosse's *Father and Son* on my knee.

"There, dear. There's the money for your horse, and the Hunt subscription as well." She placed a cheque on the arm of the chair. "It's your Christmas present," she explained. It was so unexpected that I almost forgot to thank her. But I had the grace to ask whether she could really afford it.

"Well, dear," she said, "to tell the truth, I *couldn't*. But I *can* now." And she confessed that she'd sold one of her rings for seventy-five pounds up in London. "And why not?" she asked. "I'm so delighted at your having taken up hunting again; it's such a healthy hobby for a young man, and Dixon's almost beside himself—he's so pleased with the new horse. And after all, dear, I've got no other interest in the whole world except you."

Miriam then appeared with the tea-tray, and soon afterwards I went upstairs to gloat over my good fortune.

PART SIX: THE COLONEL'S CUP

I

By the end of February I had made further progress in what I believed to be an important phase of my terrestrial experience. In other words (and aided by an exceptionally mild winter) I had averaged five days a fortnight with the hounds. I had, of course, confided in Dixon my intention of entering Cockbird for the Ringwell Heavy Weight Race. My main object now seemed to be to jump as many fences as possible before that eventful day arrived. Meets of the Dumborough had been disregarded, and a series of short visits to the Rectory had continued the "qualifying" of Cockbird. ("Qualifying" consisted in drawing the Master's attention to the horse during each day's hunting; and I did this more than conscientiously, since Stephen and I were frequently shouted at by him for "larking" over fences when the hounds weren't running.)

The problem of Harkaway's lack of stamina had been solved by Dixon when he suggested that I should box him to the Staghound meets. He told me that they generally had the best of their fun in the first hour, so I could have a good gallop and bring the old horse home early. This took me (by a very early train from Baldock Wood) to a new and remote part of the country, and some of the fun I enjoyed there is worth a few pages of description.

The Coshford Vale Stag Hunt, which had been in existence as a subscription pack for about half a century, had been kept on its legs by the devoted efforts of a group of prosperous hop-farmers and a family of brewers whose name was a household word in the district. *Gimling's Fine Ales* were a passport to popularity, and the genial activities of Mr. "Gus" Gimling, who had been Master for more years then he cared to count, had kept the Hunt flourish-

ing and assured it of a friendly reception almost everywhere
in the country over which it hunted (described in the scar-
let-covered Hunting Directory as "principally pasture with
very little plough"). This description encouraged me to
visualize an Elysium of green fields and jumpable hedges;
but the country, although it failed to come up to my pre-
conceived idea of its charms, included a nice bit of vale;
and in those days there was very little wire in the fences.

I need hardly say that, since stags were no longer indi-
genous to that part of England, the Coshford stag-hunters
kept theirs at home (in a deer paddock a few miles from the
kennels). The animal which had been selected to provide
the day's sport was carried to the meet in a mysterious-
looking van, driven by the deerkeeper, a ruddy faced Irishman in a brown velveteen jacket who had earned a reputation for humorous repartee, owing to the numerous inquiries of inquisitive persons on the roads who asked him
what he'd got in that old hearse of his.

Provincial stag-hunts are commonly reputed to be comic
and convivial gatherings which begin with an uproarious
hunt-breakfast for the local farmers. Purple faced and bold
with cherry brandy, they heave themselves on to their
horses and set off across the country, frequently falling off
in a ludicrous manner. But the Coshford sportsmen, as I
knew them, were businesslike and well-behaved; they were
out for a good old-fashioned gallop. In fact, I think of them
as a somewhat serious body of men. And since the field was
mainly composed of farmers, there was nothing smart or
snobbish about the proceedings.

I need hardly say that there was no levity in my own
attitude of mind when I set out for my first sample of this
new experiment in sportsmanship. In spite of talking big to
Dixon the night before, I felt more frightened than light-
hearted. For I went alone and knew no one when I got
there. Dixon had talked to me about Harry Buckman, who
acted as amateur huntsman and was well known as a rider
at hunt races all over the country. That was about all I'd
got to go on, and I gazed at Buckman with interest and
admiration when he tit-tupped stylishly past me at the

meet with his velvet cap cocked slightly over one ear. Buck-man was a mixture of horse dealer and yeoman farmer. In the summer he rode jumpers in the show ring. His father had hunted a pack of harriers, and it was said that when times were bad he would go without his dinner himself rather than stint his hounds of their oatmeal.

Roughly speaking, young Buckman's task as huntsman was twofold. Firstly, he was there to encourage and assist the hounds (a scratch pack—mostly dog-hounds drafted from foxhound kennels because they were over-sized) in following the trail of their unnaturally contrived quarry; secondly, he had to do everything he could to prevent his hounds from "pulling down" the deer. With this paradoxical but humane object in view he had once jumped a rail-way gate; by this feat of horsemanship he arrived in the nick of time and saved the deer's life. Fast hunts were fairly frequent, but there were slow-hunting days when scent was bad and the Coshford subscribers were able to canter along at their ease enjoying a pretty bit of hound-work. Some-times the uncarted animal got clean away from them, and there was a special interest attached to a meet when they drew for an outlying deer.

My first day with the Staghounds was on Christmas Eve and I find the following entry in my diary: "*Coshford; Pack-man's Green*. Perfect hunting day; came on wet about 2.30. Turned out at Hazelpits Farm and ran well to Wissenden, then on by Chartley Church and Henhurst down the hill and on towards Applestead. Took deer ('Miss Masterful') about 2. Nine-mile point. Harkaway in good form. Took a toss over a stile toward the end. Very nice country, especi-ally the first bit." From this concise account it may seem as if I had already mastered the Coshford topography, but I suspect that my source of information was a paragraph in a local paper.

I cannot remember how I made myself acquainted with the name of the deer which provided the nine-mile point. But in any case, how much is taken for granted and left un-recorded in that shorthand description? And how helpful it would have been now if I had written an accurately observed and detailed narrative of the day. But since the object of these pages is to supply that deficiency I must make my reminiscent deductions as best I can. And those words from my diary do seem worth commenting on— symbolic as they are of the equestrian equilibrium on which my unseasoned character was trying to pattern itself. I wrote myself down that evening as I wanted myself to be— a hard-bitten hunting man, self-possessed in his localized knowingness and stag-hunting jargon. The words might well have been penned by a middle-aged sheep-farmer, or even by Mr. "Gus" Gimling himself. "Took a toss over a stile" is the only human touch. But taking tosses was incidental to the glory of being a hard rider. What I ought to have written was—that I couldn't make up my mind whether to go at it or not, and the man behind me shouted "go on if you're going", so I felt flustered and let Harkaway rush at it anyhow and then jerked his mouth just as he was taking off, and he didn't really fall, but only pecked badly and chucked me over his head and then stood quite still waiting for me to scramble up again, and altogether it was rather an inglorious exhibition, and thank goodness Stephen wasn't there to see it. For though Stephen and I always made a joke out of every toss we took, it wouldn't have suited my dignity if he'd told me in cold blood that I was still a jolly rotten rider—the tacit assumption being that my falls were entirely due to my thrusting intrepidity.

It will be noticed that no mention is made of the method by which "Miss Masterful" was "taken", although I had witnessed that performance for the first time in my life. As far as I can recollect, Miss M. having decided that the show had lasted long enough, plunged into a small pond and stood there with only her small head appearing above the muddy water. Raucous ratings and loud whip-crackings restrained the baying hounds from splashing in after her, and then genial Mr. Gimling, assisted by one of the whiskered wiseacres of the hunt (in a weather-stained black coat which came nearly down to his knees, white cord breeches, black butcher-boots, and very long spurs), began to get busy with a long rope. After Miss M. had eluded their attempts several times they succeeded in lassooing her head and she was persuaded to emerge from the pond. She was then frog-marched away to a farm building, where she awaited the arrival of her conveyance, which was cruising about the country and usually put in an appearance much earlier than might have been expected.

It can also be inferred from my diary that the weather "came on wet" as soon as I'd started my ten-mile ride back to the railway-station and Harkaway's horse-box, and that the supporters of the Coshford Hunt departed in different directions wishing one another a merry Christmas and a happy New Year. It may also be inferred that poor Miss Masterful sweated and shivered in the barn with heaving sides and frightened eyes. It did not occur to me to sympathize with her as I stood at the entrance to watch them tie her up. I only wondered how far I was from the station and my poached eggs for tea. Any sympathy I had was reserved for Harkaway, who looked as if he'd had more galloping than was good for him. But when I was jogging back by Chartley Church, with my coat collar turned up and the rain soaking my knees, I chuckled to myself as I thought of an amusing incident which had happened earlier in the day.

We were galloping full-tilt along a road just outside a cosy village. An angry faced old parson was leaning over his garden gate, and as we clattered past he shook his fist at us and shouted "Brutes! Brutes!" in a loud unclerical voice. Excited and elated as I was, I turned in the saddle and waved my whip derisively at him. Silly old buffer! And what a contrast to that jolly sporting parson in a low-crowned top-hat who went so well and came up and talked to me so nicely while Miss Masterful was being hauled out of the pond!

I have analysed the orthodox entry in my diary more fully than I had intended. But how lifelessly I recover the breathing reality of which those words are the only relics. The night before hunting: the anxious wonderings about the weather; lying awake for a while with busy thoughts about to-morrow that grow blurred with the beginning of an untroubled sleep. And then Miriam battering on the door with "it's twenty to seven, sir", and the first look at the quiet morning greyness, and the undefinable feeling produced by the yellow candlelight and the wintry smelling air from the misty garden. Such was the impermanent fabric as it unfolded: memory enchants even the dilatory little train journey which carried my expectant simplicity into the freshness of a country seen for the first time. All the sanguine guesswork of youth is there, and the silliness; all the novelty of being alive and impressed by the urgency of tremendous trivialities.

II

The end of February became the beginning of March, and this unavoidable progression intensified my anticipations of the date in April which meant so much to me. Cockbird had done his eight qualifying days without the slightest mishap or the least sign of unsoundness. He was so delightfully easy to handle that my assurance as a rider had increased rapidly. But in the period of preparation Dixon and I, between us, carried a large invisible load of solicitude and suspense. Our conversational demeanour was jauntily portentous. But when I was alone with myself and indoors, I often felt so nervous that the month-long remoteness of the point-to-points became almost unbearable. My confidence in Cockbird's ability to carry off the Colonel's Cup served only to magnify my imaginations of what might go wrong in the race through my own lack of experience.

I consoled myself with day-dreams in which I won in every way that my limited racing repertory could contrive. There was cantering home an easy winner; and there was winning cleverly by half a length; and there was coming up with a rush to score sensationally in the last stride. Easy winner lacked intensity; I would have preferred something more spectacular and heroic. But this was difficult to manage; I couldn't win with my arm in a sling unless I started in that condition, which would be an anti-climax. On the whole I was in favour of a fine finish with Stephen, although even this seemed inappropriate because Jerry was believed to be much slower than Cockbird, and could only hope to win if I fell—a thought which reduced my suppositions to reality.

Meanwhile Cockbird existed unperturbed, munching large feeds of crushed oats (with which Dixon mixed some water, for he had an idea that this was good for his wind) and doing three hours' steady work on the road every day. Once a week we took him to a ten-acre field on a hillside, which a well-disposed farmer allowed us to use for gallops. Round and round we went with set and serious faces (Dixon riding Harkaway) until we had done three presumptive miles up and down hill. When we pulled up Dixon would jump off, and I would jump off to stand meekly by the horses' snorting heads while he fussed round Cockbird with as much solemnity and solicitude as if he were a Grand National favourite. And, so far as we were concerned, "the National" (which was to be run ten days before the Ringwell Heavy Weight Race) was quite a secondary affair, though we sometimes talked about it in an offhand way which might have led a stranger to suppose that either of us might slip up to Liverpool to see it, provided that we could spare the time. Neither of us doubted that Cockbird himself could "get round Aintree" if asked to do so. He was, we agreed, a regular National stamp of horse, and though I had never seen an Aintree fence, I was quite sure that no fence was too big for him.

On some such afternoon, (for we always went out in the afternoon, though before breakfast would have been more correct, but it would have made the day so long and empty) on some such afternoon, when Cockbird had done his gallop to our mutual satisfaction and we were jogging quietly home, with the sun making haloes on the fleeces of the sheep who watched us pass—on some such afternoon, I repeat, I was reminded of the old days when I was learning to ride the cob Sheila, and of how I used to ask Dixon to pretend to be Mr. MacDoggart winning the Hunt Cup. Such a suggestion now would have struck both of us as unseemly; this was no time for such childish nonsense as that (though, when one came to think of it, twelve years ago wasn't such a very long time and "the twenty hop-kilns" were still down there in the valley to remind me of my childish excitement about them). But the thought passed through my mind, and at the same moment the warning whistle of a train going along the Weald would remind me of that interrogative railway journey which the three of us would be making in not much more than two weeks' time —was it really as near as that now?

The thought of Mr. MacDoggart's remote victories at Dumborough Races made me wish that I could ask Dixon for some first-hand information about race-riding. But although he had once worked in a racing-stable, he'd never had an opportunity of riding in a race. And I was shy of asking him questions which would expose my ignorance of things which, for some reason, I supposed that I ought to have known; so I had to make the best of such hints as he dropped me.

And then there was the difficulty of dress, a subject on which he never offered advice. Desperately in need of information, I asked myself what I was to wear on my head. Stephen had worn some sort of cap last year, but the idea of buying a jockey-cap seemed somehow ludicrous. (I remembered the old brown corduroy one I wore on my first day with the Dumborough.)

On this particular afternoon I had shortened my stirrups by several holes. I had observed, in some steeplechasing photographs in an illustrated paper, that the jockeys rode with their knees ever so much higher than mine. This experiment caused me to feel important and professional but less secure in the saddle. And when Cockbird made a sudden swerve (quite needlessly alarmed by a blackbird that flew out of the hedge which we hugged so as to make the field as large as possible) I almost lost my balance; in fact I nearly fell off. Dixon said nothing until we were on our way home, and then he merely remarked that he'd never believed in riding very short. "They always say that for a point-to-point there's nothing like sticking to the old-fashioned hunting seat." I took the hint, which was a wise one.

Much depended on Cockbird; but much more depended on me. There were moments when I felt acutely conscious of the absolute nullity of my past as a race-rider. It wasn't easy to discuss the event when one was limited by a tacit avowal that one had no idea what it would feel like. The void in my experience caused circumlocutions. My only authority was Stephen, whose well-known narrative of last year's race I was continually paraphrasing. The fact that the Ringwell country was so far away added to the anxious significance of my attempt. How could we—humble denizens of an inglorious unhunted region—hope to invade successfully the four-day-a-week immensity which contained the Colonel and his coveted Cup?

Such was the burden of my meditations while I lugged the garden roller up and down the tennis lawn after tea, while the birds warbled and scolded among the laurels and arbutuses in the latening March twilight and Aunt Evelyn tinkled Handel's "Harmonious Blacksmith" on the piano in the drawing-room.

III

It will have been observed that, in the course of my career as a sportsman, I was never able to believe that I could do a thing until I had done it. Whatever quality it was which caused this tentative progress toward proficiency, it gave intensity to everything that I did. I do not claim that it was unusual—this nervousness of mine about my first point-to-point race. On the contrary, I am sure that it was a normal and exemplary state of mind. Anyone who cares to do so is at liberty to make fun of the trepidations which a young man carries about with him and conceals. But there is a risk in such ridicule. As I remember and write, I grin, but not unkindly, at my distant and callow self and the absurdities which constitute his chronicle. To my mind the only thing that matters is the resolve to do something. Middle-aged retrospection may decide that it wasn't worth doing; but the perceptions of maturity are often sapless and restrictive; and "the thoughts of youth are long, long thoughts", even though they are only about buying a racing-cap.

A week before the races I went to London and bought a cap with a jutting peak; it was made of black silk, with strings that hung down on each side until they had been tied in front. I had remarked, quite casually, to Stephen, that I supposed a top-hat was rather uncomfortable for racing, and he had advised me about the cap, telling me to be sure to get one which came well down over my ears, "for there's nothing that looks so unworkmanlike as to have a pair of red ears sticking out under your cap." Whereupon he pulled one of mine, which, as he said, were big enough to catch any wind there was.

I also bought a weight-cloth. The Heavy Weight Racers had to carry fourteen stone, and after Dixon had weighed me and my hunting saddle on the old weighing machine in the harness room, we came to the conclusion that, assuming our antiquated machine to be accurate, I should be required to carry twelve pounds of lead.

"Thank heaven it wasn't thirteen," I thought, as I went into the stable to give Cockbird a few well-washed carrots.

He certainly was looking an absolute picture, though Dixon said he'd like to get a shade more of the meat off him. As he nipped playfully at my sleeve I marvelled at my good fortune in being the possessor of such unparalleled perfection.

With an access of elation I ran back to the house in a hailstorm. The sun was out again by the time I was upstairs brushing my hair for luncheon. I got out my new cap and tried it on before the glass. Then Miriam bumped into the room with a can of hot water, and as I hadn't time to snatch it off I stood there with the strings hanging down, looking, no doubt, a bit of a fool.

"Oh, sir, you did give me a turn!" she ejaculated, "I'd hardly have known you in that there jockey-cap!" She added that I'd be the death of them all before I'd done.

During luncheon Aunt Evelyn remarked that she did so hope it wouldn't be wet for the point-to-points. She had never seen one in her life, but she had once been to Dumborough Races, which she considered dangerous. Fortunately for her peace of mind, she still visualized a point-to-point as a sort of paper-chase, and I had said nothing to counteract this notion, although I did not want to minimize the grandeur of next week's events. Aunt Evelyn's intense love of horses made Cockbird the object of an admiration which almost equalled my own. This, combined with her unshakeable faith in Dixon, gave her a comfortable feeling that I was quite safe on Cockbird. But when Miriam, rather tactlessly, blurted out, "Mr. George hasn't half got a lovely jockey-cap!" she showed symptoms of alarm.

"Oh, I do hope the jumps won't be very big!" she exclaimed. To which I replied, somewhat boastfully, that I meant to get over them whatever they might be like.

"I'm going over to walk round the course with Stephen on Sunday. He says it's a course that wants knowing," I said, helping myself to some more tapioca pudding.

Stephen had warned me that I shouldn't be able to stay at the Rectory for the Races, because his mother was already "in such a muck-sweat about it" that the topic was never touched on in her presence. So I bicycled to Dumbridge, took the slow train which explored Sussex on Sunday mornings, got out at a wayside station, and then bicycled another seven miles to the course. (The seven-mile ride saved me from going on to Downfield and changing on to the branch line which went to the station close by the course.) These exertions were no hardship at all on that dusty spring day; had it been necessary, I would gladly have bicycled all the whole thirty miles from Butley and back again. Nothing in my life had ever appeared more imperative than that I should walk round that "three and a half miles of fair hunting country" and memorize each obstacle in the sequence. I wanted to carry home in my cranium every inch of the land over which Cockbird would, I strenuously hoped, stride with his four legs.

In the meantime I had plenty to occupy my mind pleasantly as I pedalled seriously along the leafless lanes. I already knew that part of the Ringwell country moderately well; I could identify most of the coverts by their names, and I ruminated affectionately on the rainy February days when I had gone round and through them in a hot and flustered gallop with the mud from the man in front of me flying past my head. Eagerly I recognized the hedges and heave-gates which I had jumped, and the ruddy faces of the Ringwell sportsmen accompanied my meditations in amicable clusters.

Memories within memories; those red and black and brown coated riders return to me now without any beckoning, bringing along with them the wintry smelling freshness of the woods and fields. And how could I forget them, those evergreen country characters whom once I learnt to know by heart, and to whom I have long since waved my last farewell (as though at the end of a rattling good day). Sober faced squires, with their civil greetings and knowing eyes for the run of a fox; the landscape belonged to them and they to the homely landscape. Weather-beaten farmers, for whom the activities of the Hunt were genial interludes in the stubborn succession of good or bad seasons out of which they made a living on their low-lying clay or wind-swept downland acres. These people were the pillars of the Hunt—the landowners and the farmers. The remainder were merely subscribers; and a rich-flavoured collection of characters they were, although I only half-recognized them as such while I was with them.

There was loquacious old Mr. Dearborn; formerly a none-too-successful stockbroker, and now a gentleman of leisure, who enjoyed himself on a couple of spavined screws which (he continually asserted) were worth at least a couple of hundred apiece and as clever as cats, though he'd never given more than thirty pounds for a horse, and rarely went as high as that; both of them, as Stephen said, looked lonely without a gig behind them. Old Dearborn jabbered his way through the days, attaching himself to one group of riders after another until a fox was found; at the end of a good hunt he would always turn up again, puffing and blowing and purple in the face, but voluble with enthusiasm for the way his horse had got over "one of the ugliest places you ever saw in your life". However tedious he may have been, the Ringwell field wouldn't have been the same without him.

Many an exuberant voice and lively countenance I could revive from that vanished cavalcade. But I can't help thinking that the best man of them all was "Gentleman George", as we called him. George was a grey-haired groom; Mr. Clampton, his middle-aged master, was "something in the City"—a natty untalkative little man, who came out in queerly cut clothes and a low-crowned hat. Mr. Clampton kept three stout-hearted weight-carriers, but he seldom hunted more than one day a week. George put in as many days as possible; he called it "keeping the guv'nor's 'osses well in work". No day was too long and no fence too hairy for George and the guv'nor's 'osses. At the most remote meets he would trot up—his fine-featured open face subdued to the decorum of servitude and a jolly twinkle for ever lurking in his keen eyes. (He was a man who could condense more meaning into a single wink than most political speakers can put into a peroration.) Always he had his free and easy hail for the hunt-servants (to whom he could generally give some useful information during the day); for the gentry he reserved a respectful rap of his hat-brim and a sonorous "Mornin', sir". However curt his utterances were, the tones of his voice seemed to imply the underlying richness and vigour of his vitality. He knew every inch of the country backwards, and the short-tailed grey who was his favourite had done fourteen seasons with those hounds since Mr. Clampton first bought him as a five-year-old from a farm in County Waterford.

The great joke about George was his method of acting as second horseman when his worthy master was out hunting. This, of course, should have meant that he kept as much as possible to the roads and handed the horse over to his employer as soon as the first horse had done as much galloping and jumping as was considered good for him. Not so George, who was seldom more than two fields away from hounds however hard they ran. Times without number I have seen him come crashing through some black-looking fence and then turn to shout back at the irresolute Mr. Clampton, "Shove 'im at it, sir; there's a big old ditch on the landing side!" And at the end of a gallop, when both horses were smoking hot, he would dismount with the utmost gravity and exchange horses with his master, who had even been known to go home first, leaving his privileged retainer to knock holes in the fences in a late afternoon hunt.

In him I seem to be remembering all that was warmhearted and exhilarating in my days with the Ringwell, for he showed a special interest in Stephen Colwood and myself, and was never so well contented as when he was showing us the way over an awkward place or giving us the benefit of his ripe experience and intimate knowledge. There was something noble about him. And so (I choose to think) it was for "Gentleman George" that I kept the kindliest of my meditations as I was bicycling to the point-to-point course.

*　　　　*　　　　*

It was peaceful and pleasant to be squatting on a gate and opening the package of sandwiches that Miriam had made me. The gate opened on to a boggy lane which ran through Cruchett's Wood—a well-known covert. But Cruchett's Wood was beginning to look more idyllic than sporting now; it was dotted with primrose bunches, and the wild anemones were numerous. Although I saw them with placid appreciation my uppermost thought was that the country was drying up nicely; deep going was believed to be a disadvantage to Cockbird, who was supposed to possess a turn of speed which he would have more chance of showing if the ground were dry.

The early afternoon was quiet and Sunday-like as I sat with half a ham-sandwich in my hand; a saffron butterfly fluttered aimlessly along the hedge; miles away the grey-green barrier of the downs overlooked the inactive Weald, and I thought I'd rather like to be up there, by the old windmill on Ditchbury Beacon.

Discarding this unsportsmanlike notion I went on my way; half an hour later my uncompanioned identity had been merged in my meeting with Stephen and we were very deliberately inspecting the first few fences. There was a stake-and-bound hedge on a bank which we didn't much like the look of. While we were still planted in front of it the cheery voice of Arthur Brandwick hailed us with "That's a place where you'll have to take a pull at your old horse, Steve." With him was Nigel Croplady, wearing white gaiters and puffing a cigar; his somewhat supercilious recognition of my existence made me feel that I had no business to be there at all. Croplady was on the Point-to-Point Committee; he had helped to plan out the course and had supervised the making up and trimming of the fences.

"I'm not at all sure we oughtn't to have made the course a bit stiffer," he remarked.

Brandwick replied that he wouldn't be saying that if he were having a bump round it himself.

Croplady expressed regret that he wasn't able to ride the horse he'd entered for the Heavy Weights. "That infernal knee of mine went groggy again while I was playing golf on Thursday. But I've got 'Boots' Brownrigg to ride him for me, so he ought to be in the picture all right."

I gathered that "Boots" Brownrigg was in the "Blues" and had "ridden a clinking good finish at the Guards' Meeting at Hawthorn Hill the other day".

Brandwick told us that he'd asked Roger Pomfret to ride his young horse. "He's a mutton-fisted beggar; but the horse is a bit nappy, and young Roger'll be the man to keep him going at his fences."

Every syllable they uttered made my own private aspirations more preposterous and perishable: my optimism was at a very low ebb as we plodded across a wet pasture to the next obstacle, which had a wide ditch on the take-off side.

"There's another place where there'll be trouble for

somebody!" Brandwick's jolly voice seemed to be glorying in the prospect of horses refusing and riders shooting up their necks, or even over their ears. He turned to me. "Let's see, you're running that nice-looking bay of yours, aren't you?"

I replied, "Yes, I'm having a ride."

Croplady became knowledgeable about the entries, which had long been a subject for speculation between Stephen and myself. "Quite a hot lot for the Heavy Weights this year. Two of those Cavalry thrusters who keep their nags in Downfield. They're always rather an unknown quantity."

Stephen remarked that the Colonel's Cup was well worth winning, and Croplady agreed that it was a much better pot than the Light Weight one, and must have cost the old boy five-and-twenty quid at least.

Silent and disheartened, I longed to be alone again; the presence of the other two made it impossible for me to talk naturally to Stephen, and I couldn't help feeling that they regarded me as an entry which could be ruled out of all serious consideration. The whole affair had become bleakly detached from my previous conception of it. I was just a greenhorn. What chance had I got against Brownrigg of the "Blues", or those ferociously efficient Cavalry officers? Bicycling back to the station with only just time to catch the train, I visualized myself refusing the first fence and colliding with Roger Pomfret, who was associated in my memory with all my most timorous experiments with the Dumborough.

Aunt Evelyn found me an uncommunicative companion that evening; and it wasn't easy to talk to Dixon about the course when I went to the stable next morning. "I hear there's a very hot lot entered for the Heavy Weights," I said, as I watched him polishing away at Cockbird's glossy coat. My tone was, perhaps, a shade extenuatory. I couldn't bring myself to speak of Brownrigg of the "Blues".

Dixon straightened himself and passed his hand along Cockbird's back. "Don't you worry about that. I'll bet our horse gives some of 'em a shaking up!" he replied.

Cockbird gave a playful hoist of his hind quarters and then snatched a mouthful of hay from his rack. I wished that the confidence of my confederates was a little more infectious.

IV

The races were to be on Wednesday. After exercising our minds on the problem of how best to convey Cockbird to the course by two o'clock on that afternoon, we decided against his spending the previous night in Downfield. I suggested that he would probably sleep better in his own stable, which struck me at the time as being improperly expressed, though it was necessary that he should lie down and shut his eyes like everybody else who has something important to do next day. In this connection I should like to mention an odd fact, which is that when I dream about horses, as I often do, they usually talk like human beings, although the things they say, as in most dreams, are only confused fantasias on ordinary speech.

Anyhow, it was arranged that Dixon should ride Cockbird to Dumbridge on Wednesday morning, box him to Downfield, put him up at Whatman's "Hunting and Livery Stables" for two or three hours, and then jog him quietly out to the course, which was about four miles from Downfield. In the meantime I was to ride Harkaway to Dumbridge, (I felt that this ride would be better for me than if I drove in the dogcart) catch a later train, and find my way out to the course as best I could. The bag holding my coat, boots, cap, spurs, and weight-cloth would go by the carrier. (I mention these details because they did seem so vastly important at the time.)

Cockbird's night's rest was, I imagine, normal, and it didn't occur to me to speculate about Dixon's. My own slumbers were what I should then have considered inadequate; that is to say, I lay awake for a couple of hours and then slept like a top until Miriam called me at eight.

I came down to breakfast reticent and self-conscious.

Patient Miriam's anxiety that I should eat a good breakfast wasn't well received, and Aunt Evelyn's forced cheerfulness made me feel as if I were going to be hanged in the
afternoon. She had never made any reference to the possibility of her going to see the Races. I have no doubt that
she was as sensitive to the precarious outcome of the adventure as I was. For me the whole day, until my race started,
was pervaded by the sinking sensation which is commonly
called being in a blue funk. But when the stable-boy (his
face clearly showing his awareness that he was at close
quarters with momentous happenings) had led Harkaway
out of the stable, and I had mounted and was trotting
through the village, I was conscious of being as fit as I'd
ever been in my life, and of being in some way harmonious
with the mild, half-clouded April morning which contained
me.

The morning tasted good; but it had only one meaning:
it was the morning of the point-to-points. To have understood the gusto of that physical experience would have
been to destroy the illusion which we call youth and im-
maturity—that unforeseeing actuality which retrospection
can transmute into a lucid and orderly emotion. The April
morning, as I see it now, symbolized a stage which I had
then reached in my earthly pilgrimage.

But whatever "bright shoots of everlastingness" my
body may have felt, my ordinary mind manifested itself
only by instructing me to feel in my coat pocket for the
half-sheet of notepaper on which I had written "This is to
certify that Mr. G. Sherston's bay gelding Cockbird has
been fairly and regularly hunted with the Ringwell
Hounds"; to which the M.F.H. had appended his signa-
ture, adding the figures of the current hunting season,
which I had carelessly omitted. This document had to be
shown at the scales, although when I actually got there the
Clerk of the Scales forgot to ask me for it. When I was
making sure that it was still in my pocket I was still under
the misapprehension that unless I could produce it in the
weighing tent I should be disqualified from riding in my
race.

In the middle of the village I met John Homeward and his van. He was setting out on his monotonous expedition to the county town, and I stopped for a few words with him. His benevolent bearded face made me feel more confident, and so did his gruff voice when he took a stumpy clay pipe out of his mouth to wish me luck.

"I've asked Tom to put half a crown on for me," he said; "it'll be a great day for Butley if you win!" His blunt nod, as I left him sitting under the shadow of his hooded van, was a send-off which stiffened my faltering ambition to prove myself worthy of being the owner of Cockbird.

Remembering how I'd bicycled off to the Ringwell Meeting twelve months before, I thought how flabbergasted I should have been if I'd been told that I should be riding in a race there next year. And in spite of that persistent sinking sensation, I was thankful that, at any rate, I had got as far as "having a bump round". For whatever might happen, I was much superior to any of the spectators. Taking my cap off to two elderly ladies, the Miss Pattons, who passed me on their tricycles with bobs and smiles, I wondered whether it was going to rain. Perhaps the sun came out to show that it was going to be a fine afternoon. When I was on the main road I passed Joey, the lizard-faced stone-breaker, who looked up from his flint-hammering to salute me with a grin.

*   *   *

The sun was still shining when I got to the course; but it was now less easy to believe that I had engaged myself to contribute to the entertainment which was attracting such a crowd of cheerful country folk. I felt extraneous and forlorn. Everyone else seemed intent on having as good a time as possible on such a lovely afternoon. I had come briskly out from Downfield on a two-horse char-a-banc which was waiting outside the station. The journey cost half a crown. Several of my fellow-passengers were "bookies" and their clerks, with their name-boards and giant umbrellas; their jocosities accentuated the crudity of the impact on my mind made by the realistic atmosphere of racing. I did my best to feel as much like a "gentleman-rider" as I could, and to forget that I was making my first appearance in a race.

The air smelt of trodden turf as I lugged my bag (loaded with fourteen one-pound lead weights) into the dressing-room, which was in a farm building under some elms on the crest of the rising ground which overlooked the sparsely flagged course. After dumping the bag in a corner of the dry-mud floored barn, I went out to look for Cockbird and Dixon. They were nowhere to be seen, so I returned to the dressing-room, reminding myself that Dixon had said he wouldn't bring "our horse" out there any earlier than he was obliged to, since it would only excite him; I also realized that I should get "rattled" myself unless I kept quiet and reserved my energies for three o'clock.

The first race was run at two, and mine was the third event on the card, so I bought that absorbing document and perched myself on an old corn-bin to peruse it. "*Riders are requested to return their number-cloths to the Clerk of the Scales immediately after each race.*" I had forgotten that number-cloths existed, so that was news to me. "*These Steeplechases are held subject to National Hunt Rules as to corrupt and fraudulent practices.*" A moment's reflection convinced me that I need not worry about that admonition; it was sufficiently obvious that I had a clean sheet under National Hunt Rules, though it flattered me to feel that I was at last within their jurisdiction.

After these preliminaries I looked inside the card, at the entries. Good heavens, there were fourteen in my race! Several of the names I didn't know. Captain Silcock's "Crumpet". Mr. F. Duckwith's "Grasshopper". Those must be the soldiers who hunted from Downfield. Mr. G. Bagwell's "Kilgrubbin III". That might be—yes, of course, it was—the fat little man on the weedy chestnut, who was always refusing small timber out hunting. Not much danger from him as long as I kept well out of his way at the first fence, and probably he, and several of the others, wouldn't go to the post after all. My own name looked nice.

A blue-jowled man in a yellow waistcoat hurried in, ex-

claiming, "Can anybody lend me a weight-cloth?" I
glanced at my bag and resolved that nothing would induce
me to lend him mine (which had yet to receive its baptis-
mal instalment of sweat). Several riders were now preparing for the first race, but no one took any notice of me until
ginger-haired Roger Pomfret came in. He had been inspecting the fences, and he wiped his fleshy red face with
his sleeve as he sat down and started rummaging in his bag.
Tentatively I asked him what he thought of the course. I
was quite glad to see someone I knew, though I'd have
preferred to see someone else. He chucked me a surly nod,
which he supplemented with—"Course? I don't mind telling you, this something course would break the heart of a
blank buffalo. It's nothing but twists and turns, and there
isn't a something fence you could go fast at without risking
your something neck, and a nice hope I've got on that
blank sketchy jumper of Brandwick's!"

Before I could think of an answer his boon companion
in blasphemy, Bill Jaggett, came in (embellished with a
brown billycock hat and black and white check breeches).
Jaggett began chaffing him about the something unhealthy
ride he was going to have in the Heavy Weights. "I'll lay
you a tenner to a fiver you don't get round without falling," he guffawed. Pomfret took the bet and called him a
pimply faced bastard into the bargain.

I thought I might as well get dressed up: when I had
pulled my boots on and was very deliberately tucking the
straps in with the boot-hook, Stephen strolled in; he was
already wearing his faded pink cap, and the same elon-
gated and anxious countenance which I had seen a year
ago. No doubt my own face matched his. When we'd reassured one another about the superlative fitness of our
horses he asked if I'd had any lunch, and as I hadn't he
produced a bar of chocolate and an orange, which I was
glad to get. Stephen was always thoughtful of other people.

The shouts of the bookies were now loudening outside in
the sunlight, and when I'd slipped on my raincoat we went
out to see what we could of the Light Weight Race.

*   *   *

The first two races were little more than the clamour and commotion of a passing procession. The "Open Race" was the main excitement of the afternoon; it was run "in colours", and there were about a dozen dashing competitors, several of them well-known winners in such events.

But everything connected with this contest reached me as though from a long way off, since I was half-stupefied by yawning nervousness. They appeared to be accomplishing something incredible by galloping round the course. I had got to do it myself in half an hour; and what was worse, Dixon was relying on me to put up a creditable performance. He even expected me to give the others "a shaking up". Stephen had ceased to be any moral support at all: in spite of his success last year he was nearly as nervous as I was, and when the field for the Open Race had filed out of the hurdle-guarded enclosure, which did duty as the paddock, he disappeared in the direction of Jerry and I was left to face the future alone.

Also, as far as I knew, my horse hadn't yet arrived, and it was with a new species of alarm that I searched for him after I had seen the race start; the paddock and its environs now looked unfriendly and forsaken.

I discovered my confederates in a quiet corner under a hayrick. They seemed a discreet and unassuming pair, but Dixon greeted me with an invigorative grin. "I kept him away from the course as long as I could," he said confidentially; "he's as quiet as a sheep, but he knows what he's here for; he's staled twice since we got here." He told me that Mr. Gaffikin was about and had been looking for me. "He says our horse stands a jolly good chance with the going as good as it is."

I said there was one place, in and out of a lane, where I'd have to be careful.

We then escorted Cockbird to the paddock; by the time we were there and I'd fetched my weight-cloth, the Open Race was over and the spectators were trooping back again. Among them was Mr. Gaffikin, who hailed me companionably with "Hullo, old chap; jolly sporting of you to be having a ride!" and thereafter took complete charge of

me in a most considerate manner, going with me to the
weighing tent with the weight-cloth over his arm, while I,
of course, carried my saddle.

The winner of the Open Race was weighing in when we
arrived, and I stepped diffidently on to the machine immediately after his glorified and perspiring vacation of the
seat. Mr. Gaffikin doled out a few leads for me to slip into
the leather pouches on the dark blue cloth until I tipped
the scale at fourteen stone. The Clerk of the Scales, an un-
smiling person with a large sallow face—he was a corn-
merchant—verified my name on the card and handed me
my number-cloth and armlet; my number was seven;
under less exacting conditions I might have wondered
whether it was a lucky number, but I was pushed out of
the way by Pomfret. Arthur Brandwick (in a grey bowler)
was at his elbow, talking nineteen to the dozen; I caught a
glimpse of Stephen's serious face; Colonel Hesmon was
with him, behaving exactly the same as last year, except
that, having already "given the boy the horse", he could
no longer say that he was going to do so if he won the race.

While Dixon was putting the last testing touches to
Cockbird's straps and buckles, the little Colonel came
across to assure me that if Jerry didn't win there was no
one he'd rather see first past the judge's waggon than me.
He added that he'd taken a lot of trouble in choosing the
Cup—"very nice goblet shape—got it from Stegman &
Wilks—excellent old firm in the City". But his eye wandered away from Cockbird; his sympathies were evidently
strongly implicated in Jerry, who was as unperturbed as if
he were being put into a brougham to fetch someone from
the station.

Near him, Nigel Croplady was fussing round his horse,
with quite a crowd round him.

The terrific "Boots" Brownrigg was puffing a cigarette
with apparent unconcern; his black cap was well over his
eyes and both hands were plunged in the pockets of a short
blue overcoat; from one of the pockets protruded a short
cutting whip. His boots were perfection. Spare built and
middle-sized, he looked absolutely undefeatable; and if he

had any doubts about his own abilities he concealed them well.

Stifling another yawn, I did my best to imitate his demeanour. The bookies were bawling "Two to one bar one". Cockbird, stimulated by publicity, now began to give himself the airs of a real restive racehorse, chucking his head about, flattening his ears, and capering sideways in a manner which caused the onlookers to skip hastily out of range of his heels.

"I say, that's a classy looking quad!" exclaimed a youth who appeared to have purchased the paddock. He consulted his card, and I overheard his companion, as they turned away, saying something about "his jockey looking a bit green". "We'd better back Nigel's horse. They say he'll win for a cert."

For want of anything else to do at this critical moment I asked Dixon whether he'd put Homeward's half-crown on. He said, "Yes, sir; Mr. Gaffikin's man has just done it for me, and I've got a bit on for myself. *It's a good thing*; they're laying five to one about him. Mr. Stephen's horse is at two's."

Mr. Gaffikin chimed in with "Mikado's a hot favourite. *Two to one on*, all along the line!" Mikado was Croplady's horse.

Mr. Gaffikin then tied the strings of my cap in a very tight bow; a bell jangled and a stentorian voice shouted, "Now, then, gentlemen, I'm going down to the post." The blue sky suddenly went white; my heart bumped; I felt dazed and breathless. Then Mr. Gaffikin's remote voice said, "Let me give you a leg up, old chap"; I grabbed hold of the reins, lifted an awkward foot, and was lifted airily on to the slippery saddle: Cockbird gave one prance and then stood still; Dixon was holding him firmly by the head. Pressing my knees into the saddle I overheard Mr. Gaffikin's ultimate advice. "Don't go in front unless you can help it; but *keep well with 'em*." They both wished me luck and released me to my destiny.

I felt as if I'd never been on Cockbird's back before; everything around me appeared unreal and disconnected from all my previous experience. As I followed Stephen out of the paddock in a sort of equestrian trance I caught sight of his father's face, pale and fixed in its most strenuous expression; his eyes followed his son, on whose departure he was too intent to be able to take in anyone else. We filed through a gate under some trees: "Gentleman George" was standing by the gate; he stared up at me as I passed. "That's the 'oss for my money," was all that he said, but his measured tone somehow brought me to my senses, and I was able to look about me when we got down to the starting place.

But even then I was much more a passenger than a resolute rider with his wits about him to "pinch" a good start. There were seven others. I kept close to Stephen. We lined up uneasily; while the starter (on his dumpy grey cob) was instructing us to keep the red flags on the right and the white flags on the left (which we already knew) I noticed Pomfret, (on a well-bred, excitable brown) and Brownrigg (Croplady's bright chestnut looking very compact) already stealing forward on the side furthest from him.

When he said "Go", I went with the others; albeit with no sense of initiative. The galloping hoofs sounded strange. But Cockbird felt strong under me and he flicked over the first fence with level and unbroken stride; he was such a big jumper and so quick over his fences that I had to pull him back after each one in order to keep level with Jerry, who was going his best pace all the way. One of the soldiers (in a top-hat) was making the running with Brownrigg and Pomfret close behind him. At the awkward fifth fence (the one on a bank) Pomfret's horse jumped sideways and blundered as he landed; this caused Pomfret to address him in uncomplimentary language, and at the next obstacle (another awkward one) he ran out to the left, taking one of the soldiers with him. This, to my intense relief, was the last I saw of him. I took it at a place where a hole had been knocked in it in the previous races. The next thing I remember was the brook, which had seemed wide and intimidating when I was on foot and had now attracted a small gathering of spectators. But water jumps are deceptive things and Cockbird shot over this one beautifully. (Stephen told me afterwards that he'd "never seen a horse throw such an enormous lep".) We went on up a long slope of firm pasture-land, and I now became aware of my responsibility; my arms were aching and my fingers were numb and I found it increasingly difficult to avoid taking the lead, for after jumping a couple more fences and crossing a field of light ploughland we soared over a hedge with a big drop and began to go down the other side of the hill. Jerry was outpaced and I was level with Mikado and the Cavalry soldier who had been cutting out the work. As Stephen dropped behind he said, "Go on, George; you've got 'em stone-cold."

We were now more than three parts of the way round, and there was a sharp turn left-handed where we entered on the last half-mile of the course. I lost several lengths here by taking a wide sweep round the white flag, which Brownrigg almost touched with his left boot. At the next fence the soldier went head over heels, so it was just as well for me that I was a few lengths behind him. He and his horse were still rolling about on the ground when I landed well clear of them. Brownrigg looked round and then went steadily on across a level and rather wet field which compelled me to take my last pull at Cockbird. Getting on to better ground, I remembered Mr. Gaffikin's advice, and let my horse go after him. When I had drawn up to him it was obvious that Cockbird and Mikado were the only ones left in it. I was alone with the formidable Brownrigg. The difference between us was that he was quite self-contained and I was palpitating with excitement.

We were side by side: approaching the fourth fence from the finish he hit his horse and went ahead; this caused Cockbird to quicken his pace and make his first mistake in the race by going too fast at the fence. He hit it hard and pecked badly; Brownrigg, of course, had steadied Mikado for the jump after the quite legitimate little piece of strategy which so nearly caused me to "come unstuck". Nearly, but not quite. For after my arrival at Cockbird's ears his recovery tipped me half-way back again and he

cantered on across the next field with me clinging round
his neck. At one moment I was almost in front of his chest.
I said to myself, "I *won't* fall off", as I gradually worked
my way back into the saddle. My horse was honestly following Mikado, and my fate depended on whether I could
get into the saddle before we arrived at the next fence.
This I just succeeded in doing, and we got over somehow.
I then regained my stirrups and set off in urgent pursuit.

After that really remarkable recovery of mine, life became lyrical, beatified, ecstatic, or anything else you care
to call it. To put it tersely, I just galloped past Brownrigg,
sailed over the last two fences, and won by ten lengths.
Stephen came in a bad third. I also remember seeing
Roger Pomfret ride up to Jaggett in the paddock and inform him in a most aggressive voice that he'd got to "something well pay up and look pleasant".

Needless to say that Dixon's was the first face I was
aware of; his eager look and the way he said, "Well done",
were beyond all doubt the quintessence of what my victory
meant to me. All else was irrelevant at that moment, even
Stephen's unselfish exultation and Mr. Gaffikin's loquacious enthusiasm. As for Cockbird, no words could ever
express what we felt about him. He had become the equine
equivalent of Divinity.

*   *   *

Excited as I was, an inward voice cautioned me to control my volubility. So when I had weighed in and returned
with my saddle to find a cluster of knowing ones casting an
eye over the winner, I just waited soberly until Dixon had
rubbed him down, mounted, and ridden serenely out of
sight. The Colonel was on the spot to congratulate me on
my "nailing good performance" and, better still, to give
Dixon his due for having got Cockbird so fit. Those few
lofty minutes when he was making much of his horse were
Dixon's reward for all the trouble he had taken since Cockbird had been in his charge. He had needed no such incen-
tive, but he asked for nothing more. While he was on his
way back to Downfield he may also have thought to him-

self how he had made me into a good enough rider to have got round the course without a catastrophe. (He had yet to hear full details of the race—including my peculiar acrobatics toward the end, which had been witnessed by no one except the rider of Mikado, who had been kind enough to tell Croplady that he never saw such a thing in his life, which was, I hoped, intended as a compliment.)

When I had watched Dixon's departure I found that public interest was being focused on the Yeomanry Team Race. I was glad to slip away by myself: a few fields out in the country I relaxed my legs on a five-barred gate and contemplated my achievement with as much mental detachment as I could muster. Even in those days I had an instinct for getting the full flavour of an experience. Perhaps I was fortunate in not yet having become aware that the winner of the last race is forgotten as soon as the next one starts.

Forty minutes later I had claimed my cup. (There was no ceremony of presentation.) Having crammed the ebony pedestal into my kit-bag I came out into the paddock with the cup in my other hand. It was convenient to carry, for it had handles to it.

Good-natured Arthur Brandwick came up and offered me a lift back to Downfield. While he was patting me on the back I caught sight of a figure which seemed somehow familiar. A loose-built ruddy faced young sportsman was talking to a couple of jovial whiskered farmers; he sat on a shooting-stick with his thin neatly gaitered legs straightened; a brown felt hat was tipped well over his blunt nose, for the five o'clock sun was glaring full in his eyes. I wondered who it was he reminded me of. Brandwick answered my unspoken question.

"D'you twig who that is?" I shook my head. "Well, take another good look at him. It's our new Master, and a hell of a good lad he is, from all I've heard. Up till a month ago everyone thought the country'd have to be hunted by a Committee next season. There was something fishy about every one of the coves who'd applied for the Mastership. And then this chap wrote and offered to hunt the hounds himself and put up fifteen hundred a year if we guaranteed him another two thousand. Hardly a soul knew about it till to-day. We're lucky to get him. He's been hunting a good rough country in Ireland the last two seasons and showing rare sport. He's run across for a couple of days to look at us." As we walked away the new Master turned his head and favoured us with a slow and rather blank stare.

"What did you say his name was?" I asked, when we were out of earshot. Brandwick informed me that his name was Milden—Denis Milden—and I knew that I'd known it all the time, though I hadn't set eyes on him since I was eleven years old.

*   *   *

Aquamarine and celestial were the shoals of sunset as I hacked pensively home from Dumbridge. The Colonel's Cup clinked and joggled against my saddle. Time was irrelevant. But I was back at Butley by eight o'clock, and Cockbird, who had returned by an earlier train, was safe and sound; a little uneasily he wandered around his loose-box, rustling the deep straw, but always going back to the manger for another mouthful of clover-hay. Dixon serenely digested triumph with his tea; presently he would go out to the "Rose and Crown" to hand Homeward his multiplied half-crown and overawe the gossips with his glory.

Absolved and acquiescent was the twilight as I went quietly across the lawn and in at the garden door to the drawing-room. Aunt Evelyn's arm-chair scrooped on the beeswaxed floor as she pushed it back and stood up with her bottle of smelling-salts in her hand. For the first time since my success I really felt like a hero. And Miriam served the dinner with the tired face of a saint that seemed lit with foreknowledge of her ultimate reward. But at that time I didn't know what her goodness meant.

At the end of our evening, when they had gone upstairs with my highly coloured history of the day in their heads, I strolled out into the garden; for quite a long time I stared at the friendly lights that twinkled from the railway station and along the dark Weald. I had brought something home

with me as well as the Cup. There was this new idea of
Denis Milden as Master. For I hadn't forgotten him, and
my persistent studying of *Horse and Hound* and *The Hunting
Directory* had kept me acquainted with his career as an
amateur huntsman since he had left Oxford. A dog barked
and a train went along the Weald . . . the last train to London, I thought. . . .

Going back to the drawing-room, I lit a pair of candles
which made their miniature gold reflections on the shining
surface of the massive Cup. I couldn't keep my eyes away
from it. I looked round the shadowed room on which all
my childhood and adolescence had converged, but everything led back to the talisman; while I gazed and gazed on
its lustre I said to myself, aloud, "It can't be true that it's
really there on the table!" The photograph of Watts's
"Love and Death" was there on the wall; but it meant no
more to me than the strangeness of the stars which I had
seen without question, out in the quiet spring night. I was
secure in a cosy little universe of my own, and it had
rewarded me with the Colonel's Cup. My last thought
before I fell asleep was, "Next season I'll come out in a
pink coat."

PART SEVEN: DENIS MILDEN AS MASTER

I

All through an extra fine summer I often wondered how the new Master was getting on in the Ringwell country. But I was almost entirely ignorant of what a Master of Hounds does with himself between April and September. I saw next to nothing of Stephen, who was at Aldershot, learning how to be a Special Reserve officer in the Royal Field Artillery.

My own energies were mainly expended on club cricket matches. I managed to play in three or four matches every week; I was intent on keeping my batting average up to twenty runs per innings, which I found far from easy, though I had one great afternoon when I compiled a century for Butley against some very mediocre village bowling. Those long days of dry weather and white figures moving to and fro on green grounds now seem like an epitome of all that was peaceful in my past. Walking home across the fields from Butley, or driving back in the cool of the evening after a high-scoring game on the county ground at Dumbridge, I deplored my own failure or gloated over one of my small successes; but I never looked ahead, except when I thought about next winter's hunting. The horses were out at grass; and so, in a sense, was I.

Now and again I accompanied Aunt Evelyn to a garden-party where, as a rule, I competed in a putting tournament, which was a favourite mode of entertainment at the time. Solemnly round someone's garden I putted, partnered, perhaps, by a major's wife or a clergyman's daughter. At Squire Maundle's I won a magnifying glass, and on another occasion I carried off a carriage clock. Aunt Evelyn, who preferred croquet, was extremely pleased, and my leisurely conquests among herbaceous borders and yew

hedges accentuated the unique pride I had in my racing
Cup. In an exciting match play final on Captain Huxtable's mossy and evergreen-shaded lawn I just failed to
capture an ivory paper knife.

One week-end in July Stephen came to stay with us.
Artillery life had caused no apparent change in him. We indulged in cheerful nostalgia for the chase. After sniffing the
trussed hay in the stable-barn we contemplated Cockbird
and Harkaway in the paddock. We sighed for a nice moist
winter morning. Stephen was hoping to get "attached" to
some Gunners who were conveniently stationed in the
Ringwell country. He could tell me nothing about the new
Master, except that he was already reputed to be a tireless
worker and very well liked by the farmers. For his benefit
I unearthed my early impressions of Denis Milden as I had
seen him when he was staying at Dumborough Castle as a
boy. Already Milden was a very great man in our minds.

My memory of that summer returns like a bee that
comes buzzing into a quiet room where the curtains are
drawn on a blazing hot afternoon.

*　　　　　*　　　　　*

By the middle of September Dixon had got the horses up
from grass. Cricket matches were out of season, but there
hadn't been a spot of rain since the end of June. Robins
warbled plaintively in our apple orchard, and time hung
rather heavy on my hands. The Weald and the wooded
slopes were blue misted on sultry afternoons when I was
out for a ruminative ride on one of my indolent hunters.
Hop-picking was over early that year and the merry pick-
ers had returned to the slums of London to the strains of
the concertina or accordion. I was contemplating an expedition to the West End to order a short-skirted scarlet
coat and two pairs of white breeches from Kipward & Son;
Craxwell was to make me a pair of boots with mahogany
coloured tops. I intended to blossom out at the opening
meet as a full-fledged fox-hunter.

The autumn was a period of impatience. I longed for
falling leaves and the first of November. The luminous

melancholy of the fine September weather was a prelude
rather than an elegy. I was only half in love with mists and
mellow fruitfulness. I did not dread the dark winter as
people do when they have lost their youth and live alone in
some great city. Not wholly unconscious of the wistful
splendour, but blind to its significance, I waited for cub-
hunting to end. Europe was nothing but a name to me. I
couldn't even bring myself to read about it in the daily
paper. I could, however, read about cubbing in the Midlands; it was described at some length every week in the
columns of *Horse and Hound*. Any other interests I had are
irrelevant to these memoirs, and were in any case subsidiary to my ambition as a sportsman.

Disapproving Mr. Pennett had left me severely alone
since the previous winter, and for the time being my income seemed adequate.

Toward the end of the month Stephen asked me to stay
at the Rectory. He had escaped from Aldershot and was
about to join his new brigade, which was quartered in the
Ringwell country. Both his brothers were still serving their
country in foreign parts.

The first morning I was there we got up at four o'clock,
fortified ourselves with boiled eggs and cocoa, and set off
on bicycles to a cubbing meet about eight miles away. The
ground was still as hard as a brick, and we had decided to
save the horses' legs for later on and see what we could
"from our flat feet". Cock-crowing dimness became daylight; the road was white and dry, but the air smelt of
autumn. I saw Milden again, in the glinting rays of a quiet
scarlet-orbed sunrise; he was on a compact little roan
horse; among his hounds outside some gryphoned lodge-
gates he leant forward in diplomatic conference with a
communicative keeper. The "field" consisted of a young
lady with a cockaded groom and a farmer on an unclipped
and excited four-year-old. A few more riders turned up
later on when the hounds were chivvying an inexperienced
cub up and down a wide belt of woodland. After the first
invigorating chorus in the early morning air had evoked
our enthusiasm the day soon became sultry: pestered by

gnats and flies we panted to and fro, and then followed the hunt to another big covert.

By ten o'clock we had both of us lost our early ardour; they had killed a cub and now a brace had gone to ground in a warren. Stephen told me that the Master was mad keen on digging out foxes, which in that and many other parts of the country were too plentiful for good sport later in the season. While cheering his hounds up and down the woods he had several times passed us; but he was engrossed in his job and scarcely gave us a glance.

When we arrived at the rabbit-warren I could at first see nothing of him but the back of his old mulberry coat; his head and shoulders were half underground; he had just put a terrier in and was listening intently for muffled subterranean barkings. Stephen got into conversation with Will, the first whip, who was an old friend of his, since he'd been second whip under the previous huntsman (the ineffectual Ben Trotter). I didn't dare to hope that Milden would remember me, but when he straightened himself and swivelled a jolly red face in my direction I gazed at him with humble expectancy.

I drew his face blank; for his eyes travelled on toward the first whip and he exclaimed, with the temporary Irish brogue which he had acquired while he was hunting the Kilcurran Hounds, "They're a tarrible long time bringing those spades, Will!"

Whereupon he picked up his heavy-thonged crop and whistled some baying and inquisitive bitches away from the rabbit-hole, addressing them in the unwriteable huntsman's lingo which they appeared to understand, judging by the way they looked up at him. "Trinket . . . good ole gal . . . here; Relic; Woeful; Bonnybell; get along bike there, Gamesome . . . good little Gamesome"—with affectionate interpolations, and an aside to Will that that Windgall was entering first rate and had been right up in front all the morning . . . "throwing your tongue a treat, weren't ye, little Windgall?" Windgall jumped up at him and flourished her stern.

Soon afterwards the second whip rode through the

undergrowth encumbered with spades, and they took their coats off in the dappling sunshine for a real good dig. The crunch of delving spades and the smell of sandy soil now mingled with the redolence of the perspiring pack, the crushed bracken that the horses were munching, and the pungent unmistakeable odour of foxes. However inhumane its purpose, it was a kindly country scene.

Well enough I remember that September morning, and how, when I offered to take a turn with one of the spades, Denis Milden looked at me and said, "Haven't I seen ye somewhere before?" I answered shyly that perhaps he'd seen me at the point-to-points. It seemed providential when Will reminded him that I'd won the Hunt Heavy Weights. Milden casually remarked, "That must be a good horse of yours."

Emboldened by this, I asked whether by any chance he remembered meeting me out with the Dumborough nearly fourteen years before. But for the life of him he couldn't recollect that. "Ye see I've seen such a tarrible lot of new people since then!" he remarked cheerily, pushing his blue velvet cap up from a heated brow. Nevertheless, I toiled back to the Rectory well satisfied with the way I'd managed to remind him of my undistinguished identity, and Stephen exulted with me that the new Master was such an absolutely top-hole chap. "Not an atom of swank about him." It is quite possible that we may both of us have talked with a slight Irish accent when we were telling the attentive Rector all about it during luncheon.

II

October arrived; the drought broke with forty-eight hours' quiet rain; and Dixon had a field day with the new clipping machine, of which it is enough to say that the stable-boy turned a handle and Dixon did the rest. He had decided to clip the horses' legs this season; the Ringwell was a bad country for thorns, and these were naturally less likely to be overlooked on clipped legs, which also were more sightly and dried quicker than hairy ones.

"Only bad grooms let their horses get cracked heels", was one of his maxims. "Only lazy grooms wash the mud off with water" went without saying.

We often spoke about the new Master, who was already the sum and substance of my happy hunting-ground thirty miles away. Dixon remembered him distinctly; he had always considered him the pattern of what a young gentleman ought to be. Frequently I wished Aunt Evelyn's sedate establishment could be transplanted into that well-foxed and unstagnant county. For one thing it was pretty poor fun for Dixon if I were to be continually boxing Cockbird and Harkaway to Downfield or staying at the Rectory; but Dixon seemed satisfied by the bare fact of my being a hunting man.

Resplendent in my new red coat, and almost too much admired by Aunt Evelyn and Miriam, I went off to the opening meet by the early train from Dumbridge to Downfield. Half an hour's ride took me to the kennels, where I joined an impressive concourse, mounted, in vehicles, and on foot. The sun shone after a white frost, and everyone was anxious to have a look at the new Master. My new coat was only a single spot of colour among many, but I felt a tremendous swell all the same. Familiar faces greeted me, and when we trotted away to draw Pacey's Plantation, old Mr. Dearborn bumped along beside me in his faded red coat and blue and white spotted bird's-eye cravat. "This horse ought to have one of you young chaps on his back!" he exclaimed. "Jumps too big for an old buffer like me; never known him put a foot wrong, clever as a cat— (*hold up, will you!*)" . . . his clever hunter having tripped badly on some stones.

He presented me to an affable person on the other side of him—Mr. Bellerby, of Cowslake Manor. Mr. Bellerby was mounted on a fidgety, ewe-necked, weak-middled, dun-coloured mare. He had a straggling sandy beard and was untidily dressed in new clothes which looked all wrong. He seemed to have put them on in a hurry—baggy black coat half-unbuttoned—spurs falling back from loose-fitting patent-leather boots, starched stock with a horseshoe pin insecurely inserted—badly cut white corduroy breeches; and an absurdly long cane hunting-crop without a thong. He had a mackintosh coat rolled up and strapped on the back of his saddle. He wore moss-green worsted gloves, and his mare's bridle had a browband of yellow and black striped patent leather.

Mr. Dearborn remarked, when we lost sight of him in the crowd outside the covert, that he was a queer fish to look at, but a very warm man in Mincing Lane. "Made a pile of money out in the East; just come to live in our country; built a billiard-room on to his house, I hear; sort of man who might be good for a fifty pound subscription. Fear he's no horseman, however. That dun of his gallops like a train till she gets near a fence, and then digs her toes in. I know all about her, for he bought her in the summer from a neighbour of mine. Pity he didn't ask my advice. I'd have let him have this one for a hundred and twenty. Absolute patent-safety, this one; jump a house if you asked him to!"

Now it so happened that the new owner of Cowslake Manor provided the liveliest incident that I remember out of that day, which was "badly served by scent" as the local scribe reported in the paper. A fox was found in Pacey's Plantation (it was hinted that he'd been put there by Mr. Pacey, a hard-riding farmer who believed in showing the foot people some fun on an opening day). The majority of the field hustled round the outside of the covert, but I thought to be clever and went through by a grassy ride. A short distance in front of me galloped Mr. Bellerby; his hat bounced on his back, suspended by its string, and he was manifestly travelling quicker than he had intended. Some-one in front pushed through the gate out of the Plantation, and while we neared it the open gate was slowly swinging back again. It was uncertain which would win, Mr. Beller-by or the gate. I stole past him on his near side, got there just in the nick of time, and retarded the gate with my left hand. Mr. Bellerby bolted through the aperture, narrowly avoiding the gatepost with his right knee. It was an easily managed exploit on my part, since I had Cockbird well under control, and, as usual, he understood what we were about every bit as well as his owner. Mr. Bellerby continued his involuntary express journey across a ridge-and-furrow field, bore down on a weak hedge, swerved, shot half-way up his mare's neck, and came to a standstill while Cockbird was taking the fence in his stride.

After Mr. Pacey's fox had got into a drain half a mile further on, Mr. Bellerby reappeared and besieged me with his gratitude. He really didn't know how to thank me enough or how to congratulate me in adequate terms on what he persisted in describing as my "magnificent feat of horsemanship". It was, he asserted, the most alarming experience he'd ever had since he was run away with down a steep hill in a dogcart years ago in Surrey; he recalled his vivid emotions on that appalling occasion. "Shall I jump out, I thought, or shall I remain where I am? I jumped out! I shall never forget those awful moments!"

Embarrassed by his effusive acknowledgments I did my best to avoid him during the rest of the day, but he was constantly attaching himself to me, and everybody who happened to be near us had to hear all about my marvellous feat of horsemanship.

"Not a second to spare! I really think Mr. Sherston saved my life!" he ejaculated to Sir John Ruddimore, a stolid and rather exclusive landowner who followed the hounds very sedately with an elderly daughter. The local big-wig listened politely to the story; but I felt a fool, and was much relieved when I saw the back of Mr. Bellerby as he tit-tupped away to Cowslake Manor after pressing me to accept a cheroot about eight inches long out of a crocodile-skin case.

I returned to Butley without having exchanged a word with Milden. Whenever I saw him his face was expressionless and he seemed to be unaware of anything except his hounds and what they were doing. Nigel Croplady, however, referred to him by his christian name and led one to suppose that he had been indispensable to him since he had taken the country. But Croplady, I am afraid, was just a little bit of a snob.

For several weeks Milden remained eminently unapproachable, although I diligently went out with his hounds, enlarging my equestrian experience by taking a full thirty-five bobs' worth out of Whatman's hard-legged hirelings. My moneysworth included several heavy falls on my hat, but I took rather a pride in that, since my sole intention was to impress the Master with my keenness. Up to Christmas the hounds showed very moderate sport; scent was bad, but I overheard a lot of grumbling (mainly from unenterprising riders) about Milden being such a slow huntsman. Certainly he seemed in no hurry, but I was always quite satisfied, myself, as long as I had done plenty of jumping by the end of a day.

And our amateur huntsman, as I afterwards discovered, knew exactly what he was doing. As soon as he took over the country he had asserted his independence by getting rid of the Ringwell dog-pack, on which the members had always prided themselves so much. To the prudent protestations of the Committee he replied bluntly that although the dog-hounds were all right to listen to in the woods, they were too slow for words on the unenclosed downs, and too big and cloddy for the cramped and strongly fenced vale country. He added that Ben Trotter had got them into terrible bad habits and he wasn't going to waste his time teaching them how to hunt.

Shortly afterwards he had bought five-and-twenty couple of unentered bitches at Rugby Hound Sales; so that, when the Ringwell-bred puppies came in from walk, he began the season with no less than thirty-seven couple of unentered hounds. To those people who properly understood hunting his patient methods must have been a welcome contrast to the harum-scarum, hoicking, horn-blowing "which way'd 'e go?" performances of the late huntsman.

Denis Milden refused to lift his hounds unless he was obliged to do so, and in this way he taught them to hunt on a catchy scent without looking for help. They learned to keep their noses down, and day after day Milden watched them worrying out the barely workable line of a fox who was half an hour ahead of them; he was deaf to the cap-

tious comments of his field and the loudly offered information of would-be helpers who knew which way his fox had
gone. The result of this procedure was that after Christmas,
when scenting conditions improved, the light-boned bitches
began to hunt like blazes; in fact, as he said, "they fairly
screamed along", and of the two packs he really couldn't
make up his mind which was the better—the big bitches or
the little bitches. When the big bitches had pushed an old
dog-fox out of Basset Wood and killed him after a fast fifty
minutes with only one check, a six-mile point over all the
best of the Monday country, the little bitches went one
better with a really beautiful hunt from one of the big
gorse coverts on the hills. The grumbling contingent now
forgot that they'd ever uttered a word of criticism, and for
the moment were unable to exercise their grumbling aptitude at all. But the real wiseacres, such as Sir John Ruddimore and Fred Buzzaway, nodded conclusively to one another, as though agreeing that it was only what they'd
been expecting all the time.

Fred Buzzaway, whose name has just cropped up casually, was a totally different type of sportsman from that
reticent local magnate Sir John Ruddimore (of Rapworth
Park). Always fond of a joke, Fred Buzzaway was a blue-
jowled dog-faced bachelor, who habitually dressed as
though it were going to be a pouring wet day. Bowler hat
well down over his ears; dark whipcord coat and service-
able brown breeches; tight and skimpy stock; such was his
rig-out, wet or fine. I see him now, splashed with mud,
his coat collar turned up, and his head bent against the
driving rain. His boots were usually muddy owing to his
laudable habit of getting off his horse as often as possible
to give it a rest, and during a slow hunt he was often to be
seen leading his mount and even running beside it. He was
an active man on his feet, and when he wasn't riding to
hounds he was following a pack of foot-harriers. Stag-
hunting he despised. "Jackasses hunting a carted jackass",
he called it. In his youth Buzzaway had been called to the
Bar. His friends always said that when he got there he
asked for a bottle of "Bass" and never went back again

after he had discovered his mistake. From this it may be inferred that he had a wholesome belief in good liquor.

"Beer goes well with beagling," he would remark, "but after a fox-hunt I feel the need for something stronger."

Few of my fox-hunting acquaintances seem to have been taciturn, but Buzzaway, I am inclined to think, outwent them all in consistent chattiness. He enjoyed airing his observations, which were shrewd and homely. He was one of those men whose personal conviction as to which way the hunted fox has gone is only equalled by their expert knowledge, at the end of a gallop, of the ground he went over. His intimacy with minor local topography was unsurpassed by anyone I knew. Even when he had been out with some neighbouring pack, he could reel off the parish names like clockwork. When asked what sort of a day he'd had, he would reply: "Found in Clackett's Copse, ran a couple of rings, and then out by Hogstye, over the old fosse-way, and into Warthole Wood, where he tried the main-earths and went on into Cuddleswood Park; along the Banks and into Hawk's Rough, back by the Banks into the Park, left-handed by Warthole Wood . . ." and so on, until one could almost have believed that he'd been riding the fox himself instead of one of his low-priced and persevering hunters.

As might be imagined, he was by no means difficult to get to know. At first I was rather scared by the noises he made whenever I was anywhere near him: either he was hustling along close behind me, shouting "Forrard on", or else he was cracking his whip at a straggling hound, or bawling "Hold up" to his horse at a jump, and I felt that I should be the next one to get shouted at. But I soon discovered what a cheery customer he was, and I became one of his best listeners. Needless to say, he was on easy terms with the Master, and it was in his company that I made my first step toward knowing Milden well.

Buzzaway was one of the privileged (or pushful) people who were sometimes to be seen riding along a road beside the huntsman, although Milden's manner was abstracted and discouraging to conversation. More than once I had overtaken the hounds on their way to a meet, but I had always kept unobtrusively at the rear of the procession, which included three second-horsemen, one of them carrying a terrier in a bag. I was so shy that I scarcely ventured to say good-morning when I passed Milden at the meet. But one day in the middle of December I stayed out to the very end on one of Whatman's hirelings; as a rule I started back to Downfield a bit earlier, to catch my train, but it was getting dark early and the hounds had been running hard in the big woods all day, changing foxes several times. Milden was standing up in his stirrups and blowing his horn; the first whip was counting the hounds with little wags of his crops as though conducting a string band. Buzzaway was taking a long pull at his flask, and everyone else had gone home. Will announced that they were all there except Purity.

"Blast that Purity!" muttered Milden, whereupon Purity emerged penitently from the shades of the covert and the cavalcade moved off along the lane.

So it came about that I found myself riding mutely along in the middle of the pack with Buzzaway and the Master. In front of us "Toprail", the hunting correspondent of the *Southern Daily*, wobbled along on his bicycle and accumulated information from the second whip, a melancholy young man named Bill Durrant, whose existence was made no merrier by the horses he had to ride, especially the one he was on—a herring-gutted piebald which, as he had been heard to complain, was "something crool over timber".

"Well, Master," remarked Buzzaway, "you were devilish unlucky when that fresh fox got up in Cowleas Wood! I viewed your hunted fox going back to Danehurst Hatch, and he looked so beat I could almost have caught him myself."

Milden tucked his horn into the case on his saddle. "Beat, was he? We'll catch him next time, never you fear. And we'll hunt *you* when we get short of foxes. I'll be bound you'd leave a good smell behind you!"

Buzzaway grinned with as much pleasure as if he'd been

paid the most graceful of compliments. Jabber, jabber, jabber went his tongue, undiscouraged by the inadequate response it met with. And considering the amount of shouting he'd done during the day, it wasn't to be wondered at that Milden was somewhat silent and preferred to munch a large brown biscuit which he produced from his pocket in a twist of paper. Later on, however, he turned to me and asked if I'd got far to go. When he heard that I lived thirty miles away in the next county he said I "must be desperate keen, to come all that way", and my heart glowed with gratitude. But this was nothing compared with what I felt when he continued, "I tell you what, I can put you up at the Kennels any time you like, when you're having a day with us. It's terrible quiet there of an evening, and I'd be glad of someone to talk to. Just drop me a card the day before, and bring your horse as well if you like; or you can find your way out from Downfield somehow if you're on one of Whatman's screws." He tickled my hireling's neck with the end of his crop. "They earn their keep all right, don't they? That poor old sod was out the day before yesterday, I know, for some silly blighter from the barracks landed slap in the middle of my hounds on him. I wish some of those soldiers weren't quite so mad on jumping. It's the only thing they come out for!"

We got to Clumpton crossroads and he said good-night. Buzzaway and I trotted briskly on toward Downfield in a drizzle of rain. I could scarcely believe that I had been invited to stay at the Kennels, and I listened absent-mindedly to my companion's account of a day he'd had with the Cotswold last season when staying with his brother. Ordinarily I should have found this interesting, but the only information I gathered was that though the Cotswold was a niceish country for watching hounds work, the Ringwell needed brains as well as boldness and he asked for nothing better. I then parted from him and clattered into Whatman's cobbled yard.

III

It was close on Christmas, but the weather remained mild, and in the following week I wrote a concise letter offering myself as a guest at Ringwell after Wednesday's hunting—the meet being only a few miles from the Kennels. At home I said not a word about my sudden elevation in the sporting world, and I allowed Aunt Evelyn to take it for granted that I was going to Hoadley Rectory. After I had actually been to the Kennels I could talk about it, but not before. It was too important an event for casual conversation, and even Dixon was kept in the dark about it. Aunt Evelyn had shown the right amount of interest in Denis Milden, remembering him as such a nice-looking boy, and remembering also how she had come across his people in Northamptonshire when she was a girl—a well-known sporting family who had a large place near, she thought, Daventry. I sometimes wished that my own family was like that, for the architecture of my existence seemed meagre, and I wanted to be strongly connected with the hunting organism which at that time I thought of as the only one worth belonging to. And it *was* (though a limited one) a clearly defined world, which is an idea that most of us cling to, unless we happen to be transcendental thinkers.

Staying at the Kennels was the most significant occasion my little world could offer me, and in order that he might share my sublunary advancement I took Cockbird with me. In reply to my reserved little note I received a cheery letter from Denis: he would be delighted to see me and gave detailed instructions about my bag being called for and taken out to the Kennels from Downfield. He told me to be sure to bring a rug for my horse as he was "terrible short of clothing". My belongings were to be conveyed to the Kennels on the "flesh-cart", which would be in Downfield that day. I was surprised that he should take so much trouble, for I had yet to learn how methodical and thorough he was in everything which he undertook.

I remember nothing of that day's hunting; but the usual

terse entry in my diary perpetuates the fact that the meet was at "The Barley Mow". "Found in Pilton Shaw and Crumpton Osiers, but did little with either as scent was rotten. Weather very wet in afternoon; had quite a good hunt of nearly two hours from Trodger's Wood; hounds were stopped in Basset Wood at 4.25." The concluding words, "Stayed at the Kennels", now seem a very bleak condensation of the event. But it did not occur to me that my sporting experiences would ever be called upon to provide material for a book, and I should have been much astonished if I could have foreseen my present efforts to put the clock back (or rather the calendar) from 1928 to 1911.

Yet I find it easy enough to recover a few minutes of that grey south-westerly morning, with its horsemen hustling on in scattered groups, the December air alive with the excitement of the chase, and the dull green landscape seeming to respond to the rousing cheer of the huntsman's voice when the hounds hit off the line again after a brief check. Away they stream, throwing up little splashes of water as they race across a half-flooded meadow. Cockbird flies a fence with a watery ditch on the take-off side. "How topping", I think, "to be alive and well up in the hunt"; and I spur along the sound turf of a green park and past the front of a square pink Queen Anne house with blank windows and smokeless chimneys, and a formal garden with lawns and clipped yew hedges sloping to a sunk fence. A stone statue stares at me, and I wonder who lived there when the house was first built. "I am riding past the past," I think, never dreaming that I shall one day write that moment down on paper; never dreaming that I shall be clarifying and condensing that chronicle of simple things through which I blundered so diffidently.

But the day's hunting is ended, and I must watch myself jogging back to the Kennels, soaked to the skin but quietly satisfied in my temporary embodiment with the Hunt establishment; beneath a clean-swept sky, too, for the rain-clouds have gone on with the wind behind them. Soon we are passing the village green; a quarter of a mile from the Kennels, Denis Milden blows a long wavering blast to warn the kennelman and the head-groom that we are almost home. When we turn in at a gate under some trees there are men waiting with swinging stable-lanterns, which flicker on their red jerseys, outside the long range of portable loose-boxes which Denis has put up. He and his whips are quickly off their horses and into the kennel-yard among the jostling hounds. He has told me to find my way indoors and get my tea and a bath. Cockbird is led into a loose-box under the superior eye of Meeston, the head-groom, a gruff, uncommunicative man in a long, dirty white kennel-coat. Cockbird gives his head a shake, glad to be rid of his bridle. Then he lowers it, and I pull his ears for a while—an operation which most horses enjoy when they are tired. The place is pervaded by a smell of oatmeal and boiled horse-flesh, and the vociferations of the hounds accompany me as I tread stiffly through the darkness to a wicket-gate, and so to the front door of the old wood-built huntsman's house— "the wooden hutch", as we used to call it.

*   *   *

Welcomed by barks from an elderly Aberdeen and a slim white fox-terrier with a black head, I followed an expressionless young man-servant up the narrow staircase to my room, which was furnished with the bleakest necessities. The house creaked in the wind, and the geyser in the bathroom seemed likely to blow up at any moment. I was downstairs again and had finished my tea before Denis came in from the kennels. However late and wet he returned, he always saw his hounds fed, and it was usually about an hour before he was inside the house. No professional huntsman ever worked harder than he did, and he invariably rode to the meet and home again with his hounds.

Sitting in the poky little living-room on the ground floor, I was surrounded by all his significant personal belongings. There were a few photographs, mostly in silver frames, of his contemporaries at Eton and Oxford, all in hunting or racing clothes; the walls were hung with monotonously executed portraits of horses which he had owned, and

there was one large group of four hounds which had won a
first prize at Peterborough Hound Show. There was also a
coloured drawing of himself winning a University Steeple-
chase. A few standard sporting books (including Lindsay
Gordon's poems, and the leather-backed volumes of the
Foxhound Kennel Stud-Book) filled a small bookcase. The
letters and papers on his writing-table were very tidily
arranged. On the sideboard were racing-cups and a huge
silver tray "presented by the members of the Kilcurran
Hunt as a testimony of their appreciation of the sport he
had shown them during his Mastership". There were
several foxes' masks among the pictures, with place and
date of death in small white lettering: one or two brushes
were tucked behind picture frames, and a fox's pad was
mounted as the handle of a paper knife. Finally (and there
was only just enough room for it) an upright piano with a
pianola apparatus attached to it, demonstrated that he was
fond of a bit of music. A record of Dvořák's "New World"
Symphony appeared to be his only link with Europe. But
he had the advantage of me as regards foreign travel, since
he had once been to Budapest to play in a polo tournament. (He told me this at dinner, when we were saying
how superior the English were to all foreigners.)

It was after half-past six when he came in. He seemed to
take me for granted already, but he assured me once again
that he was "terrible pleased to have someone to talk to".
He threw off his wet hunting coat and slipped into a ragged
tweed jacket which the silent servant Henry held out for
him. As soon as he had swallowed a cup of tea he lit his
pipe and sat down at his writing-table to open a pile of letters. He handed me one, with a grimy envelope addressed
to "Mr. Milden, The Dog Kennels, Ringwell". The writer
complained that a fox had been the night before and killed
three more of his pullets, and unless he could bring the
dogs there soon there wouldn't be one left and they'd really
have to start shooting the foxes, and respectfully begging
to state that he was owed fifteen shillings by the Hunt for
compensation. Many of Denis's letters were complaints
from poultry keepers or from small farmers whose seeds or

sown ground had been ridden over when the land was wet. I asked what he did with these, and he replied that he sent them on to old McCosh, the Hunt secretary. "But when they look like being troublesome I go over and talk to them myself."

I found afterwards that he had a great gift for pacifying such people, to whom the Hunt might have been an unmitigated nuisance if it hadn't been an accepted institution. The non-hunting farmers liked to see the Hunt, but they disliked the marks it left on their land. The whole concern depended on the popularity and efficiency of the Master, and the behaviour of the people who hunted. Denis Milden's predecessor in the Mastership had been too lavish with indiscriminate five-pound notes; consequently the petitioners for compensation had begun to regard the Poultry and Damage Fund as a regular friend in need, and complaints from poultry farmers were far too frequent. To hear Denis talk about them one might have thought that hens were the enemies of society instead of being the providers of that universally respected object, the egg.

Watching him open those letters was an important step in my sporting education. Until then I had not begun to realize how much there was to be done apart from the actual chivvying of the foxes. Thenceforward I became increasingly aware that a successful day's hunting was the result of elaborate and tactful preparations, and I ceased to look upon an angry farmer with a pitchfork as something to be laughed at. In the meantime I wished he would go upstairs and change his wet clothes. But he sat there in his muddy boots for almost an hour, writing letters in his careful calligraphy and filling in his diary—a log-book of details such as which horses had been out, where foxes had been found, and so on.

It was eight-thirty by the time he'd had his bath and was shouting from the top of the stairs to Mrs. Timson, the buxom grey-haired cook: "Mrs. Timson! Tell Henry to put that dinner on."

When that dinner had been put on and eaten (there was a large joint of beef, I remember) he asked me to play some music. I treadled away at the pianola, while he dozed in a shabby arm-chair with Moll, the fox-terrier, on his knees, and a litter of newspapers at his carpet-slippered feet. I had ambled to the end of a musical comedy arrangement ("*The Geisha*" I think it was) and was bundling the perforated music-roll back again with reverse motion when he suddenly heaved himself out of the chair, yawned, remarked that he'd give anything to be able to play the piano properly, whistled to the dogs, and turned them out into the night for an airing. He then lit a couple of candles, extinguished the unshaded oil-lamp, led the way upstairs, and hoped I'd sleep all right. All this sounds humdrum, but I have since then spent many a much duller evening with people who were under the impression that they were talking brilliantly. I have never cared greatly about highly sophisticated persons, although some of them may seek to enlarge their intellectual experience by perusing my modest narrative.

Lying awake that night I listened to the wind which was making queer noises round the flimsily constructed house. Once or twice there was an outburst of hound music from the kennels. Through the thin partition wall I could hear the grunts and snores of the stablemen, whose dormitory was next to the spare room. The blind on my window flapped. I thought how different staying at Ringwell Kennels was from what I'd expected. Yet it seemed exactly like what it ought to be. I wondered whether old Cockbird was asleep out in his loose-box. Thought what an odd character the head-groom looked, and how surprised Stephen would be when I told him all about my visit. Meditated on the difference between Denis hunting the hounds (unapproachable and with "a face like a boot") and Denis indoors—homely and kind and easy to get on with; would he really want me to come and stay with him again, I wondered. And then I fell into so sound a sleep that the stablemen on the other side of the partition wall failed to awake me when they got up at some unearthly hour and went down the dark stairs with their clumping boots to begin their work in the damp December morning.

IV

I must pass rather rapidly through the remainder of that season and the one which followed it. While Denis continued to show splendid sport, my own achievements included learning to identify the majority of the hounds by their names. This I did mainly while "walking out" with them on non-hunting days. The road by the Kennels had wide green borders to it, and along these we used to loiter for an hour or two at a time; the full-fed bitches, their coats sprinkled with sulphur, were continually being spoken to by name, and in this way I silently acquired information. I cannot say that I ever became anything of a judge of their shape and make, or that my knowledge has since proved profitable; but I knew Brightness from Brevity, Ramble from Roguery, and Wavelet from Watercress, and this enabled me to show an intelligent interest and to share the Master's enthusiasm for his favourites; I could speciously agree that, although Tempest was a beautiful bitch to look at, she was by no means what she might be when it came to hunting. Peerless, on the other hand, was worthy of her appellation, and frequently hit off the line when the others were at a loss to know which way their fox had gone across a bit of cold ploughland.

My regular visits to the Kennels, and the facility with which I echoed the Master's ideas and opinions, bolstered up my self-complacence and gave me a certain reflected importance among the members of the Hunt, which I should otherwise have lacked. I now wore the Hunt button and was regarded as being "in the know"; people like Colonel Hesmon and Fred Buzzaway would ask me whether I could tell them where the meets were likely to be the week after next. A few words of praise from Denis were, however, what I most wanted. Opportunities for earning his approval were not numerous; but now and again, when he was on a sticky jumper and I happened to be with him in a run, he would shout "Go on, George". Probably there was a big brambly hedge to be got over, and I would cram at it, not caring whether I took a heavy fall so long as I had the privilege of giving him a lead; the bigger the hole I made in the hedge the better pleased he was. He was a strong and patient horseman, and since the country was for the most part rough and "trappy" and the going deep on the heavy clay soil, he rode very deliberately at the fences. While everyone else was fully occupied in keeping with the hounds at all, Denis never seemed to have half his mind on the horse he was riding. His eyes were on the hounds, and he went over the country, as we used to say, "as if it wasn't there".

During January and February in his first season I had many good days with the Ringwell, riding anything I could hire or borrow when I hadn't one of my own to bring out. Stephen hunted regularly from his barracks, and shared my appreciation of Denis. He was ready, he said, to knock anyone off his horse who uttered a word of criticism against the huntsman. His main ambition in life being to hunt a pack of hounds himself, he appointed himself a sort of amateur second whipper-in, and he was never so happy as when Denis asked him to watch the end of a covert or stop some hounds when they had divided and a few couple were away on the line of a second fox. Stephen called me a lucky old devil to be staying at the Kennels so often. He liked soldiering well enough, but the horses were his real interest. The guns, he said, were nothing but a nuisance, and he, for one, had no wish to chuck shells at anyone.

During the month of March my movements were restricted by the Coal Strike. There were no trains, and I missed some of the best hunts of the season. But I had a few days with the Dumborough and made myself conspicuous by jumping every fence I could find.

Dixon, who had been rather out of it, now came in for the solemnities of preparing Cockbird for the point-to-points. I ran him in a few "Open" races, but found that he couldn't go quite fast enough, though he jumped faultlessly and once finished third in a field of a dozen. Thanks to his reliability I was beginning to have quite a high opinion of myself. The Ringwell Races were late in April that year. Denis rode his best horse in the Heavy Weights and beat me by three lengths. His victory seemed to me quite appropriate, and everyone wanted him to win. It had never occurred to me that I should finish in front of him. Good-natured Mr. Gaffikin was there again to give me a leg-up, and he praised me for my improved handling of my horse. He assured me that if I'd won the Race two years running I should never have been able to get my hat on again—a remark which appeared to cause him extreme satisfaction, for he repeated it more than once, with a lady-killing laugh. (The inference was that I should have suffered from "a swelled head".)

I saw very little of Denis during that summer, which was a wet one, and bad for my batting average. Having made only fifteen runs in my last seven innings I was glad enough to put away my cricket-bag, and by the second week in September I was back at the Kennels for a prolonged stay. There was a new lot of horses, and Denis, who badly needed someone to talk to, always had a spare one for me to ride.

*   *   *

Ringwell cubbing days are among my happiest memories. Those mornings now reappear in my mind, lively and freshly painted by the sunshine of an autumn that made amends for the rainy weeks which had washed away the summer. Four days a week we were up before daylight. I had heard the snoring stable-hands roll out of bed with yawns and grumblings, and they were out and about before the reticent Henry came into my room with a candle and a jug of warm water. (How Henry managed to get up was a mystery.) Any old clothes were good enough for cubbing, and I was very soon downstairs in the stuffy little living-room, where Denis had an apparatus for boiling eggs. While they were bubbling he put the cocoa-powder in the cups, two careful spoonfuls each, and not a grain more. A third spoonful was unthinkable.

Not many minutes afterwards we were out by the range of loose-boxes under the rustling trees, with quiet stars overhead and scarcely a hint of morning. In the kennels the two packs were baying at one another from their separate yards, and as soon as Denis had got his horse from the gruff white-coated head-groom, a gate released the hounds —twenty-five or thirty couple of them, and all very much on their toes. Out they streamed like a flood of water, throwing their tongues and spreading away in all directions with waving sterns, as though they had never been out in the world before. Even then I used to feel the strangeness of the scene with its sharp exuberance of un-kennelled energy. Will's hearty voice and the crack of his whip stood out above the clamour and commotion which surged around Denis and his horse. Then, without any apparent lull or interruption, the whirlpool became a well-regulated torrent flowing through the gateway into the road, along which the sound of hoofs receded with a purposeful clip-clopping. Whereupon I hoisted myself on to an unknown horse—usually an excited one—and set off higgledy-piggledy along the road to catch them up. Sometimes we had as many as twelve miles to go, but more often we were at the meet in less than an hour.

The mornings I remember most zestfully were those which took us up on to the chalk downs. To watch the day breaking from purple to dazzling gold while we trotted up a deep-rutted lane; to inhale the early freshness when we were on the sheep-cropped uplands; to stare back at the low country with its cock-crowing farms and mist-coiled waterways; thus to be riding out with a sense of spacious discovery—was it not something stolen from the lie-a-bed world and the luckless city workers—even though it ended in nothing more than the killing of a leash of fox-cubs? (for whom, to tell the truth, I felt an unconfessed sympathy). Up on the downs in fine September weather sixteen years ago. . . .

It is possible that even then, if I was on a well-behaved horse, I could half forget why we were there, so pleasant was it to be alive and gazing around me. But I would be dragged out of my day dream by Denis when he shouted to me to wake up and get round to the far side of the covert;

for on such hill days we often went straight to one of the big gorses without any formality of a meet. There were beech woods, too, in the folds of the downs, and lovely they looked in the mellow sunshine, with summer's foliage falling in ever-deepening drifts among their gnarled and mossy roots.

*   *   *

"What you want is a good, hard, short-legged horse well up to your weight and able to get through the mud and do a long day," remarked Denis one afternoon in October.

We had been out from seven till four, with a good long spell of digging to finish up with. Having said this he settled himself in his chair, lit his pipe, and applied his mind to the Racing Intelligence in *The Sportsman* with an air of having settled the matter once and for all. The sort of horse he had described was the sort of horse everyone in the Ringwell country wanted; but Denis was never afraid of uttering an honest unvarnished exactitude.

I suggested that such a horse might cost more money than I could conveniently afford.

"Put a fiver on Michaelmas Daisy for the Cambridgeshire. She's at 100 to 8. I'm having a tenner on each way myself," he replied, without turning his head.

Although I'd never had more than half a sovereign on a horse in my life, and that was only at point-to-points, I risked two pounds ten shillings each way, and Michaelmas Daisy did it by half a length.

Soon afterwards Denis took me to see a dealer on the other side of the country, and there we found the very horse I wanted. The dealer (an amusing Irishman whose deportment I must for once decline to describe) was anxious to oblige the M.F.H. and knocked ten pounds off the price. Sunny Jim was mine for ninety pounds. He was a short-tailed corky-looking bay with a habit of grinding his teeth as he jogged along the roads. And that is really all I intend to say about him, except that he was well worth the money and approved of by Dixon as a real old-fashioned sort. I could just manage fifty pounds out of my own money, so my fortuitous forty pounds saved the situation. Harkaway was now transferred to Aunt Evelyn's dogcart, where he conducted himself with dignity and decorum.

The opening meet therefore, found me prosperous and complacent, exhibiting my new horse to the Rev. Colwood, Buzzaway, "Gentleman George", and all the rest of my Ringwell friends, and successfully competing with Stephen and his brother officers from the barracks. But a couple of weeks before Christmas the continuity of things was abruptly fractured by an event which caused a terrible to-do among the supporters of the Ringwell Hounds, myself included. Just as we had all settled down to a record-breaking season, the Master handed in his resignation. A lawn-meet at Rapworth Park was rendered positively funereal by the announcement, and Mr. McCosh, the stolid purple-faced Hunt secretary, swallowed a stiff brandy and soda as if a posset of poison was the sole solution for the blow which had made him so huffy.

It had been a recognized fact that for Denis Milden the Ringwell country was only a stepping-stone to higher things. Nobody had hoped that he would remain with a provincial hunt for ever. But this was sudden. He had sometimes talked to me about his prospects of getting a better country, but he could be as dumb as a post when he had a motive for silence, and he had given me no inkling of a change before the morning when he came down to breakfast with a letter in his hand and informed me that he'd been elected Master of the Packlestone. He said it with satisfied sobriety, and I did my best to seem delighted. Now the Packlestone Hunt, as I knew well enough, was away up in the Midlands. And the Midlands, to put it mildly, were a long step from Butley. So Denis, as I might have expected, was to be translated to a region which I couldn't even visualize. It meant that he was going out of my existence as completely as he had entered it. Every time I returned to the Kennels I found greater difficulty in making my voice sound convincing while I conjectured to him about the attractive qualities of his new country.

In the meantime, as if to tantalize the Ringwellites, the

bitches excelled themselves. The only consolation was that he couldn't take them with him. A new Master was secured, but no one felt much confidence in him or the future. The less they knew about him the more they shook their heads over his inevitable fallibilities. Already it was rumoured that he was the slowest amateur huntsman in England; and now he was proposing to hunt the hounds himself two days a week.

When I discussed Denis Milden's departure with people out hunting they often assumed that I should be going with him. I replied guardedly that I hadn't thought about it yet, although the truth was that I had thought of little else. I had to acclimatize myself to the disconsolate idea of a Ringwell country where I should once again be reduced to the status of a visiting nonentity. But one evening when Denis was unusually bright and communicative (after a good day in the nice bit of grass country close to the Kennels) he turned his blunt kindly face in my direction (he was at his writing-table with a lot of letters to answer), and remarked: "I'll have to get you up to Packlestone somehow. It's too sad for words to think of leaving you behind!" When he said that I knew that he intended me to go with him. And Denis had a habit of getting his own way.

PART EIGHT: MIGRATION TO THE MIDLANDS

I

When Dixon arrived at the Packlestone Kennels in the middle of October, with my four hunters and a man under him, he was realizing an ambition which must often have seemed unattainable. To break away from Butley for a season in a country which adjoined such notable names as the Quorn, the Pytchley, and Mr. Fernie's—well might he have wondered how it had been brought about! But there we were; and Aunt Evelyn had been left to drive through a lonely winter with Harkaway and the stable-boy—now nearly eighteen and promoted to the dignity of wearing Dixon's top-hat and blue livery coat.

From the moment when Denis had first suggested my going with him, I had made up my mind to do it. Nevertheless, the fact remained that I couldn't afford it. I was putting myself in a false position in more ways than one: financially, because I should be spending my whole year's income in less than six months; and socially, because the people in the Packlestone Hunt quite naturally assumed that I was much better off than I really was. I had discussed it all with Denis in April. Denis was good at making fifteen shillings do the work of a pound, and he was fond of talking about money. But when I divulged my exact income he gravely admitted that the pecuniary problem was no easy one to solve. He found it a terrible tight fit himself; it had been costing him over two thousand a year out of his own pocket to hunt the Ringwell country, and the Packlestone would be an even more expensive undertaking. When we had worked it out on paper—so much a week for my own keep while living with him in the huntsman's house, so much for keep of horses, so much for my two men's wages, and so on—the total came to more than ten pounds a week. And I had to buy two more horses into the bargain; for, as he said, I couldn't have any fun with less than four, "and it absolutely defeats me how you're going to get four days a week even then".

"I'll have one good season, anyhow, whatever happens afterwards!" I exclaimed. All that I needed, at that juncture, was a miraculous doubling of my income.

The mental condition of an active young man who asks nothing more of life than twelve hundred a year and four days a week with the Packlestone is perhaps not easy to defend. It looks rather paltry on paper. That, however, was my own mental position, and I saw nothing strange in it, although I was well aware of the sort of things the family solicitor would be saying if he were permitted to cast his eye over the half-sheet of paper on which Denis had figured out my probable expenditure. Aunt Evelyn, however, cordially approved of my project, and after consultations with Stephen (who thought it a magnificent effort) and the delighted Dixon, I bought a couple of horses in April and May, and then settled down to a summer of strict economizing. Cricket matches, at any rate, were an inexpensive occupation.

Of my new horses one was a bit of a gamble. He was a very good-looking chestnut who "roared like a bull". He had the reputation of being a wonderful performer, and I bought him, rather recklessly, for forty-three guineas, at the end of a sale at Tattersalls, after the horse I'd hoped to buy had gone for double the price I was able to bid for him. A vet. from the Ringwell country drew my attention to the handsome chestnut, assuring me that he'd heard from a safe quarter that he was a remarkable jumper. Throughout the summer Dixon and I contemplated him and speculated on his problematical capabilities (which proved to be in accordance with the information given me by the vet.).

My other new horse was the result of a chance ride in a point-to-point. He was a well-bred old horse, a great stayer, and a very bold jumper. After I had ridden him in two races, in both of which he finished strongly, though not fast enough to win, his owner offered to let me have him for thirty pounds, admitting that he found him too much of a handful out hunting. I was already aware that the old chestnut had a very hard mouth, but I took him gladly and he carried me well and kept my weight down by causing me considerable exertions by his impetuous behaviour.

When Dixon brought the horses up from benighted Butley I had already been at Packlestone the best part of a month, riding Denis's horses out cub-hunting, getting to know my way about the country, and becoming acquainted with a few of the local characters, most of whom were extremely civil to me on account of my close connection with their new Master. I did my best to live up to my too conspicuous position, mainly by saying as little as possible and looking as knowledgeable as I knew how. My acclimatization to the new conditions was made easier by the fact that not many people came out cubbing before the middle of October. We clattered out in the misty mornings to disturb the important fox coverts and the demesnes of influential personages in the Hunt, and I learned to recognize the new faces in more or less segregated instalments.

On one occasion we went to a place about twenty miles from the Kennels, had two days' routing up the cubs, and spent two nights in a large country house. The owner was away, probably at some German spa: the furniture was draped in dust-sheets, and I remember that we had our dinner in a little housekeeper's room. To be there with Denis and his hounds gave me an agreeable feeling of having got into a modernized Surtees novel (though there was little evidence of modernity in what we did and saw). Less agreeable, I remember, was our sixteen-mile ride home on a grilling September afternoon, with the famous Packlestone dog-hounds, who found the dust and heat rather more than they could manage after a long morning.

Life at the Kennels appeared to me almost perfect, especially when I was sitting with Denis in the little room in the huntsman's house and discussing the new country in all its aspects. My approach to the country had been uncritical and eagerly expectant. Once I was settled there I saw it entirely through the eyes of Denis. If he found anything amiss I at once assumed that I had already taken the imperfection into account. For instance, several of the artificial gorse coverts, he said, were very thin; and no right-minded fox would remain in some of the small woods when once the leaves were off and the vegetation had died down. I shook my head and agreed that a lot of the coverts wanted looking after. Several new gorse coverts ought to be planted in the Friday country, which was the best part for riding over. And then there was the wire, which was deplorably prevalent in places, though well marked with red boards in the hedges. In the Kennels, too, there was much to be attended to.

The Packlestone country was hunted four days a week. Its character was varied—cow-pastures and collieries being the extremes of good and bad. In some districts there were too many villages, and there were three or four biggish industrial towns. This abundance of population seemed to me an intrusion, and I wished I could clear every mean modern dwelling out of the hunt. For the most part, however, it appeared to be a paradise of jumpable fences, and compared with the well-wooded Ringwell region it was a tip-top country. For the first time in my life I was able to sit down and jump a dozen clean fences without pulling up. In fact, as Denis said, it was a place where I could jump myself silly. Also it had the charm of freshness, and I have always thought that a country becomes less enjoyable as one gets to know it better; in a strange country a twisting hunt seems like a straight one. But this is a truism which applies to many things in life besides riding to hounds.

Foxes were plentiful, except in parts of the Friday country; but there was no shortage anywhere as regards rich-flavoured Surteesian figures. Coming, as I did, from afar, and knowing nothing of their antecedents and more intimate aspects, I observed the Packlestone people with peculiar vividness. I saw them as a little outdoor world of country characters and I took them all for granted on their face value. How privileged and unperturbed they appeared—those dwellers in a sporting Elysium! Half-conscious of the sense of security and stability which they inspired, I watched them and listened to them with a comfortable feeling that here was something which no political upheaval could interrupt.

There was, however, one discordant element in life which I vaguely referred to as "those damned socialists who want to stop us hunting". Curiously enough, I didn't connect socialists with collieries, though there had been a long coal strike eighteen months before. Socialists, for me, began and ended in Hyde Park, which was quite a harmless place for them to function in. And I assured Denis that whatever the newspapers might say, the Germans would never be allowed to attack us. Officers at the barracks were only an ornament; war had become an impossibility. I had sometimes thought with horror of countries where they had conscription and young men like myself were forced to serve two years in the army whether they liked it or not. Two years in the army! I should have been astonished if I'd been told that socialists opposed conscription as violently as many fox-hunting men supported the convention of soldiering.

II

The Packlestone fox-hunters prided themselves on being hail-fellow-well-met—quite a happy family, in fact—though a large one, for there were always between a hundred and a hundred and fifty riders at a Monday meet. The Mondays, which were in the middle of the Hunt, attracted all the regular followers, whereas on Fridays there was a cutting and thrusting contingent from two adjoining hunts, and these people were rightly regarded as outsiders by the true-blue Packlestone residents.

During my October days new faces continually added themselves to the covert-side crowd, and by the time when I began to ride my own horses the fields were fairly representative, and I very soon found myself included in the friendliness for which the Hunt had a reputation, though it was some time before I could say that I felt at home, especially when I was on my old chestnut, who fairly pulled my arms out.

On a bright morning late in October, composed though slightly self-conscious on Cockbird's back outside Olton Gorse, I could look around me and identify the chief supporters of the Hunt. Prominent, owing to his official capacity, was the Field-Master, Bertie Hartby, a keen-faced man whose appointment by Denis had caused a certain amount of controversy. It was said that Hartby was always in too much of a hurry, but there he was, anyhow, intent on doing his best to keep the field in order.

Near him was a highly important personage, Captain Harry Hinnycraft, who for a vast number of years had been Honorary Secretary of the Hunt. "Dear old Captain Harry," as the young ladies called him (for on them he was wont to turn an appreciative eye), was by no means an easy old gentleman to please unless it suited him to be amiable. His unqualified approval of the new Master was balanced by an unconcealed prejudice against his Field-Master, who was, he asserted to all and sundry, "as wild as a hawk", varying this with "mad as a hatter". Compromise was a word of which Captain Hinnycraft had never mastered the meaning; massive and white-moustached on his magnificent weight-carriers, he had always ridden about the Packlestone country with the air of a monarch. He belonged to the old school of country gentlemen, ruling his estate with semi-benevolent tyranny and turning his back on all symptoms of social innovation. Under his domination the Packlestone country had been looked after on feudal system lines. His method of dealing with epistolary complaints from discontented farmers was to ignore them; in verbal intercourse he bullied them and sent them about their business with a good round oath. Such people, he firmly believed, were put there by Providence to touch their hats and do as they were told by their betters. As might be expected, he had conventional eighteenth-century ideas about what constituted masculine gallantry and sprightly conversation. Captain Harry defied all criticism because he was a complete anachronism. And as such he continued beyond his eightieth year, until he fell into a fish-pond on his estate and was buried by the parson whose existence he had spurned by his arrogance.

It may well be wondered how the Hunt had survived the despotism of this old-world grandee, with whom previous Masters had been obliged to co-operate (as "best Master we've ever had" while they reigned, and "good riddance of bad rubbish" when they resigned and left him to find someone to replace them).

An explanation of the continued prosperity of the Packlestone was largely to be found in Mrs. Oakfield of Thurrow Park, a lady who made friends wherever she went. Since her childhood she had been intimately associated with the Hunt, for her father had been Master for more than twenty years. From her large and well-managed estate she set an example of up-to-date (though somewhat expensive) farm-management, and every farmer in the country (except a few stubborn Radicals) swore by Mrs. Oakfield as the feminine gender of a jolly good fellow. As a fine judge of cattle and sheep they respected her; and to this was added her reputation for boundless generosity. The Packlestone farmers were proud to see Mrs. Oakfield riding over their land—as well they might be, for it was a sight worth going a long way to see. A fine figure of a woman she was, they all agreed, as she sailed over the fences in her tall hat and perfectly fitting black habit with a bunch of violets in her buttonhole. This brilliant horsewoman rode over the country in an apparently effortless manner: always in the first flight, she never appeared to be competing for her prominent position; quick and dashing, she was never in a hurry; allowing for the fact that she was very well mounted and knew the country by heart, she was undoubtedly a paragon of natural proficiency. John Leech would have drawn her with delight. I admired Mrs. Oakfield enormously; her quickness to hounds was a revelation to me, and in addition she was gracious and charming in manner. Whether she bowed her acknowledgment to a lifted hat at the meet or cantered easily at an awkward bit

of timber in an otherwise unjumpable hedge, she possessed
the secret of style. Needless to say, she was the only person
in the Hunt who knew how to manage Captain Harry,
who always spoke of her as "a splendid little woman".
Which brings me back to my original explanation as to
how the behaviour of that intractable old gentleman failed
to cause as much trouble as one might have expected.

While Captain Hinnycraft lived and bulked big in the
middle of the Monday country, all roads in the Wednesday
district converged on Mrs. Oakfield at Thurrow Park.
Fashionable Friday contained several good-sized estates and
many important fox-preservers and staunch supporters,
but no predominant personage. Saturday, however, had its
unmistakable magnate in Sir Jocelyn Porteus-Porteous of
Folesford Hall. The Saturday country was the least popular of the four divisions. Well-wooded, hilly, and sporadic-
ally blemished by collieries, it was considered very sporting
by those who lived in it. A Saturday hunt was a scrambling, cramped, hound-musical affair, much enjoyed by
middle-aged enthusiasts on slow horses. A minor feature
which I remember was an abundance of holly trees, which
contributed a cosy old-fashioned Christmas atmosphere to
my impression of Saturdays. Sunny Jim, my short-tailed,
short-backed, short-legged, clever performer, found Saturdays much more to his liking than the other days, with their
cut and laid fences, big ditches, and quick bursts across pasture and arable. I was very fond of Jim and I always gave
him half of the apple which I produced from my pocket
early in the afternoon. He was an artful old customer, and
sometimes when he heard me munching my apple he
would halt and turn his head to receive his portion. He did
this one day when I was loitering with a slack rein along
one of the spacious green rides which ventilated the Folesford home coverts. The august presence of Sir Jocelyn happened to be just behind me; his amusement at Sunny Jim's
intelligent behaviour is a lucky little stroke of reminiscence,
for it is not easy to describe him without seeming a shade
discourteous to Porteus-Porteous. (Note the majestic vari-
ation in spelling.)

No one could meet Sir Jocelyn and remain blind to the fact that he had a pompous manner. And when he was in the middle of the park at Folesford, with its chain of woodlands and superabundance of foxes and pheasants, he seemed just a little larger than life-size. (He was pardonably proud of the concordant profusion of those sporting incompatibles, the fox and the pheasant.) His ancestral seat (the Porteous family had sat there since Plantagenet times) was, if I remember rightly, a Gothic nucleus with Tudor and Jacobean additions. Unwelcome, from the picturesquely feudal point of view, were the rows of industrial habitations which had cropped up outside his grandiose gateway. These, with the unsightly colliery chimneys, were a lucrative element in his existence, since they represented mineral royalties for the owner of the estate. Nevertheless, his attitude toward such plebeian upstarts was lofty and impercipient: not having been introduced to them, he had not the pleasure of their acquaintance, so to speak. Sir Jocelyn was a short, thick-set, round-legged man with regular features and a moustache. It would be unfair to accuse him of looking complacent, for how could any man look otherwise than comfortable and well satisfied when he had inherited such an amply endowed existence? There was hauteur in his manner, but it was not unkindly, though it was accentuated by his unconscious habit of punctuating his utterances with regularly recurrent sniffs. In this connection I am unable to resist the temptation to reproduce a memorable remark which he once made to me out hunting.

That winter he gave a ball for the coming-out of his eldest daughter. (Mrs. Oakfield gave one in the same week —an intensely exciting week for the graceful nymphs, dashing sparks, and diamonded dowagers of the Hunt.)

"When did you last give a ball at Folesford, Sir Jocelyn?" I politely asked him, gazing bashfully at one of his dangling top-boots.

"We have no record [sniff] of any ball at Folesford [sniff]," was his rejoinder.

Why there had never been any balls at Folesford I am

still at a loss to understand. But the fact remained. It was (sniff) so. . . . And Sir Jocelyn, as I have taken trouble to indicate, was the king of the Saturday country.

III

Anything like an adequate inventory of the Packlestone subscribers is beyond the scope of my narrative—pleasant though it would be to revive so many estimable and animated equestrians. Warm-hearted memory creates a crowded gathering when one has both the dead and the living to draw upon. I have no doubt that the Packlestone field (and its similitude elsewhere) still survives in its main characteristics. Nevertheless, I adhere protectively to my sense of its uniqueness as it was when I was a unit in its hurry of hoofs and covert-side chatter. I can believe in the present-day existence of intrepid young ladies, such as were the two Miss Amingtons, who would have perished rather than see someone else jump a big fence without having a cut at it themselves on their game and not over-sound horses.

But are there still such veterans as those who went so well when I was there to watch them? Grey-bearded Squire Wingfield was over seventy, but he took the fences as they came and held his own with many a would-be thruster forty years younger. And there were two or three contemporaries of his who got over the country in a way which I remember with astonishment. Compared with such *anno Domini* defying old birds, jolly Judge Burgess (who came from London as often as his grave duties permitted) was a mere schoolboy. The Judge had returned to the hunting-field at the age of fifty, after thirty years' absence, and he had evidently made up his mind to enjoy every minute of it as he bucketed along on a hollow-backed chestnut who, he affirmed, knew a dashed sight more about hunting than his learned owner.

Regretfully I remember how incapable I was of appreciating many of the ripe-flavoured characters whom I encountered with such regularity. Obvious enough was the newly-rich manufacturer who lived in a gaudy multi-gabled mansion, and asked me, "'Ow many 'orses do *you* reckon to keep?" as he ambled along on a good-looking and confidential grey for which he had given a mint of money. Much more interesting, as I see him now, was Mr. Jariott, an exquisitely polite silver-haired gentleman, who lived alone in a shallow-roofed white-faced house in a discreetly undulating park. As owner of several good coverts, small and easy to get away from, he was a punctilious preserver of foxes. It was said that he knew all his foxes by name, and mourned the loss when one of them was killed. But he would have been horrified if his coverts had been drawn blank, and so far as I could hear, such a thing had never happened. The cut of his clothes was soberly stylish and old-fashioned, and he was shy and sparing in his utterances. I was told that he bred a certain sort of shooting-dog and knew more about that breed than any other man in England. I have an idea that the dogs were golden brown, silky-haired, and elegant. I was only inside his house once, when the hounds met there: the interior left an impression of being only half lived in; I imagined Mr. Jariott as its attentive but lonely inhabitant, and the windows looked vacantly out on the pleasant park from the box-like building.

Not far from Mr. Jariott's house there was a strip of woodland named Lady Byron's Covert. Years afterwards I discovered that the poet had lived at that house for a short time with that "moral Clytemnestra", his wife, who remained there in her aggrieved seclusion long after his departure to Italy. My knowledge of this seems to explain the impression of haunting unhappiness which the house made on my mind. I should like to know what old Mr. Jariott thought about it all.

Among the younger generation in the Packlestone Hunt the brothers Peppermore were far the most conspicuous, as they would have been in any sporting community. Jack and Charlie Peppermore were both under twenty-five and had already broken most of their bones. They were well known as amateur race-riders. Jack, the younger of the two, was in temporary retirement from racing, for he had cracked his skull in a hurdle race at the end of the previous winter. This did not prevent him from hunting, and he was usually to be seen out on some borrowed horse which had proved itself completely beyond the control of its owner. Charlie was rather more particular about what he rode, and was, correspondingly, a more reticent character. These brothers did and said pretty well what they pleased in the Packlestone Hunt; ungovernable as their exploits often were, they were always forgiven, for they were brilliant riders and had all the qualities which make a young man popular in sporting circles. They were reckless, insolent, unprincipled, and aggressively competitive; but they were never dull, frequently amusing, and, when they chose, had charming manners. In fact, they disarmed criticism, as do all people whom one cannot help admiring. And they were the last people in the world to expect excuses to be made for them. To me, at that time, they were the epitome of a proficiency and prestige to which I could not even aspire. As I remember them now they were desperately fine specimens of a genuine English traditional type which has become innocuous since the abolition of duelling. But if they were to some extent survivals from a less civilized age, they were also the most remarkable light-weight sparks I had ever seen, and as they treated me with amiable tolerance I considered myself fortunate in knowing them. Nor have I ever altered that opinion. For in their peculiar way the Peppermores were first-rate people, and I felt genuinely sorry when I read in an evening paper, a year or two ago, that Charlie Peppermore had fallen at the first fence in the Grand National when riding the favourite.

To say that the brothers were competitive is to put it mildly. Whenever it was a question of getting there first, they were absolute demons of energy, alertness, and pugnacious subtlety. In the hunting-field, however, they had little opposition to compete against, and in a fast hunt they were undefeatable. Denis Milden's arrival on the scene of their supremacy reminded them that they must look to their laurels; but Denis showed no awareness of the competitive spirit; his only purpose was to hunt the hounds, and the Peppermores very soon recognized this and did all they could to help him. To have aroused their animosity would have been no joke. Once when I was at a race meeting I happened to be standing beside Charlie Peppermore when an inferior amateur rider fell off, rather ignominiously, at a plain fence in front of the enclosure. The horse went on alone and the jockey scrambled to his feet and as he walked past us on the other side of the rails Charlie Peppermore laughed. It was the most insulting, contemptuous laugh I'd ever heard. Then he turned to me and drawled: "How I hate that man! I've been waiting years to see him break his neck."

Of the two, Denis liked Jack the better, and one Saturday in the middle of November Jack was invited to dinner, with two other young sportsmen who lived not many miles away. This was an uncommon event at the Kennels, and Mrs. Timson rolled up her sleeves and prepared a more than usually solid repast. When we came in from hunting Denis got out two bottles of champagne, and some full-bodied port. As a rule we drank water, and the quantity of champagne and port I had consumed in my whole life could easily have been contained in half a dozen bottles of each fluid.

"I'm afraid drink isn't too good for old Jack since that accident of his," remarked Denis, rubbing his forehead dubiously.

He then told the inscrutable Henry to "get that dinner on at eight o'clock" and went upstairs to dress—the occasion demanding the special effort of a dinner jacket.

Jack arrived alone in his father's brougham—a means of conveyance which seemed vaguely improbable. Peppermore senior had been a well-known figure on the Turf, and he still owned a few steeplechasers which his sons trained and rode. But he had become heavy and uncommunicative with middle age, and now devoted himself almost entirely to looking after his farms and house property (and putting the brake on his sons' transactions with bookmakers). Jack was the mainspring of the party, and his drawling voice kept us all amused with a continuous flow of chaff and chatter. I wish I could remember a single word of it, but as I am unable to do so I can only say that I made one with the other guests in compliant appreciation while Denis was an attentive host, and the champagne promoted conviviality in moderation.

After dinner we moved into the other room, which was even smaller. A decanter of port quickly became empty, and a certain rowdiness began to show itself among the company, though there was nothing to be rowdy about and very little space to be rowdy in. When Henry brought in the replenished decanter Jack picked up a small tumbler and filled it. From his demeanour it appeared that the competitive spirit was asserting itself. A few minutes afterwards he threw a chair across the room and the other young men felt it incumbent on them to imitate him. He then refilled his glass with port, standing in the middle of the room, drank it straight off, and collapsed on the floor. The little room was overheated by a roaring fire, and the air was heavy with cigar smoke. The other two guests were a bad colour, and I went to the front door to get a breath of the frosty air.

When I returned Denis was looking after the prostrate Jack; he was, I remember, making a hissing sound, as if he were grooming a horse, and I thought what a kind-hearted chap he was. He told me to go and order Jack's carriage. I went to the kitchen, and informed them in subdued tones that Mr. Peppermore was very drunk. The coachman grinned and went out to put his horse in.

I then became aware that I was very drunk myself, and soon afterwards Denis gently assisted me up the steep stairs to my room. I was glad, next morning, that I hadn't got to go out hunting. This was the first occasion on which I was authentically intoxicated.

IV

To give a detailed account of my doings during that winter would be to deviate from my design. It may be inferred, however, that I enjoyed myself wholeheartedly and lived in total immunity from all intellectual effort (a fact which may seem rather remarkable to those who recognize a modicum of mental ability in the writing of these memoirs). For more than six months I perused nothing except newspapers; my pen was employed only in a weekly scribble to Aunt Evelyn, and in copying out hound pedigrees for Denis, who had discovered that the Packlestone pedigree books had not been kept with quite that precision which was proper for such essential registers. In this manner I acquired an exact knowledge of the ancestries of Vivian, Villager, Conquest, Cottager, and various other eloquent veterans whose music had made the ploughman pause with attentive ear on many a copse-crowned upland.

Odd enough it seems now, that detached and limited segment of my human experience, when I was so completely identified with what I was doing and so oblivious to anything else. Coming in at the end of a long day, I would find Dixon giving the horses their evening feed, or brushing the mud off the horse I had ridden in the morning. Dixon was entirely in his element now, and he had the intense satisfaction of going out as my second horseman. Dignified and discreet he rode about with the other grooms, catching an occasional glimpse of me as I popped over a fence into a lane or cantered across a field toward a covert. My broken-winded chestnut had turned out to be a wonderful hunter; I could trot him up to a high post and rails in absolute assurance that he would hop over it like a deer, and on such occasions he made me look a much better rider than I really was. In spite of all the hard work he had to get through, Dixon was permanently happy that winter. He was breathing the same air as the renowned Peppermores, whose steeplechasing successes made them heroic in his eyes; and every day he was within speaking distance of Denis Milden, for whom he had a corresponding admiration. When Denis came to my loose-box and told Dixon that the horses were looking fine, Dixon was more delighted than he knew how to say; and, of course, as befitted a "perfect gentleman's servant", he said almost nothing at all.

This was all very pleasant; but when the afternoons began to lengthen and I had just paid another bill for forage I was forced to look ahead and to realize that the end of the winter would find me in no end of a fix. Fix wasn't the word for it as I thought of what Mr. Pennett's face would look like when I told him that I was £300 in debt. "Outrunning the constable" was the phrase which would leap to his lips as sure as eggs were eggs. It was certain that I should be obliged to sell two of the horses at the end of the season. I couldn't afford to keep them even if there had been room for them all in Aunt Evelyn's stable, which there wasn't (two of them had been put up in the village in the previous autumn).

Faced by the prospect of intensive economy in the summer and with no apparent hope of another season in the Midlands, my exodus from the Kennels meant disconsolate exile from all newly discovered delights. Even Denis had to admit this, but he had already more than enough to occupy his mind. The Packlestone people, too, were so pleasant to me, and so unaware of my inadequate resources, that I was frequently reminded of my forlorn future. Quite a number of them would be going to London for the season, or had houses there already, and when they hoped to see something of me in the summer I felt a very passable imitation of an impostor. Those prosperous and well-appointed lives had no connection with my economical future at Butley.

Nevertheless, I had visions of Mayfair in June, and all the well-oiled ingredients of affluence and social smartness. I saw myself sauntering about the sunlit streets, well dressed and acquainted with plenty of people with large houses in Berkeley, Grosvenor, or Portman Squares, free to attend fashionable functions and liberated from my previous provincialism. Fantasias of polite society swept through me in wave on wave of secret snobbishness; life in London when Hyde Park would be bright with flowers assumed the enchanting aspect of a chapter in an elegantly written novel about people with large incomes and aristocratic connections. Sighing for such splendours, I knew

that I was only flattening my nose against the plate-glass
window of an expensive florist's shop. Orchids were altogether beyond my income. I never doubted the authenticity of those enjoyments. My immature mind, as was
natural, conjectured something magical in such allure-
ments of prosperity. It was the spectacle of vivid life, and I
was young to it.

As for the Packlestone people and their London season
—well, it is just possible that they weren't quite as brilliant
as I imagined. Ascot, Lords, a few dances and theatres,
dull dinner-parties, one or two visits to the Opera—that
was about all. Since I have grown older I have heard the
hollow echoes in that social apparatus; but at that time I
was only aware that it was an appropriate sequel to the
smoothly moving scene in which I was involved. It was a
contrast, also, to the rigorous routine of life at the Kennels.
All this contributed to a feeling of finality in my proceedings.

The hunting season ended with an ironic glory at the
point-to-points, where the inestimable Cockbird managed
to win the Heavy Weight Race after Denis had set him an
example in the Light Weights. Everyone agreed that it was
a great day for the Kennels, and a couple of weeks afterwards I was back at Butley.

I had been away from Aunt Evelyn for nearly seven
months. I found it none too easy to tell her all about my
eventful absence from the quiet background which awaited
my return. Everything was just the same as ever at Butley;
and as such it was inevitable that I found it monotonous.
Sadly I sold my brilliant chestnut for thirty-six guineas at
Tattersalls. He was bought by a Belgian officer. I couldn't
bring myself to part with any of the others; neither could I
discuss my sporting future with Dixon, although he was
undoubtedly aware of my difficulties. After an unpalatable
interview with Mr. Pennett I succeeded in extracting an
extra hundred pounds; and so I settled down to an uneventful summer, restless and inwardly dissatisfied, unable
to make up my mind what to do next winter, and healthier
than I'd ever been in my life, which (though I wasn't

aware of it at the time) was saying a good deal from the physiological point of view.

I have said I found everything at Butley unchanged. This was not so, for faithful Miriam had retired from domestic service and her manner of doing so had been consistent with her character. During the winter Aunt Evelyn had persuaded her to go to the seaside for a fortnight's holiday, as her health had become noticeably bad. While at the seaside she unobtrusively died of heart failure. To the last, therefore, she managed to avoid being a trouble to anyone. This was a severe blow to Aunt Evelyn. She had been so much a part of the place that I had taken for granted everything she did. Now that she was gone I began to regret the occasions when I had shown her too little consideration.

Stephen Colwood, who was now a well-contented Artillery subaltern, had stayed for a week with us at the Kennels, and had departed saying that the Packlestone country was a fox-hunter's Paradise and had spoilt him for anything else.

And so my life lumbered on into July, very much with the same sedate manner of progress which characterized Homeward's carrier's van. I went to see the Hunt horses sold at Tattersalls, at the end of May, and there I encountered many of the friendly Packlestone faces. After that I avoided London: the mystery and magnificence of Mayfair remained remote from my callow comprehension of terrestrial affairs.

PART NINE: IN THE ARMY

I

Sitting in the sunshine one morning early in September, I ruminated on my five weeks' service as a trooper in the Yeomanry. Healthier than I'd ever been before, I sat on the slope of a meadow a few miles from Canterbury, polishing a cavalry saddle and wondering how it was that I'd never learned more about that sort of thing from Dixon. Below me, somewhere in the horse-lines, stood Cockbird, picketed to a peg in the ground by a rope which was already giving him a sore pastern. Had I been near enough to study his facial expression I should have seen what I already knew, that Cockbird definitely disliked being a trooper's charger. He was regretting Dixon and resenting mobilization. He didn't even belong to me now, for I had been obliged to sell him to the Government for a perfunctory fifty pounds, and I was lucky not to have lost sight of him altogether. Apart from the fact that for forty-five months he had been my most prized possession in the world, he was now my only tangible link with the peaceful past which had provided us both with a roof over our heads every night.

My present habitation was a bivouac, rigged up out of a rick-cloth and some posts, which I shared with eleven other troopers. Outside the bivouac I sat, with much equipment still uncleaned after our morning exercises. I had just received a letter, and it was lying on the grass beside me. It was from someone at the War Office whom I knew slightly; it offered me a commission, with the rank of captain, in the Remount Service. I had also got yesterday's *Times*, which contained a piece of poetry by Thomas Hardy. "What of the faith and fire within us, men who march away ere the barn-cocks say night is growing grey?"

I did not need Hardy's "Song of the Soldiers" to warn me that the Remounts was no place for me. Also the idea of my being any sort of officer in the Army seemed absurd. I had already been offered a commission in my own Yeomanry, but how could I have accepted it when everybody was saying that the Germans might land at Dover any day? I was safe in the Army, and that was all I cared about.

I had slipped into the Downfield troop by enlisting two days before the declaration of war. For me, so far, the War had been a mounted infantry picnic in perfect weather. The inaugural excitement had died down, and I was agreeably relieved of all sense of personal responsibility. Cockbird's welfare was my main anxiety; apart from that, being in the Army was very much like being back at school. My incompetence, compared with the relative efficiency of my associates, was causing me perturbed and flustered moments. Getting on parade in time with myself and Cockbird properly strapped and buckled was ticklish work. But several of the officers had known me out hunting with the Ringwell, and my presence in the ranks was regarded as a bit of a joke, although in my own mind my duties were no laughing matter and I had serious aspirations to heroism in the field. Also I had the advantage of being a better rider than a good many of the men in my squadron, which to some extent balanced my ignorance and inefficiency in other respects.

The basis of my life with the "jolly Yeo-boys" was bodily fatigue, complicated by the minor details of my daily difficulties. There was also the uncertainty and the feeling of emergency which we shared with the rest of the world in that rumour-ridden conjuncture. But my fellow troopers were kind and helpful, and there was something almost idyllic about those early weeks of the War. The flavour and significance of life were around me in the homely smells of the thriving farm where we were quartered; my own abounding health responded zestfully to the outdoor world, to the apple-scented orchards, and all those fertilities which the harassed farmer was gathering in while stupendous

events were developing across the Channel. Never before
had I known how much I had to lose. Never before had I
looked at the living world with any degree of intensity. It
seemed almost as if I had been waiting for this thing to
happen, although my own part in it was so obscure and
submissive.

I belonged to what was known as the "Service Squadron", which had been formed about three weeks after
mobilization. The Yeomanry, as a Territorial unit, had
not legitimately pledged themselves for foreign service. It
was now incumbent upon them to volunteer. The squadron commanders had addressed their mustered men eloquently on the subject, and those who were willing to lay
down their lives without delay were enrolled in the Service
Squadron which for a few weeks prided itself on being a
corps d'élite under specially selected officers. Very soon it became obvious that everyone would be obliged to go abroad
whether they wanted to or not, and the too-prudent
"Home-service" men were not allowed to forget their previous prudence.

As I sat on the ground with my half-cleaned saddle and
the War Office letter, I felt very much a man dedicated to
death. And to one who had never heard the hiss of machine-
gun bullets there was nothing imaginatively abhorrent in
the notion. Reality was a long way off; I had still to learn
how to roll my "cloak" neatly on the pommel of my saddle
and various other elementary things. Nor had I yet learned
how to clean my rifle; I hadn't even fired a shot with it.
Most of the letters I had received since enlisting had been
bills. But they no longer mattered. If the War goes on till
next spring, I ruminated, I shall be quite rich. Being in the
army was economical, at any rate!

The bugle blew for twelve o'clock "stables", and I went
down to the horse-lines to take Cockbird to the watering
trough. Everyone had been talking about the hundred
thousand Russians who were supposed to have passed
through England on their way to France. Away across the
hot mid-day miles the bells of Canterbury Cathedral refused to recognize the existence of a war. It was just a

dazzling early autumn day, and the gaitered farmer came riding in from his fields on a cob.

As I was leading Cockbird back from watering I passed Nigel Croplady, who was one of the troop leaders. He stopped to speak to me for a moment, and asked whether I had heard from Denis Milden lately; this caused me to feel slightly less *déclassé*. Calling the officers "sir" and saluting them still made me feel silly. But I got on so comfortably with the other troopers that I couldn't imagine myself living in the farmhouse with the officers. The men in my troop included two or three bank clerks, several farmers' and small tradesmen's sons, a professional steeple-chase jockey, and the son of the local M.P. (who had joined at the outbreak of war). They were all quite young. Discipline was not rigorous, but their conduct was exemplary. I soon found out, however, that they were by no means as efficient as I had expected. The annual training had been little more than a three weeks' outing. "Solidarity on parade" was not an impressive element in the Service Squadron, and squadron drill was an unsymmetrical affair. Nevertheless, we talked impressively among ourselves as though being ordered abroad was only a matter of weeks or even days, and our officers regaled us with optimistic news from the Western Front. Many of us believed that the Russians would occupy Berlin (and, perhaps, capture the Kaiser) before Christmas. The newspapers informed us that German soldiers crucified Belgian babies. Stories of that kind were taken for granted; to have disbelieved them would have been unpatriotic.

When Aunt Evelyn came over to see me one hot Sunday afternoon I assured her that we should soon be going to the Front. Her private feelings about "men who march away" had to be sacrificed to my reputability as a cavalryman. She brought with her some unnecessarily thick shirts and the news from Butley, where I was, I surmised, regarded as something of a hero. Enlistment in the Army had not yet become an inevitability. Everyone thought it splendid of me to set such an example. I shared their opinion as we went along the horse-lines to look at Cockbird. Aunt Evelyn was bearing up bravely about it all, but it was no good pretending that the War had brought any consolations for her, or for Dixon either.

Dixon had taken Cockbird to Downfield the day after mobilization, and had returned home just in time to interview some self-important persons who were motoring about the country requisitioning horses for the Army. Harkaway had been excused on grounds of old age, but the other two had been taken, at forty pounds apiece: the plump mowing-machine pony was not yet needed for a European war.

When we had finished making a fuss of Cockbird I took Aunt Evelyn up to inspect our bivouac; several of my companions were taking their Sabbath ease in the shade of the rick-cloth; they scrambled shyly to their feet and Aunt Evelyn was friendly and gracious to them; but she was a visible reminder to us of the homes we had left behind us.

As I lay awake after "lights-out", visual realizations came to me of the drawing-room at Butley, and Miriam's successor bringing in the oil-lamp; I had not liked it when I was seeing my aunt into the train at Canterbury—the slow train which took her home in the evening sunshine through that life-learned landscape, which, we all felt, was now threatened by barbaric invasion. I had never thought about her in that way while I was enjoying myself up at Packlestone, and my sympathetic feeling for her now was, perhaps, the beginning of my emancipation from the egotism of youth. I wished I hadn't told her that "we should probably be going out quite soon". She would be lying awake and worrying about it now. The ground was hard under my waterproof sheet, but I was very soon asleep.

*   *   *

The cloudless weather of that August and September need not be dwelt on; it is a hard fact in history; the spellbound serenity of its hot blue skies will be in the minds of men as long as they remember the catastrophic events which were under way in that autumn when I was raising the dust on the roads with the Yeomanry. But there was no tragic element in my own experience, though I may have seen sadness in the sunshine as the days advanced toward October and the news from France went from one extreme to the other with the retreat and advance of our expeditionary force.

I can remember the first time that I was "warned for guard", and how I polished up my boots and buttons for that event. And when, in the middle of the night, I had been roused up to take my turn as sentry, I did not doubt that it was essential that someone in a khaki uniform should stand somewhere on the outskirts of the byres and barns of Batt's Farm. My King and Country expected it of me. There was, I remember, a low mist lying on the fields, and I was posted by a gate under a walnut tree. In the autumn-smelling silence the village church clanged one o'clock. Shortly afterwards I heard someone moving in my direction across the field which I was facing. The significance of those approaching feet was intensified by my sentrified nerves. Holding my rifle defensively (and a loaded rifle, too) I remarked in an unemphatic voice: "Halt, who goes there?" There was no reply. Out of the mist and the weeds through which it was wading emerged the Kentish cow which I had challenged.

*   *   *

By the third week in September the nights were becoming chilly, and we weren't sorry when we were moved into the Workhouse, which was quite near the farm where we had been camping. Sleeping in the Workhouse seemed luxurious; but it put an end to the summer holiday atmosphere of the previous weeks, and there were moments when I felt less light-hearted than I would have admitted to myself at the time. Soon afterwards young Nunburne (the M.P.'s son) was whisked away to Sandhurst, his father having decided that he would be more suitably situated as a subaltern in the Guards. His departure made a difference but it did not convince me that I ought to become an officer myself, though Cockbird, also, had in a manner of speaking, accepted a commission.

For the daily spectacle of Cockbird's discomforts (the

most important of which was the enormous weight of equipment which he had to carry) had induced me to transfer him to the squadron commander, who was glad to get hold of such a good-looking and perfect-mannered charger. Having got a tolerably comfortable horse in exchange, I now had the satisfaction of seeing Cockbird moving easily about with a light-weight on his back and a properly trained groom to look after him. I felt proud of him as I watched his elegant and pampered appearance.

"Of course you'll be able to buy him back at the end of the War," said the squadron commander; but I knew that I had lost him; it was a step nearer to bleak realization of what I was in for. Anyhow, I thought, Dixon would hate to see old Cockbird being knocked about in the ranks. As for Cockbird, he didn't seem to know me since his promotion.

It must have been about this time that I began to be definitely bored with Yeomanry life. It was now becoming a recognized fact, even in the ranks, that we were unlikely to be sent to the Front in our present semi-efficient condition. It was said, too, that "Kitchener had got a down on our Brigade". I remember riding home from a Brigade Field Day one afternoon at the end of September. My horse had gone lame and I had been given permission to withdraw from the unconvincing operations. During three or four leisurely miles back to the Workhouse I was aware of the intense relief of being alone and, for those few miles, free. For the first time since I'd joined the Army with such ardours I felt homesick. I was riding back to a Workhouse and the winter lay ahead of me. There was no hope of sitting by the fire with a book after a good day's hunting.

I thought of that last cricket match, on August Bank Holiday, when I was at Hoadley Rectory playing for the Rector's eleven against the village, and how old Colonel Hesmon had patted me on the back because I'd enlisted on the Saturday before. Outwardly the match had been normally conducted, but there was something in the sunshine which none of us had ever known before that calamitous Monday. Parson Colwood had three sons in the service, and his face showed it. I thought of how I'd said good-bye to Stephen the next day. He had gone to his Artillery; and I had gone to stay at the hotel in Downfield, where I waited till the Wednesday morning and then put on my ill-fitting khaki and went bashfully down to the Drill Hall to join the Downfield troop. I had felt a hero when I was lying awake on the floor of the Town Hall on the first night of the War.

But the uncertainty and excitement had dwindled. And here I was, riding past the park wall of Lord Kitchener's country house and wondering how long this sort of thing was going to last. Kitchener had told the country that it would be three years. "Three years or the duration" was what I had enlisted for. My heart sank to my boots (which were too wide for my stirrups) as I thought of those three years of imprisonment and dreary discomfort. The mellow happy looking afternoon and the comfortable Kentish landscape made it worse. It wouldn't have been so bad if I'd been doing something definite. But there was nothing to write home about in this sort of existence. Raking up horse-dung before breakfast had ceased to be a new experience. And the jokes and jollity of my companions had likewise lost freshness. They were very good chaps, but young Nunburne had been the only one I could really talk to about things which used to happen before the War began. But there was burly Bob Jenner, son of a big farmer in the Ringwell Hunt; he was in my section, and had failed to get a commission on account of his having lost the sight of one eye. What I should have done without him to talk to I couldn't imagine. I had known him out hunting, so there were a good many simple memories which we could share. . . .

Escape came unexpectedly. It came about a week later. My horse was still lame and I had been going out on the chargers of various men who had special jobs in the squadron, such as the quartermaster-sergeant. One fortunate morning the farrier-sergeant asked me to take his horse out; he said the horse needed sharpening up. We went out for some field-work, and, as usual, I was detailed to act as ground scout. My notion of acting as ground scout was to go several hundred yards ahead of the troop and look for jumpable fences. But the ground was still hard and the hedges were blind with summer vegetation, and when I put the farrier-sergeant's horse at a lush-looking obstacle I failed to observe that there was a strand of wire in it. He took it at the roots and turned a somersault. My wide boots were firmly wedged in the stirrups and the clumsy beast rolled all over me. Two young men, acting as the "advance guard" of the troop, were close behind me. One of them dismounted and scrambled hurriedly through the hedge, while the other shouted to him to "shoot the horse", who was now recumbent with one of my legs under him. My well-meaning rescuer actually succeeded in extracting my rifle from its "bucket", but before he had time to make my position more perilous by loading it, Bob Jenner arrived, brought him to his senses with some strong language, and extricated me, half-stunned and very much crushed. The same day I was taken to a doctor's house in Canterbury. It would be hypocrisy to say that I was fundamentally distressed about my badly broken arm. I couldn't have got a respite from the Workhouse in any other way. But if I had been able to look into the future I should have learned one very sad fact. I had seen the last of my faithful friend Cockbird.

II

Staring at my face in a mirror two months after the accident, I compared my pallid appearance with the picture of health I used to see in a small scrap of glass when I was shaving with cold water in the Army. All my sunburnt health and hardihood had vanished with my old pair of breeches (which the nurse who looked after me had thrown away, saying that they made the room smell like a stable) but I had still got my skimpy tunic to remind me that I had signed away my freedom. Outside the doctor's house where I was lodged, another stormy December afternoon was closing in with torrents of rain. Would it ever stop raining,

I wondered. And would my right arm ever be rid of this
infernal splint? Anyhow, my December face matched the
weather in exactly the same way as it had done in August
and September.

The Yeomanry were now in a camp of huts close to the
town. Every Saturday Bob Jenner or one of the others came
to see me; while they were with me my ardour revived, but
when I was alone again I found it more and more difficult
to imagine myself sharing the discomforts which they described so lightheartedly. But I had only exchanged one
prison for another, and after reading about the War in the
newspapers for nine weeks, the "faith and fire" within me
seemed almost extinguished. My arm had refused to join
up, and I had spent more than an hour under an anæs-
thetic while the doctor screwed a silver plate on to the
bone. The fracture wobbled every time I took a deep
breath, and my arm was very much inflamed. When I was
out for a walk with my arm in a sling I felt a fraud, because
the people I passed naturally assumed that I had been to
the Front. When my squadron commander came to see me
I couldn't help feeling that he suspected me of not getting
well on purpose. I still found it impossible to imagine myself as an officer. It was only half an hour's walk to the
Yeomanry camp, but I could never get myself to go up
there.

The weather had been as depressing as the war news.
Like everybody else I eagerly assimilated the optimistic
reports in the papers about Russian victories in East
Prussia, and so on. "The Russian steam-roller"; how remote that phrase seems now! . . . Often I prayed that the
War would be over before my arm got well. A few weeks
later the doctor said the bone had united and I had another operation for the removal of the plate. In the middle
of January I was allowed to return home, with my arm still
in a splint.

Since my accident I had received a series of letters from
Stephen, who was with an ammunition column on the
Western Front and apparently in no immediate danger.
He said there wasn't an honest jumpable fence in Flanders;

his forced optimism about next year's opening meet failed
to convince me that he expected the "great contest" as he
called it, to be over by then. Denis had disappeared into a
cavalry regiment and was still in England. For him the
world had been completely disintegrated by the War, but
he seemed to be making the best of a bad job.

It was five and a half months since I had been home. I
had left Butley without telling anyone that I had made up
my mind to enlist. On that ominous July 31st I said long
and secret good-byes to everything and everyone. Late in a
sultry afternoon I said good-bye to the drawing-room. The
sun-blinds (with their cords which tapped and creaked so
queerly when there was any wind to shake them) were
drawn down the tall windows; I was alone in the twilight
room, with the glowering red of sunset peering through the
chinks and casting the shadows of leaves on a fiery patch of
light which rested on the wall by the photograph of "Love
and Death". So I looked my last and rode away to the
War on my bicycle. Somehow I knew that it was inevitable, and my one idea was to be first in the field. In fact, I
made quite an impressive inward emotional experience
out of it. It did not occur to me that everyone else would be
rushing off to enlist next week. My gesture was, so to speak,
an individual one, and I gloried in it.

And now, although Aunt Evelyn fussed over me as if I
were a real wounded soldier, I was distinctly conscious of
an anti-climax. I had looked forward to seeing Dixon again
in spite of the sad state of affairs in the stable. But before I
had been in the house five minutes Aunt Evelyn had given
me some news which took me by surprise. Dixon had gone
away to join the Army Veterinary Corps. This had happened two days ago. He was forty-three, but he hadn't a
grey hair, and he had stated his age as thirty-five. The news
had a bracing effect on me. It wasn't the first time that
Tom Dixon had given me a quiet hint as to what was expected of me.

The worst of the winter was over and my arm was mending. Aunt Evelyn talked almost gaily about my going back
to the Yeomanry in the spring. She had twigged that it

was a comparatively safe location, and I knew from her tone of voice that she was afraid I might do something worse. If she had been more subtle and sagacious she would have urged me to exchange into the Infantry. As it was she only succeeded in stiffening my resolve to make no mistake about it this time. I had made one false start, and as I'd got to go to the Front, the sooner I went the better. The instinct of self-preservation, however, made it none too easy, when I was sitting by the fire of an evening, or out for a walk on a mild February afternoon; already there were primroses in the woods, and where should I be in twelve months' time, I wondered. Pushing them up, perhaps! . . .

But I had struggled through the secret desperations of that winter, and I like to remember myself walking over one afternoon to consult Captain Huxtable about a commission in an infantry regiment. Captain Huxtable, who had always shown an almost avuncular concern for my career, had joined the Army in 1860. He was a brisk, freckled, God-fearing, cheerful little man, and although he was now over seventy, he didn't seem to have altered in appearance since I was a child. He was a wonderful man for his age. Chairman of the local bench, churchwarden, fond of a day's shooting with Squire Maundle, comfortably occupied with a moderate sized farm overlooking the Weald, he was a pattern of neighbourly qualities, and there was no one with whom Aunt Evelyn more enjoyed a good gossip. Time-honoured jokes passed between them, and his manner toward her was jovial, spruce, and gallant. He was a neat skater, and his compact homespun figure seemed to find its most appropriate setting when the ponds froze and he was cutting his neat curves on the hard, ringing surface; his apple-cheeked countenance, too, had a sort of blithe good humour which seemed in keeping with fine frosty weather. He was a man who knew a good Stilton cheese and preferred it over ripe. His shrewd and watchful eyes had stocked his mind with accurate knowledge of the countryside. He was, as he said himself, "addicted to observing the habits of a rook", and he was also a keen gardener.

Captain Huxtable was therefore an epitome of all that

was most pleasant and homely in the countrified life for which I was proposing to risk my own. And so, though neither of us was aware of it, there was a grimly jocular element in the fact that it was to him that I turned for assistance. It may be inferred that he had no wish that I should be killed, and that he would have been glad if he could have gone to the Front himself, things being as they were; but he would have regarded it as a greater tragedy if he had seen me shirking my responsibility. To him, as to me, the War was inevitable and justifiable. Courage remained a virtue. And that exploitation of courage, if I may be allowed to say a thing so obvious, was the essential tragedy of the War, which, as everyone now agrees, was a crime against humanity.

Luckily for my peace of mind, I had no such intuitions when I walked across the fields to Butley that afternoon, with four o'clock striking in mellow tones from the grey church tower, the village children straggling home from school, and the agricultural serenity of the Weald widespread in the delicate hazy sunshine. In the tall trees near Captain Huxtable's house the rooks were holding some sort of conference, and it was with a light heart that I turned in at his gate. It happened that as I rang the front-door bell an airship droned its way over the house. Every afternoon that airship passed over our parish, on its way, so it was said, to France. The Captain came out now to watch it from his doorstep, and when it had disappeared he led me into his sanctum and showed me a careful pencil drawing of it, which he had made the first time its lustrous body appeared above his garden. Under the stiff little sketch he had written, "airship over our house", and the date. It was his way of "putting on record" a significant event. Sixteen months afterwards he probably jotted down some such memorandum as this: "Between 11 and 12 this morning, while we were getting in the last load of hay, I distinctly heard the guns in France. A very faint thudding noise but quite continuous as long as it was audible." But he wasn't able to make a neat pencil drawing of the intensive preliminary bombardment on the Somme.

III

As a result of my conversation with Captain Huxtable he wrote a letter about me to the Adjutant at the Training Depot of the Royal Flintshire Fusiliers, which was his old regiment. As far as he was concerned the Flintshire Fusiliers were, as he said, ancient history; but the Adjutant happened to be the nephew of an old brother officer of his, and he jovially remarked that he would perjure himself for once in a way by giving me a good character. For him his old "corps" ranked next below religion, and to be thus almost actively in touch with the regiment gave him deep satisfaction.

His room contained many objects associated with his army life; he had seen garrison service in India; there were mementoes of that; and his little water-colour foreign sketches which I had often seen before. His sword, of course, was hanging on the wall. Everything connected with Captain Huxtable's regimental career had suddenly become significant and stimulating. The Flintshire Fusiliers, which I had so often heard him speak about (and had taken so little interest in) had become something to be lived up to. I would be a credit to him, I resolved, as I went home across the dark fields.

The local doctor had said I might take the splint off my arm next day and that was a step in the right direction. I said nothing to Aunt Evelyn about my conspiracy with her old friend until a week later, when I received a favourable letter from the Adjutant. I was to make a formal application for a Special Reserve commission. The Special Reserve was a new name for the old Militia; a temporary commission in the New Army would have been much the same, but Captain Huxtable wanted me to do the thing properly. Greatly as he admired their spirit, he couldn't help looking down a bit on those Kitchener's Army battalions.

When I broke the news to Aunt Evelyn she said that of course I was doing the right thing. "But I do hate you doing it, my dear!" she added. Should I have to go all the

way to Flintshire, she asked. I said I supposed I should, for
the depot was there.

And although I agreed with her that it would have been
nice if I'd been somewhere nearer, I had a private conviction that I wanted to make my fresh start among people
who knew nothing about me. Dixon had said (when he
brought Cockbird to Downfield the day after mobilization) that if I had to be in the ranks I ought to have done it
somewhere where I wasn't so well known. I found afterwards that there was a great deal of truth in his remark.
The Yeomanry would have been more comfortable for me
if none of the officers had known me before I joined. I now
felt strongly in favour of getting right away from my old
associations. Captain Huxtable had given me all I needed
in the way of a send-off. Aunt Evelyn was helping at the
Voluntary Aid Detachment Hospital, which, as she said,
took her mind off things.

Stephen, when I wrote and told him about it, replied
that since I was so keen on getting killed I might as well do
it properly dressed, and gave me the name of his military
tailor, which was a rather unfortunate one—Craven & Sons.
He had been expecting to get a week's leave, but it had been
"stopped owing to the big strafe" which was imminent (the
Battle of Neuve Chapelle happened soon afterwards).

Ordering my uniform from Craven & Sons was quite
enjoyable—almost like getting hunting clothes. Situated in
a by-way off Bond Street, the firm of Craven & Sons had
been established a century ago in the cathedral city of
Wintonbury. To the best of my knowledge the firm was
exclusively military, though there may have been a demure
ecclesiastical connection at the "and at Wintonbury"
shop. I was warmly welcomed by a florid gentleman with
a free and easy manner; he might almost have been a
major if he had not been so ostensibly a tailor. He spoke
affectionately of the Flintshire Fusiliers ("The Twenty-
Fifth" he called them); he had "been up at the depot only
the other day", and he mentioned a few of the first and
second battalion officers by name; one might almost have
imagined that he had played polo with them, so dashing

was his demeanour as he twirled his blond moustache. This representative of Craven & Sons was like the royal family; he never forgot a name. He must have known the Army List from cover to cover, for he had called on nearly every officers' mess in the country during the periodical pilgrimages on which the prosperity of his firm depended. Newly gazetted subalterns found themselves unable to resist his persuasive suggestions, though he may have met his match in an occasional curmudgeonly colonel. Mr. Stoving (for that was his name) chatted his way courageously through the War; "business as usual" was his watchword. Undaunted by the ever more bloated bulk of the Army List, he bobbed like a cork on the lethal inundation of temporary commissions, and when I last saw him, a few months before the Armistice, he was still outwardly unconscious of the casualty lists which had lost (and gained) him such a legion of customers.

As soon as he had put me at my ease I became as wax in his hands. He knew my needs so much better than I did that when I paid a second visit to try on my tunics, there seemed no reason why he shouldn't put me through a little squad drill. But he only made one reference to the cataclysm of military training which was in progress, and that was when I was choosing khaki shirts. "*You can't have them too dark,*" he insisted, when my eye wandered toward a paler pattern. "We have to keep those in stock—they're for the East of course—but it's quite unpermissible the way some of these New Army officers dress: really, the Provost-Marshal ought to put a stop to all these straw-coloured shirts and ties they're coming out in." He lifted his eyes in horror. . . .

A few weeks later (a second lieutenant in appearance only) I arrived at the training depot of the "Twenty-Fifth". The whole concern had recently migrated from the small peace-time barracks in Flintshire to a new camp of huts on the outskirts of Liverpool. On a fine afternoon at the end of April I got out of the local electric railway at Clitherland Station. Another evidently new officer also climbed out of the train, and we shared a cab up to the camp, with our brand new valises rolling about on the roof. My companion was far from orthodox in what he was wearing, and from his accent I judged him to be a Yorkshireman. His good-humoured face was surmounted by a cap, which was as soft as mine was stiff. His shirt and tie were more yellow than khaki. And his breeches were of a bright buff tint. His tunic was of the correct military colour, but it sat uneasily on his podgy figure. His name, he told me, was Mansfield, and he made no secret of the fact that he had chucked up a job worth £800 a year. "And a nice hope I've got of ever getting it back again!" he added.

When our luggage was unloaded we went to report ourselves at the orderly room. Everything was quiet and deserted, for the troops were drilling on a big field a few hundred yards up the road which went past the camp. We entered the orderly room. The Adjutant was sitting at a table strewn with documents. We saluted clumsily, but he did not look up for a minute or two. When he deigned to do so his eyes alighted on Mansfield. During a prolonged scrutiny he adjusted an eyeglass. Finally he leant back in his chair and exclaimed, with unreproducible hauteur, "*Christ! who's your tailor?*" This (with a reminder that his hair wanted cutting) was the regimental recognition which Mansfield received from his grateful country for having given up a good job in the woollen industry. My own reception was in accordance with the cut of my clothes and my credentials from Captain Huxtable.

IV

It is ten years since I uttered an infantry word of command: and I am only one of a multitude of men in whose minds parade ground phraseology has become as obsolete and derelict as a rusty kettle in a ditch. So much so that it seems quite illuminating to mention the fact. "At the halt on the left form platoon" now sounds to me positively peculiar, and to read *Infantry Training 1914* for a few minutes might be an almost stimulating experience. Though banished to the backs of our minds, those automatic utterances can still be recalled; but who can restore Clitherland Camp and its counterparts all over the country? Most of them were constructed on waste land; and to waste land they have relapsed. I cannot imagine any ex-soldier revisiting Clitherland in pensive pilgrimage. Apart from its deadening associations, it was in an unattractive neighbourhood. The district was industrial. Half a mile away were the chimneys of Bryant's Match Factory. Considerably closer was a hissing and throbbing inferno, which incessantly concocted the form of high explosive known as T.N.T.; when the wind was in the east the Camp got the benefit of the fumes, which caused everyone to cough. Adjoining the Camp, on the other side, was a large Roman Catholic cemetery. Frequent funeral processions cheered up the troops. The surrounding country, with its stunted dwelling-houses, dingy trees, disconsolate canal, and flat root-fields, was correspondingly unlikeable.

Unrolling my valise in a comfortless hut on that first afternoon, I was completely cut off from anything I had done before. Not a soul in the Camp had ever set eyes on me until to-day. And I was totally ignorant of all that I had to learn before I was fit to go to the Front. Fixing up my folding bed, in which I managed to pinch my finger, I listened to what this new world had to tell me. A bugle call was blown—rather out of tune—but what event it signalized I couldn't say. An officer's servant was whistling cheerfully, probably to a pair of brown shoes. A door banged and his army boots thumped hastily along the passage. Then a sedate tread passed along on the boards, evidently some senior officer. Silence filled a gap, and then I heard a dusty rhythm of marching feet; the troops were returning from the drill-field up the road. Finally, from the open space behind the officers' quarters, a manly young voice shouted: "At the halt on the left form close column of platoons." Clitherland Camp had got through another afternoon parade. I was in a soldier manufactory, although I did not see it in that way at the time.

The cell-like room was already occupied by one other officer. He transpired as an unobtrusive ex-civil-engineer—a married man, and expecting to go to France with the next draft of officers. He was friendly but uncommunicative; in the evenings, after mess, he used to sit on his bed playing patience with a pack of small cards. It must not be assumed that I found life in the Camp at all grim and unpleasant. Everything was as aggressively cheerful and alert as the ginger-haired sergeant-major who taught the new officers how to form fours and slope arms, and so on, until they could drill a company of recruits with rigid assurance. In May, 1915, the recruits were men who had voluntarily joined up, the average age of the second lieutenants was twenty-one, and "war-weariness" had not yet been heard of. I was twenty-eight myself, but I was five years younger in looks, and in a few days I was one of this outwardly light-hearted assortment, whose only purpose was to "get sent out" as soon as possible.

The significant aspects of Clitherland as it was then can now be seen clearly, and they are, I think, worth reviving. It was a community (if anything could be called a community under such convulsive conditions) which contained contrasted elements. There were the ostensibly permanent senior officers of the pre-war Special Reserve Battalion (several of whom had South African War ribbons to make them more impressive); and there were the young men whose salutes they received and for whose future efficiency at the Front they were, supposedly, responsible. For these younger men there was the contrast between the Camp at Clitherland (in the bright summer weather of that year) and the places they were booked for (such as the Battle of Loos and the Dardanelles). It was, roughly speaking, the difference between the presence of life (with battalion cricket matches and good dinners at the *hôtel de luxe* in Liverpool) and the prospect of death. (Next winter in the trenches, anyhow.) A minor (social) contrast was provided by the increasingly numerous batches of Service Battalion officers, whose arrival to some extent clashed with the more carefully selected Special Reserve commissions (like

my own) and the public-school boys who came from the
Royal Military College. I mention this "feeling" because
the "temporary gentlemen", (disgusting phrase) whose
manners and accents were liable to criticism by the Adjutant, usually turned out to be first-rate officers when they
got to the trenches. In justice to the Adjutant it must be
remembered that he was there to try and make them con-
form to the Regular "officer and gentleman" pattern
which he exemplified. And so, while improvised officers
came and went, Clitherland Camp was a sort of raft on
which they waited for the moment of embarcation which
landed them as reinforcements to the still more precarious
communities on the other side of the Channel.

Those who were fortunate enough to return, a year or
two later, would find, among a crowd of fresh faces, the
same easy-going Militia majors enjoying their port placidly
at the top of the table. For, to put it plainly, they weren't
mobile men, although they had been mobilized for the
Great War. They were the products of peace, and war had
wrenched them away from their favourite nooks and
niches. The Commanding Officer was a worthy (but somewhat fussy) Breconshire landowner. He now found himself
in charge of 3,000 men and about 100 officers, and was inundated with documents from the War Office. His second-
in-command was a tall Irishman, who was fond of snipe-
shooting. Nature had endowed him with an impressive
military appearance; but he was in reality the mildest of
men. This kind and courteous gentleman found himself
obliged to exist in a hut on the outskirts of Liverpool for an
indefinite period.

There were several more majors; three of them had been
to the Front, but had remained there only a few weeks; the
difference between a club window and a dug-out had been
too much for them. Anyhow, here they were, and there
was the War, and to this day I don't see how things could
have been differently arranged. They appeared to be un-
imaginative men, and the Colonel probably took it as all in
the day's work when he toddled out after mess on some
night when a draft was "proceeding to the Front". Out on

the Square he would find, perhaps, 150 men drawn up; discipline would be none too strict, since most of them had been fortifying themselves in the canteen. He would make his stuttering little farewell speech about being a credit to the regiment; going out to the Big Push which will end the War; and so on. And then the local clergyman would exhort them to trust in their Saviour, to an accompaniment of asides and witticisms in Welsh.

"And now God go with you," he would conclude, adding, "I will go with you as far as the station. . . ."

And they would march away in the dark, singing to the beat of drums. It wasn't impressive, but what else could the Colonel and the clergyman have said or done? . . .

Young officers were trained by efficient N.C.O.'s; the senior officers were responsible for company accounts, kit inspections, and other camp routine. And the spirit of the regiment, presumably, presided over us all. I have reason to believe that Clitherland was one of the most competently managed camps in the country; high authorities looked upon it as exemplary.

Needless to say, I felt awestruck by my surroundings as I edged my way shyly into mess on my first evening. The cheerful crowd of junior officers sat at two long tables which culminated in the one across the top, which was occupied by the impressive permanencies of whom I have been writing. Old soldiers with South African, China, and even Ashanti medal ribbons bustled in and out with plates.

Outside in the evening light, among the subalterns who waited for the Olympians to emerge from the ante-room, I had spoken to no one. Next to me now was a young man who talked too much and seemed anxious to air his social eligibility. From the first I felt that there was something amiss with him. And he was, indeed, one of the most complete failures I ever came across in the War. G. Vivian-Simpson had joined the battalion two or three months before, and for a time he was regarded as smart and promising. A bit of a bounder, perhaps, but thoroughly keen and likely to become competent. He was known among the young officers as "Pardon-me", which was his characteristic utterance. Little by little, poor "Pardon-me" was found out by everyone. His social pretensions were unmasked. (He had been an obscure bank clerk in Liverpool.) His hyphenated name became an object of ridicule. His whole spurious edifice fell to bits. He got into trouble with the Adjutant for cutting parades and failing to pass in musketry. In fact, he was found to be altogether unreliable and a complete cad. For two and a half years he remained ignominiously at the Camp. Fresh officers arrived, were fully trained, and passed away to the trenches. In the meantime guards had to be provided for the docks along the Mersey, and "Pardon-me" was usually in command of one of these perfunctory little expeditions. He must have spent some dreary days at the docks, but it was rumoured that he consoled himself with amorous adventures. Then, when he least expected it, he was actually sent to the Front. Luck was against him; he was introduced to the Ypres salient at its worst. His end was described to me as follows. "Poor old 'Pardon-me'! He was in charge of some Lewis gunners in an advance post. He crawled back to Company headquarters to get his breakfast. You remember what a greedy devil he was! Well, about an hour after he'd gone back to his shell-hole, he decided to chance his arm for another lot of eggs and bacon. A sniper got him while he was on his way, and so he never got his second breakfast!"

It was a sad story, but I make no apology for dragging it from its decent oblivion. All squalid, abject, and inglorious elements in war should be remembered. The intimate mental history of any man who went to the War would make unheroic reading. I have half a mind to write my own.

In the meantime there is nothing more to be said about my first night in mess, and the next morning I began to acquire the alphabet of infantry training. Mansfield picked it up twice as quickly as I did. For he was a competent man, in spite of his New Army style of dress. And his "word of command" had fire and ferocity; whereas mine was much as might have been expected (in spite of my having acquired a passable "view holloa" during my fox-hunting life). Learning how to be a second-lieutenant was a relief to my mind. It made the War seem further away. I hadn't time to think about it, and by the end of each day I was too healthily tired to worry about anything.

Life in the officers' mess was outwardly light-hearted. Only when news came from our two battalions in France were we vividly reminded of the future. Then for a brief while the War came quite close; mitigated by our inexperience of what it was like, it laid a wiry finger on the heart. There was the battle of Festubert in the middle of May. That made us think a bit. The first battalion had been in it and had lost many officers. Those who were due for the next draft were slightly more cheerful than was natural. The next thing I knew about them was that they had gone —half a dozen of them. I went on afternoon parade, and when I returned to the hut my fellow occupant had vanished with all his tackle. But my turn was months away yet. . . .

The following day was a Sunday, and I was detailed to take a party to church. They were Baptists and there were seven of them. I marched them to the Baptist Chapel in Bootle, wondering what on earth to do when I got them to the door. Ought I say "Up the aisle; quick march?" As far as I can remember we reverted to civilian methods and shuffled into the Chapel in our own time. At the end of the service the bearded minister came and conversed with me very cordially and I concealed the fact that it was my first experience of his religion. Sunday morning in the Baptist Chapel made the trenches seem very remote. What possible connection was there?

Next day some new officers arrived, and one of them took the place of the silent civil-engineer in my room. We had the use of the local cricket ground; I came in that evening feeling peaceful after batting and bowling at the nets for an hour. It seemed something to be grateful for— that the War hadn't killed cricket yet, and already it was a relief to be in flannels and out of uniform. Coming cheerfully into the hut I saw my new companion for the first time. He had unpacked and arranged his belongings, and was sitting on his camp-bed polishing a perfectly new pipe.

He looked up at me. Twilight was falling and there was only one small window, but even in the half-light his face surprised me by its candour and freshness. He had the obvious good looks which go with fair hair and firm features, but it was the radiant integrity of his expression which astonished me. While I was getting ready for dinner we exchanged a few remarks. His tone of voice was simple and reassuring, like his appearance. How does he manage to look like that? I thought; and for the moment I felt all my age, though the world had taught me little enough, as I knew then, and know even better now. His was the bright countenance of truth; ignorant and undoubting; incapable of concealment but strong in reticence and modesty. In fact, he was as good as gold, and everyone knew it as soon as they knew him.

Such was Dick Tiltwood, who had left school six months before and had since passed through Sandhurst. He was the son of a parson with a good family living. Generations of upright country gentlemen had made Dick Tiltwood what he was, and he had arrived at manhood in the nick of time to serve his country in what he naturally assumed to be a just and glorious war. Everyone told him so; and when he came to Clitherland Camp he was a shining epitome of his unembittered generation which gladly gave itself to the German shells and machine-guns—more gladly, perhaps, than the generation which knew how much (or how little, some would say) it had to lose. Dick made all the difference to my life at Clitherland. Apart from his cheerful companionship, which was like perpetual fine weather, his Sandhurst training enabled him to help me in mine. Patiently he heard me while I went through my repetitions of the mechanism of the rifle. And in company drill, which I was slow in learning, he was equally helpful. In return for this I talked to him about fox-hunting, which never failed to interest him. He had hunted very little, but he regarded it as immensely important, and much of the material of these memoirs became familiar to him through our conversations in the hut: I used to read him Stephen's letters from the Front, which were long and full of amusing references to the sport that for him symbolized everything enjoyable which the War had interrupted and put an end to. His references to the War were facetious. "An eight-inch landed and duly expanded this morning twenty yards from our mess, which was half-filled with earth. However, the fourth footman soon cleared it and my sausage wasn't even cracked, so I had quite a good breakfast." But he admitted that he was looking forward to "the outbreak of peace", and in one letter went so far as to say that he was "just about as bucked as I should be if I was booked for a week with the Pytchley and it froze the whole time". Dick got to know Stephen quite well, although he had never seen him, except in a little photograph I had with me. So we defied the boredom of life in the Camp, and while the summer went past us our only fear was that we might be separated when our turn came to go abroad. He gave me a sense of security, for his smooth head was no more perplexed with problems than a robin redbreast's; he wound up his watch, brushed his hair, and said his prayers morning and evening.

September arrived, and we were both expecting to get a week's leave. (It was known as "last leave".) One morning Dick came into the hut with a telegram which he handed me. It happened that I was orderly officer that day. Being orderly officer meant a day of dull perfunctory duties, such as turning out the guard, inspecting the prisoners in the guard-room, the cookhouses, the canteen, and everything else in the Camp. When I opened my telegram the orderly sergeant was waiting outside for me; we were due for a tour of the men's huts while they were having their mid-day meal. The telegram was signed Colwood; it informed me that Stephen had been killed in action. But the orderly sergeant was waiting, and away we went, walking briskly over the grit and gravel. At each hut he opened the door and shouted "Shun!" The clatter and chatter ceased and all I had to ask was "Any complaints?" There were no complaints, and off we went to the next hut. It was queer to be doing it, with that dazed feeling and the telegram in my pocket. . . . I showed Dick the telegram when I returned. I had seen Stephen when he was on leave in the spring, and he had written to me only a week ago. Reading the Roll of Honour in the daily paper wasn't the same thing as this. Looking at Dick's blank face I became aware that he would never see Stephen now, and the meaning of the telegram became clear to me.

PART TEN: AT THE FRONT

I

Dick and I were on our way to the First Battalion. The real War, that big bullying bogey, had stood up and beckoned to us at last; and now the Base Camp was behind us with its overcrowded discomforts that were unmitigated by *esprit de corps*. Still more remote, the sudden shock of being uprooted from the Camp at Clitherland, and the strained twenty-four hours in London before departure. For the first time in our lives we had crossed the Channel. We had crossed it in bright moonlight on a calm sea—Dick and I sitting together on a tarpaulin cover in the bow of the boat, which was happily named *Victoria*. Long after midnight we had left Folkestone; had changed our course in an emergency avoidance of Boulogne, (caused by the sinking of a hospital ship, we heard afterwards) had stared at Calais harbour, and seen sleepy French faces in the blear beginnings of November daylight. There had been the hiatus of uncertainty at Etaples (four sunless days of north wind among pine-trees) while we were waiting to be "posted" to our battalion. And now, in a soiled fawn-coloured first-class compartment, we clanked and rumbled along and everything in the world was behind us. . . .

Victoria Station: Aunt Evelyn's last, desperately forced smile; and Dick's father, Canon Tiltwood, proud and burly, pacing the platform beside his slender son and wearing cheeriness like a light unclerical overcoat, which couldn't conceal the gravity of a heart heavy as lead. What did they say to one another, he and Aunt Evelyn, when the train had snorted away and left an empty space in front of them? . . .

To have finished with farewells; that in itself was a burden discarded. And now there was nothing more to worry about. Everything was behind us, and the First Battalion was in front of us.

At nine o'clock we were none of us looking over bright, for we had paraded with kit at two in the morning, though the train, in its war time way, hadn't started till three hours later. There we sat, Dick and I and Mansfield (at last released from peace-time Army conventions) and Joe Barless (a gimlet-moustached ex-sergeant-major who was submitting philosophically to his elevation into officerdom and spat on the floor at frequent regular intervals). On our roundabout journey we stopped at St. Pol and overheard a few distant bangs—like the slamming of a heavy door they sounded. Barless had been out before; had been hit at the first battle of Ypres; had left a wife and family behind him; knocked his pipe out and expectorated, with a grim little jerk of his bullet head, when he heard the guns. We others looked at him for guidance now, and he was giving us all we needed, in his taciturn, matter-of-fact way, until he got us safely reported with the first battalion.

It felt funny to be in France for the first time. The sober-coloured country all the way from Etaples had looked lifeless and unattractive, I thought. But one couldn't expect much on a starved grey November morning. A hopeless hunting country, it looked. . . . The opening meet would have been last week if there hadn't been this war. . . . Dick was munching chocolate and reading the *Strand Magazine*, with its cosy reminder of London traffic on the cover. I hadn't lost sight of *him* yet, thank goodness. The Adjutant at Clitherland had sworn to do his best to get us both sent to the First Battalion. But it was probably an accident that he had succeeded. It was a lucky beginning, anyhow. What a railway-tasting mouth I'd got! A cup of coffee would be nice, though French coffee tasted rather nasty, I thought. . . . We got to Béthune by half-past ten.

*   *   *

We got to Béthune by half-past ten: I am well aware that the statement is, in itself, an arid though an accurate one. And at this crisis in my career I should surely be ready with something spectacular and exciting. Nevertheless, I must admit that I have no such episode to exhibit. The events in my experience must take their natural course. I distinctly remember reporting at battalion headquarters in Béthune. In a large dusky orderly room in—was it a wine-merchant's warehouse?—the Colonel shook hands with me. I observed that he was wearing dark brown field-boots, small in the leg, and insinuating by every supple contour that they came from Craxwell. And since the world is a proverbially small place, there was, I hope, nothing incredible in the fact that the Colonel was a distant relative of Colonel Hesmon, and had heard all about how I won the Colonel's Cup. It will be remembered that Colonel Hesmon's conversational repertoire was a limited one, so it wasn't to be wondered at that my new Commanding Officer could tell me the name of my horse, or that I was already well acquainted with *his* name, which was Winchell. For the old Colonel had frequently referred to the exploits of his dashing young relative.

I mention this mainly because my first few minutes with my unit in France transported me straight back to England and the Ringwell Hunt. Unfortunately, the migration was entirely mental; my physical feet took me straight along a *pavé* road for about three miles, to Le Hamel, where my company was in billets. Anyhow, it was to my advantage that I was already known to Colonel Winchell as a hunting man. For I always found that it was a distinct asset, when in close contact with officers of the Regular Army, to be able to converse convincingly about hunting. It gave one an almost unfair advantage in some ways.

Mansfield, (who had been received with reservations of cordiality) Dick (*persona grata* on account of his having been at Sandhurst, and also because no one could possibly help liking him at sight) and I (no comment required) were all posted to "C" company which was short of officers. The battalion had lately been much below full strength, and was now being filled up with drafts. We had arrived at a good time, for our Division was about to be withdrawn to a back area for a long rest. And the Givenchy trenches on the La Bassée Canal had taken their toll in casualties. For the time being, the Western Front received us into comparative comfort and domesticity. We found Captain Barton, the company commander, by a stove (which was smoking badly) in a small tiled room on the ground floor of a small house on the road from Béthune to Festubert. The smoke made my eyes water, but otherwise things were quite cheerful. We all slept on the floor, the hardness and coldness of which may be imagined. But then, as always, my sleeping-bag (or "flea-bag" as we called it) was a good friend to me, and we were in clover compared with the men (no one who was in the War need be reminded of that unavoidable circumstance).

Barton (like all the battalion officers except the C.O., the second-in-command, and the quartermaster, and four or five subalterns from Sandhurst) was a civilian. He was big, burly, good-natured, and easy-going; had been at Harrow and, until the War, had lived a comfortably married life on an adequate unearned income. He was, in fact, a man of snug and domesticated habits and his mere presence (wearing pince-nez) in a front-line trench made one feel that it *ought*, at any rate, to be cosy. Such an inherently amicable man as Barton was a continual reminder of the incongruity of war with everyday humanity. In the meantime he was making gallant efforts to behave professionally, and keep his end up as a company commander. But that stove had no business to be making the room uninhabitable with its suffocating fumes. It really wasn't fair on a chap like old Barton, who had always been accustomed to a bright fire and a really good glass of port. . . .

So my company received me: and for an infantry subaltern the huge unhappy mechanism of the Western Front always narrowed down to the company he was in. My platoon accepted me apathetically. It was a diminished and exhausted little platoon, and its mind was occupied with anticipations of "Divisional Rest".

To revert to my earlier fact, "got to Béthune by half-past ten", it may well be asked how I can state the time of arrival so confidently. My authority is the diary which I began to keep when I left England. Yes; I kept a diary, and intend to quote from it (though the material which it contains is meagre). But need this be amplified? . . .

"*Thursday*. Went on working-party, 3 to 10.30 p.m. Marched to Festubert, a ruined village, shelled to bits. About 4.30, in darkness and rain, started up half a mile of light-railway lines through marsh, with sixty men. Then they carried hurdles up the communication trenches, about three-quarters of a mile, which took two hours. Flares went up frequently; a few shells, high overhead, and exploding far behind us. The trenches are very wet. Finally emerged at a place behind the first- and second-line trenches, where new trenches (with 'high-command breastworks') are being dug.

"*Saturday*. Working-party again. Started 9.45 p.m. in bright moonlight and iron frost. Dug 12—2. Men got soup in ruined house in Festubert, with the moon shining through matchwood skeleton rafters. Up behind the trenches, the frost-bound morasses and ditches and old earthworks in moonlight, with dusky figures filing across the open, hobbling to avoid slipping. Home 4.15.

"*Sunday*. Same as Saturday. Dug 12—2. Very cold.

"*Monday*. Went with working-party at 3 p.m. Wet day. Awful mud. Tried to dig, till 7.30, and came home soaked. Back 9.45. Beastly night for the men, whose billets are wretched."

I can see myself coming in, that last night, with Julian Durley, a shy, stolid-faced platoon commander who had been a clerk in Somerset House. He took the men's discomforts very much to heart. Simple and unassertive, he liked sound literature, and had a sort of metropolitan turn of humour. His jokes, when things were going badly, reminded me of a facetious bus conductor on a wet winter day. Durley was an inspiration toward selfless patience. He was an ideal platoon officer, and an example which I tried to imitate from that night onward. I need hardly say that he had never hunted. He could swim like a fish, but no social status was attached to that.

II

When I had been with the battalion a week we moved away from the La Bassée sector at nine o'clock on a fine bright morning. In spite of my quite mild experiences there, I felt that I'd seen more than enough of that part of the country. Barton and Durley and young Ormand (who was now second-in-command of the company) were always talking about the Givenchy trenches and how their dug-out had been "plastered with trench-mortars and whizz-bangs". Now that they were out of it they seemed to take an almost morbid delight in remembering their escapes. No one knew where we were moving to, but the Quarter-master had told Barton that we might be going south. "New Army" battalions were beginning to arrive in France, and the British line was being extended.

On our second day's march (we had done ten kilometres to a comfortable billet the first day) we passed an infantry brigade of Kitchener's Army. It was raining; the flat dreary landscape was half-hidden by mist, and the road was liquid mud. We had fallen out for a halt when they passed us. Four after four they came, some of them wearing the steel basin-helmets which were new to the English armies then. The helmets gave them a Chinese look. To tell the truth, their faces looked sullen, wretched, and brutal as they sweated with their packs under glistening waterproof capes. Worried civilian officers on horses, young-looking subalterns in new rainproof trench-coats; and behind the trudging column the heavy transport horses plodding through the sludge, straining at their loads, and the stolid drivers munching, smoking, grinning, yelling coarse gibes at one another. It was the War all right, and they were going in the direction of it.

Late that afternoon I walked out a little way from our billets. In the brooding stillness I watched the willows and poplars, and the gleaming dykes which reflected the faint flush of a watery sunset. A heron sailed slowly away across the misty flats of ploughed land. Twilight deepened, and a flicker of star-shells wavered in the sky beyond Béthune. The sky seemed to sag heavily over Flanders; it was an oppressive, soul-clogging country, I thought, as I went back to our company mess in the squalid village street, to find Dick polishing his pipe against his nose, Ormand and Mansfield playing "nap", and Durley soberly reading *The Cloister and the Hearth* in an Everyman edition. Already we were quite a happy family. "Old Man Barton" as we called him, had gone out to invite the Quartermaster to dinner with us. Until that evening I had only seen the Q.M. from a distance, but I was already aware that he was the bed-rock of the battalion (as befitted one on whom we relied for our rations). I saw him clearly for what he was, on that first evening (though not so clearly as I can see him now).

Joe Dottrell had been quartermaster-sergeant before the War: he was now Acting Quartermaster, with the rank of captain, since the real Q.M. had faded away into a "cushy job" at Army Headquarters. (He had, in fact, found that haven before the battalion went into action at the first battle of Ypres, whence it had emerged with eighty-five men and one officer—Joe Dottrell.) Whatever might happen, Joe was always there, and he never failed to get the rations up; no bombardment could have prevented him doing that. And what those "dixies" of hot tea signified no one knows who wasn't there to wait for them. He was a small, spare man—a typical "old soldier". He had won his D.C.M. in South Africa, and had a row of ribbons to match his face, which was weather-beaten and whiskyfied to purple tints which became blue when the wind was cold.

Joe Dottrell now entered, his cap hiding his bald brow, and his British-warm coat concealing his medal ribbons, and old man Barton beaming beside him.

"I've brought Dottrell in to jolly you all up," he said, with his nervous giggle. "Have a drink, Joe," he continued, holding up a squat bottle of "Old Vatted Highland".

"Well, my lucky lads!" exclaimed Joe, in his Lanca-shire voice.

Accepting the proffered glass he wished us all "the

best", and his presence gave us just that sense of security which we were in need of. But something went wrong in the kitchen, and the dinner was a disgrace. Barton "strafed" the servants until they were falling over one another, but Dottrell said the toasted cheese wasn't too bad, and "There's worse things in the world than half-warmed Maconochie", he remarked. (Maconochie, it will be remembered, was a tinned compound of meat and vegetables; but perhaps it has survived the War. If so, it has my sympathy.)

* * *

Next day we took it easy. The day after that we travelled to our destination. I have been looking at the map. The distance, by a straight line, was fifty miles. Sixty-five, perhaps, by road; an easy three hours' drive for the Divisional General in his car. Not so easy for the rank and file, whose experiences of migration were summarized well and truly by a private soldier, in a simple sentence which once met my eye while I was censoring the correspondence of my platoon. "Our company have been for a bath to-day and had a clean shirt given us and socks. We had to march five miles each way, so we had a good walk for it, didn't we? My feet are minus all the top skin. *Everywhere we go seems such a long way.*" In those last words one infantry private speaks for them all.

Our big move to the back area began at six a.m. We had to be up by then, for our kits had to be packed and ready by half-past seven. As soon as we had eaten our bacon and eggs in the stuffy billet by the light of a candle, the officers' servants began to pack up the tin plates and dishes, and I remember how I went out alone into the first grey of the morning and up the village street with the cocks crowing. I walked slowly up to some higher ground with a view of woods and steeples and colliery chimneys; rooks were cawing in some tall trees against the faint colours of a watery daybreak, and the *curé* came out of his gate in a garden wall and said good-morning to me as he passed. It was Sunday morning, and by eight o'clock there was a sound of church bells from far and near. Then a troop of mules and horses clattered along the road at their morning exercise, some of them led by turbaned Indians. I sat on a milestone and watched the sun come out, and a thrush sang a little way off—the first I'd heard in France. But solitude was scanty and precious in the Army, and at half-past ten I was on parade.

We marched two miles into Lillers and entrained. The train started at noon. Ten hours later we detrained at a station three miles from Amiens. We had averaged four miles an hour, and it was now after ten; a dark, still night, with a little rain at times. Men, transport horses, officers' chargers, limbers, and field-kitchens (known as "the cookers") were unloaded. All this took two hours. We had some tea. . . . If I could taste that tea out of the dixies now I should write it all very much as it was. Living spontaneity would be revived by that tea, the taste of which cannot be recovered by any effort of memory.

Fifteen minutes after midnight we moved off. It was rumoured that we had only a few miles to go. On we went to the steady beat of the drums, halting for ten minutes at the end of each fifty. After the second halt the road seemed to become more hilly. About once in an hour we passed through a dark sleeping village. There was a lamp hung on a limber in the rear of the column. Twice I saw our shadows thrown on a white wall in a village. The first time it was a few colossal heads with lurching shoulders and slung rifles; and a second time, on a dead white wall, it was a line of legs; legs only; huge legs striding away from us as if jeering at our efforts to keep going. Movement became mechanical, and I found myself falling asleep as I walked. The men had the weight of their packs and equipment to keep them awake!

A little after six, just before it began to get light, we halted for the sixth time in a small town with a fine church. I sat on the steps at the church door with Dick beside me. Barton came and told us that we had another five kilometres to go "up a high hill". How we managed it I can't say, but an hour afterwards we entered a straggling village on the wooded uplands. As we hobbled in we were met by the Quartermaster, who had got there a few hours ahead of us with the Interpreter (a spindle-shanked Frenchman with a gentle soul and a large military moustache—exiled, poor man, from his jewellery shop at Pau).

As we were the first troops who had ever been billeted in the village, old Joe and Monsieur Perrineau had been having quite a lively time with the rustic inhabitants, who had been knocked up out of their beds and were feeling far from amiable as regards the Flintshire Fusiliers. Having seen the men into their ramshackle barns we sorted ourselves out into our own billets. Dick and I shared a small room in an empty cottage. My diary informs me that I slept from eleven till five. We had marched sixteen miles. It was no easy matter to move an infantry battalion fifty miles. Let those who tour the continent in their comfortable cars remember it and be thankful.

III

Dick and I and Mansfield were starting our active service with a peaceful interlude which we had no right to expect. We had "struck it lucky" as Mansfield remarked. Young Ormand made round eyes under his dark eyebrows as he gloated over the difference between Divisional Rest and those ruddy Givenchy trenches. He was a sturdy little public-school boy who made no secret of his desire to avoid appearing in the Roll of Honour. He wanted life, and he appeared capable of making good use of it, if allowed the opportunity. Dick remained silent; he usually kept his thoughts to himself, confirming other people's opinions with one of his brilliant smiles and the trustful look which he carried in his grey eyes. Julian Durley, too contented for speech, stretched his hands toward the blazing wood fire which crackled cheerfully while the wind blustered comfortably around the cottage.

We were all five of us sitting round the fire in my billet, which had a good open grate, a few pieces of old furniture, and a clock which ticked sedately, as if there were no war on. The owner of the cottage was with the French army. There wasn't a man in the village under forty, and most of them looked gaffers of seventy. They complained that the Battalion was burning all their wood, but firewood was plentiful, since the village was only half a mile from a small forest, and there were trees all round it. This, and its rural remoteness, gave it an air of avoiding conscription. While we were sitting there, my servant Flook (who had been a railway signalman in Lancashire) blundered in at the door with a huge sack of firewood, which he dropped on the tiled floor with a gasp of relief and an exclamation in the war jargon which is so difficult to remember, which made us all laugh. He explained that the people had been playing up hell to the Interpreter, so he'd slipped round to an adjacent woodstack as soon as it was dark to get some more of the "stoof" before the trouble began. Having emptied the sack in a corner he went out for another cargo.

Memories of our eight weeks at Montagne are blurred, like the war jargon which was around me then. I remember it by the light of a couple of ration candles, stuck in bottles; for our evenings were almost homely, except on the few occasions when we went out for a couple of hours of night-work. And even that was quite good fun, especially when old man Barton dropped his pince-nez in the middle of a wood. Mansfield's lurid language was another source of amusement. By daylight we were "training for open warfare". Colonel Winchell was very much on his toes and intent on impressing the Brigadier with his keenness and efficiency. He persistently preached "open warfare" at us, prophesying a "big advance" in the spring.

So we did outpost schemes at the forest's edge, and open-order attacks across wheat-fields and up the stubbled slopes, while sandy hares galloped away, and an old shepherd, in a blue frieze cloak with a pointed hood, watched us from the nook where he was avoiding the wind.

Every evening, at sunset, the battalion fifes and drums marched down the village street with martial music to signify that another day was at an end and the Flintshire

Fusiliers in occupation. Ploughmen with their grey teams drove a last furrow on the skyline; windmills spun their sails merrily; rooks came cawing home from the fields; pigeons circled above farmstead stacks with whistling sober-hued wings; and the old shepherd drove his sheep and goats into the village, tootling on a pipe. Sometimes a rampart of approaching rain would blot out the distance, but the foreground would be striped with vivid green, lit with a gleam of sun, and an arc of iridescence spanned the slate-coloured cloud. The War was fifty kilometres away, though we could hear the big guns booming beyond the horizon.

I was happy as I trudged along the lanes in the column, with my platoon chattering behind me and everything gilt with the sun's good humour. Happier still when I borrowed the little black mare no one could ride and cantered about the open country by myself, which I did two or three afternoons a week. The black mare was well bred, but had lost the use of one eye. She had a queer temper, and had earned an evil reputation by kicking various officers off or bolting back to the transport lines with them after going half a mile quite quietly. She was now used as a pack-pony for carrying ammunition, but by gentle treatment I gained her confidence and she soon became a sort of active-service echo of my old favourites. Dick rode out with me as often as he could persuade the Transport Officer to let him have a horse.

When riding alone I explored the country rather absent-mindedly, meditating on the horrors which I had yet to experience; I was unable to reconcile that skeleton certainty with the serenities of this winter landscape—clean-smelling, with larks in the sky, the rich brown gloom of distant woods, and the cloud shadows racing over the lit and dappled levels of that widespread land. And then I would pass a grey-roofed château, with its many windows and no face there to watch me pass. Only a bronze lion guarding the well in the middle of an overgrown lawn, and the whole place forlorn and deserted. Once, as I was crossing the main road from Abbeville to Beauvais, I watched the

interminable column of a French army corps which was
moving southward. For the first time I saw the famous
French field-guns—the "75's".

But even then it wasn't easy to think of dying. . . . Still
less so when Dick was with me, and we were having an
imitation hunt. I used to pretend to be hunting a pack of
hounds, with him as my whipper-in. Assuming a Denis
Milden manner, (Denis was at Rouen with the cavalry and
likely to remain there, in spite of the C.O.'s assumptions
about open warfare) I would go solemnly through a wood,
cheering imaginary hounds. After an imaginary fox had
been found, away we'd scuttle, looking in vain for a fence
to jump, making imaginary casts after an imaginary check,
and losing our fox when the horses had done enough galloping. An imaginary kill didn't appeal to me, somehow.
Once, when I was emerging rapidly from a wood with
loud shouts, I came round a corner and nearly knocked the
Brigadier off his horse. He was out for a ride with his staff-
captain; but no doubt he approved of my sporting make-
believe, and I didn't dare to stop for apologies, since the
Brigadier was a very great man indeed. Dick enjoyed these
outings enormously and was much impressed by my hunting noises. The black mare seemed to enjoy it also.

Thus, in those delusive surroundings, I reverted ficti-
tiously to the jaunts and jollities of peace time, fabricating
for my young friend a light-hearted fragment of the sport
which he had not lived long enough to share. It was queer,
though, when we met some of the black-bearded Bengal
Lancers who were quartered in one of the neighbouring
villages. What were they doing among these wooded ridges,
with the little roads winding away over the slopes toward
a low yellow sunset and the nowhere of life reprieved to
live out its allotted span?

*   *   *

Christmas came—a day of disciplined insobriety—and
the First Battalion entered 1916 in a state of health and
happiness. But it was a hand-to-mouth happiness, preyed
upon by that remote noise of artillery; and as for health—

well, we were all of us provisionally condemned to death in our own thoughts and if anyone had been taken seriously ill and sent back to "Blighty" he would have been looked upon as lucky. For anybody who allowed himself to think things over, the only way out of it was to try and feel secretly heroic, and to look back on the old life as pointless and trivial. I used to persuade myself that I had "found peace" in this new life. But it was a peace of mind which resulted from a physically healthy existence combined with a sense of irresponsibility. There could be no turning back now; one had to do as one was told. In an emotional mood I could glory in the idea of the supreme sacrifice.

But where was the glory for the obscure private who was always in trouble with the platoon sergeant and got "medicine and duty" when he went to the medical officer with rheumatism? He had enlisted "for the duration" and had a young wife at home. It was all very well for Colonel Winchell to be lecturing in the village schoolroom on the offensive spirit, and the spirit of the regiment, but everyone knew that he was booked for a brigade, and some said that he'd bought a brigadier's gold-peaked cap last time he was on leave.

When I instructed my platoon, one or two evenings a week, I confined myself to asking them easy questions out of the infantry training manual, saying that we had got to win the War (and were certain to) and reading the League Football news aloud. I hadn't begun to question the rights and wrongs of the War then; and if I had, nothing would have been gained by telling my platoon about it—apart from the grave breach of discipline involved in such heart-searchings.

Early in the New Year the first gas-masks were issued. Every morning we practised putting them on, transforming ourselves into grotesque goggle-faced creatures as we tucked the grey flannel under our tunics in flustered haste. Those masks were an omen. An old wood-cutter in high leather leggings watched us curiously, for we were doing our gas-drill on the fringe of the forest, with its dark cypresses among the leafless oaks and beeches, and a faint golden light over all.

One Sunday in January I got leave to go into Amiens.
(A rambling train took an hour and a half to do the eigh-
teen-mile journey.) Dick went with me. After a good lunch
we inspected the Cathedral, which was a contrast to the
life we had been leading. But it was crowded with sight-
seeing British soldiers; the kilted "Jocks" walked up and
down the nave as if they had conquered France, and I remember seeing a Japanese officer flit in with curious eyes.
The long capes which many of the soldiers wore gave them
a mediæval aspect, insolent and overbearing. But the background was solemn and beautiful. White columns soared
into lilies of light, and the stained-glass windows harmon-
ized with the chanting voices and the satisfying sounds of
the organ. I glanced at Dick and thought what a young
Galahad he looked (a Galahad who had got his school
colours for cricket).

Back in the company mess at Montagne we found the
Quartermaster talking to Barton, who was looking none
too bright, for old Joe seemed to think that we might be
moving back to the Line any day now.

Young Ormand had got his favourite record going on
his little gramophone. That mawkish popular song haunts
me whenever I am remembering the War in these after-
days:

> *And when I told them how wonderful you were,*
> *They wouldn't believe me; they wouldn't believe me;*
> *Your hands, your eyes, your lips, your hair,*
> *Are in a class beyond compare . . .*

and so on. His records were few, and all were of a similar
kind. I would have liked to hear a Handel violin sonata
sometimes; there was that one which Kreisler had played
the first time I heard him. . . . And I'd have liked to hear
Aunt Evelyn playing "The Harmonious Blacksmith", on
that Sunday evening when we began to pull ourselves together for "the Line". . . . In her last letter she had said
how long the winter seemed, in spite of being so busy at the
local hospital. She was longing for the spring to come
again. "Spring helps one so much in life." (In the spring,

I thought, the "Big Push" will begin.) Her chief bit of news was that Dixon was in France. Although he had enlisted in the Army Veterinary Corps he was now attached to the Army Service Corps, and was a sergeant. "He seems quite happy, as he has charge of a lot of horses," she wrote. I wondered whether there was any chance of my seeing him, but it seemed unlikely. Anyhow, I would try to find out where he was, as soon as I knew where our division was going. Dottrell thought we were for the Somme trenches, which had lately been taken over from the French.

*　　　*　　　*

But before we left Montagne Colonel Winchell sent for me and told me to take over the job of Transport Officer. This was an anti-climax, for it meant that I shouldn't go into the trenches. The late Transport Officer had gone on leave, and now news had come that he had been transferred to a reserve battalion in England. Mansfield remarked that God seemed to watch over some people. He seemed to be watching over me too. Everyone in "C" company mess expressed magnanimous approval of my appointment, which was considered appropriate, on account of my reputation as a fox-hunting man. I entered on my new duties with "new-broom" energy. And the black mare was now mine to ride every day. For the time being I remained with "C" company mess, but when we got to the Line I should live with Dottrell and the Interpreter. It was a snug little job which would have suited Barton down to the ground.

There was one thing which worried me; I disliked the idea of Dick going into the front line while I stayed behind. I said so, and he told me not to be an old chump. So we had a last ride round the woods, and the next morning, which was raw and foggy, we turned our backs on the little village. The First Battalion never had such a peaceful eight weeks again for the remainder of the War.

We crossed the Somme at Picquigny: after that we were in country unknown to us. I rode along with the rattle and rumble of limber and wagon wheels, watching the patient

dun-coloured column winding away in front; conscious of
what they were marching to, I felt myself strongly identified with this queer community, which still contained a
few survivors from the original Expeditionary Force battalion which had "helped to make history" at Ypres in October, 1914. Most of the old soldiers were on the strength of
the Transport, which numbered about sixty.

On the roll of the Transport were drivers, officers'
grooms, brakesmen, and the men with the nine pack animals which carried ammunition. Then there was the transport-sergeant (on whose efficiency my fate depended), his
corporal, and a farrier-corporal; and those minor special-
ists, the shoeing-smith, saddler, carpenter, and cook. Our
conveyances were the G.S. wagon (with an old driver who
took ceaseless pride in his horses and the shining up of his
steelwork) the mess wagon (carrying officers' kits, which
were strictly limited in weight) the company cookers
(which lurched cumbersomely along with the men's dinners stewing away all the time) the watercart, and a two-
wheeled vehicle known as "the Maltese cart" (which carried a special cargo connected with the Quartermaster's
stores and was drawn by an aged pony named Nobbie).
There were also the limbers, carrying the machine-guns
and ammunition.

The transport-sergeant was a Herefordshire man who
could easily be visualized as a farmer driving to market in
his gig. The C.O. had told me that the transport had been
getting rather slack and needed smartening up; but I was
already aware that Dottrell and the transport-sergeant
could have managed quite easily without my enthusiastic
support; they knew the whole business thoroughly, and all
I could do was to keep an eye on the horses, which were a
very moderate assortment, though they did their work well
enough.

So far I have said next to nothing about the officers outside my own company, and there is nothing to be said
about them while they are on their way to the Line, except
that their average age was about twenty-five, and that I
had known the majority of them at Clitherland. It was a

more or less untried battalion which marched across the Somme that misty morning. But somehow its original spirit survived, fortified by those company sergeant-majors and platoon sergeants whose duties were so exacting; how much depended on them only an ex-infantry officer can say for certain; according to my own experience, everything depended on them. But the Army was an interdependent concern, and when the Brigadier met us on the road Colonel Winchell's face assumed a different expression of anxiety from the one which it wore when he was riding importantly up and down the column with the Adjutant at his heels. (The Adjutant, by the way, became a Roman Catholic priest after the War, and it doesn't surprise me that he felt the need for a change of mental atmosphere.) The Brigadier, in his turn, became a more or less meek and conciliatory man when he encountered the Divisional General. And so on, up to Sir John French, who had lately been replaced by Sir Douglas Haig.

We went thirteen miles that day. I remember, soon after we started on the second day, passing the end of an avenue, at the far end of which there was an enticing glimpse of an ancient château. My heart went out to that château: it seemed to symbolize everything which we were leaving behind us. But it was a bright morning, and what had I got to complain about, riding cockily along on my one-eyed mare while Dick was trudging in front of his platoon? . . .

On the third day, having marched thirty-three miles altogether, we entered Morlancourt, a village in the strip of undulating landscape between the Somme and the Ancre rivers. This was our destination (until the next day, when the troops went up to the trenches, which were four or five miles away). It was an ominous day, but the sun shone and the air felt keen; as we marched down to Morlancourt a flock of pigeons circled above the roofs with the light shining through their wings. It was a village which had not suffered from shell-fire. Its turn came rather more than two years afterwards.

We were all kept busy that afternoon: Barton and the other company commanders were harassed by continuous

"chits" from battalion H.Q. and, as young Ormand remarked when he came to leave his gramophone in my care,
"everyone had fairly got the breeze up". The only person
who showed no sign of irritability was the Quartermaster,
who continued to chaff M. Perrineau, with whom he
stumped about the village mollifying everyone and putting
difficulties to rights.

Late in the evening I was sent off to a hamlet a mile
away to find out (from the billeting officer of the New
Army battalion we were relieving next day) certain details
of routine connected with the transport of rations to the
Line. This billeting officer recognized me before I remembered who he was. His name was Regel (which he now
pronounced Regal). I had forgotten his existence since we
were at school together. He now dictated his methodical
information, and when I had finished scribbling notes
about "water-trolley horses", "mule-stable just beyond
first barricade", and so on, we talked for a while about old
days.

"How's your cousin Willie?" I asked, for want of anything else to say. His chubby face looked embarrassed, and
he replied (in a low voice, for there were two other officers
in the room): "He's on the other side—in the artillery." . . .

I remembered then that Willie (a very nice boy) had
always gone home to Hanover for the holidays. And now
he might be sending a five-nine shell over at us for all we,
or he, knew. It was eleven o'clock when I got back to Morlancourt. Dottrell was having a glass of rum and hot water
before turning in. He had already found out all the details
which I had scribbled in my notebook.

IV

Morlancourt was tucked away among the fold of long
slopes and bare ridges of ploughland. Five roads entered
the village and each road, in its friendly convergence with
the others, had its little crop of houses. There was a church
with a slated tower and a gilt vane, round which birds

wheeled and clacked. In the hollow ground in the middle, where the five roads met, there was a congregation of farm buildings round an open space with a pond on one side of it. It seemed a comfortable village when one looked down on its red and grey roofs and its drab and ochre walls.

The long lines of the high ground hid the rest of the world: on the ridge one saw a few straggling trees, a team of greys ploughing or dredging, and some horsemen or a hooded farm-cart moving along the white edge of the sky-line. The wind piped across the open, combing the thorn bushes which grew under high banks, and soughing in isolated plane trees and aspens. It was a spacious landscape of distant objects delicately defined under an immense sky. The light swept across it in a noble progress of wind and cloud, and evening brought it mystery and sadness. At night the whole region became a dusk of looming slopes with lights of village and bivouac picked out here and there, little sparks in the loneliness of time. And always the guns boomed a few miles away, and the droning aeroplanes looked down on the white seams of the reserve trench lines with their tangle of wires and posts.

Here, while the battalion began its "tours of trenches" (six days in and four days out), I had my meals comfortably with mild M. René Perrineau and Joe Dottrell. I slept in a canvas hut close to the transport lines, falling asleep to the roar and rattle of trench warfare four miles away, and waking to see, on sunny mornings, the shadows of birds flitting across my canvas roof, and to hear the whistling of starlings from the fruit trees and gables of the farm near by. After breakfast I would sit for a while reading a book by the fire in Dottrell's billet, while the soldier cook sang "I want to go to Michigan" at the top of his voice about three yards away. But however much he wanted to go to Michigan, he was lucky not to be in the trenches, and so was I; and I knew it as I toddled down to the transport lines to confer with Sergeant Hoskins about getting some carrots and greenstuff for the horses and indenting for some new nosebags and neckpieces for the limber harness. Some of the horses were looking hide-bound, and I promised the sergeant that I'd buy a couple of hundredweight of linseed for them when I went on leave. Linseed was a cosy idea; it reminded me of peacetime conditions.

Our serious activities began after lunch. At half-past two I mounted the black mare, and old Joe soused himself into the saddle of his pony Susan (a veteran who had sustained a shrapnel wound on the near hip at the first battle of Ypres) and the transport moved off along the Bray road with the rations for the battalion. As the days lengthened the expedition started later, for we couldn't go beyond Bray until after dusk. It was a roundabout journey of seven miles, and if we started at three we were never home before ten. But home we came, to find Monsieur Perrineau solacing himself with Ormand's gramophone: "But when I told them how wonderful you were" or "Just a little love, a little kiss". (Perrineau was hoping to go on leave soon, and his wife was waiting for him at Pau.)

There were times when I felt that I ought to be somewhere else; I always went up to see my company, and when they were in the front line I was reluctant to leave them. One night (during the second time they were in) I arrived while our batteries were busily retaliating after a heavy afternoon bombardment by the Germans. I had some difficulty in getting up to the front line as the communication trenches were badly knocked about. But I found the five "C" company officers none the worse for having been "strafed" with trench-mortars, and my visit seemed to cheer them. I came home across the open country that night (which saved three miles) and it was a relief to leave it all behind me—the water-logged trenches, and men peering grimly at me from under their round helmets: riding home there was friendly gloom around me, while the rockets soared beyond the ridge and the machine-guns rattled out their mirthless laughter. I left the mare to find her way to the gap in the reserve trench line: she never hesitated though she had only been up that way once by daylight. I was seeing the War as a looker-on, it seemed.

*   *   *

I had written to Dixon, telling him all about my new job, and I now received a reply. We were, apparently, in the same army corps, so he couldn't be so very many miles away.

"I have been wondering, sir," he wrote, "whether it might possibly be fixed up for me to exchange into your battalion as transport-sergeant. You say your sergeant has been in France since the beginning, so he's done his bit all right! It would be quite like old times for me to be your transport-sergeant. That was a rotten business about Mr. Colwood being killed, sir. We shall all miss him very much when this War is over."

Dixon's letter sent me off into pleasant imaginings; to have him near me would make all the difference, I thought. Everything I had known before the War seemed to be withering away and falling to pieces: Denis seldom wrote to me, and he was trying to get a job on the Staff; but with Dixon to talk to I should still feel that the past was holding its own with the War; and I wanted the past to survive and to begin again; the idea was like daylight on the other side of this bad weather in which life and death had come so close to one another. I couldn't get used to the idea of Stephen being dead. And Denis had become so remote that I seldom remembered him, though I couldn't say why it was.

So, by the time I was showing Dottrell the letter, I had made up my mind that Dixon's exchange was as good as settled. Joe read the letter through twice. "Your old groom must be a good sport," he remarked, pouring himself out a couple of inches of O.V.H. and adding a similar amount of water. "But it would take a deal of wangling to work his exchange. And if you want my private opinion, young George, he'd far better stay where he is. We'll find ourselves in much less cushy places than this, and you say he's turned forty-five. . . ." He handed me the letter. "And you might find yourself back with 'C' company again if we had some casualties. Things change pretty quick nowadays. And I don't mind betting there'll be a few changes when Kinjack rolls up to take command of the battalion!"

I nodded wisely. For everyone now knew that Winchell had got his brigade, and Major Kinjack was expected (from the Second Battalion) in a week or two. And Kinjack had a somewhat alarming reputation as a disciplinarian. He was, according to Dottrell, who had known him since he was a subaltern, "a bloody fine soldier but an absolute pig if you got the wrong side of him". Old man Barton was in a twitter about the new C.O., his only hope being, he said, that Kinjack would send him home as incompetent. Barton came in at this moment, for the battalion had returned from the trenches the day before.

"Why, Barton," exclaimed Dottrell, "you look as if you'd just come out of quod!"

Barton's hair had been cut by an ex-barber (servant to the medical officer) who had borrowed a pair of horse-clippers to supplement his scissors. Barton giggled and rubbed his cropped cranium. He said it made him feel more efficient, and began to chaff Dick (who had come in to ask if he might go for a ride with me that afternoon) about his beautifully brushed hair. "Kinjack'll soon have the horse-clippers on your track, young man!" he said. Dick smiled and said nothing.

We arranged to go for a ride, and he went off to inspect the company's dinners. When he had gone Barton remarked that he wished he could get Dick to take more care of himself up in the Line. "I sent him out on a short patrol two nights ago, but he stayed out there nearly an hour and a half and went right up to the Boche wire." Old Joe agreed that he was a rare good lad: no cold feet about him; the country couldn't afford to lose many more like that. . . .

And he got on to his favourite subject—"The Classes and the Masses". For Joe had been brought up in the darkest part of Manchester, and he prided himself on being an old-fashioned socialist. But his Socialism was complicated by his fair-minded cognizance of the good qualities of the best type of the officer class, with whom he had been in close contact ever since he enlisted. He clenched a knotted fist. "This war", he exclaimed in his husky voice, "is being carried on by the highest and the lowest in the land—the blue-blooded upper ten and the poor unfortunate people that some silly bastard called 'the Submerged Tenth'. All the others are making what they can out of it and shirking the dirty work. Selfish hogs! And the politicians are no better."

"That's right, Joe. That's the stuff to give 'em!" said Barton.

And they both drank damnation to the (enigmatic) part of the population which was leaving all the dirty work to the infantry. Their generalizations, perhaps, were not altogether fair. There was quite a lot of blue blood at G.H.Q. and Army Headquarters. And Mansfield and Durley, to name only two of our own officers, were undoubtedly members of "the middle class", whatever that may be.

*　　　*　　　*

My ride with Dick was a great success. Over the rolling uplands and through an occasional strip of woodland, with the sun shining and big clouds moving prosperously on a boisterous north-west wind, we rode to a village six or seven miles away, and had tea at an unbelievable shop where the cakes were as good as anything in Amiens. I wouldn't like to say how many we ate, but the evening star shone benevolently down on us from among a drift of rosy clouds while we were cantering home to Morlancourt. But about a fortnight later, when Dick was up in the trenches, I received a letter in reply to the one I had sent Dixon. Someone informed me that Sergeant Dixon had died of pneumonia. Major Kinjack arrived to take command a day or two afterwards.

V

Lieutenant-Colonel Kinjack (to give him his new rank) exceeded all our expectations. He was the personification of military efficiency. Personal charm was not his strong point, and he made no pretension to it. He was aggressive and blatant, but he knew his job, and for that we respected him and were grateful. His predecessor had departed in his Brigadier's cap without saying good-bye to anyone. For that we were less grateful; but as Dottrell said: "He'd had Brigadier on the brain ever since he came back off leave, and now he'd never be satisfied till he'd got a Division and another decoration to go with it." Dottrell had just got his D.S.O., so he had no cause to feel jealous, even if he had been capable of that feeling, which he wasn't. His only complaint was that they didn't make his "acting rank" permanent. He aired that grievance several evenings a week, especially when he had got back late with the ration party, and his references to the "permanent" Quartermaster (at Army Headquarters) were far from flattering.

Colonel Kinjack stopped one night in Morlancourt, and on the following afternoon I guided him up to the Line, going by the short cut across the open country and the half-dug and feebly wired reserve trench which, we hoped, would never be utilized. The new C.O. had inspected the Transport in the morning without active disapproval, but he was less pleased when our appearance on the ridge (half a mile behind the front line) attracted a few shells, none of which exploded near us. This was considered quite a good joke in the battalion, and I was often reminded afterwards of how I'd got Kinjack welcomed with whizz-bangs.

"The Boches saw Kinjack coming all right. The Transport Officer made sure of that!" Barton would say, with a chuckle.

For in spite of my easy job, it was supposed that I could be a bit of a daredevil if I liked. Not that I wanted to be, that afternoon; Kinjack frightened the life out of me, and was so sceptical of my ability to find the way that I began to feel none too sure about it myself. . . . It is, however, just conceivable that at that time I didn't care what happened to the new Colonel or anybody else. . . .

That same day, at about midnight, I was awakened by Dottrell, who told me that I was to go on leave next morning. I drove to the station in the Maltese cart; the train started at 9.30, crawled to Havre, and by ten o'clock next

day I was in London. I had been in France less than four
months. As regards war experience I felt a bit of an impostor. I had noticed that officers back from their ten days'
leave were usually somewhat silent about it. Then, after a
few weeks, they began to look forward to their next leave
again, and to talk about this future fact. But there wasn't
much to be said about mine, for it was bitterly cold and a
heavy fall of snow knocked my hopes of hunting on the
head. So I remained quietly with Aunt Evelyn at Butley,
telling myself that it was a great luxury to have a hot bath
every day, and waiting for a thaw. If it thawed I should
have two or three days with the Ringwell on Colonel Hesmon's horses. And I should stay at Hoadley Rectory. But
no thaw came, and I returned to France without having
been to the Rectory, which had been a painful idea in any
case. The Rector evidently felt the same, for he wrote me a
sad letter in which he said "as I think of all the suffering
and death, the anxieties and bereavements of this terrible
struggle, I feel that in our ignorance we can only rest on
the words, 'What I do thou knowest not now but thou
shalt know hereafter'. Obedience and self-sacrifice for right
and truth in spite of suffering and death is Christianity.
. . ." I received this letter on my last day at Butley. Sitting
alone in the schoolroom late at night, I felt touched by the
goodness and patience of my old friend, but I was unable
to accept his words in the right spirit. He spoke too soon.
I was too young to understand. And England wasn't what
it used to be. I had been over to say good-bye to Captain
Huxtable that afternoon; but the War was making an old
man of him, though he did his best to be bright. And kind
Aunt Evelyn talked bitterly about the Germans and called
them "hell-hounds". I found myself defending them,
although I couldn't claim acquaintance with a single one
of them (except Willie Regel, and I shouldn't have known
him by sight if I'd met him).

Looking round the room at the enlarged photographs of
my hunters, I began to realize that my past was wearing a
bit thin. The War seemed to have made up its mind to
obliterate all those early adventures of mine. Point-to-

point cups shone, but without conviction. And Dixon was
dead. . . .

Perhaps, after all, it was better to be back with the battalion. The only way to forget about the War was to be on
the other side of the Channel. But the fire burnt brightly
and the kettle was hissing on the hob. It was nice to be
wearing my old civilian clothes, and to make myself a cup
of tea. Old Joe will be on his way home with the transport
now, I thought, contrasting my comfort with him joggling
along the Bray road in this awful weather. His bronchitis
had been bad lately, too. Dick was a thought which I repressed. He would be getting his leave soon, anyhow. . . .
The Rector said we were fighting for right and truth; but
it was no use trying to think it all out now. There were
those things to take back for the others—a bottle of old
brandy for Dottrell and some smoked salmon for "C"
company mess—I mustn't make any mistake about that
when I get to town in the morning, I thought. . . .

And the next evening I was on the boat at Southampton; the weather had turned mild again; it was a quiet
evening; I watched the red and green lights across the harbour, and listened to the creaking cries of the gulls, like the
sound of windlasses and pulleys, as they swooped in circles
or settled on the smooth dusk of the water. From the town
came the note of a bugle, a remote call, like the last thought
of home. And then we were churning across the dark sea,
to find France still under snow.

*   *   *

There was a continuous rumble and grumble of bombardment while we were going up with the rations on the
day after I got back from leave. As we came over the hill
beyond Bray the darkness toward Albert was lit with the
glare of explosions that blinked and bumped. Dottrell remarked that there seemed to be a bit of a mix-up, which
was his way of saying that he didn't altogether like the
look of things that evening.

When we arrived at the ration dump the quartermaster-
sergeant told us that the battalion had been standing to for

the past two hours. It was possible that the Boches might be coming across. "C" company was in the front line. The noise was subsiding, so I went up there, leaving Joe to pay his nightly call at battalion headquarters.

Stumbling and splashing up a communication trench known as Canterbury Avenue, with the parcel of smoked salmon stuffed into my haversack, I felt that smoked salmon wasn't much of an antidote for people who had been putting up with all that shell-fire. Still, it was something. . . . Round the next corner I had to flatten myself against the wall of that wet ditch, for someone was being carried down on a stretcher. An extra stretcher-bearer walking behind told me it was Corporal Price of "C" company. "A rifle-grenade got him . . . looks as if he's a goner. . . ." His face was only a blur of white in the gloom; then, with the drumming of their boots on the trench-boards, Corporal Price left the War behind him. I remembered him vaguely as a quiet little man in Durley's platoon. No use offering *him* smoked salmon, I thought, as I came to the top of Canterbury Avenue, and, as usual, lost my way in the maze of saps and small trenches behind the front line. Watling Street was the one I wanted. Finding one's way about the trenches in the dark was no easy job when one didn't live up there. I passed the dug-outs of the support company at Maple Redoubt. Candles and braziers glinted through the curtain-flaps and voices muttered gruffly from the little underground cabins (which would have been safer if they had been deeper down in the earth). Now and again there was the splitting crack of a rifle-shot from the other side, or a five-nine shell droned serenely across the upper air to burst with a hollow bang; voluminous reverberations rolled along the valley. The shallow blanching flare of a rocket gave me a glimpse of the mounds of bleached sand-bags on the Redoubt. Its brief whiteness died downward, leaving a dark world; chilly gusts met me at corners, piping drearily through crannies of the parapet; very different was the voice of the wind that sang in the cedar tree in the garden at home. . . .

Pushing past the gas-blanket, I blundered down the

stairs to the company headquarters' dug-out. There were twenty steps to that earthy smelling den, with its thick wooden props down the middle and its precarious yellow candlelight casting wobbling shadows. Barton was sitting on a box at the rough table, with a tin mug and a half-empty whisky bottle. His shoulders were hunched and the collar of his trench-coat was turned up to his ears. Dick was in deep shadow, lying on a bunk (made of wire-netting with empty sandbags on it). It was a morose cramped little scene, loathsome to live in as it is hateful to remember. The air was dank and musty; lumps of chalk fell from the "ceiling" at intervals. There was a bad smell of burnt grease, and the frizzle of something frying in the adjoining kennel that was called the kitchen was the only evidence of ordinary civilization—that and Barton's shining pince-nez, and the maps and notebooks which were on the table. . . .

Smoked salmon from Piccadilly Circus was something after all. It cheered Barton immensely. He unpacked it; he sniffed it; and no doubt it brought the lights of London into his mind.

"Gosh, if only this war would stop!" he exclaimed. "I'd be off to Scott's oyster-bar like a streak of light and you'd never get me away from it again!"

He held the smoked salmon under Dick's nose and told him what a lucky young devil he was to be going on leave in two or three days' time. Dick wasn't as bright as usual; he'd got a rotten headache, he said. Barton told him he'd better let Ormand go out with the wiring-party instead of him. But he said no, he'd be all right by then, and Ormand had been out last night. Barton told me they'd had a lively time with the C.O. lately: "He gave orders for the whole of the front line to be re-wired; we've been at it every night, but he came up this morning with his big periscope, strafing like hell about the gaps along by the mine-craters. He says the wire isn't strong enough to stop a wheelbarrow— why a wheelbarrow God knows!" He laughed, rather hysterically; his nerves were on edge, and no wonder. . . . For, as he said, what with the muck everything was in since the snow melted, and being chivvied by Kinjack, and then being "crumped" all the afternoon, life hadn't been worth living lately. The odd thing was that good old Barton seemed equally concerned because the snowy weather had prevented me from having any hunting while on leave. And Dick agreed that it had been very rough on me.

Mansfield and Ormand came in at that moment; these two were very good friends, and they always seemed to be cheering one another up. They had left Durley on duty in the front trench. They wanted to hear all about the "shows" I had been to in London, but I couldn't tell them anything (though I wished I could) for I hadn't been to a theatre, and it was no use talking about the Symphony Concert at Queen's Hall, which now made me feel rather a prig.

Dick was still lying in his dark corner when I said good-night and groped my way up the steps, leaving them to make the most of the smoked salmon. Going down Canterbury Avenue it was so pitch black that I couldn't see my own hand; once or twice a flare went up in the spectral region on the shoulder of the hill behind me; lit by that unearthly glare the darkness became desolation.

*   *   *

Coming up from the transport lines at twelve o'clock next morning I found Joe Dottrell standing outside the Quartermaster's stores. His face warned me to expect bad news. No news could have been worse. Dick had been killed. He had been hit in the throat by a rifle bullet while out with the wiring-party, and had died at the dressing-station a few hours afterwards. The battalion doctor had been a throat specialist before the War, but this had not been enough.

The sky was angry with a red smoky sunset when we rode up with the rations. Later on, when it was dark, we stood on the bare slope just above the ration dump while the Brigade chaplain went through his words; a flag covered all that we were there for; only the white stripes on the flag made any impression on the dimness of the night. Once the chaplain's words were obliterated by a prolonged burst of machine-gun fire; when he had finished, a trench-mortar "canister" fell a few hundred yards away, spouting the earth up with a crash. . . . A sack was lowered into a hole in the ground. The sack was Dick. I knew Death then.

*　　　*　　　*

A few days later, when the battalion was back at Morlancourt, and Kinjack was having a look round the Transport lines, he remarked that he wasn't sure that I wasn't rather wasted as Transport Officer. "I'd much rather be with 'C' Company, sir." Some sort of anger surged up inside me as I said it. . . . He agreed. No doubt he had intended me to return to my platoon.

VI

Easter was late in April that year; my first three tours of trenches occupied me during the last thirty days of Lent. This essential season in the Church calendar was not, as far as I remember, remarked upon by anyone in my company, although the name of Christ was often on our lips, and Mansfield (when a canister made a mess of the trench not many yards away from him) was even heard to refer to our Saviour as "murry old Jesus!" These innocuous blasphemings of the holy name were a peculiar feature of the War, in which the principles of Christianity were either obliterated or falsified for the convenience of all who were engaged in it. Up in the trenches every man bore his own burden; the Sabbath was not made for man; and if a man laid down his life for his friends it was no part of his military duties. To kill an enemy was an effective action; to bring in one of our own wounded was praiseworthy, but unrelated to our war-aims. The Brigade chaplain did not exhort us to love our enemies. He was content to lead off with the hymn "How sweet the name of Jesus sounds"!

I mention this war-time dilemma of the Churches because my own mind was in rather a muddle at that time. I went up to the trenches with the intention of trying to kill someone. It was my idea of getting a bit of my own back. I did not say anything about it to anyone; but it was this feeling which took me out patrolling the mine-craters whenever an opportunity offered itself. It was a phase in my war experience—no more irrational than the rest of the proceedings, I suppose; it was an outburst of blind bravado which now seems paltry when I compare it with the behaviour of an officer like Julian Durley, who did everything that was asked of him as a matter of course.

Lent, as I said before, was not observed by us. But Barton got somewhere near observing it one evening. We had just returned to our dug-out after the twilight ritual of "standing-to". The rations had come up, and with them the mail. After reading a letter from his wife he looked at me and said: "O Kangar, how I wish I were a cathedral organist!" (I was known as "the Kangaroo" in "C" company.) His remark, which had no connection with any religious feeling, led us on to pleasant reminiscences of cathedral closes. Nothing would be nicer, we thought, than to be sauntering back, after Evensong, to one of those snug old houses, with a book of anthems under our arms—preferably on a mild evening toward the end of October. (In his civilian days Barton had attended race meetings regularly; his musical experience had been confined to musical comedy.)

The mail that evening had brought me a parcel from Aunt Evelyn, which contained two pots of specially good jam. Ration jam was usually in tins, and of tins it tasted. Barton gazed affectionately at the coloured label, which represented a cherry-growing landscape. The label was a talisman which carried his mind safely to the home counties of England. He spoke of railway travelling. "Do you remember the five-thirty from Paddington? What a dear old train it was!" Helping himself to a spoonful of cherry jam he mentally passed through Maidenhead in a Pullman carriage. . . . The mail had also brought me the balance sheet of the Ringwell Hunt. These Hunt accounts made me feel homesick. And it appeared that the late Mr. S. Colwood had subscribed ten pounds. He must have sent it early in September, just before he was killed. No doubt he wrote the cheque in a day dream about hunting. . . .

In the meantime we were down in that frowsty smelling dug-out, listening to the cautious nibbling of rats behind the wooden walls; and above ground there was the muffled boom of something bursting. And two more officers had been killed. Not in our company though. The Germans had put up another mine that afternoon without doing us any damage. Their trenches were only a hundred and fifty yards from ours; in some places less than fifty. It was a sector of the line which specialized in mines; more than half of our 750-yard frontage was pitted with mine-craters, some of them fifty feet deep. . . .

"They were digging in front of Bois Français Trench again last night," I remarked.

Barton had just received a message from battalion head-quarters saying that the company front was to be tho-roughly patrolled.

"I'll take O'Brien out with me to-night," I added.

Barton's ruddy face had resumed the worried expression which it wore when messages came from Kinjack or the Adjutant.

"All right, Kangar; but do be careful. It puts the fear of God into me when you're out there and I'm waiting for you to come in."

It put the fear of God into me too, but it was the only escape into freedom which I could contrive, up in those trenches opposite Fricourt and Mametz. And I was angry with the War.

*   *   *

Memory eliminates the realities of bodily discomfort which made the texture of trench-life what it was. Mental activity was clogged and hindered by gross physical actu-alities. It was these details of discomfort which constituted the humanity of an infantryman's existence. Being in the trenches meant among other things having a "trench-mouth".

I can see myself sitting in the sun in a nook among the

sandbags and chalky débris behind the support line. There is a strong smell of chloride of lime. I am scraping the caked mud off my wire-torn puttees with a rusty entrenching tool. Last night I was out patrolling with Private O'Brien, who used to be a dock labourer at Cardiff. We threw a few Mills' bombs at a German working-party who were putting up some wire and had no wish to do us any harm. Probably I am feeling pleased with myself about this. Now and again a leisurely five-nine shell passes overhead in the blue air where the larks are singing. The sound of the shell is like water trickling into a can. The curve of its trajectory sounds peaceful until the culminating crash. A little weasel runs past my outstretched feet, glancing at me with tiny bright eyes, apparently unafraid. One of our shrapnel shells, whizzing over to the enemy lines, bursts with a hollow crash. Against the clear morning sky a cloud of dark smoke expands and drifts away. Slowly its dingy wrestling vapours take the form of a hooded giant with clumsy expostulating arms. Then, with a gradual gesture of acquiescence, it lolls sideways, falling over into the attitude of a swimmer on his side. And so it dissolves into nothingness. Perhaps the shell has killed someone. Whether it has or whether it hasn't, I continue to scrape my puttees, and the weasel goes about his business. The sun strikes the glinting wings of an aeroplane, forging away westward. Somewhere on the slope behind me a partridge makes its unmilitary noise—down there where Dick was buried a few weeks ago. Dick's father was a very good man with a gun, so Dick used to say. . . .

*   *   *

Down in the reserve line I was sitting in the gloom of the steel hut (like being inside a boiler) reading a novel by candlelight while Barton and Mansfield snored on their beds and my servant Flook sang "Dixieland" in some adjoining cubby-hole. Being in reserve was a sluggish business; in the front line we were much less morose. Outside there was a remote rumble going on, like heavy furniture being moved about in a room overhead. But the little

wooden weather-vane on the roof kept on spinning and
rattling as though nothing were amiss with the world. Then
the patter of rain began, and I shivered and turned chilly
and thought of home and safety. It was time to be going up
with that working-party. We should be out from eight till
midnight, piling sandbags on the parapet of the front-line
trench, which had suffered from the wet weather.

It was a pitch dark night. As we were going up across the
open to the support line, the bombardment, about two
miles away in the low country on our left, reached a climax.
The sky winked and flickered like a thunderstorm gone
crazy. It was a battle seen in miniature against a screen of
blackness. Rocket-lights, red and white, curved upward; in
the rapid glare of bursting explosives the floating smoke
showed rufous and tormented; it was like the last hour of
Gomorrah; one couldn't imagine anything left alive there.
But it was only a small local attack—probably a raid by
fifty men, which would be reported in two lines of the
G.H.Q. communiqué. It would soon be our turn to do a
raid. The Brigadier had made it quite clear that he
"wanted a prisoner". One would be enough. He wanted
to make certain what troops were in front of us.

*   *   *

For identification purposes a dead body would be better
than nothing, Kinjack said. O'Brien and I went out one
moonlight night into a part of no-man's-land where there
were no mine-craters. We had been instructed to bring in a
dead body which (so our Observation Officer said) was
lying out there. The Germans had been across the night
before, cutting our wire, and the Lewis-gun officer was certain that he had inflicted severe casualties on them. Anyhow, a pair of boots could be seen sticking up out of a
shell-hole. But when we arrived at the boots we found
them attached to the body of a French soldier who had
been there several months. I didn't like this much; but
O'Brien whispered to me: "T'Colonel shall have t'boot,"
and the boot, with half a leg on it, was sent down to Kinjack, as a proof of our efficiency.

Prisoners were seldom seen at that time. I never saw one myself until the Somme battle began in the summer. The landscape was in front of us; similar in character to the one behind us, but mysterious with its unknown quality of being "behind the Boche line". We could see the skeleton villages of Fricourt and Mametz, and the ruinous cemetery (which the men called "the rest camp"). But the enemy was invisible. On still nights our sleepy sentries heard him cough from the far side of the craters. He patrolled, and we patrolled. Often, when I was crawling about on my belly, I imagined a clod of earth to be a hostile head and shoulders watching me from a shell-hole. But patrols had a sensible habit of avoiding personal contact with one another. Men in the Tunnelling Company who emerged, blinking and dusty white, from the mine-shafts, had heard the enemy digging deep underground. They may even have heard the muffled mutter of German voices. But, apart from the projectiles he sent us, the enemy was, as far as we were concerned, an unknown quantity. The Staff were the people who knew all about him. . . .

*　　　*　　　*

Spring arrived late that year. Or was it that spring kept away from the front line as long as possible? Up there it seemed as though the winter would last for ever. On wet days the trees a mile away were like ash-grey smoke rising from the naked ridges, and it felt very much as if we were at the end of the world. And so we were; for that enemy world (which by daylight we saw through loopholes or from a hidden observation post) had no relation to the landscape of life. It had meant the end of the world for the man whose helmet was still lying about the trench with a jagged hole through it. Steel hats (which our Division had begun to wear in February) couldn't keep out a rifle bullet. . . .

By five o'clock on a frosty white morning it would be daylight. Trees and broken roofs emerged here and there from the folds of mist that drifted in a dense blur; above them were the white shoals and chasms of the sky flushed with the faint pink of dawn. Standing-to at dawn was a desolate affair. The men stamped their feet and rats scurried along the crannied parapets. But we'd had our tot of rum, and we were to be relieved that afternoon. . . . Dandelions had begun to flower along the edges of the communication trenches. This was a sign of spring, I thought, as we filed down Canterbury Avenue, with the men making jokes about the estaminet in Morlancourt. Estaminet! What a memory-evoking word! . . . It was little enough that they had to go back to.

As for me, I had more or less made up my mind to die; the idea made things easier. In the circumstances there didn't seem to be anything else to be done. I only mention the fact because it seems, now, so strange that I should have felt like that when I had so much of my life to lose. Strange, too, was the thought of summer. It meant less mud, perhaps, but more dust; and the "big push" was always waiting for us.

Safe in Morlancourt, I slept like a log. Sleep was a wonderful thing when one came back from the Line; but to wake was to remember. Talking to Joe Dottrell did me good. A new transport officer had arrived—a Remount man from England. It was said that he had been combed out of a cushy job. I was glad I'd given up the transport. Glad, too, to be able to ride out on the black mare.

After the ugly weather in the trenches a fine afternoon in the wood above Méaulte was something to be thankful for. The undergrowth had been cut down, and there were bluebells and cowslips and anemones, and here and there a wild-cherry tree in blossom. Teams of horses, harrowing the uplands, moved like a procession, their crests blown by the wind. But the rural spirit of the neighbourhood had been chased away by supply sheds and R.E. stores and the sound of artillery on the horizon. Albert, (where Jules Verne used to live) with its two or three chimney-stacks and the damaged tower of the basilica, showed above a line of tall trees along the riverside; a peaceful medley of roofs as I watched it, but in reality a ruined and deserted town. And in the foreground Bécourt church tower peeped above a shoulder of hill like a broken tooth.

Anyhow the black mare had got the better of the new transport officer. That was something, I thought, as I jogged home again.

* * *

My faithful servant Flook always contrived to keep me supplied with oranges when we were up in the trenches. An orange, and taking my sodden boots off whenever I got the chance, (though it was against the rules) were my two favourite recreations in the front line. Flook called me (with an orange) at two in the morning; I had to relieve Ormand, who had been on duty since midnight. The orange woke me up. But it was a wet night, and I'd been out with the wiring-party from ten till twelve. Lugging coils of concertina wire along a narrow trench swilling with mud and water wasn't much fun. Stumbling with it over shell-holes and trip-wires was worse. However, we had got quite a lot out. . . .

Once I'd shaken off my stupor it wasn't so bad to be out in the night air. The rain had stopped and Ormand had nothing to report. For the next two hours I should loiter up and down with my knobkerrie in my hand; now and again I had a whack at a rat running along the parados. From one "bay" to another I went, stopping for a word in an undertone with the sentries; patient in their waterproof sheets they stood on the firestep, peering above the parapet until bleak daylight began to show itself. The trench was falling in badly in places after the rain. . . .

Then there was the bombing-post up a sap which went thirty or forty yards out into no-man's-land. Everything had been very quiet, the bombers muttered. . . .

Back in the main trench, I stood on the firestep to watch the sky whitening. Sad and stricken the country emerged. I could see the ruined village below the hill and the leafless trees that waited like sentries up by Contalmaison. Down in the craters the dead water took a dull gleam from the sky. I stared at the tangles of wire and the leaning posts, and there seemed no sort of comfort left in life. My steel hat was heavy on my head while I thought how I'd been on leave last month. I remembered how I'd leant my elbows on Aunt Evelyn's front gate. (It was my last evening.) That twilight, with its thawing snow, made a comfortable picture now. John Homeward had come past with his van, plodding beside his weary horse. He had managed to make his journey, in spite of the state of the roads. . . . He had pulled up for a few minutes, and we'd talked about Dixon, who had been such an old friend of his. "Ay; Tom was a good chap; I've never known a better. . . ." He had said good-bye and good-night and set his horse going again. As he turned the corner the past had seemed to go with him. . . .

And here I was, with my knobkerrie in my hand, staring across at the enemy I'd never seen. Somewhere out of sight beyond the splintered tree-tops of Hidden Wood a bird had begun to sing. Without knowing why, I remembered that it was Easter Sunday. Standing in that dismal ditch, I could find no consolation in the thought that Christ was risen. I sploshed back to the dug-out to call the others up for "stand-to".

MEMOIRS OF
AN INFANTRY OFFICER

PART ONE: AT THE ARMY SCHOOL

I

I have said that Spring arrived late in 1916, and that up in the trenches opposite Mametz it seemed as though Winter would last for ever. I also stated that *as for me, I had more or less made up my mind to die* because *in the circumstances there didn't seem anything else to be done*. Well, we came back to Morlancourt after Easter, and on the same evening a message from the Orderly Room instructed me to proceed to the Fourth Army School next morning for a month's refresher-course. Perhaps Colonel Kinjack had heard that I'd been looking for trouble. Anyhow, my personal grievance against the Germans was interrupted for at least four weeks, and a motor-bus carried me away from all possibility of dying a murky death in the mine-craters.

Barton saw me off at the crossroads in the middle of the village. It was a fine day and he had recovered his good spirits. "Lucky Kangaroo—to be hopping away for a holiday!" he exclaimed, as I climbed into the elderly bus. My servant Flook hoisted up my bulging valise, wiped his red face with his sleeve, and followed me to the roof. "Mind and keep Mr. Sherston well polished up and punctual on parade, Flook!" said Barton. Flook grinned; and away we went. Looking back, I saw Barton's good-natured face, with the early sun shining on his glasses.

There were several of us on board (each Battalion in our Brigade was sending two officers) and we must have stopped at the next village to pick up a few more. But memory tries to misinform me that Flook and I were alone on that omnibus, with a fresh breeze in our faces and our minds "making a separate peace" with the late April landscape. With sober satisfaction I watched a train moving out of a station with rumble and clank of wheels while we waited at the crossing gates. Children in a village street surprised me: I saw a little one fall, to be gathered, dusted, cuffed and cherished by its mother. Up in the line one somehow lost touch with such humanities.

The War was abundantly visible in supply-convoys, artillery horse-lines, in the dirty white tents of a Red Cross camp, or in troops going placidly to their billets. But everyone seemed to be off duty; spring had arrived and the fruit trees were in blossom; breezes ruffled the reedy pools and creeks along the Somme, and here and there a peaceful fisherman forgot that he was a soldier on active service. I had been in close contact with trench warfare, and here was a demonstration of its contrast with cosy civilian comfort. One has to find things out as one goes along, I thought; and I was wholeheartedly grateful for the green grass and a miller's wagon with four horses, and the spire of Amiens Cathedral rising above the congregated roofs of an undamaged city.

*   *   *

The Fourth Army School was at Flixécourt, a clean little town exactly halfway between Amiens and Abbeville. Between Flixécourt and the War (which for my locally experienced mind meant the Fricourt trenches) there were more than thirty English miles. Mentally, the distance became immeasurable during my first days at the School. Parades and lectures were all in the day's work, but they failed to convince me of their affinity with our long days and nights in the Front Line. For instance, although I was closely acquainted with the mine-craters in the Fricourt sector, I would have welcomed a few practical hints on how to patrol those God-forsaken cavities. But the Army School instructors were all in favour of Open Warfare, which was sure to come soon, they said. They had learnt all about it in peace-time; it was essential that we should be taught to "think in terms of mobility". So we solved tactical schemes in which the enemy was reported to have occupied some village several miles away, and with pencil and paper made arrangements for unflurried defence or blank-cartridged skirmishing in a land of field-day make-believe.

Sometimes a renowned big-game hunter gave us demonstrations of the art of sniping. He was genial and enthusiastic; but I was no good at rifle-shooting, and as far as I was concerned he would have been more profitably employed in reducing the numerical strength of the enemy. He was an expert on loopholes and telescopic-sights; but telescopic-sights were a luxury seldom enjoyed by an infantry battalion in the trenches.

The Commandant of the School was a tremendous worker and everyone liked him. His motto was "always do your utmost", but I dare say that if he had been asked his private opinion he would have admitted that the School was in reality only a holiday for officers and N.C.O.s who needed a rest. It certainly seemed so to me when I awoke on the first morning and became conscious of my clean little room with its tiled floor and shuttered windows. I knew that the morning was fine; voices passed outside; sparrows chirped and starlings whistled; the bell in the church tower tolled and a clock struck the quarters. Flook entered with my Sam Browne belt and a jug of hot water. He remarked that we'd come to the right place, for once, and regretted that we weren't there for the duration. Wiping my face after a satisfactory shave, I stared out of the window; on the other side of the street a blossoming apple-tree leant over an old garden wall, and I could see the friendly red roof of a dovecot. It was a luxury to be alone, with plenty of space for my portable property. There was a small table on which I could arrange my few books. Hardy's *Far from the Madding Crowd* was one of them. Also Lamb's *Essays* and *Mr. Sponge's Sporting Tour*. Books about England were all that I wanted. I decided to do plenty of solid reading at the Army School.

Near by was the Mess Room where fourteen of us had our meals. A jolly-faced Captain from the Ulster Division had undertaken the office of Mess President and everyone was talkative and friendly. With half an hour to spare after breakfast, I strolled up the hill and smoked my pipe under a quick-set hedge. Loosening my belt, I looked at a chestnut tree in full leaf and listened to the perfect performance of a nightingale. Such things seemed miraculous after the desolation of the trenches. Never before had I been so intensely aware of what it meant to be young and healthy in fine weather at the outset of summer. The untroubled notes of the nightingale made the Army School seem like some fortunate colony which was, for the sake of appearances, pretending to assist the struggle from afar. It feels as if it's a place where I might get a chance to call my soul my own, I thought, as I went down the hill to my first parade. If only they don't chivvy us about too much, I added. . . . It was not unlike the first day of a public school term, and my form-master (we were divided into classes of twenty-eight) was a youngish Major in the Oxford and Bucks Light Infantry. He was an even-tempered man, pleasant to obey, and specially likeable through a certain shyness of manner. I cannot remember that any of us caused him any annoyance, though he more than once asked me to try and be less absent-minded. Later in the year he was commanding a battalion, and I don't doubt that he did it excellently.

*   *   *

Every afternoon at half-past five the School assembled to listen to a lecture. Eyeing an audience of about 300 officers and N.C.O.s, I improved my knowledge of regimental badges, which seemed somehow to affect the personality of the wearer. A lion, a lamb, a dragon or an antelope, a crown, a harp, a tiger or a sphinx, these devices differentiated men in more ways than one. But the regimental names were probably the potent factor, and my meditations while waiting for the lecturer would lead me along pleasant associative lanes connected with the English counties—the difference between Durham and Devon for instance. There was food for thought also in the fact of sitting between a Connaught Ranger and a Seaforth Highlander, though both were likely to have been born in Middlesex. Queer, too, was the whole scene in that schoolroom, containing as it did a splendid sample of the Fourth Army which began the Somme Battle a couple of months afterwards. It was one of those peaceful war pictures which have vanished for ever and are rarely recovered even in imaginative retrospect.

My woolgatherings were cut short when the lecturer cleared his throat; the human significance of the audience was obliterated then, and its outlook on life became restricted to destruction and defence. A gas expert from G.H.Q. would inform us that "gas was still in its infancy". (Most of us were either dead or disabled before gas had had time to grow up.) An urbane Artillery General assured us that high explosive would be our best friend in future battles, and his ingratiating voice made us unmindful, for the moment, that explosives often arrived from the wrong direction. But the star turn in the schoolroom was a massive sandy-haired Highland Major whose subject was "The Spirit of the Bayonet". Though at that time undecorated, he was afterwards awarded the D.S.O. for lecturing. He took as his text a few leading points from the *Manual of Bayonet Training*.

To attack with the bayonet effectively requires Good Direction, Strength and Quickness, during a state of wild excitement and probably physical exhaustion. The bayonet is essentially an offensive weapon. In a bayonet assault all ranks go forward to kill or be killed, and only those who have developed skill and strength by constant training will be able to kill. The spirit of the bayonet must be inculcated into all ranks, so that they go forward with that aggressive determination and confidence of superiority born of continual practice, without which a bayonet assault will not be effective.

He spoke with homicidal eloquence, keeping the game alive with genial and well-judged jokes. He had a Sergeant to assist him. The Sergeant, a tall sinewy machine, had been trained to such a pitch of frightfulness that at a moment's warning he could divest himself of all semblance of humanity. With rifle and bayonet he illustrated the Major's ferocious aphorisms, including facial expression. When told to "put on the killing face", he did so, combining it with an ultra-vindictive attitude. "To instil fear into the opponent" was one of the Major's main maxims. Man, it seemed, had been created to jab the life out of Germans. To hear the Major talk, one might have thought that he did it himself every day before breakfast. His final words were: "Remember that every Boche you fellows kill is a point scored to our side; every Boche you kill brings victory one minute nearer and shortens the war by one minute. Kill them! Kill them! There's only one good Boche, and that's a dead one!"

Afterwards I went up the hill to my favourite sanctuary, a wood of hazels and beeches. The evening air smelt of wet mould and wet leaves; the trees were misty-green; the church bell was tolling in the town, and smoke rose from the roofs. Peace was there in the twilight of that prophetic foreign spring. But the lecturer's voice still battered on my brain. "The bullet and the bayonet are brother and sister." "If you don't kill him, he'll kill you." "Stick him between the eyes, in the throat, in the chest." "Don't waste good steel. Six inches are enough. What's the use of a foot of steel sticking out at the back of a man's neck? Three inches will do for him; when he coughs, go and look for another."

II

Whatever my private feelings may have been after the Major's lecture, the next morning saw me practising bayonet-fighting. It was all in the day's work; short points, long points, parries, jabs, plus the always-to-be-remembered importance of "a quick withdrawal". Capering over the obstacles of the assault course and prodding sacks of straw was healthy exercise; the admirable sergeant-instructor was polite and unformidable, and as I didn't want him to think me a dud officer, I did my best to become proficient. Obviously it would have been both futile and inexpedient to moralize about bayonet-fighting at an Army School.

There is a sense of recovered happiness in the glimpse I catch of myself coming out of my cottage door with a rifle slung on my shoulder. There was nothing wrong with life on those fine mornings when the air smelt so fresh and my body was young and vigorous, and I hurried down the white road, along the empty street, and up the hill to our training ground. I was like a boy going to early school, except that no bell was ringing, and instead of Thucydides or Virgil, I carried a gun. Forgetting, for the moment, that I was at the Front to be shot at, I could almost congratulate myself on having a holiday in France without paying for it.

I also remember how I went one afternoon to have a hot bath in the Jute Mill. The water was poured into a dyeing vat. Remembering that I had a bath may not be of much interest to anyone, but it was a good bath, and it is my own story that I am trying to tell, and as such it must be received; those who expect a universalization of the Great War must look for it elsewhere. Here they will only find an attempt to show its effect on a somewhat solitary-minded young man.

At that time I was comfortably aware that the British Expeditionary Force in France was a prosperous concern. I have already remarked that the officers and N.C.O.s at the School epitomized a resolute mass of undamaged material; equally impressive was the equine abundance which I observed one afternoon when we were on our way to a "demonstration" at the Army Bombing School. Hundreds of light and heavy draft horses were drawn up along a road for an inspection by the Commander-in-Chief (a bodily presence which the infantry mind could not easily imagine). The horses, attached to their appropriate vehicles and shining in their summer coats, looked a picture of sleekness and strength. They were of all sorts and sizes but their power and compactness was uniform. The horsehood of England was there with every buckle of its harness brightened. There weren't many mules among them, for mules were mostly with the Artillery, and this was a slap-up Army Service Corps parade, obviously the climax of several weeks' preparation. I wished that I could have spent the afternoon inspecting them; but I was only a second-lieutenant, and the bus carried me on to study explosions and smoke-clouds, and to hear a lecture about the tactical employment of the Mills' Bomb.

*   *   *

News of the Battalion came from the Quartermaster, to whom I had sent an account of my "cushy" existence. Dottrell wrote that things had been quiet up in the Line, but advised me to make the most of my rest-cure, adding that he'd always noticed that the further you got from the front line the further you got from the War. In accordance with my instructions he was making good progress with the box of kippers (which Aunt Evelyn sent me twice a month); ditto the Devonshire cream, though some of it hadn't stood the journey well. His letter put me in the right frame of mind for returning to tours of trenches, though I should be sorry to say good-bye to young Allgood, with whom I was spending most of my spare time.

Allgood was quiet, thoughtful, and fond of watching birds. We had been to the same public school, though there were nearly ten years between us. He told me that he hoped to be a historian, and I listened respectfully while he talked about the Romans in Early Britain, which was his favourite subject. It was easy to imagine him as an undergraduate at Cambridge; travelling in Germany during the Long Vacation and taking a good Degree. But his Degree had been postponed indefinitely. He said he'd always wanted to go to Germany, and there seemed nothing incongruous in the remark; for the moment I forgot that every German we killed was a point scored to our side. Allgood never grumbled about the war, for he was a gentle soul, willing to take his share in it, though obviously unsuited to homicide. But there was an expression of veiled melancholy on his face, as if he were inwardly warned that he would never see his home in Wiltshire again. A couple of months afterwards I saw his name in one of the long lists of killed, and it seemed to me that I had expected it.

*   *   *

Our last day at the School was hot and cloudless. In the morning English and French Generals rolled up in their cars; there must have been about a hundred of them; it was not unlike an army of uniformed Uncles on Prize-giving Day. There were no prizes, naturally. But we did our best to show them how efficient we were, by running round the assault course in teams, stabbing the straw sacks. We also competed in putting up screw-pickets and barbed wire with rapidity and precision. Our exertions ended with a march past the Army Commander, and then we fell out to witness the explosion of two small mines. Earth and chalk heaved up at the blue sky, the ground vibrated, and there was a noise like a mad rainstorm, caused by the whizzing descent of clods and stones and the hiss of smaller particles. Finally, a fountain of dingy smoke arose and drifted away from the débris, and the Generals retired to have luncheon in the white château; and there, let us hope, they let their belts out a hole or two and allowed themselves a little relaxation from intellectual effort. Allgood said that he thought the French Generals looked much brainier than the British ones; but I told him that they must be cleverer than they looked, and anyhow, they'd all got plenty of medal-ribbons.

PART TWO: THE RAID

I

I came back from the Army School at the end of a hot Saturday afternoon. The bus turned off the bumpy main road from Corbie and began to crawl down a steep winding lane. I looked, and there was Morlancourt in the hollow. On the whole I considered myself lucky to be returning to a place where I knew my way about. It was no use regretting the little room at Flixécourt where I had been able to sit alone every night, reading a good book and calling my soul my own. . . . Distant hills and hazy valleys were dazzled with sun-rays and the glaring beams made a fiery mist in the foreground. It was jolly fine country, I thought. I had become quite fond of it, and the end-of-the-world along the horizon had some obscure hold over my mind which drew my eyes to it almost eagerly, for I could still think of trench warfare as an adventure. The horizon was quiet just now, as if the dragons which lived there were dozing.

The Battalion was out of the line, and I felt almost glad to be back as I walked up to our old Company Mess with Flook carrying my valise on his back. Flook and I were very good friends, and his vigilance for my personal comfort was such that I could more easily imagine him using his rifle in defence of my valise than against the Germans.

Nobody was in when I got to our billets, but the place had improved since I last saw it; the horse-chestnut in front of the house was in flower and there were a few peonies and pink roses in the neglected little garden at the back.

Dusk had fallen when I returned from a stroll in the fields; the candles were lit, there was a smell of cooking, and the servants were clattering tin plates in the sizzling kitchen. Durley, Birdie Mansfield, and young Ormand were sitting round the table, with a new officer who was meekly reading the newspaper which served as tablecloth. They all looked glum, but my advent caused some pumped-up cheeriness, and I was introduced to the newcomer whose name was Fewnings. (He wore spectacles and in private life had been a schoolmaster.) Not much was said until the end of the steak and onions; by then Mansfield had lowered the level of the whisky bottle by a couple of inches, while the rest of us drank lime-juice. Tinned peaches appeared, and I inquired where Barton was—with an uneasy feeling that something might have happened to him. Ormand replied that the old man was dining at Battalion Head-quarters. "And skiting to Kinjack about the Raid, I'll bet," added Mansfield, tipping some more whisky into his mug. "The Raid!" I exclaimed, suddenly excited, "I haven't heard a word about it." "Well, you're the only human being in this Brigade who hasn't heard about it." (Mansfield's remarks were emphasized by the usual epi-thets.) "But what about it? Was it a success?" "Holy Christ! Was it a success? The Kangaroo wants to know if it was a success!" He puffed out his plump cheeks and gazed at the others. "This god-damned Raid's been a funny story for the last fortnight, and we've done every-thing except send word over to the Fritzes to say what time we're coming; and now it's fixed up for next Thursday, and Barton's hoping to get a D.S.O. out of it for his execu-tive ability. I wish he'd arrange to go and fetch his (some-thing) D.S.O. for himself!" From this I deduced that poor Birdie was to be in charge of the Raiding Party, and I soon knew all there was to be known. Ormand, who had obvi-ously heard more than enough lately, took himself off, vocally announcing that he was "Gilbert the filbert, the Nut with a K, the pride of Piccadilly, the blasé roué".

*　　　*　　　*

Barton was still up at Headquarters when I went across the road to my billet. Flook had spread my "flea-bag" on the tiled floor, and I had soon slipped into it and blown out my candle. Durley, on the other side of the room, was asleep in a few minutes, for he'd been out late on a working-party the night before. I was now full of information about the Raid, and I could think of nothing else. My month at Flixécourt was already obliterated. While I was away I had almost forgotten about the Raid; but it seemed now that I'd always regarded it as my private property, for when it had begun to be a probability in April, Barton had said that I should be sure to take charge of it. My feeling was much the same as it would have been if I had owned a horse and then been told that someone else was to ride it in a race.

Six years before I had been ambitious of winning races because that had seemed a significant way of demonstrating my equality with my contemporaries. And now I wanted to make the World War serve a similar purpose, for if only I could get a Military Cross I should feel comparatively safe and confident. (At that time the Doctor was the only man in the Battalion who'd got one.) Trench warfare was mostly monotonous drudgery, and I preferred the exciting idea of crossing the mine-craters and getting into the German front line. In my simple-minded way I had identified myself with that strip of no-man's-land opposite Bois Français; and the mine-craters had always fascinated me, though I'd often feared that they'd be the death of me.

Mansfield had gloomily remarked that he'd something-well go on the razzle if he got through Thursday night with his procreative powers unimpaired. Wondering why he had been selected for the job, I wished I could take his place. I knew that he had more common-sense ability than I had, but he was podgily built and had never been an expert at crawling among shell-holes in the dark. He and Ormand and Corporal O'Brien had done two patrols last week but the bright moonlight had prevented them from properly inspecting the German wire. Birdie's language about moonlight and snipers was a masterpiece, but he hadn't a ghost of an idea whether we could get through the Boche wire. Nevertheless I felt that if I'd been there the patrolling would have been profitable, moon or no moon. I wouldn't mind going up there and doing it now, I thought, for I was wideawake and full of energy after my easy life at the Army School. . . . *Doing it now?* The line was quiet to-night. Now and again the tapping of a machine-gun. But the demented night-life was going on all the time and the unsleeping strangeness of it struck my mind silent for a moment, as I visualized a wiring-party standing stock still while a flare quivered and sank, silvering the bleached sandbags of the redoubt.

Warm and secure, I listened to the gentle whisper of the aspens outside the window, and the fear of death and the horror of mutilation took hold of my heart. Durley was muttering in his sleep, something rapid and incoherent, and then telling someone to get a move on; the war didn't allow people many pleasant dreams. It was difficult to ima-gine old Julian killing a German, even with an anonymous bullet. I didn't want to kill any Germans myself, but one had to kill people in self-defence. Revolver shooting wasn't so bad, and as for bombs, you just chucked them and hoped for the best. Anyhow I meant to ask Kinjack to let me go on the Raid. Supposing he *ordered* me to go on it? How should I feel about it then? No good thinking any more about it now. With some such ponderings as these I sighed and fell asleep.

II

Next morning I went to the other end of the village to have a chat with my friend the Quartermaster. Leaning against a bit of broken wall outside his billet, we exchanged a few observations about the larger aspects of the war and the possibilities of peace. Joe was pessimistic as ever, airing his customary criticisms of profiteers, politicians, and those whose military duties compelled them to remain at the Base and in other back areas. He said that the permanent staff at Fourth Army Headquarters now numbered any-thing up to four thousand. With a ribald metaphor he speculated on what they did with themselves all day. I said that some of them were busy at the Army School. Joe supposed there was no likelihood of their opening a rest-cure for Quartermasters.

When I asked his opinion about the Raid he looked serious, for he liked Mansfield and knew his value as an officer. "From all I hear, Kangar," he said, "it's a baddish place for a show of that kind, but you know the ground better than I do. My own opinion is that the Boches would have come across themselves before now if they'd thought it worth trying. But Brigade have got the idea of a raid hot and strong, and they've nothing to lose by it one way or the other, except a few of our men." I asked if these raids weren't a more or less new notion, and he told me that our Battalion had done several small ones up in Flanders during the first winter; Winchell, our late Colonel, had led one when he was still a company commander. The idea had been revived early this year, when some Canadian toughs had pulled off a fine effort, and since then such entertainments had become popular with the Staff. Our Second Battalion had done one, about a month ago, up at Cuinchy; their Quartermaster had sent Joe the details; five officers and sixty men went across, but casualties were numerous and no prisoners were brought back. He sighed and lit a cigarette. "It's always the good lads who volunteer for these shows. One of the Transport men wanted to send his name in for this one; but I told him to think of his poor unfortunate wife, and we're pushing him off on a transport-course to learn cold-shoeing."

Prodding the ground with my stick, I stared at the Transport lines below us—a few dirty white bell-tents and the limbers and wagons and picketed horses. I could see the horses' tails switching and the men stooping to groom their legs. Bees hummed in the neglected little garden; red and grey roofs clustered round the square church tower; everything looked Sunday-like and contented with the fine weather. When I divulged my idea of asking Kinjack to let me go on the Raid, Joe remarked that he'd guessed as much, and advised me to keep quiet about it as there was

still a chance that it might be washed out. Kinjack wasn't
keen about it and had talked pretty straight to the Brigade
Major; he was never afraid of giving the brass-hats a bit of
his mind. So I promised to say nothing till the last moment,
and old Joe ended by reminding me that we'd all be over
the top in a month or two. But I thought, as I walked
away, how silly it would be if I got laid out by a stray
bullet, or a rifle-grenade, or one of those clumsy "canis-
ters" that came over in the evening dusk with a little trail
of sparks behind them.

*   *   *

We went into the line again on Tuesday. For the first
three days Barton's Company was in reserve at 71. North,
which was an assortment of dug-outs and earth-covered
shelters about a thousand yards behind the front line. I
never heard anyone ask the origin of its name, which for
most of us had meant shivering boredom at regular intervals since January. Some map-making expert had chris-
tened it coldly, and it had unexpectedly failed to get itself
called the Elephant and Castle or Hampton Court. Anyhow it was a safe and busy suburb of the front line, for the
dug-outs were hidden by sloping ground and nicely tucked
away under a steep bank. Shells dropped short or went well
over; and as the days of aeroplane aggressiveness had not
yet arrived, we could move about by daylight with moderate freedom. A little way down the road the Quartermaster-sergeant ruled the ration dump, and every evening
Dottrell arrived with the ration-limbers. There, too, was
the dressing station where Dick Tiltwood had died a couple
of months ago; it seemed longer than that, I thought, as I
passed it with my platoon and received a cheery greeting
from our Medical Officer, who could always make one feel
that Harley Street was still within reach.

The road which passed 71. North had once led to Fricourt; now it skulked along to the British Front Line,
wandered evilly across no-man's-land, and then gave itself
up to the Germans. In spite of this, the road had for me a
queer daylight magic, especially in summer. Though grass-

patched and derelict, something of its humanity remained.
I imagined everyday rural life going along it in pre-war
weather, until this businesslike open-air inferno made it an
impossibility for a French farmer to jog into Fricourt in his
hooded cart.

There was a single line railway on the other side of the
road, but the only idea which it suggested to Barton was
that if the war lasted a few more years we should be coming
to the trenches every day by train like city men going to
the office. He was due for leave next week and his mind
was already half in England. The Raid wasn't mentioned
now, and there was little to be done about it except wait
for Thursday night. Mansfield had become loquacious
about his past life, as though he were making a general
audit of his existence. I remember him talking about the
hard times he'd had in Canada, and how he used to get a
meal for twelve cents. In the meantime I made a few notes
in my diary.

" *Tuesday evening, 8.30. At Bécordel crossroads*. On a working party. A small bushy tree against a pale yellow sky;
slate roofs gleaming in the half-light. A noise of carts coming along with rations. Occasional bang of our guns close
to the village. The church tower, gloomy, only the front
remains; more than half of it shot away and most of the
church. In the foreground two broken barns with skeleton
roofs. A quiet cool evening after a shower. Stars coming
out. The R.E. stores are dumped around French soldier-
cemetery. Voices of men in the dusk. Dull rattle of machine-
guns on the left. Talking to a Northumberland Fusilier
officer who drops aitches. Too dark to write. . . .

" *Wednesday, 6.15 p.m. On Crawley Ridge*. Ormand up here
in the Redoubt with a few men. I relieve him while he goes
down to get his dinner. Very still evening; sun rather hazy.
Looking across to Fricourt; trench mortars bursting in the
cemetery; dull white smoke slowly floats away over grey-
green grass with buttercups and saffron weeds. Fricourt; a
huddle of reddish roofs; skeleton village; church tower,
almost demolished, a white patch against green of Fricourt
wood (full of German batteries). North, up the hill, white

scams and heapings of trenches dug in chalk. Sky full of
lark songs. Sometimes you can count thirty slowly and
hear no sound of a shot; then the muffled pop of a rifle or a
slamming 5.9 or one of our 18-pounders. Then a burst of
machine-gun fire. Westward the yellow sky with a web of
filmy cloud half across the sun; the ridges with blurred outlines of trees. An aeroplane droning overhead. A thistle
sprouting through the chalk on the parapet; a cockchafer
sailing through the air. Down the hill, the Bray-Fricourt
road, white and hard. A partridge flies away, calling. Lush
grass and crops of nettles; a large black slug out for his
evening walk (doing nearly a mile a month)."

III

At ten o'clock on Thursday night I was alone with Durley
in the sack-cloth smelling dug-out at 71. North. Rain was
falling steadily. Everything felt fateful and final. A solitary
candle stood on the table in its own grease, and by its golden glimmer I had just written a farewell letter to Aunt
Evelyn. I did not read it through, and I am glad I cannot
do so now, for it was in the "happy warrior" style and my
own fine feelings took precedence of hers. It was not humanly possible for me to wonder what Aunt Evelyn was doing
while I wrote; to have done so would have cramped my
style. But it is possible that she was calling her black Persian cat in from the dripping summer garden; when it
scampered in from the darkness she would dry it carefully
with a towel, whistling under her breath, while she did so,
some indeterminate tune. Poor Aunt Evelyn was still comfortingly convinced that I was transport officer, though I
had given up that job nearly three months ago. Having
licked and fastened the flimsy envelope I handed it to Durley, with a premonition that it would be posted. Durley
received it with appropriate gravity.

In the meantime Mansfield was making a final reconnaissance of the ground with Sergeant Miles and Corporal
O'Brien, while Barton (unaware of my intentions) was

administering a drop of whisky to the raiding party in the large dug-out just along the road. It was time to be moving; so I took off my tunic, slipped my old raincoat on over my leather waistcoat, dumped my tin hat on my head, and picked up my nail-studded knobkerrie. Good old Durley wished me luck and economically blew out the candle. As we went along the road he remarked that it was lucky the night was dark and rainy.

Entering the other dug-out I was slightly startled, for I had forgotten that the raiders were to have blacked faces (to avoid the danger of their mistaking one another for Germans). Exchanging boisterous jokes, they were putting the finishing touches to their make-up with bits of burnt cork. Showing the whites of their eyes and pretending not to recognize one another, those twenty-five shiny-faced nigger minstrels might almost have been getting ready for a concert. Everyone seemed to expect the entertainment to be a roaring success. But there were no looking-glasses or banjos, and they were brandishing knobkerries, stuffing Mills' bombs into their pockets and hatchets into their belts, and "Who's for a Blighty one to-night?" was the stock joke (if such a well-worn wish could be called a joke).

At 10.30 there was a sudden silence, and Barton told me to take the party up to Battalion Headquarters. It surprises me when I remember that I set off without having had a drink, but I have always disliked the flavour of whisky, and in those days the helpfulness of alcohol in human affairs was a fact which had not yet been brought home to me. The raiders had been given only a small quantity, but it was enough to hearten them as they sploshed up the communication trench. None of us could know how insignificant we were in the so-called "Great Adventure" which was sending up its uneasy flares along the Western Front. No doubt we thought ourselves something very special. But what we thought never mattered; nor does it matter what sort of an inflated fool I was when I blundered into Kinjack's Headquarters at Maple Redoubt to report the presence of the raiders and ask whether I might go across with them. "Certainly not," said the Colonel, "your job is to stop in our trench and count the men as they come back." He spoke with emphasis and he was not a man who expected to have to say a thing twice. We stared at one another for a moment; some freak of my brain made me remember that in peace time he had been an enthusiastic rose-grower—had won prizes with his roses, in fact; for he was a married man and had lived in a little house near the barracks.

My thought was nipped in the bud by his peremptory voice telling Major Robson, his second-in-command, to push off with the party. We were about 400 yards from the front line, and Robson now led us across the open to a point in the support trench, from which a red electric torch winked to guide us. Then up a trench to the starting point, the men's feet clumping and drumming on the duck-boards. This noise, plus the clinking and drumming and creaking of weapons and equipment, suggested to my strained expectancy that the enemy would be well warned of our arrival. Mansfield and his two confederates now loomed squatly above us on the parapet; they had been laying a guiding line of lime across the craters. A gap had been cut in our wire, and it was believed that some sort of damage had been done to the German wire which had been "strafed" by trench mortars during the day.

The raiders were divided into four parties of five men; operation orders had optimistically assumed that the hostile trenches would be entered without difficulty; "A" party would go to the left, "B" party to the right, and so on and so forth. The object of the raid was to enter the enemy loop on the edge of the crater; to enter Kiel Trench at two points; to examine the portions of trench thus isolated, capture prisoners, bomb dug-outs, and kill Germans. An "evacuating party" (seven men carrying two ten-foot ladders and a red flash lamp) followed the others. The ladders were considered important, as the German front trench was believed to be deep and therefore difficult to get out of in a hurry. There were two mine-craters a few yards from our parapet; these craters were about fifty yards in diameter and about fifty feet deep; their sides were steep and composed of thin soft soil; there was water at the bottom of them. Our men crossed by a narrow bridge of earth between the craters; the distance to the German wire was about sixty yards.

It was now midnight. The five parties had vanished into the darkness on all fours. It was raining quietly and persistently. I sat on the parapet waiting for something to happen. Except for two men at a sentry post near by (they were now only spectators) there seemed to be no one about. "They'll never keep that —— inside the trench," muttered the sentry to his mate and even at that tense moment I valued the compliment. Major Robson and the stretcher-bearers had been called away by a message. There must be some trouble further along, I thought, wondering what it could be, for I hadn't heard a sound. Now and again I looked at my luminous watch. Five, ten, fifteen minutes passed in ominous silence. An occasional flare, never near our craters, revealed the streaming rain, blanched the tangles of wire that wound away into the gloom, and came to nothing, bringing down the night. Unable to remain inactive any longer, I crawled a little way out. As I went, a few shells began to drone across in their leisurely way. Our communication trench was being shelled. I joined the evacuating party; they were lying on the lip of the left-hand crater. A flare fizzed up, and I could see the rest of the men lying down, straight across the ridge, and was able to exchange a grimace with one of the black-faced ladder-carriers. Then some "whizz-bangs" rushed over to our front trench; one or two fell on the craters; this made the obstinate silence of Kiel Trench more menacing. Soon afterwards one of the bayonet men came crawling rapidly back. I followed him to our trench where he whispered his message. "They can't get through the second belt of wire; O'Brien says it's a washout; they're all going to throw a bomb and retire."

I suppose I ought to have tried to get the ladder-carriers in before the trouble started; but the idea didn't strike me as I waited with bumping heart; and almost immediately the explosions began. A bomb burst in the water of the left-hand crater, sending up a phosphorescent spume. Then a concentration of angry flashes, thudding bangs, and cracking shots broke itself up in a hubbub and scurry, groans and curses, and stampeding confusion. Stumbling figures loomed up from below, scrambling clumsily over the parapet; black faces and whites of eyes showed grotesque in the antagonistic shining of alarm flares. Dodging to and fro, I counted fourteen men in; they all blundered away down the trench. I went out, found Mansfield badly hit, and left him with two others who soon got him in. Other wounded men were crawling back. Among them was a grey-haired lance-corporal, who had one of his feet almost blown off; I half carried him in, and when he was sitting on the firestep he said: "Thank God Almighty for this; I've been waiting eighteen months for it, and now I can go home." I told him we'd get him away on a stretcher soon, and then he muttered: "Mick O'Brien's somewhere down in the craters."

All this had been quick work and not at all what I'd expected. Things were slowing down now. The excitement was finished, and O'Brien was somewhere down in the craters. The bombing and rifle fire had slackened when I started out to look for him. I went mechanically, as though I were drowning myself in the darkness. This is no fun at all, was my only thought as I groped my way down the soft clogging side of the left-hand crater; no fun at all, for they were still chucking an occasional bomb and firing circumspectly. I could hear the reloading click of rifle bolts on the lip of the crater above me as I crawled along with mud-clogged fingers, or crouched and held my breath painfully. Bullets hit the water and little showers of earth pattered down from the banks. I knew that nothing in my previous experience of patrolling had ever been so grim as this, and I lay quite still for a bit, miserably wondering whether my number was up; then I remembered that I was wearing my pre-war raincoat; I could feel the pipe and tobacco pouch in my pocket and somehow this made me less forlorn, though life seemed much further away than the low mumble of voices in our trench. A flare would have helped my searchings, but they had stopped sending them up; pawing the loose earth and dragging my legs after me, I worked my way round the crater. O'Brien wasn't there, so I got across into the other one, which was even more precipitous and squashy. Down there I discovered him. Another man was crouching beside him, wounded in one arm and patiently waiting for help. O'Brien moaned when I touched him; he seemed to have been hit in several places. His companion whispered huskily: "Get a rope." As I clambered heavily up the bank I noticed that it had stopped raining. Robson was peering out of the trench; he sent someone for a rope, urging him to be quick for already there was a faint beginning of daylight. With the rope, and a man to help, I got back to O'Brien, and we lifted him up the side of the crater.

It was heavy work, for he was tall and powerfully built, and the soft earth gave way under our feet as we lugged and hoisted the limp shattered body. The Germans must have seen us in the half light, but they had stopped firing; perhaps they felt sorry for us.

At last we lowered him over the parapet. A stretcher-bearer bent over him and then straightened himself, taking off his helmet with a gesture that vaguely surprised me by its reverent simplicity. O'Brien had been one of the best men in our Company. I looked down at him and then turned away; the face was grotesquely terrible, smeared with last night's burnt cork, the forehead matted with a tangle of dark hair.

I had now accounted for everyone. Two killed and ten wounded was the only result of the raid. In the other Company sector the Germans had blown in one of our mine-galleries, and about thirty of the tunnelling company had been gassed or buried. Robson had been called there with the stretcher-bearers just as the raid began.

Nothing now remained for me to do except to see Kinjack on my way back. Entering his dug-out I looked at him with less diffidence than I'd ever done before. He was sitting on his plank bed, wearing a brown woollen cap with a tuft on the top. His blond face was haggard; the last few hours had been no fun for him either. This was a Kinjack

I'd never met before, and it was the first time I had ever shared any human equality with him. He spoke kindly to me in his rough way, and in doing so made me very thankful that I had done what I could to tidy up the mess in no-man's-land.

Larks were shrilling in the drizzling sky as I went down to 71. North. I felt a wild exultation. Behind me were the horror and the darkness. Kinjack had thanked me. It was splendid to be still alive, I thought, as I strode down the hill, skirting shell-holes and jumping over communication trenches, for I wasn't in a mood to bother about going along wet ditches. The landscape loomed around me, and the landscape was life, stretching away and away into freedom. Even the dreary little warren at 71. North seemed to await me with a welcome, and Flook was ready with some hot tea. Soon I was jabbering excitedly to Durley and old man Barton, who told me that the Doctor said Mansfield was a touch and go case, but already rejoicing at the prospect of getting across to Blighty, and cursing the bad wire-cutters which had been served out for the raid. I prided myself on having pulled off something rather heroic; but when all was said and done it was only the sort of thing which people often did during a fire or a railway accident.

*   *   *

Nothing important had happened on the British Front that night, so we were rewarded by a mention in the G.H.Q. *communiqué*. "*At Mametz we raided hostile trenches. Our party entered without difficulty and maintained a spirited bombing fight, and finally withdrew at the end of twenty-five minutes.*" This was their way of telling England. Aunt Evelyn probably read it automatically in her *Morning Post*, unaware that this minor event had almost caused her to receive a farewell letter from me. The next night our Company was in the front line and I recovered three hatchets and a knob-kerrie from no-man's-land. Curiously enough, I hadn't yet seen a German. I had seen dim figures on my dark patrols; but no human faces.

PART THREE: BEFORE THE PUSH

I

One evening about a fortnight later I was down in that too familiar front-line dug-out with Barton, who had just returned from leave and was unable to disguise his depression. I wasn't feeling over bright myself after tramping to and fro in the gluey trenches all day. A little rain made a big difference to life up there, and the weather had been wet enough to make the duckboards wobble when one stepped on them. I'd got sore feet and a trench mouth and food tasted filthy. And the Boche trench-mortars had been strafing us more than usual that evening. Probably I've been smoking too much lately, I thought, knocking my pipe out against one of the wooden props which held up the cramped little den, and staring irritably at my mud-encumbered boots, for I was always trying to keep squalor at bay, and the discomfort of feeling dirty and tickly all over was almost as bad as a bombardment. It certainly wasn't much of a place to be low-spirited in, so I tried reading the paper which the Company-Sergeant-Major had just delivered when he came down for the rum ration. The rum jar lived under Barton's bed; having been poured into some tin receptacle, the rum was carried cautiously upstairs to be tipped into the men's tea-dixies.

"Fancy Kitchener being drowned in the North Sea!" I remarked, looking up from the *Daily Mail* which was making the most of that historic event. (It seemed a long time since I rode past his park wall in Kent when I was with the Yeomanry; it would be two years next September, though it wasn't much use looking as far ahead as that, with all these preparations going on for the "Big Push".) Barton was scribbling away with his indelible pencil—filling in all that bosh which made Brigade think they were busy. "If

you want my opinion," he grumbled, "I believe those
damned Irish had a hand in Kitchener being drowned.
I'd like to see that fatuous island of theirs sunk under the
sea." Barton had an irrational dislike of the Irish, and he
always blamed anything on them if he could. He wouldn't
even admit that Ireland was an agricultural country, and
since the Easter Rebellion in Dublin it wasn't safe to show
him a bottle of Irish whisky. "I've never met an Irishman
with any more sense than that mouse!" he exclaimed. A
mouse was standing on its head in the sugar basin, which
was made of metal and contained soft sugar. He eyed the
mouse morosely, as though accusing it of Irish ancestry.
"This time three nights ago my wife and I were having
dinner at the Café Royal. Upstairs at the Café Royal—
best food in London, and as good as ever even now. I tell
you, Kangar, it's too much of a bloody contrast, coming
back to all this." There was a muffled "Wump" and both
candles went out. Something heavy had burst outside our
door. Lighting the candles, I thought I'd just as soon be
upstairs as down in this musty limbo. In about an hour I
should be out with the wiring-party, dumping concertina
wire in the shell-holes along the edge of the craters. I wondered if I should ever get a Blighty wound. One of our best
officers had been hit last night while out with the wirers.
This was Bill Eaves, who had been a Classical Scholar at
Cambridge and had won medals there for writing Greek
and Latin epigrams. Now he'd got a nice bullet wound
in the shoulder, with the muscles damaged enough to
keep him in England several months. And two nights
ago Ormand and a Sandhurst boy named Harris had
been hit while on a working party. Ormand's was a
"cushy" shell splinter; but Harris had got his knee
smashed up, and the doctor said he would probably be
out of the war for good. It was funny to think of young
Harris being hit in the first twenty-four hours of his first
tour of trenches.

Anyhow we were due for Divisional Rest, which would
take us to the back area for three weeks, and the clogging
monotony of life in the line would be cleaned out of our

minds. And you never knew—perhaps the war would end in those three weeks. The troops were beginning to need a rest badly, for most of them had been doing tours of trenches ever since the end of January, and even when we were at Morlancourt there was a working party every second night, which meant being out from seven o'clock till after midnight. And Miles, my platoon sergeant, hadn't been quite his usual self since the raid; but he'd been in France nearly a year, which was longer than most men could stick such a life. The chances are, I thought, that if Sergeant Miles is still here a few months hence, and I'm not, some fresh young officer from England will be accusing him of being windy. Sooner or later I should get windy myself. It was only a question of time. But could this sort of thing be measured by ordinary time, I wondered (as I lay on a bunk wishing to God Barton would stop blowing on his spectacles, which surely didn't need all that polishing). No; one couldn't reckon the effect of the war on people by weeks and months. I'd noticed that boys under twenty stood it worst, especially when the weather was bad. Mud and boredom and discomfort seemed to take all the guts out of them. If an officer crumpled up, Kinjack sent him home as useless, with a confidential report. Several such officers were usually drifting about at the Depot, and most of them ended up with safe jobs in England. But if a man became a dud in the ranks, he just remained where he was until he was killed or wounded. Delicate discrimination about private soldiers wasn't possible. A "number nine pill" was all they could hope for if they went sick. Barton sometimes told me that I was too easy-going with the men when we were out of the Line, but it often seemed to me that I was asking them to do more than could be fairly expected of them. It's queer, I thought, how little one really knows about the men. In the Line one finds out which are the duds, and one builds up a sort of comradeship with the tough and willing ones. But back in billets the gap widens and one can't do much to cheer them up. I could never understand how they managed to keep as cheery as they did through such drudgery and discomfort, with nothing to look forward to but going over the top or being moved up to Flanders again.

*　　　*　　　*

Next evening, just before stand-to, I was watching a smouldering sunset and thinking that the sky was one of the redeeming features of the war. Behind the support line where I stood, the shell-pitted ground sloped sombrely into the dusk; the distances were blue and solemn, with a few trees grouped on a ridge, dark against the deep-glowing embers of another day endured. I was looking westward, away from the war, and the evening star twinkled serenely. Guns were grumbling miles away. Cartwheels could be heard on the roads behind Fricourt; it still made me feel strange when I remembered that they were German cartwheels.

Moments like those are unreproducible when I look back and try to recover their living texture. One's mind eliminates boredom and physical discomfort, retaining an incomplete impression of a strange, intense, and unique experience. If there be such a thing as ghostly revisitation of this earth, and if ghosts can traverse time and choose their ground, I would return to the Bois Français sector as it was then. But since I always assume that spectral presences have lost their sense of smell (and I am equally uncertain about their auditory equipment) such hauntings might be as inadequate as those which now absorb my mental energy. For trench life was an existence saturated by the external senses; and although our actions were domineered over by military discipline, our animal instincts were always uppermost. While I stood there then, I had no desire to diagnose my environment. Freedom from its oppressiveness was what I longed for. Listening to the German cartwheels rumbling remotely, I thought of an old German governess I had known, and how she used to talk about "dear old Moltke and Bismarck" and her quiet home in Westphalia where her father had been a Protestant pastor. I wondered what sort of a place Westphalia was, and wished I'd seen more of the world before it became so busy with bloodshed. For until I came out to the war I had only the haziest notion of anything outside England.

Well, here I was, and my incomplete life might end any minute; for although the evening air was as quiet as a cathedral, a canister soon came over quite near enough to shatter my meditations with its unholy crash and cloud of black smoke. A rat scampered across the tin cans and burst sandbags, and trench atmosphere reasserted itself in a smell of chloride of lime. On my way to the dug-out, to fetch my revolver and attend the twilight ceremony of stand-to and rifle inspection, I heard the voice of Flook; just round a bend of the support trench he was asking one of the company bombers if he'd seen his officer bloke go along that way. Flook was in a hurry to tell me that I was to go on leave. I didn't wait to inspect my platoon's rifles and not many minutes later I was on my way down the Old Kent Road trench. Maple Redoubt was getting its usual evening bombardment, and as a man had been killed by a whizz-bang in the Old Kent Road a few minutes earlier, I was glad when I was riding back to Morlancourt with Dottrell; glad, too, to be driving to Méricourt station behind the sluggish pony next morning; to hear the mellow bells of Rouen on the evening air while the leave train stood still for half an hour before making up its mind to lumber on to Havre. And thus the gradations of thankfulness continued, until I found myself in a quiet house in Kensington where I was staying the night with an old friend of Aunt Evelyn's.

To be there, on a fine Sunday evening in June, with the drawing-room windows open and someone playing the piano next door, was an experience which now seemed as queer as the unnatural conditions I had returned from. Books, pictures, furniture, all seemed kind and permanent and unrelated to the present time and its troubles. I felt detached from my surroundings—rather as if I were in a doctor's waiting-room, expecting to be informed that I had some incurable disease. The sound of the piano suggested that the specialist had a happy home life of his own, but it

had no connection with my coming and going. A sense of
gentle security pervaded the room; but I could no longer
call my life my own. The pensive music had caught me off
my guard; I was only an intruder from the Western Front.
But the room contained one object which unexpectedly reminded me of the trenches—a silent canary in a cage. I had
seen canaries in cages being carried by the men of the tunnelling company when they emerged from their mine
galleries.

II

Correspondingly queer (though I didn't consciously observe it at the time) was the experience of returning to
France after sleeping seven nights in a proper bed and
wearing civilian clothes. The personal implications were
obvious, since everybody at home seemed to know that the
long-planned offensive was due to "kick off" at the end of
June. Officers going on leave had been cautioned to say
nothing about it, but even Aunt Evelyn was aware of the
impending onslaught. I was disinclined to talk about the
trenches; nevertheless I permitted myself to drop a few
heavy hints. No one had any notion what the Big Push
would be like, except that it would be much bigger than
anything which had happened before. And somehow those
previous battles hadn't divulged themselves very distinctly
to anyone except the actual participators, who had so far
proved inarticulate reporters.

As regards my own adventures, I had decided to say
nothing to my aunt about the raid. Nevertheless it all
slipped out on the second evening, probably after she had
been telling me how splendidly Mrs. Ampney's nephew
had done out in Mesopotamia. Also I didn't omit to mention that I had been recommended for a Military Cross.
"But I thought you were only looking after the horses,"
she expostulated, clutching my hand; her anxious face
made me wish I'd held my tongue about it. Of course,
Aunt Evelyn wanted me to do well in the war, but she

couldn't enjoy being reminded that "do be careful to wear your warm overcoat, dearie", was no precaution against German bombs and bullets. Afterwards I excused myself by thinking that she was bound to find out sooner or later, especially if I got killed.

Next day I walked across the fields to Butley and had tea with my old friend Captain Huxtable. I found him chubby-cheeked as ever, and keeping up what might be called a Justice of the Peace attitude toward the war. Any able-bodied man not serving in H.M. Forces should be required to show a thundering good reason for it, and the sooner conscription came in the better. That was his opinion; in the meantime he was working his farm with two elderly men and a boy; "and that's about all an old crock like me can do for his country." I gave him to understand that it was a jolly fine life out at the Front, and, for the moment, I probably believed what I was saying. I wasn't going to wreck my leave with facing facts, and I'd succeeded in convincing myself that I really wanted to go back. Captain Huxtable and I decided, between us, that the Push would finish the war by Christmas. While we talked, pacing to and fro in the garden, with his surly black retriever at our heels, the rooks cawed applaudingly in the clump of elms near by as though all were well with England on that June afternoon. I knew that the Captain would have asked nothing better than to go over the top with his old regiment, if only he'd been thirty years younger, and I wished I could have told him so, when we were standing at his gate. But English reticence prohibited all that sort of thing, and I merely remarked that Aunt Evelyn's lightning-conductor had been blown off the chimney in the spring and she said it wasn't worth while having it put up again. He laughed and said she must be getting war-weary; she had always been so particular about the lightning-conductor. "We old 'uns can't expect to be feeling very cock-a-hoop in these days," he added, wrinkling up his shrewd and kindly little eyes and giving my hand a farewell squeeze which meant more than he could say aloud.

*   *   *

When Aunt Evelyn wondered whether I'd like anyone to come to dinner on my last evening (she called it Friday night) I replied that I'd rather we were alone. There were very few to ask, and, as she said, people were difficult to get hold of nowadays. So, after a dinner which included two of my favourite puddings, we made the best of a bad job by playing cribbage (a game we had been addicted to when I was at home for my school holidays) while the black Persian cat washed his face with his paw and blinked contentedly at the fire which had been lit though there was no need for it, the night being warm and still. We also had the grey parrot brought up from the kitchen. Clinging sideways to the bars of his cage Popsy seemed less aware of the war than anyone I'd met. But perhaps he sensed the pang I felt when saying good-bye to him next morning; parrots understand more than they pretend to, and this one had always liked me. He wasn't much of a talker, though he could imitate Aunt Evelyn calling the cats.

Next morning she contrived to be stoically chatty until I had seen her turn back to the house door and the village taxi was rattling me down the hill. She had sensibly refrained from coming up to London to see me off. But at Waterloo Station I was visibly reminded that going back for the Push was rather rough on one's relations, however incapable they might be of sharing the experience. There were two leave trains and I watched the people coming away after the first one had gone out. Some sauntered away with assumed unconcern; they chatted and smiled. Others hurried past me with a crucified look; I noticed a well-dressed woman biting her gloved fingers; her eyes stared fixedly; she was returning alone to a silent house on a fine Sunday afternoon.

But I had nobody to see me off, so I could settle myself in the corner of a carriage, light my pipe and open a Sunday paper (though goodness knows what it contained, apart from *communiqués*, casualty lists, and reassuring news from Galicia, Bukovina, and other opaque arenas of war). It would have been nice to read the first-class cricket averages for a change, and their absence was an apt epitome of the life we were condemned to. While the train hurried out of London I watched the flitting gardens of suburban houses. In my fox-hunting days I had scorned the suburbs, but now there was something positively alluring in the spectacle of a City man taking it easy on his little lawn at Surbiton. Woking Cemetery was a less attractive scene, and my eyes recoiled from it to reassure themselves that my parcels were still safe on the rack, for those parcels were the important outcome of my previous day's shopping.

Armed with Aunt Evelyn's membership ticket (posted back to her afterwards) I had invaded the Army and Navy Stores and procured a superb salmon, two bottles of old brandy, an automatic pistol, and two pairs of wire-cutters with rubber-covered handles. The salmon was now my chief concern. I was concerned about its future freshness, for I had overstayed my leave by twenty-four hours. A rich restaurant dinner followed by a mechanical drawing-room comedy hadn't made the risk of Kinjack's displeasure seem worth while; but I felt that the salmon spelt safety at Battalion Headquarters. Probably the word *smelt* also entered my apprehensive mind. The brandy claimed that it had been born in 1838, so one day more or less couldn't affect its condition, as long as I kept an eye on it (for such bottles were liable to lose themselves on a leave boat). The wire-cutters were my private contribution to the Great Offensive. I had often cursed the savage bluntness of our Company's wire-cutters, and it occurred to me, in the Army and Navy Stores, that if we were going over the top we might want to cut our own wire first, to say nothing of the German wire (although our artillery would have made holes in that, I hoped). So I bought these very civilized ones, which looked almost too good for the Front Line. The man in the Weapon Department at the Stores had been persuasive about a periscope (probably prismatic) but I came to the conclusion that a periscope was a back number in my case. I shouldn't be in the trench long enough to need it. Apart from the wire-cutters and the pistol, all other "trench requisites" appeared redundant.

I couldn't see myself leading my platoon with *Mortleman's Patent Sound Absorbers* plugged in my ears, and a combined Compass-Barometer also failed to attract me. The automatic pistol wasn't "warranted to stop a man", but it could be slipped into the pocket. It was only a plaything, but I was weary of my Colt revolver, with which I knew I couldn't hit anything, although I had blazed it off a few times in the dark when I was pretending to be important in no-man's-land. The only object I could be sure of hitting was myself, and I decided (in the Army and Navy Stores) that I might conceivably find it necessary to put myself out of my misery, if the worst came to the worst and I was lying out in a shell-hole with something more serious than a Blighty wound. To blow one's brains out with that clumsy Colt was unthinkable. The automatic pistol, on the other hand, was quite a charming little weapon. Not that I'd ever been fond of firearms. I had never shot at a bird or an animal in my life, though I'd often felt that my position as a sportsman would be stronger if I were "a good man with a gun".

The truth was that the only explosive weapon I owned before the war was a toy pistol which made a noise but discharged nothing. Sitting in the wrong-way leave train I remembered how, when about nine years old, I used to go up to the little sweet shop in the village and buy "three penn'orth of percussion caps" for my pistol; and how the buxom old woman used to ask briskly, "Anything else to-day, Master George?" Whereupon I would be compelled to decide between clove and peppermint bulls' eyes, with a bar of chocolate-cream to make it up to sixpence. Twenty years was a long time ago; but already the village green as I saw it last week was beginning to seem almost as remote. . . . However, it was no use dreaming about all that now; Kinjack's salmon was my immediate problem, and as soon as I was on board the crowded boat, I consulted an obliging steward and my fishy insurance policy was providentially accommodated in the cold-storage cupboard. Consequently my mind was unperturbed when we steamed out of Southampton Water. I watched the woods on the Isle of

Wight, hazily receding in the heat. And when the Isle of Wight was out of sight—well, there was nothing to be done about it.

*   *   *

At Havre I was instructed, by the all-knowing authority responsible for my return, to get out of the train at Corbie. Havre was a glitter of lights winking on dark slabbing water. Soon the glumly-laden train was groaning away from the wharves, and we nodded and snored through the night. Daylight came, and we crawled past green landscapes blurred with drizzling rain. Of my compartment companions I remember nothing except that one of them talked irrepressibly about his father's farm in Suffolk. His father, he said, owned a bull who had produced sixty black and white calves. This information was received with apathy. The Battalion was at Bussy, a three-mile walk in late afternoon sunshine. I kept to the shady side of the road, for the salmon in its hamper was still my constant care. Bussy came in sight as a pleasant little place on a tributary of the Ancre. A few of our men were bathing, and I thought how young and light-hearted they looked, splashing one another and shouting as they rocked a crazy boat under some lofty poplars that shivered in a sunset breeze. How different to the trudging figures in full marching order; and how difficult to embody them in the crouching imprisonment of trench warfare!

With an unsoldierly sigh I picked up my packages and plodded on in search of C Company, who were billeted in some buildings round a friendly farmhouse. There I found Flook and despatched him to Kinjack's Headquarters with the hamper and a bottle of brandy. Barton, to whom I entrusted the second bottle, told me that I was a cunning old Kangaroo, and then regaled me with all the rumours about next week's operations. "The bombardment begins on Saturday," he said, "so we're having Battalion Sports tomorrow, in case we get moved back to Morlancourt." Then Durley came in with Jenkins, one of the new officers who had been posted to the Battalion while I was away. Fewn-

ings, the gentle ex-schoolmaster, had been appointed
Lewis gun officer, but he still messed with us; he now
entered with the air of a man who had been teaching
Euclid and Algebra all day. The Brigadier, he remarked,
had ticked him off that afternoon, because he was wearing
a light-coloured shirt; but no fault had been found with his
Lewis gun team organization, and, as he remarked, it
wouldn't make much odds what sort of shirt he was wearing in a week or two. Neither Durley nor I had ever been
favoured with a word from our Brigadier, perhaps because
our shirts were the orthodox colour. It was odd, how seldom those graduated autocrats found time to realize that a
few kind words could make a platoon commander consider
them jolly good Generals.

But there was harmony in our Company Mess, as if our
certainty of a volcanic future had put an end to the occasional squabblings which occurred when we were on one
another's nerves. A rank animal healthiness pervaded our
existence during those days of busy living and inward foreboding. The behaviour of our servants expressed it; they
were competing for the favours of a handsome young woman in the farmhouse, and a comedy of primitive court-
ship was being enacted in the kitchen. Death would be
lying in wait for the troops next week, and now the flavour
of life was doubly strong. As I went to my room across the
road, the cool night smelt of mown grass and leafy gardens.
Away toward Corbie there was the sound of a train, and
bull-frogs croaked continuously in the marshes along the
river. I wasn't sorry to be back; I was sure of that; we'd all
got to go through it, and I was trying to convert the idea of
death in battle into an emotional experience. Courage, I
argued, is a beautiful thing, and next week's attack is what
I have been waiting for since I first joined the army. I am
happy to-night, and I don't suppose I'll be dead in a
month's time. Going into my billet I almost fell over a goat
which was tethered among some currant bushes in the
garden.

*   *   *

Five days passed us by. We did easy field-training; the

Battalion Sports were a great success, and we were de-
feated, in an officers' tug-of-war, by our 9th Battalion who
were resting a few miles away. Saturday evening brought a
feeling of finality, for we were moving up to Morlancourt
on Monday and the intense bombardment had begun that
morning. Barton and I (and our bottle of '38 brandy) dined
at Battalion Headquarters. Kinjack was full of confidence;
he told us that the French were holding on well at Verdun,
which would make all the difference. But the doctor looked
thoughtful, and even the brandy couldn't make Barton
optimistic about his ability to command a company in
open warfare.

PART FOUR: BATTLE

I

On the morning of a Battalion move I made it my business to keep out of the way until the last moment. At the end of a march I had my definite duties, but before we started Barton was always in such a stew that my absence was a positive advantage to him. So on Monday, after bolting my breakfast while Flook waited to pack the mugs and plates in the mess-box, I left Barton shouting irritably for the Sergeant-Major and wandered away to sit by the river until the whistles began to blow. Durley and Jenkins had gone to make sure that the billets were being left clean and tidy. In the green orchard behind the farm buildings the men were putting their kits together, their voices sounding as jolly as though they were off for a summer holiday. For me it was a luxury to be alone for a few minutes, watching the yellow irises, and the ribbon weeds that swayed like fishes in the dimpling stream. I was sorry to be saying good-bye to the Marais and its grey-green pools and creeks and the congregation of poplar stems that upheld a cool whispering roof. Water-haunting birds whistled and piped, swinging on the bulrushes and tufted reeds, and a tribe of little green and gold frogs hopped about in the grass without caring whether they arrived anywhere. All this was obviously preferable to a battle, and it was a perfect morning to be reading a book beside the river.

But on the horizon the bombardment bumped and thudded in a continuous bubbling grumble. After a long stare at sun-flecked foliage and idly reflective alleys I bustled back to the farmyard to find my platoon all present and correct. Before I'd finished my formal inspection Barton emerged from the house with bulging pockets, his burly figure hung like a Christmas tree with haversack, water-bottle, revolver, field-glasses, gas-mask, map-case, and other oddments. The Battalion moved off at eight o'clock; by twelve-thirty it was at Morlancourt, which was now congested with infantry and supply columns, and "lousy with guns" as the saying was. A colony of camouflage-daubed tents had sprung up close to the village; this was the New Main Dressing Station. We were in our usual billets—Durley and I in the room containing a representation of the Eiffel Tower and a ludicrous oleograph of our Saviour preaching from a boat, which we always referred to as jocular Jesus. After a sultry dinner, the day ended with torrents of rain. While I lay on the floor in my flea-bag the blackness of the night framed in the window was lit with incessant glare and flash of guns. But I fell asleep to the sound of full gutters and rainwater gurgling and trickling into a well; and those were comfortable noises, for they signified that I had a roof over my head. As for my flea-bag, it was no hardship; I have never slept more soundly in any bed.

*   *   *

Operation Orders were circulated next morning. They notified us that Thursday was "Z" (or zero) day. The Seventh Division Battle Plan didn't look aggressively unpleasant on paper as I transcribed it into my notebook. Rose Trench, Orchard Alley, Apple Alley, and Willow Avenue, were among the first objectives in our sector, and my mind very properly insisted on their gentler associations. Nevertheless this topographical Arcadia was to be seized, cleared, and occupied when the historic moment arrived and in conjunction with the French the Fourth Army took the offensive, establishing as a primary objective a line Montauban-Pozières, passing to the south of Mametz Wood. There wasn't going to be any mistake about it this time. We decided, with quite a glow of excitement, that the Fourth Army was going to fairly wipe the floor with the Boches. In the meantime our Corps Intelligence Summary (known as *Comic Cuts*) reported on June 27th that three enemy balloons had been set on fire and

destroyed on the previous afternoon; also that a large number of enemy batteries had been silenced by our artillery.
The anonymous humorist who compiled *Comic Cuts* was
also able to announce that the Russians had captured a
redoubt and some heavy guns at Czartovijsk, which, he
explained, was forty-four miles north-east of Luck. At
Martinpuich a large yellowish explosion had been observed. On Tuesday afternoon I went up to the Line with
Durley on some preliminary errand, for we were to relieve
a battalion of the Border Regiment next day, in the sector in
front of Fricourt Cemetery. Our Batteries were firing strenuously all along the countryside, with very little retaliation.

As we passed the gun-pits where some Heavies were hidden in a hollow called Gibraltar, I remarked on a sickly
sweet smell which I attributed to the yellow weeds which
were abundant there, but Durley explained that it was the
lingering aroma of gas-shells. When we rode down the
slope to 71. North, that familiar resort appeared much the
same as usual, except for the impressive accumulations of
war material which were dumped along the road. Durley
remarked that he supposed the old spot would never be the
same again after this week; and already it seemed to us as
if the old days when Mansfield and Ormand were with our
company had become an experience to be looked back on
with regret. The Bois Français sector had been a sort of
village, but we should soon be leaving it behind us in our
vindictive explorations of Rose Trench, Apple Alley, and
Willow Avenue.

On our way up to the Front Line we met a staff-officer
who was wearing well-cut riding boots and evidently in a
hurry to rejoin his horse. Larks were rejoicing aloft, and the
usual symbolic scarlet poppies lolled over the sides of the
communication trench; but he squeezed past us without so
much as a nod, for the afternoon was too noisy to be idyllic,
in spite of the larks and poppies which were so popular with
war-correspondents. "I suppose those brass-hats do know
a hell of a lot about it all, don't they, Julian?" I queried.
Durley replied that he hoped they'd learnt something since
last autumn when they'd allowed the infantry to educate

themselves at Loos, regardless of expense. "They've got to learn their job as they go along, like the rest of us," he added sagely. Five sausage balloons were visible beyond the sky-line, peacefully tethered to their mother earth. It was our duty to desire their destruction, and to believe that Corps Intelligence had the matter well in hand. What we did up in the Front Line I don't remember; but while we were remounting our horses at 71. North two privates were engaged in a good-humoured scuffle; one had the other's head under his arm. Why should I remember that and forget so much else?

*   *   *

Wednesday morning was miserably wet. Junior officers, being at a loss to know where to put themselves, were continually meeting one another along the muddy street, and gathering in groups to exchange cheerful remarks; there was little else to be done, and solitude produced the sinking sensation appropriate to the circumstances. The men were in their billets, and they too were keeping their spirits up as vocally as they could. At noon Barton came back from the Colonel's final conference of company commanders. A couple of hours later the anti-climax arrived. We were told that all arrangements for the show were in temporary abeyance. A popular song, *All dressed up and nowhere to go*, provided the obvious comment, and our confidence in Operation Orders oozed away. Was it the wet weather, we wondered, or had the artillery preparation been inadequate? Uncertainty ended with an inanimate message; we were to go up to the line that evening. The attack was postponed forty-eight hours. No one knew why.

At five o'clock C Company fell in, about eighty strong. The men were without packs; they carried extra ammunition, two Mills' bombs, two smoke helmets, and a waterproof sheet with a jersey rolled inside; their emergency rations consisted of two tins of bully beef, eight hard biscuits, and canteen packed with grocery ration. In spite of the anti-climax (which had made us feel that perhaps this was only going to be a second edition of the Battle of Loos)

my personal impression was that we were setting out for
the other end of nowhere. I had slipped a book into my
haversack and it was a comfort to be carrying it, for
Thomas Hardy's England was between its covers. But if
any familiar quotation was in my mind during the bustle
of departure, it may well have been "we brought nothing
into this world, and it is certain we can carry nothing out
of it". We had trudged that way up to the Citadel and 71.
North many times before; but never in such a blood-red
light as now, when we halted with the sunset behind us and
the whole sky mountainous with the magnificence of retreating rainclouds. Tours of trenches had been routine,
with an ordinary chance of casualties. But this time we
seemed to have left Morlancourt behind us for ever, and
even a single company of Flintshire Fusiliers (with a ten
minute interval between it and B and D Companies) was
justified in feeling that the eyes of Europe were upon it. As
for myself, I felt nothing worth recording—merely a sense
of being irrevocably involved in something bigger than had
ever happened before. And the symbolism of the sunset
was wasted on the rank and file, who were concerned with
the not infrequent badness of their boots, the discomfort
caused by perspiration, and the toils and troubles of keeping pace with what was required of them till further notice.
By nine o'clock we had relieved the Border Regiment. The
mud was bad, but the sky was clear. The bombardment
went on steadily, with periods of intensity; but that infernal shindy was taken for granted and was an aid to optimism. I felt rather lonely without Durley, who had been left
behind with the dozen officers who were in reserve.

New Trench, which we took over, had been a good deal
knocked about, but we passed an unharassed night. We
were opposite Sunken Road Trench, which was 300 yards
away up a slope. Gaps had been cut in our wire for the
attacking battalion to pass through. Early on the next
afternoon Kinjack came up to inspect the gaps. With the
assistance of his big periscope he soon discovered that the
wire wasn't properly cut. It must be done that night, he
said. Barton brought me the news. I was huddled up in a

little dog-kennel of a dug-out, reading *Tess of the D'Urber-villes* and trying to forget about the shells which were hur-rying and hurrooshing overhead. I was meditating about England, visualizing a grey day down in Sussex; dark green woodlands with pigeons circling above the tree-tops; dogs barking, cocks crowing, and all the casual tappings and twinklings of the countryside. I thought of the hunts-man walking out in his long white coat with the hounds; of Parson Colwood pulling up weeds in his garden till tea-time; of Captain Huxtable helping his men get in the last load of hay while a shower of rain moved along the blurred Weald below his meadows. It was for all that, I supposed, that I was in the front-line with soaked feet, trench mouth, and feeling short of sleep, for the previous night had been vigilant though uneventful. Barton's head and shoulders butting past the gas-blanket in the dug-out doorway wrecked my reverie; he wanted me to come out and have a squint at the uncut wire, which was no day dream since it was going to affect the fortunes of a still undiminished New Army Battalion. Putting *Tess* in my pocket, I followed him to the fire-trench, which was cumbered with gas-cylinders and boxes of smoke-bombs. A smoke-cloud was to be let off later in the afternoon, for no special reason (except, perhaps, to make us cough and wipe our eyes, since what wind there was blew the smoke along our trench). Shells were banging away on the rising ground behind Fricourt and the low ridge of Contalmaison. A young yellow-hammer was fluttering about in the trench, and I wondered how it had got there: it seemed out of place, perching on a body which lay trussed in a water-proof sheet. As for the gaps in the wire, they looked too bad for words and only one night remained for widening them.

When I was back in the dug-out I found myself fingering with pardonable pride my two pairs of wire-cutters from the Army and Navy Stores. It is possible that I over-esti-mated their usefulness, but their presence did seem provi-dential. Any fool could foresee what happened when troops got bunched up as they left their trench for a daylight attack; and I knew that, in spite of obstinate indentations to the source of supplies, we hadn't got a decent pair of wire cutters in the Battalion.

The big-bugs back at Brigade and Divisional H.Q. were studying trench-maps with corrugated brows, for the "greatest battle in history" was timed to explode on Saturday morning. They were too busy to concern themselves with the ant-like activities of individual platoon commanders, and if they sent a sympathetic Staff Captain up to have a look round he couldn't produce wire-cutters like a conjurer. But the fact remained that insistence on small (and often irrelevant) details was a proverbial characteristic of Staff organization, and on the eve of battle poor old Barton would probably be filling in a "return" stating how many men in his company had got varicose veins or married their deceased wife's sister. In the meantime my casual purchase at "the Stores" had, perhaps, lessened the likelihood of the Manchesters getting bunched up and mown down by machine-guns when they went over the top to attack Sunken Road Trench. And what would the Manchesters say about the Flintshire Fusiliers if the wire wasn't properly cut? So it seemed to me that our prestige as a Regular Battalion had been entrusted to my care on a front of several hundred yards.

Anyhow, I was ready with my party as soon as it began to be dark. There were only eight of them (mostly from the other companies) and we were unable to do anything before midnight owing to rather lively shelling. I remember waiting there in the gloom and watching an unearthly little conflagration caused by some phosphorus bombs up the hill on our right. When we did get started I soon discovered that cutting tangles of barbed wire in the dark in a desperate hurry is a job that needs ingenuity, even when your wire-cutters have rubber-covered handles and are fresh from the Army and Navy Stores. More than once we were driven in by shells which landed in front of our trench (some of them were our own dropping short); two men were wounded and some of the others were reluctant to resume work. In the first greying of dawn only three of us were still at it. Kendle (a nineteen year old lance-corporal

from my platoon) and Worgan (one of the tough characters of our company) were slicing away for all they were
worth; but as the light increased I began to realize the un-
impressive effect of the snippings and snatchings which had
made such a mess of our leather gloves. We had been working three and a half hours but the hedge hadn't suffered
much damage, it seemed. Kendle disappeared into the
trench and sauntered back to me, puffing a surreptitious
Woodbine. I was making a last onslaught on a clawing
thicket which couldn't have been more hostile if it had
been put there by the Germans. "We can't do any more in
this daylight," said Kendle. I straightened my stiff and
weary back and looked at him. His jaunty fag-smoking
demeanour and freckled boyish face seemed to defy the
darkness we had emerged from. That moment has impressed itself strongly on my memory; young Kendle was
remarkable for his cheerfulness and courage, and his cheeky
jokes. Many a company had its Kendle, until the war broke
his spirit. . . . The large solicitous countenance of old man
Barton now appeared above the parapet; with almost aunt-
like anxiety he urged us to come in before we got sniped.
But there had been no sniping that night, and the machine-
gun at Wing Corner had been silent. Wing Corner was at
the edge of the skeleton village of Fricourt, whose ruinous
church tower was now distinctly visible against the dark
green wood. The Germans, coming up from their foundering dug-outs, would soon be staring grimly across at us
while they waited for the relentless bombardment to begin
again. As we got down into the trench young Kendle remarked that my new wire-cutters were a fair treat.

*   *   *

Next day, in warm and breezy weather, we moved to
our battle-assembly position. For C Company "battle-
assembly position" meant being broken up into ammunition carrying parties, while Barton, Jenkins, and myself
occupied an inglorious dug-out in the support line. The
Manchesters were due to relieve us at 9 a.m., but there was
still no sign of them at 10.30, so Barton, who was in a free

and easy mood, (caused by our immunity from to-morrow's attack) led the company away and left New Trench to look after itself. I had made up my mind to have another cut at the wire, which I now regarded with personal enmity, enjoying at the same time a self-admiring belief that much depended on my efforts. Worgan stayed behind with me. Kendle was unwilling to be left out of the adventure, but two of us would be less conspicuous than three, and my feeling for Kendle was somewhat protective. It was queer to be in an empty front-line trench on a fine morning, with everything quite peaceful after a violent early bombardment. Queerer still to be creeping about in the long grass (which might well have been longer, I thought) and shearing savagely at the tangles which had bewildered us in the dark but were now at our mercy. As Worgan said, we were giving it a proper hair-cut this journey.

Lying on my stomach I glanced now and again at the hostile slope which overlooked us, wondering whether anyone would take a pot-shot at us, or speculating on a possible visitation of machine-gun bullets from Wing Corner. Barton's ignorance of what we were doing made it seem like an escapade, and the excitement was by no means disagreeable. It was rather like going out to weed a neglected garden after being warned that there might be a tiger among the gooseberry bushes. I should have been astonished if someone could have told me that I was an interesting example of human egotism. Yet such was the truth. I was cutting the wire by daylight because commonsense warned me that the lives of several hundred soldiers might depend on it being done properly. I was excited and pleased with myself while I was doing it. And I had entirely forgotten that to-morrow six Army Corps would attack, and whatever else happened, a tragic slaughter was inevitable. But if I had been intelligent enough to realize all that, my talents would have been serving in some more exalted place, probably Corps Intelligence Headquarters. Anyhow, at the end of an hour and a half the gaps were real good ones, and Barton's red face and glittering pince-nez were bobbing up and down beyond the parapet with *sotto-*

voce incitements to prudence. Soon afterwards we dropped into the trench and the Manchesters began to arrive. It had been great fun, I said, flourishing my wire-cutters.

*   *   *

Early in the afternoon the Doctor bustled up from Battalion Headquarters to tell me that my M.C. had come through. This gratifying little event increased my blindness to the blood-stained future. Homeliness and humanity beamed in Barton's congratulations; and the little doctor, who would soon be dressing the wounds of moaning men, unpicked his own faded medal-ribbon, produced a needle and thread, and sewed the white and purple portent on to my tunic. For the rest of the day and, indeed, for the remainder of my military career, the left side of my chest was more often in my mind than the right—a habit which was common to a multitude of wearers of Military Cross ribbons. Books about war psychology ought to contain a chapter on "medal-reflexes" and "decoration complexes". Much might be written, even here, about medals and their stimulating effect on those who really risked their lives for them. But the safest thing to be said is that nobody knew how much a decoration was worth except the man who received it. Outwardly the distribution of them became more and more fortuitous and debased as the War went on; and no one knew it better than the infantry, who rightly insisted that medal-ribbons earned at the Base ought to be a different colour.

But I must return to June 30th, which ended with a sullen bombardment from the British guns and a congestion of troops in the support-trench outside our dug-out. They had lost their way, and I remember how the exhausted men propped themselves against the sides of the trench while their exasperated Adjutant and a confused civilian Colonel grumbled to Barton about the ambiguity of their operation orders. They were to attack on our left, and they vanished in that direction, leaving me with my Military Cross and a foreboding that disaster awaited them. Since they came within the limited zone of my observations I can

record the fact that they left their trench early next morning at a wrong zero hour and got badly cut up by the artillery support which ought to have made things easy for them.

II

On July the first the weather, after an early morning mist,
was of the kind commonly called heavenly. Down in our
frowsty cellar we breakfasted at six, unwashed and apprehensive. Our table, appropriately enough, was an empty
ammunition box. At six-forty-five the final bombardment
began, and there was nothing for us to do except sit round
our candle until the tornado ended. For more than forty
minutes the air vibrated and the earth rocked and shud-
dered. Through the sustained uproar the tap and rattle of
machine-guns could be identified; but except for the whistle
of bullets no retaliation came our way until a few 5.9 shells
shook the roof of our dug-out. Barton and I sat speechless,
deafened and stupefied by the seismic state of affairs, and
when he lit a cigarette the match flame staggered crazily.
Afterwards I asked him what he had been thinking about.
His reply was "Carpet slippers and kettle-holders". My
own mind had been working in much the same style, for
during that cannonading cataclysm the following refrain
was running in my head:

> *They come as a boon and a blessing to men,*
> *The Something, the Owl, and the Waverley Pen.*

For the life of me I couldn't remember what the first one
was called. Was it the Shakespeare? Was it the Dickens?
Anyhow it was an advertisement which I'd often seen in
smoky railway stations. Then the bombardment lifted and
lessened, our vertigo abated, and we looked at one another
in dazed relief. Two Brigades of our Division were now
going over the top on our right. Our Brigade was to attack
"when the main assault had reached its final objective".
In our fortunate role of privileged spectators Barton and I
went up the stairs to see what we could from Kingston

Road Trench. We left Jenkins crouching in a corner, where he remained most of the day. His haggard blinking face haunts my memory. He was an example of the paralysing effect which such an experience could produce on a nervous system sensitive to noise, for he was a good officer both before and afterwards. I felt no sympathy for him at the time, but I do now. From the support-trench, which Barton called "our opera box", I observed as much of the battle as the formation of the country allowed, the rising ground on the right making it impossible to see anything of the attack towards Mametz. A small shiny black notebook contains my pencilled particulars, and nothing will be gained by embroidering them with afterthoughts. I cannot turn my field-glasses on to the past.

*   *   *

7.45. The barrage is now working to the right of Fricourt and beyond. I can see the 21st Division advancing about three-quarters of a mile away on the left and a few Germans coming to meet them, apparently surrendering. Our men in small parties (not extended in line) go steadily on to the German front-line. Brilliant sunshine and a haze of smoke drifting along the landscape. Some Yorkshires a little way below on the left, watching the show and cheering as if at a football match. The noise almost as bad as ever.

9.30. Came back to the dug-out and had a shave. 21st Division still going across the open, apparently without casualties. The sunlight flashes on bayonets as the tiny figures move quietly forward and disappear beyond mounds of trench débris. A few runners come back and ammunition parties go across. Trench-mortars are knocking hell out of Sunken Road Trench and the ground where the Manchesters will attack soon. Noise not so bad now and very little retaliation.

9.50. Fricourt half-hidden by clouds of drifting smoke, blue, pinkish and grey. Shrapnel bursting in small bluish-white puffs with tiny flashes. The birds seem bewildered; a lark begins to go up and then flies feebly along, thinking better of it. Others flutter above the trench with querulous

cries, weak on the wing. I can see seven of our balloons, on
the right. On the left our men still filing across in twenties
and thirties. Another huge explosion in Fricourt and a
cloud of brown-pink smoke. Some bursts are yellowish.

10.5. I can see the Manchesters down in New Trench,
getting ready to go over. Figures filing down the trench.
Two of them have gone out to look at our wire gaps! Have
just eaten my last orange. . . . I am staring at a sunlit picture of Hell, and still the breeze shakes the yellow weeds,
and the poppies glow under Crawley Ridge where some
shells fell a few minutes ago. Manchesters are sending forward some scouts. A bayonet glitters. A runner comes back
across the open to their Battalion Headquarters close here
on the right. 21st Division still trotting along the skyline
toward La Boisselle. Barrage going strong to the right of
Contalmaison Ridge. Heavy shelling toward Mametz.

12.15. Quieter the last two hours. Manchesters still waiting. Germans putting over a few shrapnel shells. Silly if I
got hit! Weather cloudless and hot. A lark singing confidently overhead.

1.30. Manchesters attack at 2.30. Mametz and Montauban reported taken. Mametz consolidated.

2.30. Manchesters left New Trench and apparently took
Sunken Road Trench, bearing rather to the right. Could
see about 400. Many walked casually across with sloped
arms. There were about forty casualties on the left (from
machine-gun in Fricourt). Through my glasses I could see
one man moving his left arm up and down as he lay on his
side; his face was a crimson patch. Others lay still in the
sunlight while the swarm of figures disappeared over the
hill. Fricourt was a cloud of pinkish smoke. Lively machine-
gun fire on the far side of the hill. At 2.50 no one to be seen
in no-man's-land except the casualties (about half-way
across). Our dug-out shelled again since 2.30.

5.0. I saw about thirty of our A Company crawl across
to Sunken Road from New Trench. Germans put a few big
shells on the Cemetery and traversed Kingston Road with
machine-gun. Manchester wounded still out there. Remainder of A Company went across—about 100 altogether.

Manchesters reported held up in Bois Français Support. Their Colonel went across and was killed.

8.0. Staff Captain of our Brigade has been along. Told Barton that Seventh Division has reached its objectives with some difficulty, except on this Brigade front. Manchesters are in trouble, and Fricourt attack has failed. Several hundred prisoners brought in on our sector.

9.30. Our A Company holds Rectangle and Sunken Road. Jenkins gone off in charge of a carrying-party. Seemed all right again. C Company now reduced to six runners, two stretcher-bearers, Company Sergeant-Major, signallers, and Barton's servant. Flook away on carrying-party. Sky cloudy westward. Red sunset. Heavy gun-fire on the left.

2.30. (Next afternoon.) Adjutant has just been up here, excited, optimistic, and unshaven. He went across last night to ginger up A Company who did very well, thanks to the bombers. About 40 casualties; only 4 killed. Fricourt and Rose Trench occupied this morning without resistance. I am now lying out in front of our trench in the long grass, basking in sunshine where yesterday there were bullets. Our new front-line on the hill is being shelled. Fricourt is full of troops wandering about in search of souvenirs. The village was a ruin and is now a dust heap. A gunner (Forward Observation Officer) has just been along here with a German helmet in his hand. Said Fricourt is full of dead; he saw one officer lying across a smashed machine-gun with his head bashed in—"a fine looking chap," he said, with some emotion, which rather surprised me.

8.15. Queer feeling, seeing people moving about freely between here and Fricourt. Dumps being made. Shacks and shelters being put up under skeleton trees and all sorts of transport arriving at Cemetery Cross Roads. We stay here till to-morrow morning. Feel a bit of a fraud.

III

Early next morning we took leave of our subterranean sanctuary in Kingston Road, joined the Battalion at 71. North, and marched a couple of miles to a concentration point between Mametz and Carnoy. There, in a wide hollow, the four units of our Brigade piled arms, lay down on the grass, and took their boots off. Most of them had been without sleep for two nights and the immediate forecast was "murky". But every man had a waterproof sheet to sit on, helmets were exchanged for woollen caps, unshaven faces felt gratitude for generous sunshine, and bare feet stretched contented toes. Our Division having done well, there was a confident feeling in the air. But we had heard of partial and complete failures in other parts of the line, and the name of Gommecourt had already reached us with ugly implications. It was obvious that some of us would soon be lacing up our boots for the last time, and the current rumour, "They say we've got to attack some Wood or other", could not fail to cause an uneasy visceral sensation. However, one felt that big things were happening, and my Military Cross was a comfort to me. It was a definite personal possession to be lived up to, I thought. I watched the men dozing in odd ungainly attitudes, half listened to their talk about the souvenirs they'd picked up in the German trenches, or stared at some captured guns being brought down the lane which led to Mametz.

A few of the men were wandering about, and my meditations were disturbed by Kinjack, who had given orders that everyone was to rest all day. "Tell those men to lie down," he shouted, adding—as he returned to his bivouac on the slope —"The bastards'll be glad to before they're much older." It was believed that his brusque manners had prevented him getting promotion, but everyone knew that it would be a bad day for the Battalion when Kinjack got his Brigade.

Evening fell calm and overcast, with a blurred orange sunset. Sitting among rank grass and thistles I stared pensively down at the four battalions grouped in the hollow. Thin smoke rose from the little bivouac fires which had been used for tea making; among the gruff murmuring which came up with the smoke, the nasal chant of a mouth organ did its best to "keep the home fires burning". In front of the hollow the open ground sloped treeless to Bazentin Ridge, dull green and striped with seams of trenches cut in the chalky soil. Field-guns were firing on the right and some aeroplanes hummed overhead. Beyond that hill our future awaited us. There would be no turning back from it. . . . I would have liked Flook to bring me an orange, but he was away with Jenkins and the carrying-party, and oranges were almost as remote as the sunset. Poor Flook will be awfully worried about not being with his officer bloke, I thought, imagining his stolid red face puffing along under a box of ammunition. . . . I went down the hill just in time to hear that we'd got orders to go up and dig a trench somewhere in front of Mametz.

For a few minutes the hollow was full of the subdued hubbub and commotion of troops getting into their equipment. Two battalions had been called out; the Royal Irish moved off ahead of us. As we went up the lane toward Mametz I felt that I was leaving all my previous war experience behind me. For the first time I was among the débris of an attack. After going a very short distance we made the first of many halts, and I saw, arranged by the roadside, about fifty of the British dead. Many of them were Gordon Highlanders. There were Devons and South Staffordshires among them, but they were beyond regimental rivalry now—their fingers mingled in blood-stained bunches, as though acknowledging the companionship of death. There was much battle gear lying about, and some dead horses. There were rags and shreds of clothing, boots riddled and torn, and when we came to the old German front-line, a sour pervasive stench which differed from anything my nostrils had known before. Meanwhile we made our continually retarded progress up the hill, and I scrutinized these battle effects with partially complacent curiosity. I wanted to be able to say that I had seen "the horrors of war"; and here they were, nearly three days old.

No one in the glumly halted column knew what was delaying us. After four hours we had only progressed 1,500 yards and were among some ruined buildings on the outskirts of the village. I have dim remembrance of the strangeness of the place and our uneasy dawdling in its midnight desolation. Kinjack was somewhere ahead of us with a guide. The guide, having presumably lost his way, was having a much hotter time than we were. So far we had done nothing except file past a tool-dump, where the men had collected picks, shovels, coils of wire, and corkscrew stakes. At 2 a.m. we really began to move, passing through Mametz and along a communication trench. There were some badly mangled bodies about. Although I'd been with the Battalion nearly eight months, these were the first newly dead Germans I had seen. It gave me a bit of a shock when I saw, in the glimmer of daybreak, a dumpy, baggy-trousered man lying half sideways with one elbow up as if defending his lolling head; the face was grey and waxen, with a stiff little moustache; he looked like a ghastly doll, grotesque and undignified. Beside him was a scorched and mutilated figure whose contorted attitude revealed bristly cheeks, a grinning blood-smeared mouth and clenched teeth. These dead were unlike our own; perhaps it was the strange uniform, perhaps their look of butchered hostility. Anyhow they were one with the little trench direction boards whose unfamiliar lettering seemed to epitomize that queer feeling I used to have when I stared across no-man's-land, ignorant of the humanity which was on the other side.

Leaving the trench we filed across the open hillside with Mametz Wood looming on the opposite slope. It was a dense wood of old trees and undergrowth. The Staff of our Division had assumed that the near side was now unoccupied. But as soon as we had halted in a sunken road an uproar broke out at the edge of the wood, which demonstrated with machine-guns and bombs that the Staff had guessed wrong.

Kinjack promptly ordered A Company forward to get in touch with the Royal Irish, whose covering parties were having a bombing fight in the Wood. Our men were fired on as they went along the road and forced to take cover in a quarry. I remember feeling nervous and incompetent while I wondered what on earth I should do if called on to lead a party out "into the blue". But the clouds were now reddening, and we were fed up with the whole performance. Messages went back and our guns chucked a lot of shrapnel which burst over the near side of the Wood and enabled the Irish to withdraw. We then, as Kinjack described it afterwards, "did a guy"; but it was a slow one for we weren't back at our camping ground until 8.30 a.m. The expedition had lasted nearly eleven hours and we had walked less than three miles, which was about all we could congratulate ourselves on. The Royal Irish had had sixty casualties; we had one killed and four wounded. From a military point of view the operations had enabled the Staff to discover that Mametz Wood was still full of Germans, so that it was impossible to dig a trench on the bluff within fifty yards of it, as had been suggested. It was obvious now that a few strong patrols could have clarified the situation more economically than 1,000 men with picks and shovels. The necessary information had been obtained, however, and the Staff could hardly be expected to go up and investigate such enigmas for themselves. But this sort of warfare was a new experience for all of us, and the difficulties of extempore organization must have been considerable.

*   *   *

During the morning we were a silent battalion, except for snoring. Some eight-inch guns were firing about 200 yards from the hollow, but our slumbers were inured to noises which would have kept us wide awake in civilian life. We were lucky to be dry, for the sky was overcast. At one o'clock our old enemy the rain arrived in full force. Four hours' deluge left the troops drenched and disconsolate, and then Dottrell made one of his providential appearances with the rations. Dixies of hot tea, and the rum issue, made all the difference to our outlook. It seemed to me that the Quartermaster symbolized that region of temporary security which awaited us when our present adversities were ended. He had a cheery word for everyone, and his jocularity was judicious. What were the jokes he made, I wonder? Their helpfulness must be taken for granted. I can only remember his chaffing an officer named Woolman, whose dumpy figure had bulged abnormally since we came up to the battle area. Woolman's young lady in England had sent him a bullet-proof waistcoat; so far it had only caused its wearer to perspire profusely; and although reputed to be extremely vulnerable, it had inspired a humorist in his company to refer to him as "Asbestos Bill".

Time seems to have obliterated the laughter of the war. I cannot hear it in my head. How strange such laughter would sound, could I but recover it as it was on such an evening as I am describing, when we all knew that we'd got to do an attack that night; for short-sighted Barton and the other company commanders had just returned from a reconnaissance of the ground which had left them little wiser than when they started. In the meantime we'd got some rum inside us and could find something to laugh about. Our laughter leapt up, like the flames of camp fires in the dusk, soon to be stamped out, or extinguished by our impartial opponent, the rain. The consoling apparition of Dottrell departed, and I don't suppose he did much laughing once he was alone with his homeward rattling limbers.

Zero hour was forty-five minutes after midnight. Two companies were to attack on a 600-yard front and the Royal Irish were to do the same on our right. Barton's company was to be in reserve; owing to the absence of the carrying-party it could only muster about thirty men.

At nine o'clock we started up the sunken road to Mametz. As a result of the rain, yesterday's dry going had been trodden to a quagmire. Progress was slow owing to the congestion of troops in front. We had only a couple of thousand yards to go, but at one time it seemed unlikely that the assaulting companies would be in position by zero hour. It was pitch dark as we struggled through the mud, and we got there with fifteen minutes to spare, having taken three and a half hours to go a mile and a quarter.

Barton arranged his men along a shallow support trench on the edge of Bottom Wood, which was a copse just to the left of the ground we'd visited the night before. Almost at once the short preliminary bombardment began and the darkness became diabolic with the din and flash of the old old story. Not for the first time—I wondered whether shells ever collided in the air. Silence and suspense came after. Barton and I talked in undertones; he thought I'd better borrow his electric torch and find out the nearest way to Battalion Headquarters.

Everyone was anonymous in the dark, but "It's me, Kendle, sir," from a looming figure beside me implied an intention to share my explorations. We groped our way into the wood, and very soon I muttered that unless we were careful we'd get lost, which was true enough, for my sense of direction had already become uncertain. While we hesitated, some shells exploded all round us in the undergrowth with an effect of crashing stupidity. But we laughed, encouraging each other with mutual bravado, until we found a path. Along this path came someone in a hurry. He bumped into me and I flashed the torch on his face. He was an officer who had joined us the week before. He had now lost all control of himself and I gathered from his incoherent utterances that he was on his way to Headquarters to tell Kinjack that his Company hadn't moved yet because they didn't know which way to go to find the Germans. This wasn't surprising; but I felt alarmed about his reception at Headquarters, for Kinjack had already got an idea that this poor devil was "cold-footed". So, with an assumption of ferocity, I pulled out my automatic pistol, gripped him by the shoulder, and told him that if he didn't go straight back to "Asbestos Bill" I'd shoot him, adding that Kinjack would certainly shoot him if he rolled up at Headquarters with such a story and in such a state of "wind-up". This sobered him and he took my advice, though I doubt whether he did any damage to the Germans. (Ten days later he was killed in what I can only call a *bona fide* manner.) So far, I thought, my contribution to this attack is a queer one; I have saved one of our officers from being court-martialled for cowardice. I then remarked to Kendle that this seemed to be the shortest way to Battalion Headquarters and we found our own way back to Barton without further incident. I told Barton that "Asbestos Bill" seemed to be marking time, in spite of his bullet-proof waistcoat.

The men were sitting on the rough-hewn fire-step, and soon we were all dozing. Barton's bulky figure nodded beside me, and Kendle fell fast asleep with his head against my shoulder. We remained like this until my luminous watch indicated twenty past two. Then a runner arrived with a verbal message. "C Company bombers to go up at once." With a dozen men behind me I followed him through Bottom Wood. Darkness was giving way to unrevealing twilight as we emerged from the trees and went up a shell-pitted slope. It was about 500 yards across the open to the newly captured Quadrangle Trench. Just before we got there a second runner overtook us to say that my bombers were to go back again. I sent them back. I cannot say why I went on myself; but I did, and Kendle stayed with me.

*　　　　*　　　　*

There wasn't much wire in front of Quadrangle Trench. I entered it at a strong point on the extreme left and found three officers sitting on the fire-step with hunched shoulders and glum unenterprising faces. Two others had gone away wounded. I was told that Edmunds, the Battalion Observation Officer had gone down to explain the situation to Kinjack; we were in touch with the Northumberland Fusiliers on our left. Nevertheless I felt that there must be something to be done. Exploring to the right I found young Fernby, whose demeanour was a contrast to the apathetic trio in the sand-bagged strong-point. Fernby had only been out from England a few weeks but he appeared quite at home in his new surroundings. His face showed that he was exulting in the fact that he didn't feel afraid. He told me that no one knew what had happened on our right; the Royal Irish were believed to have failed. We went along the trench which was less than waist deep. The Germans had evidently been digging when we attacked, and had left their packs and other equipment ranged along the reverse edge of the trench. I stared about me; the smoke-drifted twilight was alive with intense movement, and there was a wild strangeness in the scene which somehow excited me. Our men seemed a bit out of hand and I couldn't see any of the responsible N.C.O.s; some of the troops were firing excitedly at the Wood; others were rummaging in the German packs. Fernby said that we were being sniped from the trees on both sides. Mametz Wood was a menacing wall of gloom, and now an outburst of rapid thudding explosions began from that direction. There was a sap from the Quadrangle to the Wood, and along this the Germans were bombing. In all this confusion I formed the obvious notion that we ought to be deepening the trench. Daylight would be on us at once, and we were along a slope exposed to enfilade fire from the Wood. I told Fernby to make the men dig for all they were worth, and went to the right with Kendle. The Germans had left a lot of shovels, but we were making no use of them. Two tough-looking privates were disputing the ownership of a pair of field-glasses, so I pulled out my pistol and urged them, with ferocious objurations, to chuck all that fooling and dig. I seemed to be getting pretty handy with my pistol, I thought, for the conditions in Quadrangle Trench were giving me a sort of angry impetus. In some places it was only a foot deep, and already men were lying wounded and killed by sniping. There were high-booted German bodies, too, and in the blear beginning of daylight they seemed as much the victims of a catastrophe as the men who had attacked them. As I stepped over one of the Germans an impulse made me lift him up from the miserable ditch. Propped against the bank, his blond face was undisfigured, except by the mud which I wiped from his eyes and mouth with my coat sleeve. He'd evidently been killed while digging, for his tunic was knotted loosely about his shoulders. He didn't look to be more than eighteen. Hoisting him a little higher, I thought what a gentle face he had, and remembered that this was the first time I'd ever touched one of our enemies with my hands. Perhaps I had some dim sense of the futility which had put an end to this good-looking youth. Anyhow I hadn't expected the Battle of the Somme to be quite like this. . . . Kendle, who had been trying to do something for a badly wounded man, now rejoined me, and we continued, mostly on all fours, along the dwindling trench. We passed no one until we came to a bombing post—three serious-minded men who said that no one had been further than that yet. Being in an exploring frame of mind, I took a bag of bombs and crawled another sixty or seventy yards with Kendle close behind me. The trench became a shallow groove and ended where the ground overlooked a little valley along which there was a light railway line. We stared across at the Wood. From the other side of the valley came an occasional rifle-shot, and a helmet bobbed up for a moment. Kendle remarked that from that point anyone could see into the whole of our trench on the slope behind us. I said we must have our strong-post here and told him to go back for the bombers and a Lewis gun. I felt adventurous and it seemed as if Kendle and I were having great fun together. Kendle thought so too. The helmet bobbed up again. "I'll just have a shot at him," he said, wriggling away from the crumbling bank which gave us cover. At this moment Fernby appeared with two men and a Lewis gun. Kendle was half kneeling against some broken ground; I remember seeing him push his tin hat back from his forehead and then raise himself a few inches to take aim. After firing once he looked at us with a lively smile; a second later he fell sideways. A blotchy mark showed where the bullet had hit him just above the eyes.

The circumstances being what they were, I had no justification for feeling either shocked or astonished by the sudden extinction of Lance-Corporal Kendle. But after blank awareness that he was killed, all feelings tightened and contracted to a single intention—to "settle that sniper" on the other side of the valley. If I had stopped to think, I shouldn't have gone at all. As it was, I discarded my tin hat and equipment, slung a bag of bombs across my shoulder, abruptly informed Fernby that I was going to find out who *was* there, and set off at a downhill double. While I was running I pulled the safety-pin out of a Mills' bomb; my right hand being loaded, I did the same for my left. I mention this because I was obliged to extract the second

safety-pin with my teeth, and the grating sensation reminded me that I was half way across and not so reckless
as I had been when I started. I was even a little out of
breath as I trotted up the opposite slope. Just before I
arrived at the top I slowed up and threw my two bombs.
Then I rushed at the bank, vaguely expecting some sort of
scuffle with my imagined enemy. I had lost my temper with
the man who had shot Kendle; quite unexpectedly, I
found myself looking down into a well-conducted trench
with a great many Germans in it. Fortunately for me, they
were already retreating. It had not occurred to them that
they were being attacked by a single fool; and Fernby,
with presence of mind which probably saved me, had
covered my advance by traversing the top of the trench
with his Lewis gun. I slung a few more bombs, but they fell
short of the clumsy field-grey figures, some of whom half
turned to fire their rifles over the left shoulder as they ran
across the open toward the wood, while a crowd of jostling
helmets vanished along the trench. Idiotically elated, I
stood there with my finger in my right ear and emitted a
series of "view-holloas" (a gesture which ought to win the
approval of people who still regard war as a form of outdoor sport). Having thus failed to commit suicide, I proceeded to occupy the trench—that is to say, I sat down on
the fire-step, very much out of breath, and hoped to God
the Germans wouldn't come back again.

The trench was deep and roomy, with a fine view of our
men in the Quadrangle, but I had no idea what to do now
I had got possession of it. The word "consolidation" passed
through my mind; but I couldn't consolidate by myself.
Naturally, I didn't under-estimate the magnitude of my
achievement in capturing the trench on which the Royal
Irish had made a frontal attack in the dark. Nevertheless,
although still unable to see that my success was only a
lucky accident, I felt a bit queer in my solitude, so I reinforced my courage by counting the sets of equipment
which had been left behind. There were between forty and
fifty packs, tidily arranged in a row—a fact which I often
mentioned (quite casually) when describing my exploit

afterwards. There was the doorway of a dug-out, but I only peered in at it, feeling safer above ground. Then, with apprehensive caution, I explored about half way to the Wood without finding any dead bodies. Apparently no one was any the worse for my little bombing demonstration. Perhaps I was disappointed by this, though the discovery of a dead or wounded enemy might have caused a revival of humane emotion. Returning to the sniping post at the end of the trench I meditated for a few minutes, somewhat like a boy who has caught a fish too big to carry home (if such an improbable event has ever happened). Finally I took a deep breath and ran headlong back by the way I'd come.

Little Fernby's anxious face awaited me, and I flopped down beside him with an outburst of hysterical laughter. When he'd heard my story he asked whether we oughtn't to send a party across to occupy the trench, but I said that the Germans would be bound to come back quite soon. Moreover my rapid return had attracted the attention of a machine-gun which was now firing angrily along the valley from a position in front of the Wood. In my excitement I had forgotten about Kendle. The sight of his body gave me a bit of a shock. His face had gone a bluish colour; I told one of the bombers to cover it with something. Then I put on my web-equipment and its attachments, took a pull at my water-bottle, for my mouth had become suddenly intolerably dry, and set off on my return journey, leaving Fernby to look after the bombing post. It was now six o'clock in the morning, and a weary business it is, to be remembering and writing it down. There was nothing likeable about the Quadrangle, though it was comfortable, from what I have heard, compared with the hell which it became a few days afterwards. Alternately crouching and crawling, I worked my way back. I passed the young German whose body I had rescued from disfigurement a couple of hours before. He was down in the mud again and someone had trodden on his face. It disheartened me to see him, though his body had now lost all touch with life and was part of the wastage of the war. He and Kendle had cancelled one another out in the process called "attrition of man-power". Further along I found one of our men dying slowly with a hole in his forehead. His eyes were open and he breathed with a horrible snoring sound. Close by him knelt two of his former mates; one of them was hacking at the ground with an entrenching tool while the other scooped the earth out of the trench with his hands. They weren't worrying about souvenirs now.

Disregarding a written order from Barton, telling me to return, I remained up in Quadrangle Trench all the morning. The enemy made a few attempts to bomb their way up the sap from the Wood and in that restricted area I continued to expend energy which was a result of strained nerves. I mention this because, as the day went on, I definitely wanted to kill someone at close quarters. If this meant that I was really becoming a good "fighting man", I can only suggest that, as a human being, I was both exhausted and exasperated. My courage was of the cock-fighting kind. Cock-fighting is illegal in England, but in July, 1916 the man who could boast that he'd killed a German in the Battle of the Somme would have been patted on the back by a bishop in a hospital ward.

German stick-bombs were easy to avoid; they took eight seconds to explode, and the throwers didn't hang on to them many seconds after pulling the string. Anyhow, my feverish performances were concluded by a peremptory message from Battalion H.Q. and I went down to Bottom Wood by a half-dug communication trench whose existence I have only this moment remembered (which shows how difficult it is to recover the details of war experience).

It was nearly two o'clock, and the daylight was devoid of mystery when I arrived at Kinjack's headquarters. The circumstances now made it permissible for me to feel tired and hungry, but for the moment I rather expected congratulations. My expectation was an error. Kinjack sat glowering in a surface dug-out in a sand-pit at the edge of Bottom Wood. I went in from the sunlight. The overworked Adjutant eyed me sadly from a corner of an ammunition box table covered with a grey blanket, and the Colonel's face caused me to feel like a newly captured pri-

soner. Angrily he asked why I hadn't come back with my
company bombers in the early morning. I said I'd stayed
up there to see what was happening. Why hadn't I consolidated Wood Trench? Why the hell hadn't I sent back a
message to let him know that it had been occupied? I made
no attempt to answer these conundrums. Obviously I'd
made a mess of the whole affair. The Corps Artillery bombardment had been held up for three hours because Kinjack couldn't report that "my patrol" had returned to
Quadrangle Trench, and altogether he couldn't be blamed
for feeling annoyed with me, especially as he'd been ticked
off over the telephone by the Brigadier (in Morse Code
dots and dashes, I suppose). I looked at him with a sulky
grin, and went along to Barton with a splitting headache
and a notion that I ought to be thankful that I was back
at all.

*   *   *

In the evening we were relieved. The incoming battalion numbered more than double our own strength (we
were less than 400) and they were unseasoned New Army
troops. Our little trench under the trees was inundated by
a jostling company of exclamatory Welshmen. Kinjack
would have called them a panicky rabble. They were mostly undersized men, and as I watched them arriving at the
first stage of their battle experience I had a sense of their
victimization. A little platoon officer was settling his men
down with a valiant show of self-assurance. For the sake of
appearances, orders of some kind had to be given, though
in reality there was nothing to do except sit down and hope
it wouldn't rain. He spoke sharply to some of them, and I
felt that they were like a lot of children. It was going to be
a bad look-out for two such bewildered companies, huddled up in the Quadrangle, which had been over-garrisoned
by our own comparatively small contingent. Visualizing
that forlorn crowd of khaki figures under the twilight of the
trees, I can believe that I saw then, for the first time, how
blindly war destroys its victims. The sun had gone down
on my own reckless brandishings, and I understood the
doomed condition of these half trained civilians who had

been sent up to attack the Wood. As we moved out, Barton exclaimed, "By God, Kangar, I'm sorry for those poor devils!" Dimly he pitied them, as well he might. Two days later the Welsh Division, of which they were a unit, was involved in massacre and confusion. Our own occupation of Quadrangle Trench was only a prelude to that pandemonium which converted the green thickets of Mametz Wood to a desolation of skeleton trees and blackening bodies.

In the meantime we willingly left them to their troubles and marched back twelve miles to peace and safety. Mametz was being heavily shelled when we stumbled wearily through its ruins, but we got off lightly, though the first four miles took us four hours, owing to congestion of transport and artillery on the roads round Fricourt. On the hill above Bécordel we dozed for an hour in long wet grass, with stars overhead and guns booming and flashing in the valleys below. Then, in the first glimmer of a cold misty dawn, we trudged on to Heilly. We were there by eight o'clock, in hot sunshine. Our camp was on a marsh by the river Ancre—not a good camp when it rained (as it did before long) but a much pleasanter place than the Somme battlefield. . . . After three hours' sleep I was roused by Flook. All officers were required to attend the Brigadier's conference. At this function there was no need for me to open my mouth, except for an occasional yawn. Kinjack favoured me with a good-humoured grin. He only made one further comment on my non-consolidation of that fortuitously captured trench. He would probably leave me out of the "next show" as a punishment, he said. Some people asserted that he had no sense of humour, but I venture to disagree with them.

IV

Nobody had any illusions about the duration of our holiday at Heilly. Our Division had been congratulated by the Commander-in-Chief, and our Brigadier had made it clear that further efforts would be required of us in the near future. In the meantime the troops contrived to be cheerful; to be away from the battle and in a good village was all that mattered, for the moment. Our casualties had not been heavy (we had lost about 100 men but only a dozen of them had been killed). There was some grumbling on the second day, which was a wet one and reduced our camp to its natural condition—a swamp; but the Army Commander paid us a brief (and mercifully informal) visit, and this glimpse of his geniality made the men feel that they had done creditably. Nevertheless, as he squelched among the brown tents in his boots and spurs, more than one voice might have been heard muttering, "Why couldn't the old —— have dumped us in a drier spot?" But the Fourth Army figure-head may well have been absent-minded that afternoon, since the Welsh Division had attacked Mametz Wood earlier in the day, and he must already have been digesting the first reports, which reached us in wild rumours next morning.

Basking in the sunshine after breakfast with Barton and Durley, I felt that to-day was all that concerned us. If there had been a disastrous muddle, with troops stampeding under machine-gun fire, it was twelve miles away and no business of ours until we were called upon to carry on the good work. There were no parades to-day, and we were going into Amiens for lunch—Dottrell and the Adjutant with us. Barton, with a brown field-service notebook on his knee, was writing a letter to his wife. "Do you always light your pipe with your left hand, Kangar?" he asked, looking up as he tore another leaf out. I replied that I supposed so, though I'd never noticed it before. Then I rambled on for a bit about how unobservant one could be. I said (knowing that old man Barton liked hearing about such things) "We've got a grandfather clock in the hall at home and for years and years I thought the maker's name was *Thos. Verney, London*. Then one day I decided to give the old brass face a polish up and I found that it was *Thos. Vernon, Ludlow!*" Barton thought this a pleasing coincidence because he lived in Shropshire and had been to Ludlow Races. A square mile of Shropshire, he asserted, was worth the whole of France. Durley (who was reading *Great*

Expectations with a face that expressed release from reality) put in a mild plea for Stoke Newington, which was where he lived; it contained several quaint old corners if you knew where to look for them, and must, he said, have been quite a sleepy sort of place in Dickens's days. Reverting to my original topic, I remarked, "We've got an old barometer, too, but it never works. Ever since I can remember, it's pointed to *Expect Wet from N.E.* Last time I was on leave I noticed that it's not *Expect* but *Except*—though goodness knows what that means!" My companions, who were disinclined to be talkative, assured me that with such a brain I ought to be on the Staff.

Strolling under the aspens that shivered and twinkled by the river, I allowed myself a little day dream, based on the leisurely ticking of the old Ludlow clock. . . . Was it only three weeks ago that I had been standing there at the foot of the staircase, between the barometer and the clock, on just such a fine summer morning as this? Upstairs in the bathroom Aunt Evelyn was putting sweet-peas and roses in water, humming to herself while she arranged them to her liking. Visualizing the bathroom with its copper bath and basin, (which "took such a lot of cleaning") its lead floor, and the blue and white Dutch tiles along the walls, and the elder tree outside the window, I found these familiar objects almost as dear to me as Aunt Evelyn herself, since they were one with her in my mind (though for years she'd been talking about doing away with the copper bath and basin).

Even now, perhaps, she was once again carrying a bowl of roses down to the drawing-room while the clock ticked slow, and the parrot whistled, and the cook chopped something on the kitchen table. There might also be the shortwinded snorting of a traction-engine labouring up the hill outside the house. . . . Meeting a traction-engine had been quite an event in my childhood, when I was out for rides on my first pony. And the thought of the cook suggested the gardener clumping in with a trug of vegetables, and the gardener suggested birds in the strawberry nets, and altogether there was no definite end to that sort of day dream of an England where there was no war on and the village cricket ground was still being mown by a man who didn't know that he would some day join "the Buffs", migrate to Mesopotamia, and march to Bagdad.

*   *   *

Amiens was eleven miles away and the horses none too sound; but Dottrell had arranged for us to motor the last seven of the miles—the former Quartermaster of our battalion (who had been Quartermaster at Fourth Army Headquarters ever since the Fourth Army had existed)— having promised to lend us his car. So there was nothing wrong with the world as the five of us jogged along, and I allowed myself a momentary illusion that we were riding clean away from the War. Looking across a spacious and untroubled landscape chequered with ripening corn and blood-red clover, I wondered how that calm and beneficent light could be spreading as far as the battle zone. But a Staff car overtook us, and as it whirled importantly past in a cloud of dust I caught sight of a handcuffed German prisoner—soon to provide material for an optimistic paragraph in Corps Intelligence Summary, and to add his story to the omniscience of the powers who now issued operation orders with the assertion that we were "pursuing a beaten enemy". Soon we were at Querrieux, a big village cosily over-populated by the Fourth Army Staff. As we passed the General's white château Dottrell speculated ironically on the average income of his personal staff, adding that they must suffer terribly from insomnia with so many guns firing fifteen miles away. Leaving our horses to make the most of a Fourth Army feed, we went indoors to pay our respects to the opulent Quartermaster, who had retired from Battalion duties after the First Battle of Ypres. He assured us that he could easily spare his car for a few hours since he had the use of two; whereupon Dottrell said he'd been wondering how he managed to get on with only one car.

In Amiens, at the well-known Godbert Restaurant, we lunched like dukes in a green-shuttered private room. "God only knows when we'll see a clean tablecloth again," remarked Barton, as he ordered langoustes, roast duck, and two bottles of their best "bubbly". Heaven knows what else the meal contained; but I remember talking with a loosened tongue about sport, and old Joe telling us how he narrowly escaped being reduced to the ranks for "making a book" when the Battalion was stationed in Ireland before the war. "There were some fine riders in the regiment then; they talked and thought about nothing but hunting, racing, and polo," he said; adding that it was lucky for some of us that horsemanship wasn't needed for winning the war, since most mounted officers now looked as if they were either rowing a boat or riding a bicycle uphill. Finally, when with flushed faces we sauntered out into the sunshine, he remarked that he'd half a mind to go and look for a young lady to make his wife jealous. I said that there was always the cathedral to look at, and discovered that I'd unintentionally made a very good joke.

V

Two days later we vacated the camp at Heilly. The aspens by the river were shivering and showing the whites of their leaves, and it was good-bye to their cool showery sound when we marched away in our own dust at four o'clock on a glaring bright afternoon. The aspens waited, with their indifferent welcome, for some other dead beat and diminished battalion. Such was their habit, and so the war went on. It must be difficult, for those who did not experience it, to imagine the sensation of returning to a battle area, particularly when one started from a safe place like Heilly. Replenished by an unpromising draft from a home service battalion, our unit was well rested and, supposedly, as keen as mustard. Anyhow it suited everyone, including the troops themselves, to believe that victory was somewhere within sight. Retrospectively, however, I find it difficult to conceive them as an optimistic body of men, and it is certain that if the men of the new draft had any illusions about modern warfare, they would shortly lose them.

My exiguous diary has preserved a few details of that

nine-mile march. Field-Marshal Haig passed us in his
motor; and I saw a doctor in a long white coat standing in
the church door at Morlancourt. Passing through the village, we went on by a track, known as "the Red Road",
arrived at the Citadel "in rich yellow evening light", and
bivouacked on the hill behind the Fricourt road. Two
hours later we "stood-to", and then started for Mametz,
only to be brought back again after going half a mile. I fell
asleep to the sound of heavy firing toward La Boisselle,
rattling limbers on the Citadel road, and men shouting and
looking for their kits in the dark. There are worse things
than falling asleep under a summer sky. One awoke stiff
and cold, but with a head miraculously clear.

Next day I moved to the Transport Lines, a couple of
miles back, for I was one of eight officers kept in reserve.
There I existed monotonously while the Battalion was engaged in the Battle of Bazentin Ridge. My boredom was
combined with suspense, for after the first attack I might
be sent for at any moment, so I could never wander far
from the Transport Lines.

The battle didn't begin till Friday at dawn, so on Thursday Durley and I were free and we went up to look at the
old Front Line. We agreed that it felt queer to be walking
along no-man's-land and inspecting the old German
trenches in a half-holiday mood. The ground was littered
with unused ammunition, and a spirit of mischievous destruction possessed us. Pitching Stokes mortar shells down
the dark and forbidding stairs of German dug-outs, we
revelled in the boom of subterranean explosions. For a few
minutes we felt as if we were getting a bit of our own back
for what we'd endured opposite those trenches, and we
chanced to be near the mine craters where the raid had
failed. But soon we were being shouted at by an indignant
Salvage Corps Officer, and we decamped before he could
identify us. Thus we "put the lid on" our days and nights
in the Bois Français sector, which was now nothing but a
few hundred yards of waste ground—a jumble of derelict
wire, meaningless ditches, and craters no longer formidable. There seemed no sense in the toil that had heaped

those mounds of bleaching sandbags, and even the 1st of July had become an improbable memory, now that the dead bodies had been cleared away. Rank thistles were already thriving among the rusty rifles, torn clothing, and abandoned equipment of those who had fallen a couple of weeks ago.

*   *   *

That evening we heard that our Second Battalion had bivouacked about half a mile from the camp. Their Division had been brought down from Flanders and was on its way up to Bazentin. Returning from an after dinner stroll I found that several Second Battalion officers had come to visit us. It was almost dark; these officers were standing outside our tent with Durley and the others, and it sounded as if they were keeping up their courage with the volubility usual among soldiers who knew that they would soon be in an attack. Among them, big and impulsive, was David Cromlech, who had been with our Battalion for three months of the previous winter. As I approached the group I recognized his voice with a shock of delighted surprise. He and I had never been in the same Company, but we were close friends, although somehow or other I have hitherto left him out of my story. On this occasion his face was only dimly discernible, so I will not describe it, though it was a remarkable one. An instinct for aloofness which is part of my character caused me to remain in the background for a minute or two, and I now overheard his desperately cheerful ejaculations with that indefinite pang of affection often felt by a detached observer of such spontaneous behaviour. When I joined the group we had so much to tell one another that I very soon went back with him to his tentless hillside. On the way I gave him a breathless account of my adventures up at Mametz Wood, but neither of us really wanted to talk about the Somme Battle. We should probably get more than enough of it before we'd finished. He had only just joined the Second Battalion, and I was eager to hear about England. The men of his platoon were lying down a little way off; but soon their recumbent mutterings had ceased, and all around us in the gloom were sleeping soldiers and the pyramids of piled rifles. We knew that this might be our last meeting, and gradually an ultimate strangeness and simplicity overshadowed and contained our low-voiced colloquies. We talked of the wonderful things we'd do after the war; for to me David had often seemed to belong less to my war experience than to the freedom which would come after it. He had dropped his defensive exuberance now, and I felt that he was rather luckless and lonely—too young to be killed up on Bazentin Ridge. It was midnight when I left him. First thing in the morning I hurried up the hill in hope of seeing him again. Scarcely a trace remained of the battalion which had bivouacked there, and I couldn't so much as identify the spot where we'd sat on his ground sheet, until I discovered a scrap of silver paper which might possibly have belonged to the packet of chocolate we had munched while he was telling me about the month's holiday he'd had in Wales after he came out of hospital.

When I got back to our tent in the Transport Lines I found everyone in a state of excitement. Dottrell and the ration party had returned from their all-night pilgrimage with information about yesterday's attack. The Brigade had reached its first objectives. Two of our officers had been killed and several wounded. Old man Barton had got a nice comfortable one in the shoulder. Hawkes (a reliable and efficient chap who belonged to one of the other companies) had been sent for to take command of C Company, and was even now completing his rapid but methodical preparations for departure.

*   *   *

The reserve Echelon was an arid and irksome place to be loafing about in. Time hung heavy on our hands and we spent a lot of it lying in the tent on our outspread valises. During the sluggish mid-afternoon of the same Saturday I was thus occupied in economizing my energies. Durley had nicknamed our party "the eight little nigger boys", and there were now only seven of us. Most of them were feeling more talkative than I was, and it happened that I emerged from a snooze to hear them discussing "that queer bird Cromlech". Their comments reminded me, not for the first time, of the diversified impressions which David made upon his fellow Fusiliers.

At his best I'd always found him an ideal companion, although his opinions were often disconcerting. But no one was worse than he was at hitting it off with officers who distrusted cleverness and disliked unreserved utterances. In fact he was a positive expert at putting people's backs up unintentionally. He was with our Second Battalion for a few months before they transferred him to "the First", and during that period the Colonel was heard to remark that young Cromlech threw his tongue a hell of a lot too much, and that it was about time he gave up reading Shakespeare and took to using soap and water. He had, however, added, "I'm agreeably surprised to find that he isn't windy in trenches."

David certainly was deplorably untidy, and his absent-mindedness when off duty was another propensity which made him unpopular. Also, as I have already hinted, he wasn't good at being "seen but not heard". "Far too fond of butting in with his opinion before he's been asked for it," was often his only reward for an intelligent suggestion. Even Birdie Mansfield (who had knocked about the world too much to be intolerant) was once heard to exclaim, "Unless you watch it, my son, you'll grow up into the most bumptious young prig God ever invented!"—this protest being a result of David's assertion that all sports except boxing, football, and rock climbing were snobbish and silly.

From the floor of the tent, Holman (a spick and span boy who had been to Sandhurst and hadn't yet discovered that it was unwise to look down on temporary officers who "wouldn't have been wanted in the Regiment in peace time") was now saying, "Anyhow, I was at Clitherland with him last month, and he fairly got on people's nerves with his hot air about the Battle of Loos, and his brain-waves about who really wrote the Bible." Durley then philosophically observed, "Old Longneck certainly isn't the sort of man you meet every day. I can't always follow his theories myself, but I don't mind betting that he'll go a long way—provided he isn't pushing up daisies when Peace breaks out." Holman (who had only been with us a few days and soon became more democratic) brushed Durley's defence aside with "The blighter's never satisfied unless he's turning something upside down. I actually heard him say that Homer was a woman. Can you beat that? And if you'll believe me he had the darned sauce to give me a sort of pi-jaw about going out with girls in Liverpool. If you ask me, I think he's a rotten outsider, and the sooner he's pushing up daisies the better." Whereupon Perrin (a quiet man of thirty-five who was sitting in a corner writing to his wife) stopped the discussion by saying, "Oh, dry up, Holman! For all we know the poor devil may be dead by now."

* * *

Late that night I was lying in the tent with *The Return of the Native* on my knee. The others were asleep, but my candle still guttered on the shell-box at my elbow. No one had mumbled "For Christ's sake put that light out"; which was lucky, for I felt very wide awake. How were things going at Bazentin, I wondered? And should I be sent for to-morrow? A sort of numb funkiness invaded me. I didn't want to die—not before I'd finished reading *The Return of the Native* anyhow. "The quick-silvery glaze on the rivers and pools vanished; from broad mirrors of light they changed to lustreless sheets of lead." The words fitted my mood; but there was more in them than that. I wanted to explore the book slowly. It made me long for England, and it made the War seem waste of time. Ever since my existence became precarious I had realized how little I'd used my brains in peace time, and now I was always trying to keep my mind from stagnation. But it wasn't easy to think one's own thoughts while on active service, and the outlook of my companions was mostly mechanical; they dulled everything with commonplace chatter and made even the vividness of the War ordinary. My encounter with

David Cromlech—after three months' separation—had re-awakened my relish for liveliness and originality. But I had no assurance of ever seeing him again, or of meeting any-one who could stir up my dormant apprehensions as he did. Was it a mistake, I wondered, to try and keep intelligence alive when I could no longer call my life my own? In the brown twilight of the tent I sat pondering with my one golden candle flame beside me. Last night's talk with David now assumed a somewhat ghostlike character. The sky had been starless and clouded and the air so still that a lighted match needed no hand to shield it. Ghosts don't strike matches, of course; and I knew that I'd smoked my pipe, and watched David's face—sallow, crooked, and whimsical—when he lit a cigarette. There must have been the usual noises going on; but they were as much a part of our surroundings as the weather, and it was easy to ima-gine that the silence had been unbroken by the banging of field batteries and the remote tack-tack of rifles and machine-guns. Had that sombre episode been some pre-monition of our both getting killed? For the country had loomed limitless and strange and sullenly imbued with the Stygian significance of the War. And the soldiers who slept around us in their hundreds—were they not like the dead, among whom in some dim region where time survived in ghostly remembrances, we two could still cheat ourselves with hopes and forecasts of a future exempt from antago-nisms and perplexities? . . . On some such sonorous cadence as this my thoughts halted. Well, poor old David was up in the battle; perhaps my mind was somehow in touch with his (though he would have disparaged my "fine style", I thought). More rationally reflective, I looked at my com-panions, rolled in their blankets, their faces turned to the earth or hidden by the folds. I thought of the doom that was always near them now, and how I might see them lying dead, with all their jollity silenced, and their talk, which had made me impatient, ended for ever. I looked at gallant young Fernby; and Durley, that kind and sensitive soul; and my own despondency and discontent released me. I couldn't save them, but at least I could share the dangers and discomforts they endured. "Outside in the gloom the guns are shaking the hills and making lurid flashes along the valleys. Inevitably, the War blunders on; but among the snoring sleepers I have had my little moment of magnanimity. What I feel is no more than the candle which makes tottering shadows in the tent. Yet it is something, perhaps, that one man can be awake there, though he can find no meaning in the immense destruction which he blindly accepts as part of some hidden purpose." . . . Thus (rather portentously, perhaps) I recorded in my diary the outcome of my ruminations.

*   *   *

For another five days my war experience continued to mark time in that curious camp. I call the camp curious, for it seemed so, even then. There was a makeshift effect of men coming and going, loading and unloading limbers and wagons, carrying fodder, shouting at horses and mules, attending to fires, and causing a smell of cooking. A whiff from a certain sort of wood fire could make me see that camp clearly now, since it was strewn and piled with empty shell-boxes which were used for fuel, as well as for building bivouacs. Along the road from Fricourt to Méaulte, infantry columns continually came and went, processions of prisoners were brought down, and small parties of "walking wounded" straggled thankfully toward the Casualty Clearing Station. The worn landscape looked parched and shabby; only the poppies made harsh spots of red, matching the head caps of the Indian cavalry who were camped near by.

Among all this activity time passed sluggishly for me. Inside our tent I used to stare at the camouflage paint smears which showed through the canvas, formulating patterns and pictures among which the whiteness of the sky showed in gaps and rents. The paint smears were like ungainly birds with wide spread wings, fishes floating, monkeys in scarecrow trees, or anything else my idle brain cared to contrive. In one corner a fight was going on (in a Futuristic style) and a figure brandished a club while his adversary took a side-leap, losing an arm and a leg from a bomb explosion. Then someone would darken the doorway with a rumour that the Battalion had been moved up to attack High Wood—a new name, and soon afterwards an ugly one. Night would fall, with the others playing "Nap" and talking stale war stuff out of the *Daily Mail*, and the servants singing by a bright shell-box fire in the gusty twilight. And I would think about driving home from cricket matches before the War, wondering whether I'd ever go back to that sort of thing again.

I remember another evening (it was the last one I spent in that place) when the weather seemed awaiting some spectacular event in this world of blundering warfare. Or was it as though the desolation of numberless deaths had halted the clouded sky to an attitude of brooding inertia? I looked across at Albert; its tall trees were flat grey-blue outlines, and the broken tower of the basilica might have been a gigantic clump of foliage. Above this landscape of massed stillness and smoky silhouettes the observation balloons were swaying slowly, their noses pointing toward the line of battle. Only the distant thud of gun-fire disturbed the silence—like someone kicking footballs—a soft bumping, miles away. Walking along by the river I passed the horse-lines of the Indian cavalry; the barley field above couldn't raise a rustle, so still was the air. Low in the west, pale orange beams were streaming down on the country that receded with a sort of rich regretful beauty, like the background of a painted masterpiece. For me that evening expressed the indeterminate tragedy which was moving, with agony on agony, toward the autumn.

I leant on a wooden bridge, gazing down into the dark green glooms of the weedy little river, but my thoughts were powerless against unhappiness so huge. I couldn't alter European history, or order the artillery to stop firing. I could stare at the War as I stared at the sultry sky, longing for life and freedom and vaguely altruistic about my fellow-victims. But a second-lieutenant could attempt nothing—except to satisfy his superior officers; and altogether, I concluded, Armageddon was too immense for my solitary understanding. Then the sun came out for a last reddening look at the War, and I turned back to the camp with its clustering tents and crackling fires. I finished the day jawing to young Fernby about fox-hunting.

*   *   *

The Division had now been in action for a week. Next day they were to be relieved. Late in the afternoon Dottrell moved the Transport back about three miles, to a hill above Dernancourt. Thankful for something to do at last, I busied myself with the putting up of tents. When that was done I watched the sun going down in glory beyond the main road to Amiens. The horizon trees were dark blue against the glare, and the dust of the road floated in wreaths; motor-lorries crept continuously by, while the long shadows of trees made a sort of mirage on the golden haze of the dust. The country along the river swarmed with camps, but the low sun made it all seem pleasant and peaceful. After nightfall the landscape glowed and glinted with camp-fires, and a red half-moon appeared to bless the combatant armies with neutral beams. Then we were told to shift the tents higher up the hill and I became active again; for the Battalion was expected about midnight. After this little emergency scramble I went down to the crossroads with Dottrell, and there we waited hour after hour. The Quartermaster was in a state of subdued anxiety, for he'd been unable to get up to Battalion Head-quarters for the last two days. We sat among some barley on the bank above the road, and as time passed we conversed companionably, keeping ourselves awake with an occasional drop of rum from his flask. I always enjoyed being with Dottrell, and that night the husky-voiced old campaigner was more eloquent than he realized. In the simplicity of his talk there was a universal tone which seemed to be summing up all the enduring experience of an Infantry Division. For him it was a big thing for the Battalion to be coming back from a battle, though, as he said, it was a new Battalion every few months now.

An hour before dawn the road was still an empty picture

of moonlight. The distant gun-fire had crashed and rumbled all night, muffled and terrific with immense flashes, like waves of some tumult of water rolling along the horizon. Now there came an interval of silence in which I heard a horse neigh, shrill and scared and lonely. Then the procession of the returning troops began. The camp-fires were burning low when the grinding jolting column lumbered back. The field guns came first, with nodding men sitting stiffly on weary horses, followed by wagons and limbers and field-kitchens. After this rumble of wheels came the infantry, shambling, limping, straggling and out of step. If anyone spoke it was only a muttered word, and the mounted officers rode as if asleep. The men had carried their emergency water in petrol-cans, against which bayonets made a hollow clink; except for the shuffling of feet, this was the only sound. Thus, with an almost spectral appearance, the lurching brown figures flitted past with slung rifles and heads bent forward under basin-helmets. Moonlight and dawn began to mingle, and I could see the barley swaying indolently against the sky. A train groaned along the riverside, sending up a cloud of whitish fiery smoke against the gloom of the trees. The Flintshire Fusiliers were a long time arriving. On the hill behind us the kite balloon swayed slowly upward with straining ropes, its looming bulbous body reflecting the first pallor of daybreak. Then, as if answering our expectancy, a remote skirling of bagpipes began, and the Gordon Highlanders hobbled in. But we had been sitting at the crossroads nearly six hours, and faces were recognizable, when Dottrell hailed our leading Company.

Soon they had dispersed and settled down on the hillside, and were asleep in the daylight which made everything seem ordinary. None the less I had seen something that night which overawed me. It was all in the day's work —an exhausted Division returning from the Somme Offensive—but for me it was as though I had watched an army of ghosts. It was as though I had seen the War as it might be envisioned by the mind of some epic poet a hundred years hence.

PART FIVE: ESCAPE

I

On Saturday afternoon we made a short train journey and then marched four easy miles to a village called La Chaussée. Twenty-four hours' rest and a shave had worked the usual miracle with the troops (psychological recovery was a problem which no one had time to recognize as existent) and now we were away from the Line for at least a fortnight. It was a dusty golden evening, and the road led us through quiet green country. Delusively harmonious, perhaps, is that retrospective picture of the Battalion marching at ease along an unfrequented road, at the end of a July afternoon, with Colonel Kinjack riding rather absentmindedly in front, or pulling up to watch us go past him —his face thoughtful and indulgent and expressing something of the pride and satisfaction which he felt.

So it will go on, I thought; in and out, in and out, till something happens to me. We had come along the same road last January. Only five officers of that lot were with us now: not many of them had been killed, but they had "faded away" somehow or other, and my awareness of this created a deceptive sense of "the good old days". Yesterday afternoon I'd heard that Cromlech had been killed up at High Wood. This piece of news had stupefied me, but the pain hadn't begun to make itself felt yet, and there was no spare time for personal grief when the Battalion was getting ready to move back to Divisional Rest. To have thought about Cromlech would have been calamitous. "Rotten business about poor old 'Longneck'," was the only comment that Durley, Dottrell and the others allowed themselves. And after all he wasn't the only one who'd gone west lately. It was queer how the men seemed to take their victimization for granted. In and out; in and out; singing and whistling, the column swayed in front of me, much the same length as usual, for we'd had less than a hundred casualties up at Bazentin. But it was a case of every man for himself, and the corporate effect was optimistic and untroubled. A London editor driving along the road in a Staff car would have remarked that the spirit of the troops was amazing. And so it was. But somehow the newspaper men always kept the horrifying realities of the War out of their articles, for it was unpatriotic to be bitter, and the dead were assumed to be gloriously happy. However, it was no use worrying about all that; I was part of the Battalion, and now I'd got to see about getting the men settled into billets.

Some Australians had been in the billets at La Chaussée, and (if they will pardon me for saying so) had left them in a very bad state. Sanitation had been neglected, and the inhabitants were complaining furiously that their furniture had been used for firewood. Did the Australians leave anything else behind them, I wonder? For some of them had been in Gallipoli, and it is possible that dysentery germs were part of the legacy they left us.

The fact remains that I awoke on Monday morning feeling far from well and, after a mechanical effort to go on parade in a glare of sunlight, took refuge in the cavernous bedroom which I occupied alone. Feeling worse and worse, in the evening I remembered that I possessed a thermometer, which had been handed over to me when I was Transport Officer. I had never taken the temperatures of any of the horses, but I now experimented shakily on myself. When I saw that it indicated 105° I decided that the thing was out of order; but next morning I was confusedly aware that Flook had fetched the doctor, and by the afternoon I was unbelievably at the New Zealand Hospital, which was in a substantial old building in the middle of Amiens.

*   *   *

The advantages of being ill were only too obvious. Lying awake in the large lofty ward on my fourth night, I was aware that I was feeling rather run down, but much better —almost too well, in fact. That evening my temperature had been normal, which reminded me that this change from active service to invalidism was an acute psychological experience. The door to safety was half open, and though an impartial New Zealand doctor decided one's destiny, there was a not unnatural impulse to fight for one's own life instead of against the Germans. Less than two weeks ago I'd been sitting in a tent thinking noble thoughts about sharing the adversities of my fellow Fusiliers. But that emotional defence wouldn't work now, and the unutterable words "wangle my way home" forced their way obstinately to the foreground, supported by a crowd of smug-faced excuses.

Durley and the Adjutant had visited me that afternoon; they'd joked with me about how well I was looking. While they were with me I had talked about coming back in a few days, and I'd genuinely felt as if I wanted to. But they took my fortitude away with them, and now I was foreseeing that another night's rest would make me look indecently healthy for a man in a hospital. "I suppose they'll all think I'm swinging the lead," I thought. Turning the last few months over in my mind, I argued with myself that I had done all that was expected of me. "Oh God," I prayed, "do get me sent down to the Base!" (How often was that petition whispered during the War?) To-day I had seen young Allgood's name in the Roll of Honour—a bit of news which had slammed the door on my four weeks at the Army School and provided me with a secondary sorrow, for I was already feeling sufficiently miserable about my friend Cromlech. I sympathized with myself about Allgood, for I had been fond of him. But he was only one among thousands of promising young men who had gone west since the 1st of July. Sooner or later I should probably get killed too. A breath of wind stirred the curtains, blowing them inward from the tall windows with a rustling sigh. The wind came from the direction of the Somme, and I could hear the remote thudding of the guns. Everyone in the ward seemed to be asleep except the boy whose bed had screens round it. The screens were red and a light glowed through them. Ever since he was brought in he'd been continually calling to the nurse on duty. Throughout the day this had gradually got on everyone's nerves, for the ward was already full of uncontrollable gasps and groans. Once I had caught a glimpse of his white face and miserable eyes. Whatever sort of wound he'd got he was making the most of it, had been the opinion of the man next to me (who had himself got more than he wanted, in both legs). But he must be jolly bad, I thought now, as the Sister came from behind the screen again. His voice went on, in the low, rapid, even tone of delirium. Sometimes I could catch what he said, troubled and unhappy and complaining. Someone called Dicky was on his mind, and he kept on crying out to Dicky. "Don't go out, Dicky; they snipe like hell!" And then, "Curse the Wood. . . . Dicky, you fool, don't go out!" . . . All the horror of the Somme attacks was in that raving; all the darkness and the dreadful daylight. . . . I watched the Sister come back with a white-coated doctor; the screen glowed comfortingly; soon the disquieting voice became inaudible and I fell asleep. Next morning the screens had vanished; the bed was empty, and ready for someone else.

*   *   *

Not that day, but the next one, my supplication to the Almighty was put to the test. The doctor came along the ward on his cheerful morning inspection. Arriving at my bed he asked how I was feeling. I stared up at him, incapable of asserting that I felt ill and unwilling to admit that I felt well. Fortunately he didn't expect a reply. "Well, we'll have to be moving you on," he said with a smile; and before my heart had time to beat again he turned to the nurse with, "Put him down for the afternoon train." The nurse made a note of it, and my mind uttered a spontaneous Magnificat. Now, with any luck, I thought, I'll get a couple of weeks at one of those hospitals on the coast, at Étretat or Le Tréport, probably. The idea of reading a book by the seaside was blissful. No one could blame me for that, and I should be back with the Battalion by the end of August, if not earlier.

In my hurried exodus from my billet at La Chaussée, some of my belongings had been left behind, and good old Flook had brought them to the hospital next day. He had come treading in with clumsy embarrassment to deposit the packful of oddments by my bed, announcing in a hoarse undertone, "Ah've brought the stoof," and telling me that the lads in C Company were hoping to see me back soon. Somehow Flook, with his rough and ready devotion, had seemed my strongest link with the Battalion. When I shook his hand and said good-bye, he winked and advised me, confidentially, not to be in too much of a hurry about getting back. A good rest would do me no harm, he said; but as he tiptoed away I wondered when he himself would get a holiday, and whether he would ever return to his signal-box on the railway.

The details of my journey to the Base were as follows. First of all I was carried carefully down the stairs on a stretcher (though I could easily have walked to the ambulance, or even to the railway station, if such an effort had been demanded of me). Then the ambulance took me to Corbie, and from there the train (with 450 casualties on board) rumbled sedately to Rouen; we did the sixty miles in ten hours, and at two o'clock in the morning I was carried into No. 2 Red Cross Hospital. I remember that particular hospital with affection. During the morning a genial doctor came along and had a look at me. "Well, my lad, what's wrong with you?" he asked. "They call it enteritis," I replied, with an indefinite grin. He had a newspaper in his hand as he glanced at the descriptive chart behind my bed. My name caused him to consult *The Times*. "Is this you?" he asked. Sure enough, my name was there, in a list of Military Crosses which chanced to have appeared that day. The doctor patted me on the shoulder and informed me that I should be going across to England next day. Good luck had "wangled me home". Even now I cannot think of that moment without believing that I was involved in one of the lesser miracles of the Great War. For I am certain that I should have remained at Rouen if that observant and kind-hearted doctor hadn't noticed my name among the decorations. And in that case I should have been back with the Battalion in nice time for their operations at Delville Wood, which might quite conceivably have qualified my name for a place on the Butley village War Memorial.

*   *   *

The Hospital Ship left Rouen about midday. While we steamed down the Seine in fine weather I lay watching the landscape through a porthole with a sense of thankfulness which differed from any I had ever known before. A label was attached to me; I have kept that label, and it is in my left hand as I write these words. It is marked *Army Form W* 3083, though in shape and substance it is an ordinary civilian luggage label. It is stamped *Lying Train and Ship* in blue letters, with *Sick P.U.O.* on the other side. On the boat, my idle brain wondered what *P.U.O.* meant. There must, I thought, be a disease beginning with P. Perhaps it was "Polypipsis unknown origin". Between Rouen and Havre I devised several feebly funny solutions, such as "Perfectly undamaged officer". But my final choice was "Poorly until October".

At noon next day we reached Southampton. Nothing could be better than this, I thought, while being carried undeservedly from the ship to the train; and I could find no fault with Hampshire's quiet cornfields and unwarlike woods in the drowsy August afternoon. At first I guessed that we were on our way to London; but when the journey showed signs of cross-countrihood I preferred not to be told where we were going. Recumbent, I gazed gloatingly at England. Peaceable stay-at-homes waved to the Red Cross Train, standing still to watch it pass. It was nice to think that I'd been fighting for them, though exactly what I'd done to help them was difficult to define. An elderly man, cycling along a dusty road in a dark blue suit and a straw hat, removed one hand from the handle-bars to wave comprehensive gratitude. Everything seemed happy and homely. I was delivered from the idea of death, and that other thing which had haunted me, the dread of being blinded. I closed contented eyes, became sleepy, and awoke to find myself at Oxford. By five o'clock I was in a small white room on the ground floor of Somerville College. Listening to the tranquil tolling of Oxford bells and someone strumming melodiously on a piano across the lawn, with a glimpse of tall chestnut trees swaying against the blue sky, I whispered the word Paradise. Had I earned it? I was too grateful to care.

II

In Oxford lived Mr. Farrell, an old friend of Aunt Evelyn's. Some years before the War he had lived near Butley, and he now came to pay me an afternoon visit at the Hospital, where I was reclining under a tree on the lawn, still keeping up appearances as an invalid officer. He sat beside me and we conversed rather laboriously about Aunt Evelyn and her neighbourhood. He was Irish and a voluble talker, but he seemed to have lost much of his former vivacity. I noticed that he was careful to keep the conversation safely on this side of the Channel, probably out of consideration for my feelings, although I wouldn't have minded telling him a thing or two about the Somme. Mr. Farrell was a retired Civil Servant and an authority on Military Records. He had written the lives of several famous Generals and an official History of the Indian Mutiny. But he showed no curiosity about the military operations of the moment. He was over seventy, and his face was unlit and fatigued as he talked about food restrictions in England. "Sugar is getting scarce," he remarked, "but that doesn't affect me; my doctor knocked me off sugar several years ago." I looked at his noticeably brown teeth, and then averted my eyes as if he could read my thoughts, for I was remembering how Aunt Evelyn used to scold me for calling him "sugar-teeth"; his untidy teeth did look like lumps of sugar soaked in tea. . . .

Dear old Mr. Farrell, with his red tie and the cameo ring round it, and his silver hair and ragged tobacco-stained moustache! As his large form lumbered away across the lawn, I thought that his clothes had got too big for him, though he'd always worn them rather baggy. Could it be possible that scrupulous people at home were getting thin while the soldiers got fat on their good rations at the Front? I began to suspect that England wasn't quite what it used to be. But my mind soon wandered indolently into the past which the veteran military historian had brought with him into the college garden. I remembered summer evenings when I was a little boy overhearing, from in bed upstairs, the mumble of voices down in the drawing-room, where Aunt Evelyn was having an after-dinner chat with Mr. Farrell and Captain Huxtable, who had walked across the fields from Butley in the twilight. Sometimes I tiptoed down the stairs and listened at the door (rather hoping to hear them saying something complimentary about myself) but they were nearly always gassing about politics, or India. Mr. Farrell had been in India for ages, and Captain Huxtable had been out there too; and Aunt Evelyn loved to hear about it. When we went to see Mr. Farrell he used to show us delightful old books with coloured plates of Indian scenes. What queer old codgers they were, sipping tea and puffing their cigars (which smelt quite nice) and talking all that rot about Lord Salisbury and his Government. "Her-her-her," laughed Mr. Farrell whenever he finished another of his funny stories which always ended with what someone had said to someone else or how he'd scored off someone at his club. They'd go on talking just the same, whatever happened; even if a Death's Head Hawk Moth flew into the room they wouldn't be a bit excited about it. It would be rather fun, I thought, if I were to fire my percussion-cap pistol outside the drawing-room door, just to give them a surprise. As I crept upstairs again in my nightgown, I wondered if I should ever be like that myself. . . . Mr. Farrell was fond of playing tennis; he used to serve underhand, holding the ball a few inches above the ground as he struck it. . . .

Emerging from my retrospective reverie, I felt that this. war had made the past seem very peculiar. People weren't the same as they used to be, or else I had changed. Was it because I had experienced something that they couldn't share or imagine? Mr. Farrell had seemed diffident that afternoon, almost as if he were talking to a survivor from an incomprehensible disaster. Looking round me I began to feel that I wanted to be in some place where I needn't be reminded of the War all the time. For instance, there was that tall well-preserved man pushing his son very slowly across the lawn in a long wheeled bed. The son was sallow and sulky, as he well might be, having lost one of his legs. The father was all solicitude, but somehow I inferred that the pair of them hadn't hit it off too well before the War. More than once I had seen the son look at his father as though he disliked him. But the father was proud of his disabled son, and I heard him telling one of the nurses how splendidly the boy had done in the Gommecourt attack, showing her a letter, too, probably from the boy's colonel. I wondered whether he had ever allowed himself to find out that the Gommecourt show had been nothing but a massacre of good troops. Probably he kept a war map with little flags on it; when Mametz Wood was reported as captured he moved a little flag an inch forward after breakfast. For him the Wood was a small green patch on a piece of paper. For the Welsh Division it had been a bloody nightmare. . . . "Is the sun too strong for you here, Arthur?" Arthur shakes his head and frowns up at the sky. Then the father, with his neatly-trimmed beard and elegant buff linen waistcoat, begins to read him Haig's latest despatch. "There is strong evidence that the enemy forces engaged on the battle-front have been severely shaken by the repeated successes gained by ourselves and our Allies. . . ." The level cultivated voice palavers on until the nurse approaches brightly with a spouted feeding-cup. "Time for some more beef-tea!" Nourishment is administered under approving parental eyes.

III

During my last week I was allowed out of the hospital in the afternoons, and I used to go up the Cherwell in a canoe. I found this recreation rather heavy work, for the water was a jungle of weeds and on the higher reaches progress had become almost impossible. Certainly the Great War had made a difference to the charming River Cherwell. But I had been feeling much more cheerful lately, for my friend Cromlech had risen again from the dead. I had seen his name in the newspaper list of killed, but soon afterwards someone telegraphed to tell me that he was in a London hospital and going on well. For fully a fortnight I had accustomed myself to the idea that his dead body was somewhere among the Somme shell-holes and it was a queer experience, to be disentangling myself from the mental obituary notices which I had evolved out of my luminous memories of our companionship in the First Battalion. "Silly old devil," I thought affectionately; "he always manages to do things differently from other people."

By the end of August I was back at Butley with a month's sick leave and the possibility of an extension. So for the first week or two I forgot the future and enjoyed being made a fuss of by Aunt Evelyn. My outlook on the War was limited to the Battalion I had served with. After being kept out of the Line for nearly five weeks, they were expecting to be moved up at any moment. This news came in a letter from Durley. Suppressing such disquietude as it caused me, I put the letter in my pocket and went out to potter round the garden. It was a fine early September morning—almost my favourite sort of weather, I thought. The garden was getting wild and overgrown, for there was only one old man working in it now. The day before I had begun an attempt to recivilize the tangled tennis-lawn, but it had been too much like canoeing on the Cherwell, and to-day I decided to cut dead wood out of the cedar. While I climbed about in the tree with a bill-hook in my hand I could hear old Huckett trundling the water-tank along the kitchen garden. Then Aunt Evelyn came along with her flower-basket full of dahlias; while she was gazing up at me another brittle bough cracked and fell, scaring one of the cats who followed her about. She begged me to be careful, adding that it would be no joke to tumble out of such a big tree.

Later in the morning I visited the stables. Stagnation had settled there; nettles were thick under the apple-trees and the old mowing-machine pony grazed in shaggy solitude. In Dixon's little harness room, saddles were getting mouldy and there were rust-spots on the bits and stirrup-irons which he had kept so bright. A tin of *Harvey's Hoof Ointment* had obviously been there since 1914. It would take Dixon a long time to get the place straightened up, I thought, forgetting for a moment that he'd been dead six months. . . . It wasn't much fun, mooning about the stables. But a robin trilled his little autumn song from an apple-tree; beyond the fruit-laden branches I could see the sunlit untroubled Weald, and I looked lovingly at the cowls of hop-kilns which twinkled across those miles that were the country of my childhood. I could smell autumn in the air, too, and I thought I must try to get a few days' cubbing before I go back to the Depot. Down in Sussex there were a few people who would willingly lend me a horse, and I decided to write to old Colonel Hesmon about it. I went up to the schoolroom to do this; rummaging in a drawer for some note-paper, I discovered a little pocket mirror—a relic of my days in the ranks of the Yeomanry. Handling it absent-mindedly, I found myself using it to decipher the blotting paper, which had evidently been on the table some time, for the handwriting was Stephen Colwood's. "*P.S. The Old Guvnor is squaring up my annual indebtedness. Isn't he a brick?*" Stephen must have scribbled that when he was staying with us in the summer of 1914. Probably he had been writing to his soldier brother in Ireland. I imagined him adding the postscript and blotting it quickly. Queer how the past crops up, I thought, sadly, for my experience of such poignant associations was "still in its infancy", as someone had said of Poison Gas when lecturing to cannon-fodder at the Army School.

Remembering myself at that particular moment, I realize the difficulty of recapturing war-time atmosphere as it was in England then. A war historian would inform us that "the earlier excitement and suspense had now abated, and the nation had settled down to its organization of man-power and munition making". I want to recover something more intimate than that, but I can't swear to anything unusual at Butley except a derelict cricket field, the absence of most of the younger inhabitants, and a certain amount of talk about food prospects for the winter. Two of our nearest neighbours had lost their only sons, and with them their main interest in life; but such tragedies as those remained intimate and unobtrusive. Ladies worked at the Local Hospital and elderly gentlemen superintended Recruiting Centres and Tribunals; but there was little outward change and no military training-camp within a radius of ten miles. So I think I am accurate when I say that Aunt Evelyn was jogging along much as usual (now that her mind was temporarily at rest about my own active service career). She was, of course, a bit intolerant about the Germans, having swallowed all the stories about atrocities in Belgium. It was her duty, as a patriotic Englishwoman, to agree with a certain prelate when he preached the axiom that "every man who killed a German was performing a Christian act". Nevertheless, if Aunt Evelyn had found a wounded Prussian when she was on her way to the post office, she would undoubtedly have behaved with her natural humanity (combined with enthusiasm for administering first aid). In the meantime we avoided controversial topics (such as that all Germans were fiends in human form) and while I was writing my letter to Colonel Hesmon she entered the schoolroom with her arms full of lavender which she strewed along the floor under the window. The sun would dry it nicely there, she said, adding that I must find her a very dull old party nowadays, since she had no conversation and seemed to spend all her time trying to catch a new housemaid. I assured her that it was a great relief after being incessantly ordered about in the Army, to be with someone who had no conversation.

But after dinner that evening I did find myself a bit dull, so I walked across the fields for a chat with Protheroe, a middle-aged bachelor who lived in a modest old house with his quiet sister. Before I started my aunt implored me to be careful about extinguishing the oil lamp in the drawing-room when I got back. Oil lamps were far from safe—downright dangerous, in fact!

The night was very still; as I went along the field path I was almost sure I could hear the guns. Not that I wanted to; but the newspapers reported that a new offensive had been started at Guillemont, and I couldn't help feeling that our Division was in it. (I still thought of it as "our Division".) Our village was quiet enough, anyhow, and so was Protheroe's white-faced house, with its creaking gate and red-blinded windows. I rapped with the knocker and Miss Protheroe came to the door, quite surprised to see me, though I'd seen her a few hours before when she called to return last month's *Blackwood's Magazine*. Protheroe was in the middle of a game of chess with the village doctor, a reticent little man whose smallest actions were aways extremely deliberate. The doctor would make up his mind to move one of his men, grasp it resolutely, become hesitative, release it, and then begin his cogitative chin-rubbing and eye-puckering all over again, while Protheroe drummed his fingers on the table and stared at a moth which was bumping softly against the ceiling of the snug little parlour, and his sister, with gentle careworn face, knitted something woollen for the brother who, though past forty, was serving as a corporal in the infantry in France. My arrival put a stop to the doctor's perplexities; and since I was welcomed rather as a returned hero, I was inclined to be hearty. I slapped Protheroe on the back, told him he'd got the best dug-out in Butley, and allowed myself to be encouraged to discuss the War. I admitted that it was pretty bad out there, with an inward feeling that such horrors as I had been obliged to witness were now something to be proud of. I even went so far as to assert that I wouldn't have missed this War for anything. It brought things home to one somehow, I remarked, frowning portentously as I lit my pipe, and forgetting for the moment what a mercy it had been when it brought me home myself. Oh yes, I knew all about the Battle of the Somme, and could assure them that we should be in Bapaume by October. Replying to their tributary questions, I felt that they envied me my experience.

While I was on my way home, I felt elated at having outgrown the parish boundaries of Butley. After all, it was a big thing, to have been in the thick of a European War, and my peace-time existence had been idle and purposeless. It was bad luck on Protheroe and the doctor; they must hate being left out of it. . . . I suppose one must give this damned War its due, I thought, as I sat in the school-room with one candle burning. I felt comfortable, for Miss Protheroe had made me a cup of cocoa. I took Durley's letter out of my pocket and had another look at it; but it wasn't easy to speculate on its implications. The War's all right as long as one doesn't get killed or smashed up, I decided, blowing out the candle so that I could watch the moonlight which latticed the floor with shadows of the leaded windows. Where the moonbeams lay thickest they touched the litter of drying lavender. I opened the window and sniffed the autumn-smelling air. An owl hooted in the garden, and I could hear a train going along the Weald. Probably a hospital-train from Dover, I thought, as I closed the window and creaked upstairs on tiptoe so as not to disturb Aunt Evelyn.

*   *   *

About a week afterwards I received two letters from Dottrell, written on consecutive days, but delivered by the same post. The first one began: "The old Batt. is having a rough time. We were up in the front a week ago, and lost 200 men in three days. The aid-post, a bit of a dug-out hastily made, was blown in. At the time it contained 5 wounded men, 5 stretcher-bearers, and the doctor. All were killed except the Doc. who was buried in the débris. He was so badly shaken when dug out that he had to be sent down, and will probably be in England by now. It is a hell of a place up there. The Batt. is attacking to-day. I hope they have better luck. The outlook is not rosy. Very glad to hear you are sitting up and taking nourishment. A lot of our best men have been knocked out recently. We shall soon want another Battn. All the boys send their love and best wishes in which your humble heartily joins."

The second letter, which I chanced to open and read first, was the worst of the two.

"Dear Kangaroo. . . . Just a line to let you know what rotten bad luck we had yesterday. We attacked Ginchy with a very weak Battn. (about 300) and captured the place but were forced out of half of it—due to the usual thing. Poor Edmunds was killed leading his Coy. Also Perrin. Durley was badly wounded, in neck and chest, I think. It is terrible to think of these two splendid chaps being cut off, but I hope Durley pulls through. Asbestos Bill died of wounds. Fernby, who was O.C. Bombers, very badly hit and not expected to live. Several others you don't know also killed. Only two officers got back without being hit. C.S.M. Miles and Danby both killed. The Battn. is *not now* over strength for rations! The rest of the Brigade suffered in proportion. Will write later. Very busy." . . .

I walked about the room, whistling and putting the pictures straight. Then the gong rang for luncheon. Aunt Evelyn drew my attention to the figs, which were the best we'd had off the old tree that autumn.

IV

October brought an extension of my sick leave and some mornings with the hounds. By the time I received another letter from Dottrell, Delville Wood had more or less buried its dead, in my mind if not altogether in reality. The old Quartermaster let off steam in a good grumble from which I quote a specimen.

"Well, we have been out at rest about 10 kilos from the place we were at last Xmas. We expected to be there three weeks but after 8 days have had sudden orders to move to the old spot with a *Why*. Kinjack left us to take command of a Brigade; a great loss to the Battn. They all come and go; stay in the Batt. long enough to get something out of it, and then disappear and will hardly give a thought to the men and officers who were the means of getting them higher rank. It's a selfish world, my friend. All successive C.O.'s beg me to stay with the old Battalion they love so well. I do. So do they, till they get a better job. They neither know nor care what happens to me (who at their special request have stuck to 'the dear old Corps') when I leave the Service on a pension of 30s. a week."

I am afraid I wasn't worrying overmuch about "the dear old Corps" myself, while out with the Ringwell Hounds on Colonel Hesmon's horses. In spite of the War, hunting was being carried on comfortably, though few people came out. "The game was being kept alive for the sake of the boys at the Front", who certainly enjoyed the idea (if they happened to be keen fox-hunters and were still alive to appreciate the effort made on their behalf). As for me, I was armed with my uniform and the protective colouring of my Military Cross, and no one could do enough for me. I stayed as long as I liked with Moffat, the genial man who now combined the offices of Master and Secretary, and for a few weeks the pre-war past appeared to have been conjured up for my special benefit. It was difficult to believe that the misty autumn mornings, which made me free of those well-known woods and farms and downs, were simultaneously shedding an irrelevant brightness on the Ypres Salient and on Joe Dottrell riding wearily back with the ration-party somewhere near Plug Street Wood. I don't think I could see it quite like that at the time. What I am writing now is the result of a bird's-eye view of the past, and the cub-hunting subaltern I see there is part of the "selfish world" to which his attention had been drawn. He is listening to Colonel Hesmon while the hounds are being blown out of a big wood—hearing how well young Winchell has done with his Brigade (without wondering how many of them have been "blown out" of their trenches) and being assured by the loquacious old Colonel that the German Count who used to live at Puxford Park was undoubtedly a spy and only hunted with the Ringwell for that reason; the Colonel now regretted that he didn't ride over to Puxford Park and break all the windows before war was declared. He also declared that any man under forty who wasn't wearing the King's uniform was nothing but a damned shirker. I remarked to Moffat afterwards that the Colonel seemed to be overdoing it a bit about the War. Moffat told me that the old boy was known to have practised revolver shooting in his garden, addressing insults to individual tree trunks and thus ventilating his opinion of Germany as a whole. He had been much the same about vulpicides and socialists in peace time. "It's very odd; for Hesmon's an extraordinarily kind-hearted man," said Moffat, who himself regarded the War as an unmitigated nuisance, but didn't waste his energy abusing it or anybody else. He had enough to do already, for he found it far from easy to keep the Hunt on its legs, and what the hounds would get to eat next year he really didn't know. He added that "the Missus's dachshunds only just escaped being interned as enemy aliens".

*   *   *

Sport in Sussex was only a makeshift exhilaration, and early in November I went to London for a final Medical Board. At the Caxton Hall in Westminster I spent a few minutes gazing funereally round an empty waiting-room. Above the fireplace (there was no fire) hung a neatly-framed notice for the benefit of all whom it might concern. It stated the scale of prices for artificial limbs, with instructions as to how officers could obtain them free of cost. The room contained no other ornament. While I was adjusting my mind to what a journalist might have called "the grim humour" of this footnote to Army life, a Girl Guide stepped in to say that Colonel Crossbones (or whatever his cognomen was) would see me now. A few formalities "put paid to" my period of freedom, and I pretended to be feeling pleased as I walked away from Westminster, though wondering whether the politicians had any expectations that hostilities would be concluded by Christmas, and eyeing the Admiralty with a notion that it must be rather nice to be in the Navy.

Good-byes began all over again. A last day with the Ringwell ended at the crossroads by the old Harcombe point-to-point course. I went one way and the hounds went another. Jogging down the lane, they disappeared in the drizzling dusk. Moffat's "Best of luck, old boy!" left me to ride on, alone with the creak of the saddle. I was due back at the Depot next day, but we'd had a good woodland hunt with one quite nice bit in the open, and I'd jumped a lot of timber and thoroughly enjoyed my day. Staring at the dim brown landscape I decided that the War was worth while if it was being carried on to safeguard this sort of thing. Was it? I wondered; and if a doubt arose it was dismissed before it had been formulated. Riding into Downfield where I was leaving the horse which had been lent me, I remembered how I'd slept on the floor of the Town Hall on the day war was declared. Two years and three months ago I had enlisted for "three years or the duration". It was beginning to look as if I had enlisted for a lifetime (though the word was one which had seen better days). Under the looming shadow of the hills the lights of the town twinkled cosily. But a distant bugle-call from some camp seemed to be summoning the last reluctant farm labourer. "You'll all have to go in the end," it seemed to say, and the comfortless call was being sounded far across Europe. . . .

On my way home in the train I read about Roumania in the paper. Everyone, Aunt Evelyn included, had been delighted when Roumania came in on our side in August. But the results had not been reassuring. I couldn't help feeling annoyed with the Roumanian Army for allowing their country to be overrun by the Germans. They really might have put up a better show than that!

PART SIX: AT THE DEPOT

I

Clitherland Camp had acquired a look of coercive stability; but this was only natural, since for more than eighteen months it had been manufacturing Flintshire Fusiliers, many of whom it was now sending back to the Front for the second and third time. The Camp was as much an essential co-operator in the national effort as Brotherhood & Co.'s explosive factory, which flared and seethed and reeked with poisonous vapours a few hundred yards away. The third winter of the War had settled down on the lines of huts with calamitous drabness; fog-bleared sunsets were succeeded by cavernous and dispiriting nights when there was nothing to do and nowhere to do it.

Crouching as close as I could to the smoky stove in my hut I heard the wind moaning around the roof, feet clumping cheerlessly along the boards of the passage, and all the systematized noises and clatterings and bugle-blowings of the Camp. Factory-hooters and ships' fog-horns out on the Mersey sometimes combined in huge unhappy dissonances; their sound seemed one with the smoke-drifted munition works, the rubble of industrial suburbs, and the canal that crawled squalidly out into blighted and forbidding farmlands which were only waiting to be built over.

Except for the permanent staff, there weren't many officers I had known before this winter. But I shared my hut with David Cromlech, who was well enough to be able to play an energetic game of football, in spite of having had a bit of shell through his right lung. Bill Eaves, the Cambridge scholar, had also returned and was quietly making the most of his few remaining months. (He was killed in February while leading a little local attack.) And there was young Ormand, too, pulling wry faces about his next Medical Board, which would be sure to pass him for General

Service. I could talk to these three about "old times with the First Battalion", and those times had already acquired a delusive unobnoxiousness, compared with what was in store for us; for the "Big Push" of last summer and autumn had now found a successor in "the Spring Offensive" (which was, of course, going to "get the Boches on the run").

Mess, at eight o'clock, was a function which could be used for filling up an hour and a half. While Ormand was making his periodic remark—that his only reason for wanting to go out again was that it would enable him to pay off his overdraft at Cox's Bank—my eyes would wander up to the top table where the Colonel sat among those good-natured easy-going Majors who might well have adopted as their motto the ditty sung by the troops: "We're here because we're here because we're here because we're here." At nine-thirty the Colonel went to the ante-room for his game of Bridge. But the second-in-command, Major Macartney, would sit on long afterwards, listening to one or two of his cronies and slowly imbibing port with a hand that trembled nervously. Probably his mind was often back in Ireland, snipe shooting and salmon fishing. There was nothing grim about the Major, though his features had a certain severity, slightly reminiscent of the late Lord Kitchener. He was a reserved and dignified man, much more so than the other Majors. These convivial characters were ostensibly directing the interior economy of the Camp, and as the troops were well fed and looked after they must be given credit for it. The training of recruits was left to sergeant-instructors, most of whom were Regular N.C.O.s of the best pattern, hard-worked men who were on their legs from morning to night, and strict because they had to be strict. The raw material to be trained was growing steadily worse. Most of those who came in now had joined the Army unwillingly, and there was no reason why they should find military service tolerable. The War had become undisguisedly mechanical and inhuman. What in earlier days had been drafts of volunteers were now droves of victims. I was just beginning to be aware of this.

*　　　　*　　　　*

But Clitherland had accessible compensations. One of them was the Golf Course at Formby. The electric train took only twenty minutes to get there, and Formby was famous for its bracing air, comfortable Club House, and superlatively good war-time food. I went there at least one afternoon a week; usually I played alone, and often I had the links to myself, which was no disadvantage, since I have always been considerably addicted to my own company.

My main purpose, however, was a day with the hounds. For this I was readily given leave off Saturday morning duties, since an officer who wanted to go out hunting was rightly regarded as an upholder of pre-war regimental traditions. The Saturday Meets of the Cheshire Hounds were a long way off, but nothing short of impossibility deterred me, and the working out of my plans was an effective antidote to war-weariness. It was, in fact, very like achieving the impossible, when I sat in my hut of an evening, cogitating with luxurious deliberation, consulting a map and calculating how my hireling could meet me at such and such a station, measuring the distance from there to the meet, and so on in the manner known to enthusiastic young sportsmen. On such Saturdays I would get up in the dark with joyful alacrity. Leaving Liverpool by an early train, I would eagerly observe the disconsolate beginnings of a dull December day, encouraging as far as I could the illusion that I was escaping from everything associated with the uniform which I wore, and eyeing my brown Craxwell field-boots affectionately.

Under such conditions no day could be a bad one, and although more than one Saturday's hunting was stopped by frost, I derived singular consolation from the few hunts I had. My consolations included a heavy fall over some high timber which I ought to have had more sense than to tackle, since my hireling was a moderate though willing performer. Anyhow, the contrast between Clitherland Camp and the Cheshire Saturday country was like the difference between War and Peace—especially when—at the end of a good day—I jogged a few miles homeward with the hounds, conversing with the cheery huntsman in my best pre-war style.

Apart from these compensations I had the companionship of David who was now quite the "old soldier" and as argumentative as ever. In fact, while I pored over my one-inch-to-the-mile map of Cheshire after dinner, he was usually sitting on in the Mess and taking an active part in the wordy warfare of other "old soldiers", among whom he was now listened to as one having authority. It was something to have been in the Battle of the Somme; but to have been at the Battle of Loos as well made him feel quite a big gun. In our hut, however, we sought fresher subjects than bygone battles and obliterated trenches. I enjoyed talking about English literature, and listened to him as to an oracle which I could, now and then, venture to contradict. Although he was nine years younger than I was, I often found myself reversing our ages, since he knew so much more than I did about almost everything except fox-hunting. He made short work of most books which I had hitherto venerated, for David was a person who consumed his enthusiasms quickly, and he once fairly took my breath away by pooh-poohing *Paradise Lost* as "that moribund academic concoction". I hadn't realized that it was possible to speak disrespectfully about Milton. Anyhow, John Milton was consigned to perdition, and John Skelton was put forward as "one of the few really good poets". But somehow I could never quite accept his supremacy over Milton as an established fact. At that period Samuel Butler was the source of much of David's ingenuity at knocking highly-respected names and notions off their perches.

Anyhow, I was always ready to lose another literary illusion, for many of my friend's quiddities were as nicely rounded, and as evanescent, as the double smoke rings he was so adroit at blowing. He was full of such entertaining little tricks, and I never tired of hearing him imitate the talk of excitable Welshmen. He was fond of music, too; but it was a failure when we went to an orchestral concert in Liverpool. David said that it "upset him psychologically". It was no good as music either. No music was really any

good except the Northern Folk-Ballad tunes which he was
fond of singing at odd moments. "The Bonny Earl of
Murray" was one of his favourites, and he sang it in agreeably melancholy style. But much though I admired these
plaintive ditties I could not believe that they abolished
Beethoven's Fifth Symphony, which we'd heard at the
Concert. I realize now that what I ought to have said was
"Oh rats, David!" Instead of which I clumsily tried to
explain the merits of various composers other than the in-
ventors of *The Minstrelsy of the Border,* which was exactly
what he wanted me to do. Sometimes he made me quite
angry. I remember one morning when he was shaving with
one hand and reading *Robinson Crusoe* in the other. Crusoe
was a real man, he remarked; fox-hunting was the sport of
snobs and half-wits. Since it was too early in the day for
having one's leg pulled, I answered huffily that I supposed
Crusoe was all right, but a lot of people who hunted were
jolly good sorts, and even great men in their own way. I
tried to think of someone to support my argument, and
after a moment exclaimed: "Anthony Trollope, for instance! He used to hunt a lot, and you can't say he was a
half-wit." "No, but he was probably a snob!" I nearly lost
my temper while refuting the slur on Trollope's character,
and David made things worse by saying that I had no idea
how funny I was when I reverted to my peace-time self.
"I had an overdose of the hunting dope when I was with
the Second Battalion in '15," he added. "If I'd been able
to gas about Jorrocks and say I'd hunted with the Bedfordshire Hounds all my life, the Colonel and the Adjutant
would have behaved quite decently to me." "You can't be
certain of that," I replied, "and anyway, there's no such
thing as 'the Bedfordshire Hounds'. Bedfordshire's mostly
the Oakley, and that isn't a first-class country either. You
might as well get the names right when you're talking
through your hat about things you don't understand."
What did it matter to David whether the Oakley was bor-
dered by the Grafton, Fitzwilliam, and Whaddon Chase—
none of which I'd ever hunted with, but I knew they were
good countries and I didn't pretend that I wasn't interested

in them, and I strongly objected to them being sneered at by a crank—yes, a fad-ridden crank—like David. "You're a fad-ridden crank," I remarked aloud. But as he always took my admonitions for what they were worth, the matter ended amicably, and a minute later I was able to remind him that he was going on parade without a tie.

I have already said that, as a rule, we avoided war-talk. Outwardly our opinions did not noticeably differ, though his sense of "the regimental tradition" was stronger than mine, and he "had no use for anti-war idealism". But each of us had his own attitude toward the War. My attitude (which had not always been easy to sustain) was that I wanted to have fine feelings about it. I wanted the War to be an impressive experience—terrible, but not horrible enough to interfere with my heroic emotions. David, on the other hand, distrusted sublimation and seemed to want the War to be even uglier than it really was. His mind loathed and yet attached itself to rank smells and squalid details. Like his face (which had a twist to it, as though seen in a slightly distorting mirror) his mental war-pictures were a little uncouth and out of focus. Though in some ways more easily shocked than I was, he had, as I once informed him, "a first-rate nose for anything nasty". It is only fair to add that this was when he'd been discoursing about the ubiquity of certain establishments in France. His information was all second-hand; but to hear him talk —round-eyed but quite the man of experience—one might have imagined that Amiens, Abbeville, Béthune, and Armentières were mainly illuminated by "Blue Lamps" and "Red Lamps", and that for a good young man to go through Havre or Rouen was a sort of Puritan's Progress from this world to the next.

II

Going into Liverpool was, for most of us, the only antidote to the daily tedium of the Depot. Liverpool usually meant the Olympic Hotel. This palatial contrast to the Camp was the chief cause of the overdrafts of Ormand and other

young officers. Never having crossed the Atlantic, I did not
realize that the Hotel was an American importation, but I
know now that the whole thing might have been brought
over from New York in the mind of a first-class passenger.
Once inside the Olympic, one trod on black and white
squares of synthetic rubber, and the warm interior smelt of
this pseudo-luxurious flooring. Everything was white and
gilt and smooth; it was, so to speak, an air-tight Paradise
made of imitation marble. Its loftiness made resonance
languid; one of its attractions was a swimming-bath, and
the whole place seemed to have the acoustics of a swimming-bath; noise was muffled and diluted to an aqueous
undertone, and even the languishing intermezzos of the
string band throbbed and dilated as though a degree removed from ordinary audibility. Or so it seemed to the
Clitherland subaltern who lounged in an ultra-padded
chair eating rich cakes with his tea, after drifting from
swimming-bath to hairdresser, buying a few fiction-maga-
zines on his way. Later on the cocktail bar would claim
him; and after that he would compensate himself for
Clitherland with a dinner that defied digestion.

"Fivers" melted rapidly at the Olympic, and many of
them were being melted by people whose share in the
national effort was difficult to diagnose. In the dining-
room I began to observe that some non-combatants were
doing themselves pretty well out of the War. They were
people whose faces lacked nobility, as they ordered lobsters
and selected colossal cigars. I remember drawing Durley's
attention to some such group when he dined with me
among the mirrors and mock magnificence. They had con-.
cluded their spectacular feed with an ice-cream concoction, and now they were indulging in an afterthought—
stout and oysters. I said that I supposed they must be profiteers. For a moment Durley regarded them with unspecu-
lative eyes, but he made no comment; if he found them
incredible, it wasn't surprising; both his brothers had been
killed in action and his sense of humour had suffered in
proportion. I remarked that we weren't doing so badly
ourselves and replenished his champagne glass. Durley

was on sick leave and had come to Liverpool for a night
so as to see me and one or two others at the Depot. The
War was very much on his mind, but we avoided discussing it during dinner. Afterwards, when we were sitting in
a quiet corner, he gave me an account of the show at Delville Wood on September 3rd. Owing to his having been
wounded in the throat, he spoke in a strained whisper. His
narrative was something like this:

"After our first time up there—digging a trench in front
of Delville Wood—we came back to Bonté Redoubt and
got there soon after daylight on the 30th. That day and the
next we were being shelled by long-range guns. About ten
o'clock on the night of the 31st, Kinjack decided to shift
camp. That took us two hours, though it was only 1,500
yards away, but it was pitch dark and pouring with rain.
I'd got into 'slacks' and was just settling down in a bell-
tent when we got the order to move up to Montauban in
double quick time. Kinjack went on ahead. You can imagine the sort of mix-up it was—the men going as fast as they
could, getting strung out and losing touch in the dark, and
the Adjutant galloping up and down cursing everyone; I
never saw him in such a state before—you know what a
quiet chap he usually is. We'd started in such a hurry that
I'd got my puttees on over my 'slacks'! It must have been
nearly five miles, but we did it in just over the hour. When
we got there no one could say what all the 'wind-up' was
about; we were in reserve all next day and didn't move up
to the Wood till the evening after that. We were to attack
from the right-hand corner of the Wood, with the East
Surreys covering our left and the Manchesters attacking
Ginchy on our right. Our objective was Pint Trench, taking Bitter and Beer and clearing Ale and Vat, and also
Pilsen Lane in which the Brigade thought there were some
big dug-outs. When I showed the battle-plan to the Sergeant-Major, all he said was 'We'll have a rough house
from Ale Alley'. But no one had any idea it was going to be
such a schimozzle as it was! . . . Anyhow by 8.30 on the
night of September 2nd I got C Company inside the Wood,

with Perrin and his Company just in front of us. A lot of
the trees were knocked to splinters and most of the undergrowth had gone, so it wasn't difficult to get about. But
while we were getting into position in shell-holes and a
trench through the Wood there were shells coming from
every direction and Véry lights going up all round the
Wood, and more than once I had to get down and use my
luminous compass before I could say which side was which.
Young Fernby and the Battalion bombers were on my
right, and I saw more of him than of Perrin during the
night; he was quite cheerful; we'd been told it was going to
be a decent show. The only trouble we struck that night
was when a shell landed among some men in a shell-hole;
two of the stretcher-bearers were crying and saying it was
bloody murder.

"Next day began grey and cheerless; shells screeching
overhead, the earth going up in front of the Wood, and
twigs falling on my tin hat. When it got near zero, the
earth was going up continuously. Boughs were coming
down. You couldn't hear the shells coming—simply felt
the earth quake when they arrived. There was some sort of
smoke-screen but it only let the Boches know we were coming. No one seems to be able to explain exactly what happened, but the Companies on the left never had a hope.
They got enfiladed from Ale Alley, so the Sergeant-Major
was right about the 'rough house'. Edmunds was killed
almost at once and his Company and B were knocked to
bits as soon as they came out of the Wood. I took C along
just behind Perrin and his crowd. We advanced in three
rushes. It was nothing but scrambling in and out of shell-
holes, with the ground all soft like potting-mould. The
broken ground and the slope of the hill saved us a bit from
their fire. Bitter Trench was simply like a filled-in ditch
where we crossed it. The contact-aeroplane was just over
our heads all the time, firing down at the Boches. After the
second rush I looked round and saw that a few of the men
were hanging back a bit, and no wonder, for a lot of them
were only just out from England! I wondered if I ought to
go back to them, but the only thing I'd got in my head was

a tag from what some instructor had told me when I was a private in the Artists' Rifles before the War. *In an attack always keep going forward!* Except for that, I couldn't think much; the noise was appalling and I've never had such a dry tongue in my life. I knew one thing, that we must keep up with the barrage. We had over 500 yards to go before the first lift and had been specially told we must follow the barrage close up. It was a sort of cinema effect; all noise and no noise. One of my runners was shot through the face from Ale Alley; I remember something like a half-brick flying over my head, and the bullets from the enfilade fire sort of smashing the air in front of my face. I saw a man just ahead topple over slowly, almost gracefully, and thought 'poor little chap, that's his last Cup Tie'. Anyhow, the two companies were all mixed up by the time we made the third rush, and we suddenly found ourselves looking down into Beer Trench with the Boches kneeling below us. Just on my left, Perrin, on top, and a big Boche, standing in the trench, fired at one another; down went the Boche. Then they cleared off along Vat Alley, and we blundered after them. I saw one of our chaps crumpled up, with a lot of blood on the back of his neck, and I took his rifle and bandolier and went on with Johnson, my runner. The trench had fallen in in a lot of places. They kept turning round and firing back at us. Once, when Johnson was just behind me, he fired (a cool careful shot—both elbows rested) and hit one of them slick in the face; the red jumped out of his face and up went his arms. After that they disappeared. Soon afterwards we were held up by a machine-gun firing dead on the trench where it was badly damaged, and took refuge in a big shell-hole that had broken into it. Johnson went to fetch Lewis guns and bombers. I could see four or five heads bobbing up and down a little way off so I fired at them and never hit one. The rifle I'd got was one of those 'wirer's rifles' which hadn't been properly looked after, and very soon nothing happened when I pressed the trigger which had come loose somehow and wouldn't fire the charge. I reloaded and tried again, then threw the thing away and got back into the trench. There was a man kneeling with his rifle sticking up, so I thought I'd use that; but as I was turning to take it another peace-time tag came into my head—*Never deprive a man of his weapon in a post of danger!*

"The next thing I knew was when I came to and found myself remembering a tremendous blow in the throat and right shoulder, and feeling speechless and paralysed. Men were moving to and fro above me. Then there was a wild yell—'They're coming back!' and I was alone. I thought 'I shall be bombed to bits lying here' and just managed to get along to where a Lewis gun was firing. I fell down and Johnson came along and cut my equipment off and tied up my throat. Someone put my pistol in my side pocket, but when Johnson got me on to my legs it was too heavy and pulled me over so he threw it away. I remember him saying, 'Make way; let him come,' and men saying 'Good luck, sir'—pretty decent of them under such conditions! Got along the trench and out at the back somehow—everything very hazy—drifting smoke and shell-holes—down the hill—thinking 'I must get back to Mother'—kept falling down and getting up—Johnson always helping. Got to Battalion Headquarters; R.S.M. outside; he took me very gently by the left hand and led me along, looking terribly concerned. Out in the open again at the back of the hill I knew I was safe. Fell down and couldn't get up any more. Johnson disappeared. I felt it was all over with me till I heard his voice saying, 'Here he is,' and the stretcher-bearers picked me up. . . . When I was at the dressing-station they took a scrap of paper out of my pocket and read it to me. 'I saved your life under heavy fire'; signed and dated. The stretcher-bearers do that sometimes, I'm told!"

He laughed huskily, his face lighting up with a gleam of his old humour. . . .

I asked whether the attack had been considered successful. He thought not. The Manchesters had failed, and Ginchy wasn't properly taken till about a week later. "When I was in hospital in London," he went on, "I talked to a son of a gun from the Brigade Staff; he'd been slightly gassed. He told me we'd done all that was expected of us; it was only a holding attack in our sector, so as to stop the Boches from firing down the hill into the backs of our men who were attacking Guillemont. They knew we hadn't a hope of getting Ale Alley."

He had told it in a simple unemphatic way, illustrating the story with unconscious gestures—taking aim with a rifle, and so on. But the nightmare of smoke and sunlight had been in his eyes, with a sense of confusion and calamity of which I could only guess at the reality. He was the shattered survivor of a broken battalion which had "done all that was expected of it".

I asked about young Fernby. Durley had been in the same hospital with him at Rouen and had seen him once. "They were trying to rouse him up a bit, as he didn't seem to recognize anybody. They knew we'd been in the same Battalion, so I was taken into his ward one night. His head was all over shrapnel wounds. I spoke to him and tried to get him to recognize me, but he didn't know who I was; he died a few hours later."

Silence was the only comment possible; but I saw the red screens round the bed and Durley whispering to Fernby's bandaged head and irrevocable eyes, while the nurse stood by with folded hands.

III

At the beginning of January David got himself passed for General Service abroad. I was completely taken by surprise when he came back and told me. Apparently the doctor asked him whether he wanted some more home service, but a sudden angry pride made him ask to be given G.S. A couple of weeks later he'd had his final leave and I was seeing him off at Liverpool Station.

A glum twenty-one-year-old veteran (unofficially in charge of a batch of young officers going out for the first time) he butted his way along the crowded platform with shoulders hunched, collar turned up to his ears, and hands plunged in pockets. A certain philosophic finality was combined with the fidgety out-of-luck look which was not unusual with him. "I've reduced my kit to a minimum this time. No revolver. I've worked it out that the chances are about five to one against my ever using it," he remarked, as he stood shuffling his feet to try and keep them warm. He hadn't explained how he'd worked the chances out, but he was always fond of a formula. Then the train began to move and he climbed awkwardly into his compartment. "Give my love to old Joe when you get to the First Battalion," was my final effort at heartiness. He nodded with a crooked smile. Going out for the third time was a rotten business and his face showed it.

"I ought to be going with him," I thought, knowing that I could have got G.S. at my last Board if I'd had the guts to ask for it. But how could one ask for it when there was a hope of getting a few more days with the Cheshire and the weather was so perishing cold out in France? "What a queer mixture he is," I thought, as I wandered absent-mindedly away from the station. Nothing could have been more cheerless than the rumbling cobbled street by the Docks, with dingy warehouses shutting out the dregs of daylight and an ash-coloured sky which foretold some more snow.

I remember going back to the hut that night after Mess. There was snow on the ground, and the shuttered glare and muffled din of the explosive works seemed more than usually grim. Sitting by the stove I began to read a magazine which David had left behind. It was a propagandist weekly containing translations from the Foreign Press. A Copenhagen paper said: "The sons of Europe are being crucified on the barbed wire because the misguided masses are shouting for it. They do not know what they do, and the statesmen wash their hands. They dare not deliver them from their martyr's death. . . ." Was this really the truth, I wondered; wild talk like that was new to me. I thought of Dick Tiltwood, and how he used to come into this hut with such shining evidences of youth in his face; and of dark-haired little Fernby who was just such another; and of Lance-Corporal Kendle, and all those others whose violent deaths had saddened my experience. David was now returning to be a candidate for this military martyrdom, and so (I remembered it with a sick assurance) was I.

Lying awake while the stove-light died redly in the corner of the room, I remembered the wine-faced Army Commander with his rows of medal-ribbons, and how young Allgood and I had marched past him at the Army School last May, with the sun shining and the band playing. He had taken the salute from four hundred officers and N.C.O.s of his Army. How many of them had been killed since then, and how deeply was he responsible for their deaths? Did he know what he was doing, or was he merely a successful old cavalryman whose peace-time popularity had pushed him up on to his present perch?

It was natural that I should remember Flixécourt. Those four weeks had kept their hold on my mind, and they now seemed like the First Act of a play—a light-hearted First Act which was unwilling to look ahead from its background of sunlight and the glorying beauty of beech forests. Life at the Army School, with its superb physical health, had been like a prelude to some really conclusive sacrifice of high-spirited youth. Act II had carried me along to the fateful First of July. Act III had sent me home to think things over. The autumn attacks had been a sprawling muddle of attrition and inconclusiveness. In the early summer the Fourth Army had been ready to advance with a new impetus. Now it was stuck in the frozen mud in front of Bapaume, like a derelict tank. And the story was the same all the way up to Ypres. Bellicose politicians and journalists were fond of using the word "crusade". But the "chivalry" (which I'd seen in epitome at the Army School) had been mown down and blown up in July, August, and September, and its remnant had finished the year's "crusade" in a morass of torment and frustration. Yet I was haunted by the memory of those Flixécourt weeks—almost as though I were remembering a time when I'd been in love. Was it with life that I'd been in love then?—for the days had seemed saturated with the fecundity of physical health and fine weather, and it had been almost as if my own germinant aliveness were interfused with some sacrificial rite which was to celebrate the harvest. "Germinating and German-hating," I thought, recovering my sense of reality with a feeble joke. After that I fell asleep.

*   *   *

I had an uncomfortable habit of remembering, when I woke up in the morning, that the War was still going on and waiting for me to go back to it; but apart from that and the times when my inmost thoughts got the upper hand of me, life at the Camp was comparatively cheerful, and I allowed myself to be carried along by its noisy current of good-humoured life. At the end of each day I found conso-lation in the fact that I had shortened the winter, for the new year had begun with a spell of perishing cold weather. Our First Battalion, which had been up to its neck in mud in front of Beaumont-Hamel, was now experiencing fifteen degrees of frost while carrying on minor operations con-nected with straightening the line. Dottrell wrote that they "weren't thinking beyond the mail and the rum ration", and advised me to stay away until the weather improved. It wasn't difficult to feel like following his advice; but soon afterwards I went into Liverpool for what I knew to be my final Medical Board. It was a dark freezing day, and all the officers in the waiting-room looked as if they wanted to feel their worst for the occasion. A sallow youth confided in me that he'd been out on the razzle the night before and was hoping to get away with another four weeks' home service.

There were two silver-haired Army doctors sitting at a table, poring over blue and white documents. One, with a waxed moustache, eyed me wearily when I came into the office. With a jerk of the head he indicated a chair by the table. "Feel fit to go out again?" "Yes; quite well, thank you." His pen began to move across the blue paper. "Has been passed fit for General Ser. . . ." He looked up irrit-ably. "Don't shake the table!" (I was tapping it with my fingers.) The other Colonel gazed mildly at me over his pince-nez. Waxed moustache grunted and went on writing. Shaking the table wouldn't stop that pen of his!

PART SEVEN: ROUEN IN FEBRUARY

I

Sometime in the second week of February I crossed to Havre on a detestable boat named *Archangel*. As soon as the boat began to move I was aware of a sense of relief. It was no use worrying about the War now; I was in the Machine again, and all responsibility for my future was in the haphazard control of whatever powers manipulated the British Expeditionary Force. Most of us felt like that, I imagine, and the experience was known as "being for it again". Apart from that, my only recollection of the crossing is that someone relieved me of my new trench-coat while I was asleep.

At nine o'clock in the evening of the next day I reported myself at the 5th Infantry Base Depot at Rouen. The journey from London had lasted thirty-three hours (a detail which I record for the benefit of those who like slow-motion war-time details). The Base Camp was a couple of miles from the town, on the edge of a pine forest. In the office where I reported I was informed that I'd been posted to our Second Battalion; this gave me something definite to grumble about, for I wanted to go where I was already known, and the prospect of joining a strange battalion made me feel more homeless than ever. The 5th I.B.D. Adjutant advised me to draw some blankets; the store-room was just round the corner, he said. After groping about in the dark and tripping over tent ropes I was beginning to lose my temper when I opened a door and found myself in a Guard Room. A man, naked to the waist, was kneeling in the middle of the floor, clutching at his chest and weeping uncontrollably. The Guard were standing around with embarrassed looks, and the Sergeant was beside him, patient and unpitying. While he was leading me to the blanket store I asked him what was wrong. "Why, sir, the man's been under detention for assaulting the military police, and now 'e's just 'ad news of his brother being killed. Seems to take it to 'eart more than most would. 'Arf crazy, 'e's been, tearing 'is clothes off and cursing the War and the Fritzes. Almost like a shell-shock case, 'e seems. It's his third time out. A Blighty one don't last a man long nowadays, sir." As I went off into the gloom I could still hear the uncouth howlings.

"Well, well; this is a damned depressing spot to arrive at!" I thought, while I lay awake trying to keep warm and munching a bit of chocolate, in a narrow segment of a canvas shed about four feet high. Beyond the army-blanket which served as a partition, two officers were chattering interminably in rapid Welsh voices. They were comparing their experiences at some squalid pleasure house in Rouen, and their disclosures didn't make the War seem any jollier. It was, in fact, the most disgusting little conversation I'd ever listened to. But what right had I to blame the poor devils for trying to have a good time before they went up to the Line? . . . Nevertheless, the War seemed to be doing its best to make me feel unheroic.

Next day I found the 5th I.B.D. Mess dispiriting. I knew nobody, and it wasn't a place where people felt inclined to be interested in one another, since none of them were there for more than a few days. They agreed in grumbling about the alcoholic R.C. padre who managed the mess; the food was bad, and four and threepence a day was considered an exorbitant charge. When they weren't on the training ground (known as "the Bull Ring") officers sat about in the Mess Room playing cards, cursing the cold weather, and talking tediously about the War with an admixture of ineffective cynicism which hadn't existed twelve months before. I watched them crowding round the notice board after a paper had been pinned to it. They were looking to see if their names were on the list of those going up to the Line next day. Those who were on the list laughed harshly and sat down, with simulated unconcern, to read a stale picture paper. On the same notice board were the names of three private soldiers who had been shot for cowardice since the end of January. "The sentence was duly carried out. . . ." In the meantime we could just hear the grumbling of the guns and there was the Spring Offensive to look forward to.

I was feeling as if I'd got a touch of fever, and next morning the doctor told me I'd got German measles. So I transferred myself ingloriously to No. 25 Stationary Hospital, which was a compound of tents with a barbed wire fence round it, about 300 yards from the Camp. There were six in the tent already and my arrival wasn't popular. An extra bed had to be brought in, and the four card players huddled against a smoky stove were interrupted by a gust of Arctic wind. There was snow on the ground and the tent was none too warm at the best of times. "Now, Mr. Parkins, I'm afraid you must shift round a bit to make room for the new patient," said the nurse. While my bed was being lugged into position by an orderly, Mr. Parkins made it plain that six had been company in that tent and seven was an inconvenience. One of his opponents told him to stop chewing the rag and deal again. The cards had been blown off the table and Parkins had lost what, he said, was the first decent hand he'd held that morning. But the additional overcrowding soon ceased to be a grievance, and I didn't spoil their well established circle by offering to butt in at bridge, for I was content to read a book and observe my fellow-invalids.

The quietest of them was Strangford, a specimen of adolescent simplicity, lanky and overgrown and credulous. He wore a kilt, but came of good North Irish stock. Though barely nineteen, he had done several months in the trenches. His father kept a pack of harriers in County Down, and his face would light up when I encouraged him to tell me about them. But unless he was talking or had some little job to keep him busy, his brain appeared to cease working altogether. He would sit on the edge of his bed, slowly rubbing his knee which had a bad sore on it; a mop of untidy brown hair hung over his forehead, and his huge clumsy hands and red wrists had outgrown his tunic.

After rubbing his knee, he takes a letter from his breast pocket, bending his gawky, unformed face over it; once he smiles secretly, but when he has read it through he is solemn—wondering, perhaps, when he will see his home and the harriers again.

Parkins was an obvious contrast to this modest youth. Pent up in the accidental intimacy of army life, men were usually anxious to exhibit themselves to the best advantage, particularly as regards their civilian antecedents. "I'll bet he was jolly well-dressed before the war," was a type of remark frequently made by young platoon commanders. Parkins was about thirty, and often reminded us that he had been to Cambridge; in private life he had been a schoolmaster. Plausible at first, he soon revealed his defects, for the slovenly tedium of that tent brought greed and selfishness to the surface. With his muddy eyes and small dark moustache, he wasn't a man one took to. But he was self-satisfied, and did his best to amuse us with indecent rhymes and anecdotes. He was also fond of using certain stilted expressions, such as "for the nonce" and "anent". "I've no complaints to make anent this hand," he would say when playing cards. He posed as a gay dog, chaffing the nurses when they brought in the food, and quoting Omar Khayyám at them—"a jug of wine, a loaf of bread and thou beside me, singing in the Wilderness"— and referring to the tent as "this battered Caravanserai whose portals are alternate Night and Day". Parkins did not conceal his dislike of the Front Line, and was now in hopes of getting a job as Railway Transport Officer. But he was the sort of man who would get killed in some unutterably wretched attack after doing his best to dodge it.

Young Holt was another second-rate character, plump, smooth-faced and spuriously smart. He had escaped from the Infantry into the Balloon Section, and now fancied himself in a leather overcoat with a fur collar—playing at "being in the Royal Flying Corps". He felt that R.F.C. officers had a social superiority to the Infantry. Being up in a balloon elevated a man in more ways than one, and he often aired his discrimination in such matters. Speaking of the Artillery, he would say: ' Yes, there's more *tone* in the R.F.A.—much more tone than you find in the Garrison Gunners!'' Holt was a harmless easy-going creature, but we got very tired of his incessant repetition of a stale joke which consisted in saying in a loud voice, *I will arise and will go unto my father and will say unto him: Father, stand-at-ease!*

Then there was White, a sensible Territorial Captain who had been in charge of Heavy Trench Mortars. Short and thick-set, with a deep, humorous voice, he talked in a muddled way about the War—sardonic about English methods, but easily impressed by notable "public names" of politicians and generals. He liked discussing Trench Mortar technicalities, and from the way he spoke about his men I knew that he had earned their gratitude.

There was another youngish man who had been a clerk in the Colonial Office and had gone to Egypt as a Yeomanry Sergeant before getting his Infantry commission. He talked to me, in a cockney accent, about his young wife, and was evidently kindly and reliable, though incapable of understanding an original idea. Two days after I'd seen the last of him, I couldn't remember either his face or his name.

The last of my six companions was Patterson, aged nineteen and fresh from Edinburgh University with a commission in the Field Artillery. His home was in Perth and he admitted that he loved porridge, when asking the nurse to try and wangle him a second helping of it. He talked broad Scots and made simple-minded war jokes, and then surprised me by quoting Milton and Keats. Self-reliant with a sort of pleasant truculence, he was thorough and careful in everything he did. With his crisp fair hair, grey eyes, and fresh complexion, he was a pattern of charming youthfulness. If he lived, he would be a shrewd, kindly man. Did he live, I wonder? . . .

After the first few days I used to slip through the wire fence and walk in the clean-smelling pine-woods. The surf-like sighing of the lofty colonnades could tranquillize my thoughts after the boredom of the tent and the chatter of the card players crouching by the stove. The pine-trees are patiently waiting for the guns to stop, I thought, and I felt less resentment against the War than I had done since I left England. . . . One afternoon I followed an alley which led downhill to a big shuttered house. Blackbirds were scolding among the bushes as I trespassed in the untidy garden, and someone was chopping timber in a brown copse below the house. A dog barked from the stable-yard; hens clucked, and a cow lowed. Such homely sounds were comforting when one was in the exile of army life. I thought of the lengthening spring twilights and the lovely wakening of the year, forgetful of the "Spring Offensive". But it was only for a short while, and the bitter reality returned to me as I squeezed myself through the hospital's barbed wire fence. I was losing my belief in the War, and I longed for mental acquiescence—to be like young Patterson, who had come out to fight for his country undoubting, who could still kneel by his bed and say his simple prayers, steadfastly believing that he was in the Field Artillery to make the world a better place. I had believed like that, once upon a time, but now the only prayer which seemed worth uttering was Omar Khayyám's:

> *For all the Sin wherewith the face of Man*
> *Is blackened—Man's forgiveness give—and take.*

II

Back at the Infantry Base Depot after my ten days of German measles, I stared at the notice board on nine successive mornings before my own name (typewritten and slightly misspelt Sharston) caused me to saunter away with the correct air of unconcern. At that moment the Medical Officer came in, shaking some snow off his coat. Sturdy, pink-faced and chubby, he looked a typical optimist. He had been two years with a fighting battalion and was now down at the Base for good, with a well earned D.S.O. He and I got on well together, but his appearance was deceptive, for he was a profound pessimist. He now exclaimed, rather crustily, that he supposed there'd only be one more winter out here, if we were lucky. I'd heard this remark from him before, and the first time had made me feel gloomy, for I had been hoping that the War would be over by next autumn. When the Mess waiter had brought him a whisky I ventured to ask his opinion about the German withdrawal on the Ancre; for at that time they were retiring to the Hindenburg Line, and sanguine subalterns were rejoicing over this proof that we'd "got them on the run". The Doctor assured me that the Germans were "pulling our legs properly". The idea seemed to please him; he always looked his brightest when he was announcing that we were certain to lose the War. We were now joined by a Rifle Brigade Major with an Irish brogue, who had been a cavalryman in the South African War. He had got his skull fractured by a bit of shell at the first battle of Ypres, but in spite of this he was a resolute optimist and was delighted to be back in France as second-in-command of a New Army Battalion. England, he said, was no place for an honest man; the sight of all those dirty dogs swindling the Government made him sick. When the Doctor grumbled about the rotten outlook, the Major would say: "Yes, things couldn't be much worse, but another two or three years ought to see the job finished." I found him surly and contradictory at first, but he softened when he got to know me, though he wasn't an easy man to discuss anything with, for he simply stated his opinions in a loud voice and only listened to one's replies in a detached one-eared way (which was literally true, since he was stone deaf on one side of his head, and had only got himself passed for active service after a tussle with the War Office). His rough and ready philosophy was refreshing, and he was a wholesome example of human inconsistency. He was a good-hearted man, I felt; but his attitude toward Conscientious Objectors was frankly brutal. He described, with evident relish, his methods of dealing with two of them who had turned up at the Rifle Brigade Depot. One had been a tough nut to crack, for he was a well-educated man, and the authorities were afraid of him. But the Major had got him run in for two years' hard labour. He'd have knocked him about a bit if he'd been allowed to, he said. The other one was some humble inarticulate wretch who refused to march. So the Major had him tied to the back of a wagon and dragged along a road until he was badly cut about. "After a few hundred yards he cried enough, and afterwards turned out to be quite a decent soldier. Made good, and was killed in the trenches." He smiled grimly. Discipline had to be enforced by brutality, said the Major; and, as I have already remarked, he wasn't amenable to argument.

I hadn't formed any opinion about Conscientious Objectors, but I couldn't help thinking that they must be braver men than some I'd seen wearing uniforms in safe places and taking salutes from genuine soldiers.

*　　　*　　　*

Resolved to make the most of my last day at the Base, I went down to Rouen early in the afternoon without having wasted any time in applying for leave from the Adjutant. A tram took me most of the way; the city looked fine as we crossed the river. There wasn't so very much to be done when I got there, but the first thing was to have a hair-cut. I'd had one a week ago, but this one might have to last me a longish while, for I wasn't keen on Battalion barbers. So I told the man to cut off as much as he could, and while he clipped and snipped I gazed gloomily at myself in the glass, speculating prosaically on the probabilities of my head of hair ever needing another trim up. A captain in the next chair had been through the whole repertoire—hair-cut, shave, shampoo, face-massage, and friction. "Now I feel a quid better," he remarked when he got up to go. He was wearing trench boots and was evidently on his way to the Line. I had heard him treating the barber, who spoke English, to a panegyric on the prospects of an Allied success in the Spring. "We're going to give them the knock all right this journey!" The barber asked him about a long scar which seamed his head. He smiled: "A souvenir of Devil's Wood." I wondered how much longer he would retain his enthusiasm for the Western Front. Personally I preferred rambling around Rouen and pretending that I was an ordinary peace-time tourist. In the old quarters of the town one could stroll about without meeting many English soldiers.

Later on I was going to the Hôtel de la Poste for a valedictory bath and dinner. In the meantime I was content to stare at shop-windows and explore side streets. It was a Saturday afternoon and the people were busy marketing. At the end of my wanderings I went into the Cathedral, leaving behind me the bustling Square and the sallow gusty sunset which flared above the roofs. In the Cathedral, perhaps, I could escape from the War for a while, although the Christian Religion had apparently no claim to be regarded as a Benevolent Neutral Power.

It was some Saint's Day, and the nave was crowded with drifting figures, their footfalls echoing in the dusk. Sometimes a chair scrooped when a worshipper moved away. Candles burned in clear clusters, like flickering gold flowers, in the shrines where kneeling women gazed and whispered and moved their hands devoutly. In the pulpit a priest was urging the Lenten significance of "Jésu", tilting his pallid square face from side to side and gesticulating mechanically. A congregation sat or stood to hear him; among them, at my elbow, a small child stared up at the priest with stupid innocent eyes. That child couldn't understand the sermon any more than it understood the War. It saw a man, high up and alone, clenching his hands and speaking vehemently; it also saw the figures of people called soldiers who belonged to something that made a much bigger noise than the preacher, who now stopped suddenly, and the monotonous chanting began again in front of the altar (sounding, I thought, rather harsh and hopeless).

The preacher, I inferred, had been reminding us that we ought to love one another and be like little children. "Jésu" had said so, and He had died to save us (but not to save the Germans or the Austrians or any of that lot). It was no good trying to feel uplifted, when such thoughts grimaced at me; but there was a certain consolation in the solemnity of the Cathedral, and I remained there after the service had ended. Gradually, the glory faded from the rose-window above the organ. I looked at all the windows, until their lights were only blurs and patches, and the prophets and martyrs robed in blue and crimson and green were merged in outer darkness.

* * *

The Hôtel de la Poste hadn't altogether modernized its interior, but it contained much solid comfort and supplied the richest meals in Rouen. Consequently it was frequented by every British officer employed in the district, and had become a sort of club for those indispensable residents—so much so that strong suggestions had been advanced by senior officers to the effect that the *Poste* should be put out of bounds for all Infantry subalterns on their way to the Line. The place, they felt, was becoming too crowded, and the deportment of a "temporary gentleman" enjoying his last decent dinner was apt to be more suitable to a dug-out than a military club.

Leaning back in a wicker chair, I enjoyed the after-effects of a hot bath and wondered what I'd have for dinner. The lift came sliding down from nowhere to stop with a dull bump. A bulky grey-haired Colonel, with green tabs and a Coronation Medal, stepped heavily out, leaning on a stick and glaring around him from under a green and gold cap and aggressive eyebrows. His disapproval focused itself on a group of infantry subalterns whose ungainly legs were cumbered with high trench boots; trench-coats and haversacks were slung untidily across their chairs; to-night, or to-morrow, or "some old time or other" they'd be crawling up to the War in an over-ventilated reinforcement train, gazing enviously at the Red Cross trains which passed them—going the other way—and disparaging the French landscape, "so different to good old Blighty". Compared with "the troops", who travelled in vans designed for horses and cattle, they were in clover. The Colonel, on the other hand, probably supervised an office full of clerks who made lists of killed, wounded, and reinforcements. I had visited such a place myself in an attempt to get my name transferred to the First Battalion, and had been received with no civility at all. They were all much too busy to rearrange the private affairs of a dissatisfied second-lieutenant, as might have been expected. But the contrast between the Front Line and the Base was an old story, and at any rate the Base Details were at a disadvantage as regards the honour and glory which made the War such an uplifting experience for those in close contact with it. I smiled sardonically at the green and gold Colonel's back view. The lift ascended again, leaving a confused murmur of male voices and a clatter of feet on the polished wood floor. Officers pushed through the swing-doors in twos and threes, paused to buy an English paper from the concierge, vanished to hang up their overcoats, and straddled in again, pulling down their tunics and smoothing their hair, conscious of gaiters, neatly-fitting or otherwise. Young cavalrymen were numerous, their superior social connections demonstrated by well-cut riding boots and predominantly small heads. Nice-looking young chaps with nice manners, they sipped cocktails and stood up respectfully when a Cavalry Brigadier strode past them. The Cavalry were still waiting for their chance on the Western Front. . . . Would they ever get it, I wondered. Personally, I thought it would be a pity if they did, for I disliked the idea of a lot of good horses being killed and wounded, and I had always been soft-hearted about horses. By the time I'd finished my dinner and a bottle of Burgundy, I felt soft-hearted about almost everything. The large dining-room was full of London Clubmen dressed as Colonels, Majors, and Captains with a conscientious objection to physical discomfort. But, after all, somebody had to be at the Base; modern warfare offered a niche for everyone, and many of them looked better qualified for a card-table than a military campaign. They were as much the victims of circumstances as the unfortunate troops in the trenches. Puffing a cigar, I decided that there was a tolerant view to be taken about almost everybody, especially after a good dinner at the Hôtel de la Poste.

PART EIGHT: THE SECOND BATTALION

I

Although the War has been described as the greatest event in history, it could be tedious and repetitional for an ordinary Infantry Officer like myself.

From Corbie Station the War had started me on my home journey in a Hospital Train. Rather more than seven months later, at midnight, it again deposited me at Corbie Station after eight hours in an unlit and overcrowded carriage which had no glass in its windows. My valise was on a truck and though I made a scrambling attempt to get it unloaded the train clanked away into the gloom with all my belongings on board. We slept on the floor of the Field Ambulance Hut outside the station; my companions grumbled a good deal, for several of them were out again after being wounded last year, and one of them claimed to have been hit in both lungs. Two cadet-officers were going with me to the Second Battalion, but I had little in common with them except our lost valises, which were returned to us a week later (with one sample of everything abstracted by someone at the Army Service Corps Dump). Next morning, after glumly congratulating myself that I'd packed my safety razor in my haversack, I walked to my new unit, which was seven miles away. I was wearing my best friends, a pair of greased marching boots whose supple strength had never failed to keep the water out; how much those boots meant to me can only be understood by persons who have shared my type of experience; I can only say that they never gave me sore feet; and if this sounds irrelevant, I must remind the reader that a platoon commander's feet were his fortune.

The Second Battalion of the Flintshire Fusiliers had recently returned from two months in the Cléry sector of the Somme Front, where they had endured some of the severest weather of the War. Battalion records relate that there were no braziers in the trenches, fuel was so scarce that wooden crosses were taken from casual graves, and except for the tepid tea that came up in tins wrapped in straw, food was mostly cold. Major-General Whincop, who commanded the Division, had made himself obnoxiously conspicuous by forbidding the Rum Ration. He was, of course, over anxious to demonstrate his elasticity of mind, but the "No Rum Division" failed to appreciate their uniqueness in the Expeditionary Force. He also thought that smoking impaired the efficiency of the troops and would have liked to restrict their consumption of cigarettes. General Whincop had likewise demonstrated his independence of mind earlier in the War by forbidding the issue of steel helmets to his Division. His conservative objection (which was based on a belief that this new War Office luxury would weaken the men's fighting spirit—"make them soft", in fact) was, of course, only a flash in the pan (or brain-pan) and Whincop's reputation as an innovator was mainly kept alive by his veto on the Rum Ration. G.O.C.s, like platoon commanders, were obliged to devise "stunts" to show their keenness, and opportunities for originality were infrequent. But since 1918 Generals have received their full share of ridicule and abuse, and it would not surprise me if someone were to start a Society for the Prevention of Cruelty to Great War Generals. If such a Society were formed, I, for one, would gladly contribute my modest half-guinea per annum; for it must be remembered that many an unsuccessful General had previously been the competent Colonel of an Infantry Battalion, thereby earning the gratitude and admiration of his men.

Anyhow, the frost had been intense, and owing to the rationing of coal in England the issue to the Army had been limited and coke-issues had caused many cases of coke-fume poisoning where the men slept in unventilated dug-outs. After this miserable experience (which had ended with a thaw and a hundred cases of trench-feet) the Second

Battalion was now resting at Camp 13, about two miles from Morlancourt. The huts of Camp 13 had been erected since last summer; they disfigured what I had formerly known as an inoffensive hollow about half a mile from the reedy windings of the Somme. No one had a good word for the place. The Battalion was in low spirits because the Colonel had been wounded a few weeks before, and he had been so popular that everyone regarded him as irreplaceable. His successor was indulgent and conciliatory, but it seemed that greater aggressiveness would have been preferable. Contrasting him with the rough-tongued efficiency of Kinjack, I began to realize that, in a Commanding Officer, amiability is not enough.

Meanwhile we were in what was called "Corps Reserve", and Colonel Easby had issued the order "carry on with platoon training" (a pronouncement which left us free to kill time as best we could). No. 8 Platoon, which was my own compact little command, was not impressive on parade. Of its thirty-four N.C.O.s and men, eight were Lewis gunners and paraded elsewhere. Eight was likewise the number of Private Joneses in my platoon, and my first difficulty was to differentiate between them. The depleted Battalion had been strengthened by a draft from England, and these men were mostly undersized, dull-witted, and barely capable of carrying the heavy weight of their equipment. As an example of their proficiency, I can say that in one case platoon training began with the man being taught how to load his rifle. Afterwards I felt that he would have been less dangerous in his pre-existing ignorance.

It was difficult to know what to do with my bored and apathetic platoon. I wasn't a competent instructor, and my sergeant was conscientious but unenterprising. *Infantry Training*, which was the only manual available, had been written years before trench-warfare "came into its own" as a factor in world affairs, and the condensed and practical *Handbook for the Training of Platoons* was not issued until nearly twelve months afterwards. One grey afternoon, when we had gone through all our monotonous exercises and the men's eyes were more than usually mindless, I had a bright unmilitary idea and ordered them to play hide-and-seek among some trees. After a self-conscious beginning they livened up and actually enjoyed themselves. When I watched them falling in again with flushed and jolly faces I was aware that a sense of humanity had been restored to them, and realized how intolerable the ordinary exercises were unless the instructor was an expert. Even football matches were impossible, since there was no suitable ground.

The main characteristics of Camp 13 were mud and smoke. Mud was everywhere. All the Company officers lived in one long gloomy draughty hut with an earth floor. Smoke was always drifting in from the braziers of the adjoining kitchen. After dark we sat and shivered in our "British Warm" coats, reading, playing cards, and writing letters with watering eyes by the feeble glimmer of guttering candles. Orderlies brought in a clutter of tin mugs and plates, and Maconochie stew was consumed in morose discomfort. It was an existence which suffocated all pleasant thoughts; nothing survived except animal cravings for warmth, food, and something to break the monotony of Corps Rest routine.

The only compensation for me was that my body became healthy, in spite of lesser discomforts such as a continuous cold in the head. The landscape was a compensation too, for I liked its heaving grey and brown billows, dotted with corn-stacks, patched and striped by plough and stubble and green crops, and crossed by bridle tracks and lonely wandering roads. Hares and partridges hurried away as I watched them. Along the horizon the guns still boomed and thudded, and bursting shells made tiny puffs of smoke above ridges topped by processions of trees, with here and there the dark line of woods. But from some windy upland I looked down on villages, scattered in the folds of hill and valley like handfuls of pebbles, grey and dull red, and from such things I got what consolation I could.

One Sunday afternoon I walked across to Heilly. I'd been there for a few days with the First Battalion last July, before we marched back to the Line in dust and glare. The water still sang its undertones by the bridge and went twinkling to the bend, passing the garden by the house where the Field Cashier used to hand us our money. I remembered going there with Dick Tiltwood, just a year ago. Ormand was with me this time, for he had joined the Second Battalion soon after I did. He had still got his little gramophone, and we reminded ourselves how Mansfield and Barton used to be for ever "chipping" him about it. "I must say I used to get jolly fed-up with them sometimes; they overdid it, especially about that record *Lots of Loving*." He laughed, rolling his good-humoured eyes round at me under the strongly marked black eyebrows which indicated that he had a strong temper when roused. The joke about *Lots of Loving* had consisted in the others pretending that it contained an unprintable epithet. On one occasion they conspired with the Adjutant, who asked Ormand to play *Lots of Loving* and then simulated astonishment at a certain adjective which was indistinct owing to the worn condition of the disc. Whereupon Ormand explained angrily, "I ask you, is it bloody likely that 'His Master's Voice' would send out a record with the word —— in it?"

As we trudged back from Heilly the sun was sinking red beyond the hazy valleys, a shrewd wind blowing, and plough teams turning a last furrow along the ridges. We'd had quite a good afternoon, but Ormand's cheerfulness diminished as we neared the Camp. He didn't fancy his chance in the Spring Offensive and he wanted to be back with the "good old First Battalion", though he wouldn't find many of the good old faces when he got there. He spoke gloomily about his longing for an ordinary civilian career and his hatred of "this silly stunt which the blasted Bishops call the Great Adventure". He had been on a Court Martial the day before, and though nothing had been required of him except to make up the quorum of officers trying the case, he had been upset by it. Some poor wretch had been condemned to be shot for cowardice. The court had recommended the prisoner to mercy, but the proceedings had been bad for young Ormand. However, he relieved the situation by exclaiming, "And to-morrow I've got to have my . . . anti-typhoid injection!" and I reminded him that he was reducing his overdraft at Cox's by being at the Front. So our walk ended; we passed the looming aerodrome, and the lines of lorries under the trees along the main road, and the sentry who stood by a glowing brazier at the crossroads. Down in the hollow crouched the Camp; a disgusting dinner in the smoky hut and then early to bed, was all it could offer us. "Summer time" began at midnight, which meant one hour less sleep and absolutely nothing else.

II

Palm Sunday was on April 1st that year. On April 2nd we left Camp 13. No one wanted to see it again, and as we went up hill to the Corbie road the smoke from the incinerators made the place look as if we had set fire to it.

I had a feeling that we were marching away to a better land. Camp 13 had clogged our minds, but the troops were in better spirits to-day and the Battalion seemed to have recovered its consciousness as a unit. The wind was blowing cold enough for snow, but the sun shone and wintry weather couldn't last much longer. Where were we walking to, I wondered; for this was known to be the first stage of a longish migration northwards. Arras, perhaps; rumours of an impending battle there had been active lately. As second-in-command of the Company I went along behind it, rather at my ease. Watching the men as they plodded patiently on under their packs, I felt as if my own identity was becoming merged in the Battalion. We were on the move and the same future awaited all of us (though most of the men had bad boots and mine were quite comfortable).

More light-hearted than I'd been for some time, I contemplated my Company Commander, who was in undisputed occupation of a horse which looked scarcely up to his weight. Captain Leake had begun by being rude to me. I never discovered the reason. But he had been a Special Reserve officer before the War, and he couldn't get certain regimental traditions out of his head. In the good old days, all second-lieutenants had been called "warts", and for their first six months a senior officer never spoke to them, except on parade. Leake evidently liked the idea, for he was a man who enjoyed standing on his dignity; but such behaviour was inappropriate to active service, and six months at the Front usually sufficed to finish the career of a second-lieutenant. On my second morning at Camp 13 Leake had remarked (for my special benefit) that "these newly joined warts were getting too big for their boots". This was incorrect, for I was bemoaning the loss of my valise, and the M.O. had just given me my anti-typhoid injection. Leake also resented the fact that I had served with the First Battalion, which he appeared to regard as a hated rival. He thawed gradually after my first week, and was now verging on cordiality, which I did my best to encourage. The other Company Commanders had been friendly from the first, for I had known them at Clitherland in 1915.

Then there was the Doctor, who was now away on leave but would certainly be back before things became lively. Captain Munro had been with the Second Battalion about eighteen months. The first time I saw him was when he gave me my anti-typhoid injection. I looked at him with interest, for he was already known to me by reputation. "Hullo, here's Sherston, the man who did stunts with the First Battalion," he remarked, as I unbuttoned my shirt for the perforation process. He was giving double injections, so as to save us the trouble of feeling unwell twice. "That'll keep you quiet for forty-eight hours," he observed; and I retired, with a sickly grin. The M.O. was a famous character in the Battalion, and I was hoping to get to know him better. (At the time of writing I can indeed claim to have achieved my hope. But the Doctor is a man adverse to the idea of being applauded in print, and he would regard any reference to his local renown as irrelevant to this narrative.)

Equally popular was Bates, the Quartermaster, who was a burlier prototype of Joe Dottrell, with fewer political prejudices. When, at Camp 13, there had been rumours of a Divisional Race Meeting, Bates had asked me to ride his mare. The Races had been cancelled, but the notion had delighted me for a day or two. This mare could gallop quite well and was the apple of the Quartermaster's eye. It was said that on one occasion, when the Transport was having a rough time, Bates had rigged up a tarpaulin shelter for his mare and slept out in the open himself. I was mentally comparing Bates and Dottrell, to their mutual credit, when we came to the end of our first fifty minutes and the men fell out at the side of the road and slipped their packs off. A gang of red and blue capped German prisoners was at work on the road close by, and their sullen under-nourished faces made our own troops look as if they were lucky in some sort of liberty. But whistles blew, pack straps were adjusted, and on we went. By half-past one the Battalion was in its billets in Corbie.

*   *   *

Before dinner Ralph Wilmot came round to our Company Mess to suggest that Leake and myself should join "a bit of a jolly" which he'd arranged for that evening. Wilmot was a dark, monocled young man, mature for his years. His war experience had begun with despatch riding on a motor-bicycle in 1914. Afterwards he had gone to Gallipoli, where he had survived until the historic Evacuation. He had now done a long spell of service in France, and was a popular character in the Second Battalion. He had the whimsical smile which illuminated a half-melancholy temperament, and could give an amusing twist to the sorriest situation, since he liked to see life as a tragi-comedy and himself as a debonair philosopher, a man with a gay past who had learned to look at the world more in sorrow than in anger. His unobtrusive jests were enunciated with a stammer which somehow increased their effect. With some difficulty he now told us that he had discovered a place where we could "buy some bubbly and tickle the

ivories". The ivory-tickling would be his own contribution, for he had a passion for playing the piano. So we
spent the evening in a sparsely furnished little parlour on
the ground-floor of a wine-merchant's house. The wine-
merchant's wife, a sallow silent woman, brought in bottle
after bottle of "bubbly" which, whatever its quality, produced conviviality. We drank farewell to civilization with
an air of finality, while Wilmot performed on an upright
piano, the tone of which was meretriciously agreeable, like
the flavour of the champagne. He played, mostly by ear,
familiar passages from *Tosca* and *Bohème*, musical comedy
extracts, and sentimental ballads. We all became confidential and almost emotional. I felt that at last I was really
getting on good terms with Leake; every glass of wine made
us dislike one another a little less. Thus the proceedings
continued until after midnight, while Wilmot became more
and more attached to a certain popular song. We sang the
chorus over and over again:

> *Moon, moon, see-reen-ly shy-ning,*
> *Don't go home too soo-oon;*
> *You've such a charm about you*
> *That we—can't get—on with-out you.*
> *Da-da-da, de-dum . . . etc.*

The atmosphere of the room had become tropical, for we
had all been smoking like chimneys. But Wilmot couldn't
tear himself away from that piano, and while he caressed
the keys with lingering affection, the wine-merchant's wife
received I don't know how many francs and we all wrote
our names in her album. From the number of shaky signa-
tures in it I judged that she must have made a handsome
profit out of the War.

Out in the white moonlight, Leake and I meandered
along the empty street, accompanied by our tipsy shadows.
At the door of my billet we shook hands "sholemnly", and
I assured him that he could always rely on me to "blurry
well do my damndest for him". He vanished heavily, and
I spent several minutes prodding at the key-hole of the
greengrocer's shop. Once inside the door, my difficulties

were almost ended. I remember balancing myself in the
dark little shop, which was full of strong-smelling vegetables, and remarking aloud, "Well, old boy, here you are,
and now you gotter get up the stairs." My room was an
unventilated cupboard which reeked of onions; the stairs
were steep, but my flea-bag was on the floor and I fell
asleep fully dressed. What with the smell of onions and the
bad champagne, I awoke feeling like nothing on earth, and
to say that Leake was grumpy at breakfast would be to put
it mildly. But we were on the march by nine, in cold bright
weather, and by the first halt I was feeling surprisingly
clear-headed and alert.

We had halted on some high ground above Pont Noyelles:
I can remember the invigorating freshness of the air and
the delicate outlines of the landscape towards Amiens, and
how I gazed at a line of tall trees by the river beyond which
not two miles away, was the village of Bussy where I'd
been last June before the Somme battle began. At such a
moment as that the War felt quite a friendly affair and I
could assure myself that being in the Infantry was much
better than loafing about at home. And at the second halt
I was able to observe what a pleasant picture the men
made, for some of them were resting in warm sunlight
under a crucifix and an old apple-tree. But by midday the
march had become tedious; the road was dusty, the sun
glared down on us, and I was occupied in preventing exhausted men from falling out. It was difficult to keep some
of them in the ranks, and by the time we reached Villers-
Bocage (nearly fourteen miles from Corbie) I was pushing
two undersized men along in front of me, another one
staggered behind hanging on to my belt, and the Company
Sergeant-Major was carrying three rifles as well as his own.
By two o'clock they were all sitting on dirty straw in a sun-
chinked barn, with their boots and socks off. Their feet
were the most important part of them, I thought, as I made
my sympathetic inspection of sores and blisters. The old
soldiers grinned at me philosophically, puffing their Woodbines. It was all in the day's work, and the War was the
War. The newly-joined men were different; white and

jaded, they stared up at me with stupid trusting eyes. I wished I could make things easier for them, but I could do nothing beyond sending a big batch of excruciating boots to the Battalion boot-menders, knowing that they'd come back roughly botched, if anything were done to them at all. But one Company's blisters were a small event in the procession of sore feet that was passing through Villers-Bocage. The woman in my billet told me in broken English that troops had been going through for fifteen days, never stopping more than one night and always marching towards Doullens and Arras. My only other recollection of Villers-Bocage is the room in which our Company's officers dined and slept. It contained an assortment of stuffed and mouldy birds with outspread wings. There was a stork, a jay, and a sparrow-hawk; also a pair of squirrels. Lying awake on the tiled floor I could watch a seagull suspended by a string from the ceiling; very slowly it revolved in the draughty air; and while it revolved I fell asleep, for the day had been a long one.

*   *   *

Next day's march took us to Beauval, along a monotonous eight-mile stretch of the main road from Amiens to St. Pol. Wet snow was falling all the way. We passed into another "Army area"; the realm of Rawlinson was left behind us and our self-sacrificing exertions were now to be directed by Allenby. Soon after entering the Allenby Area we sighted a group of mounted officers who had stationed themselves under the trees by the roadside. Word was passed back that it was the Corps Commander. Since there were only three Corps Commanders in each Army they were seldom seen, so it was with quite a lively interest that we put ourselves on the alert to eyes-left this one. While we were trudging stolidly nearer to the great man, Colonel Easby detached himself from the head of the column, rode up to the General, and saluted hopefully. The Corps Commander (who was nothing much to look at, for his interesting accumulation of medal-ribbons was concealed by a waterproof coat) ignored our eyes-lefting of him; he was too busy bellowing at poor Colonel Easby, whom he welcomed thus. *C.G.* "Are you stuck to that bloody horse?" *Col. E.* "No, sir." (Dismounts hastily and salutes again.) As Leake's Company went by, the General was yelling something about why the hell hadn't the men got the muzzles of their rifles covered (this being one of his "special ideas"). "Pity he don't keep his own muzzle covered," remarked someone in the ranks, thereby voicing a prevalent feeling. The Corps Commander was equally abusive because the "Cookers" were carrying brooms and other utilitarian objects. Also the Companies were marching with fifty yard intervals between them (by a special order of the late Rawlinson). In Allenby's Army the intervals between Companies had to be considerably less, as our Colonel was now finding out. However, the episode was soon behind us and the "Cookers" rumbled peacefully on their way, brooms and all, emitting smoke and stewing away at the men's dinners. Very few of us ever saw the Corps Commander again. It was a comfort to know that Allenby, at any rate, could be rude to him if he wanted to.

*　　　*　　　*

We started from Beauval at four o'clock on a sunny afternoon and went another eight miles to a place called Lucheux. . . . There is nothing in all this, the reader will expostulate. But there was a lot in it, for us. We were moving steadily nearer to the Spring Offensive; for those who thought about it the days had an ever intensifying significance. For me, the idea of death made everything seem vivid and valuable. The War could be like that to a man, until it drove him to drink and suffocated his finer apprehensions.

Among the troops I observed a growing and almost eager expectancy; their cheerfulness increased; something was going to happen to them; perhaps they believed that the Arras Battle would end the War. It was the same spirit which had animated the Army before the Battle of the Somme. And now, once again, we could hear along the horizon that blundering doom which bludgeoned armies into material for military histories. "That way to the Sausage Machine!" some old soldier exclaimed as we passed a signpost marked *Arras, 32 k.* We were entering Doullens with the brightness of the setting sun on our faces. As we came down the hill our second-in-command (a gentle middle-aged country solicitor) was walking beside me, consoling himself with reminiscences of cricket and hunting.

Thus the Battalion slogged on into an ominous Easter, and every man carried his own hazardous hope of survival. Overshadowed by the knowledge of what was ahead of us, I became increasingly convinced that a humble soldier holding up a blistered foot could have greater dignity than a blustering Corps Commander.

That night we were in huts among some wooded hills. I can remember how we had supper out in the moonlight sitting round a brazier with plates of ration stew on our knees. The wind was from the east and we could hear the huge bombardment up at Arras. Brown and leafless, the sombre woods hemmed us in. Soon the beeches would be swaying and quivering with the lovely miracle of spring. How many of us will return to that, I wondered, forgetting my hatred of the War in a memory of all that April had ever meant for me. . . .

On Good Friday morning I woke with sunshine streaming in at the door and broad Scots being shouted by some Cameronians in the next hut. Someone was practising the bagpipes at the edge of the wood, and a mule contributed a short solo from the Transport Lines.

*   *   *

On Saturday afternoon we came to Saulty, which was only ten miles from Arras and contained copious indications of the Offensive, in the form of ammunition and food dumps and the tents of a Casualty Clearing Station. A large Y.M.C.A. canteen gladdened the rank and file, and I sent my servant there to buy a pack full of Woodbines for an emergency which was a certainty. Canteens and *estaminets* would be remote fantasies when we were in the devastated area. Twelve dozen packets of Woodbines in a pale green cardboard box were all that I could store up for the future consolation of B Company; but they were better than nothing and the box was no weight for my servant to carry.

Having seen the men settled into their chilly barns and sheds, I stuffed myself with coffee and eggs and betook myself to a tree stump in the peaceful park of a white château close to the village. Next day we were moving to our concentration area, so I was in a meditative mood and disposed to ask myself a few introspective questions. The sun was just above the tree-tops; a few small deer were grazing; a rook flapped overhead; and some thrushes and blackbirds were singing in the brown undergrowth. Nothing was near to remind me of the War; only the enormous thudding on the horizon and an aeroplane humming across the clear sky. For some obscure reason I felt confident and serene. My thoughts assured me that I wouldn't go back to England to-morrow if I were offered an improbable choice between that and the battle. Why should I feel elated at the prospect of the battle, I wondered. It couldn't be only the coffee and eggs which had caused me to feel so acquiescent. Last year, before the Somme, I hadn't known what I was in for. I knew now; and the idea was giving me emotional satisfaction! I had often read those farewell letters from second-lieutenants to their relatives which the newspapers were so fond of printing. "Never has life brought me such an abundance of noble feelings," and so on. I had always found it difficult to believe that these young men had really felt happy with death staring them in the face, and I resented any sentimentalizing of infantry attacks. But here I was, working myself up into a similar mental condition, as though going over the top were a species of religious experience. Was it some suicidal self-deceiving escape from the limitless malevolence of the Front Line? . . . Well, whatever it was, it was some compensation for the loss of last year's day dreams about England (which I could no longer indulge in, owing to an indefinite hostility to "people at home who couldn't understand "). I was beginning to feel rather arrogant toward "people at home". But my mind was in a muddle; the War was too big an event for one man to stand alone in. All I knew was that I'd lost my faith in it and there was nothing left to believe in except "the Battalion spirit". The Battalion spirit meant living oneself into comfortable companionship with the officers and N.C.O.s around one; it meant winning the respect, or even the affection, of platoon and company. But while exploring my way into the War I had discovered the impermanence of its humanities. One evening we could be all together in a cosy room in Corbie, with Wilmot playing the piano and Dunning telling me about the eccentric old ladies who lived in his mother's boarding house in Bloomsbury. A single machine-gun or a few shells might wipe out the whole picture within a week. Last summer the First Battalion had been part of my life; by the middle of September it had been almost obliterated. I knew that a soldier signed away his independence; we were at the front to fight, not to think. But it became a bit awkward when one couldn't look even a week ahead. And now there was a steel curtain down between April and May. On the other side of the curtain, if I was lucky, I should meet the survivors, and we should begin to build up our little humanities all over again.

That was the bleak truth, and there was only one method of evading it; to make a little drama out of my own experience—that was the way out. I must play at being a hero in shining armour, as I'd done last year; if I didn't, I might crumple up altogether. (Self-inflicted wounds weren't uncommon on the Western Front, and brave men had put bullets through their own heads before now, especially when winter made trench warfare unendurable.) Having thus decided on death or glory, I knocked my pipe out and got up from the tree stump with a sense of having solved my problems. The deer were still grazing peacefully in the park; but the sun was a glint of scarlet beyond the strip of woodland and the air was turning chilly. Along the edge of the world that infernal bang-

ing was going on for all it was worth. Three Army Corps
were to attack on Easter Monday.

*   *   *

On a sunny Easter morning we moved another seven
miles, to Basseux, a village which had been quite close to
the trenches before the Germans withdrew to the Hindenburg Line. The Sausage Machine was now only eight
miles away from us, and the preliminary bombardment
was, as someone in the ranks remarked, "a fair bloody
treat to listen to". We insisted on being optimistic. The
Tanks were going to put the fear of God into the Boches,
and the Cavalry would get their opportunity at last. We
passed a squadron of Lancers on the road. Oh yes, they
were massing for a break-through. Allenby knew what he
was up to all right. And our Divisional General had told
someone that it would be a walk-over for the infantry this
time.

That afternoon I strolled out to inspect our old front-
line trenches. As usual they gave me a queer feeling; it
would be almost accurate to say that they fascinated me.
Derelict ditches as they now were, battalion after battalion
had endured intensities of experience in that intensified
strip of territory. Night after night the tea-dixies had been
carried up that twisting communication trench. Night
after night sentries had stared over sodden parapets until
the sky reddened and the hostile territory emerged, familiar and yet foreign. Not a very good sector to hold, I
thought, observing how our cramped trench system had
been overlooked by the Germans. That mile-and-a-bit
back to Basseux hadn't been so easy a couple of months
ago.

In peace time the village must have been quite a pretty
little place, and even now it wasn't very badly damaged.
All our officers were billeted in a dilapidated white château, which I now explored until I was sitting with my feet
out of the window of an attic. Down in the courtyard Ormand and Dunning and one or two others were playing
cricket with a stump and a wooden ball, using an old

brazier as a wicket. Wilmot had found a ramshackle piano
from which he was extracting his favourite melodies.
Pigeons fluttered around the red tiled roofs and cooed in
the warm evening sunshine. Three yellow balloons were
visible. Then the little Adjutant bustled across the courtyard with a bunch of papers in his hand. There was no
time for relaxation in the orderly room, for after to-day we
were under orders to move at the shortest notice. . . .
Young Ormand shouted up at me, "Come down and have
a knock at the nets."

*   *   *

The Battle of Arras began at 5.30 next morning. For two
days we hung about the château, listening to the noise (of
Military History being manufactured regardless of expense) and waiting for the latest rumours. With forced uneasy gaiety we talked loudly about the successes reported
from the Line. "Our objectives gained at Neuville-
Vitasse", "five thousand prisoners taken", and so on. But
every one of us had something in his mind which he
couldn't utter, even to his best friend.

Meanwhile the weather was misbehaving itself badly.
Snow showers passed by on a bitterly cold wind, and I
began an intimate battle in which a chill on the intestines
got the better of me. It wasn't so easy to feel like a happy
warrior turning his necessities to glorious gain, when
doomed to go in company with gastritis, a sore throat, and
several festering scratches on each hand. No more clean
socks or handkerchiefs either. A big mail came in on Tuesday—the first we'd had for a week—and this kept us quiet
for an interval of flimsy consolation. My only letter was
from Aunt Evelyn, who apologized as usual for having so
little to say. She had been reading *The Life of Disraeli*—
"such a relief to get away from all these present-day horrors. What a wonderful man he was. Are you still in the
Rest Camp? I do hope so." She added that spring-cleaning
had been going on vigorously, with the usual floods of conversation from the maids. . . . This didn't help my gastritis,
which was getting beyond a joke. The M.O. wasn't back

from leave yet, but one of his orderlies handed me an opium pill of such constipating omnipotence that my intestines were soon stabilized to a condition suitable for open warfare.

In the middle of Wednesday afternoon we were having an eleven-a-side single-brazier cricket match on a flat piece of ground in the château garden. The sun was shining between snow showers, and most of the men were watching from the grassy bank above. One of the Company Sergeant-Majors was playing a lively innings, though the ball was beginning to split badly. Then a whistle blew and the match ended abruptly. Less than an hour later the Battalion marched away from Basseux.

III

A heavy snowstorm set in soon after we started. A snowstorm on April 11th was the sort of thing that one expected in the War and it couldn't be classed as a major misfortune. Nevertheless we could have done without it, since we were marching away from all comfort and safety; greatcoats had been left behind and we had nothing but what we stood up in. As we slogged along narrow winding lanes the snow melted on the shiny waterproof sheets which kept the men uncomfortably warm. We were now in the devastated area; villages had been levelled to heaps of bricks; fruit trees, and even pollard-willows, had been hacked down, and there was still a chance that we might be the victims of a booby trap in the shape of a dynamite charge under a causeway. A signpost pointed to Blairville; but a couple of inches of snow was enough to blot out Blairville. The next village was Ficheux (the men called it "Fish Hooks"—any joke being better than none in that snowstorm); but Ficheux wasn't there at all; it had vanished from the landscape.

The snow had stopped when, after marching eight miles, we bivouacked in the dregs of daylight by a sunken road near Mercatel, a place which offered no shelter except the humanity of its name. After dark I found my way into a small dug-out occupied by a Trench Mortar Sergeant-Major and two signallers who were working a field telephone. With Shirley (one of our Company officers) I considered myself lucky to be there, crouching by a brazier, while the Sergeant-Major regaled us, in omniscient tones, with rumours about the desperate fighting at Wancourt and Heninel, names which meant nothing to me. I dozed through the night without ever being unaware of the coke fumes from the brazier and the tick-tack of the telephone.

Daylight discovered us blear-eyed and (to abbreviate a contemporary phrase) "fed up and far from home". We got through the morning somehow and I issued some of my "emergency Woodbines". Rifle-cleaning and inspection was the only occupation possible. Early in the afternoon the Battalion moved on four miles to St. Martin-Cojeul. The snow had melted, leaving much mud which rain made worse. St. Martin was a demolished village about a mile behind the battle-line. As we entered it I noticed an English soldier lying by the road with a horribly smashed head; soon such sights would be too frequent to attract attention, but this first one was perceptibly unpleasant. At the risk of being thought squeamish or even unsoldierly, I still maintain that an ordinary human being has a right to be momentarily horrified by a mangled body seen on an afternoon walk, although people with sound common sense can always refute me by saying that life is full of gruesome sights and violent catastrophes. But I am no believer in wild denunciations of the War; I am merely describing my own experiences of it; and in 1917 I was only beginning to learn that life, for the majority of the population, is an unlovely struggle against unfair odds, culminating in a cheap funeral. Anyhow, the man with his head bashed in had achieved theoretical glory by dying for his country in the Battle of Arras, and we who marched past him had an excellent chance of following his example.

We took over an old German reserve trench (captured on Easter Monday). Company Headquarters was a sort of rabbit-hole, just wide enough to accommodate Leake, a tiny stove, and myself. Leake occupied himself in enlarging it with a rusty entrenching tool. When dusk was falling I went out to the underground dressing-station to get my festering fingers attended to. I felt an interloper, for the place was crowded with groaning wounded. As I made my way back to our trench a few shells exploded among the ruinous remains of brickwork. All this, I thought, is disgustingly unpleasant, but it doesn't really count as war experience. I knew that if I could get the better of my physical discomforts I should find the War intensely interesting. B Company hadn't arrived at the groaning stage yet; in fact, they were grimly cheerful, though they'd only had one meal that day and the next was to-morrow morning. Leake and I had one small slice of ration bacon between us; I was frizzling my fragment when it fell off the fork and disappeared into the stove. Regardless of my unfortunate fingers I retrieved and ate it with great relish.

The night was cold and sleep impossible, since there was no space to lie down in. Leake, however, had a talent for falling asleep in any position. Chiselling away at the walls by candlelight, I kept myself warm, and in a couple of hours I had scooped out sufficient space for the other two officers. They were a well contrasted couple. Rees was a garrulous and excitable little Welshman; it would be flattery to call him anything except uncouth, and he made no pretensions to being "a gentleman". But he was good-natured and moderately efficient. Shirley, on the other hand, had been educated at Winchester and the War had interrupted his first year at Oxford. He was a delicate-featured and fastidious young man, an only child, and heir to a comfortable estate in Flintshire. Rees rather got on our nerves with his table manners, and Shirley deprecated the way he licked his thumb when dealing the cards for their games of nap. But social incompatibilities were now merged in communal discomfort. Both of them were new to the line, so I felt that I ought to look after them, if possible. I noticed that Rees kept his courage up by talking incessantly and making jokes about the battle; while Shirley, true to the traditions of his class, simulated nonchalance, discussing with Leake (also an Oxford man) the comparative merits of Madgalen and Christ Church, or Balliol and New College. But he couldn't get the nonchalance into his eyes. . . . Both Shirley and Rees were killed before the autumn.

*   *   *

From our obsolete trench we looked toward the naked ground which rose to the ridge. Along that ridge ran the Hindenburg Line (a mile and a half away) from which new attacks were now being attempted. There was another attack next morning. Rees was detailed for an ammunition-carrying party, and he returned noisier than ever. It had been his first experience of shell-fire. Narrating his numerous escapes from hostile explosives, he continually invoked the name of the founder of his religion; now that it was all over he enjoyed the retrospective excitement, roaring with laughter while he told us how he and his men had flung themselves on their faces in the mud. Rees never minded making himself look ridiculous, and I began to feel that he was capable of taking care of himself. Shirley raised his eyebrows during the recital, evidently disapproving of such volubility and not at all sure that officers ought to throw themselves flat on their faces when shells burst. Later in the day I took him for a walk up the hill; I wanted to educate him in unpleasant sights. The wind had dropped and the sunset sky was mountainous with calm clouds. We inspected a tank which had got stuck in the mud while crossing a wide trench. We succeeded in finding this ungainly monster interesting. Higher up the hill the open ground was dotted with British dead. It was an unexpectedly tidy scene, since most of them had been killed by machine-gun fire. Stretcher-bearers had been identifying the bodies and had arranged them in happy warrior attitudes, hands crossed and heads pillowed on haversacks. Often the contents of a man's haversack were scattered around him. There were letters lying about; the pathos of those last letters from home was obvious enough. It was a queer thing, I thought, that I should be taking a young Oxford man for this conducted tour of a battlefield on a fine April evening. Here we were, walking about in a sort of visible fraction of the Roll of Honour, and my pupil was doing his best to behave as if it were all quite ordinary and part of the public-school tradition. He was being politely introduced to the horrors of war, and he made no comment on them. Earlier in the day an attack on Fontaine-les-Croiselles had fizzled out in failure. Except for the intermittent chatter of machine-guns, the country ahead of us was quiet. Then, somewhere beyond the ridge, a huge explosion sent up a shapeless tower of yellow vapour. I remarked sagely that a German dump had probably been blown up. Shirley watched it intently as though the experience would be of use to him during future operations.

*   *   *

At five-thirty next morning our Brigade renewed the attack on Fontaine-les-Croiselles, but we remained in reserve. Enveloped by the din of the bombardment I leaned my elbows on the parapet and looked at the ridge. A glowering red sun was rising; the low undulant hills were grey-blue and deeply shadowed; the landscape was full of gun flashes and drifting smoke. It was a genuine battle picture, and I was aware of its angry beauty. Not much more than a mile away, on the further side of that menacing slope, lines of muttering men were waiting, strained to an intolerable expectancy, until the whistles blew and the barrage crept forward, and they stumbled across the open with the good wishes of General Allenby and the bad wishes of the machine-guns in the German strong-posts. Perhaps I tried to visualize their grim adventure. In my pocket I had a copy of a recent *communiqué* (circulated for instructive purposes) and I may as well quote it now. "That night three unsuccessful bombing attacks were made on the Tower at Wancourt. During the Battalion relief next night the enemy opened a heavy bombardment on the Tower and its immediate vicinity, following it up with an attack which succeeded, mainly owing to the relief being in progress. A local counter-attack delivered by the incoming battalion failed owing to the darkness, pouring rain, and lack of knowledge of the ground. It was then decided that nothing could be done till daylight." The lesson to be drawn from this episode was, I think, that lack of Artillery preparation is a mistake. . . . The Wancourt Tower was only a couple of miles away on our left, so I felt vaguely impressed by being so close to events which were, undoubtedly, of historic importance in the annals of the War. And anyone who has been in the front line can amplify that *communiqué* for himself.

IV

On Saturday afternoon the order to move up took us by surprise. Two days of stagnation in the cramped little trench had relaxed expectancy, which now renewed itself in our compact preparations for departure. As usual on such occasions, the Company Sergeant-Major was busier than anybody else. I have probably said so before, but it cannot be too often repeated that C.S.M.s were the hardest worked men in the infantry; everything depended on them, and if anyone deserved a K.C.B. it was a good C.S.M.

At 9 p.m. the Company fell in at the top of the ruined street of St. Martin. Two guides from the outgoing battalion awaited us. We were to relieve some Northumberland Fusiliers in the Hindenburg Trench—the companies going up independently.

It was a grey evening, dry and windless. The village of St. Martin was a shattered relic; but even in the devastated area one could be conscious of the arrival of spring, and as I took up my position in the rear of the moving column there was something in the sober twilight which could remind me of April evenings in England and the Butley cricket field where a few of us had been having our first knock at the nets. The cricket season had begun. . . . But the Company had left the shell-pitted road and was going uphill across open ground. Already the guides were making the pace too hot for the rear platoon; like most guides they were inconveniently nimble owing to their freedom from accoutrement, and insecurely confident that they knew the way. The muttered message "pass it along—steady the pace in front" was accompanied by the usual muffled clinkings and rattlings of arms and equipment. Unwillingly retarded, the guides led us into the deepening dusk. We hadn't more than two miles to go, but gradually the guides grew less authoritative. Several times they stopped to get their bearings. Leake fussed and fumed and they became more and more flurried. I began to suspect that our progress was circular.

At a midnight halt the hill still loomed in front of us; the guides confessed that they had lost their way, and Leake decided to sit down and wait for daylight. (There were few things more uncomfortable in the life of an officer than to be walking in front of a party of men all of whom knew that he was leading them in the wrong direction.) With Leake's permission I blundered experimentally into the gloom, fully expecting to lose both myself and the Company. By a lucky accident, I soon fell headlong into a sunken road and found myself among a small party of Sappers who could tell me where I was. It was a case of "Please, can you tell me the way to the Hindenburg Trench?" Congratulating myself on my cleverness I took one of the Sappers back to poor benighted B Company, and we were led to our Battalion rendezvous.

The rendezvous took some finding, since wrong map references had been issued by the Brigade Staff; but at last, after many delays, the Companies filed along to their ordained (and otherwise anathematized) positions.

We were at the end of a journey which had begun twelve days before, when we started from Camp 13. Stage by stage, we had marched to the life-denying region which from far away had threatened us with the blink and growl of its bombardments. Now we were groping and stumbling along a deep ditch to the place appointed for us in the zone of inhuman havoc. There must have been some hazy moonlight, for I remember the figures of men huddled against the sides of communication trenches; seeing them in some

sort of ghastly glimmer (was it, perhaps, the diffused whiteness of a sinking flare beyond the ridge?) I was doubtful
whether they were asleep or dead, for the attitudes of many
were like death, grotesque and distorted. But this is nothing new to write about, you will say; just a weary company, squeezing past dead or drowsing men while it sloshes
and stumbles to a front-line trench. Nevertheless that night
relief had its significance for me, though in human experience it had been multiplied a millionfold. I, a single human
being with my little stock of earthly experience in my head,
was entering once again the veritable gloom and disaster
of the thing called Armageddon. And I saw it then, as I see
it now—a dreadful place, a place of horror and desolation
which no imagination could have invented. Also it was a
place where a man of strong spirit might know himself
utterly powerless against death and destruction, and yet
stand up and defy gross darkness and stupefying shell-fire,
discovering in himself the invincible resistance of an animal or an insect, and an endurance which he might, in
after days, forget or disbelieve.

Anyhow, there I was, leading that little procession of
Flintshire Fusiliers many of whom had never seen a front-
line trench before. At that juncture they asked no compensation for their efforts except a mug of hot tea. The tea
would have been a miracle, and we didn't get it till next
morning, but there was some comfort in the fact that it
wasn't raining.

It was nearly four o'clock when we found ourselves in
the Hindenburg Main Trench. After telling me to post the
sentries, Leake disappeared down some stairs to the Tunnel (which will be described later on). The Company we
were relieving had already departed, so there was no one
to give me any information. At first I didn't even know for
certain that we were in the Front Line. The trench was a
sort of gully, deep, wide, and unfinished looking. The sentries had to clamber up a bank of loose earth before they
could see over the top. Our Company was only about
eighty strong and its sector was fully 600 yards. The distance between the sentry-posts made me aware of our in-

adequacy in that wilderness. I had no right to feel homeless, but I did; and if I had needed to be reminded of my forlorn situation as a living creature I could have done it merely by thinking of a Field Cashier. Fifty franc notes were comfortable things, but they were no earthly use up here, and the words "Field Cashier" would have epitomized my remoteness from snugness and security, and from all assurance that I should be alive and kicking the week after next. But it would soon be Sunday morning; such ideas weren't wholesome, and there was a certain haggard curiosity attached to the proceedings; combined with the self-dramatizing desperation which enabled a good many of us to worry our way through much worse emergencies than mine.

When I had posted the exhausted sentries, with as much cheeriness as I could muster, I went along to look for the Company on our left. Rather expecting to find one of our own companies, I came round a corner to a place where the trench was unusually wide. There I found myself among a sort of panic party which I was able to identify as a platoon (thirty or forty strong). They were jostling one another in their haste to get through a cavernous doorway, and as I stood astonished one of them breathlessly told me that "the Germans were coming over". Two officers were shepherding them downstairs and before I'd had time to think the whole lot had vanished. The Battalion they belonged to was one of those amateur ones which were at such a disadvantage owing to lack of discipline and the absence of trained N.C.O.s. Anyhow, their behaviour seemed to indicate that the Tunnel in the Hindenburg Trench was having a lowering effect on their *morale*.

Out in no-man's-land there was no sign of any German activity. The only remarkable thing was the unbroken silence. I was in a sort of twilight, for there was a moony glimmer in the low-clouded sky; but the unknown territory in front was dark, and I stared out at it like a man looking from the side of a ship. Returning to my own sector I met a runner with a verbal message from Battalion H.Q. B Company's front was to be thoroughly patrolled at once.

Realizing the futility of sending any of my few spare men out on patrol (they'd been walking about for seven hours and were dead beat) I lost my temper, quietly and inwardly. Shirley and Rees were nowhere to be seen and it wouldn't have been fair to send them out, inexperienced as they were. So I stumped along to our right-flank post, told them to pass it along that a patrol was going out from right to left, and then started sulkily out for a solitary stroll in no-man's-land. I felt more annoyed with Battalion Headquarters than with the enemy. There was no wire in front of the trench, which was, of course, constructed for people facing the other way. I counted my steps; 200 steps straight ahead; then I began to walk the presumptive 600 steps to the left. But it isn't easy to count your steps in the dark among shell-holes, and after a problematic 400 I lost confidence in my automatic pistol, which I was grasping in my right-hand breeches pocket. Here I am, I thought, alone out in this god-forsaken bit of ground, with quite a good chance of bumping into a Boche strong-post. Apparently there was only one reassuring action which I could perform; so I expressed my opinion of the War by relieving myself (for it must be remembered that there are other reliefs beside Battalion reliefs). I insured my sense of direction by placing my pistol on the ground with its muzzle pointing the way I was going. Feeling less lonely and afraid, I finished my patrol without having met so much as a dead body, and regained the trench exactly opposite our left-hand post, after being huskily challenged by an irresolute sentry, who, as I realized at the time, was the greatest danger I had encountered. It was now just beginning to be more daylight than darkness, and when I stumbled down a shaft to the underground trench I left the sentries shivering under a red and rainy-looking sky.

There were fifty steps down the shaft; the earthy smell of that triumph of Teutonic military engineering was strongly suggestive of appearing in the Roll of Honour and being buried until the Day of Judgment. Dry-mouthed and chilled to the bone, I lay in a wire-netting bunk and listened to the dismal snorings of my companions. Along the Tunnel the air blew deathly cold and seasoned with mephitic odours. In vain I envied the snorers; but I was getting accustomed to lack of sleep, and three hours later I was gulping some peculiar tea with morose enjoyment. Owing to the scarcity of water (which had to be brought up by the Transport who were eight miles back, at Blairville) washing wasn't possible; but I contrived a refreshing shave, utilizing the dregs of my tea.

By ten o'clock I was above ground again, in charge of a fatigue party. We went half-way back to St. Martin, to an ammunition dump, whence we carried up boxes of trench mortar bombs. I carried a box myself, as the conditions were vile and it seemed the only method of convincing the men that it had to be done. We were out nearly seven hours; it rained all day and the trenches were a morass of glue-like mud. The unmitigated misery of that carrying party was a typical infantry experience of discomfort without actual danger. Even if the ground had been dry the boxes would have been too heavy for most of the men; but we were lucky in one way; the wet weather was causing the artillery to spend an inactive Sunday. It was a yellow corpse-like day, more like November than April, and the landscape was desolate and treeless. What we were doing was quite unexceptional; millions of soldiers endured the same sort of thing and got badly shelled into the bargain. Nevertheless I can believe that my party, staggering and floundering under its loads, would have made an impressive picture of "Despair". The background, too, was appropriate. We were among the débris of the intense bombardment of ten days before, for we were passing along and across the Hindenburg Outpost Trench, with its belt of wire (fifty yards deep in places); here and there these rusty jungles had been flattened by tanks. The Outpost Trench was about 200 yards from the Main Trench, which was now our front line. It had been solidly made, ten feet deep, with timbered fire-steps, splayed sides, and timbered steps at intervals to front and rear and to machine-gun emplacements. Now it was wrecked as though by earthquake and eruption. Concrete strong-posts were smashed and tilted sideways; everywhere the chalky soil was pocked and pitted with huge shell-holes; and wherever we looked the mangled effigies of the dead were our *memento mori*. Shell-twisted and dismembered, the Germans maintained the violent attitudes in which they had died. The British had mostly been killed by bullets or bombs, so they looked more resigned. But I can remember a pair of hands (nationality unknown) which protruded from the soaked ashen soil like the roots of a tree turned upside down; one hand seemed to be pointing at the sky with an accusing gesture. Each time I passed that place the protest of those fingers became more expressive of an appeal to God in defiance of those who made the War. Who made the War? I laughed hysterically as the thought passed through my mud-stained mind. But I only laughed mentally, for my box of Stokes gun ammunition left me no breath to spare for an angry guffaw. And the dead were the dead; this was no time to be pitying them or asking silly questions about their outraged lives. Such sights must be taken for granted, I thought, as I gasped and slithered and stumbled with my disconsolate crew. Floating on the surface of the flooded trench was the mask of a human face which had detached itself from the skull.

V

Plastered with mud and soaked to the skin, the fatigue-party clumped down the steps to the Tunnel. The carrying job was finished; but a stimulating surprise awaited me, for Leake was just back from Battalion H.Q. (somewhere along the Tunnel) and he breezily informed me that I'd been detailed to take command of a hundred bombers in the attack which had been arranged for next morning. "Twenty-five bombers from each Company; you're to act as reserve for the Cameronians," he remarked. I stared at him over my mug of reviving but trench-flavoured tea (made with chlorinated water) and asked him to tell me some more. He said: "Well, they're a bit hazy about it at Headquarters, but the General is frightfully keen on our doing an underground attack along the Tunnel, as well as along the main trench up above. You've got to go and discuss the tactical situation with one of the Company commanders up in the Front Line on our right." All that I knew about the tactical situation was that if one went along the Tunnel one arrived at a point where a block had been made by blowing it in. On the other side one bumped into the Germans. Above ground there was a barrier and the situation was similar. Bombing along a Tunnel in the dark. . . . Had the War Office issued a text book on the subject? . . . I lit my pipe, but failed to enjoy it, probably because the stewed tea had left such a queer taste in my mouth.

Ruminating on the comfortless responsibility imposed on me by this enterprise, I waited until nightfall. Then a superbly cheerful little guide bustled me along a maze of waterlogged ditches until I found myself in a small dug-out with some friendly Scotch officers and a couple of flame-wagging candles. The dug-out felt more like old times than the Hindenburg Tunnel, but the officers made me feel incompetent and uninformed, for they were loquacious about local trench topography which meant nothing to my newly-arrived mind. So I puffed out my Military Cross ribbon, (the dug-out contained two others) nodded my head knowingly, and took an acquiescent share in the discussion of the strategic situation. Details of organization were offered me and I made a few smudgy notes. The Cams didn't think that there was much chance of my party being called on to support them, and they were hoping that the underground attack would be eliminated from operation orders.

I emerged from the desperation jollity of their little den with only a blurred notion of what it was all about. The objective was to clear the trench for 500 yards while other battalions went over the top on our left to attack Fontaine-les-Croiselles. But I was, at the best of times, only an opportunist officer; technical talk in the Army always made me feel mutely inefficient. And now I was floundering home in the dark to organize my command, put something plausible on paper, and take it along to the Adjutant. If only I could consult the Doctor, I thought; for he was back from leave, though I hadn't seen him yet. It seemed to me, in my confused and exhausted condition, that I was at a crisis in my military career; and, as usual, my main fear was that I should make a fool of myself. The idea of making a fool of oneself in that murderous mix-up now appears to me rather a ludicrous one; for I see myself merely as a blundering flustered little beetle; and if someone happens to put his foot on a beetle, it is unjust to accuse the unlucky insect of having made a fool of itself. When I got back to Leake and Rees and Shirley I felt so lost and perplexed that I went straight on to Battalion H.Q.

The Tunnel was a few inches higher than a tall man walking upright; it was fitted with bunks and recessed rooms; in places it was crowded with men of various units, but there were long intervals of unwholesome-smelling solitude. Prying my way along with an electric torch, I glimpsed an assortment of vague shapes, boxes, tins, fragments of broken furniture and frowsy mattresses. It seemed a long way to Headquarters, and the Tunnel was memorable but not fortifying to a fatigued explorer who hadn't slept for more than an hour at a stretch or taken his clothes off since last Tuesday. Once, when I tripped and recovered myself by grabbing the wall, my tentative patch of brightness revealed somebody half hidden under a blanket. Not a very clever spot to be taking a nap, I thought as I stooped to shake him by the shoulder. He refused to wake up, so I gave him a kick. "God blast you, where's Battalion Headquarters?" My nerves were on edge; and what right had he to be having a good sleep, when I never seemed to get five minutes' rest? . . . Then my beam settled on the livid face of a dead German whose fingers still clutched the blackened gash on his neck. . . . Stumbling on, I could only mutter to myself that this was really a bit too thick. (That, however, was an exaggeration; there is nothing remarkable about a dead body in a European War, or a squashed beetle in a cellar.) At Headquarters I found the Adjutant alone, worried and preoccupied with clerical work. He had worked in an office, at accountancy, I believe, before the War; and now most of his fighting was done in writing, though he had served his apprenticeship as a brave and indefatigable platoon commander. He told me that the underground attack had been washed out by a providential counter-order from Division, and asked me to send my organization scheme along as soon as possible. "Right-O!" I replied, and groped my way back again feeling the reverse of my reply. By a stroke of luck I discovered Ralph Wilmot, sitting by himself in a small recessed room—his dark hair smoothly brushed and his countenance pensive but unperturbed. He might conceivably have been twiddling a liqueur glass in a Piccadilly restaurant. Unfortunately he had no liquid refreshment to offer, but his philosophic way of greeting me was a consolation and in him I confided my dilemma. With an understanding air he assumed his monocle, deliberated for a while, snuffed the candle wick, and wrote out an authoritative looking document headed "Organization of F.F. Parties". The gist of it was "15 Bombers (each carrying 5 grenades). 5 Carriers (also act as bayonet men). 1 Full Rank." There wasn't much in it, he remarked, as he appended "a little bit of skite about consolidation and defensive flanks". It certainly looked simple enough when it was done, though I had been at my wits' end about it.

While he was fixing up my future for me I gazed around and thought what a queer refuge I'd found for what might possibly be my final night on earth. Dug-out though it was, the narrow chamber contained a foggy mirror and a clock. The clock wasn't ticking, but its dumb face stared at me, an idiot reminder of real rooms and desirable domesticity. Outside the doorless doorway people were continually passing in both directions with a sound of shuffling feet and mumbling voices. I caught sight of a red-capped Staff Officer, and a party of sappers carrying picks and shovels. The Tunnel was a sort of highway and the night had brought a considerable congestion of traffic. When we'd sent my document along to the Adjutant there was nothing more to be done except sit and wait for operation orders. It was now about ten o'clock.

As evidence of my own soldierly qualities I would like to be able to declare that we eagerly discussed every aspect of the situation as regards next morning's attack. But the truth is that we said nothing at all about it. The thing had to be attempted and there was an end of it (until zero hour). The Brigadier and his Staff (none too bright at map-references) were hoping to satisfy (vicariously) General Whincop (who'd got an unpopular bee in his bonnet about the Rum Ration, and had ordered an impossible raid, two months ago, which had been prevented by a providential thaw and caused numerous deaths in a subsequently sacrificed battalion).

Whincop was hoping to satisfy the Corps Commander, of whom we knew nothing at all, except that he had insulted our Colonel on the Doullens road. The Corps Commander hoped to satisfy the Army Commander, who had as usual informed us that we were "pursuing a beaten enemy", and who had brought the Cavalry up for a "break-through". (It is worth mentioning that the village which was now our Division's objective was still held by the Germans eight months afterwards.) And the Army Commander, I suppose, was in telephonic communication with the Commander-in-Chief, who, with one eye on Marshal Foch, was hoping to satisfy his King and Country. Such being the case, Wilmot and myself were fully justified in leaving the situation to the care of the military caste who were making the most of their Great Opportunity for obtaining medal-ribbons and reputations for leadership; and if I am being caustic and captious about them I can only plead the need for a few minutes' post-war retaliation. Let the Staff write their own books about the Great War, say I. The Infantry were biased against them, and their authentic story will be read with interest.

As for our conversation between ten o'clock and midnight (when my operation orders arrived from the Adjutant) I suppose it was a form of drug, since it was confined to pleasant retrospections of peace. Wilmot was well acquainted with my part of the world and he'd come across many of our local worthies. So we were able to make a little tour of the Kentish Weald and the Sussex border, as though on a couple of mental bicycles. In imagination we cycled along on a fine summer afternoon, passing certain milestones which will always be inseparable from my life history. Outside Squire Maundle's park gate we shared a distinct picture of his angular attitudes while he addressed his golf-ball among the bell-tinklings and baaings of sheep on the sunny slopes above Amblehurst (always followed by a taciturn black retriever). Much has been asserted about the brutalized condition of mind to which soldiers were reduced by life in the Front Line; I do not deny this, but I am inclined to suggest that there was a proportionate amount of simple-minded sentimentality. As far as I was concerned, no topic could be too homely for the trenches.

Thus, while working parties and machine-gunners filed past the door with hollow grumbling voices, our private recess in the Hindenburg Tunnel was precariously infused with evocations of rural England and we challenged our surroundings with remembrances of parish names and farm-houses with friendly faces. A cottage garden was not an easy idea to recover convincingly. . . . Bees among yellow wall-flowers on a warm afternoon. The smell of an apple orchard in autumn. . . . Such details were beyond our evocation. But they were implied when I mentioned Squire Maundle in his four-wheeled dogcart, rumbling along the Dumbridge Road to attend a County Council Meeting.

*   *   *

"*Secret*. The Bombing Parties of 25 men will rendezvous at 2.30 a.m. to-morrow morning, 16th inst. in shafts near C Coy. H.Q. The greatest care will be taken that each separate Company Party keeps to one side of the Shaft and that the Dump of Bombs be in the trench at the head of these shafts, suitably split. The necessity of keeping absolute silence must be impressed on all men. These parties (under 2nd Lt. Sherston) will come under the orders of O.C. Cameronians at ZERO minus 10. Lt. Dunning and 2 orderlies will act liaison and report to O.C. Cameronians at ZERO minus 5. While the parties are in the shaft they must keep a free passage way clear for runners, etc."

Such was the document which (had I been less fortunate) would have been my passport to the Stygian shore. In the meantime, with another two hours to sit through, we carried on with our world without end conversation. We were, I think, on the subject of Canterbury Cricket Week when my watch warned me that I must be moving on. As I got up from the table on which we'd been leaning our elbows, a blurred version of my face looked at me from the foggy mirror with an effect of clairvoyance. Hoping that this was an omen of survival, I went along to the rendezvous-shaft and satisfied myself that the Bombing Parties were sitting on the stairs in a bone-chilling draught, with my two subordinate officers in attendance.

Zero hour was at 3 a.m. and the prefatory uproar was already rumbling overhead. Having tightened my mud-caked puttees and put my tie straight (there was no rule against wearing a tie in an attack) diffidently I entered the Cameronian H.Q. dug-out, which was up against the foot of the stairs. I was among strangers, and Zero minus 10 wasn't a time for conversational amenities, so I sat self-consciously while the drumming din upstairs was doing its utmost to achieve a reassuring climax. Three o'clock arrived. The tick-tacking telephone-orderly in a corner received a message that the attack had started. They were over the barrier now, and bombing up the trench. The Cameronian Colonel and his Adjutant conversed in the constrained undertones of men who expect disagreeable news. The Colonel was a fine looking man, but his well-disciplined face was haggard with anxiety. Dunning sat in another corner, serious and respectful, with his natural jollity ready to come to the surface whenever it was called for.

At the end of twenty minutes' tension the Colonel exclaimed abruptly, "Good God, I wish I knew how they're doing!" . . . And then, as if regretting his manifestation of feeling, "No harm in having a bit of cake, anyhow." There was a large home-made cake on the table. I was offered a slice, which I munched with embarrassment. I felt that I had no business to be there at all, let alone helping to make a hole in the Colonel's cake, which was a jolly good one. I couldn't believe that these competent officers were counting on me to be of any use to them if I were required to take an active part in the proceedings upstairs. Then the telephone-orderly announced that communication with Captain Macnair's headquarters had broken down; after that the suspense continued monotonously. I had been sitting there about two and a half hours when it became evident that somebody was descending the steps in a hurry. H.Q. must have kept its cooking utensils on the stairs, for the visitor arrived outside the doorway in a clattering cascade of pots and pans. He was a breathless and dishevelled sergeant, who blurted out an incoherent statement about their having been driven back after advancing a short distance. While the Colonel questioned him in a quiet and controlled voice I rose stiffly to my feet. I don't remember saying anything or receiving any orders; but I felt that the Cameronian officers were sensitive to the delicacy of my situation. There was no question of another slice of home-made cake. Their unuttered comment was, "Well, old chap, I suppose you're for it now."

Leaving them to get what satisfaction they could from the sergeant's story, I grinned stupidly at Dunning, popped my helmet on my head, and made for the stairway. It must have been a relief to be doing something definite at last, for without pausing to think I started off with the section of twenty-five who were at the top of the stairs. Sergeant Baldock got them on the move at once, although they were chilled and drowsy after sitting there for over three hours. None of them would have been any the worse for a mouthful of rum at that particular moment. In contrast to the wearisome candlelight of the lower regions, the outdoor world was bright and breezy; animated also by enough noise to remind me that some sort of battle was going on. As we bustled along, the flustered little contingent at my heels revived from its numbness. I had no idea what I was going to do; our destination was in the brain of the stooping

Cameronian guide who trotted ahead of me. On the way
we picked up a derelict Lewis gun, which I thought might
come in handy though there was no ammunition with it.
At the risk of being accused of "taking the wrong half of
the conversation" (a favourite phrase of Aunt Evelyn's) I
must say that I felt quite confident. (Looking back on that
emergency from my arm-chair, I find some difficulty in
believing that I was there at all.) For about ten minutes we
dodged and stumbled up a narrow winding trench. The
sun was shining; large neutral clouds voyaged willingly
with the wind; I felt intensely alive and rather out of
breath. Suddenly we came into the main trench, and where
it was widest we met the Cameronians. I must have picked
up a bomb on the way, for I had one in my hand when I
started my conversation with young Captain Macnair. Our
encounter was more absurd than impressive. Macnair and
his exhausted men were obviously going in the wrong direction, and I was an incautious newcomer. Consequently I
had the advantage of him while he told me that the Germans were all round them and they'd run out of bombs.
Feeling myself to be, for the moment, an epitome of Flintshire infallibility, I assumed an air of jaunty unconcern;
tossing my bomb carelessly from left hand to right and
back again, I inquired, "But where *are* the Germans?"—
adding "I can't see any of them." This effrontery had its
effect (though for some reason I find it difficult to describe
this scene without disliking my own behaviour). The Cameronian officers looked around them and recovered their
composure. Resolved to show them what intrepid reinforcements we were, I assured Macnair that he needn't
worry any more and we'd soon put things straight. I then
led my party past his, halted them, and went up the trench
with Sergeant Baldock—an admirably impassive little man
who never ceased to behave like a perfectly trained and
confidential man-servant. After climbing over some sort of
barricade, we went about fifty yards without meeting anyone. Observing a good many Mills' bombs lying about in
little heaps, I sent Baldock back to have them collected and
carried further up the trench. Then, with an accelerated

heart beat, I went round the corner by myself. Unexpectedly, a small man was there, standing with his back to me, stockstill and watchful, a haversack of bombs slung over his left shoulder. I saw that he was a Cameronian corporal; we did not speak. I also carried a bag of bombs; we went round the next bay. There my adventurous ardour experienced a sobering shock. A fair-haired Scotch private was lying at the side of the trench in a pool of his own blood. His face was grey and serene, and his eyes stared emptily at the sky. A few yards further on the body of a German officer lay crumpled up and still. The wounded Cameronian made me feel angry, and I slung a couple of bombs at our invisible enemies, receiving in reply an egg-bomb, which exploded harmlessly behind me. After that I went bombing busily along, while the corporal (more artful and efficient than I was) dodged in and out of the saps —a precaution which I should have forgotten. Between us we created quite a demonstration of offensiveness, and in this manner arrived at our objective without getting more than a few glimpses of retreating field-grey figures. I had no idea where our objective was, but the corporal informed me that we had reached it, and he seemed to know his business. This, curiously enough, was the first time either of us had spoken since we met.

The whole affair had been so easy that I felt like pushing forward until we bumped into something more definite. But the corporal had a cooler head and he advised discretion. I told him to remain where he was and started to explore a narrow sap on the left side of the trench. (Not that it matters whether it was on the left side or the right, but it appears to be the only detail I can remember; and when all is said and done, the War was mainly a matter of holes and ditches.) What I expected to find along that sap, I can't say. Finding nothing, I stopped to listen. There seemed to be a lull in the noise of the attack along the line. A few machine-guns tapped, spiteful and spasmodic. High up in the fresh blue sky an aeroplane droned and glinted. I thought what a queer state of things it all was, and then decided to take a peep at the surrounding country. This was a mistake which ought to have put an end to my terrestrial adventures, for no sooner had I popped my silly head out of the sap than I felt a stupendous blow in the back between my shoulders. My first notion was that a bomb had hit me from behind, but what had really happened was that I had been sniped from in front. Anyhow my foolhardy attitude toward the Second Battle of the Scarpe had been instantaneously altered for the worse. I leant against the side of the sap and shut my eyes. . . . When I reopened them Sergeant Baldock was beside me, discreet and sympathetic, and to my surprise I discovered that I wasn't dead. He helped me back to the trench, gently investigated my wound, put a field-dressing on it, and left me sitting there while he went to bring up some men.

After a short spell of being deflated and sorry for myself, I began to feel rabidly heroical again, but in a slightly different style, since I was now a wounded hero, with my arm in a superfluous sling. All my seventy-five men were now on the scene (minus a few who had been knocked out by our own shells, which were dropping short). I can remember myself talking volubly to a laconic Stokes-gun officer, who had appeared from nowhere with his weapon and a couple of assistants. I felt that I must make one more onslaught before I turned my back on the War and my only idea was to collect all available ammunition and then renew the attack while the Stokes-gun officer put up an enthusiastic barrage. It did not occur to me that anything else was happening on Allenby's Army Front except my own little show. My over-strained nerves had wrought me up to such a pitch of excitement that I was ready for any suicidal exploit. This convulsive energy might have been of some immediate value had there been any objective for it. But there was none; and before I had time to inaugurate anything rash and irrelevant Dunning arrived to relieve me. His air of competent unconcern sobered me down, but I was still inflamed with the offensive spirit and my impetuosity was only snuffed out by a written order from the Cameronian Colonel, who forbade any further advance owing to the attack having failed elsewhere. My ferocity fizzled out then, and I realized that I had a raging thirst. As I was starting my return journey (I must have known then that nothing could stop me till I got to England) the M.O. came sauntering up the trench with the detached demeanour of a gentle botanist. "Trust him to be up there having a look round," I thought. Within four hours of leaving it I was back in the Tunnel.

*   *   *

Back at Battalion Headquarters in the Tunnel I received from our Colonel and Adjutant generous congratulations on my supposedly dashing display. In the emergency candlelight of that draughty cellar recess I bade them good-bye with voluble assurances that I should be back in a few weeks; but I was so overstrained and excited that my assurances were noises rather than notions. Probably I should have been equally elated without my wound; but if unwounded, I'd have been still up at the Block with the bombing parties. In the meantime, nothing that happened to me could relieve Battalion H.Q. of its burdens. The Adjutant would go on till he dropped, for he had an inexhaustible sense of duty. I never saw him again; he was killed in the autumn up at Ypres. . . . I would like to be able to remember that I smiled grimly and departed reticently. But the "bombing show" had increased my self-importance, and my exodus from the Front Line was a garrulous one. A German bullet had passed through me leaving a neat hole near my right shoulder-blade and this patriotic perforation had made a different man of me. I now looked at the War, which had been a monstrous tyrant, with liberated eyes. For the time being I had regained my right to call myself a private individual.

The first stage of my return journey took me to the Advanced Dressing Station at Henin. My servant went with me, carrying my haversack. He was a quiet clumsy middle-aged man who always did his best and never complained. While we picked our way along the broken ground of Henin Hill I continued talkative, halting now and again to recover breath and take a last stare at the blighted slope where yesterday I had stumbled to and fro with my working party.

The sky was now overcast and the landscape grey and derelict. The activities of the attack had subsided, and we seemed to be walking in a waste land where dead men had been left out in the rain after being killed for no apparent purpose. Here and there, figures could be seen moving toward the Dressing Station, some of them carrying stretchers.

It was the mid-day stagnation which usually followed an early morning attack. The Dressing Station was a small underground place crowded with groaning wounded. Two doctors were doing what they could for men who had paid a heavy price for their freedom. My egocentricity diminished among all that agony. I remember listening to an emotional padre who was painfully aware that he could do nothing except stand about and feel sympathetic. The consolations of the Church of England weren't much in demand at an Advance Dressing Station. I was there myself merely to go through the formality of being labelled "walking wounded". I was told to go on to a place called "B. Echelon", which meant another three miles of muddy walking. Beat to the world, I reached B. Echelon, and found our Quartermaster in a tent with several officers newly arrived from the Base and one or two back from leave. Stimulated by a few gulps of whisky and water, I renewed my volubility and talked nineteen to the dozen until the kind Quartermaster put me into the mess-cart which carried me to a cross road where I waited for a motor bus. There, after a long wait, I shook hands with my servant, and the handshake seemed to epitomize my good-bye to the Second Battalion. I thanked him for looking after me so well; but one couldn't wish a man luck when he was going back to the Hindenburg Trench. It may be objected that my attitude toward the Western Front was too intimate; but this was a question of two human beings, one of whom was getting out of it comfortably while the other went back to take his chance in the world's worst war. . . .
In the bus, wedged among "walking wounded", I was

aware that I had talked quite enough. For an hour and a half we bumped and swayed along ruined roads till we came to the Casualty Clearing Station at Warlencourt. It was seven o'clock and all I got that night was a cup of Bovril and an anti-tetanus injection.

The place was overcrowded with bad cases and I had to wait until after midnight for a bed. I remember sitting in a chair listening to the rain pelting on the roof of the tent and the wailing of a wintry wind. I was too exhausted to sleep; my head had lost control of its thoughts, which continued to re-echo my good-bye garrulities; the injection had made me feel chilly and queer, and my wound began to be painful. But I was able to feel sorry for "the poor old Battalion" (which was being relieved that night) and to be thankful for my own lucky escape.

What I'd been through was nothing compared with the sort of thing that many soldiers endured over and over again; nevertheless I condoled with myself on having had no end of a bad time.

Next afternoon a train (with 500 men and 35 officers on board) conveyed me to a Base Hospital. My memories of that train are strange and rather terrible, for it carried a cargo of men in whose minds the horrors they had escaped from were still vitalized and violent. Many of us still had the caked mud of the war zone on our boots and clothes, and every bandaged man was accompanied by his battle experience. Although many of them talked lightly and even facetiously about it, there was an aggregation of enormities in the atmosphere of that train. I overheard some slightly wounded officers who were excitedly remembering their adventures up at Wancourt, where they'd been bombed out of a trench in the dark. Their jargoning voices mingled with the rumble and throb of the train as it journeyed—so safely and sedately—through the environing gloom. The Front Line was behind us; but it could lay its hand on our hearts, though its bludgeoning reality diminished with every mile. It was as if we were pursued by the Arras Battle which had now become a huge and horrible idea. We might be boastful or sagely reconstructive about

our experience, in accordance with our different characters. But our minds were still out of breath and our inmost
thoughts in disorderly retreat from bellowing darkness and
men dying out in shell-holes under the desolation of returning daylight. We were the survivors; few among us
would ever tell the truth to our friends and relations in
England. We were carrying something in our heads which
belonged to us alone, and to those we had left behind us in
the battle. There were dying men, too, on board that Red
Cross train, men dying for their country in comparative
comfort.

We reached our destination after midnight, and the next
day I was able to write in my diary: "I am still feeling war-
like and quite prepared to go back to the Battalion in a few
weeks; I am told that my wound will be healed in a fortnight. The doctor here says I am a lucky man as the bullet
missed my jugular vein and spine by a fraction of an inch.
I know it would be better for me not to go back to England,
where I should probably be landed for at least three months
and then have all the hell of returning again in July or
August." But in spite of my self-defensive scribble I was
in London on Friday evening, and by no means sorry to be
carried through the crowd of patriotic spectators at Charing Cross Station. My stretcher was popped into an ambulance which took me to a big hospital at Denmark Hill. At
Charing Cross a woman handed me a bunch of flowers and
a leaflet by the Bishop of London who earnestly advised me
to lead a clean life and attend Holy Communion.

PART NINE: HOSPITAL AND CONVALESCENCE

I

The first few days were like lying in a boat. Drifting, drifting, I watched the high sunlit windows or the firelight that flickered and glowed on the ceiling when the ward was falling asleep. Outside the hospital a late spring was invading the home-service world. Trees were misty green and sometimes I could hear a blackbird singing. Even the screech and rumble of electric trams was a friendly sound; trams meant safety; the troops in the trenches thought about trams with affection. With an exquisite sense of languor and release I lifted my hand to touch the narcissi by my bed. They were symbols of an immaculate spirit— creatures whose faces knew nothing of War's demented language.

For a week, perhaps, I could dream that for me the War was over, because I'd got a neat hole through me and the nurse with her spongings forbade me to have a bath. But I soon emerged from my mental immunity; I began to think; and my thoughts warned me that my second time out in France had altered my outlook (if such a confused condition of mind could be called an outlook). I began to feel that it was my privilege to be bitter about my war experiences; and my attitude toward civilians implied that they couldn't understand and that it was no earthly use trying to explain things to them. Visitors were, of course, benevolent and respectful; my wound was adequate evidence that I'd "been in the thick of it", and I allowed myself to hint at heroism and its attendant horrors. But as might have been expected my behaviour varied with my various visitors; or rather it would have done so had my visitors been more various. My inconsistencies might become tedious if tabulated collectively, so I will confine myself to the following imaginary instances.

Some Senior Officer under whom I'd served: Modest, politely subordinate, strongly imbued with the "spirit of the Regiment" and quite ready to go out again. "Awfully nice of you to come and see me, sir." Feeling that I ought to jump out of bed and salute, and that it would be appropriate and pleasant to introduce him to "some of my people" (preferably of impeccable social status). Willingness to discuss active service technicalities and revive memories of shared front-line experience.

Middle-aged or elderly Male Civilian: Tendency (in response to sympathetic gratitude for services rendered to King and Country) to assume haggard facial aspect of one who had "been through hell". Inclination to wish that my wound was a bit worse than it actually was, and have nurses hovering round with discreet reminders that my strength mustn't be overtaxed. Inability to reveal anything crudely horrifying to civilian sensibilities. "Oh yes, I'll be out there again by the autumn." (Grimly wan reply to suggestions that I was now honourably qualified for a home-service job.) Secret antagonism to all uncomplimentary references to the German Army.

Charming Sister of Brother Officer: Jocular, talkative, debonair, and diffidently heroic. Wishful to be wearing all possible medal-ribbons on pyjama jacket. Able to furnish a bright account of her brother (if still at the front) and suppressing all unpalatable facts about the War. "Jolly decent of you to blow in and see me."

Hunting Friend (a few years above Military Service Age): Deprecatory about sufferings endured at the front. Tersely desirous of hearing all about last season's sport. "By Jingo, that must have been a nailing good gallop!" Jokes about the Germans, as if throwing bombs at them was a tolerable substitute for fox-hunting. A good deal of guffawing (mitigated by remembrance that I'd got a bullet hole through my lung). Optimistic anticipations of next season's Opening Meet and an early termination of hostilities on all fronts.

Nevertheless my supposed reactions to any one of these hypothetical visitors could only be temporary. When alone with my fellow patients I was mainly disposed toward self-pitying estrangement from everyone except the troops in the Front Line. (Casualties didn't count as tragic unless dead or badly maimed.)

When Aunt Evelyn came up to London to see me I felt properly touched by her reticent emotion; embitterment against civilians couldn't be applied to her. But after she had gone I resented her gentle assumption that I had done enough and could now accept a safe job. I wasn't going to be messed about like that, I told myself. Yet I knew that the War was unescapable. Sooner or later I should be sent back to the Front Line, which was the only place where I could be any use. A cushy wound wasn't enough to keep me out of it.

I couldn't be free from the War; even this hospital ward was full of it, and every day the oppression increased. Outwardly it was a pleasant place to be lazy in. Morning sunshine slanted through the tall windows, brightening the grey-green walls and the forty beds. Daffodils and tulips made spots of colour under three red-draped lamps which hung from the ceiling. Some officers lay humped in bed, smoking and reading newspapers; others loafed about in dressing-gowns, going to and from the washing room where they scraped the bristles from their contented faces. A raucous gramophone continually ground out popular tunes. In the morning it was rag-time—*Everybody's Doing it* and *At the Fox-Trot Ball*. (*Somewhere a Voice is calling, God send you back to me*, and such-like sentimental songs were reserved for the evening hours.) Before midday no one had enough energy to begin talking war shop, but after that I could always hear scraps of conversation from around the two fireplaces. My eyes were reading one of Lamb's Essays, but my mind was continually distracted by such phrases as "Barrage lifted at the first objective", "shelled us with heavy stuff", "couldn't raise enough decent N.C.O.s", "first wave got held up by machine-guns", and "bombed them out of a sap".

There were no serious cases in the ward, only flesh wounds and sick. These were the lucky ones, already washed clean of squalor and misery and strain. They were lifting their faces to the sunlight, warming their legs by the fire; but there wasn't much to talk about except the War.

In the evenings they played cards at a table opposite my bed; the blinds were drawn, the electric light was on, and a huge fire glowed on walls and ceiling. Glancing irritably up from my book I criticized the faces of the card-players and those who stood watching the game. There was a lean airman in a grey dressing-gown, his narrow whimsical face puffing a cigarette below a turban-like bandage; he'd been brought down by the Germans behind Arras and had spent three days in a bombarded dug-out with Prussians, until our men drove them back and rescued him. The Prussians hadn't treated him badly, he said. His partner was a swarthy Canadian with a low beetling forehead, sneering wide-set eyes, fleshy cheeks, and a loose heavy mouth. I couldn't like that man, especially when he was boasting how he "did in some prisoners". Along the ward they were still talking about "counter-attacked from the redoubt", "permanent rank of captain", "never drew any allowances for six weeks", "failed to get through their wire". . . . I was beginning to feel the need for escape from such reminders. My brain was screwed up tight, and when people came to see me I answered their questions excitedly and said things I hadn't intended to say.

From the munition factory across the road, machinery throbbed and droned and crashed like the treading of giants; the noise got on my nerves. I was being worried by bad dreams. More than once I wasn't sure whether I was awake or asleep; the ward was half shadow and half sinking firelight, and the beds were quiet with huddled sleepers. Shapes of mutilated soldiers came crawling across the floor; the floor seemed to be littered with fragments of mangled flesh. Faces glared upward; hands clutched at neck or belly; a livid grinning face with bristly moustache peered at me above the edge of my bed; his hands clawed at the sheets. Some were like the dummy figures used to deceive snipers; others were alive and looked at me reproachfully, as though envying me the warm safety of life which they'd longed for when they shivered in the gloomy dawn, waiting for the whistles to blow and the bombardment to lift. . . . A young English private in battle equipment pulled himself painfully toward me and fumbled in his tunic for a letter; as he reached forward to give it to me his head lolled sideways and he collapsed; there was a hole in his jaw and the blood spread across his white face like ink spilt on blotting paper. . . .

Violently awake, I saw the ward without its phantoms. The sleepers were snoring and a nurse in grey and scarlet was coming silently along to make up the fire.

II

Although I have stated that after my first few days in hospital I "began to think", I cannot claim that my thoughts were clear or consistent. I did, however, become definitely critical and inquiring about the War. While feeling that my infantry experience justified this, it did not occur to me that I was by no means fully informed on the subject. In fact I generalized intuitively, and was not unlike a young man who suddenly loses his belief in religion and stands up to tell the Universal Being that He doesn't exist, adding that if He does, He treats the world very unjustly. I shall have more to say later on about my antagonism to the World War; in the meantime it queered my criticisms of it by continually reminding me that the Adjutant had written to tell me that my name had been "sent in for another decoration". I could find no fault with this hopeful notion, and when I was allowed out of hospital for the first time my vanity did not forget how nice its tunic would look with one of those (still uncommon) little silver rosettes on the M.C. ribbon, which signified a Bar; or, better still, a red and blue D.S.O.

It was May 2nd and warm weather; no one appeared to be annoyed about the War, so why should I worry? Sitting on the top of a bus, I glanced at the editorial paragraphs of the *Unconservative Weekly*. The omniscience of this ably written journal had become the basis of my provocative views on world affairs. I agreed with every word in it and was thus comfortably enabled to disagree with the bellicose patriotism of the *Morning Post*. The only trouble was that an article in the *Unconservative Weekly* was for me a sort of divine revelation. It told me what I'd never known but now needed to believe, and its ratiocinations and political pronouncements passed out of my head as quickly as they entered it. While I read I concurred; but if I'd been asked to restate the arguments I should have contented myself with saying "It's what I've always felt myself, though I couldn't exactly put it into words."

The Archbishop of Canterbury was easier to deal with. Smiling sardonically, I imbibed his "Message to the Nation about the War and the Gospel". "Occasions may arise", he wrote, "when exceptional obligations are laid upon us. Such an emergency having now arisen, the security of the nation's food supply may largely depend upon the labour which can be devoted to the land. This being so, we are, I think, following the guidance given in the Gospel if in such a case we make a temporary departure from our rule. I have no hesitation in saying that in the need which these weeks present, men and women may with a clear conscience do field-work on Sundays." Remembering the intense bombardment in front of Arras on Easter Sunday, I wondered whether the Archbishop had given the sanction of the Gospel for that little bit of Sabbath field-work. Unconscious that he was, presumably, pained by the War and its barbarities, I glared morosely in the direction of Lambeth Palace and muttered, "Silly old fossil!" Soon afterwards I got off the bus at Piccadilly Circus and went into the restaurant where I had arranged to meet Julian Durley.

With Durley I reverted automatically to my active-service self. The war which we discussed was restricted to the doings of the Flintshire Fusiliers. Old So-and-so had been wounded; poor old Somebody had been killed in the Bullecourt show; old Somebody Else was still commanding B

Company. Old jokes and grotesquely amusing trench incidents were re-enacted. The Western Front was the same treacherous blundering tragi-comedy which the mentality of the Army had agreed to regard as something between a crude bit of fun and an excuse for a good grumble. I suppose that the truth of the matter was that we were remaining loyal to the realities of our war experience, keeping our separate psychological secrets to ourselves, and avoiding what Durley called "his dangerous tendency to become serious". His face, however, retained the haunted unhappy look which it had acquired since the Delville Wood attack last autumn, and his speaking voice was still a hoarse whisper.

When I was ordering a bottle of hock we laughed because the waiter told us that the price had been reduced since 1914, as it was now an unpopular wine. The hock had its happy effect, and soon we were agreeing that the Front Line was the only place where one could get away from the War. Durley had been making a forlorn attempt to enter the Flying Corps, and had succeeded in being re-examined medically. The examination had started hopefully, as Durley had confined himself to nods and headshakings in reply to questions. But when conversation became inevitable the doctor had very soon asked angrily, "Why the hell don't you stop that whispering?" The verdict had been against his fractured thyroid cartilage; though, as Durley remarked, it didn't seem to him to make much difference whether you shouted or whispered when you were up in an aeroplane. "You'll have to take some sort of office job," I said. But he replied that he hated the idea, and then illogically advised me to stay in England as long as I could. I asserted that I was going out again as soon as I could get passed for General Service, and called for the bill as though I were thereby settling my destiny conclusively. I emerged from the restaurant without having uttered a single anti-war sentiment.

When Durley had disappeared into his aimless unattached existence, I sat in Hyde Park for an hour before going back to the hospital. What with the sunshine and the effect of the hock, I felt rather drowsy, and the columns of the *Unconservative Weekly* seemed less stimulating than usual.

On the way back to Denmark Hill I diverted my mind by observing the names on shops and business premises. I was rewarded by Pledge (pawnbroker), Money (solicitor), and Stone (builder). There was also an undertaker named Bernard Shaw. But perhaps the most significant name was Fudge (printing works). What use, I thought, were printed words against a war like this? Durley represented the only reality which I could visualize with any conviction. People who told the truth were likely to be imprisoned, and lies were at a premium. . . . All my energy had evaporated and it was a relief to be back in bed. After all, I thought, it's only sixteen days since I left the Second Battalion, so I've still got a right to feel moderately unwell. How luxurious it felt, to be lying there, after a cup of strong tea, with daylight diminishing, and a vague gratitude for being alive at the end of a fine day in late spring. Anyhow the War had taught me to be thankful for a roof over my head at night. . . .

Lying awake after the lights were out in the ward, it is possible that I also thought about the Second Battalion. Someone (it must have been Dunning) had sent me some details of the show they'd been in on April 23rd. The attack had been at the place where I'd left them. A little ground had been gained and lost, and then the Germans had retreated a few hundred yards. Four officers had been killed and nine wounded. About forty other ranks killed, including several of the best N.C.O.s. It had been an episode typical of uncountable others, some of which now fill their few pages in Regimental Histories. Such stories look straightforward enough in print, twelve years later; but their reality remains hidden; even in the minds of old soldiers the harsh horror mellows and recedes.

Of this particular local attack the Second Battalion Doctor afterwards wrote, "The occasion was but one of many when a Company or Battalion was sacrificed on a limited objective to a plan of attack ordered by Division or some higher Command with no more knowledge of the

ground than might be got from a map of moderate scale."
But for me (as I lay awake and wondered whether I'd have
been killed if I'd been there) April 23rd was a blurred picture of people bombing one another up and down ditches;
of a Company stumbling across open ground and getting
mown down by machine-guns; of the Doctor out in the
dark with his stretcher-bearers, getting in the wounded;
and of an exhausted Battalion staggering back to rest-bil-
lets to be congratulated by a genial exculpatory Major-
General, who explained that the attack had been ordered
by the Corps Commander. I could visualize the Major-
General all right, though I wasn't aware that he was
"blaming it on the Corps Commander". And I knew for
certain that Ralph Wilmot was now minus one of his arms,
so my anti-war bitterness was enabled to concentrate itself
on the fact that he wouldn't be able to play the piano
again. Finally, it can safely be assumed that my entire
human organism felt ultra-thankful to be falling asleep in
an English hospital. Altruism is an episodic and debatable
quality; the instinct for self-preservation always got the last
word when an infantryman was lying awake with his
thoughts.

*   *   *

With an apology for my persistent specifyings of chronology, I must relate that on May 9th I was moved on to a
Railway Terminus Hotel which had been commandeered
for the accommodation of convalescent officers. My longing to get away from London made me intolerant of the
Great Central Hotel, which was being directed by a mind
more military than therapeutic. The Commandant was a
non-combatant Brigadier-General, and the convalescents
grumbled a good deal about his methods, although they
could usually get leave to go out in the evenings. Many of
them were waiting to be invalided out of the Army, and
the daily routine orders contained incongruous elements.
We were required to attend lectures on, among other
things, Trench Warfare. At my first lecture I was astonished to see several officers on crutches, with legs amputated, and at least one man had lost that necessary faculty

for trench warfare, his eyesight. They appeared to be accepting the absurd situation stoically; they were allowed to smoke. The Staff Officer who was drawing diagrams on a black-board was obviously desirous of imparting information about the lesson which had been learnt from the Battle of Neuve Chapelle or some equally obsolete engagement. But I noticed several faces in the audience which showed signs of tortured nerves, and it was unlikely that their efficiency was improved by the lecturer who concluded by reminding us of the paramount importance of obtaining offensive ascendancy in no-man's-land.

In the afternoon I had an interview with the doctor who was empowered to decide how soon I went to the country. One of the men with whom I shared a room had warned me that this uniformed doctor was a queer customer. "The blighter seems to take a positive pleasure in tormenting people," he remarked, adding, "He'll probably tell you that you'll have to stay here till you're passed fit for duty." But I had contrived to obtain a letter from the Countess of Somewhere, recommending me for one of the country houses in her Organization; so I felt fairly secure. (At that period of the War people with large houses received convalescent officers as guests.)

The doctor, a youngish man dressed as a temporary Captain, began by behaving quite pleasantly. After he'd examined me and the document which outlined my insignificant medical history, he asked what I proposed to do now. I said that I was hoping to get sent to some place in the country for a few weeks. He replied that I was totally mistaken if I thought any such thing. An expression, which I can only call cruel, overspread his face. "You'll stay here; and when you leave here, you'll find yourself back at the front in double-quick time. How d'you like that idea?" In order to encourage him, I pretended to be upset by his severity; but he seemed to recognize that I wasn't satisfactory material for his peculiar methods, and I departed without having contested the question of going to the country. I was told afterwards that officers had been known to leave this doctor's room in tears. But it must not be supposed that I regard his behaviour as an example of Army brutality. I prefer to think of him as a man who craved for power over his fellow men. And though his power over the visiting patients was brief and episodic, he must have derived extraordinary (and perhaps sadistic) satisfaction from the spectacle of young officers sobbing and begging not to be sent back to the front.

I never saw the supposedly sadistic doctor again; but I hope that someone gave him a black eye, and that he afterwards satisfied his desire for power over his fellow men in a more public-spirited manner.

Next morning I handed the letter of the Countess to a slightly higher authority, with the result that I only spent three nights in the Great Central Hotel, and late on a fine Saturday afternoon I travelled down to Sussex to stay with Lord and Lady Asterisk.

III

Nutwood Manor was everything that a wounded officer could wish for. From the first I was conscious of a kindly welcome. It was the most perfect house I'd ever stayed in. Also, to put the matter plainly, it was the first time I'd ever stayed with an Earl. "Gosh! This is a slice of luck," I thought. A reassuring man-servant conducted me upstairs. My room was called "The Clematis Room"; I noticed the name on the door. Leaning my elbows on the window-sill, I gazed down at the yew hedges of a formal garden; woods and meadows lay beyond and below, glorious with green and luminous in evening light; far away stood the Sussex Downs, and it did my heart good to see them. Everything in the pretty room was an antithesis to ugliness and discomfort. Beside the bed there was a bowl of white lilac and a Bible. Opening it at random to try my luck, I put my finger on the following verse from the Psalms: "The words of his mouth were smoother than butter, but war was in his heart." Rather an odd coincidence, I thought, that the word "war" should turn up like that; but the Old

Testament's full of fighting. . . . While I was changing
into my best khaki uniform I could hear quiet feet and
murmurous voices moving about the house; doors closed
discreetly on people about to dress for dinner. Still almost
incredulous at my good fortune I went downstairs, to be
greeted by a silver-haired and gracious hostess, and introduced to three other officers, all outwardly healthy and
gentlemanly-looking. I was presented to Lord Asterisk,
over eighty and crippled with rheumatism, but resolutely
holding on to a life which had been devoted to useful public service. Respectfully silent, I listened to his urbane eloquence and felt sufficiently at my ease to do justice to a
very good dinner. The port wine went its round; and afterwards, in the drawing-room, I watched Lady Asterisk
working at some embroidery while one of the officers played
Gluck and Handel on the piano. Nothing could have been
more tranquil and harmonious than my first evening at
Nutwood Manor. Nevertheless I failed to fall asleep in the
Clematis Room. Lying awake didn't matter much at first;
there was plenty to ruminate about; the view across the
Weald at sunset had revived my memories of "the good
old days when I hunted with the Ringwell". I had escaped
from the exasperating boredom of hospital life, and now
for a few weeks I could forget about the War. . . . But the
War insisted on being remembered, and by 3 a.m. it had
become so peremptory that I could almost believe that
some of my friends out in France must be waiting to go over
the top. One by one, I thought of as many of them as I
could remember. . . .

I'd overheard Lady Asterisk talking about spiritualism
to one of the officers; evidently she was a strong believer in
the "unseen world". Perhaps it was this which set me
wondering whether, by concentrating my mind on, say,
young Ormand (who was still with the Second Battalion)
I might be able to receive some reciprocal communication.
At three o'clock in the morning a sleepless mind can welcome improbabilities and renounce its daylight scepticism.
Neither voice nor vision rewarded my expectancy.

But I was rewarded by an intense memory of men whose

courage had shown me the power of the human spirit—
that spirit which could withstand the utmost assault. Such
men had inspired me to be at my best when things were
very bad, and they outweighed all the failures. Against the
background of the War and its brutal stupidity those men
had stood glorified by the thing which sought to destroy
them. . . .

I went to the window and leant out. The gables of the
house began to loom distinct against a clear sky. An owl
hooted from the woods; cocks were crowing from distant
farms; on the mantelpiece a little clock ticked busily.
Oppressed by the comfort of my surroundings, I felt an
impulse to dress and go out for a walk. But Arras and the
Somme were a long way off; I couldn't walk there and
didn't want to; but they beckoned me with their bombardments and the reality of the men who endured them. I
wanted to be there again for a few hours, because the
trenches really were more interesting than Lady Asterisk's
rose-garden. Seen from a distance, the War had a sombre
and unforgettable fascination for its bondsmen. I would
have liked to go and see what was happening, and perhaps
take part in some exciting little exploit. I couldn't gainsay
certain intense emotional experiences which I'd lived
through in France. But I also wanted to be back at Nutwood Manor for breakfast. . . . Returning to my bed I
switched on the yellow shaded light. Yes; this was the
Clematis Room, and nothing could be less like the dug-out
where I'd sat a month ago talking about Sussex with Ralph
Wilmot. Through the discurtained window the sky was
deep nocturnal blue. I turned out the lamp, and the window became a patch of greyish white, with tree-tops dark
and still in the strange quietude before dawn. I heard the
cuckoo a long way off. Then a blackbird went scolding
along the garden.

*   *   *

I awoke to a cloudless Sabbath morning. After breakfast
Lady Asterisk led me into the garden and talked very kindly for a few minutes.

"I am sure you have had a very trying time at the front", she said, "but you must not allow yourself to be worried by unpleasant memories. We want our soldier-guests to forget the War while they are with us."

I replied, mumbling, that in such surroundings it wouldn't be easy to worry about anything; and then the old Earl came out on to the terrace, pushing the wheeled apparatus which enabled him to walk.

Often during the next three weeks I was able to forget about the War; often I took refuge in the assuasive human happiness which Nutwood Manor's hospitality offered me. But there were times when my mental mechanism was refractory, and I reverted to my resolution to keep the smoke-drifted battle memories true and intense, unmodified by the comforts of convalescence. I wasn't going to be bluffed back into an easy-going tolerant state of mind, I decided, as I opened a daily paper one morning and very deliberately read a despatch from "War Correspondents' Headquarters".

"I have sat with some of our lads, fighting battles over again, and discussing battles to be," wrote some amiable man who had apparently mistaken the War for a football match between England and Germany. "One officer—a mere boy—told me how he'd run up against eleven Huns in an advanced post. He killed two with a Mills' bomb ('Grand weapon, the Mills'!' he laughed, his clear eyes gleaming with excitement) wounded another with his revolver, and marched the remainder back to our own lines. . . ." I opened one of the illustrated weeklies and soon found an article on "War Pictures at the Royal Academy". After a panegyric about "Forward the Guns!" (a patriotic masterpiece by a lady who had been to the Military Tournament in pre-War days) the following sentence occurred: "I think I like Mr. Blank's 'Contalmaison' picture best. He almost makes one feel that he must have been there. The Nth Division are going over the second line I expect—the tips of their bayonets give one this impression —and it is a picture which makes one's pulse beat a lot faster. . . ."

"The tips of their bayonets give one that impression."
... Obviously the woman journalist who wrote those words
was deriving enjoyment from the War, though she may not
have been aware of the fact. I wondered why it was necessary for the Western Front to be "attractively advertised"
by such intolerable twaddle. What *was* this camouflage
War which was manufactured by the press to aid the imaginations of people who had never seen the real thing?
Many of them probably said that the papers gave them a
sane and vigorous view of the overwhelming tragedy.
"Naturally", they would remark, "the lads from the front
are inclined to be a little morbid about it; one expects that,
after all they've been through. Their close contact with the
War has diminished their realization of its spiritual aspects." Then they would add something about "the heal-
ing of Nations". Such people needed to have their noses
rubbed in a few rank physical facts, such as what a company of men smelt like after they'd been in action for a
week. .... The gong rang for luncheon, and Lady Asterisk
left off reading a book by Tagore (whose mystical philo-
sophies had hitherto seemed to me nebulous and unsatis-
fying).

*   *   *

It must not be supposed that I was ungrateful for my
good luck. For several days on end I could feel obliviously
contented, and in weaker moments there was an absurd
hope that the War might be over before next autumn.
Rambling among woods and meadows, I could "take
sweet counsel" with the country-side; sitting on a grassy
bank and lifting my face to the sun, I could feel an intensity of thankfulness such as I'd never known before the
War; listening to the little brook that bubbled out of a
copse and across a rushy field, I could discard my personal
relationship with the military machine and its ant-like
armies. On my way home I would pass old Mr. Jukes leaning on his garden gate, or an ancient labourer mending
gaps in a hedge. I would stop to gaze at the loveliness of
apple-blossom when the sun came out after a shower. And

the protective hospitality of Nutwood Manor was almost bewildering when compared with an average twenty-four hours in a front-line trench.

All this was well enough; but there was a limit to my season of sauntering; the future was a main road where I must fall into step and do something to earn my "pay and allowances". Lady Asterisk liked to have serious helpful little talks with her officers, and one evening she encouraged me to discuss my immediate horizon. I spoke somewhat emotionally, with self-indulgence in making a fine effect rather than an impartial resolve to face facts. I suggested that I'd been trying to make up my mind about taking a job in England, admitting my longing for life and setting against it the idea of sacrifice and disregard of death. I said that most of my friends were assuring me that there was no necessity for me to go out for the third time. While I talked I saw myself as a noble suffering character whose death in action would be deeply deplored. I saw myself as an afflicted traveller who had entered Lady Asterisk's gates to sit by the fire and rest his weary limbs. I did not complain about the War; it would have been bad form to be bitter about it at Nutwood Manor; my own "personal problem" was what I was concerned with. . . .

We were alone in the library. She listened to me, her silver hair and handsome face bent slightly forward above a piece of fine embroidery. Outwardly emotionless, she symbolized the patrician privileges for whose preservation I had chucked bombs at Germans and carelessly offered myself as a target for a sniper. When I had blurted out my opinion that life was preferable to the Roll of Honour she put aside her reticence like a rich cloak. "But death is nothing," she said. "Life, after all, is only the beginning. And those who are killed in the War—they help us from up there. They are helping us to win." I couldn't answer that; this "other world", of which she was so certain, was something I had forgotten about since I was wounded. Expecting no answer, she went on with a sort of inflexible sympathy (almost "as if my number was already up", as I would have expressed it), "It isn't as though you were heir to a great name. No; I can't see any definite reason for your keeping out of danger. But, of course, you can only decide a thing like that for yourself."

I went up to the Clematis Room feeling caddishly estranged and cynical; wondering whether the Germans "up there" were doing anything definite to impede the offensive operations of the Allied Powers. But Lady Asterisk wasn't hard-hearted. She only wanted me "to do the right thing". . . . I began to wish that I could talk candidly to someone. There was too much well-behaved acquiescence at Nutwood Manor; and whatever the other officers there thought about the War, they kept it to themselves; they had done their bit for the time being and were conventional and correct, as if the eye of their Colonel was upon them.

*   *   *

Social experience at Nutwood was varied by an occasional visitor. One evening I sat next to the new arrival, a fashionable young woman whose husband (as I afterwards ascertained) was campaigning in the Cameroons. Her manner implied that she was ready to take me into her confidence, intellectually; but my responses were cumbersome and uneasy, for her conversation struck me as containing a good deal of trumped-up intensity. A fine pair of pearls dangled from her ears, and her dark blue eyes goggled emptily while she informed me that she was taking lessons in Italian. She was "dying to read Dante", and had already started the Canto about Paolo and Francesca; adored D'Annunzio, too, and had been reading *his* Paolo and Francesca (in French). "Life is so wonderful—so great—and yet we waste it all in this dreadful War!" she exclaimed. Rather incongruously, she then regaled me with some typical gossip from high quarters in the Army. Lunching at the Ritz recently, she had talked to Colonel Repington, who had told her—I really forget what, but it was excessively significant, politically, and showed that there was no need for people to worry about Allenby's failure to advance very far at Arras. Unsusceptible to her outward attractions, I came to the conclusion that she wasn't the stamp of woman for whom I was willing to make the supreme sacrifice. . . .

Lord Asterisk had returned that evening from London, where he'd attended a dinner at the House of Lords. The dinner had been in honour of General Smuts (for whom I must parenthetically testify my admiration). This name made me think of Joe Dottrell, who was fond of relating how, in the Boer War, he had been with a raiding party which had nocturnally surprised and almost captured the Headquarters of General Smuts. I wondered whether the anecdote would interest Lord Asterisk; but (the ladies having left the table) he was embarking on his customary after-dinner oratory, while the young officer guests sipped their port and coffee and occasionally put in a respectful remark. The old fellow was getting very feeble, I thought, as I watched the wreckage of his fine and benevolent face. He sat with his chin on his chest; his brow and nose were still firm and authoritative. Sometimes his voice became weak and querulous, but he appeared to enjoy rolling out his deliberate parliamentary periods. Talking about the War, he surprised me by asserting the futility of waiting for a definite military decision. Although he had been a Colonial Governor, he was "profoundly convinced of the uselessness of some of our Colonies", which, he said, might just as well be handed over to the Germans. He turned to the most articulate officer at the table. "I declare to you, my dear fellow" (voice sinking to a mumble), "I declare to you" (louder), "have you any predominating awareness" (pause) "of—*Sierra Leone?*"

As for Belgium, he invoked the evidence of history to support him in his assertion that its "redemption" by the Allies was merely a manifestation of patriotic obliquity. The inhabitants of Belgium would be just as happy as a German Subject-State. To the vast majority of them their national autonomy meant nothing. While I was trying to remember the exact meaning of the word autonomy, he ended the discussion by remarking, "But I'm only an old dotard!" and we pretended to laugh, naturally, as if it were quite a good joke. Then he reverted to a favourite subject of his, viz., the ineffectiveness of ecclesiastical administrative bodies. "Oh what worlds of dreary (mumble) are hidden by the hats of our episcopal dignitaries! I declare to you, my dear fellow, that it is my profound conviction that the preponderance of mankind is entirely— yes, most grievously indifferent to the deliberations of that well-intentioned but obtuse body of men, the Ecclesiastical Commissioners!" Slightly sententious, perhaps; but no one could doubt that he was a dear old chap who had done his level best to leave the world in better order than he'd found it.

*   *   *

There were times when I felt perversely indignant at the "cushiness" of my convalescent existence. These reactions were mostly caused by the few letters which came to me from the front. One of Joe Dottrell's hastily pencilled notes could make me unreasonably hostile to the cheerful voices of croquet players and inarticulately unfriendly to the elegant student of Italian when she was putting her pearl necklace out in the sun, "because pearls do adore the sun so!"

It wasn't easy to feel animosity against the pleasant-mannered neighbours who dropped in to tea. Nibbling cucumber sandwiches, they conceded full military honours to any officer who had been wounded. They discussed gardening and joked about domestic difficulties; they talked about war-work and public affairs; but they appeared to be refusing to recognize the realities which were implied by a letter from an indomitable quartermaster in France. "The Battalion has been hard at it again and had a rough time, but as usual kept their end up well—much to the joy of the Staff, who have been round here to-day like flies round a jam-pot, congratulating the Colonel and all others concerned. I am sorry to say that the Padre got killed. . . . He was up with the lads in the very front and got sniped in the stomach and died immediately. I haven't much room for his crowd as a rule, but he was the finest

parson I've ever known, absolutely indifferent to danger.
Young Brock (bombing officer—he said he knew you at
Clitherland) was engaging the Boche single-handed when
he was badly hit in the arm, side, and leg. They amputated
his left leg, but he was too far gone and we buried him to-
day. Two other officers killed and three wounded. Poor
Sergeant Blaxton was killed. All the best get knocked over.
. . . The boys are now trying to get to Amiens to do a bit of
courting." Morosely I regarded the Clematis Room. What
earthly use was it, ordering boxes of kippers to be sent to
people who were all getting done in, while everyone at
home humbugged about with polite platitudes? . . . Birdie
Mansfield wrote from Yorkshire; he had been invalided
out of the Army. "I'm fed to the teeth with wandering
around in mufti and getting black looks from people who
pass remarks to the effect that it's about time I joined up.
Meanwhile I exist on my provisional pension (3s. a day).
A few days' touring round these munition areas would give
you food for thought. The average conversation is about
the high cost of beer and the ability to evade military service by bluffing the Tribunals."

I looked at another letter. It was from my servant (to
whom I'd sent a photograph of myself and a small gramophone). "Thank you very much for the photo, which is like
life itself, and the men in the Company say it is just like
him. The gramophone is much enjoyed by all. I hope you
will pardon my neglect in not packing the ground-sheet
with your kit." What could one do about it? Nothing short
of stopping the War could alter the inadequacy of kippers
and gramophones or sustain my sense of unity with those
to whom I sent them.

*   *   *

On the day before I departed from Nutwood Manor I
received another letter from Dottrell. It contained bad
news about the Second Battalion. Viewed broadmindedly,
the attack had been quite a commonplace fragment of the
War. It had been a hopeless failure, and with a single exception all officers in action had become casualties. None

of the bodies had been brought in. The First and Second Battalions had been quite near one another, and Dottrell had seen Ormand a day or two before the show. "He looked pretty depressed, though outwardly as jolly as ever." Dunning had been the first to leave our trench; had shouted "Cheerio" and been killed at once. Dottrell thanked me for the box of kippers. . . .

Lady Asterisk happened to be in the room when I opened the letter. With a sense of self-pitying indignation I blurted out my unpleasant information. Her tired eyes showed that the shock had brought the War close to her, but while I was adding a few details her face became self-defensively serene. "But they are safe and happy now," she said. I did not doubt her sincerity, and perhaps they *were* happy now. All the same, I was incapable of accepting the deaths of Ormand and Dunning and the others in that spirit. I wasn't a theosophist. Nevertheless I left Nutwood with gratitude for the kindness I had received there. I had now four weeks in which to formulate my plans for the future.

PART TEN: INDEPENDENT ACTION

I

At daybreak on June 7th the British began the Battle of Messines by exploding nineteen full-sized mines. For me the day was made memorable by the fact that I lunched with the editor of the *Unconservative Weekly* at his club. By the time I entered that imposing edifice our troops had advanced more than two miles on a ten-mile front and a great many Germans had been blown sky-high. To-morrow this news would pervade clubland on a wave of optimism and elderly men would glow with satisfaction.

In the meantime prospects on the Russian Front were none too bright since the Revolution; but a politician called Kerensky ("Waiter, bring me a large glass of light port") appeared to be doing his best for his country and one could only hope that the Russian Army would—humph—stick to its guns and remember its obligations to the Allies and their War Aims.

My luncheon with Mr. Markington was the result of a letter impulsively written from Nutwood Manor. The letter contained a brief outline of my War service and a suggestion that he ought to publish something outspoken so as to let people at home know what the War was really like. I offered to provide such details as I knew from personal experience. The style of my letter was stilted, except for a postscript: "I'm fed up with all the hanky-panky in the daily papers." His reply was reticent but friendly, and I went to his club feeling that I was a mouthpiece for the troops in the trenches. However, when the opportunity for altruistic eloquence arrived, I discovered, with relief, that none was expected of me. The editor took most of my horrifying information on trust, and I was quite content to listen to his own acrimonious comments on contemporary affairs. Markington was a sallow spectacled man with earnest uncompromising eyes and a stretched sort of mouth which looked as if it had ceased to find human follies funny. The panorama of public affairs had always offered him copious occasions for dissent; the Boer War had been bad enough, but this one had provided almost too much provocation for his embitterment. In spite of all this he wasn't an alarming man to have lunch with; relaxing into ordinary humanity, he could enjoy broad humour, and our conversation took an unexpected turn when he encouraged me to tell him a few army anecdotes which might be censored if I were to print them. I felt quite fond of Markington when he threw himself back in his chair in a paroxysm of amusement. Most of his talk, however, dealt with more serious subjects, and he made me feel that the world was in an even worse condition than my simple mind had suspected. When I questioned him about the probable duration of the War he shrugged his shoulders. The most likely conclusion that he could foresee was a gradual disintegration and collapse of all the armies. After the War, he said, conditions in all countries would be appalling, and Europe would take fifty years to recover. With regard to what I suggested in my letter, he explained that if he were to print veracious accounts of infantry experience his paper would be suppressed as prejudicial to recruiting. The censorship officials were always watching for a plausible excuse for banning it, and they had already prohibited its foreign circulation. "The soldiers are not allowed to express their point of view. In war-time the word patriotism means suppression of truth," he remarked, eyeing a small chunk of Stilton cheese on his plate as if it were incapable of agreeing with any but ultra-Conservative opinions. "Quite a number of middle-aged members of this club have been to the front," he continued. "After a dinner at G.H.Q. and a motor drive in the direction of the trenches, they can talk and write in support of the War with complete confidence in themselves. Five years ago they were probably saying that modern civilization had made a European War unthinkable. But their principles are purchasable. Once they've been invited to visit G.H.Q. they never look back. Their own self-importance is all that matters to them. And any lie is a good lie as long as it stimulates unreasoning hatred of the enemy."

He listened with gloomy satisfaction to my rather vague remarks about incompetent Staff work. I told him that our Second Battalion had been almost wiped out ten days ago because the Divisional General had ordered an impossible attack on a local objective. The phrase "local objective" sounded good, and made me feel that I knew a hell of a lot about it. . . .

On our way to the smoking-room we passed a blandly Victorian bust of Richard Cobden, which caused Markington to regret that the man himself wasn't above ground to give the present Government a bit of his mind. Ignorant about Cobden's career, I gazed fixedly at his marble whiskers, nodded gravely, and inwardly resolved to look up a few facts about him. "If Cobden were alive now," said Markington, "the *Morning Post* would be anathematizing him as a white-livered defeatist! You ought to read his speeches on International Arbitration—not a very popular subject in these days!"

I was comfortably impressed by my surroundings, for the club was the Mecca of the Liberal Party. From a corner of the smoking-room I observed various eminent-looking individuals who were sipping coffee and puffing cigars, and I felt that I was practically in the purlieus of public life. Markington pointed out a few Liberal politicians whose names I knew, and one conspicuous group included a couple of novelists whose reputations were so colossal that I could scarcely believe that I was treading the same carpet as they were. I gazed at them with gratitude; apart from their eminence, they had provided me with a great deal of enjoyment, and I would have liked to tell them so. For Markington, however, such celebrities were an everyday occurrence, and he was more interested in my own sensations while on active service. A single specimen of my eloquence will be enough. "As a matter of fact I'm almost sure that the War doesn't seem nearly such a bloody rotten show when one's out there as it does when one's back in England. You see as soon as one gets across the Channel one sort of feels as if it's no good worrying any more—you know what I mean—like being part of the Machine again, with nothing to be done except take one's chance. After that one can't bother about anything except the Battalion one's with. Of course, there's a hell of a lot of physical discomfort to be put up with, and the unpleasant sights seem to get worse every year; but apart from being shelled and so on, I must say I've often felt extraordinarily happy even in the trenches. Out there it's just one thing after another, and one soon forgets the bad times; it's probably something to do with being in the open air so much and getting such a lot of exercise. . . . It's only when one gets away from it that one begins to realize how stupid and wasteful it all is. What I feel now is that if it's got to go on there ought to be a jolly sound reason for it, and I can't help thinking that the troops are being done in the eye by the people in control." I qualified these temperate remarks by explaining that I was only telling him how it had affected me personally; I had been comparatively lucky, and could now see the War as it affected infantry soldiers who were having an infinitely worse time than I'd ever had—particularly the privates.

When I inquired whether any peace negotiations were being attempted, Markington said that England had been asked by the new Russian Government, in April, to state definitely her War Aims and to publish the secret treaties made between England and Russia early in the War. We had refused to state our terms or publish the treaties. "How damned rotten of us!" I exclaimed, and I am afraid that my instinctive reaction was a savage desire to hit (was it Mr. Lloyd George?) very hard on the nose. Markington was bitter against the military caste in all countries. He said that all the administrative departments in Whitehall were trying to get the better of one another, which resulted in muddle and waste on an unprecedented scale. He told me that I should find the same sort of things described in Tolstoy's *War and Peace*, adding that if once the common soldier became articulate the War couldn't last a month. Soon afterwards he sighed and said he must be getting back to the office; he had his article to write and the paper went to press that evening. When we parted in Pall Mall he told me to keep in touch with him and not worry about the War more than I could help, and I mumbled something about it having been frightfully interesting to meet him.

As I walked away from Markington my mind was clamorous with confused ideas and phrases. It seemed as if, until to-day, I had been viewing the War through the loop-hole of a trench parapet. Now I felt so much "in the know" that I wanted to stop strangers in the street and ask them whether they realized that we ought to state our War Aims. People ought to be warned that there was (as I would have expressed it) some dirty work going on behind their backs. I remembered how sceptical old Lord Asterisk had been about the redemption of "gallant little Belgium" by the Allies. And now Markington had gloomily informed me that our Aims were essentially acquisitive, what we were fighting for was the Mesopotamian Oil Wells. A jolly fine swindle it would have been for me, if I'd been killed in April for an Oil Well! But I soon forgot that I'd been unaware of the existence of the Oil Wells before Markington mentioned them, and I conveniently assimilated them as part of my evidential repertoire.

* * *

Readers of my pedestrian tale are perhaps wondering how soon I shall be returning to the temperate influence of Aunt Evelyn. In her latest letter she announced that a Zeppelin had dropped a bomb on an orchard about six miles away; there had also been an explosion at the Powder Mills at Dumbridge, but no one had been hurt. Nevertheless Butley was too buzzing and leisurely a background for my mercurial state of mind; so I stayed in London for another fortnight, and during that period my mental inquietude achieved some sort of climax. In fact I can safely say that my aggregated exasperations came to a head; and, naturally enough, the head was my own. The prime cause of this psychological thunderstorm was my talk with Markington, who was unaware of his ignitionary effect until I called on him in his editorial room on the Monday after our first meeting. Ostensibly I went to ask his advice; in reality, to release the indignant emotions which his editorial utterances had unwittingly brought to the surface of my consciousness. It was a case of direct inspiration; I had, so to speak, received the call, and the editor of the *Unconservative Weekly* seemed the most likely man to put me on the shortest road to martyrdom. It really felt very fine, and as long as I was alone my feelings carried me along on a torrent of prophetic phrases. But when I was inside Markington's office (he sitting with fingers pressed together and regarding me with alertly mournful curiosity) my internal eloquence dried up and I began abruptly. "I say, I've been thinking it all over, and I've made up my mind that I ought to do something about it." He pushed his spectacles up on to his forehead and leant back in his chair. "You want to do something?" "About the War, I mean. I just can't sit still and do nothing. You said the other day that you couldn't print anything really outspoken, but I don't see why I shouldn't make some sort of statement—about how we ought to publish our War Aims and all that and the troops not knowing what they're fighting about. It might do quite a lot of good, mightn't it?" He got up and went to the window. A secretarial typewriter tick-tacked in the next room. While he stood with his back to me I could see the tiny traffic creeping to and fro on Charing Cross Bridge and a barge going down the river in the sunshine. My heart was beating violently. I knew that I couldn't turn back now. Those few moments seemed to last a long time; I was conscious of the stream of life going on its way, happy and untroubled, while I had just blurted out something which alienated me from its acceptance of a fine day in the third June of the Great War. Returning to his chair, he said, "I suppose you've realized what the results of such an action would be, as regards yourself?" I replied that I didn't care two damns what they did to me as long as I got the thing off my chest. He laughed, looking at me with a gleam of his essential kindness. "As far as I am aware, you'd be the first soldier to take such a step, which would, of course, be welcomed by the extreme pacifists. Your service at the front would differentiate you from the conscientious objectors. But you must on no account make this gesture—a very fine one if you are really in earnest about it—unless you can carry it through effectively. Such an action would require to be carefully thought out, and for the present I advise you to be extremely cautious in what you say and do." His words caused me an uncomfortable feeling that perhaps I was only making a fool of myself; but this was soon mitigated by a glowing sense of martyrdom. I saw myself "attired with sudden brightness, like a man inspired", and while Markington continued his counsels of prudence my resolve strengthened toward its ultimate obstinacy. After further reflection he said that the best man for me to consult was Thornton Tyrrell. "You know him by name, I suppose?" I was compelled to admit that I didn't. Markington handed me *Who's Who* and began to write a letter while I made myself acquainted with the details of Tyrrell's biographical abridgement, which indicated that he was a pretty tough proposition. To put it plainly he was an eminent mathematician, philosopher, and physicist. As a mathematician I'd never advanced much beyond "six from four you can't, six from fourteen leaves eight"; and I knew no more about the functions of a physicist than a cat in a kitchen. "What sort of a man is he to meet?" I asked dubiously. Markington licked and closed the envelope of his rapidly written letter. "Tyrrell is the most uncompromising character I know. An extraordinary brain, of course. But you needn't be alarmed by that; you'll find him perfectly easy to get on with. A talk with him ought to clarify your ideas. I've explained your position quite briefly. But, as I said before, I hope you won't be too impetuous."

I put the letter in my pocket, thanked him warmly, and went soberly down the stairs and along the quiet side-street into the Strand. While I was debating whether I ought to buy and try to read one of Tyrrell's books before going to see him, I almost bumped into a beefy Major-General. It was lunch-time and he was turning in at the Savoy Hotel entrance. Rather grudgingly, I saluted. As I went on my way, I wondered what the War Office would say if it knew what I was up to.

II

Early in the afternoon I left the letter at Tyrrell's address in Bloomsbury. He telegraphed that he could see me in the evening, and punctually at the appointed hour I returned to the quiet square. My memory is not equal to the effort of reconstructing my exact sensations, but it can safely be assumed that I felt excited, important, and rather nervous. I was shown into an austere-looking room where Tyrrell was sitting with a reading lamp at his elbow. My first impression was that he looked exactly like a philosopher. He was small, clean-shaven, with longish grey hair brushed neatly above a fine forehead. He had a long upper lip, a powerful ironic mouth, and large earnest eyes. I observed that the book which he put aside was called *The Conquest of Bread* by Kropotkin, and I wondered what on earth it could be about. He put me at my ease by lighting a large pipe, saying as he did so, "Well, I gather from Markington's letter that you've been experiencing a change of heart about the War." He asked for details of my career in the Army, and soon I was rambling on in my naturally inconsequent style. Tyrrell said very little, his object being to size me up. Having got my mind warmed up, I began to give him a few of my notions about the larger aspects of the War. But he interrupted my "and after what Markington told me the other day, I must say", with, "Never mind about what Markington told you. It amounts to this, doesn't it—that you have ceased to believe what you are told about the objects for which you supposed yourself to be fighting?" I replied that it did boil down to something like that, and it seemed to me a bloody shame, the troops getting killed all the time while people at home humbugged themselves into believing that everyone in the trenches enjoyed it. Tyrrell poured me out a second cup of tea and suggested that I should write out a short personal statement based on my conviction that the War was being unnecessarily prolonged by the refusal of the Allies to publish their war aims. When I had done this we could discuss the next step to be taken. "Naturally I should help you in every way possible," he said. "I have always regarded all wars as acts of criminal folly, and my hatred of this one has often made life seem almost unendurable. But hatred makes one vital, and without it one loses energy. 'Keep vital' is a more important axiom than 'love your neighbour'. This act of yours, if you stick to it, will probably land you in prison. Don't let that discourage you. You will be more alive in prison than you would be in the trenches." Mistaking this last remark for a joke, I laughed, rather half-heartedly. "No; I mean that seriously," he said. "By thinking independently and acting fearlessly on your moral convictions you are serving the world better than you would do by marching with the unthinking majority who are suffering and dying at the front because they believe what they have been told to believe. Now that you have lost your faith in what you enlisted for, I am certain that you should go on and let the consequences take care of themselves. Of course your action would be welcomed by people like myself who are violently opposed to the War. We should print and circulate as many copies of your statement as possible. . . . But I hadn't intended to speak as definitely as this. You must decide by your own feeling and not by what anyone else says." I promised to send him my statement when it was written and walked home with my head full of exalted and disorderly thoughts. I had taken a strong liking for Tyrrell, who probably smiled rather grimly while he was reading a few more pages of Kropotkin's *Conquest of Bread* before going upstairs to his philosophic slumbers.

*   *   *

Although Tyrrell had told me that my statement needn't be more than 200 words long, it took me several days to formulate. At first I felt that I had so much to say that I didn't know where to begin. But after several verbose failures it seemed as though the essence of my manifesto could be stated in a single sentence: "I say this War ought to stop." During the struggle to put my unfusilierish opinions into some sort of shape, my confidence often diminished. But there was no relaxation of my inmost resolve, since I was in the throes of a species of conversion which made the prospect of persecution stimulating and almost enjoyable. No; my loss of confidence was in the same category as my diffidence when first confronted by a Vickers Machine-Gun and its Instructor. While he reeled off the names of its numerous component parts, I used to despair of ever being able to remember them or understand their workings. "And unless I know all about the Vickers Gun I'll never get sent out to the front," I used to think. Now, sitting late at night in an expensive but dismal bedroom in Jermyn Street, I internally exclaimed, "I'll never be able to write out a decent statement and the whole blasted protest will be a washout! Tyrrell thinks I'm quite brainy, but when he reads this stuff he'll realize what a dud I am."

What could I do if Tyrrell decided to discourage my candidature for a court martial? Chuck up the whole idea and go out again and get myself killed as quick as possible? "Yes," I thought, working myself up into a tantrum, "I'd get killed just to show them all I don't care a damn." (I didn't stop to specify the identity of "them all"; such details could be dispensed with when one had lost one's temper with the Great War.) But common sense warned me that getting sent back was a slow business, and getting killed on purpose an irrelevant gesture for a platoon commander. One couldn't choose one's own conditions out in France. . . . Tyrrell had talked about "serving the world by thinking independently". I must hang on to that idea and remember the men for whom I believed myself to be interceding. I tried to think internationally; the poor old Boches must be hating it just as much as we did; but I couldn't propel my sympathy as far as the Balkan States, Turks, Italians, and all the rest of them; and somehow or other the French were just the French and too busy fighting and selling things to the troops to need my intervention. So I got back to thinking about "all the good chaps who'd been killed with the First and Second Battalions since I left them". . . . Ormand, dying miserably out in a shell-hole. . . . I remembered his exact tone of voice when saying that if his children ever asked what he did in the Great War, his answer would be, "No bullet ever went quick enough to catch me;" and how he used to sing 'Rock of ages cleft for me, let me hide myself in thee," when we were being badly shelled. I thought of the typical Flintshire Fusilier at his best, and the vast anonymity of courage and cheerfulness which he represented as he sat in a frontline trench cleaning his mess-tin. How could one connect him with the gross profiteer whom I'd overheard in a railway carriage remarking to an equally repulsive companion that if the War lasted another eighteen months he'd be able to retire from business? . . . How could I co-ordinate such diversion of human behaviour, or believe that heroism was its own reward? Something must be put on paper, however, and I re-scrutinized the rough notes I'd been making: *Fighting men are victims of conspiracy among (a) politicians; (b) military caste; (c) people who are making money out of the War.* Under this I had scribbled, *Also personal effort to dissociate myself from intolerant prejudice and conventional complacence of those willing to watch sacrifices of others while they sit safely at home.* This was followed by an indignant afterthought. *I believe that by taking this action I am helping to destroy the system of deception, etc., which prevents people from facing the truth and demanding some guarantee that the torture of humanity shall not be prolonged unnecessarily through the arrogance and incompetence of.* . . . Here it broke off, and I wondered how many c's there were in "unnecessarily". *I am not a conscientious objector. I am a soldier who believes he is acting on behalf of soldiers.* How inflated and unconvincing it all looked! If I wasn't careful I should be yelling like some crank on a barrel in Hyde Park. Well, there was nothing for it but to begin all over again. I couldn't ask Tyrrell to give me a few hints. He'd insisted that I must be independent-minded, and had since written to remind me that I must decide my course of action for myself and not be prompted by anything he'd said to me.

Sitting there with my elbows on the table I stared at the dingy red wallpaper in an unseeing effort at mental concentration. If I stared hard enough and straight enough, it seemed, I should see through the wall. Truth would be revealed, and my brain would become articulate. *I am making this statement as an act of wilful defiance of military authority because I believe that the War is being deliberately prolonged by those who have the power to end it.* That would be all right as a kick-off, anyhow. So I continued my superhuman cogitations. Around me was London with its darkened streets; and far away was the War, going on with wave on wave of gunfire, devouring its victims, and unable to blunder forward either to Paris or the Rhine. The air-raids were becoming serious, too. Looking out of the window at the searchlights, I thought how ridiculous it would be if a bomb dropped on me while I was writing out my statement.

III

Exactly a week after our first conversation I showed the statement to Tyrrell. He was satisfied with it as a whole and helped me to clarify a few minor crudities of expression. Nothing now remained but to wait until my leave had expired and then hurl the explosive document at the Commanding Officer at Clitherland (an event which I didn't permit myself to contemplate clearly). For the present the poor man only knew that I'd applied for an instructorship with a Cadet Battalion at Cambridge. He wrote that he would be sorry to lose me and congratulated me on what he was generous enough to describe as my splendid work at the front. In the meantime Tyrrell was considering the question of obtaining publicity for my protest. He introduced me to some of his colleagues on the "Stop the War Committee" and the "No Conscription Fellowship". Among them was an intellectual conscientious objector (lately released after a successful hunger-strike). Also a genial veteran Socialist (recognizable by his red tie and soft grey hat) who grasped my hand with rugged good wishes. One and all, they welcomed me to the Anti-War Movement, but I couldn't quite believe that I had been assimilated. The reason for this feeling was their antipathy to everyone in a uniform. I was still wearing mine, and somehow I was unable to dislike being a Flint-shire Fusilier. This little psychological dilemma now seems almost too delicate to be divulged. In their eyes, I suppose, there was no credit attached to the fact of having been at the front; but for me it had been a supremely important experience. I am obliged to admit that if these anti-war enthusiasts hadn't happened to be likeable I might have secretly despised them. Any man who had been on active service had an unfair advantage over those who hadn't. And the man who had really endured the War at its worst was everlastingly differentiated from everyone except his fellow soldiers.

Tyrrell (a great man and to be thought of as "in a class by himself") took me up to Hampstead one hot afternoon to interview a member of Parliament who was "interested in my case". Walking alongside of the philosopher I felt as if we were a pair of conspirators. His austere scientific intellect was far beyond my reach, but he helped me by his sense of humour, which he had contrived, rather grimly, to retain, in spite of the exasperating spectacle of European civilization trying to commit suicide. The M.P. promised to raise the question of my statement in the House of Commons as soon as I had sent it to the Colonel at Clitherland, so I began to feel that I was getting on grandly. But except for the few occasions when I saw Tyrrell, I was existing in a world of my own (in which I tried to keep my courage up to protest-pitch). From the visible world I sought evidence which could aggravate my quarrel with acquiescent patriotism. Evidences of civilian callousness and complacency were plentiful, for the thriftless licence of war-time behaviour was an unavoidable spectacle, especially in the Savoy Hotel Grill Room which I visited more than once in my

anxiety to reassure myself of the existence of bloated profiteers and uniformed jacks in office. Watching the guzzlers
in the Savoy (and conveniently overlooking the fact that
some of them were officers on leave) I nourished my righteous hatred of them, anathematizing their appetites with
the intolerance of youth which made me unable to realize
that comfort-loving people are obliged to avoid self-know-
ledge—especially when there is a war on. But I still believe
that in 1917 the idle, empty-headed, and frivolous ingredients of Society were having a tolerably good time, while
the officious were being made self-important by nicely
graded degrees of uniformed or un-uniformed war-emer-
gency authority. For middle-aged persons who faced the
War bleakly, life had become unbearable unless they persuaded themselves that the slaughter was worth while.
Tyrrell was comprehensively severe on everyone except inflexible pacifists. He said that the people who tried to resolve the discords of the War into what they called "a
higher harmony" were merely enabling themselves to contemplate the massacre of the young men with an easy conscience. "By Jingo, I suppose you're right!" I exclaimed,
wishing that I were able to express my ideas with such
comprehensive clarity.

*　　*　　*

Supervising a platoon of Cadet Officers at Cambridge
would have been a snug alternative to "general service
abroad" (provided that I could have bluffed the cadets
into believing that I knew something about soldiering). I
was going there to be interviewed by the Colonel and
clinch my illusory appointment; but I was only doing this
because I considered it needful for what I called "strengthening my position". I hadn't looked ahead much, but
when I did so it was with an eye to safeguarding myself
against "what people would say".

When I remarked to Tyrrell that "people couldn't say I
did it so as to avoid going back to France if I had been
given a job in England", he pulled me up short.

"What people say doesn't matter. Your own belief in

what you are doing is the only thing that counts." Know-ing that he was right, I felt abashed; but I couldn't help regretting that my second decoration had failed to materi-alize. It did not occur to me that a Bar to one's Military Cross was a somewhat inadequate accretion to one's quali-fications for affirming that the War was being deliberately prolonged by those who had the power to end it. Except for a bullet-hole in my second best tunic, all that I'd got for my little adventure in April consisted of a gilt-edged card on which the Divisional General had inscribed his con-gratulations and thanks. This document was locally re-ferred to as "one of Whincop's Bread Cards", and since it couldn't be sewn on to my tunic I did my best to feel that it was better than nothing.

Anyhow, on a glaring hot morning I started to catch a train to Cambridge. I was intending to stay a night there for it would be nice to have a quiet look round and perhaps go up to Grantchester in a canoe. Admittedly, next month was bound to be ghastly; but it was no good worrying about that. . . . Had I enough money on me? Probably not; so I decided to stop and change a cheque at my bank in Old Broad Street. Changing a cheque was always a com-forting performance. "Queer thing, having private means," I thought. "They just hand you out the money as if it was a present from the Bank Manager." It was funny, too, to think that I was still drawing my Army pay. But it was the wrong moment for such humdrum cogitations, for when my taxi stopped in that narrow thoroughfare, Old Broad Street, the people on the pavement were standing still, staring up at the hot white sky. Loud bangings had begun in the near neighbourhood, and it was obvious that an air-raid was in full swing. This event could not be ignored; but I needed money and wished to catch my train, so I decided to disregard it. The crashings continued, and while I was handing my cheque to the cashier a crowd of women clerks came wildly down a winding stairway with vociferations of not unnatural alarm. Despite this commotion the cashier handed me five one-pound notes with the stoical politeness of a man who had made up his mind to go down with the ship. Probably he felt as I did—more indignant than afraid; there seemed no sense in the idea of being blown to bits in one's own bank. I emerged from the building with an air of soldierly unconcern; my taxi-driver, like the cashier, was commendably calm, although another stupendous crash sounded as though very near Old Broad Street (as indeed it was). "I suppose we may as well go on to the station," I remarked, adding, "it seems a bit steep that one can't even cash a cheque in comfort!" The man grinned and drove on. It was impossible to deny that the War was being brought home to me. At Liverpool Street there had occurred what, under normal conditions, would be described as an appalling catastrophe. Bombs had been dropped on the station and one of them had hit the front carriage of the noon express to Cambridge. Horrified travellers were hurrying away. The hands of the clock indicated 11.50; but railway time had been interrupted; for once in its career, the imperative clock was a passive spectator. While I stood wondering what to do, a luggage trolley was trundled past me; on it lay an elderly man, shabbily dressed, and apparently dead. The sight of blood caused me to feel quite queer. This sort of danger seemed to demand a quality of courage dissimilar to front-line fortitude. In a trench one was acclimatized to the notion of being exterminated and there was a sense of organized retaliation. But here one was helpless; an invisible enemy sent destruction spinning down from a fine weather sky; poor old men bought a railway ticket and were trundled away again dead on a barrow; wounded women lay about in the station groaning. And one's train didn't start. . . . Nobody could say for certain when it *would* start, a phlegmatic porter informed me; so I migrated to St. Pancras and made the journey to Cambridge in a train which halted good-naturedly at every station. Gazing at sleepy green landscapes, I found difficulty in connecting them (by the railway line) with the air-raid which (I was afterwards told) had played hell with Paternoster Avenue. "It wouldn't be such a bad life", I thought, "if one were a station-master on a branch line in Bedfordshire". There was something attractive, too, in the idea of being a commercial traveller, creeping about the country and doing business in drowsy market towns and snug cathedral cities.

If only I could wake up and find myself living among the parsons and squires of Trollope's Barsetshire, jogging easily from Christmas to Christmas, and hunting three days a week with the Duke of Omnium's Hounds. . . .

The elms were so leafy and the lanes invited me to such rural remoteness that every time the train slowed up I longed to get out and start on an indefinite walking tour— away into the delusive Sabbath of summer—away from air-raids and inexorable moral responsibilities and the ever-increasing output of munitions.

But here was Cambridge, looking contented enough in the afternoon sunshine, as though the Long Vacation were on. The Colleges appeared to have forgotten their copious contributions to the Roll of Honour. The streets were empty, for the Cadets were out on their afternoon parades —probably learning how to take compass-bearings, or pretending to shoot at an enemy who was supposedly advancing from a wood nine hundred yards away. I knew all about that type of training. "Half-right; haystack; three fingers left of haystack; copse; nine hundred; AT THE COPSE, ten rounds rapid, FIRE!" There wasn't going to be any musketry-exercise instructing for me, however. I was only "going through the motions" of applying for a job with the Cadet Battalion. The orderly room was on the ground floor of a college. In happier times it had been a library (the books were still there) and the Colonel had been a History Don with a keen interest in the Territorials. Playing the part of respectful young applicant for instructorship in the Arts of War, I found myself doing it so convincingly that the existence of my "statement" became, for the moment, an improbability. "Have you any specialist knowledge?" inquired the Colonel. I told him that I'd been Battalion Intelligence Officer for a time (suppressing the fact that I'd voluntarily relinquished that status after three days of inability to supply the necessary eye-wash reports). "Ah, that's excellent. We find the majority of men very weak in map-reading," he replied, adding, "our main object, of course, is to instil first-rate morale. It isn't always easy to impress on these new army men what we mean by the tradition of the pre-War regimental officer. . . . Well, I'm sure you'll do very good work. You'll be joining us in two or three weeks, I think? Good-bye till then." He shook my hand rather as if I'd won a History Scholarship, and I walked out of the college feeling that it was a poor sort of joke on him. But my absence as an instructor was all to the good as far as he was concerned, and I was inclined to think that I was better at saying the War ought to stop than at teaching cadets how to carry it on. Sitting in King's Chapel I tried to recover my conviction of the nobility of my enterprise and to believe that the pen which wrote my statement had "dropped from an angel's wing". I also reminded myself that Cambridge had dismissed Tyrrell from his lectureship because he disbelieved in the War. "Intolerant old blighters!" I inwardly exclaimed. "One can't possibly side with people like that. All they care about is keeping up with the other colleges in the casualty lists." Thus refortified, I went down to the river and hired a canoe.

IV

Back at Butley, I had fully a fortnight in which to take life easily before tackling "wilful defiance of military authority". I was, of course, compelled to lead a double life, and the longer it lasted the less I liked it. I am unable to say for certain how far I was successful in making Aunt Evelyn believe that my mind was free from anxiety. But I know that it wasn't easy to sustain the evangelistic individuality which I'd worked myself up to in London. Outwardly those last days of June progressed with nostalgic serenity. I say nostalgic, because in my weaker moods I longed for the peace of mind which could have allowed me to enjoy having tea out in the garden on fine afternoons. But it was no use trying to dope my disquiet with Trollope's novels or any of my favourite books. The purgatory I'd let myself in for always came between me and the pages; there was no escape for me now. Walking restlessly about the garden at night I was oppressed by the midsummer silence and found no comfort in the twinkling lights along the Weald. At one end of the garden three poplars tapered against the stars; they seemed like sentries guarding a prisoner. Across the uncut orchard grass, Aunt Evelyn's white beehives glimmered in the moonlight like bones. The hives were empty, for the bees had been wiped out by the Isle of Wight disease. But it was no good moping about the garden. I ought to be indoors improving my mind, I thought, for I had returned to Butley resolved to read for dear life—circumstances having made it imperative that I should accumulate as much solid information as I could. But sedulous study only served to open up the limitless prairies of my ignorance, and my attention was apt to wander away from what I was reading. If I could have been candid with myself I should have confessed that a fortnight was inadequate for the completion of my education as an intellectual pacifist. Reading the last few numbers of Markington's weekly was all very well as a tonic for disagreeing with organized public opinion, but even if I learnt a whole article off by heart I should only have built a little hut on the edge of the prairie. "I must have all the arguments at my fingers' ends," I had thought when I left London. The arguments, perhaps, were epitomized in Tyrrell's volume of lectures ("given to me by the author," as I had written on the flyleaf). Nevertheless those lectures on political philosophy, though clear and vigorous in style, were too advanced for my elementary requirements. They were, I read on the first page, "inspired by a view of the springs of action which has been suggested by the War. And all of them are informed by the hope of seeing such political institutions established in Europe as shall make men averse from war —a hope which I firmly believe to be realizable, though not without a great and fundamental reconstruction of economic and social life." From the first I realized that this was a book whose meanings could only be mastered by dint of copious underlining. *What integrates an individual life is a consistent creative purpose or unconscious direction.* I underlined that, and then looked up "integrate" in the dictionary. Of course, it meant the opposite to *disintegrate*, which was what the optimists of the press said would soon happen to the Central Powers of Europe. Soon afterwards I came to the conclusion that much time would be saved if I underlined the sentences which *didn't* need underlining. The truth was that there were too many ideas in the book. I was forced to admit that nothing in Tyrrell's lectures could be used for backing up my point of view when I was being interrogated by the Colonel at Clitherland. . . . The thought of Clitherland was unspeakably painful. I had a vague hope that I could get myself arrested without going there. It would be so much easier if I could get my case dealt with by strangers.

*　　　*　　　*

Aunt Evelyn did her best to brighten the part of my double life which included her, but at meal times I was often morose and monosyllabic. Humanly speaking, it would have been a relief to confide in her. As a practical proposition, however, it was impossible. I couldn't allow my protest to become a domestic controversy, and it was obviously kinder to keep my aunt in the dark about it until she received the inevitable shock. I remember one particular evening when the suspense was growing acute. At dinner Aunt Evelyn, in her efforts to create cheerful conversation, began by asking me to tell her more about Nutwood Manor. It was, she surmised, a very well-arranged house, and the garden must have been almost perfection. "Did azaleas grow well there?" Undeterred by my gloomily affirmative answer, she urged me to supply further information about the Asterisks and their friends. She had always heard that old Lord Asterisk was such a fine man, and must have had a most interesting life, although, now she came to think of it, he'd been a bit of a Radical and had supported Gladstone's Home Rule Bill. She then interrupted herself by exclaiming: "Naughty, naughty, naughty!" But this rebuke was aimed at one of the cats who was sharpening his claws on the leather seat of one of the Chippendale chairs. Having thrown my napkin at the cat, I admitted that Lord Asterisk was a dear old chap, though unlikely to live much longer. Aunt Evelyn expressed concern about his infirmity, supplementing it with her perennial "Don't eat so fast, dear; you're simply bolting it down. You'll ruin your digestion." She pressed me to have some more chicken, thereby causing me to refuse, although I should have had some more if she'd kept quiet about it. She now tried the topic of my job at Cambridge. What sort of rooms should I live in? Perhaps I should have rooms in one of the colleges which would be very nice for me—much nicer than those horrid huts at Clitherland. Grumpily I agreed that Cambridge was preferable to Clitherland. A bowl of strawberries, perhaps the best ones we'd had that summer, created a diversion. Aunt Evelyn regretted the unavoidable absence of cream, which enabled me to assure her that some of the blighters I'd seen in London restaurants weren't denying themselves much; and I went off into a diatribe against profiteers and officials who gorged at the Ritz and the Savoy while the poorer classes stood for hours in queues outside food shops. Much relieved at being able to agree with me about something, Aunt Evelyn almost overdid her indignant ejaculations, adding that it was a positive scandal—the disgracefully immoral way most of the young women were behaving while doing war-work. This animation subsided when we got up from the table. In the drawing-room she lit the fire "as the night felt a bit chilly and a fire would make the room more cheerful". Probably she was hoping to spend a cosy evening with me; but I made a bad beginning, for the lid fell off the coffee-pot and cracked one of the little blue and yellow cups, and when Aunt Evelyn suggested that we might play one of our old games of cribbage or halma, I said I didn't feel like that sort of thing. Somehow I couldn't get myself to behave affectionately toward her, and she had irritated me by making uncomplimentary remarks about Markington's paper, a copy of which was lying on the table. (She said it was written by people who were mad with their own self-importance and she couldn't understand how I could read such a paper.) Picking it up I went grumpily upstairs and spent the next ten minutes trying to teach Popsy the parrot how to say "Stop the War". But he only put his head down to be scratched, and afterwards obliged me with his well-known rendering of Aunt Evelyn calling the cats. On her way up to bed she came in (with a glass of milk) and told me that she was sure I wasn't feeling well. Wouldn't it be a good thing if I were to go to the seaside for a few days' golf? But this suggestion only provided me with further evidence that it was no earthly use expecting her to share my views about the War. Games of golf indeed! I glowered at the glass of milk and had half a mind to throw it out of the window. Afterwards I decided that I might as well drink it, and did so.

*   *   *

Late on a sultry afternoon, when returning from a mutinous-minded walk, I stopped to sit in Butley Churchyard. From Butley Hill one looks across a narrow winding valley, and that afternoon the woods and orchards suddenly made me feel almost as fond of them as I'd been when I was in France. While I was resting on a flat-topped old tombstone I recovered something approximate to peace of mind. Gazing at my immediate surroundings, I felt that "joining the great majority" was a homely—almost a comforting— idea. Here death differed from extinction in modern warfare. I ascertained from the nearest headstone that *Thomas Welfare, of this Parish, had died on October* 20th, 1843, *aged* 72. "*Respected by all who knew him.*" *Also Sarah, wife of the above.* "*Not changed but glorified.*" Such facts were resignedly acceptable. They were in harmony with the simple annals of this quiet corner of Kent. One could speculate serenely upon the homespun mortality of such worthies, whose lives had "taken place" with the orderly and inevitable progression of a Sunday service. They made the past seem pleasantly prosy in contrast with the monstrous emergencies of to-day. And Butley Church, with its big-buttressed square tower, was protectively permanent. One could visualize it there for the last 599 years, measuring out the unambitious local chronology with its bells, while English history unrolled itself along the horizon with coronations and rebellions and stubbornly disputed charters and covenants. Beyond all that, the "foreign parts" of the world widened incredibly toward regions reported by travellers' tales. And so outward to the windy universe of astronomers and theologians. Looking up at the battlemented tower, I improvised a clear picture of some morning—was it in the seventeenth century? Men in steeple-crowned hats were surveying a rudimentary-looking landscape with anxious faces, for trouble was afoot and there was talk of the King's enemies. But the insurgence always passed by. It had never been more than a rumour for Butley, whether it was Richard of Gloucester or Charles the First who happened to be losing his kingdom. It was difficult to imagine that Butley had contributed many soldiers for the Civil Wars, or even for Marlborough and Wellington, or that the village carpenter of those days had lost both his sons in Flanders. Between the church door and the lych gate the plump yews were catching the rays of evening. Along that path the coffined generations had paced with sober church-going faces. There they had stood in circumspect groups to exchange local gossip and discuss the uncertainly reported events of the outside world. They were a long way off now, I thought—their names undecipherable on tilted headstones or humbly oblivioned beneath green mounds. For the few who could afford a permanent memorial, their remoteness from posterity became less as the names became more legible, until one arrived at those who had watched the old timbered inn by the churchyard being burnt to the ground—was it forty years ago? I remembered Captain Huxtable telling me that the catastrophe was supposed to have been started by the flaring up of a pot of glue which a journeyman joiner had left on a fire while he went to the tap-room for a mug of beer. The burning of the old Bull Inn had been quite a big event for the neighbourhood; but it wouldn't be thought much of in these days; and my mind reverted to the demolished churches along the Western

Front, and the sunlit inferno of the first day of the Somme
Battle. There wouldn't be much Gray's Elegy atmosphere
if Butley were in the Fourth Army area!

Gazing across at the old rifle butts—now a grassy indenta-
tion on the hillside half a mile away—I remembered the
volunteers whose torchlight march-past had made such a
glowing impression on my nursery-window mind, in the
good old days before the Boer War. Twenty years ago there
had been an almost national significance in the fact of a
few Butley men doing target practice on summer evenings.

Meanwhile my meditations had dispelled my heavy-
heartedness, and as I went home I recovered something of
the exultation I'd felt when first forming my resolution. I
knew that no right-minded Butley man could take it upon
himself to affirm that a European war was being needlessly
prolonged by those who had the power to end it. They
would tap their foreheads and sympathetically assume that
I'd seen more of the fighting than was good for me. But I
felt the desire to suffer, and once again I had a glimpse of
something beyond and above my present troubles—as
though I could, by cutting myself off from my previous
existence, gain some new spiritual freedom and live as I
had never lived before.

"They can all go to blazes," I thought, as I went home
by the field path. "I know I'm right and I'm going to do
it," was the rhythm of my mental monologue. If all that
senseless slaughter had got to go on, it shouldn't be through
any fault of mine. "It won't be any fault of mine," I muttered.

A shaggy farm horse was sitting in the corner of a field
with his front legs tucked under him; munching placidly,
he watched me climb the stile into the old green lane with
its high thorn hedges.

V

Sunshade in one hand and prayer-book in the other, Aunt
Evelyn was just starting for morning service at Butley. "I
really must ask Captain Huxtable to tea before you go

away. He looked a little hurt when he inquired after you last Sunday," she remarked. So it was settled that she would ask him to tea when they came out of church. "I really can't think why you haven't been over to see him," she added, dropping her gloves and then deciding not to wear them after all, for the weather was hot and since she had given up the pony cart she always walked to church. She put up her pink sunshade and I walked with her to the front gate. The two cats accompanied us, and were even willing to follow her up the road, though they'd been warned over and over again that the road was dangerous. Aunt Evelyn was still inclined to regard all motorists as reckless and obnoxious intruders. The roads were barely safe for human beings, let alone cats, she exclaimed as she hurried away. The church bells could already be heard across the fields, and very peaceful they sounded.

July was now a week old. I had overstayed my leave several days and was waiting until I heard from the Depot. My mental condition was a mixture of procrastination and suspense, but the suspense was beginning to get the upper hand of the procrastination, since it was just possible that the Adjutant at Clitherland was assuming that I'd gone straight to Cambridge.

Next morning the conundrum was solved by a telegram, *Report how situated*. There was nothing for it but to obey the terse instructions, so I composed a letter (brief, courteous, and regretful) to the Colonel, enclosing a typewritten copy of my statement, apologizing for the trouble I was causing him, and promising to return as soon as I heard from him. I also sent a copy to Dottrell, with a letter in which I hoped that my action would not be entirely disapproved of by the First Battalion. Who else was there, I wondered, feeling rather rattled and confused. There was Durley, of course, and Cromlech also—fancy my forgetting him! I could rely on Durley to be sensible and sympathetic; and David was in a convalescent hospital in the Isle of Wight, so there was no likelihood of his exerting himself with efforts to dissuade me. I didn't want anyone to begin interfering on my behalf. At least I hoped that I didn't; though there were weak moments later on when I wished they would. I read my statement through once more (though I could have recited it only too easily) in a desperate effort to calculate its effect on the Colonel. "*I am making this statement as an act of wilful defiance of military authority, because I believe that the War is being deliberately prolonged by those who have the power to end it. I am a soldier, convinced that I am acting on behalf of soldiers. I believe that this War, upon which I entered as a war of defence and liberation, has now become a war of aggression and conquest. I believe that the purposes for which I and my fellow soldiers entered upon this War should have been so clearly stated as to have made it impossible to change them, and that, had this been done, the objects which actuated us would now be attainable by negotiation. I have seen and endured the sufferings of the troops, and I can no longer be a party to prolong these sufferings for ends which I believe to be evil and unjust. I am not protesting against the conduct of the War, but against the political errors and insincerities for which the fighting men are being sacrificed. On behalf of those who are suffering now I make this protest against the deception which is being practised on them; also I believe that I may help to destroy the callous complacency with which the majority of those at home regard the continuance of agonies which they do not share, and which they have not sufficient imagination to realize.*" It certainly sounds a bit pompous, I thought, and God only knows what the Colonel will think of it.

Thus ended a most miserable morning's work. After lunch I walked down the hill to the pillar-box and posted my letters with a feeling of stupefied finality. I then realized that I had a headache and Captain Huxtable was coming to tea. Lying on my bed with the window curtains drawn, I compared the prospect of being in a prison cell with the prosy serenity of this buzzing summer afternoon. I could hear the cooing of the white pigeons and the soft clatter of their wings as they fluttered down to the little bird-bath on the lawn. My sense of the life-learned house and garden enveloped me as though all the summers I had ever known were returning in a single thought. I had felt the same a year ago, but going back to the War next day hadn't been as bad as this.

Theoretically, to-day's tea-party would have made excellent material for a domestic day-dream when I was at the front. I was safely wounded after doing well enough to be congratulated by Captain Huxtable. The fact that the fighting men were still being sacrificed needn't affect the contentment of the tea-party. But everything was blighted by those letters which were reposing in the local pillar-box, and it was with some difficulty that I pulled myself together when I heard a vigorous ring of the front-door bell, followed by the firm tread of the Captain on the polished wood floor of the drawing-room, and the volubility of Aunt Evelyn's conversational opening alternating with the crisp and cheery baritone of her visitor. Captain Huxtable was an essentially cheerful character ("waggish" was Aunt Evelyn's favourite word for him) and that afternoon he was in his most jovial mood. He greeted me with a reference to Mahomet and the Mountain, though I felt more like a funeral than a mountain, and the little man himself looked by no means like Mahomet, for he was wearing brown corduroy breeches and a white linen jacket, and his face was red and jolly after the exertion of bicycling. His subsequent conversation was, for me, strongly flavoured with unconscious irony. Ever since I had joined the Flintshire Fusiliers our meetings always set his mind alight with memories of his "old corps", as he called it; I made him, he said, feel half his age. Naturally, he was enthusiastic about anything connected with the fine record of the Flintshires in this particular war, and when Aunt Evelyn said, "Do show Captain Huxtable the card you got from your General," he screwed his monocle into his eye and inspected the gilt-edged trophy with intense and deliberate satisfaction. I asked him to keep it as a souvenir of his having got me into the Regiment—(bitterly aware that I should soon be getting myself out of it pretty effectively!). After saying that I couldn't have given him anything which he'd value more highly, he suggested that I might do worse than adopt the Army as a permanent career (forgetting that I was nearly ten years too old for such an idea to be feasible). But no doubt I was glad to be going to the Depot

for a few days, so as to have a good crack with some of my
old comrades, and when I got to Cambridge I must make
myself known to a promising young chap (a grandson of
his cousin, Archdeacon Crocket) who was training with the
Cadet Battalion. After a digression around this year's fruit
crop, conversation turned to the Archbishop of Canterbury's message to the nation about Air Raid Reprisals. In
Captain Huxtable's opinion the Church couldn't be too
militant, and Aunt Evelyn thoroughly agreed with him.
With forced facetiousness I described my own air-raid experience. "The cashier in the bank was as cool as a cucumber," I remarked. There were cucumber sandwiches on the
table, but the implications of the word "cashier" were
stronger, since for me it was part of the price of martyrdom, while for the Captain it epitomized an outer darkness of dishonour. But the word went past him, innocent of
its military meaning, and he referred to the increasing
severity of the German air-raids as "all that one can expect from that gang of ruffians". But there it was, and we'd
got to go through with it; nothing could be worse than a
patched-up peace; and Aunt Evelyn "could see no sign of
a change of heart in the German nation".

The Captain was delighted to see in to-day's *Times* that
another of those cranky pacifist meetings had been broken
up by some Colonial troops; and he added that he'd like to
have the job of dealing with a "Stop the War" meeting in
Butley. To him a conscientious objector was the antithesis
of an officer and a gentleman, and no other point of view
would have been possible for him. The Army was the
framework of his family tradition; his maternal grandfather had been a Scotch baronet with a distinguished military career in India—a fact which was piously embodied
in the Memorial Tablet to his mother in Butley Church.
As for his father—"old Captain Huxtable"—(whom I
could hazily remember, white-whiskered and formidable)
he had been a regular roaring martinet of the gouty old
school of retired officers, and his irascibilities were still
legendary in our neighbourhood. He used to knock his
coachman's hat off and stamp on it. "The young Captain,"

as he was called in former days, had profited by these paroxysms, and where the parent would have bellowed "God damn and blast it all" at his bailiff, the son permitted himself nothing more sulphurous than "con-found", and would have thought twice before telling even the most red-hot Socialist to go to the devil.

Walking round the garden after tea—Aunt Evelyn drawing his attention to her delphiniums and he waggishly affirming their inferiority to his own—I wondered whether I had exaggerated the "callous complacency" of those at home. What could elderly people do except try and make the best of their inability to sit in a trench and be bombarded? How could they be blamed for refusing to recognize any ignoble elements in the War except those which they attributed to our enemies?

Aunt Evelyn's delphinium spires were blue against the distant blue of the Weald and the shadows of the Irish yews were lengthening across the lawn. . . . Out in France the convoys of wounded and gassed were being carried into the Field Hospitals, and up in the Line the slaughter went on because no one knew how to stop it. "Men are beginning to ask for what they are fighting," Dottrell had written in his last letter. Could I be blamed for being one of those at home who were also asking that question? Must the War go on in order that colonels might become brigadiers and brigadiers get Divisions, while contractors and manufacturers enriched themselves, and people in high places ate and drank well and bandied official information and organized entertainments for the wounded? Some such questions I may have asked myself, but I was unable to include Captain Huxtable and Aunt Evelyn in the indictment.

VI

I had to wait until Thursday before a second Clitherland telegram put me out of my misery. Delivered early in the afternoon and containing only two words, *Report immediately*, it was obviously a telegram which did not need to be read twice. But the new variety of suspense which it created was an improvement on what I'd been enduring, because I could end it for certain by reporting at Clitherland within twenty-four hours. All considerations connected with my protest were now knocked on the head. It no longer mattered whether I was right or whether I was wrong, whether my action was public-spirited or whether it was preposterous. My mind was insensible to everything but the abhorrent fact that I was in for an appalling show, with zero hour fixed for to-morrow when I arrived at the Depot.

In the meantime I must pack my bag and catch the five-something train to town. Automatically I began to pack in my usual vacillating but orderly manner; then I remembered that it would make no difference if I forgot all the things I needed most. By this time to-morrow I shall be under arrest, I thought, gloomily rejecting my automatic pistol, water bottle, and whistle, and rummaging in a drawer for some khaki socks and handkerchiefs. A glimpse of my rather distracted-looking face in the glass warned me that I must pull myself together by to-morrow. I must walk into the Orderly Room neat and self-possessed and normal. Anyhow the parlourmaid had given my tunic buttons and belt a good rub up, and now Aunt Evelyn was rapping on the door to say that tea was ready and the taxi would be here in half an hour. She took my abrupt departure quite as a matter of course, but it was only at the last moment that she remembered to give me the bundle of white pigeons' feathers which she had collected from the lawn, knowing how I always liked some for pipe-cleaners. She also reminded me that I was forgetting to take my golf clubs; but I shouldn't get any time for golf, I said, plumping myself into the taxi, for there wasn't too much time to catch the train.

The five-something train from Baldock Wood was a slow affair; one had to change at Dumbridge and wait forty minutes. I remember this because I have seldom felt more dejected than I did when I walked out of Dumbridge Station and looked over the fence of the County Cricket Ground. The afternoon was desolately fine and the ground, with its pavilion and enclosures, looked blighted and forsaken. Here, in pre-eminently happier times, I had played in many a club match and had attentively watched the varying fortunes of the Kent Eleven; but now no one had even troubled to wind up the pavilion clock.

Back in the station I searched the bookstall for something to distract my thoughts. The result was a small red volume which is still in my possession. It is called *The Morals of Rousseau*, and contains, naturally enough, extracts from that celebrated author. Rousseau was new to me and I cannot claim that his morals were any help to me on that particular journey or during the ensuing days when I carried him about in my pocket. But while pacing the station platform I remembered a certain couplet, and I mention this couplet because, for the next ten days or so, I couldn't get it out of my head. There was no apparent relevancy in the quotation (which I afterwards found to be from Cowper). It merely persisted in saying:

> *I shall not ask Jean Jacques Rousseau*
> *If birds confabulate or no.*

London enveloped my loneliness. I spent what was presumably my last night of liberty in the bustling dreariness of one of those huge hotels where no one ever seems to be staying more than a single night. I had hoped for a talk with Tyrrell, but he was out of town. My situation was, I felt, far too serious for theatre going—in fact I regarded myself as already more or less under arrest; I was going to Clitherland under my own escort, so to speak. So it may be assumed that I spent that evening alone with J. J. Rousseau.

*   *   *

Next morning—but it will suffice if I say that next morning (although papers announced *Great Russian Success in Galicia*) I had no reason to feel any happier than I had done the night before. I am beginning to feel that a man can write too much about his own feelings, even when "what he felt like" is the nucleus of his narrative. Nevertheless I cannot avoid a short summary of my sensations while on the way to Liverpool. I began by shutting my eyes and refusing to think at all; but this effort didn't last long. I tried looking out of the window; but the sunlit fields only made me long to be a munching cow. I remembered my first journey to Clitherland in May 1915. I had been nervous then—diffident about my ability to learn how to be an officer. Getting out to the Front had been an ambition rather than an obligation, and I had aimed at nothing more than to become a passably efficient second-lieutenant. Pleasantly conscious of my new uniform and anxious to do it credit, I had felt (as most of us did in those days) as if I were beginning a fresh and untarnished existence. Probably I had travelled by this very train. My instant mental transition from that moment to this (all intervening experience excluded) caused me a sort of vertigo. Alone in that first-class compartment, I shut my eyes and asked myself out loud what this thing was which I was doing; and my mutinous act suddenly seemed outrageous and incredible. For a few minutes I completely lost my nerve. But the express train was carrying me along; I couldn't stop it, any more than I could cancel my statement. And when the train pulled up at Liverpool I was merely a harassed automaton whose movements were being manipulated by a typewritten manifesto. To put it plainly, I felt "like nothing on earth" while I was being bumped and jolted out to the Camp in a ramshackle taxi.

It was about three o'clock when the taxi passed the gates of Brotherhood's Explosive Works and drew up outside the officers' quarters at Clitherland. The sky was cloudless and the lines of huts had an air of ominous inactivity. Nobody seemed to be about, for at that hour the troops were out on the training field. A bored sentry was the only witness of my arrival, and for him there was nothing remarkable in a second-lieutenant telling a taxi-man to dump his luggage down outside the officers' mess. For me, however, there now seemed something almost surreptitious about my return. It was as though I'd come skulking back to see how much damage had been caused by that egregious projectile, my protest. But the camp was exactly as it would have been if I'd returned as a dutiful young officer. It was I who was desolate and distracted; and it would have been no consolation to me if I could have realized that, in my mind, the familiar scene was having a momentary and ghastly existence which would never be repeated.

For a few moments I stared wildly at the huts, conscious (though my brain was blank) that there was some sort of climax in my stupefied recognition of reality. One final wrench, and all my obedient associations with Clitherland would be shattered.

It is probable that I put my tie straight and adjusted my belt-buckle to its central position between the tunic buttons. There was only one thing to be done after that. I walked into the Orderly Room, halted in front of a table, and saluted dizzily.

After the glaring sunlight, the room seemed almost dark. When I raised my eyes it was not the Colonel who was sitting at the table, but Major Macartney. At another table, ostensibly busy with Army forms and papers, was the Deputy-Assistant-Adjutant (a good friend of mine who had lost a leg in Gallipoli). I stood there, incapable of expectation. Then, to my astonishment, the Major rose, leant across the table, and shook hands with me.

"How are you, Sherston? I'm glad to see you back again." His deep voice had its usual kindly tone, but his manner betrayed acute embarrassment. No one could have been less glad to see me back again than he was. But he at once picked up his cap and asked me to come with him to his room, which was only a few steps away. Silently we entered the hut, our feet clumping along the boards of the passage. Speechless and respectful, I accepted the chair which he offered me. There we were, in the comfortless little room which had been his local habitation for the past twenty-seven months. There we were; and the unfortunate Major hadn't a ghost of an idea what to say.

He was a man of great delicacy of feeling. I have seldom known as fine a gentleman. For him the interview must have been as agonizing as it was for me. I wanted to make things easier for him; but what could I say? And what could he do for me, except, perhaps, offer me a cigar? He did so. I can honestly say that I have never refused a cigar with anything like so much regret. To have accepted it would have been a sign of surrender. It would have meant that the Major and myself could have puffed our cigars and debated—with all requisite seriousness, of course—the best way of extricating me from my dilemma. How blissful that would have been! For my indiscretion might positively have been "laughed off" (as a temporary aberration brought on, perhaps, by an overdose of solitude after coming out of hospital). No such agreeable solution being possible, the Major began by explaining that the Colonel was away on leave. "He is deeply concerned about you, and fully prepared to overlook the"—here he hesitated— "the paper which you sent him. He has asked me to urge you most earnestly to—er—dismiss the whole matter from your mind." Nothing could have been more earnest than the way he looked at me when he stopped speaking. I replied that I was deeply grateful but I couldn't change my mind. In the ensuing silence I felt that I was committing a breach, not so much of discipline as of decorum.

The disappointed Major made a renewed effort. "But, Sherston, isn't it *possible* for you to reconsider your—er— ultimatum?" This was the first time I'd heard it called an ultimatum, and the locution epitomized the Major's inability to find words to fit the situation. I embarked on a floundering explanation of my mental attitude with regard to the War; but I couldn't make it sound convincing, and at the back of my mind was a misgiving that I must seem to him rather crazy. To be telling the acting-Colonel of my regimental Training Depot that I had come to the conclusion that England ought to make peace with Germany —was this altogether in focus with rightmindedness? No; it was useless to expect him to take me seriously as an ultimatumist. So I gazed fixedly at the floor and said, "Hadn't you better have me put under arrest at once?"—thereby causing poor Major Macartney additional discomfort. My remark recoiled on me, almost as if I'd uttered something unmentionable. "I'd rather die than do such a thing!" he exclaimed. He was a reticent man, and that was his way of expressing his feeling about those whom he had watched, month after month, going out to the trenches, as he would have gone himself had he been a younger man.

At this point it was obviously his duty to remonstrate with me severely and to assert his authority. But what fulminations could be effective against one whose only object was to be put under arrest? . . . "As long as he doesn't really think I'm dotty!" I thought. But he showed no symptom of that, as far as I was aware; and he was a man who made one feel that he trusted one's integrity, however much he might disagree with one's opinions.

No solution having been arrived at for the present, he now suggested—in confidential tones which somehow implied sympathetic understanding of my predicament—that I should go to the Exchange Hotel in Liverpool and there await further instructions. I gladly acquiesced, and we emerged from the hut a little less funereally than we had entered it. My taxi-man was still waiting, for in my bewilderment I had forgotten to pay him. Once more the Major grasped my hand, and if I did not thank him for his kindness it was because my gratitude was too great. So I trundled unexpectedly back to Liverpool; and although, in all likelihood, my troubles were only just starting, an immense load had been lifted from my mind. At the Exchange Hotel (which was quiet and rarely frequented by the Clitherland officers) I thoroughly enjoyed my tea, for I'd eaten nothing since breakfast. After that I lit my pipe and thought how nice it was not to be under arrest. I had got over the worst part of the show, and now there was nothing to be done except stick to my statement and wait for the M.P. to read it out in the House of Commons.

VII

For the next three days I hung about the Exchange Hotel in a state of mind which need not be described. I saw no one I knew except a couple of Clitherland subalterns who

happened to be dining in the Hotel. They cheerily enquired when I was coming out to the Camp. Evidently
they were inquisitive about me, without suspecting anything extraordinary, so I inferred that Orderly Room had
been keeping my strange behaviour secret. On Tuesday my
one-legged friend, the Deputy-Assistant-Adjutant, came to
see me. We managed to avoid mentioning everything connected with my "present situation", and he regaled me
with the gossip of the Camp as though nothing were wrong.
But when he was departing he handed me an official document which instructed me to proceed to Crewe next day
for a Special Medical Board. A railway warrant was en-
closed with it.

Here was a chance of turning aside from the road to
court-martialdom, and it would be inaccurate were I to
say that I never gave the question two thoughts. Roughly
speaking, two thoughts were exactly what I did give to it.
One thought urged that I might just as well chuck the
whole business and admit that my gesture had been futile.
The other one reminded me that this was an inevitable
conjuncture in my progress, and that such temptations
must be resisted inflexibly. Not that I ever admitted the
possibility of my accepting the invitation to Crewe; but I
did become conscious that acceptance would be much
pleasanter than refusal. Submission being impossible, I
called in pride and obstinacy to aid me, throttled my warm
feelings toward my well-wishers at Clitherland Camp and
burnt my boats by tearing up both railway warrant and
Medical Board instructions.

On Wednesday I tried to feel glad that I was cutting the
Medical Board, and applied my mind to Palgrave's *Golden
Treasury of Songs and Lyrics*. I was learning by heart as many
poems as possible, my idea being that they would be a help
to me in prison, where, I imagined, no books would be
allowed. I suppose I ought to try and get used to giving up
tobacco, I thought, but I went on smoking just the same
(the alternative being to smoke as many pipes as I could
while I'd got the chance).

On Thursday morning I received an encouraging letter

from the M.P. who urged me to keep my spirits up and was hoping to raise the question of my statement in the House next week. Early in the afternoon the Colonel called to see me. He found me learning Keats's *Ode to a Nightingale*. "I cannot see what flowers are at my feet, Nor what soft. . . ." What soft was it, I wondered, re-opening the book. But here was the Colonel, apparently unincensed, shaking my hand, and sitting down opposite me, though already looking fussed and perplexed. He wasn't a lively-minded man at the best of times, and he didn't pretend to understand the motives which had actuated me. But with patient common-sense arguments, he did his best to persuade me to stop wanting to stop the War. Fortified by the M.P.'s letter in my pocket, I managed to remain respectfully obdurate, while expressing my real regret for the trouble I was causing him. What appeared to worry him most was the fact that I'd cut the Medical Board. "Do you realize, Sherston, that it had been specially arranged for you and that an R.A.M.C. Colonel came all the way from London for it?" he ejaculated ruefully, wiping the perspiration from his forehead. The poor man—whose existence was dominated by documentary instructions from "higher quarters", had probably been blamed for my non-appearance; and to disregard such an order was, to one with his habit of mind, like a reversal of the order of nature. As the interview dragged itself along, I began to feel quite optimistic about the progress I was making. The Colonel's stuttering arguments in support of "crushing Prussian militarism" were those of a middle-aged civilian; and as the overworked superintendent of a reinforcement manufactory, he had never had time to ask himself why North Welshmen were being shipped across to France to be gassed, machine-gunned, and high explosived by Germans. It was absolutely impossible, he asserted, for the War to end until it ended—well, until it ended as it ought to end. Did I think it right that so many men should have been sacrificed for no purpose? "And surely it stands to reason, Sherston, that you must be wrong when you set your own opinion against the practically unanimous feeling of the whole British Empire." There was no answer I could make to that, so I remained silent, and waited for the British Empire idea to blow over. In conclusion he said, "Well, I've done all I can for you. I told Mersey Defences that you missed your Board through a misunderstanding of the instructions, but I'm afraid the affair will soon go beyond my control. I beg you to try and reconsider your refusal by to-morrow, and to let us know at once if you do."

He looked at me almost irately, and departed without another word. When his bulky figure had vanished I felt that my isolation was perceptibly increasing. All I needed to do was to wait until the affair had got beyond his control. I wished I could have a talk with Tyrrell. But even he wasn't infallible, for in all our discussions about my plan of campaign he had never foreseen that my senior officers would treat me with this kindly tolerance which was so difficult to endure.

During the next two days my mind groped and worried around the same purgatorial limbo so incessantly that the whole business began to seem unreal and distorted. Sometimes the wording of my thoughts became incoherent and even nonsensical. At other times I saw everything with the haggard clarity of insomnia.

So on Saturday afternoon I decided that I really must go and get some fresh air, and I took the electric train to Formby. How much longer would this ghastly show go on, I wondered, as the train pulled up at Clitherland Station. All I wanted now was that the thing should be taken out of my own control, as well as the Colonel's. I didn't care how they treated me as long as I wasn't forced to argue about it any more. At Formby I avoided the Golf Course (remembering, with a gleam of woeful humour, how Aunt Evelyn had urged me to bring my "golf sticks", as she called them). Wandering along the sand dunes I felt outlawed, bitter, and baited. I wanted something to smash and trample on, and in a paroxysm of exasperation I performed the time-honoured gesture of shaking my clenched fists at the sky. Feeling no better for that, I ripped the M.C. ribbon off my tunic and threw it into the mouth of the Mersey.

Weighted with significance though this action was, it would have felt more conclusive had the ribbon been heavier. As it was, the poor little thing fell weakly on to the water and floated away as though aware of its own futility. One of my point-to-point cups would have served my purpose more satisfyingly, and they'd meant much the same to me as my Military Cross.

Watching a big boat which was steaming along the horizon, I realized that protesting against the prolongation of the War was about as much use as shouting at the people on board that ship.

*   *   *

Next morning I was sitting in the hotel smoking-room in a state of stubborn apathy. I had got just about to the end of my tether. Since it was Sunday and my eighth day in Liverpool I might have chosen this moment for reviewing the past week, though I had nothing to congratulate myself on except the fact that I'd survived seven days without hauling down my flag. It is possible that I meditated some desperate counter-attack which might compel the authorities to treat me harshly, but I had no idea how to do it. "Damn it all, I've half a mind to go to church," I thought, although as far as I could see there was more real religion to be found in the *Golden Treasury* than in a church which only approved of military-aged men when they were in khaki. Sitting in a sacred edifice wouldn't help me, I decided. And then I was taken completely by surprise; for there was David Cromlech, knobby-faced and gawky as ever, advancing across the room. His arrival brought instantaneous relief, which I expressed by exclaiming: "Thank God you've come!"

He sat down without saying anything. He, too, was pleased to see me, but retained that air of anxious concern with which his eyes had first encountered mine. As usual he looked as if he'd slept in his uniform. Something had snapped inside me and I felt rather silly and hysterical. "David, you've got an enormous black smudge on your forehead," I remarked. Obediently he moistened his handkerchief with his tongue and proceeded to rub the smudge off, tentatively following my instructions as to its whereabouts. During this operation his face was vacant and childish, suggesting an earlier time when his nurse had performed a similar service for him. "How on earth did you manage to roll up from the Isle of Wight like this?" I inquired. He smiled in a knowing way. Already he was beginning to look less as though he were visiting an invalid; but I'd been so much locked up with my own thoughts lately that for the next few minutes I talked nineteen to the dozen, telling him what a hellish time I'd had, how terribly kind the depot officers had been to me, and so on. "When I started this anti-war stunt I never dreamt it would be such a long job, getting myself run in for a court martial," I concluded, laughing with somewhat hollow gaiety.

In the meantime David sat moody and silent, his face twitching nervously and his fingers twiddling one of his tunic buttons. "Look here, George," he said, abruptly, scrutinizing the button as though he'd never seen such a thing before, "I've come to tell you that you've got to drop this anti-war business." This was a new idea, for I wasn't yet beyond my sense of relief at seeing him. "But I can't drop it," I exclaimed. "Don't you realize that I'm a man with a message? I thought you'd come to see me through the court martial as 'prisoner's friend'." We then settled down to an earnest discussion about the "political errors and insincerities for which the fighting men were being sacrificed". He did most of the talking, while I disagreed defensively. But even if our conversation could be reported in full, I am afraid that the verdict of posterity would be against us. We agreed that the world had gone mad; but neither of us could see beyond his own experience, and we weren't life-learned enough to share the patient selfless stoicism through which men of maturer age were acquiring anonymous glory. Neither of us had the haziest idea of what the politicians were really up to (though it is possible that the politicians were only feeling their way and trusting in providence and the output of munitions to solve their problems). Nevertheless we argued as though the secret confabulations of Cabinet Ministers in various countries were as clear as daylight to us, and our assumption was that they were all wrong, while we, who had been in the trenches, were far-seeing and infallible. But when I said that the War ought to be stopped and it was my duty to do my little bit to stop it, David replied that the War was bound to go on till one side or the other collapsed, and the Pacifists were only meddling with what they didn't understand. "At any rate Thornton Tyrrell's a jolly fine man and knows a bloody sight more about everything than you do," I exclaimed. "Tyrrell's only a doctrinaire", replied David, "though I grant you he's a courageous one." Before I had time to ask what the hell he knew about doctrinaires, he continued, "No one except people who've been in the real fighting have any right to interfere about the War; and even they can't get anything done about it. All they can do is to remain loyal to one another. And you know perfectly well that most of the conscientious objectors are nothing but skrimshankers." I retorted that I knew nothing of the sort, and mentioned a young doctor who'd played Rugby Football for Scotland and was now in prison although he could have been doing hospital work if he'd wanted to. David then announced that he'd been doing a bit of wire-pulling on my behalf and that I should soon find that my Pacifist M.P. wouldn't do me as much good as I expected. This put my back up. David had no right to come butting in about my private affairs. "If you've really been trying to persuade the authorities not to do anything nasty to me", I remarked, "that's about the hopefullest thing I've heard. Go on doing it and exercise your usual tact, and you'll get me two years' hard labour for certain, and with any luck they'll decide to shoot me as a sort of deserter." He looked so aggrieved at this that I relented and suggested that we'd better have some lunch. But David was always an absent-minded eater, and on this occasion he prodded disapprovingly at his food and then bolted it down as if it were medicine.

A couple of hours later we were wandering aimlessly

along the shore at Formby, and still jabbering for all we were worth. I refused to accept his well-meaning assertion that no one at the Front would understand my point of view and that they would only say that I'd got cold feet. "And even if they do say that", I argued, "the main point is that by backing out of my statement I shall be betraying my real convictions and the people who are supporting me. Isn't that worse cowardice than being thought cold-footed by officers who refuse to think about anything except the gentlemanly traditions of the Regiment? I'm not doing it for fun, am I? Can't you understand that this is the most difficult thing I've ever done in my life? I'm not going to be talked out of it just when I'm forcing them to make a martyr of me." "They won't make a martyr of you," he replied. "How do you know that?" I asked. He said that the Colonel at Clitherland had told him to tell me that if I continued to refuse to be "medically-boarded" they would shut me up in a lunatic asylum for the rest of the War. Nothing would induce them to court martial me. It had all been arranged with some big bug at the War Office in the last day or two. "Why didn't you tell me before?" I asked. "I kept it as a last resort because I was afraid it might upset you," he replied, tracing a pattern on the sand with his stick. "I wouldn't believe this from anyone but you. Will you swear on the Bible that you're telling the truth?" He swore on an imaginary Bible that nothing would induce them to court martial me and that I should be treated as insane. "All right, then, I'll give way." As soon as the words were out of my mouth I sat down on an old wooden breakwater.

So that was the end of my grand gesture. I ought to have known that the blighters would do me down somehow, I thought, scowling heavily at the sea. It was appropriate that I should behave in a glumly dignified manner, but already I was aware that an enormous load had been lifted from my mind. In the train David was discreetly silent. He got out at Clitherland. "Then I'll tell Orderly Room they can fix up a Board for you to-morrow," he remarked, unable to conceal his elation. "You can tell them anything you bloody well please!" I answered ungratefully. But as soon as I was alone I sat back and closed my eyes with a sense of exquisite relief. I was unaware that David had, probably, saved me from being sent to prison by telling me a very successful lie. No doubt I should have done the same for him if our positions had been reversed.

*   *   *

It was obvious that the less I said to the Medical Board the better. All the necessary explanations of my mental condition were contributed by David, who had been detailed to give evidence on my behalf. He had a long interview with the doctors while I waited in an ante-room. Listening to their muffled mumblings, I felt several years younger than I'd done two days before. I was now an irresponsible person again, absolved from any obligation to intervene in world affairs. In fact the present performance seemed rather ludicrous, and when David emerged, solemn and concerned, to usher me in, I entered the "Bird Room" assuring myself that I should not ask Jean Jacques Rousseau if birds confabulated or no. The Medical Board consisted of a Colonel, a Major, and a Captain. The Captain was a civilian in uniform, and a professional neurologist. The others were elderly Regular Army doctors, and I am inclined to think that their acquaintance with Army Forms exceeded their knowledge of neurology.

While David fidgeted about the ante-room I was replying respectfully to the stereotyped questions of the Colonel, who seemed slightly suspicious and much mystified by my attitude to the War. Was it on religious grounds that I objected to fighting, he inquired. "No, sir; not particularly," I replied. "Fighting on religious grounds" sounded like some sort of a joke about the Crusades. "Do you consider yourself qualified to decide when the War should stop?" was his next question. Realizing that he was only trying to make me talk rubbish, I evaded him by admitting that I hadn't thought about my qualifications, which wasn't true. "But your friend tells us that you were very good at bombing. Don't you still dislike the Germans?" I have forgotten how I answered that conundrum. It didn't matter what I said to him, as long as I behaved politely. While the interrogations continued, I felt that sooner or later I simply must repeat that couplet out loud—"if birds confabulate or no". Probably it would be the best thing I could do, for it would prove conclusively and comfortably that I was a harmless lunatic. Once I caught the neurologist's eye, which signalled sympathetic understanding, I thought. Anyhow, the Colonel (having demonstrated his senior rank by asking me an adequate number of questions) willingly allowed the Captain to suggest that they couldn't do better than send me to Slateford Hospital. So it was decided that I was suffering from shell-shock. The Colonel then remarked to the Major that he supposed there was nothing more to be done now. I repeated the couplet under my breath. "Did you say anything?" asked the Colonel, frowning slightly. I disclaimed having said anything and was permitted to rejoin David.

When we were walking back to my hotel I overheard myself whistling cheerfully, and commented on the fact. "Honestly, David, I don't believe I've whistled for about six weeks!" I gazed up at the blue sky, grateful because, at that moment, it seemed as though I had finished with the War.

Next morning I went to Edinburgh. David, who had been detailed to act as my escort, missed the train and arrived at Slateford War Hospital several hours later than I did. And with my arrival at Slateford War Hospital this volume can conveniently be concluded.

SHERSTON'S PROGRESS

*" I told him that I was a Pilgrim going to the
Celestial City."*

PART ONE: RIVERS

I

To be arriving at a shell-shock hospital in a state of un-militant defiance of military authority was an experience peculiar enough to stimulate my speculations about the immediate future. In the train from Liverpool to Edin-burgh I speculated continuously. The self-dramatizing ele-ment in my mind anticipated something sensational. After all, a mad-house would be only a few degrees less grim than a prison, and I was still inclined to regard myself in the role of a "ripe man of martyrdom". But the unhistrionic part of my mind remembered that the neurologist member of my medical board had mentioned someone called Rivers. "Rivers will look after you when you get there." I inferred, from the way he said it, that to be looked after by Rivers was a stroke of luck for me. Rivers was evidently some sort of great man; anyhow his name had obvious free associ-ations with pleasant landscapes and unruffled estuaries.

Slateford War Hospital was about twenty minutes in a taxi from Edinburgh. In peace-time it had been a "hydro", and it was a gloomy cavernous place even on a fine July afternoon. But before I'd been inside it five minutes I was actually talking to Rivers, who was dressed as an R.A.M.C. captain. There was never any doubt about my liking him. He made me feel safe at once, and seemed to know all about me. What he didn't know he soon found out.

Readers of my previous volumes will be aware that I am no exception to the rule that most people enjoy talking about themselves to a sympathetic listener. Next morning I went to Rivers' room as one of his patients. In an hour's talk I told him as much as I could about my perplexities. Forgetting that he was a doctor and that I was an "inter-esting case", I answered his quiet impartial questions as clearly as I could, with a comfortable feeling that he understood me better than I understood myself.

For the first few days, we had one of these friendly confabulations every evening. I had begun by explaining that my "attitude", as expressed in my "statement", was unchanged. "Just because they refused to court martial me, it doesn't make any difference to my still being on strike, does it?" I remarked. (This fact was symbolized by my tunic, which was still minus the M.C. ribbon that I had thrown into the River Mersey!)

Rivers replied that my safest plan would be to mark time for a few weeks; meanwhile the hospital authorities would allow me all the freedom I wanted and would rely on me not to do anything imprudent. One evening I asked whether he thought I was suffering from shell-shock.

"Certainly not," he replied.

"What *have* I got, then?"

"Well, you appear to be suffering from an anti-war complex." We both of us laughed at that. Rivers never seemed elderly; though there were more than twenty years between us, he talked as if I were his mental equal, which was very far from being the case.

Meanwhile my main problem was how to fill up my time. Everything possible was done to make the hospital pleasant for its inmates, but the fact remained that most of the "other patients" weren't feeling as happy as they used to do. The place was a live museum of war neuroses—in other words the hospital contained about 150 officers who had been either shattered or considerably shaken by their war experience. I shared a room with a cheerful young Scotch captain who showed no symptom of eccentricity, though I gradually ascertained that he had something on his mind—was it some hallucination about his having been shot at by a spy?—I have forgotten, and only remember that he was a thoroughly nice man. On the whole, I felt happier outside the hydro than in it, so I went for long walks on the Pentland Hills, which really did seem unaware that there was a war on, while retaining their commemorative associations with Robert Louis Stevenson. But at the end of my first week at Slateford my career as a public character was temporarily resuscitated by my "statement" being read out in the House of Commons. Referring to Hansard's *Parliamentary Debates*, 30th July, 1917, I find that the episode occurred at 7 p.m. There, I think, it may safely be allowed to remain at rest, unless I decide to reprint the proceedings as an appendix to this volume, which is improbable. I will only divulge that the debate ended by Mr. Bryce saying "We know that the Croats, the Serbs, the Slovaks, the Slovenes, and the Czechs are all opposed to it." (What they were opposed to was the Austrian dynasty, not my statement.) Oddly enough, the name of the commandant of Slateford Hospital was also Bryce, which only shows what a small place the world is.

As far as I was concerned the only visible result was a batch of letters from people who either agreed or disagreed with my views. But I needed a holiday from that sort of thing. The intensity of my individual effort to influence the Allied Governments had abated.

At intervals I reminded myself that my enormous gesture was still, so to speak, "on show", but I unconsciously allowed myself to relax the mental effort required to sustain it. My "attitude" was, indeed, unchanged; it had merely ceased to be aggressive. I didn't even feel annoyed when a celebrated novelist (for whose opinion I had asked) wrote: "Your position cannot be argumentatively defended. What is the matter with you is spiritual pride. The overwhelming majority of your fellow-citizens are against you." Anyhow a fellow-citizen (who was an equally famous novelist) wrote that it was a "very striking act", and I was grateful for the phrase. (How tantalizing of me to omit their names! But somehow I feel that if I were to put them on the page my neatly contrived little narrative would come sprawling out of its frame.) Grateful I was, and not annoyed; nevertheless it was obvious that I couldn't perform that sort of striking act more than once and in the meantime I acted on the advice of Rivers and wired to Aunt Evelyn for my golf clubs, which arrived next day, maybe accelerated by three very fully addressed labels, all inscribed "urgent". Simultaneously arrived a postcard from one of the overwhelming majority of my fellow-citizens who kept his name dark, but expressed his opinion that "Men like you who are willing to shake the bloody hand of the Kaiser are not worthy to call themselves Britons". This struck me as unjust; I'd never offered to shake the old Kaiser's hand, though I should probably have been considerably impressed if he'd offered to shake mine, for an emperor is an emperor all the world over even if he has done his best to wipe you off the face of the earth with high-explosive shells. As regards Aunt Evelyn, (who had a pretty poor opinion of the Kaiser) the *Morning Post* had now put her in full possession of the facts about my peace-propagating manifesto. No doubt she was delighted to know that I was well out of harm's way. The Under-Secretary of State had informed the House of Commons that I was suffering from a nervous breakdown and not responsible for my actions, which was good enough for Aunt Evelyn, and, as Rivers remarked, very much what I might have expected. Very soon I was slicing my tee-shots into the long grass on the nearest golf course. "I don't know what I'm doing," I exclaimed (referring to my swing and not to my recent political activity).

*   *   *

For me, the War felt as if it were a long way off while the summer of 1917 was coming to an end. Except for keeping an eye on the casualty lists, I did my best to turn my back on the entire business. Once, when I saw that one of my best friends had been killed, I lapsed into angry self-pity, and told myself that the War was "a sham and a stinking lie", and succeeded in feeling bitter against the unspecific crowd of non-combatants who believed that to go through with it to the end was the only way out. But on the whole I was psychologically passive—content to mark time on the golf links and do some steady reading after dinner. The fact remained that, when I awoke in the morning, my first conscious thought was no longer an unreprieved awareness that the War would go on indefinitely and that sooner or later I should be killed or mutilated. The prospect of being imprisoned as a war-resister had also evaporated. To wake up knowing that I was going to bicycle off to play two rounds of golf was not a penance. It was a reward. Three evenings a week I went along to Rivers' room to give my anti-war complex an airing. We talked a lot about European politicians and what they were saying. Most of our information was derived from a weekly periodical which contained translations from the foreign Press. What the politicians said no longer matters, as far as these memoirs of mine are concerned, though I would give a lot for a few gramophone records of my talks with Rivers. All that matters is my remembrance of the great and good man who gave me his friendship and guidance. I can visualize him, sitting at his table in the late summer twilight, with his spectacles pushed up on his forehead and his hands clasped in front of one knee; always communicating his integrity of mind; never revealing that he was weary as he must often have been after long days of exceptionally tiring work on those war neuroses which demanded such an exercise of sympathy and detachment combined. Remembering all that, and my egotistic unawareness of the possibility that I was often wasting his time and energy, I am consoled by the certainty that he did, on the whole, find me a refreshing companion. He liked me and he believed in me.

As an R.A.M.C. officer, he was bound to oppose my "pacifist tendency", but his arguments were always indirect. Sometimes he gently indicated inconsistencies in my impulsively expressed opinions, but he never contradicted me. Of course the weak point about my "protest" had been that it was evoked by personal feeling. It was an emotional idea based on my war experience and stimulated by the acquisition of points of view which I accepted uncritically. My intellect was not an ice-cold one. It was, so to speak, suffering from trench fever. I could only see the situation from the point of view of the troops I had served with; and the existence of supposedly iniquitous war aims among the Allies was for that reason well worth believing in—and inveighing against. Rivers suggested that peace at that time would constitute a victory for Pan-Germanism and nullify all the sacrifices we had made. He could see no evidence that militarism was yet discredited in Germany. On one occasion, when the pros and cons had got me well out of my depth as a debater, I exclaimed, "It doesn't seem to me to matter much what one does so long as one believes it is right!" In the silence that ensued I was aware that I had said something particularly fatuous, and hurriedly remarked that the people in Germany must be getting jolly short of food. I was really very ignorant, picking up my ideas as I went along, and rather like the man who said that he couldn't think unless he was wearing his spectacles. But Rivers always led me quietly past my blunders (though he looked a bit pained when I inadvertently revealed that I did not know the difference between "intuition" and "instinct"—which was, I suppose, one of the worst mistakes I could have made when talking to an eminent psychologist).

*   *   *

Among the wholesome activities of the hospital was a monthly magazine, aptly named *The Hydra*. In the September number, of which I have preserved a copy, the editorial begins as follows: "Many of us who came to the hydro slightly ill are now getting dangerously well. In this excellent concentration camp we are fast recovering from the shock of coming to England."

Outwardly, Slateford War Hospital was rather like that —elaborately cheerful. Brisk amusements were encouraged, entertainments were got up, and serious cases were seldom seen downstairs. The patients were of course unaware of the difficulties with which the medical staff had to contend. A handful of highly-qualified civilians in uniform were up against the usual red-tape ideas. War hospitals for nervous disorders were few, and the military authorities regarded them as experiments which needed careful watching and firm handling. After the War Rivers told me that the local Director of Medical Services nourished a deep-rooted prejudice against Slateford, and actually asserted that he "never had and never would recognize the existence of such a thing as shell-shock". When inspecting the hospital he "took strong exception" to the fact that officers were going about in slippers. I mention this to show how fortunate I was to have escaped contact with less enlightened army doctors, some of whom might well have aggravated me into extreme cussedness.

It was perhaps excusable that the War Office looked on Slateford with a somewhat fishy eye. The delicate problem of "lead-swingers" was involved; and in the eyes of the War Office a man was either wounded or well unless he had some officially authorized disease. Damage inflicted on the mind did not count as illness. If "war neuroses" were indiscriminately encouraged, half the expeditionary force might go sick with a touch of neurasthenia. Apparently it did not occur to the Director of Medical Services that Rivers and his colleagues were capable of diagnosing a "lead-swinger". In any case I don't think there were many of them at Slateford, and the doubtful ones were mostly men who had failed to stay the course through lack of stamina. Too much had been asked of them.

And there was I, a healthy young officer, dumped down among nurses and nervous wrecks. During my second month at the hydro I think I began to feel a sense of humiliation. (Was it "spiritual pride", I wonder, or merely the remains of *esprit de corps*?)

With my "fellow-breakdowns" I avoided war talk as far as was possible. Most of them had excellent reasons for disliking that theme; others talked about it because they couldn't get it off their minds, or else spoke of it facetiously in an effort to suppress their real feelings. Sometimes I had an uncomfortable notion that none of them respected one another; it was as though there were a tacit understanding that we were all failures, and this made me want to reassure myself that I wasn't the same as the others. "After all, I haven't broken down; I've only broken out," I thought, one evening at the end of September, as I watched the faces opposite me at the dinner table. Most of them were average types who appeared to be getting "dangerously well". But there were some who looked as if they wouldn't have had much success in life at the best of times. I was sitting between two bad stammerers—victims of "anxiety neurosis" as the saying went—(one could easily imagine "anxiety neurosis" as a staple front-line witticism). Conversation being thus impeded, I could devote my mind to wondering why I'd been playing my mashie shots so atrociously that afternoon. Up at the top table I could see Rivers sitting among the staff. He never seemed to be giving more than half his attention to what he was eating. He looked rather as though he needed a rest and I wondered how I should get on while he was away on his two weeks' leave which was due to begin next day. I supposed it would give me a chance to think out my position, which was becoming a definite problem. So far my ten weeks' respite had been mainly a pilgrimage in pursuit of a ball, and I had familiarized myself with the ups and downs of nearly all the golf courses around Edinburgh. The man I played with most days was an expert. He had been submarined on a hospital ship, but this didn't prevent him playing a good scratch game. His temper wasn't quite normal when things went wrong and he looked like losing his half-crown, but that may have been a peace-time failing also. Anyhow he was exercising a greatly improving influence on my iron shots, which had always been a weak point, and I take this opportunity of thanking him for many most enjoyable games. The way in which he laid his short approach shots stone-dead was positively fiendish.

As a purely public character I was now a complete back-number. Letters no longer arrived from utter strangers who also wanted the War to stop. The only one I'd had lately was from someone whose dottiness couldn't be whole-heartedly denied. "My dear Boy, or Man," it began, "on August 4th, 1914, I received a message from Heaven in broad daylight, which told me that Germany must go down for ever and Russia will become rich. I have thirty relations fighting and my business is ruined." He didn't tell me what his business was. I wondered how he'd got hold of my address. . . .

The man opposite me, an habitual humorist, remarked

to the orderly who was handing him a plate of steamed pudding, "Third time this week! I shall write to the War Office and complain." I felt a sudden sense of the unreality of my surroundings. Reality was on the other side of the Channel, surely.

After dinner I went straight up to my room as usual, intending to go on with Barbusse's book which I was reading in the English translation. I will not describe the effect it was creating in my mind; I need only say that it was a deeply stimulating one. Someone was really revealing the truth about the Front Line. But that evening I failed to settle down to *Under Fire*. The room felt cheerless and uncomfortable; the unshaded light from the ceiling annoyed my eyes; very soon I found myself becoming internally exasperated with everything, myself included. It was one of those occasions when one positively enjoys hating something. So I sat there indulging in acute antagonism toward anyone whose attitude to the War was what I called "complacent"—people who just accepted it as inevitable and then proceeded to do well out of it, or who smugly performed the patriotic jobs which enabled them to congratulate themselves on being part of the National Effort.

At this point the nurse on duty whisked into the room to make sure that everything was all right and that I was keeping cheerful. She too was part of the national effort to remain bright and not give way to war neuroses. Continuing my disgruntled ruminations, I decided that I didn't dislike violent Jingos as much as acquiescent moderates, though my pacifism was strong enough to make me willing to punch the nose of anyone who disagreed with me. (Was that steamed pudding disagreeing with the boiled beef, by the way?) I thought, with ill-humoured gratitude, of the people who were contending against the cant which was current about the War, comparing their unconformity with the aggravating omniscience of the novelist whose letter had assured me that "for various reasons we civilians are better able to judge the War as a whole than you soldiers. There is no sort of callousness in this." "Business as usual" was his motto. The War had stimulated rather than discouraged his output of journalism and fiction. They all knew how to win the War—in their highly paid articles! Damn them, I thought; and then painfully remembered how much I had liked that particular novelist when I met him in London. And here I was, doing my best to hate him! (Rivers would probably say that hate was a "definitely physiological condition".)

But my unprofitable meditations were now conclusively interrupted by the arrival of my room companion—not the cheerful young Scot in tartan breeches, but an older man who had replaced him a few weeks before. I will call him the Theosophist, since he was of that way of thinking (and overdid it a bit in conversation). The Theosophist was a tall fine-looking man with iron-grey hair and rather handsome eyes. His attitude toward me was avuncular, tolerant, and at times slightly tutorial. In peace time he had been to some extent a man about town. He had, I assumed, come back from the front suffering from not being quite young enough to stand the strain, which doesn't surprise me now that I am old enough to compare his time of life with my own.

Anyhow he sauntered amiably in, wearing his monocle and evidently feeling all the better for his rubber or two of bridge. Unfortunately he "came in for" the aftermath of my rather morose ruminations, for I was fool enough to begin grumbling about the War and the state of society in general.

The Theosophist responded by assuring me that we were all only on the great stairway which conducts us to higher planes of existence, and when I petulantly enquired what he thought about conscripted populations slaughtering one another, on the great stairway, in order to safeguard democracy and liberty, he merely replied: "Ah, Sherston, that is the Celestial Surgeon at work upon humanity." "Look here," I answered with unusual brilliance, "you say that you won a lot of prizes with your Labradors. Did the president of Cruft's Dog Show encourage all the exhibits to bite one another to death?"

This irreverent repartee reduced him to a dignified

silence, after which he made a prolonged scrutiny of his front teeth in the shaving glass. Next day, no doubt, I made (and he accepted with old-world courtesy) what he would have called the "amende honorable".

*   *   *

Autumn was asserting itself, and a gale got up that night. I lay awake listening to its melancholy surgings and rumblings as it buffeted the big building. The longer I lay awake the more I was reminded of the troops in the line. There they were, stoically enduring their roofless discomfort while I was safe and warm. The storm sounded like a vast lament and the rain was coming down in torrents. I thought of the Ypres salient, that morass of misery and doom. I'd never been there, but I almost wished I was there now. It was, of course, only an emotional idea induced by the equinoctial gale; it was, however, an idea that had its origins in significant experience. One didn't feel like that for nothing.

It meant that the reality of the War had still got its grip on me. Those men, so strangely isolated from ordinary comforts in the dark desolation of murderously-disputed trench-sectors, were more to me than all the despairing and war-weary civilians.

Just as it was beginning to get light I awoke from an uneasy slumber. The storm had ceased and an uncertain glimmer filtered faintly into the room through the tall thinly-curtained window. In this semi-twilight I saw a figure standing near the door.

I stared intently, wondering who on earth it could be at that hour, and possibly surmising that one of the patients was walking in his sleep. The face and head were undiscernible, but I identified a pale buff-coloured "British Warm" coat. Young Ormand always wore a coat like that up in the line, and I found myself believing that Ormand was standing by the door. But Ormand was killed six months ago, I thought. Then the Theosophist, who was always a bad sleeper, turned over in his bed on the other side of the room. I was sitting up, and I could see him looking across at me. While I waited a long minute I could hear his watch ticking on the table. The figure by the door had vanished. "Did you see anyone come into the room?" I asked. He hadn't seen anyone. Perhaps I hadn't either. But it was an odd experience.

II

While composing these apparently interminable memoirs there have been moments when my main problem was what to select from the "long littleness"—or large untidiness—of life. Although a shell-shock hospital might be described as an epitome of the after-effects of the "battle of life" in its most unmitigated form, nevertheless while writing about Slateford I suffer from a shortage of anything to say. The most memorable events must have occurred in my cranium. While Rivers was away on leave only one event occurred which now seems worth recording. The sun was shining brightly and I was giving my golf clubs a rub up after breakfast, when an orderly brought me a mysterious message. Doctor Macamble had called to see me. I had no notion who he was, but I was told that he was waiting in the entrance hall. Let me say at once that I do not know for certain whether Doctor Macamble has "passed to where beyond these voices there is peace". But, whatever his whereabouts may be at the moment of writing, in October 1917 he was, to put it plainly, a quiet-looking man who talked too much. I will go even further and suggest that at least half the time he was talking through his hat—that brown and broad-brimmed emblem of a cerebral existence —which he was holding in his left hand when I first encountered his luminous eye in the hall of the hospital.

"Second-Lieutenant Sherston?" He grasped my hand retentively.

Now to be addressed as "Second-Lieutenant" when one happens to be drawing army pay for refusing to go on being one was not altogether appropriate; and the—for him—undiffuse greeting struck me as striking an unreal note. Had he said, "Dr. Livingstone, I presume," I should have accepted his hand with a fuller conviction that he was a kindred spirit. But he went from bad to worse and did it again. "Second-Lieutenant Sherston," he continued in a voice which more than "filled the hall"; "I am here to offer you my profoundest sympathy and admiration for the heroic gesture which has made your name such a . . ." (here he hesitated, and I wondered if he was going to say "by-word") . . . "such a bugle-call to your brother pacifists." Here, ignoring my sister pacifists, he relinquished my hand and became confidential. "My name is Macamble. I venture to hope that it is not altogether unknown to you. And I have been so bold as to call on you, in the belief that I can be of some assistance to you in the inexpressibly painful confinement to which you are being subjected." At this juncture the man with whom I was going to play golf paraded impatiently past us, clattering his clubs. "What you must have endured!" he went on, moderating his voice at last, as if he had just remembered that we might be "overheard by an unfriendly ear". "More than two months among men driven mad by gun-fire! I marvel that you have retained your reason." (I might have reminded him that he hadn't yet ascertained that I really had retained it; but I merely glanced furtively at my golfing partner, whose back-view, with legs wide apart, was to be seen on the strip of grass in front of the hydro, solemnly swinging a brassy at an imaginary ball.) Doctor Macamble now proposed that we should take a little walk together; he very much wanted to discuss the whole question of the "Stop-the-War Campaign". But I very much wanted to stop being talked to by Doctor Macamble, so I said that I'd got to go and see my doctor. "Ah, the famous Dr. Rivers!" he murmured, with what appeared to be a conspiratorial glance. He then invited me to go down to Edinburgh and continue our conversation, and I agreed to do so on the following afternoon. I couldn't very well refuse point-blank, and in any case I was due there for a hair-cut.

*　　　*　　　*

The aforementioned assignation was fixed for five o'clock in the lounge of the Caledonian Hotel; but I came down from Slateford by an early afternoon tramcar and spent a couple of hours strolling contentedly about the city, which happened to be looking its best in the hazy sunshine of one of those mild October days which induce mellow meditations. After my monastical existence at the hospital I found Princes Street a very pleasant promenading place. The War did not seem to have deprived Edinburgh of any of its delightful dignity; and when I thought of Liverpool, where I wandered about with my worries in July, my preference for Edinburgh was beyond question. The town-dweller goes out into the country to be refreshed by the stillness, and whatever else he may find there in the way of wild flowers, woods, fields, far-off hills, and the nobly-clouded skies which had somehow escaped his notice while he walked to and fro with his eyes on the ground. Those who live on the land come into the city and—if they are sensible people with an aptitude for experiencing—see it as it really is. It always pleases me to watch simple country people loitering about the London pavements, staring at everything around them and being bumped into by persons pressed for time who are part of that incessant procession which is loosely referred to as "the hive of human activity". All this merely indicates that although I arrived in Edinburgh with a couple of hours to spare and had nothing definite to do except to have a hair-cut, nevertheless I found no difficulty in filling up the time by gazing at shop-windows, faces, and architectural vistas, while feeling that I was very lucky to be alive on that serenely sunlit afternoon.

Waiting for Doctor Macamble in the lounge of the Caledonian Hotel wasn't quite such good value. Life was there, of course, offering itself ungrudgingly as material to be observed and ultimately transmuted into memoirs; but it was lounge life, and the collop of it which I indiscriminately absorbed was—well, I will record it without labouring the metaphor any further. (The word collop, by the way, is inserted for the sake of its Caledonian associations.) I sat myself down within easy hearing distance of a well-dressed yellow-haired woman with white eyelashes; she was having tea with an unemphatic-looking major with a sandy moustache. The subjects undergoing discussion were Socialism, Pacifism, Ramsay MacDonald, and Snowden, and the major was acting as audience. His fair companion was "fairly on her hind-legs" about it all. Pacifists, she complained, were worse than the Germans. As for MacDonald and Snowden—"I only hope that if they do start their beloved revolution," she exclaimed, "they'll both be strung up to the nearest lamp-post by the soldiers they are now trying to betray."

"Well, Mabel, I suppose you're old enough to know your own mind," replied the stalwart and sleepy-eyed major.

"And what will *you* do, Archie, if there's ever a revolution?" she enquired.

"Oh, hide, I suppose," he answered.

"Really, Archie, I sometimes wonder how you came to be my cousin!" She handed him back his automatic cigarette-lighter, which he closed with a click, looking as if he'd prefer to be competing for the scratch medal at Prestwick or Muirfield instead of hearing pacifists consigned to perdition. The hotel musicians then struck up with Mendelssohn's (German) Spring Song, to which she was supplying a self-possessed and insouciant tra-la-la when Doctor Macamble trotted in with profuse apologies for being late.

The outspoken utterances of Mabel had at all events made me feel decidedly "pro-Macamble", but I took the wise precaution of moving him a few tables further away from her. I assumed that after hearing even a modicum of his anti-war eloquence she would be more than likely to join in, and might conceivably order her cousin Archie to frog-march the doctor out of the lounge; in fact, I feared that she might regard it as her duty to break up our little pacifist meeting, thinly attended though it was.

Before rendering my account of the meeting I must explain that Macamble was a doctor not of medicine but of philosophy—a Ph.D. in fact—which may have been the cause of his being so chock-full of ideas and adumbrations. Urbanely regarding him across an interval of eighteen years I find him quite unobnoxious; but I must candidly confess that I obtained no edification while bearing the brunt of his fussy and somewhat muddled enthusiasm. After listening to him for about an hour and a half I could be certain of one thing only—that he believed himself to be rather a great man. And like so many of us who maintain that belief, he had so far found very few people to agree with him in his optimistic self-estimate. I suspect that he looked on me as a potential disciple; anyhow he urgently desired to shepherd me along the path to a salvation which was, unquestionably, the exact antithesis to army life. Transmogrified into a music-hall ditty, Macamble's attitude to army officers would have worked out something like this:

> *I couldn't shake hands with a Colonel*
> *And Majors I muchly detest:*
> *All Captains to regions infernal*
> *I consign with both gusto and zest:*
> *To Subalterns blankly uncivil,*
> *I pronounce as my final belief*
> *That the man most akin to the " divvle "*
> *Is that fiend—the Commander-in-Chief.*

I could manage to be amused by that sort of artless intolerance; but when "about the second hour" he became disposed to speak disparagingly of Rivers, I realized that he was exceeding the limit. How much he knew about Rivers I didn't enquire. What he did was to imply that a subtly disintegrating influence was at work on my pacifist zealotry, and after these preliminaries he disclosed the plan which he had formulated for my liberation from the machinations of that uniformed pathologist. With all the good-will in the world, Doctor Macamble advised me to abscond from Slateford. I had only to take a train to London, and once I was there he would arrange for me to be examined by an "eminent alienist" who would infallibly certify that I was completely normal and entirely responsible for my actions. The word "alienist" was one of many whose exact meaning I had never identified in the dictionary. (I dimly associated it with a celebrated Italian named Lombroso who probably wasn't an alienist at all.) Macamble's man, he explained, was well known through his articles in the Press; but unfortunately it transpired that it was the popular rather than the pathological Press—the *Daily Mail*, in fact. I suppose I ought to have waxed indignant, but all I thought was, "Good Lord, he's trying to persuade me to do the dirty on Rivers!" Keeping this thought to myself, I remained reticent and parted from him with the heartiest of handshakes. Did I ever see him again, I wonder? And have I been too hard on him? Well, I can only say that nothing I can do to Doctor Macamble could be worse than his advice to me—had I been imbecile enough to act on it.

* * *

On a pouring wet afternoon a day or two later I was in the entrance hall of the hospital, indulging in some horseplay with another young officer who happened to be feeling "dangerously well" at the moment. It was the hour when visitors came to see patients, and my somewhat athletic sense of humour had focused itself on a very smug-looking brown felt hat, left to take care of itself while the owner conversed with elaborate cheerfulness to some "poor fellow" upstairs. I had just given this innocuous headgear a tremendous kick and was in the middle of a guffaw when I turned and saw Rivers standing just inside the door with a heavy bag in his hand. He was just back from leave. The memory of this little episode brings me a living picture of him, slightly different from his usual self. A spontaneous remembrance of Rivers would reveal him alert and earnest in the momentum of some discussion. (When walking he moved very fast, talking hard, and often seeming forgetful that he was being carried along by his own legs.) Standing there in the failing light of that watery afternoon, he had the half-shy look of a middle-aged person intruding on the segregative amusements of the young. For a moment he re-

garded me with an unreprimanding smile. Then he remarked, "Go steady with that hat, Sherston," and went
rapidly along the corridor to his workroom.

The hat, as I picked it up and restored its contours to
their normal respectability, looked somehow as though it
might have belonged to Doctor Macamble.

III

I have previously remarked that I would give a good deal
for a few gramophone records of my "interchanges of
ideas" with Rivers. I now reiterate the remark because at
the moment of writing I feel very much afraid of reporting
our confabulations incorrectly. In later years, while mud-
dling on toward maturity, I have made it my business to
find out all I can about the mechanism of my spontaneous
behaviour; but I cannot be sure how far I had advanced in
that art—or science—in 1917. I can only suggest that my
definite approach to mental maturity began with my contact with the mind of Rivers.

If he were alive I could not be writing so freely about
him. I might even be obliged to call him by some made-up
name, which would seem absurd. But he has been dead
nearly fourteen years now and he exists only in vigilant
and undiminished memories, continuously surviving in
what he taught me. It is that intense survival of his human
integrity which has made me pause perplexed. Can I hope
to pass the test of that invisible presence, that mind which
was devoted to the service of exact and organized research?
What exactitude would he find in such a representation of
psychological experience as this, and how far would he approve my attempt to describe him? Well, I can only trust
that he would smile at my mistakes and decide that I am
tolerably accurate about the essentials of the story.

Of one thing, at any rate, I can be certain.

In 1917 the last thing he expected me to be capable of
saying to him was—"Such knowledge as I have of the why
and wherefore of this War is only enough to make me feel

that I know nothing at all." He would have said it of him-self, though, since he was merely a plain scientist, and not an omniscient politician or political writer. And he would have added that it pained him deeply to feel that he was "at war" with German scientists. (At that time I did not know that he had studied at Heidelberg.)

As regards the "larger aspects" of the War, my method was to parade such scraps of information as I possessed, always pretending to know more than I did. Even Rivers could not cure me of the youthful habit (which many people never unlearn at all) of being conversationally dis-honest. All he could do was to make me feel uncomfortable when I thought about it afterwards—which was, anyhow, a step in the right direction. For instance he would be say-ing something about the Franco-Prussian War, and I would bluff my way through, pretending to know quite a lot about the Alsace-Lorraine question (though all I knew was that I'd once been introduced to a prebendary called Loraine, who subsequently became a canon, and who had prepared Aunt Evelyn for confirmation somewhere about the year 1870). Worse still, I would talk about some well-known person as if I knew him quite well instead of having only met him once. Since then I have entirely altered my procedure, and when in doubt I pretend to know less than I really do. The knowledge thus gained is part of my in-debtedness to Rivers.

*　　　*　　　*

In 1917 it did not occur to me that golf would one day be regarded as a predominant national occupation rather than a pastime. Nevertheless I did not like the game to be treated with levity; in fact I played it somewhat seriously. (My friend Cromlech had once insisted on trying to defeat me in a game in which he used nothing but a niblick; and to my great annoyance he performed such astonishing feats with it as to cause me some disquietude, though I won quite comfortably in the end.)

When played seriously, even golf can, I suppose, claim to be "an epitome of human life". Anyhow, in that fourth

October of the War I was a better golfer than I'd ever been before—and, I may add, a better one than I've ever been since.

I must admit, though, that I wasn't worrying much about the War when I'd just hit a perfect tee-shot up the charming vista which was the fairway to the first green at Mortonhall. How easy it felt! I scarcely seemed to be gripping the club at all. Afternoon sunshine was slanting through the golden-brown beeches and at last I knew what it was like to hit the ball properly. "I suppose I'm getting too keen on the game," I thought, as I bicycled home to the hydro at the end of some such afternoon, when I'd been sampling one of the delightfully unfrequented links which the War had converted into Arcadian solitudes. It was all very well, but this sort of thing couldn't go on for ever. Sooner or later I must let Rivers know my intentions. Had I been an ordinary patient I should have been due for a medical board long before now, and even Rivers couldn't postpone it indefinitely. And if I were to refuse to go before a board the situation would become awkward again. He had allowed me to drift on for twelve weeks, and so far he hadn't asked me what I intended to do or put the slightest pressure on me about it. Now that he was back from leave he would probably tackle the question. Perhaps he would do so that very evening.

Meanwhile I went up to my room and sat there cleaning my clubs. After a bit the Theosophist came in to smarten himself up before going into Edinburgh for dinner. When in good spirits he had a habit of addressing me in literary language, usually either tags of Shakespeare or locutions reminiscent of Rider Haggard's romances. If I remarked that the way the windows rattled and creaked was enough to keep one awake all night, he would reply, "True, O King," or "Thou hast uttered wise words, O great white chief." He now informed me, while rubbing his face with a towel, that he had been engaged on "enterprises of great pith and moment".

"To-day, toward the going down of the sun, O Sherston, the medicine men put forth their powers upon me, and soothfully I say unto you, they have passed me for permanent home service." Where would he go to, I enquired.

"I shall sit in an office, O man of little faith, wearing blue tabs upon my tunic and filling in Army Forms whereof no man knoweth the mysterious meaning," he replied, and left me wondering what occupation I ought to find for my disillusioned self.

*   *   *

Writing about it so long afterwards, one is liable to forget that while the War was going on nobody really knew when it would stop. For ordinary infantry officers like myself there was always what we called "a faint bloody hope that it may be over in six months from now". And at Slateford there was always a suppressed awareness which reminded me that I was "shortening the War" for myself every week that I remained there. No one but an expert humbug would now deny that some such awareness existed in most of us who were temporarily "out of it" but destined sooner or later to find ourselves in a front-line trench again.

While I continued to clean my clubs, some inward monitor became uncomfortably candid and remarked "This heroic gesture of yours—'making a separate peace'—is extremely convenient for you, isn't it? Doesn't it begin to look rather like dodging the Kaiser's well-aimed projectiles?" Proper pride also weighed in with a few well-chosen words. "Twelve weeks ago you may have been a man with a message. Anyhow you genuinely believed yourself to be one. But unless you can prove to yourself that your protest is still effective, you are here under false pretences, merely skrimshanking snugly along on what you did in the belief that you would be given a bad time for doing it."

Against this I argued that, having pledged myself to an uncompromising attitude, I ought to remain consistent to the abstract idea that the War was wrong. Intellectual sobriety was demanded of me. But the trouble was that I wasn't an "intellectual" at all; I was only trying to become one. I was also, it seemed, trying to become a good golfer. Rivers had never played golf in his life, though he approved of it as a healthy recreation. It would mean nothing to him if I told him that I'd been round North Berwick in one under bogey (which I hadn't done). There were many other subjects we could discuss, of course, but after the first six weeks or so there had seemed less and less to be said about my "mental position". And it was no use pretending that I'd come to Slateford to talk to him about contemporary novelists or even the incalculability of European Chancelleries. Sooner or later he would ask me straight out what I intended to do. My own reticence on the subject had been caused by the fact that I hadn't known what I did intend to do.

I was now trying to find out, while rubbing away, with oil and sandpaper, at an obstinate patch of rust on my niblick. . . .

At this point in my cogitations there was a commotion of thudding feet along the passage past my door, and I heard a nurse saying, "Now, now, you mustn't get upset like this." The sound of someone sobbing like a child receded and became inaudible after the shutting of a door. That sort of thing happened fairly often at the hydro. Men who had "done their bit in France" crying like children. One took it for granted, of course; but how much longer could I stay there among so many haunted faces and "functional nervous disorders"? Outwardly normal though a lot of them were, it wasn't an environment which stimulated one's "intellectual sobriety"!

I felt in my pocket for a little talisman which I always carried about with me. It was a lump of fire-opal clasped on a fine gold chain. Someone whose friendship I valued highly had given it to me when I went to France and I used to call it "my pocket sunset".

I had derived consolation from its marvellous colours during the worst episodes of my war experiences. In its small way it had done its best to mitigate much squalor and despondency. My companions in dismal dug-outs had held it in their hands and admired it.

I could not see its fiery colours now, for the room was almost dark.

But it brought back the past in which I had made it an emblem of successful endurance, and set up a mood of reverie about the old Front Line, which really did feel as if it had been a better place than this where I now sat in bitter safety surrounded by the wreckage and defeat of those who had once been brave.

Had I really enjoyed those tours of trenches up in the Bois Français sector? For it was that period, before the Somme battles began, which now seemed to have acquired an insidious attractiveness. No; in their reality I had intensely disliked those times—except, perhaps, the excitement of my night-patrols. It hadn't been much fun when we relieved the Manchesters—sploshing and floundering up "the Old Kent Road" at midnight; posting the sentries and machine-gunners and that bombing-post at the end of the sap; taking over the familiar desolation of soggy firesteps and sniped-at parapets and looking out again across that nothing-on-earth-like region beyond the tangled thickets of wire. And then diving under the gas-blanket in the doorway of our dug-out and groping down the steps to find Barton sitting moodily at the table with his bottle of whisky, worrying over his responsibilities while his batman cooked him some toasted cheese in the smoky recess which served as a kitchen. Up there we had arrived at the edge of the world and everything pleasant was far behind us. To be dozing doggedly on the mud-caked sandbags of a wire-netting bunk, with bits of chalk falling on one's face, was something achieved for King and Country, but it wasn't enjoyable. There was no sense, I thought, in allowing oneself to sentimentalize the smells of chloride of lime and dead rats, or in idealizing the grousings of Ormand and Mansfield because the jam ration was usually inferior, seldom Hartley's, and never Crosse and Blackwell's. But we'd all done our best to help one another, and it was good to remember Durley coming in with one of his wryfaced stories about a rifle-grenade exploding on the parados a few yards away from him—Durley demonstrating just how he'd dodged it, and creating an impression that it had been quite a funny German practical joke. Yes, we'd all of us managed to make jokes—mostly family jokes—for a company could be quite a happy family party until someone got killed. Cheerfulness under bad conditions was by no means the least heroic element of the war. Wonderful indeed had been that whimsical fortitude of the men who accepted an intense bombardment as all in the day's work and then grumbled because their cigarette ration was one packet short! But C Company Mess, as it was in the first half of 1916, could never be reassembled. Its ingredients were now imbued with ghostliness. Mansfield and Durley were disabled by wounds, and Ormand was dead. Barton was the only one of us who was functioning at the front now; he'd gone back last spring and had survived the summer and autumn without getting a scratch. Poor old devil, I thought, he must be qualifying for a spell at Slateford by now, for he'd been out there eighteen months before he was wounded the first time. . . . No, there wasn't much sense in feeling exiled from a family party which had ceased to exist; and the Bois Français sector itself had become ancient history, as remote and obsolete as the first winter of the War. Everything would be different if I went back to France now—different even from what it was last April. Gas was becoming more and more of a problem—one might almost say, more of a nightmare. Hadn't I just spent an afternoon playing golf with a man who'd lost half his company in a gas-bombardment a couple of months ago? . . . It seems to amount to this, I ruminated, twirling my putter as I polished its neck—that I'm exiled from the troops as a whole rather than from my former fellow-officers and men. And I visualized an endless column of marching soldiers, singing "Tipperary" on their way up from the back-areas; I saw them filing silently along ruined roads, and lugging their bad boots through mud until they came to some shell-hole and pillar-box line in a landscape where trees were stumps and skeletons and no Quartermaster on earth could be certain of getting the rations up. . . . "From sunlight to the sunless land". . . . The idea of going back there was indeed like death.

I suppose I ought to have concluded my strenuous woolgatherings by adding that death is preferable to dishonour. But I didn't. Humanity asserted itself in the form of a sulky little lapse into exasperation against the people who pitied my "wrong-headedness" and regarded me as "not quite normal". In their opinion it was quite right that I should be safely out of it and "being looked after". How else could I get my own back on them but by returning to the trenches? Killed in action in order to confute the Under-Secretary for War, who had officially stated that I wasn't responsible for my actions. What a truly glorious death for a promising young pacifist! . . .

By these rather peculiar methods I argued it out with myself in the twilight. And when the windows were dark and I could see the stars, I still sat there with my golf bag between my knees, alone with what now seemed an irrefutable assurance that going back to the War as soon as possible was my only chance of peace.

*   *   *

As I went along to see Rivers that evening I felt rather as if I were about to make a grand gesture. I may even have felt like doing it in the grand manner. Anyhow I was full of bottled-up emotion and conscious of the significance of the occasion. Looking back from to-day, however, I am interested, not in what my own feelings were, but in what Rivers had been thinking about the decision which he had left me so entirely free to make. Had he been asked, he would probably have replied, in his driest manner, that he considered it to be his duty, as an army medical officer, to "cure me of my pacifist errors" (though one of our jokes had been about the humorous situation which would arise if I were to convert him to my point of view). Whatever he had been thinking while away on leave, he was there, with his gentle assurance of helpfulness, and all my grand gesture exuberance faded out at once. It was impossible not to be natural with Rivers. All I knew was that he was my father-confessor, as I called him, and that at last I really had got something to tell him which wasn't merely a discursive amplification of my "marking time for a few weeks" policy. As a "lead-up" to a more definite disclosure I began by telling him about the odd experience I'd had during the night before he went on leave. I knew that he was scientifically sceptical about psychic phenomena, so I laid stress on the fact that it was probably a visual delusion caused by thinking about the Western Front in stormy weather. Though I described it diffidently, the strong emotion underlying my narrative must have been apparent. But I was so full of myself and my new-made determination that I was quite surprised when I saw that my story had affected him strongly, and that it had caused him to remove his spectacles and rub them rather more than was necessary. He said little, however, and waited for me to continue. With a bumping heart I asked him what would happen if I persisted in my pacifist attitude.

"You will be kept here until the end of the War," he replied quietly. I then asked what would happen if I went before a board for reconsideration of my "mental condition". "I could only tell them that you are not suffering from any form of psycho-neurosis," he answered, adding that if I asked for permanent home service I should probably get it. I then overheard myself—as though I were a third person in the room—saying, rather hurriedly and not at all in the grand manner, "I was getting things into focus a bit while you were away and I see now that the only thing for me to do is to get back to the front as quick as I can. But what worries me is that I'm afraid of the War Office doing me down somehow and shunting me off on to some home-service job, and if I can't be passed for G.S. I won't be passed for anything at all." I could see that he was pleased; but he said that I must think it over and make quite sure that I meant it. We could then discuss our plan of campaign to wangle things with the War Office.

(He didn't actually use the word "wangle", but he implied that it might not be altogether easy to "work it" for me.) We then talked for a bit about other things and did our best to forget that there was a war on.

IV

My previous chapter began with a little exordium on the needfulness for exactitude when one is remembering and writing down what occurred a decade or two ago. At the present moment I am—to be exact—exactly 936 weeks away from my material; but that sort of accuracy is, of course, merely a matter of chronological arithmetic. Since what I am about to relate is only an interlude, I propose to allow my fantasies more freedom than is my conscientious habit. Don't assume, though, that I am about to describe something which never happened at all. Were I to do that I should be extending the art of reminiscence beyond its prescribed purpose, which is, in my case, to show myself as I am now in relation to what I was during the War.

Allow yourself then to imagine that the before-mentioned 936 weeks have not yet intervened between "now" and the autumn of 1917. You will at once observe what I can only call "one George Sherston" going full speed up a hill on the outskirts of Edinburgh. The reason for his leg-loco-motive velocity is that he is keeping pace with that quick walker, W. H. R. Rivers. The clocks of Edinburgh are an-nouncing the hour of "One" (which we shall, I fear, some day be obliged by law to call "Thirteen", though I myself intend, for an obvious reason, to compromise by referring to it as "12A"). Up that hill we go, talking (and walking) as hard as we can. For we, a couple of khaki-clad figures in (do you doubt my veracity?) "the mellow rays of an Octo-ber sun", are on our way to have luncheon with an astro-nomer; and not an ordinary astronomer either, since this one was—to put it plainly—none other than the Astro-nomer Royal of Scotland. That, so far, was all I knew and all I needed to know, my ignorance of astronomy being what it was. Rivers was taking me up there, and it pro-mised to be a very agreeable outing, and quite a contrast to that Mecca of psycho-neuroses, Slateford War Hospital.

       *   *   *

Anybody who desires to verify my observations on the observatory is—or ought to be—at liberty to go there and see it for himself. But it will be one-sided verification, since I am unable to visualize, even vaguely, the actual observatory. Let us therefore assume it to be a building in all respects worthy of the lofty investigations which were why it was there—or, if you prefer it, "to which it was dedicated". Arrival and admittance having followed one another in accordance with immemorial usage, the Astronomer Royal welcomed us with the cordiality of a man who has plenty to spare for his fellow-men—no cordiality being required of him by the constellations, comets, and other self-luminous bodies which he had spent so much of his time in scrutinizing. I have known people who would probably have improvised some such conversational opening as "Well, sir, and how are the stars? Any new ones lately?"—but I was too shy to say anything at all to a man so widely acquainted with the universe. We were introduced to the fourth member of the quartet, a jocular-looking parson who rejoiced in the name of Father Rosary, and was, I inferred, a priest. We then sat down to luncheon. As I glanced around the room, which had eighteenth-century charm, I no longer felt shy and was completely prepared to enjoy myself. This feeling may have been brought on by Father Rosary, who was evidently an artist at creating a pleasant impression and following it up by being the best possible company. What did he talk about, I wonder, during that luncheon which has now become a memory of indistinct delightfulness—as all such luncheons should?

He told us amusing stories; witty stories, well worth remembering; but I have forgotten them. He spoke of entrancing places in foreign countries; but I had never seen them and they were only names which made me wish I'd been less unenterprising, instead of waiting for a European war to transport me abroad. He talked, without ostentation, about famous people whom he'd known. Who were they, I wonder? I rather think he mentioned Walter Pater (whose cadenced prose I had read with more awareness of its music than of its instructive ingredients) and if he didn't, he ought to have done. There was indeed an untranslatably Paterish quality about Father Rosary when he was being eloquently urbane. I suppose one should call it "an aroma of humanism"—which means that his religious vocation had not prevented him from being helpfully interested in everything that men think and do.

He was, so to speak, a connoisseur in the wisdom of the ages, and I can imagine his rich voice rolling out that fine passage of Pater's which cannot be quoted too often: "For the essence of humanism is that belief of which he seems never to have doubted, that nothing which has ever interested living men and women can wholly lose its vitality— no language they have spoken, nor oracle beside which they have hushed their voices, no dream which has once been entertained by actual human minds, nothing about which they have ever been passionate, or expended time and zeal."

Meanwhile our lively host had uncorked a bottle of ancient champagne. It might be a century old, he said, or it might be less. But it was probably the most absurdly obsolete bottle of champagne in Edinburgh, and might, he added, be a bit insipid. He had discovered it in his cellar; some previous astronomer had left it there, and by miraculous oversight it had survived to be sniffed and inspected by Father Rosary and finally subjected to the tasting test of his impeccable palate for wine. Rivers, who was a good judge of water, sipped it respectfully and (after admiring the delicate old glass from which it was fulfilling its destiny by being at last imbibed) remarked that he'd never tasted anything like it in his life. Father Rosary commented on its "solemn stillness", and then, he alone knew why, began talking about Tennyson. "Do you young men read Tennyson?" he asked me, and quoted "Now sleeps the crimson petal, now the white" with the subdued relish of an epicure. The astronomer, however, hadn't much use for poetry. Astronomy made it seem a bit unnecessary, he thought. "*Now slides the silent meteor on*—pretty enough— but if he'd known what I do about meteors he wouldn't have put it into a poem."

"But I thought he took a great interest in astronomy," I ventured.

"Yes; but he used it to suit his own game of idealizing the universe, and never really faced those ghastly immensities I'm always staring at," he replied, revealing for a moment the "whatever brute or blackguard made the world" outlook which showed itself in his face when he wasn't cracking jokes with Father Rosary, whose personality seemed to imply that Heaven was an invisible Vatican, complete with library, art-collection, and museum. Rivers, who wasn't a great poetry reader (he was handicapped by having no visual memory) remarked that he had an indistinct recollection of some poem by Tennyson in which he had to some extent "seen eye to eye" with the astronomer. There was no copy of Tennyson's works up at the observatory, but had we consulted one we should have found that Rivers was right. The line "These are Astronomy and Geology, terrible Muses" can scarcely be classed as an idealization of those two realities.

Father Rosary now recreated harmonious gaiety by seating himself at the piano and trolling out a series of delightful ditties. After that he led us yet further from uncomfortable controversies by playing some classical and nobly serious pieces, for he loved the old Italian masters. And when, at the final chords, I looked across the room, the ultimate serenity of the music seemed to be at rest in the face of my friend.

V

Sitting myself down at the table to resume this laborious task after twenty-four hours' rest, I told myself that I was "really feeling fairly fresh again". And I could have sworn that I heard the voice of Rivers say "Good!" I mention this just to show the way my mind works, though I suppose one ought not to put that sort of "aside" into a book, especially as I am always reminding myself to be ultra-careful to keep my story "well inside the frame". But I begin to feel as if I were inside the frame myself, and that

being so, I don't see why Rivers shouldn't be inside it too—
in more ways than one.

Well—to continue the chronicle—there were moments,
after I'd emerged from my anti-war imbroglio (forgive the
phrase, it amuses me) when I felt not unnaturally upset at
the idea of returning to the good old trenches, though I did
what I could to sublimate that "great adventure" into
something splendid. The whole business was now safely
settled and the date of my medical board was early in
November. Rivers had made an expedition to London on
my behalf, had interviewed two influential personages, and
had obtained the required guarantee that no obstacles
would be placed in my road back to regions where bombs,
mustard-gas, box-barrages, and similar enjoyments were
awaiting me.

He showed me a letter from one of them (a devoted
"public servant" with whom I'd often played cricket in
the old days, and whom no one but a maniac could possibly have disliked) in which the writer referred to me (in
collaboration with his typist) as "our poor friend", which
thereafter became our favourite term for alluding to me.

In weaker moments, as I said before, "our poor friend"
somewhat bleakly realized what he had let himself in for,
and, without actually wishing he hadn't done it, felt an
irrepressible hankering for some sort of reprieve. Since
mid-October mental detachment had been made easier by
my having been given a small room to myself—an insidious
privilege which allowed me to ruminate without interruption. Bad weather prevented me from playing golf all day
and every day, and my brain became more active in the
evenings. I spent ambrosial hours with favourite authors,
and a self-contained, "dug-in" state of mind ensued.

My temperamental tendency to day-dreaming asserted
itself and I realized how much I craved for solitude and
mental escape from my surroundings.

When cold weather came I was allowed a scuttle of coal
and could lie in bed watching the firelight flickering on the
walls and the embers glowing in the grate. On such nights
I remembered untroubled days and idealized my child-

hood, returning to the times when I was recovering from some illness and could dwell in realms of reverie, as when one surrenders to the spell of a book which evokes summers long ago and people transmuted by the author's mind to happy phantoms. Imagination recreated Aunt Evelyn reading aloud to me—her voice going lullingly on and on with one of R. L. Stevenson's stories, until she decided that it was time for some more medicine, for she was fond of amateur doctoring, and soon she would be busy with the medicine dropper, preparing one of her homeopathic remedies. Now I come to think of it, Aunt Evelyn's world was divided into "Homeopats" and "Allopats", who were much the same as Conservatives and Liberals; and the "Allopats" were in the same category as Radicals in whom no virtue resided. In other words, my reveries went back to the beginning of these memoirs, living them over again until August 1914 pulled me up short.

This was a permissible self-indulgence, for the past was still there to be used as a sedative in discreet doses—three drops in half a wine glass of water, so to speak. Looking at the future was quite a different matter.

There had been times since I came to Slateford when I had, rather guardedly, given myself a glimpse of an *après la guerre* existence, but I hadn't done any cosy day-dreaming about it. My talks with Rivers had increased my awareness of the limitations of my pre-war life. He had shown that he believed me to be capable of achieving something useful. He had set me on the right road and made me feel that if the War were to end to-morrow I should be starting on a new life's journey in which point-to-point races and cricket matches would no longer be supremely important and a strenuous effort must be made to take some small share in the real work of the world.

If the War were to end to-morrow! . . . That was where I remembered that my future was unlikely to happen at all. The fireproof curtain was still lowered in front of the stage on which post-war events would be enacted; and life, with an ironic gesture, had contrived that the man who had lit up my future with a new eagerness to do well in it should now be instrumental in sending me back to an even-money chance of being killed.

Here was I, in my little room, with a fire burning brightly and a dozen of the world's literary masterpieces tidily arranged on my table. Where should I be by the end of November? I wondered; for I was expecting that, since I was such a "special case", I should be sent back without much delay. The contrast, as regards comfort, between where I was now and where I might be in a few weeks' time needed no stressing. Realizing how much I wanted not to lose that chance of a "new life", I experienced a sort of ordeal by self-immolation. Immolation for what? I asked myself. I should be returning to the War with no belief in what I was doing; I should go through with it in a spirit of loneliness and detachment because there was no alternative. Going back was the only way out of an impossible situation. At the front I should at least find forgetfulness. And I would rather be killed than survive as one who had "wangled" his way through by saying that the War ought to stop. Better to be in the trenches with those whose experience I had shared and understood than with this medley of civilians who, when one generalized about them intolerantly, seemed either being broken by the War or enriched and made important by it. Whatever the soldiers might be as individuals, they seemed a more impressive spectacle as a whole in their endurance of what was imposed on them. But then there was my freedom to be considered. After all I had been under no one's orders lately, and at the best of times a platoon commander's life was just one damned thing after another. It's got to be done, I thought. That was about all I'd got to keep me up to scratch, and I went through some fairly murky moments in that little room of mine. It was, in fact, not at all unlike a renunciation of life and all that it had to offer me. As regards being dead, however, one of my main consolations has always been that I have the strongest intention of being an extremely active ghost. Let nobody make any mistake about that.

*   *   *

It must have been just before my medical board was due to take place that the great administrative crisis occurred at Slateford. The details of this event were as follows. The commandant (or head doctor) who had won the gratitude and affection of everyone whose opinion was worth anything, was duly notified, several weeks in advance, that the chief medical mandarin from the War Office would inspect the hospital. This, of course, signified automatically that elaborate efforts must be made to ensure that he should see Slateford as it had never been before and never would be again. The spit and polish process should, I suppose, have been applied even to the patients, on whom it was incumbent that they should be looking their best. "Always remember that you belong to the smartest shell-shock hospital in the British Army" should have been the order of the day.

But the commandant had his own ideas about eyewash, and he decided that the general should, just for once, see a war hospital as it really was.

He did this as a matter of principle, since in his opinion a shell-shock hospital was not the same thing as a parade ground. But administrative inspectorship failed to see the point of that sort of thing, and the mandarin was genuinely shocked by what he inspected. He went into the kitchen and found that he couldn't see his face reflected in a single frying-pan. You couldn't eat your dinner off the bathroom floors, and Sam Browne belts were conspicuous by their absence. Worst of all, most of the medical staff were occupied with their patients, instead of standing about and wasting their time for an hour or two while awaiting the arrival of their supreme therapeutic war-lord. Profoundly displeased, he departed. The place was a disgrace, and only showed what happened when civilians in uniform were allowed to run a war hospital in their own way. The commandant was notified that someone else would take over his commandancy, and the rest of the staff sent in their resignations as a demonstration of loyalty to him. These after-effects, as far as I can remember, were as yet unknown to the patients. Had I been aware that Rivers would soon be leaving the hospital I am sure I should not have done the very stupid thing which I am about to describe.

* * *

There are two ways of telling a good story well—the quick way and the slow way. Personally I prefer a good story to be told slowly. What I am about to tell is not a good story. It is merely an episode which cannot be left out. A certain abruptness is therefore appropriate.

On the appointed afternoon I smartened myself up and waited to be called before the medical board. I was also going to tea with the astronomer, who had promised to let me have a look at the moon through his telescope. But I was feeling moody and irritable, and I had to wait my turn, which was a long time in coming. Gradually I became petulant and impatient. After an hour and a half I looked at my watch for the last time, said to myself that the medical board could go to blazes, and then (I record it with regret) went off to have tea with the astronomer. It was one of those self-destructive impulses which cause people, in sheer cussedness, to do things which are to their own disadvantage. I suddenly felt "fed up with being mucked about by the War"—as I should have expressed it—and forgot all about Rivers and everything that I owed him.

Seeking some explanation of my behaviour I have wondered whether I was feeling ill without being aware of it. But I don't remember developing an influenza-cold afterwards; and if I did it would have been a poorish excuse.

In these days of incalculable dictators, by the way, (and in my humble opinion the proper place for a dictator is a parenthesis) one cannot help wondering whether an acute Continental crisis could not quite conceivably be caused by an oncoming chill. May I therefore be allowed to suggest that before hurling explosive ultimatums, all dictators should be persuaded to have their temperatures taken. One pictures the totalitarian tyrant with fountain-pen poised above some imperious edict, when the human touch intervenes in the form of a trained nurse-secretary (also a dead shot with a revolver) who slips a thermometer into that ever-open mouth. One figures him, with eyes dynamically dilated, breathing stertorously through the nose during this test of his sense of supreme responsibility for the well-being of the world. . . . "Just half a minute more, to make quite sure". . . . With a bright smile she hands the tiny talisman to a gravely-expectant medicine man, who, it may be, shakes his head and murmurs, "Nine-nine point nine. Your Supremacy should sign no documents till to-morrow morning." Poof! What a relief for Europe! . . .

To return to my insignificant self: before I was half-way to Edinburgh on the top of a tram I realized that I had done something unthinkably foolish. But it was too late now. The stars looked down on me, and soon I should be making the most of them through the largest telescope in Scotland. But the document which might have a conclusive effect on my earthly career was still unsigned.

Of my tea with the astronomer, I only remember that he couldn't get the telescope to work properly. He pushed and pulled, swivelled it and swore at it, and finally gave it up as a bad job. So even the moon was a washout. Downstairs he took me into a darkened room and showed me a delicate instrument which I can only describe by saying that it contained a small blob of luminosity, which was, I rather think, radium. What was the instrument for? I asked. He told me that it was used for measuring infinitesimal fractions of a second. He then explained how it did it.

*   *   *

Rivers, as I have already attempted to indicate, was a wonderful man. He certainly made me aware of it after I'd offered him my wretched explanation. It was, thank heaven, the only time I ever saw him seriously annoyed with me. As might be expected, he looked not only annoyed, but stern. The worst part was that he looked thoroughly miserable. With averted eyes I mumbled out my story; how I'd lost my temper because I was kept waiting; how I really didn't know why I'd done it; and how it was nothing to do with backing out of my decision to give up being a pacifist. When he heard this his face changed. He looked relieved. My eyes met his; and when I dolefully exclaimed "And now I suppose I've dished the whole thing, just through having said I'd go to tea with the astronomer!" he threw his head back and laughed in that delightful way of his. For me it was about the best laugh he ever indulged in, for it meant that he'd put the whole board-cutting business behind him and was ready to repair the damage without delay. Not a word of reproach did he utter. I was causing him a lot of extra trouble, but he merely remarked that he might find some difficulty in getting my papers past the new commandant, whose arrival was imminent. This officer was believed to be ultra-conventional in his ideas about the mental deportment of young officers, and it was feared that his attitude toward the psychoses would be somewhat adamantine. Whether it really was adamantine I am unable to say, for I don't seem to remember much about those three weeks which concluded my career at Slateford.

Oddly enough, the agitation created by board-cutting produced an ableptical effect on my introspectiveness. The episode provided a sort of bridge between psychological disquietude and a calm acceptance of "the inevitable". In other words, I ceased to worry.

When—at the end of that period of which I can only remember that I wanted it to be over quickly—I was actually waiting to go in and "be boarded", I felt self-confident but a little nervous about the result. My cranium, however, contained nothing definite except the first two lines of "Locksley Hall". (Something similar had happened when I was being "boarded" at Liverpool the previous July.) "*Comrades, leave me here a little, while as yet 'tis early morn*" (it was after lunch, and I was reclining on a dingy red plush sofa in the lofty but depressing saloon). "*Leave me here, and when you want me blow upon the bugle-horn*" ... What was the connection? Was it because they'd talked about Tennyson up at the observatory, or was "Locksley Hall" something to do with being under lock and key, or was it merely because the bugle-horn was about to blow me back to the army? One thing was obvious, at any rate. I must not ask the medical board to solve this enigma for me. When the moment arrived for me to take a deep breath and step discreetly in, I found Rivers looking as solemn as a judge, sitting at a table where he'd been telling the other two as much of my case as he deemed good for them. In a manner which was, I hoped, a nice blend of deference and self-assurance, I replied to a few perfunctory questions about my health. There was a fearsome moment when the commandant picked up my "dossier"; but Rivers diverted his attention with some remark or other and he put the papers down again. The commandant looked rather as if he wanted his tea. I was then duly passed for general service abroad—an event which seldom happened from Slateford. But that was not all. Without knowing it, two-thirds of the medical board had restored me to my former status. I was now "an officer and a gentleman", again.

*   *   *

Next morning I had my last look at the hydro before departing to entrain for Liverpool. Feeling no inclination to request my comrades to leave me there a little, I became quite certain that I never wanted to see the place again.

I had said good-bye to Rivers. Shutting the door of his room for the last time, I left behind me someone who had helped and understood me more than anyone I had ever known. Much as he disliked speeding me back to the trenches, he realized that it was my only way out. And the longer I live the more right I know him to have been.

And now, before conveying myself away from Slateford, I must add a few final impressions. The analysis and inter-pretation of dreams was an important part of the work which Rivers did; and, as everyone ought to know, his con-tributions to that insubstantial field of investigation were extremely valuable.

About my own dreams he hadn't bothered much, but as there may be someone who needs to be convinced that I wasn't suffering from shell-shock, I am offering a scrap of dream evidence, which for all I know may prove that I was!

Since the War I have experienced two distinct and recurrent specimens of war-dream. Neither of them expressed any dislike of high-explosive. I have never had nightmares about being shelled, though I must confess to a few recent ones about being bombed from the air, but that was probably caused by reading the newspapers.

The two recurrent dreams were, (1): I was with my battalion in some slough of despond, from which it seemed there was no way back. We were all doomed to perish in the worst possible of all most hopeless "dud shows". Our only enemy was mud. This was caused by hearing about the Ypres salient, and by the haunting fear that sooner or later I should find myself in some such "immortal morass", as it might be designated by one of those lofty-minded persons who prefer to let bygones be bygones—one might call them "the Unknown Warrior School of Unrealists"—"these men perished miserably, but the spirit in which they did it lives for ever", and so on. Measured in terms of unmitigated horror, this dream was, I think, quite good peace propaganda. But the queer thing about it was that while in the thick of my dream-despair, I sometimes thought "Anyhow I am adding a very complete piece of war experience to my collection". This dream did not recur after I had written my account of military service.

The second dream still recurs, every two or three months. It varies in context and background, but always amounts to the same thing. The War is still going on and I have got to return to the front. I complain bitterly to myself because it hasn't stopped yet. I am worried because I can't find my active-service kit. I am worried because I have forgotten how to be an officer. I feel that I can't face it again, and sometimes I burst into tears and say "It's no good. I can't do it." But I know that I can't escape going back, and search frantically for my lost equipment.

Sometimes I actually find myself "out there" (though the background is always in England—the Germans have usually invaded half Kent). And, as in the first dream, I am vaguely gratified at "adding to my war experience". I take out a patrol and am quite keen about it.

This dream obviously dates from the autumn of 1917,

when I made the choice which seemed like a "potential death-sentence". If it proves anything it is this; the fact that it was everybody's business to be prepared to die for his country did not alter the inward and entirely personal grievance one had against being obliged to do it. The instinct of self-preservation automatically sank below all arguments put forward by one's "higher self". "I don't want to die," it insisted. "I want to be a middle-aged man writing memoirs, and not a 'glorious name' living for evermore on a block of stone subject to the inevitable attritions and obfuscations caused by climate." "But your deathless name will be invisibly inscribed in the annals of your imperishable race" argued some celestial leader-writer. "I prefer to peruse to-morrow's *Times* in normal decrepitude" replied ignoble self-preservation.

*   *   *

It would be an exaggeration if I were to describe Slateford as a depressing place by daylight. The doctors did everything possible to counteract gloom, and the wrecked faces were outnumbered by those who were emerging from their nervous disorders. But the War Office had wasted no money on interior decoration; consequently the place had the melancholy atmosphere of a decayed hydro, redeemed only by its healthy situation and pleasant view of the Pentland Hills. By daylight the doctors dealt successfully with these disadvantages, and Slateford, so to speak, "made cheerful conversation".

But by night they lost control and the hospital became sepulchral and oppressive with saturations of war experience. One lay awake and listened to feet padding along passages which smelt of stale cigarette-smoke; for the nurses couldn't prevent insomnia-ridden officers from smoking half the night in their bedrooms, though the locks had been removed from all doors. One became conscious that the place was full of men whose slumbers were morbid and terrifying—men muttering uneasily or suddenly crying out in their sleep. Around me was that underworld of dreams haunted by submerged memories of warfare and its intolerable shocks and self-lacerating failures to achieve the impossible. By daylight each mind was a sort of aquarium for the psychopath to study. In the daytime, sitting in a sunny room, a man could discuss his psycho-neurotic symptoms with his doctor, who could diagnose phobias and conflicts and formulate them in scientific terminology. Significant dreams could be noted down, and Rivers could try to remove repressions. But by night each man was back in his doomed sector of a horror-stricken Front Line, where the panic and stampede of some ghastly experience was re-enacted among the livid faces of the dead. No doctor could save him then, when he became the lonely victim of his dream disasters and delusions.

Shell-shock. How many a brief bombardment had its long-delayed after-effect in the minds of these survivors, many of whom had looked at their companions and laughed while inferno did its best to destroy them. Not then was their evil hour, but now; now, in the sweating suffocation of nightmare, in paralysis of limbs, in the stammering of dislocated speech. Worst of all, in the disintegration of those qualities through which they had been so gallant and selfless and uncomplaining—this, in the finer types of men, was the unspeakable tragedy of shell-shock; it was in this that their humanity had been outraged by those explosives which were sanctioned and glorified by the Churches; it was thus that their self-sacrifice was mocked and maltreated—they, who in the name of righteousness had been sent out to maim and slaughter their fellow-men. In the name of civilization these soldiers had been martyred, and it remained for civilization to prove that their martyrdom wasn't a dirty swindle.

PART TWO: LIVERPOOL AND LIMERICK

I

It is not impossible that on my way back to Clitherland I compared my contemporary self with previous Sherstons who had reported themselves for duty there.

First the newly-gazetted young officer, who had yet to utter his first word of command—anxious only to become passably efficient for service at the front. (How young I had been then—not much more than two and a half years ago!) Next came the survivor of nine months in France (the trenches had taught *him* a thing or two anyhow) less diffident, and inclined, in a confused way, to ask the reason why everyone was doing and dying under such soul-destroying conditions. Thirdly arrived that somewhat incredible mutineer who had made up his mind that if a single human being could help to stop the War by making a fuss, he was that man.

There they were, those three Sherstons; and here was I —the inheritor of their dim renown. Reporting for duty again, that was all it boiled down to, after making a proper fool of myself instead of just carrying on and taking the cushy job which I could have had for the asking without anyone uttering a word against me.

Driving out to the camp in a taxi, however, I didn't doubt that I should be received with heartiness—albeit tinged with embarrassment. I must try not to think about it, I thought; and anyhow it was a comfort not to be arriving there with a bee in my bonnet; which was, I supposed, what they'd all been saying about my behaviour. But my arrival turned out to be an anti-climax. A surprise awaited me. Only a few days before, the Depot had been transplanted to Ireland on account of the troubles there. Clitherland Camp was to be taken over by an Irish battalion. In the meantime it was occupied by the Assistant-Adjutant and a few dozen "details", plus a couple of hundred recruits and men returned from hospital. So everything was quite easy. What did my concerns matter when the whole Depot had been revolutionized? The Assistant-Adjutant, who had been permanently disabled early in the War, was a much-loved institution. Warmly welcomed by him, I passed a pleasant evening discussing everything except people with pacifist opinions, and on the whole I felt quite pleased to be back inside the sheepfold.

But when I was alone—that was where the difficulty began. What was it—that semi-suicidal instinct which haunted me whenever I thought about going back to the line? Did I really feel an insidious craving to be killed, or am I only imagining it now? Was it "spiritual pride", or was it just war-weariness and repressed exasperation?

What I mean is this—that being alone with oneself is not the same thing as succeeding in being a good-natured and unpretentious person while talking to one's friends. With the Assistant-Adjutant I was "the same old Sherston as ever" —adapting himself to other people's notions and doing his best to be cheerful. But in spite of my reliance on Rivers and my resolve to remain, through his influence, sensible and unimpulsive, none the less in what, for the sake of exposition I will call my soul, (Grand Soul Theatre; performances nightly) protagonistic performances were keeping the drama alive. (I might almost say that there was a bit of "ham" acting going on at times.)

For my soul had rebelled against the War, and not even Rivers could cure it of that. To feel in some sort of way heroic—that was the only means I could devise for "carrying on". Hence, when I arrived at Clitherland, my tragedian soul was all ready to start back for the trenches with a sublime gesture of self-sacrifice. But it was an angry soul, with no inclination to be nice to anyone except its fellow-soldiers. It wanted to see itself dominating the audience (mainly civilians) and dying defiantly in some lime-lighted shell-hole; "martyred because he could not save mankind," as his platoon-sergeant remarked afterwards, in a

burst of blank-verse eloquence of which he had hitherto
believed himself incapable.

The Orderly Room, however, was unconscious of all
this. After spending three idle days at the camp, I was instructed to proceed—not to "some corner of a foreign
field"—but wherever I wanted to go during ten days'
leave. I was unofficially told I could make it twelve if I
liked.

*　　　　　*　　　　　*

My memories of that bit of leave are distinctly hazy. It
goes without saying that the object of going on leave was
to enjoy oneself. This I determined to do. I also made up
my mind to be as brainless as I could, which may account
for my not being able to remember much of it now, since
it is only natural that the less you think about what you are
doing the less there is to remember.

Butley, with its unavoidable absence of liveliness, did
make me to some extent cerebrally aware of what was happening to me. Through no fault of its own, it suffered from
the disadvantage of being "just the same as ever"—except
that all the life seemed to have gone out of it. And I was
merely my old self, on final leave, with Aunt Evelyn doing
her level best to make things bright and comfortable for
me. The pathos of her efforts needs no emphasizing, though
thinking of it gives me a heartache, even now. A strong smell
of frying onions greeted my arrival. This, anyhow, gave
me a chance to say how fond I was of that odour—as indeed I still am. "Steaks are quite difficult to get now, dear,
so I do hope it's a tender one,' she remarked. And afterwards, while we were eating it, " Much as it disagrees with
me I never can resist the merry onion."

Her tired face was just about as merry as an onion. And
the steak, of course, was tough. We hadn't much to tell one
another either. Conversation about Slateford was restricted
to my saying what a good place it was for golf, and there
was an awkwardness even in telling her what a wonderful
man Dr. Rivers was, since his name at once raised the
spectre of my "protest", which neither of us desired to discuss.

No doubt she had hoped and prayed that I might get a home-service job; but now she just accepted the fact that I'd got to go out again.

Naturally, I didn't include Aunt Evelyn among the people on whom I wanted to get my own back by being killed. But I knew that she disapproved of people being pacifists when there was a war to be won. So she suffered in silence; and if I said anything at all it was probably in the "don't much care what happens to me" style which young people go in for when in contact with elderly and anxious relatives. So Aunt Evelyn had nothing to console her except her one form of optimism, which was to try and believe that the Germans were doing so badly that very soon there would be none left.

And the only news she could think of was that dear old Mrs. Hawthorn was dead, which didn't lead to anything except the fact that she had been nearly ninety. Yet if I'd heard about it when I was in my little room at Slateford I should have indulged in quite a pleasant reverie about old Mrs. Hawthorn and the children's parties I used to go to at her house, and how she used to sit there like a queen, her artificial complexion so perfectly put on that nobody minded in the least, though in a younger person it would have been thought highly improper. But that was before the Boer War, and now the "Great One" had killed both Mrs. Hawthorn's great-nephews—those handsome boys of whom she had been so proud when she gave parties for them.

Sitting here in my omniscience I am inclined to blame Aunt Evelyn and myself for not realizing that the only solution for "final leave" was to open a bottle of champagne. But there was no champagne in the house. From patriotic principles, Aunt Evelyn preferred Empire wines. (I don't wish to libel South African hock, but the vine which produced Aunt Evelyn's vintage must have been first cousin to an aloe.) Meanwhile we did our best to be communicative, and after keeping introspection at arm's length from Friday till Tuesday, I went off to Sussex and stayed with the Moffats, who knew all about opening bottles of bubbly; and there I had a couple of days with the hounds and succeeded in being authentically jolly. I can remember one good hunt along the vale below the downs. I hadn't felt so happy since I didn't know when, I thought; which merely meant that while galloping and jumping on a good horse everything else was forgotten—for forty-five minutes of the best, anyhow. And there was no sense in feeling morbid about the dead; they were well out of the war, anyway; and they wouldn't grudge me my one good day in the vale.

After that there was London with its good dinners and an air-raid and seeing a few friends and going to a few theatres, and before I knew where I was, Clitherland Camp had claimed me for its own again.

I was feeling much more cheerful, and I told myself that I intended to lead a life of light-hearted stupidity. At Slate-ford I had been an individual isolated from outside influences, with plenty of time for thinking things over and finding out who I was. Now I was back in the brain-fuddling existence which did its best to prevent my thinking at all. I had to knock out my pipe and go on parade. My time was no longer my own. My military duties, however, were more a matter of killing time than of using it, and we were all merely waiting tó move across to Ireland. So for about three weeks after I came back from leave I was in much the same position as the man in the comic song:

> *I'd got lots of time to do it; but there wasn't much to do*
> *When I was made head-keeper—of the pheasants at the Zoo.*

II

While writing these memoirs, my interest in each chapter has been stimulated by the fact that I nearly always saw myself engaged in doing something for the first time. Even if it was only "going back to Butley", I wasn't quite the same as when I'd last left it, so one hoped that monotony was being avoided. All this, I suspect, has been little more than the operation known as the pilgrimage from the cradle to the grave, but I have had a comfortable feeling that, however ordinary my enterprises may have been, they had at any rate the advantage of containing, for me, an element of sustained unfamiliarity. I am one of those persons who begin life by exclaiming that they've "never seen anything like it before" and die in the hope that they may say the same of heaven.

Time has taught me that this talent for experiencing everyday life with ever-renewed freshness and intensity is the best qualification for making one's memoirs readable. Professional ruminator though I admittedly am, I cannot accuse myself of lacking interest in life, and my main difficulty has been that I absorb so much that I am continually asking to be allowed to sit still and digest the good (and bad) things which life has offered me. A ruminator really needs two lives; one for experiencing and another for thinking it over. Knowing that I *need* two lives and am only allowed one, I do my best to *lead* two lives; with the inevitable consequence that I am told by the world's busybodies that I am "turning my back on the contemporary situation". Such people are usually so busy trying to crowd the whole of life into their daily existence that they get very little of it permanently inside their craniums. My own idea is that it is better to carry the best part of one's life about in one's head for future reference.

As the reader already knows, I have seldom gone out in search of adventurous material. My procedure has always been to allow things to happen to me in their own time. The result was that when anything unexpected did happen to me it impressed itself on my mind as being significant. I can therefore claim that my terrestrial activities have been either accidental in origin or else part of the "inevitable sequence of events". Had there been no Great War I might quite conceivably have remained on English soil till I was buried in it. Others have done the same, so why not Sherston? The fact remains that up to the end of 1917 I had never been to Ireland.

Outwardly it was a dismal journey, for I left Liverpool

late at night and the weather was wintry. Crewe station at midnight was positively Plutonian. Waiting for the Holyhead express to come in, I listened to echoing clangour and hissing steam; people paced the platform with fixedly dejected faces, while glaring lights and gloom and vapour intermingled above them. Crewe station and everyone inside it seemed to be eternally condemned to the task of winning the War by moving men, munitions, and material to the places appointed for them in the outer darkness of Armageddon. This much I observed as I stood with hunched-up shoulders, feeling sombrely impressed by the strangeness of the scene. Then I boarded the Holyhead train, remembering how I used to ride along the Watling Street with the Packlestone Hounds and see "Holyhead, 200 miles" on a signpost; this memory led me to wonder whether I should get a day's hunting in Ireland. After that an "inevitable sequence of events" carried me across to Dublin, and thence to Limerick. There was snow on the ground and the Emerald Isle was cold and crunchy underfoot.

*   *   *

By the time I had been at Limerick a week I knew that I had found something closely resembling peace of mind. My body stood about for hours on parade, watching young soldiers drill and do physical training, and this made it easy for me to spend my spare time refusing to think. I felt extraordinarily healthy, and I was seldom alone. There had been no difficulty in reverting to what the people who thought they knew me would have called my "natural self". I merely allowed myself to become what they expected me to be. As someone good-naturedly remarked, I had "given up lecturing on the prevention of war-weariness"—(which meant, I suppose, that the only way to prevent it was to stop the War). The "New Barracks", which had been new for a good many years, were much more cheerful than the huts at Clitherland, and somehow made me feel less like a temporary soldier. Looking at the lit windows of the barrack square on my first evening in Ireland, I felt profoundly thankful that I wasn't at Slateford. And the curfew-tolling bells of Limerick Cathedral sounded much better than the factory hooters around Clitherland Camp. I had been talking to four officers who had been with me in the First Battalion in 1916, and we had been reviving memories of what had become the more or less good old days at Mametz. Two of them had been wounded in the Ypres battle three months before, and their experiences had apparently made Mametz Wood seem comparatively pleasant, and the "unimaginable touch of time" had completed the mellowing process.

Toward the end of my second week the frost and snow changed to soft and rainy weather. Onc afternoon I walked out to Adare and saw for the first time the Ireland which I had imagined before I went there. Quite unexpectedly I came in sight of a wide shallow river, washing and hastening past the ivied stones of a ruined castle among some ancient trees. The evening light touched it all into romance, and I indulged in ruminations appropriate to the scene. But this was not enough, and I soon began to make enquiries about the meets of the Limerick Hounds.

No distance, I felt, would be too great to go if only I could get hold of a decent hireling. Nobody in the barracks could tell me where to look for one. The genial majors permanent at the Depot were fond of a bit of shooting and fishing, but they had no ambition to be surmounting stone walls and big green banks with double ditches. Before long however, I had discovered a talkative dealer out at Croome, and I returned from my first day's hunting feeling that I'd had more than my money's worth. The whole thing had been most exhilarating. Everyone rode as if there wasn't a worry in the world except hounds worrying foxes. Never had I galloped over such richly verdant fields or seen such depth of blue in distant hills. It was difficult to believe that such a thing as "trouble" existed in Ireland, or that our majors were talking in apprehensive undertones about being sent out with mobile columns—the mere idea of our mellow majors going out with mobile columns seemed slightly ludicrous.

But there it was. The Irish were being troublesome—extremely troublesome—and no one knew much more than that, except that our mobile columns would probably make them worse.

Meanwhile there was abundance of real dairy butter, and I sent some across to Aunt Evelyn every week.

At the end of the third week in January my future as an Irish hunting man was conclusively foreshortened. My name came through on a list of officers ordered to Egypt. After thinking it over, I decided, with characteristic imbecility, that I would much rather go to France. I had got it fixed in my mind that I was going to France, and to be informed that I was going to Egypt instead seemed an anticlimax. I talked big to myself about Palestine being only a side-show; but I also felt that I should put up a better performance with a battalion where I was already known. So I wired to the C.O. of our second battalion asking him to try and get me posted to them; but my telegram had no result, and I heard afterwards that the C.O. had broken his leg the day after it arrived, riding along a frost-slippery street in Ypres. I don't suppose that the War Office would have posted me to him in any case; and I only record it as one of life's little contrasts—that while I was enjoying myself with the Limerick Hounds, one of our most gallant and popular senior officers—himself a fine horseman—was being put out of action while riding quietly along a road in the town which held the record for being knocked to ruins by crumps.

A day or two later, greatly to my disgust, I was despatched to Cork to attend an anti-gas course. I didn't take my studies very seriously, as I'd heard it all before and there was nothing new to learn. So on the fourth and last day I cut the exam. and had a hunt with the Muskerry Hounds. I had introduced myself to a well-known horse-dealer in Cork who hunted the hounds, and the result was that I had a nice little scramble over a rough country about eighteen miles away from the army hut where I ought to have been putting on paper such great thoughts as "gas projectors consist of drums full of liquid gas fired by trench-mortars set at an angle of forty-five degrees".

In the afternoon the hounds were drawing slowly along some woods above the river which flowed wide and rain-swollen down long glens and reaches in a landscape that was all grey-green and sad and lonely. I thought what a haunted ancient sort of land it was. It seemed to go deep into my heart while I looked at it, just as it had done when I gazed at the castle ruins at Adare.

In the county club that evening I got into conversation with a patrician-faced old parson. We were alone by the smoking-room fire, and after he'd been reminiscing delightfully about hunting it transpired that he had a son in the Cameronians. And I discovered that this son of his had been one of the officers in the headquarters dug-out in the Hindenburg trench while I was waiting to go up to the bombing attack in which I was wounded.

We agreed that this was a remarkable coincidence. It certainly felt like a queer little footnote to my last year's experience, and the old gentleman laughed heartily when I said to him "If life was like *Alice in Wonderland*, I suppose I should have said to your son—not 'I think I once met your father in Ireland' but 'I think in nine months' time I shall be talking to your father in the county club at Cork'." We then decided that on the whole it was just as well that the Almighty had arranged that *homo sapiens* should be denied the power of foreseeing the future.

*   *   *

Next day I was back at Limerick by the middle of the afternoon. Going into the ante-room I found no one there except Kegworthy. It was Sunday, and the others were all out or having a bit of extra sleep.

"There's been an old boy up here asking for you. He said he'd come back again later," said Kegworthy, adding as an afterthought, "Have a drink."

I mention the afterthought because it was a too-frequent utterance of his. Kegworthy was one of the most likeable men at the Depot; there were only two formidable things about him: his physique—he was a magnificent heavy-weight boxer—and his mess bill for drinks. I had seen several fine men trying to drown the War in whisky, but never a more good-humoured one than Kegworthy. There were no half-measures about him, however, and it was really getting rather serious. Anyhow the mess-waiter brought him another large one, and I left him to it.

On my way across the barrack square I saw someone coming through the gateway. He approached me. He was elderly, stoutish, with a pink face and a small white moustache; he wore a bowler hat and a smart blue overcoat. His small light blue eyes met mine and he smiled. He looked an extraordinarily kind old chap, I thought. We stood there, and after a moment or two he said "Blarnett". Not knowing what he meant, I remained silent. It sounded like some sort of Irish interjection. Observing my mystification, he amplified it slightly: "I'm Blarnett," he remarked serenely. So I knew that much about him. His name was Blarnett. But how did he know who I was? But perhaps he didn't.

I have recorded this little incident in its entirety because it was typical of him. Mr. Blarnett was a man who assumed that everyone knew who he was. It seldom occurred to him that many things in this world need prefatory explanation. And on this occasion he apparently took it for granted that the word Blarnett automatically informed me that he had seen me out hunting, had heard that I was very keen to come out again, that the hounds were meeting about four miles away to-morrow, that he had come to offer me a mount on one of his horses, and that he would call for me at the Barracks as punctual as the sun. The word Blarnett was, in fact, a key which unlocked for me the door into the County Limerick hunting world. All I had to do was to follow Mr. Blarnett, and the *camaraderie* of the chase made the rest of it as easy as falling off a log, or falling off one of Mr. Blarnett's horses (though these seldom "put a foot wrong", which was just as well for their owner, who rode by balance and appeared to remain on the top of his horse through the agency of a continuous miracle, being a remarkably good bad rider).

He departed, having communicated all that was necessary, and nothing else. His final words were "Mrs. O'Donnell hopes you'll take tea with her after hunting." I said I should be delighted. "A grand woman, Mrs. O'Donnell," he remarked, and toddled away, leaving me to find out for myself who she was and where he lived. No doubt he unconsciously assumed that I knew. And somehow he made one take it all as a matter of course.

Returning to the ante-room I told Kegworthy how "the old boy" had turned out to be a trump card; "And now look here," I added, "I'd already got a hireling for to-morrow, and you've jolly well got to ride it."

My suggestion seemed to cause him momentary annoyance, for he was, I regret to say, in that slightly "sozzled" state when people are apt to be irrationally pugnacious. "But, you bloody bastard, I've never been out hunting in my life. D'you want me to break my bloody neck?"

"Oh, I'm sorry, old chap, I'd no idea you were so nervous about horses."

"What's that? Are *you* telling me I'm nervous? Show me the something Irishman who says that and I'll knock his something head off."

His competitive spirit having been stimulated, it was easy to persuade him that he would enjoy every minute of it, and it was obvious that a day in the country would do him no harm at all. I told him that I'd already hired a wild Irishman with a ramshackle Ford car to take me to the meet, so he could go in that. I assumed that Mr. Blarnett and his horses would call at the Barracks, as he'd said nothing about any other arrangements. So the next morning I was waiting outside the gates in good time. After forty minutes I was still waiting and the situation looked serious when Kegworthy joined me—the Ford car being now just about due to arrive. Shortly afterwards it did arrive, and Mr. Blarnett was in it, wearing a perfectly cut pink hunting coat, with a bunch of violets in his buttonhole. He looked vaguely delighted to see us, but said nothing, so we climbed in, and the car lurched wildly away to the meet, the driver grinning ecstatically round at us when he missed a donkey and cart by inches when swerving round a sharp corner. Mr. Blarnett did not trouble himself to tell us how he came to be sharing Kegworthy's conveyance. With top hat firmly on his head and a white apron over his knees to keep his breeches from getting dirty, he sat there like a child that has been instructed to keep itself clean and tidy until it arrives at the party. And after all, what was there for him to explain? We were being bumped and jolted along a rough road at forty miles an hour, and this obviously implied that the horses had been sent on to the meet. We passed them just before we got there, and Mr. Blarnett revealed their identity by leaning out of the car and shouting "I have me flask" to the groom, who grinned and touched his hat. The flask, which had been brandished as ocular proof, was very large, and looked like a silver-stoppered truncheon.

It was a fine morning and there was quite a large crowd at the cross roads, where the hounds were clustering round the hunt servants on a strip of grass in front of an inn.

Having pulled up with a jerk which nearly shot us out of our seats, we alighted, and Mr. Blarnett, looking rather as if he'd just emerged from a cold dip in the ocean, enquired "Am I acquainted with your officer friend?" A formal introduction followed. "My friend Kegworthy is riding one of Mike Shehan's horses. He's having his first day's hunting," I explained, and then added, "His first day's hunting in Ireland"; hoping thereby to give Kegworthy a fictitious advantage over his total lack of experience.

Mr. Blarnett, in a confidential undertone, now asked, "Will you take something before we start?" Powerless to intervene I followed them to the inn. Mr. Blarnett's popularity became immediately apparent. Everyone greeted him like a long-lost brother, and I also became aware that he was universally known as "The Mister".

They all seemed overjoyed to see The Mister, though most of them had seen him out hunting three days the week before; and The Mister responded to their greetings with his usual smiling detachment. He took it for granted that everybody liked him, and seemed to attribute it to their good nature rather than to his own praiseworthiness.

But was it altogether advisable, I wondered, that he should confer such a large and ill-diluted glass of whisky on such a totally inexperienced man to hounds as Kegworthy? For the moment, however, his only wish seemed to be that the whole world should drink his health. And they did. And would have done so once again had time permitted. But the hounds were about to move off, and The Mister produced his purse with a lordly air, and the landlord kept the change, and we went out to find our horses.

Had I been by myself I should have been sitting on my hireling in a state of subdued excitement and eagerness, scrutinizing the hounds with a pseudo-knowing eye, and observing everyone around me with the detached interest of a visiting stranger. But I was with The Mister, and he made it all feel not quite serious and almost dreamlike. It couldn't have been the modicum of cherry brandy I'd sipped for politeness' sake which made the proceedings seem a sort of extravaganza of good-humoured absurdity.

There was The Mister, solemnly handing his immense flask to the groom, who inserted it in a leather receptacle attached to the saddle. And there was Kegworthy, untying the strings of The Mister's white apron; he looked happy and rather somnolent, with his cap on one side and his crop projecting from one of his trench boots.

Even The Mister's horses seemed in a trance-like condition, although the bustle and fluster of departure was in full swing around them. The Mister having hoisted himself into the saddle, I concentrated on launching Kegworthy into the unforeseeable. I had ridden the hireling before and knew it to be quiet and reliable. But before I had time to offer any advice or assistance, he had mounted heavily, caught the horse by the head, and was bumping full-trot down the road after the rest of the field. His only comment had been: "Tell Mother I died bravely."

"You'll be following to bring him home," said The Mister to our motor-driver, who replied that sure to God it was the grandest hunt we'd be having from the Gorse. We then jogged sedately away.

"Will you be staying long in Limerick?" he asked. I told

him that I might be ordered off to Egypt any day—perhaps to-morrow, perhaps not for a couple of weeks. This seemed to surprise him. "To Egypt? Will you be fighting the Egyptians then?" No, it was the Turks, I told him. "Ah, the Turks, bad luck to them! It crossed me mind when I said it that I had it wrong about the Egyptians."

A quarter of a mile away the tail end of the field could be seen cantering up a green slope to the Gorse. It was a beautiful still morning and the air smelt of the earth.

"'Ark!" exclaimed The Mister, pulling up suddenly. (Dropped aitches were with him a sure sign of cerebral excitement.) From the far side of the covert came a long-drawn view-halloa, which effectively set The Mister in motion. "Go on, boy, go on! Don't be waiting about for me. Holy Mother, you'll be getting no hunting with them Egyptians!" So I went off like a shot out of a gun, leaving him to ride the hunt in his own time. My horse was a grand mover; luckily the hounds turned toward me, and soon I was in the same field with them. Of the next forty minutes I can only say that it was all on grass and the banks weren't too formidable, and the pace just good enough to make it exciting. There was only one short check, and when they had marked their fox to ground I became aware that he had run a big ring and we were quite near the Gorse where we found him. I had forgotten all about Kegworthy, but he now reappeared, perspiring freely and considerably elated. "How did you manage it?" I asked. He assured me that he'd shut his eyes and hung on to the back of the saddle at every bank and the horse had done the rest. The Mister was now in a glow of enthusiasm and quite garrulous. "Sure that mare you're riding is worth five hundred guineas if she's worth a penny bun," he ejaculated, and proceeded to drink the mare's health from that very large flask of his.

*   *   *

As I have already suggested, there was something mysterious about The Mister—a kind of innocence which made people love him and treat him as a perennial joke. But, so far, I knew next to nothing about him, since he took it for granted that one knew everything that he knew; and the numerous hunting people to whom he'd introduced me during a rather dull and uneventful afternoon's sport took everything about The Mister for granted; so on the whole very little definite information about anything had emerged.

"How the hell did he make his money?" asked Kegworthy, as we sat after dinner comparing our impressions of the day's sport and social experience. "Men like The Mister get rid of their money quick enough, but they don't usually make any," he added.

"He certainly gives one the impression of being 'self-made'," I remarked. "Perhaps he won fifty thousand in a sweepstake. But if he'd done that he'd still be telling everyone about it, and would probably have given most of it away by now."

"Perhaps he's in the hands of trustees," suggested Kegworthy. I agreed that it might be so, and nominated Mrs. O'Donnell as one of them. Of Mrs. O'Donnell at any rate, we knew for certain that she had given us a "high-tea" after hunting which had made dining in the mess seem almost unthinkable. It had been a banquet. Cold salmon and snipe and unsurpassable home-made bread and honey had indeed caused us to forget that there was a war on; while as for Mrs. O'D. herself, in five minutes she made me feel that I'd known her all my life and could rely on her assistance in any emergency. It may have been only her Irish exuberance, but it all seemed so natural and homely in that solid plainly-furnished dining-room where everything was for use and comfort more than for ornament.

The house was a large villa, about a mile from the barracks—just outside the town. There I sat, laughing and joking, and puffing my pipe, and feeling fond of the old Mister who had reached an advanced stage of cronydom with Kegworthy, while between them they diminished a decanter of whisky. And then Mrs. O'Donnell asked me whether I played golf; but before I could reply the maid called her out of the room to the telephone, which enabled the word "golf" to transport me from Ireland to Scotland

and see myself cleaning my clubs in my room at the hydro, and deciding that the only thing to do was to go back to the War again. How serious that decision had been, and how blithely life was obliterating it until this visualized memory evoked by the mention of "golf" had startled me into awareness of the oddity of my surroundings!

*   *   *

Every day that I went out with the Limerick Hounds was, presumably, my last; but I was able to make several farewell appearances, and I felt that each day was something to the good; these were happy times, and while they lasted I refused to contemplate my Egyptian future. Mentally, I became not unlike The Mister, whose motto—if he ever formulated anything so definite as a motto—was "we may all of us be dead next week so let's make the best of this one". He took all earthly experience as it came and allowed life to convey him over its obstacles in much the same way as his horses carried him over the Irish banks. His vague geniality seemed to embrace the whole human species. One felt that if Hindenburg arrived in Limerick The Mister would receive him without one tedious query as to his credentials. He would merely offer to mount him, and proudly produce him at the meet next morning. "Let me introduce me friend Marshal Hindenbird," he would say, riding serenely up to the Master. And if the Master demurred, The Mister would remark, "Be reasonable, Master. Isn't the world round, and we all on it?"

He was a man who had few forethoughts and no afterthoughts, and I am afraid that this condition was too often artificially induced. He and Kegworthy had this in common; they both brimmed over with *bonhomie*, and (during the period when I knew them) neither could have told me much about the previous evening. In The Mister's case it didn't matter much; he was saddled with no responsibilities, and what he felt like next morning was neither here nor there. He looked surprisingly well on this regime, and continued to take the world into his confidence. (He was either solemnly sober or solemnly tipsy; his intermediate state was chatty, though his intermediate utterances weren't memorable.) But Kegworthy's convivialities were a serious handicap to his efficiency as an officer, though so far it had been "overlooked".

He did not make a second appearance in the saddle. But about a week after his début, when I was getting formal permission from the Assistant-Adjutant to go out hunting the next day, he suggested that I should take Kegworthy with me and get him, to put it candidly, sobered down. The meet was twenty-three miles away, which made it all the better for the purpose. So it was arranged. The Mister was mounting me, and we were to call for him with the erratic Ford car at Mrs. O'Donnell's house (which was where he lived).

It was a pouring wet morning and blowing half a gale. Kegworthy, who said he was feeling like hell, was unwilling to start, but I assured him that the rain would soon blow over. Mrs. O'Donnell came out on to her doorstep, and while we were waiting under the porch for The Mister, she asked me to try and bring him straight home after hunting. "The O'Hallorans are coming to dinner—and of course we are expecting you and Mr. Kegworthy to join us. But Mrs. O'Halloran's a bit stiff and starched; and The Mister's such a terrible one for calling on his friends on the way back; and it isn't barley water they offer him." At this moment The Mister came out, looking very festive in his scarlet coat and canary waistcoat. He was optimistic about the weather and I tried to feel hopeful that I should bring him and Kegworthy home "the worse" for nothing stronger than water.

The maid now appeared carrying The Mister's hat box and flask; he was helped into an enormous overcoat with an astrakhan collar which Mrs. O'Donnell turned up for him so that his countenance was almost completely concealed. He then put on an immense pair of fur gloves, pulled his voluminous tweed cap down over his nose, and gave Mrs. O'Donnell a blandly humorous look which somehow suggested that he knew that whatever he did she couldn't be angry with him. And he was right, for he really was a most likeable man. "Now Mister," she said, "bear it well in your mind that Mrs. O'Halloran and her daughter are dining with us this evening."

"Be easy about that," he replied. "Don't I know that Mrs. O'Halloran is like Limerick itself? Would you think I'm one to overlook the importance of her?" With these words he plunged deliberately under the low hood of the car, settled himself down, and remained silent until we were about half-way to the meet. Kegworthy, hunched up in his corner, showed no sign of expecting his day in the country to be a success. But the driver was getting every ounce out of his engine, through the din of which he occasionally addressed some lively and topically-local comment to The Mister, who nodded philosophically from his astrakhan enclosure. As we proceeded, the road became rough and the surroundings hilly. And the weather, if possible, grew worse.

"What sort of country is it we're going to to-day?" I enquired of the driver.

"Sure it's the wildest place you ever set eyes on. There's rocks and crags where a jackass could get to ground and sleep easy," he replied, adding, "I'm thinking, Mr. Blarnett, that the dogs'll do better to stay at home on such a day as this."

The Mister opened one eye and remarked that it would sure be madness to go up on the hills in such weather. "But me friend Tom Philipson will give us a bite to eat," he added serenely, "and you'll travel far before you find the like of the old brandy that he'll put in your glass." He nudged Kegworthy with his elbow, and I inwardly hoped that Tom Philipson's hospitality wouldn't be too alcoholic.

For it was my solemn purpose that we should travel away from brandy rather than that it should be an object of pilgrimage. Tom Philipson, it transpired, was the owner of a big house; he also owned some of the surrounding country, the aspect of which fully justified its reputation for roughness and infertility. The village which was part of his property appeared to be an assortment of stone hovels in very bad repair.

I may as well say at once that when we arrived at Tom Philipson's the M.F.H. had already decided that hunting was out of the question, and was about to go home. The hounds had already departed. Hospitality was all that awaited us, and after all there was nothing wrong with an early luncheon in a spacious and remote old Irish mansion. There was nothing wrong with Tom Philipson either. He was middle-aged, a famous character in that part of the world, and had something of the grand manner about him. My recollection of him is that he was extremely good company, and full of rich-flavoured Irish talk. What could have been more delightful than to sit in a dignified dining-room and listen to such a man, while the rain pelted against the windows and a wood fire glowed and blazed in the immense fireplace, and the fine old burnished silver shone reflectively on the mahogany table? I can imagine myself returning to the barracks after such an experience, my visit having been prolonged late into the afternoon while Tom Philipson showed me the treasures of his house. What charm it all had, ruminates my imagined self, remembering that evocative portrait of Tom Philipson's grandmother by Sir Thomas Lawrence, and the stories he'd told me about the conquests she made in Dublin and afterwards in London. Yes, I imagine myself soaking it all up and taking it all home with me to digest, rejoicing in my good fortune at having acquired such a pleasant period-example of an Irish country mansion, where one's host reticently enjoyed showing his heirlooms to an appreciative visitor. I should remember a series of dignified seldom-used rooms smelling of the past; and a creaking uneven passage with a window-seat at the end of it and a view of the wild green park beyond straggling spiral yews, and the evening clouds lit with the purplish bloom of rainy weather.

And then a door would be opened for me with a casual, "I'm not a great reader, but the backs of old books are companionable things for a man who sits alone in the evenings"—and there would be—an unravished eighteenth and early nineteenth-century library, where obsolete Sermons and Travels in mellow leather bindings might be neighboured by uncut copies of the first issues of Swift and Goldsmith, and Jane Austen might be standing demurely on a top shelf in her original boards. And Tom Philipson would listen politely while one explained that his first editions of Smollett's novels were really in positively mint condition. . . .

But this is all such stuff as dreams are made of. What authentically happened was that we had a hell of a good lunch and Tom Philipson told some devilish good stories, and The Mister was enchanted, and Kegworthy enjoyed every minute of it, and both of them imbibed large quantities of Madeira, Moselle, port wine and brandy and became very red in the face in consequence. This made me feel uneasy, especially as they seemed quite likely to sit there all the afternoon; the fact remained that at half-past three Kegworthy was lighting his second large cigar and Tom Philipson was pressing him to try some remarkable old Jamaica rum, though neither he nor the now semi-intoxicated Mister needed any "pressing" at all. I felt a bit hazy in the head myself.

Our host, however, was a man who knew how to handle an inconclusive situation. His manner stiffened perceptibly when Kegworthy showed signs of becoming argumentative about Irish politics and also addressed him as "old bean". Daylight was diminishing through the tall windows and Tom Philipson strolled across to observe that the bad weather had abated, adding that our drive back to Limerick was a long one. This hint would have been lost on my companions, so I clinched it by asking for our motor. In the entrance hall, which bristled with the horned heads of sporting trophies, The Mister gazed wonderingly around him while he was being invested with his overcoat. "Mother of God, it must have been a grand spectacle, Tom, when you were pursuing the wild antelope across the prairie with your gun," he remarked, putting up a gloved hand to stroke the nose of a colossal elk. We then said grateful good-byes to the elk's owner, and our homeward journey was begun.

I say "begun", because it wasn't merely a matter of being bundled through the gloom until we arrived at Mrs. O'Donnell's door. About half-way home, The Mister—who had said nothing since his tribute to Tom Philipson's glory as a gunman—suddenly said to the driver, "Stop at O'Grady's."

Soon afterwards we drew up, and The Mister led the way into a comfortless little house, where Mr. O'Grady made us welcome in a bleak front room, glaringly lit by a lamp which caused a strong smell of paraffin oil to be the keynote of the atmospheric conditions. There seemed no special reason why we were calling on O'Grady, but he handed each of us a tumbler containing three parts raw whisky to one part water. While I was wondering how on earth I could dispose of mine without drinking it, my companions swallowed the fiery fluid unblenchingly, and did not say "No" to a second dose. O'Grady sustained the conversation with comments on what the hounds had been doing lately and what the foxes had been doing to his poultry. The Mister blinked at the lamp and made noises which somewhat suggested a meditative hen. When we got up to go, he remarked in confidential tones to O'Grady, "I have yet to make up me mind about the little red horse that ye desire to sell me." This, apparently, epitomized the object of our visit to O'Grady. My head ached, but the night air was refreshing, though I had some doubts as to its effect on my obviously "half-seas-over" friends. Hope died in me when The Mister, after getting into the car, instructed the driver to "stop at Finnigan's".

I did not ask The Mister why he wanted to stop at Finnigan's, nor did I ask him not to. At the best of times he wasn't a man whose wishes one felt inclined to frustrate, and he was now alcoholically impervious to suggestion. He had it in mind that he wanted to stop at Finnigan's, and he had nothing else in mind, one concluded. The only information he volunteered was that Finnigan was an old friend of his. "I knew him when I had but one coat to my back." It would have been useless to remind him that his dinner-coat awaited him at Mrs. O'Donnell's, and that his heavily-enveloped form had been by no means steady

on its legs when he emerged from O'Grady's. There was
nothing now that I could do except assist him out of the
car and steer him through Finnigan's front door, which was
open to all-comers, since it was neither more nor less than a
village pub. In the bar-parlour about a dozen Irish characters were increasing the sale of malted spirits and jabbering with vehement voices. They welcomed The Mister like
one of themselves, and his vague wave of a fur-gloved hand
sufficed to signify "whiskies all round" and a subsequent
drinking of The Mister's health. "Long life to ye, Mister
Blarnett," they chorused, and The Mister's reply was
majestic. "Long life to ye all, and may I never in me grandeur forget that I was born no better than any one of you
and me money made in America." His voice was husky,
but the huskiness was not induced by emotion. The air was
thick with bad tobacco smoke and I was longing to be back
in Limerick, but there was something very touching in the
sight of the tipsy old Mister. There he sat in his scarlet coat,
nodding his white head and beaming hazily around him,
every bit as glad to be among these humble people as he
had been in Tom Philipson's fine house. More at home,
perhaps, in his heart of hearts, and dimly aware of his
youth and those hard times before he went to the States
and—Heaven knows how—made, and failed to be swindled
out of—his fortune. Kegworthy and I were completely out
of the picture (I, because I felt shy, and Kegworthy because he was in a condition verging on stupor). Meanwhile
Finnigan, elderly and foxy-faced, leant his elbows on the
bar and held forth about the troubled state of the country.
"There'll be houses burnt and lives lost before the year's
ended," he said, "and you officers, friends of Mr. Blarnett's though you be, had better be out of Ireland than in
it, if you set value on your skins." A gruff murmur greeted
this utterance, and I took a sip of my whisky, which half-
choked me and tasted strong of smoke. But The Mister remained seraphically unperturbed. He rose unsteadily, was
helped into his overcoat, and then muttered the following
valediction: "I'd be remaining among you a while longer,
boys, but there's company expected at Mrs. O'Donnell's,

and it's my tuxedo I'll be wearing to-night and the pearl studs to my shirt." Swaying slightly, he seemed to be collecting his thoughts for a final effort of speech; having done so, he delivered the following cryptic axiom: "In politics and religion, be pleasant to both sides. Sure, we'll all be dead drunk on the Day of Judgment." Table-thumpings and other sounds of approval accompanied him as he staggered to the door, having previously emptied all his loose silver into the hand of his old friend Finnigan. During the last stage of the journey he was warblesome, singing to himself in a tenor crooning that seemed to come from a long way off. I entered Mrs. O'Donnell's door with one of them on each arm.

Explanations were unnecessary when she met us in the hall. A single glance showed her how the day's hunting had ended. I had brought them back, and they were both of them blind to the world.

This was unfortunate, and should have precluded their presence at the dinner-table. But Mrs. O'Donnell had already got herself into a dark green bespangled evening dress and was deciding to be undaunted. I was about to suggest that I should take Kegworthy straight home, when she drew me aside and said in an urgent undertone, "They've three-quarters of an hour in which to recover themselves. For the love of God make Kegworthy put his head in cold water, and I'll be getting The Mister up to his room." Her large and competent presence created optimism, so I carried out her instructions and then deposited Kegworthy in the drawing-room. His manner was now muzzily morose, and I couldn't feel any confidence in him as a social asset. Mrs. O'Donnell bustled back, and she and I kept up appearances gallantly until Mrs. O'Halloran and her daughter were announced. Mrs. O'Halloran was what one might call a semi-dowager; the first impression she made on me was one of almost frumpishly constrained dignity, and the impression remained unaltered throughout the evening. She moved in an aura of unhurrying chaperonage and one felt disapproval in the background of her mind. She began by looking very hard at my field boots, whereupon Mrs. O'Donnell enlivened the situation with a fluent and even florid account of the day's adventures.

"Miles and miles they went in the wild weather, and the hounds not able to hunt—God be praised for that, for my heart was in my mouth when I thought of The Mister destroying himself over those bogs and boulders on the Mullagharier Mountains. And then what must Clancy's car do but break down twice on the way home and they five miles from anywhere." Mrs. O'Halloran signified her acceptance of the story by a stiff inclination of her head, which was surmounted by two large lacquered combs and an abbreviated plume dyed purple. She herself seemed to have travelled many miles that evening—from the end of the eighteenth century perhaps—drawn over rough roads at a footpace in some lumbering, rumbling family coach. This notion had just crossed my mind when The Mister made his appearance, which was impeccable except for the fact that he was carrying in one hand a glass of something which I assumed to be whisky.

By some Misterish miracle he had recovered his equilibrium—or leguilibrium—and was quite the grand seigneur in his deportment. His only social disadvantage was that he seemed incapable of articulate utterance. Whenever a remark was made he merely nodded like a mandarin. Kegworthy also was completely uncommunicative, but looked less amiable. We followed the ladies into the dining-room, and thus began a dinner which largely consisted of awful silences. At one end of the table sat The Mister; Mrs. O'Halloran was to the right of him and Miss O'Halloran was to the left of him. Next to Miss O'Halloran sat me; Mrs. O'Donnell, of course, faced The Mister, so Kegworthy's position may be conjectured. He was, beyond all conjecture, sitting beside Mrs. O'Halloran.

Mrs. O'Donnell and I did all the work. Kegworthy being a non-starter, she talked across him to Mrs. O'Halloran, while I made heavy weather with Miss O'Halloran, who relied mainly on a nervous titter, while her mamma relied entirely on monosyllabic decorum. As the meal went on I became seriously handicapped by the fact that I got

what is known as "the giggles". Every time I looked across
at Mrs. O'Halloran her heavily powdered face set me off
again, and I rather think that Mrs. O'Donnell became
similarly affected. The Mister only addressed two remarks
to Mrs. O'Halloran. The first one referred to the European
war. "Tom Philipson was telling me to-day that we should
be putting more pressure on Prussia." Mrs. O'Halloran
glacially agreed, but it led to nothing further, as her attention was distracted by Kegworthy, who, in attacking a slab
of stiff claret jelly, shot a large piece off his plate, chased it
with his spoon, and finally put it in his mouth with his fingers. This gave me an excuse to laugh aloud, but Mrs.
O'Halloran didn't even smile. When the port had been
round once The Mister raised his glass and said, with a
vague air of something special being expected of him. "If
there's one man in Limerick I esteem, sure to God it's your
husband. Long life to Mr. O'Halloran." At this, Kegworthy, who had been looking more morose than ever,
made his only audible contribution to the festive occasion.

"Who the hell's O'Halloran?" he enquired. His intonation implied hostility. There was, naturally enough, a
ghastly pause in the proceedings. Then Mrs. O'Donnell
arose and ushered her guests out of the room in good order.

There I sat, and for a long time neither of my companions moved. Closing my eyes, I thought about that
dinner-party, and came to the conclusion that it had been
funny.

When I opened them again I ascertained that both The
Mister and Kegworthy were fast asleep. Nothing more remains to be told, except that soon afterwards I took Kegworthy home and put him to bed.

*   *   *

On my last day in Ireland I went out in soft sunshiny
weather for a final half-day with the hounds. The meet was
twelve miles off and I'd got to catch the 4.30 train to Dublin, so I had to keep a sharp eye on my watch. The Mister
was mournful about my departure, and anathematized the
Egyptians wholeheartedly, for he couldn't get rid of his

notion that it was they who were requiring my services as a soldier. I felt a bit mournful myself as my eyes took in the country with its distant villages and gleams of water, its green fields and white cottages, and the hazy transparent hills on the horizon—sometimes silver-grey and sometimes that deep azure which I'd seen nowhere but in Ireland.

We had a scrambling hunt over a rough country, and I had all the fun I could find, but every stone wall I jumped felt like good-bye for ever to "this happy breed of men, this little world", in other words the Limerick Hunt, which had restored my faith in my capacity to be heedlessly happy. How kind they were, those friendly fox-hunters, and how I hated leaving them.

At half-past two The Mister and I began to look for Clancy's car, which contained his groom and was to take us home. But the car was on the wrong side of a big covert, and while we were following it, it was following us. Much flustered, we at last succeeded in encountering it, and Clancy drove us back to Mrs. O'Donnell's in a wild enthusiastic spurt.

Mrs. O'Donnell had a woodcock ready for my tea, and I consumed it in record time. Then there was a mad rush to the station, where my baggage was awaiting me, plus a group of Fusilier friends. The Assistant-Adjutant was at his post, assuring the engine driver that he must on no account start without me, mail-train or no mail-train. With thirty seconds to spare I achieved my undesirable object, and the next thing I knew was that I was leaning out of the carriage window and waving good-bye to them all—waving good-bye to warm-hearted Mrs. O'Donnell— waving good-bye to the dear old Mister.

PART THREE: SHERSTON'S DIARY:
FOUR MONTHS

I

Wednesday, February 13th. Left Southampton on Monday evening and got to Cherbourg by 2 a.m. Stayed last night at Rest Camp about three miles out, close to large château, used as Red Cross hospital. It is a mild grey morning, with thrushes singing like spring. I am a little way from the camp, sitting on a bundle of brushwood under a hedge. The country round, with its woods of pine, oak, and beech, and its thorn and hazel hedges, might be anywhere in the home counties—Surrey for preference.

I came up on deck on the *Antrim* on Tuesday morning at 6.30, and found we were in Cherbourg harbour.

It was just before dawn—everything asleep and strange, with lights burning round the harbour and on shore. Slowly the dark water became steel-grey and the clouded sky whitened, and the foreign hills and houses emerged from obscurity. All the while the ship hissed and steamed and the wind hummed in the rigging. This is the third time in three years that I've been in France on February 13th. A magpie is scolding among the beeches, and the wind (south-west) bustles among the bare twigs. I have just recaptured that rather pleasant feeling of detachment from all worldly business which comes when one is "back at the War". Nothing much to worry and distract one except the usual boredoms and irritations of "being mucked about" by the army.

To-day we start our 1446-mile train journey to Taranto. It takes more than a week. My companions are Hooper, Howell and Marshall. Camp-commandant (promoted from sergeant-major to major?) asked us: "Anythink else you officers may wish to partake of? . . ."

Have just picked a primrose. Wonder when I shall see another.

February 14th. 6.30 p.m. Have been twenty-seven hours in the train. Not much room to move in our compartment, what with kit and boxes for provisions, which we use as tables and put our candles on. Marshall, very good at finding out things beforehand, bought primus stoves, café-au-lait, and all sorts of useful things at Cherbourg. M. is the best of the three. About 21: big and capable; pockets usually bulging; hopes to be a doctor. Sort of chap who never grumbles—always willing to be helpful. I read most of the time, and they play cards continuously. . . . "Twist; stick", etc. . . . Halt at Bourges to draw rations. Have been reading Pater on Leonardo da Vinci! Funny mixture of crude reality and inward experience. Feel much more free to study other people than last time I was doing this sort of thing. More detached and selfless, somehow. But perhaps it's only because I don't play "Nap" and have been reading Pater—"this sense of the splendour of our experience and its awful brevity".

February 15th. Awoke to find a bright frosty morning and the train in a station for an hour's halt. Crawled on to St. Germain (15 kilos from Lyons). Got there at 12.30 after going through fine country, fir-wooded hills and charming little valleys threaded by shallow rivers. Saw some oxen hauling a tree and a boy standing looking down at the train. The sun shone gloriously and warmed my face as I craned from the window to take in as much of this new part of France as I could. We stay at a rest camp near the station. Bath and lunch and then I went marketing with Marshall. The blue Saône or Rhône—don't know which it is—flowing nobly along. We leave again to-night. Am writing this in Y.M.C.A. hut after dinner. Entertainment going on. Jock sergeant reciting poem by R. W. Service; nervous lance-corporal sang "The truth or a lie, which shall it be?" in a weak voice without any emphasis.

February 17th. 1.30 p.m. Train crawling toward Italian frontier. Bright sun and cold wind. Hard frost last two nights. Feeling ill with fever and chill on insides. Left St.

Germain 2 a.m. yesterday. Bitterly cold in the train. Went through Avignon, Cannes, Nice, etc., and along by the sea in late afternoon. A gaudy parched-looking tourist region. Flowers thrown to the troops and general atmosphere of Cook's tour. Groups of black soldiers in red fez and blue uniform seen at street-ends in brassy sunshine. Beyond Nice the sea looked less "popular", softly crashing on the brimming rocks in the dusk, and I heard it at times during the night, half-sleeping on the seat with my feet somewhere near Marshall's face. Daylight, red and frosty, found us beyond Genoa after much rumbling and clanking through short tunnels in the dark.

February 18th. (Monday morning.) Through Novi and Vochera, where we halt for lunch. Funny way of seeing Italy for the first time, but better than nothing, and inexpensive. Glaring sunlight and cold wind. All the afternoon we crawl through vinelands, with low, blue, delicate-edged hills a few miles away till the sun goes down and leaves an amethyst glow on the horizon, and at 7.30 we reach Bologna.

Jolly companionship of the journey, in spite of animal squalor and so on. Hooper rather hipped and fussy—bad campaigner I fear. Youthful charm and good looks but absence of guts. Howell sensible and philosophic. Was a schoolmaster and played football for Wales. Marshall an absolute marvel, with his jolly face and simple jokes. Tells Hooper to come off his perch and put the kettle on, which isn't well received by the golden-haired one.

February 19th. After a night journey of freezing gloom, the train stopping occasionally at cavernous stations and my insides still behaving atrociously, we reached Faenza about 3 a.m. Turned out at 8 to a sunlit morning and soon found ourselves washing and drinking coffee in a hotel, moderately comfortable. Tall clean narrow streets; market place full of gossip and babble of cloaked and hooded unshaven middle-aged men, with a sprinkling of soldiers in grey with yellow collars. The fountain was festooned with ice, like melted lead.

February 20th. Left Faenza 9 p.m. and began the journey

along the Adriatic coast. Cold morning; snow lying thin and half-melting; grey sky. On our right the low hills streaked with white. On the left (how accurate I am) the flat lavender sea, flecked and broken with foam, and the slate-coloured horizon. Breakfast at Castellamarie.

Foggia about 11 p.m. Still very cold.

February 21st. Awoke in twilight to find we were going through olive orchards (hoary ancients bent and twisted), with rough stone walls. First time I've seen olive trees. Then the sun came up and dazzled me through almond blossom, with delicate glimpses of the Adriatic a mile or two away. Quite idyllic.

About noon, we come to Brindisi (about which I know nothing except Edward Lear's limerick), and I take a shower bath and dry myself in the sun and a bracing breeze, in a garden near the railway where "ablution-sheds", etc. are put up among fig trees, vine-pergola, and almond trees, with a group of umbrella pines at one end shadowing an old stone seat for summer afternoons. Felt like staying there.

On again about 3—the final stage to Taranto—crossing a flat cultivated plain fringed and dotted with tufts and cloudy haze of pink and white blossom, with green of prickly pears(?) and young corn, the wind swaying the dull silver of tossing olive trees—all in the glare of spring sunshine. Bare fig trees are the most naked trees I've ever seen.

At sunset we passed Grottaglie, a town on a hill; flat-roofed white houses, one above another, and an old brown castle with a tower and sheer wall at the top of it all. Orchards in bloom below, already invaded by shadow. The town faced west, and seemed lit from within, smouldering and transparent and luminous like a fire-opal. It looked like a dream city. (Probably a damned smelly place for all that.) Arrived Taranto about 9, in moonlight.

Friday, February 22nd, 6 p.m. In a tent; rest camp. Walked along the harbour after lunch in glaring sunshine and shrewd wind. Blue water; rusty parched hills away on the other side. Towns far away like heaps of white stones. Glad of my good field-glasses, I sat on a rock and listened to the slapping gurgle of the water (clear as glass), while the other three straddled along the path, swinging their sticks and looking rather out of place without a pier. This journey will always come back to me when I think of an absurd song which everyone sings, hums, whistles, and shouts incessantly. "Good-bye-ee; don't cry-ee; wipe the tear, baby dear, from your eye-ee," etc. There is something a bit grown-up-babyish about Marshall's good-humoured face; the song suits him somehow!

Slept in the train again last night—alongside the station platform—and had my watch stolen. (I'd put it on my box-table near the window, so the thief had only to put his hand in.) Luckily my fire-opal was round my neck, but losing one's watch is pretty serious. All sorts of officers here —many on their way home on leave. Not many intelligent sensitive faces. (The doctors look different from the others, mostly with wise, kind faces.) The usual crowd playing poker in the mess all the time. Staff-officers, colonels, majors, Australians, flying-men—all sorts—their eyes meet one's own for a moment and then slide down to look for a medal-ribbon.

After dinner I came out into the chilly moonlight; the moonlight-coloured bell-tents had tracery of shadows on them from the poor old olive trees that are left high and dry in this upstart camp, like wise old men being mobbed. Someone was strumming on a piano in the concert marquee behind our tent-lines. I lifted a flap and peered into fantastic dimness where a few lights made a zany-show of leaping shadows and swaying whiteness. On the stage (looked at from behind) a group was rehearsing. A big man was doing a bit of gag before stepping back two paces to begin his song. "Give 'em a bit of Fred Emney!" someone shouted. Then a small man jumped into the light and did some posturing—chin out and curved Hebrew beak coming down to a thin-lipped mouth.

Another little Jew whispered to me (I was now inside the tent) "That's Sid Whelan—the other's his brother Albert" —evidently expecting me to be thrilled. They must have been well-known comedians. (All of them belong to the Jewish Battalion, which is awaiting embarkation here.)

Rumour in the mess to-night that "Jericho has fallen".

February 24th. Am now on board the P. and O. boat *Kashgar*. Lying in my bunk alone with Conrad's *Chance* and feeling all the better for being comfortable. Across the cabin steals a patch of dusty evening sunshine. Feet pace the deck above; cabin doors slam down below. The swish of the sea and the drone of a gusty breeze; and me in the middle of the longest journey of my life. Boat still in harbour.

February 26th. 7 a.m. Feeling much better this morning after headache and feverishness since Sunday night. Boat got under way yesterday afternoon and has since been ploughing the smooth Mediterranean—very well-behaved voyage so far. When going on deck for boat-drill, officers sing "Nearer my God to Thee". Can't say I've observed anything interesting so far. The sea is rather like a Royal Academy picture and the officer-conversations dull beyond description. I don't feel much sympathy for them. (I've felt pretty rotten, though, since Sunday.) But they seem so self-satisfied, with their card-playing and singing "Chu-Chin-Chow", etc. Outside the saloon door one passes from cheap cigarette smoke to what Conrad calls "the brilliant evidence of the awful loneliness of the hopeless obscure insignificance of our globe lost in the splendid revelation of a glittering soulless universe". (A bit over-written surely! Must avoid that sort of thing myself.)

The Gulf of Taranto was a level steel-blue plain. Low on the horizon, the mountainous coast was like a soft rain-cloud on the sea—a ragged receding line of hills extending to dim capes and shoals which merged themselves in the hazy romance of sunset. This was the last I saw of Italy. On the other side of the ship it was already night, with a full moon dancing on the waves.

That was written by me (not Conrad) on Monday evening. But I really must try not to be so bloody serious.

February 27. Weather fine. Brain refuses to work. Still feeling rather seedy.

February 28. Arrived Alexandria after exactly three days' voyage.

A clear, gentle-coloured afternoon; blue sea; creamy, brick-red, terra-cotta, and grey city; wharves and docks with drifting smoke and thickets of masts and funnels. Sunshine, not glaring. Everything breezy, cheerful, and busy.

British officers watch it all for a while, nonchalantly—then go below for tea. I also; no more excited than the rest of them. . . .

Shall I find anything tremendous and heroic out here, I wonder? Troops in a warm-climate sideshow. Urbane, compared with France. Rather the same sort of thing as this dock with its glassy dark water and mild night air; stars, gold moon, dark ships, quiet lights, and sound of soldiers singing—safe in port once more.

March 2. Left Alexandria 10.30 last night. Arrived Base Camp, Kantara, 10 this morning. Bought a watch in Alexandria. It is hexagonal and was very expensive. If anything like the face of the dago who sold it to me, it will let me down badly as regards time-keeping.

Same day. (No. 1 Base Depot.) Lying in tent. Valise spread on sand. Glare of sunshine outside. Splitting headache (inside).

Sounds. Thrumming of piano in officers' mess—not quite out of earshot.

Lorries rumbling along road fifty yards away. Troops marching and whistling. Bagpipes—a long way off. (So is Scotland.) Egyptian labourers go past, singing a monotonous chorus, which seems to go up into the light, somehow.

Officers' Mess; analysis. Drinks; drinks. Writing some letters. Someone says "Only one mail in the last three weeks." Bored men reading stale *Bystanders* and other illustrated papers. Amy Woodforde Finden's oriental popularities being pot-pourri'd on the tin-kettle piano. Otherwise anteroom quite cool and pleasant. Slim grey birds chirping in the roof. Onions for lunch. Why put that down, I wonder? . . . Wounded officer back from hospital said to me "They bung you back quick enough nowadays. I can hardly walk!"

This morning. Suez Canal from train. Garden at Ismalia

—a bit of blossom and greenery among sandy wastes. Waiting at Canal bridge for two big ships to go by. Talked to two Irish officers in the train. One knew Ledwidge the poet, and said "he could imitate birds and call them to him"—a tiny glimpse of "real life" in this desert of officer mentality. Am feeling ill and keep on coughing.

March 4. Marshall and I posted to 25th Battalion to-day. Moved across to Yeomanry Base Camp (half a minute's walk!). Another day of arid sunshine and utter blankness. The sand and the tents and the faces—all seem meaningless. Just a crowd of people killing time. Time wasted in waste places. People go up to the Line almost gladly, feeling that there's some purpose in life after all. Those who remain here scheme to get leave; and having got it, go aimlessly off to Cairo, Port Said or Ismalia, to spend their money on eating and drinking and being bored. One hears a certain amount of "war-shop" being talked, but it hasn't the haggard intensity of Western Front war-shop. The whole place has the empty clearness of a moving-picture. Movements of men and munitions against a background of soulless drought. The scene is drawn with unlovely distinctness. Every living soul is here against his will. And when the War ends the whole thing will vanish and the sand will blot out all traces of the men who came here.

Along the main road that runs through the camp, parties of Turkish prisoners march, straggling and hopeless—slaves of war, guarded by a few British soldiers with fixed bayonets. They too are killing time. One of them was shot last week, for striking an officer.

March 8. Went to Port Said for the day with Marshall. A dreary place; but it takes more than Port Said to depress M. Bought Tolstoy's *War and Peace* and Scott's *Antiquary*. ("Everyman" editions were all they had.) Funny books to buy at Port Said of all places in the world. Seems funny to me, anyhow. Sort of thing that would amuse Rivers.

Watching sunset waves foaming and coming in rather grandly with a breeze blowing across from Asia Minor (rather nice idea, that), I thought of Rivers—I don't quite know why.

Thinking of him always helps. . . . Port Said also provided me with a dozen wire pipe-cleaners at a penny each.
Marshall quite indignant at such profiteering. "No one
here except swindlers" he said.

March 10. Left Kantara yesterday evening. Thirteen
officers in a cattle truck. Got to Gaza after being bumped
and rattled for twelve hours.

March 11. Reached Railhead (Ludd) at 2.30 p.m. Olive
trees and almond orchards. Fine hills inland, not unlike
Scotland. Last night we went through flat sandy places.
About daybreak the country began to be green. Tents
among crops and trees all the way up from Gaza. Weather
warm and pleasant, with clouds. Thousands of camels in
one camp. A few Old Testament pictures of people and villages. Inhabitants seem to live by selling enormous oranges
to the troops on the train.

March 12. Just off to Jerusalem, after sleeping in tent at
rest camp about a mile from Ludd Station. Self and M.
dined in Canteen tent. Talked to Mountain-Battery Major
who'd ridden down from Bethlehem. "Don't go to the
Garden of Gethsemane," he said. "It's the duddest show
I've ever seen!"

First night in Palestine quite pleasant, anyhow. Looked
out last thing at calm stars and clouds and quiet candle-
glow of bell-tents among olive trees. Large black-headed
tits among cactuses. Also a sort of small rook (made same
noise as a rook, anyway). Rain in the night. Then sunshine
and larks singing. Soft warm air, like English summer.
Early this morning, rumble of gun-fire miles away, for
about ten minutes. Nothing grim about this Front so far.
France was grim, even at Rouen.

Same day. Ramallah. Started at 9.30. (Twelve officers and
baggage in a lorry.) Reached 74th Division H.Q. at 4.30.
The road climbed and twisted among the hills, which are
wild and desolate, strewn with rocks and stones like thousands of sheep. Tractors going up with six-inch howitzers.
Ambulances coming down. Leaving Ludd we passed a long
procession of grey donkeys loaded with blankets for the
troops. At the first halt (Latron, at the foot of the hills) I

munched my food in a ruined garden by a stream; frogs croaking and strange notes of birds; wild flowers out.

About 2.30 we entered Jerusalem. Not a very holy looking place. Went straight through into another region of desolate looking hills. Marshall remarked that he wished he'd brought his ruddy Bible with him now. Ramallah is 8 miles north of Jerusalem, on the top of a hill. Taken by us two months ago. Divisional H.Q. a large house with a line of cypresses. Weather cold, grey, and rainy. Yellow flaring sunset. Hills faint purple. Strange medley of soldiers and inhabitants in the narrow village street at dusk. Some of the Hebrews very handsome. Lonely glens and ravines all around, sad and silent, and the hilltops hoary in the twilight. No sound of artillery. In the muddy road I stopped and talked to a man I hadn't seen since I was in the Yeomanry, now a sergeant attached to Divn. H.Q. When I last saw him we were both privates, and in the same troop. That was nearly three and a half years ago, and seems a longish time. They have been made into Infantry, like the battalion I am joining.

March 13. Very wet morning. Our little tent became flooded and miserable, so I went out. Sat in a tent for nearly an hour talking to a private (Middlesex Regiment) while it rained. Told me he'd been twelve years in America with a circus, training trick horses. Gave a gloomy account of the Line here. Very bad country for troops, great hardships, and not much to eat! About noon the sun came out and I walked away from the village. With the better weather the country showed itself as much nicer than it had looked from a distance. Along the stony terraces there are innumerable wild flowers. Red anemones, cyclamen, and others I don't know the names of. Went back along a glen with a cheerful stream, small but companionable. Birds came down there to drink. Sitting on a stone I watched 2 men and 2 women (Arabs) driving some small black and white cattle and two donkeys along the other side of the stream. The cattle turned and looked at me and their owners shouted greetings. I waved back and shouted "Cheeroh!" The cattle-bells sounded just right. Back in the village, lorries, limbers, camel-columns, etc. coming and going, and the same old business grinding on. But I felt as if I'd escaped it all for a few hours.

March 14. Marshall and I walked up to Divisional Supply Depot, about six miles. Then on to 25th Battalion, another three miles through the usual wild hills where the Division have been advancing lately. Fine day. Got there about four o'clock. They are bivouacked on a hillside, along rocky terraces. The Colonel greeted us genially. He is a real live lord. (Something to live up to!) I must now pull myself together and try to be a keen young officer. Colonel evidently thinks me efficient, owing to my M.C. and service in France. Am second in command of "C" Company. Only one other officer. (Company commander in England on leave.)

March 15. Out from 9 till 4, with the Company, working at roadmending. Got very wet. Before we started the Brigadier addressed the Battalion; he stood on the terrace above us, leaning on a five-foot pole. He praised the men for their recent exploits in chasing "Johnny Turk" over the hills and ended by saying that he hoped our efforts would soon get him a Division. The latter remark did him no good at all.

March 17. Heavy rain the last two days. Am sitting in this canvas shelter with my one candle. Men's voices sing and talk gruffly in the bivouacs below. Some are singing hymns. (It is Sunday evening.) Two (B Company) officers here. One an Oxford man (Magdalen); about 25; gentle and diffident; reads good books; not a strong character; I imagine him repeating Kipling's poem "If" to himself and hoping to be a better man for it. The other is an ex-commercial traveller from Welshpool; aged 35, with a broken nose and a slight stammer. A considerable character; very garrulous and amusing.

March 23. Battalion moved 3 miles down the Nablus road to new camp (on terraces among fig trees). Hot day. Thousands of small purple iris out.

March 26. Seem to be getting on all right. Very easy life, mending roads.

The Battalion Doctor has made all the difference to me

lately (mentally). Different species from the other officers. Lean, grimy and brown, he goes grubbing up roots on the hills; knows every bird; rather like a bird himself. Before the war used to cruise about on rivers and canals and remote streams studying wild life. Eyes like brown pools; scrubby moustache; foul pipe; voice somehow suggests brown water flowing. Feels kind about animals (instead of shooting them).

Am learning about birds from him. Went out yesterday and was shown Critchmar's Bunting, Nubian Shrike, Syrian Jay, Lesser Whitethroat, Redstart, Arabian Wheatear, Goldfinch, and Blackcap. Also a Kestrel and some Egyptian Vultures. Can't think what I should do without the Doctor!

March 28. Late afternoon. Quiet and warm. Frogs croaking in the wet ground up the wadi. Small thorn trees make clumps of young green up the terraces. At the end of the wadi there is a water spring; small rills sing their way down among the stones and over slabs of rock. Pippits and wheatears flit and chirp among the bushes, perch on rocks, or are busy in the olive branches. On my way home from a walk, a gazelle got up and fled uphill among the boulders; stood quite still about 500 yards away, watching me. Then trotted quietly away. A free creature.

Evening. Warm dusk. The hills looming dark and solemn all around. Here and there a single dark tree on the skyline. The moon comes up hazy and clouded with silver-grey drifts A warm wind blows across the darkening heights. Below me, the camp is a shrouded glitter of tiny lights scattered on the dusk. Sounds of voices and rattling wheels which come far-off and clear, small sounds of life in the vast silence of the night and the hills. Then an eerie yelping, suddenly breaking off again. Must have been jackals.

I look down on the dim olive-trees where the terraces wind and climb—wild labyrinthine gardens. Huge headstones, slabs, and crags glimmer anciently in the clouded moonlight, like the tombs of giants, heaved and tilted sideways. Some are like enormous well-heads; others are cleft and piled to form narrow caves. Ghosts might inhabit them. But they are older than men, older than wars. They are as man first found them. Now they are ramparts of rock tufted with flowers, tangled with clematis and honeysuckle and briar. Thus I describe my sense of peace and freedom. And as I finish writing, someone comes excitedly into the tent with the latest news from France.

The bulletins are getting steadily worse. Names which mean nothing to the others make me aware that the Germans have recaptured all the ground gained in the Somme battles.

March 31. (*Easter Sunday.*) Out all the afternoon with the Doc. Rain came on and blotted the landscape. (We were on a hill from which the Mountains of Moab are visible on a clear day—rather like a herd of elephants, they look.)

In a ruined tower in a vineyard we smoked our pipes by a blazing fire of dry olive branches. He makes most of the other officers seem purblind, mentally. Says very little about them, and regards them with tolerant and good-humoured detachment. He spotted at once what a good chap Marshall is; but Marshall is being transferred to another Battalion with which he has some previous connection. He will probably be happier there; but I shall miss him.

When I'm alone in the tent I feel a bit heavy-hearted about the news from France, which gets more ominous every day though no one else seems to be worrying much. I read *War and Peace* of an evening; a grand and consoling book—a huge panorama of life and suffering humankind which makes the present troubles easier to endure and the loneliness of death a little thing. I keep my books in a Turkish bomb-box which my servant found for me. It just holds them nicely and the transport officer will be told that it contains "messing utensils". I should be in the soup without something to read!

April 3. 9 a.m. Alone with my notebook on a thyme-scented terrace close to the camp, with the sun warming my face and large white clouds moving slowly across the blue. Bees and flies drone peacefully about the grey rocks; butterflies ramble and settle on thick white clover where a few late scarlet anemones still make a spot of colour. People tell me that the climate of Judea gets bad later on, but it is like Paradise now. A little way off an Orphean Warbler sings delightfully from a thorn bush, producing the most liquid and delicate fantasia anyone could ask for. Old vines are half hidden by the spring growth of weeds and grass. A tiny fly-catcher perches six feet away on a bush, and a redstart preens himself near by. Files of camels plod along the road far below, and limber-wheels crush the stones as they clatter along. (Eight mules to each limber.) Fig trees have a few young leaves. Clematis is over; wild roses are beginning, on big bushes. Down the hill some gunners are busy around their sixty-pounders, turning some sort of wheel with a rattling noise. I watch their tiny arms working like piston-rods. Then the unmechanical warbler begins again with a low liquid phrase, and a pair of buntings flutter on to a crab-apple tree near the ledge of rock where I'm sitting.

Then a whistle blows down by the battery; a motor bike goes along the rough road; machine-gun fire taps and echoes to crashings away among the hills—probably only practice-firing. It is a heavenly morning and a heavenly place. The war is quite subsidiary to the landscape; not a sprawling destructive monster like it is in France. Am now second-in-command of A Company. (C Company commander is back from leave.)

April 4. A hot cloudless day. Saw a lot of griffon vultures; also a flock of what the Doc. says must have been black storks, moving steadily northward—rather like aeroplanes. Wonder where they were making for.

Everyone has quite decided that we are going to France. Probably untrue.

These hills are more lovely every day with everything bursting into flower and leaf. We move down to Ludd on Sunday. I don't want to leave these hills.

Perhaps we shall return. I wonder how I should stand another dose of France. Funny to think that I *tried* to get sent there in January.

April 5. Last night after dinner (we all have it together in a big Mess Tent) there was an episode which is worth recording. The Colonel announced that he was going to have "a selling sweep on where we are going to". The procedure for a "selling sweep" was unknown to me, but there seemed to be a general notion that it was rather a dashing affair to take part in. We all sat round the table and the C.O. acted as auctioneer. First of all everyone took a ticket and then there was a "draw" and the lucky ones drew a bit of paper with a word on it. (France, Salonika, Mesopotamia, Italy, Palestine, Ireland, Submarined and Home were the words.) The whole thing put my back up properly and the C.O. looked none too pleased when I declined to take a ticket. (Now I come to think of it, it must have been the first time I've been really annoyed since I left England! The auction then started, and I must say he did it in a most lifelike manner, with appropriate witticisms delivered in flashy style. Most of the junior officers have no money except their pay, but they felt it incumbent on them to bid, either through a sycophantic desire to please, or because they dared not refuse. France fetched £15; Home £14; and Palestine £20. When he put up Submarined there was a pause, and then I bid ten pounds for it (which was my one bid during the auction). There was no advance on this and it became my exasperating property. At the end there was £94 in the pool, and France had been bought by Major Evans (Second-in-Command) who had also drawn it. (Being a thoroughly decent man he will probably pay back all the money spent by those who can't afford it.) Behind it one felt that they all dreaded going to the Western Front and would have paid anything to stay in Palestine.

It was a sort of raffish attempt to turn the whole thing into a joke and a "smart Yeomanry Regiment" gamble. Everyone knows now that we *are* going to France. All maps were handed in to-day and hot-weather kit cancelled. The M.O. evidently felt as I did, for he went quietly out before the show began.

April 7. (Sunday.) 6.45 a.m. A quiet warm morning; clouds low on the hilltops and the sun shining through. Blue smoke rises from the incinerators of our camp and the one on the far side of the Nablus road. Everyone busy clearing up among the fig trees which are now misty green. To-day we begin our 45-mile march down to Ludd. It is also the first day of our journey to France, or wherever it is we are going to.

These war diaries of mine contain many a note scribbled in that hour of departure when the men are loading limbers or putting on their packs and everyone is in a fuss, except perhaps the present writer, who invariably slopes off to some secluded spot outside the camp or village. From there he hears the noise of bustling preparation—high shouts, clatter of tins, sounds of hurrying feet, "come on; fall in, headquarters"; and so on.

Birds whistle and pipe small in the still morning air, flitting among the clematis and broom, alighting on fig branches or bright green thorn bushes. The hillside feels more like a garden than ever before—an everlasting garden just outside the temporary habitations of men. In half an hour I shall be trudging along behind the column with a lot of baggage mules, trudging away from Arcadia, with not much more liberty than a mule myself.

April 7. 8 p.m. In my bivouac on a hillside near Suffa, after two days' marching. (About ten miles each day.) This morning we started from a point near Ramallah, over 3000 feet up. The early morning sky was clear; low grey banks of clouds like snow mountains above the hills toward the sea. Up at 5.15 and away by 7.40. Reached here 1.30. Passed General Allenby on the way. Hot sun and a breeze from the sea. Pink and white rock roses along the wadis. From this hill I can see a city of tiny lights below and on the opposite slope, where the rest of the Brigade are camped. Stars overhead and sound of men's voices singing and chattering: they seem contented with their lot. Away in the twilight jackals howl, and some night bird calls.

My bivouac is pitched in a tangle of large yellow daisies. (My servant is a marvel; very quiet man who never forgets anything.) A mule brays among the murmur of men's voices (probably saying what it thinks about the war). We are almost in the plains again, at the foot of the grey stony hills. Horrid smell of dead camels in places along the road this morning. Saw a Syrian Pied Woodpecker this evening. Grey with scarlet head and tail. Also a White Stork and a Hoopoe. (Doc. pointed out all three; my eyes would be useless without his help.)

Later. Reading Hardy's *Woodlanders*. Like going into a cool parlour with green reflections on wall and ceiling— after the dust and sweat of marching.

April 9. 10.45 a.m. Latron. (Exactly four weeks ago I was here on my way up.) Started 6.45 this morning. Clear dawn; its cool stillness became very hot by 8. Got here 10. Camp is on a bare sweltering slope near the dusty main road with droning lorries and files of pack animals passing. Low, rolling country, rather brown and treeless; mostly vines and corn. The sea, hazy and distant, shown by a line of sand-hills. After seeing the Company settled down I have escaped to the shadow of a thin belt of small fir trees. Tents, camps, and horse-lines only a couple of hundred yards away, but the place is cool and green, drowsy with the hum of insects and the midday chirping of a few sparrows and crested larks. Out in the vinefield, brimstone yellow with weeds, some Latronians are hoeing busily, thereby increasing my enjoyment of sitting still. Dull march to-day. Ten yards away a patriarchal person is sitting under a tree, regarding me gravely and evidently having nothing else to do. According to Old Testament topography we are now in the tribe of Dan, and I can best describe this old gent by saying that I think he looks exactly like what I think Dan ought to have looked like. After a while a welcome breeze comes from the sea, swaying the firs to an ocean murmur. Then a bird (possibly a bulbul) gives us—me and Dan— a charming flute solo. Dan dozes, and so shall I.

Evening. Out after tea, I found a charming garden beside a clear quick-flowing stream with willows and tall reeds. The garden belongs to a French monastery. Oranges, lemons, and bananas growing. Also some small apple-like fruit with large seeds in them. During a dumb-show conversation, I asked the Arab-looking gardener what these were and he said they were "askadinias" (which sounds like some sort of joke).

Came home wading through huge golden daisies among cactus-like hedges.

April 10. Up at 3.30. Started 5.30. Reached camping ground at Ludd about noon. Clear dawn with larks singing; large morning star and thin slice of moon above dim blue hills. Firefly lights of camp below.

Starting off like that in the grey-green morning is delicious. One feels so fresh, with one's long shadow swaying on, and for the first two hours the country is green and pleasant. After Ramleh (a white town with olives and fruit trees and full of British) it was very hot and the road terribly dusty. No shadow at all now and one ached all over and felt footsore—marching between cactus-hedges with motors passing all the time and clouds of dust. At lunch the C.O. told a story about some friend of his who was in charge of a camp of Turkish prisoners; they gave trouble, so he turned a machine-gun on them and killed a lot. This was received with sycophantic ha-ha's from the captains. Queer man, his lordship.

Note. Sensations of a private on the march. Left, left; left-right, left. 110 paces to the minute.∙ Monotonous rhythm of marching beats in his brain. The column moves heavily on; dust hangs over it; dust and the glaring discomfort of the sky. Going up a hill the round steel helmets sway from side to side with the lurch of heavily-laden shoulders. Vans and lorries drone and grind and blunder along the road; cactus-hedges are caked with dust. The column passes some Turkish prisoners in dingy dark uniform and red fez, guarded by Highlanders. "Make the ——s work, Jock!" someone shouts from the ranks. . . . Through the sweat-soaked exhaustion that weighs him down, he sees and hears these things; his shoulders are a dull ache; his feet burn hot and clumsy with fatigue; his eyes are tormented by the white glare of the airless road. Men in front, men behind; no escape. "Fall out on the right of the road". . . . He collapses into a dry ditch until the whistle blows again.

Evening. April 12. Kantara. Left camp 1 p.m. yesterday with advance party. Very hot; scent of orange blossom. Train left Ludd about 5 and reached Kantara at 9 this morning. When I left here a month ago I hoped I'd seen the last of it for a long time! Felt horribly tired yesterday and wasn't much improved by sixteen hours of jolting and excruciating noise of railway truck.

Every time I woke up my face was thick with sand and grime from the engine. But it was warm, and I had my valise.

It feels positive agony to leave those Palestine hills. Here I sit, in a flapping tent close to the main road through the camp. Strong wind, and sand blowing everywhere. Nearest tree God knows where! Remainder of Battalion arrives to-morrow morning. Our party was getting tents up this morning.

After one o'clock I escaped to a lake, about a mile away in the salt marshes where nothing grows. It was quite solitary except for an aeroplane overhead and a flock of flamingoes. Kantara's tents and huts were a sand-coloured blur on the edge of the hot quivering afternoon. Blown by the wind, the water came merrily in wavelets. I had a bathe in the shallow salt water with deep mud below, and the sun and wind were quite pleasant as I ran up and down— happy, because there wasn't a soul within a mile of me, though it was a dreary sort of place when one came to think of it. Miles of flat sand; dry bushes here and there, but nothing green, and the dried mud glistening with salt. But the water was blue-green; and the flamingoes had left a few feathers on the edge of the lake before they flapped away with the light shining through their rosy wings.

April 15. 9 p.m. Another day over and wasted. Endless small tiresome details to be worried through; and at the end of the day exhaustion, exasperation, and utter inability to think clearly or collect any thoughts worth putting down.

Two men, going on leave to Cairo to-morrow, have just been into my tent for their pay; their happy excited faces the only human thing worth recording from the past 15 hours.

April 19. A week at Kantara gone by. One bad sand-storm. Company training every day 6.30-10 and in afternoon. Sand; sunlight. Haven't been half a mile from camp all the time. Last Sunday night I took a party down to get their clothes and blankets boiled. Waited 2 hours for the boilers to be disengaged, and then 100 stark naked men stood about for an hour while most of their worldly possessions were stewed.

The little Doc. goes away to-morrow to join the 10th Division who are staying in Palestine. I shall miss his birdlore and his whimsical companionship very much.

April 23. Lying in my little bivouac (a new idea which enables me to be alone) I watch dim shapes going along the dusty white road in blue dusk and clouded moonlight. As they pass I overhear scraps of their talk. Many of them thick-voiced and full of drink. Others flit past silently. Confused shouts and laughter from the men's tents behind; from the road the sound of tramping boots. The pallor of the sand makes the sky look blue. A few stars are visible, framed in the triangle of my door, with field-glasses and haversack slung against the pole on the middle. Sometimes a horse goes by, or a rumbling lorry. So I puff my pipe and watch the world, ruminating on what exists within the narrow bivouac of my philosophy, lit by the single lanterncandle of my belief in things like *War and Peace* and *The Woodlanders.*

Since last year I seem to be getting outside of things a bit better. Recognizing the futility of war as much as ever, I dimly realize the human weakness which makes it possible. For I spend my time with people who are, most of them, too indolent-minded to think for themselves. Selfishly, I long for escape from the burden that is so much more difficult than it was two or three years ago. But the patience and simple decency which I find in the ordinary soldier, these make it possible to go on somehow. I feel sorry for them—that's what it is.

For in our Division considerably more than half the N.C.O.s and men have been on active service without leave since September 1915, when they went to Gallipoli. And now, as a nice change of air, they are being shipped back to the Western Front to help check the new German offen-

sives. Obviously they have sound reasons for feeling a bit
fed-up.

"Of course they have! That is why we are so grateful to
them and so proud of them" reply the people at home.
What *else* do they get, besides this vague gratitude? Company football matches, beer in the canteens, and one mail
in three weeks.

I felt all this very strongly a few evenings ago when a
Concert Party gave an entertainment to the troops. It
wasn't much; a canvas awning; a few footlights; two blue-
chinned actors in soft felt hats—one of them jangling rag-
time tunes on a worn-out upright; three women in short
silk skirts singing the old, old, soppy popular songs; and all
five of them doing their best with their little repertoire.

They were unconscious, it seemed to me, of the intense
impact of their audience—that dim brown moonlit mass of
men. Row beyond row, I watched those soldiers, listening
so quietly, chins propped on hands, to the songs which epitomized their "Blighty hunger", their longing for the
gaiety and sentiment of life.

In the front rows were half-lit ruddy faces and glittering
eyes; those behind sloped into dusk and indistinctness, with
here and there the glowing spark of a cigarette. And at the
back, high above the rest, a few figures were silhouetted
against the receding glimmer of the desert. And beyond
that was the starry sky. It was as though these civilians
were playing to an audience of the dead and the living—
men and ghosts who had crowded in like moths to a lamp.
One by one they had stolen back, till the crowd seemed
limitlessly extended. And there, in that half-lit oasis of
Time, they listen to "Dixieland" and "It's a long, long
trail", and "I hear you calling me". But it was the voice
of life that "joined in the chorus, boys"; and very powerful
and impressive it sounded.

*   *   *

May 1st. (*S.S. Malwa. P. & O.* 10,838 tons, after leaving
Alexandria for Marseilles. Three Battalions on board; also
Divisional General, four Brigadiers, and numerous staff-

officers. 3300 "souls" altogether not counting the boat's crew. Raft accommodation for about 1000. Six other boats in the convoy, escorted by destroyers.)

Scraps of conversation float up from the saloon below the gallery where I am sitting. "I myself believe. . . . I think, myself. . . . My own opinion is. . . ."

The speaker continues to enunciate his opinion in a rather too well-bred voice. The War—always the War— and world politics, plus a few other matters of supreme importance, are being discussed, quite informally, by a small group of staff-officers. (I know it is unreasonable, but I am prejudiced against staff-officers—they are so damned well dressed and superior!) After a while they drift away, and their superior talk is superseded by a jingle of knives, forks, and spoons; the stewards are preparing the long tables for our next meal.

S.S. Malwa (not a name that inspires confidence—I don't know why), cleaving the level water with a perturbed throbbing vibration, carries us steadily away from the unheeding warmth and mystery of Egypt. Leaving nothing behind us, we are bound for the heavily-rumoured grimness of the battles in France. The troops are herded on the lower decks in stifling, dim-lit messrooms, piled and hung with litter of equipment. Unlike the Staff, they have no smart uniforms, no bottles of hair-oil, and no confidential information with which to make their chatter important and intriguing. *John Bull* and ginger beer are their chief facilities for passing the time pleasantly. They do not complain that the champagne on board is inferior and the food only moderate. In fact they make me feel that Dickens was right when he wrote so warm-heartedly about "the poor". They are only a part of the huge dun-coloured mass of victims which passes through the shambles of war into the gloom of death where even generals "automatically revert to the rank of private". But in the patience and simplicity of their outward showing they seem like one soul. They are the tradition of human suffering and endurance, stripped of all the silly self-glorifications and embellishments by which human society seeks to justify its conventions.

May 3. I get intolerant and contemptuous about the officers on board and all that they represent. While I'm sitting in a corner reading Tolstoy (how priggish it sounds!) they come straddling in to sprawl on wicker chairs and padded seats—their faces crimson from over-drinking. Fortunately the fact that the Western Front is two thousand miles nearer Piccadilly Circus than Palestine seems to console them. But one gets an occasional glimpse of disquiet in the emergence of a haunted look or a bitter, uneasy laugh. Haunted by secret fear of what awaits them in France (plus the chance of my *Submarined* ticket winning the "selling sweep") they are to be pitied. But the pity needs to be vast, to encompass them all. No little human patronizing pity, like mine, is any use.

I too am tortured, but I begin to see that the War has re-made me and done away with a lot of my ideas that were no good. So I am really better for it, in spite of scowling bitterly at it.

Their trouble is that they can't understand why they are being made miserable by deprivation of everything in life which they want. So their suffering doesn't help them, and they hide from their despair in drinks and oblivion. And life becomes an obscene thing, as it is on this boat. Obscene terror invades the overcrowded ship when those on board awake in the morning and remember their present peril. And I wonder how many of these officers are facing the future undaunted? I mean the young ones—not the middle aged, who will be mostly safe when once ashore. I believe that there is submerged horror in their souls. They cannot think; they dare not think it out. The situation appals them. So they try to forget, and this passes for courage. Their hectic gaiety is the stuff that stimulates war-correspondents to enthusiasm.

Thus I sit and try to reason it out—evolving my notions from scraps of talk and flushed faces that are becoming gross with years of war.

Then my mental equilibrium is restored by a man I used to hunt with in Kent, who comes along and talks about the old days and what fun we used to have. But there is a look in his eyes which reminds me of something. It comes back to me quite clearly; he looked like that when he was waiting to go down to the post for his first point-to-point. And he told me afterwards that he'd been so nervous that he really didn't think he could face doing it again. And, being a shrewd sort of character, he never did.

May 4. Am still studying the psychology of the average officer on board. (Have just been wondering what Rivers would say about it.) One can only pick up surface hints and clues from talk and general behaviour, but I am inclined to suppose that they possess a protective apparatus in lazy-mindedness. "Thank goodness! Civilization again!" they murmur leaning back in a padded P. & O. chair. Cards and drinks and light fiction carry them through. Physically healthy, they know that they are "for it", and hope for a Blighty wound with a cushy job to follow. It is every man for himself. In a battle most of them would be splendid, one hopes. But army life away from the actual front is demoralizing. Remembrance of Rivers warns me against intolerance; but isn't this boat-load a sample of the human folly which can accept war as an inevitable and useful element in the routine of life? Old man Tolstoy says "the most difficult and the most meritorious thing in life is to love it in spite of all its undeserved suffering". But who cares for Tolstoy's wisdom here? Only me, apparently.

During the day I watch the men lying about on the decks in the sunlight, staring idly at the glittering glorious blue sea and the huge boats ploughing along in line—six of us, with about ten destroyers in the offing. (Coming up on deck early this morning I saw one of the destroyers firing at something, so I suppose we are being chased all the time.) Leaning against one another in indolent attitudes, the men seem much nearer the realities of life than the average officer.

I must, however, put in a word for the Divisional General, who has a very kind face and appears to be the best type of reticent regular officer. He is also reputed to be a good general. I watched him playing bridge last night in the gallery above the dining-saloon. He asked the band to play "The Rosary" a second time. "It may be hack-neyed," he exclaimed, "but I love it!"

May 5. In the circular gallery above the dining-saloon a few electric lamps glow with a subdued and golden sobriety which reveals vulgar oak panelling and carved balustrades, bilious green curtains, and a tawdry gilt and painted ceiling adorned with meaningless patterns. The skylight—an atrocity in blue and green glass with the steamship company's crest—is invisible owing to absence of light from above, but the lunette wall spaces below are made alluring by a pair of oleographic representations of simpering sirens doing some dancing. Electric fans revolve and hum, hurling dim whizzing shadows on the walls like ghostly wings. The boat throbs and quivers and creaks—straining onward as though conscious of her own danger which keeps every light shrouded from exterior gloom; the buzzing air is vitiated and oppressive. The smoking-room, with its convivial crowd of tipsy jabberers, is no place to write descriptive prose in. Out here it is quieter. In the saloon below some officers are playing cards; others are occupied with a small roulette-wheel. I gaze down at their well-oiled heads, where they bend over the green tables; I listen to the chink of coins and the jargon of their ejaculative comments on the game, while dusky stewards continually bring them drinks. These are the distractions which drug their exasperation and alarm; for like the boat they are straining forward to safety, environed by the menace of submarines.

Having watched all this for a while, I stumble from a dim passage into blustering darkness and invigorating air. Out there the sea is darker than the sky, but the escorting destroyers are seen like long shadows—scarcely more than a blur on the water, stealing forward all the time.

Gradually getting used to the gloom, I see a sentry looming by the davits, silent above the recumbent sleepers, while the sea races backward cavernous and chill with spray.

All along the decks the troops are sleeping, huddled close together under their blankets. And on their defence-lessness a gleam of stars looks down.

Nothing is heard but the sluicing of the waves and the throb of the engines.

Within are chart-rooms and engine-rooms, and the wireless operator in his little den, and the captain in his stateroom, and all the rest of them whose dutifulness may at any moment become a futile contention with disaster. And outside, the mystery and unpitying hugeness of the sea; and the soldiers whose sleeping forms remind me of the dead.

May 7. A quiet morning with rain clouds and sunshine. We came into Marseilles harbour about 8.30 a.m. It is said that the captain of the boat celebrated our safe arrival by bursting into tears on the bridge.

May 8. Musso. (Rest camp outside Marseilles.) Yesterday afternoon we marched away from the docks at 3.15 and got here at 6.30. The troops were childishly excited by seeing a European city after being in the East so long. The bright green plane trees along the streets gave them particular pleasure. Everyone seems delighted and refreshed also by being able to read yesterday's *Daily Mail*. But it doesn't cheer me to read that "we advanced our line a little nearer Morlancourt, a position of great tactical importance". Two years ago we were living there, and it was five miles behind our Front Line.

Marseilles is a very pleasant looking place with its climbing streets and the grey hills behind. I went there this afternoon. Inspected the Zoological Gardens, as I couldn't think of anywhere else to go! Not much there, owing to the War. In one of the aviaries, among a lot of bright-plumaged little birds, there was a blackbird; looking rather the worse for wear, he sat and sang his heart out, throwing his head back and opening his yellow bill wide, quite oblivious of the others. Somehow he made me think of a prisoner of war.

May 10. (*11 p.m.*) The Battalion entrained and left Marseilles yesterday afternoon. The train has been rumbling along all day through the Rhône country, green and lovely with early summer. Now it goes on in the dark, emitting eldritch shrieks which echo along the valleys. It was a blue and white day and nightingales were singing from every bush and thicket. I hear one now, while the train has stopped, warbling in the gloom to an orchestral accompaniment of croaking frogs. Muttering voices of officers in the next compartment. In here, the other three are asleep in various ungainly attitudes. Young Howitt looks as if he were dead.

Monday, May 13. (Domvast, a village 13 k. from Abbeville.) Early yesterday morning we detrained at Noyelles, near Abbeville. On Saturday evening we were on some high ground while passing the environs of Paris. Gazing out across that city I wondered whether I shall ever go there as a civilian. It looked rather romantic and mysterious somehow, and a deep-toned bell was tolling slowly. Four hours' march from Noyelles. Got here 6.30. Into billets—farmyard smells—all just like two years ago. Weather fine, with a breeze behind us all the way. Country looking very beautiful. But May is a deceptive time of year to arrive anywhere; it creates an illusion of youth and prosperity, as though the world were trying to be friendly, and happiness somewhere ahead of one.

Domvast is a straggling village lying low among orchards with the forest of Crécy a mile away to the west. I went up there this morning in the rain. Endless avenues and vistas of green—very comforting when compared with Kantara.

I feel rather ghost-like, returning to the familiar country and happenings. Buying eggs and butter from Madame in the billets. The servants in the kitchen stammering Expeditionary Force French to the girls. The men in barns still rather pleased with their new surroundings. All the queer Arcadian business of settling down in a village still unspoilt by continuous billeting and a good 30 or 40 miles from the War.

May 14. Sitting in the Company Mess on a fine breezy afternoon copying out and assimilating a lecture on Consolidation of Captured Trenches, which I shall spout to the Company as though it came out of my head, though it is all from the recently issued *Manual for the training and employment of Platoons* which I spent yesterday evening in studying. I now feel rather "on my toes" about being in France, and am resolved to make a good job of it this time. The

manual (a 32 page pamphlet) is a masterpiece of common
sense, clearness, and condensation, and entirely supersedes
the academic old *Infantry Training 1914* which was based on
Boer War experience and caused me much mystification.
Having just evolved an alliterative axiom—"clear com-
mands create complete control"—I sit at the window
watching soldiers going up and down the lane; now and
then a lorry passes, or a peasant with a grey horse. On the
opposite side of the road is a fine hawthorn hedge and an
orchard containing two brown cows munching lush grass.
A little way off, the church bell begins tolling. I tell myself
that I simply must become an efficient company commander. It is the only way I can do the men any good, and
they are such a decent well-behaved lot that it is a pleasure
to work with them and do what one can for their comfort.

This morning we went up to the Forest and did a little
training under the beech trees. "It's like being at home
again, sir," one of the sergeants said to me.

It was nice to watch the groups of men under the green
branches, although they were doing "gas-drill" and bayonet fighting—loathsome exercises. Nice also, to walk home
a breezy mile or two with the column—the men chattering
gaily and cloud shadows floating across the spacious landscape. In the hornbeam hedge on the edge of the forest a
blackcap was singing, and a crow sat watching me from the
young wheat.

Along that ridge, 572 years ago, the Battle of Crécy was
fought!

May 15. Another golden day, fine and warm. In the
afternoon we listened to the famous lecture on "The Spirit
of the Bayonet". The brawny Scotchman, now a Colonel,
addressed two Battalions from a farm-wagon in a bright
green field. His lecture is the same as it was two years ago,
but for me it fell rather flat. His bloodthirsty jokes went
down well with the men, but his too-frequent references to
the achievements with the bayonet of the Colonial troops
were a mistake. Anyhow his preaching of the offensive
spirit will have to be repeated *ad nauseam* by me in my
company training perorations. Such is life!

I have just been out for a stroll in the warm dusk along twilight lanes, past farms with a few yellow-lit windows, and the glooming trees towering overhead. Nightingales were singing beautifully. Beyond the village I could see the dark masses of the copses on the hill, and the stars were showing among a few thin clouds. But the sky winked and glowed with swift flashes of the distant bombardments at Amiens and Albert, and there was a faint rumbling, low and menacing. And still the nightingales sang on. O world God made!

May 17. Took 180 men to Brigade Baths, at Nouvions. Beautiful weather, but much too far; and baths very inadequate. It was 2½ hours' march to get there, and Brigade had told us to go in full marching-order, as the Brigadier wanted the men to do plenty of route-marching. Quite a useful way of sending them to get a clean shirt! I made a row with the Adjutant and got this cancelled, which made all the difference for the troops, who quite enjoyed their outing. But their feet got soft during the journey from Egypt and the hardening process is painful!

May 18. Have just been down the lane to see the Company Sergeant-Major about the armourer inspecting rifles. I feel very paternal when I watch the men sitting about outside their barn—gobbling stew out of canteen-lids, scribbling letters, chattering and smoking or lying asleep in the long grass under the apple-trees, while blankets are spread out everywhere to dry and old shirts and socks hung on currant bushes after being washed. The two company cooks, begrimed and busy with the "cooker", and the orderly sergeant making a list of something on a packing-case. (The Quartermaster's stores are in our yard.)

Some of them look up as I pick my way among them. I think they begin to realize that I am doing my best for them.

I am now "censoring" some of their letters, so I will transcribe a few typical extracts.

1. "Well, lad, this is a top-hole country, some difference to Palestine. It gives a chap a new inside to see some fields and hedges again. Just like old Blighty! . . . There is great talk of leave just now. In fact a party goes to-morrow.

Time-expired men first. I'm a *duration* man. What hopes! Never mind, Cheer-oh!"

2. "Well dear I dont sea any sighn of my leave but if we dont get it soon it will be a grate disapointment to us all for we all expected to get one when we came to England."

3. "The weather has been lovely since I came here: we are nowhere near the line yet. I've been going to the doctor these last few days, *sore feet*, so all I do now is going round these farms buying eggs for myself, so you see I'm not doing so bad."

Sunday. May 19. People send me the weekly reviews from England, but reading political journalism doesn't make much impression on my mind. Life is conditioned by the effort of campaigning, and I can see no further than the moment when I have got this Company back from its first "show" on the Western Front. All my efforts are centred on that, and I have, for the time being, escaped from my own individuality (except when I am writing my diary!) This is not a bad state to arrive at. War has its compensations—for the conscientious officer! . . .

Written as I lie on my bed after lunch. Mice trickling about among the kit strewn on the dusty floor of this ramshackle room with its musty old cupboards, in which the mice live among old black dresses and other rubbish. Handsome Howitt asleep on the floor, with his moody sensual face and large limbs. (As usual he looks as if he were dead.) He is a shy, simple, rather uncouth boy—brave and reliable, I foresee.

"Stiffy" Roberts, the other 19-year-old officer, is stocky and self-possessed and full of fun. Both are inclined to indolence, but very good lads. The other platoon commander is Harry Jones; nearly 40, clean-shaven and saturnine and fluent with jokes and stories. Has knocked about the world, in East Africa and Cardiff. Result—a ruined digestion and a lot of good sense. A knowing old bird. Am not sure how much he can be trusted. Our fourth officer is on leave. (Promoted from the ranks and not very promising.)

Later. It is now 5.30 and I have left them all scribbling down the notes on training which I've given them. The sun blazes from a clear sky; in the orchard where I am sitting the trees begin to lengthen their shadows on the green and gold and white floor of grass, buttercups, and daisies. Aeroplanes drone overhead; but the late afternoon is full of tranquillity and beauty. No one can take this loveliness from my heart.

May 20. This afternoon we marched over to Cauchy, a couple of miles away; hot sun; green wheat, and barley and clover; occasional whiffs of hawthorn smell along the narrow lanes; two red may trees over a wall, and the hawthorn whitening the landscape everywhere.

Our Brigade formed a hollow square on the green hillside above the red-roofed village snug among its trees. The Brigadier stalked on to the scene, followed by the modest Major-General who received the salute of a small forest of flashing bayonets. The General, speaking loud and distinct but rather fast, told us that he'd never been more honoured, proud, and pleased than to-day when he had come to do honour to one of the most gallant men he'd ever known. He felt sure we were all equally proud and honoured. (The men had come along using awful language owing to their having been turned out for this show before they'd finished their midday meal.) He then read out the exploits which had won Corporal Whiteway the V.C. Nothing was finer in the whole history of the British Army. The Corporal had captured a machine-gun post single-handed, shot and bayonetted the whole team (who were Turks) and redeemed the situation on his Battalion front. The General then called for Corporal Whiteway (of the Shropshire Light Infantry) and a clumsily-built squat figure in a round steel helmet doubled out of the front rank of his Company, halted, and saluted. The General then pinned something on his breast (after dropping the pin, which the Brigade-Major adroitly recovered from the long grass). He then, in a loud voice, wished Whiteway a long and happy life in which to wear his decoration, and wrung him by the hand. The little Corporal turned about and was hurriedly escaping to the shelter of the bayonet-forest, but was called back to stand beside the General who called for the General

Salute—"to do honour to Whiteway" Three cheers were then given, and that was, officially, the end of the Turkish machine-gun team till the Day of Judgment.

No doubt the deed was magnificent, but the spectacle wasn't impressive.

One felt it was all done to raise the morale of the troops. The Army is kept together by such stunts. . . . There is a "General Routine Order" which reads as follows: "It has been ruled by the Army Council that the act of voluntarily supplying blood for transfusion to a comrade, although ex-emplifying self-sacrifice and devotion, does not fall within the qualification 'Acts of gallantry or distinguished con-duct'." In other words, blood must be spilt, not transfused. But I am bound to admit that the bayonet fighting lecture and this V.C. parade have had a stimulating effect on the troops. Good weather, rations, and billets have been even better aids to morale, however!

I sometimes wonder whether this diary is worth writing. But there can't be any harm in the truth, can there? And my diary is the only person I can talk to quite openly.

May 21. Another cloudless day. In the morning I lec-tured the Company for fifteen minutes on "Morale and Offensive Spirit". Couldn't help thinking how amused Rivers would have been if he'd been there. What wouldn't I give for an hour with him now! (But the test is that I've got to get through it all without him.) After tea I gave the senior N.C.O.s a forty-minute talk under the apple-trees, and really felt as if I were quite a good instructor. The feel-ing that they like and trust me "gives me a new inside". And I have this advantage, that my predecessor was dead-stale and not at all active-minded. So these splendid N.C.O.s respond to what I try to tell them and are really keen. After lunch we did two hours (full marching order) in the forest. Very pleasant in there among the green glory of the beeches with sunshine filtering through. Prolonged wearing of gas-masks in company training rather trying. It is now 10.30 on a moonlight night with hawthorn scents and glimmerings and nightingale songs. The Boches are overhead, dropping bombs on neighbouring villages. Shattering din and organ-drone of planes going on now. They have been hammering Abbeville heavily lately. Sleeping badly lately, but nothing matters except the Company.

May 22. Cloudless weather again. Quiet day's training. Yesterday I began to read Duhamel's *Vie des Martyres* (a grand book well translated). I expect *he* felt he was in a groove while he wrote it—patiently studying the little world of his hospital with such immense compassion. While reading I suddenly realized the narrowness of the life a soldier leads on active service.

The better the soldier, the more limited is his outlook.

I am learning to understand soldiers and their ideas; intelligent instruction of them teaches me a lot. But I find them very difficult to put on paper. And in these days of hawthorn blossom and young leaves they seem like a part of the passing of the year. Autumn will bring many of them to oblivion. "It is written that you should suffer without purpose and without hope. But I will not let all your sufferings be lost in the abyss," wrote Duhamel. That is how I feel too; but all I can do for them is to try and obtain them fresh vegetables with my own money, and teach them how to consolidate shell-holes, and tell them that "the soul of defence lies in offence"!

To-morrow morning we leave Domvast. Somewhere between Arras and St. Pol will be our area for "intensive training".

Magnicourt. May 24. "Yesterday" began at 2.30 a.m. and ended at 11 p.m. when the Company were safely settled down in billets after 20 miles' marching and 5 hours in the train. (Covered trucks.) We marched away from Domvast at 5 a.m. A warm, still morning with a quiet sunrise glinting behind us beyond the trees and the village. Crossing the Abbeville-St. Omer road, we went through Crécy Forest for about 8 miles. There had been some rain in the night and the air smelt of damp leaves and dust.

Entrained at Rue, one o'clock, and reached St. Pol about 6.30. Marched 5 miles to billets. Strong breeze; much colder. It has rained all to-day and the men have been resting (the whole Company in one huge lofty barn, with nice clean straw). I have got a room up a lane, with churchyard view (!) and a clock ticking peacefully on a shelf. Have just received orders to move again to-morrow.

Sitting here I glance over my right shoulder at the little row of books, red and green and blue, which stand waiting for my hand, offering their accumulated riches. I think of the years that *may* be in store for me, and of all the pages I *may* turn. Then I look out at the falling rain and the grey evening beyond the churchyard wall and wonder if anything awaits me that will be more truly human than my sense of satisfaction yesterday at Rue railway station. What did I do to gain that feeling? . . . There were five of my men who had come too late to get any tea. Disconsolately they stood at the empty dixy—tired out by the long march and herded into a dirty van to be carried a bit nearer to hell. But I managed to get some hot tea for them. Alone I did it. Without me they would have got none. And for the moment the War seemed worth while! . . . That sort of thing reminds me of my servant and the numberless small worries and exasperations which he has saved me from in the past ten weeks. Nothing could be better than the way he does things, quiet and untiring. He is simple, humble, patient, and brave. He is reticent yet humorous. How many of us can claim to possess these qualities and ask no reward but a smile? It might have been of him that Duhamel wrote—"he waged his own war with the divine patience of a man who had waged the great world-war, and who knows that victory will not come right away." His name is 355642 Pte. John Bond. I write it here in case I am killed.

Little ginger-haired Clements, our shy Company clerk, who works so hard, goes home for a month's leave to-morrow. Funny to think that some of us may be dead when he comes back to his documents and "returns". About 150 strong and healthy men, all wondering how soon they'll get killed and hoping it will be someone else. Obvious, I suppose, but a peculiar notion to have in one's head!

May 25. Habarcq. (12 k. from Arras.) We left Magnicourt at 9 a.m. Warm day. Beastly march of ten miles;

very slow, owing to congestion of troops. This is a large
village but very much overcrowded with troops.

A girl watching us pass through a village to-day cried
out in astonishment—"*Ne pas des anciens!*" We certainly
are a fine body of men.

One of our platoons is billeted close to a burial ground,
which they refer to as "the rest camp". "No reveilles and
route-marches there!" remarked a tall, tired-looking man
with a walrus moustache. Getting near the line is working
me up into the same old feeling of confidence and freedom
from looking far ahead. Is it self-defensive, or what?

Sunday, May 26. Very tired to-night. Guns making a noise
eight miles away. I am alone in a large room in the Château—a barrack of a place. Small things have conspired to
exasperate me to-day. But I will read *Lamb's Letters* and
then go to sleep. My window looks out on tree-tops and a
large cedar. (I am on the third storey.)

May 28. Too tired to read or think after two days' hard
work with the Company. Devilish noise last night when the
next village was being bombed and anti-aircraft guns firing. They are over again to-night.

May 29. Inspection by Divisional General. He made a
very pleasant impression, and talked very niccly to the
men. No complaints about my Company, anyhow! . . .
Letters from England seem to come from another world.
Aunt Evelyn wants to know when I shall be coming home
on leave. Damn leave; I don't want it. And I don't want
to be wounded and wangle a job at home. I want the next
six weeks, and success. Do I want death? I don't know yet.
Anyhow the War is outside of life, and I'm in the War.
"Those we loved were merely happy shadows." (Duhamel
again.)

Sunday, June 2. Cloudless weather continues. On Friday
I took the Company to fire on the range; eight miles each
way; out 7.30 to 6. Fired five rounds myself; a bull's-eye,
two inners, and a magpie were duly signalled. My private
opinion is that I never hit the target at all, and I rather
think the Sergeant-Major winked at me when handing me
the rifle!

Yesterday we paraded at 6 a.m. and went seven miles to take part in a Brigade Field Day. Back at 4.30. The men's feet are very much knocked about and boots getting bad. I keep on worrying the Quartermaster about it, but he can do nothing except "indent" for boots which never arrive. Morale of Company very good, in spite of being put through it so intensively. Only three have gone on leave since we got to France. One goes next week; and the rest are *hoping*.

This morning at 8.30 I was shaving (up before 5 the last two days). Below my window a voluntary service was in progress, and about 20 voices struck up dolefully with "How sweet the name of Jesus sounds". It seemed funny, somehow—Jesus being a name which crops up fairly often on Brigade Field Days and elsewhere! Later on the Padre was preaching about the "spiritual experiences of the righteous".

After breakfast I sat under the apple-blossom behind our Mess and read a Homeric Ode to Hermes (not in Greek). It felt a great relief after a week of incessant toil over small details. But it was only a half-hour's respite from being worried by the Orderly Room. Anyhow I feel strong and confident in the security of a sort of St. Martin's Summer of Happy-Warriorism. We are now on G.H.Q. Reserve and liable to move at 24-hours' notice.

After a hasty lunch I spent 1½ hours at a "Company Officers' Conference" and listened to a lecture on Trench Warfare and a discussion of yesterday's Field Day. The Brigadier has warned us to expect "the fall of Paris". (The Germans are on the Marne and claim 45,000 more prisoners.)

But I have my large airy upper-chamber in the Château where I can be alone sometimes. From the window one sees the tops of big trees; a huge cedar, two fine ashes, a walnut, and some chestnuts. All towering up very magnificently. Birds chirp; the guns rumble miles away; and my servant has picked some syringa and wild roses, which are in a bowl by my bed. A jolly young lance-corporal (headquarters signaller) came in to cut my hair this morning; he chattered away about the Germans and so on. Likes

France, but thinks the War can't be ended by fighting. Very sensible. Then he clattered down the stairs (echoing boards) whistling "Dixieland".

After tea the mail came in; a good one for me as it contained de la Mare's new book of poems. I went out and read some of them under a thorn hedge, sitting in the long grass with a charming glimpse of the backs of barns and men sitting in the sun, and the graveyard. All the graves are of men killed in the war—mostly French. But there are flowers—white pinks and pansies.

Then I watched the Company playing football, and getting beaten. And now I must do the accounts of our Company mess.

June 4. Out 7.15 till 4.15. Did a Battalion attack. After lunch a gas lecture, and then we were bombarded with smoke and gas. I was feeling jumpy and nerve-ridden all day. It would be a relief to shed tears now. But I smoke on my bed, and the Divisional brass band is tootling on the grass outside the Château.

I will read de la Mare and try to escape from feeling that after all I am nothing but what the Brigadier calls "a potential killer of Huns". . . .

> *Beyond the rumour even of Paradise come,*
> *There, out of all remembrance, make our home.*

*   *   *

June 5. (*9.30 p.m.*) Yesterday was the first bad day I've had for several weeks and I finished up feeling terribly nervy. This morning I got up, with great difficulty, at 6.30, and at 7.45 we started out for a Brigade Field Day. Did an attack from 10.30 to 2.30, but it wasn't a strenuous one for me as I was told to "become a casualty" soon after the 3000-yard assault began, and I managed to make my way unobtrusively to an old windmill on a ridge near by. There I lay low as long as I dared, and thoroughly enjoyed myself. Below the hill I could see the troops advancing by rushes over the rye-grass of some luckless farmer. Larks were singing overhead and the sunlit countryside was swept by the coursing shadows of great white clouds. I'd escaped from soldiering for an hour, and was utterly content to sit up there among the rafters, watching the beams that filtered through chinks and listening to the creaking silence —alone in that place which smelt of old harvests, and where the rumour of war was a low rumble of guns, very far away. So I am in good spirits again this evening, and my nerve-furies have sailed away into the blue air.

When I rode into the transport-lines this afternoon I saw young Stonethwaite drudging at cleaning a limber, supervised by a military policeman.

He has still got ten days to do, of his 28 days "Field Punishment No. 2" for coming on parade drunk at Marseilles. I gave him a cheery nod and a grin, and he smiled back at me as he stood there in his grimy slacks and blue jersey. I hadn't spoken to him since I "talked to him like a father" when he was awaiting his court martial. He was in the other Company I was with for a time in Palestine, and I took an interest in him, partly because he'd served with our First Battalion in France, and partly because of the noticeably nice look in his face. (He was the sort of chap that no one could help liking.) There was something purposeful and promising about him, even when he was only sitting on a rock in Judea trying to mend one of his rotten boots. I remember watching him playing football at Kantara, and he seemed the embodiment of youthful enterprise. But some of the old toughs got him blind to the world at Marseilles, and when I heard about it I felt quite miserable. So I went into the shed at Domvast where he was shut up and talked to him about making a fresh start and so on. And I suppose he felt grateful to me, standing there with his white face and his eyes full of tears. Seeing him there this afternoon I felt very glad I'd been kind to him. And he is being transferred to the Machine-Gun Corps, where he can begin all over again and be as popular as ever. I mention this little story because it has struck me as such a contrast to that V.C. investment parade.

June 6. (*10.30 p.m.*) Was summoned this evening to an emergency meeting of Company officers in the Colonel's room downstairs.

Large gloomy room, not much lit by a few candles.

C.O., sitting at the end of a long table, looking solemn and portentous, broke the news to us that we are shortly to take over the Neuville-Vitasse sector from the Second Canadian Division. He spoke in hushed tones (as though the Germans might overhear him). As I sat there I thought of the "selling sweep", to which this seemed a natural sequel! Anyhow I am going up to the line for three days tomorrow, with the C.O. and one of the other Company Commanders, to obtain a little experience of the sector we shall take over, and ought to be able to find out quite a lot.

June 8. (In the Front Line, near Mercatel.) Yesterday morning, in fine weather, we rode to Avesnes, and were conveyed thence in a lorry to Basseux (which was the last billet I was in with the Second Battalion). Then on to Agny and lunched at Brigade H.Q. Two mile walk from there up to Battalion H.Q. The devastated area looking dried-up and as devastated as ever. Canadian Colonel with a V.C.— evidently a terrific fire-eater but very pleasant. A guide brought me up to B Company H.Q. in the Front Line, which I reached about 7.30. The Company Commander, Captain Duclos, has been wounded twice and in France 21 months. If he gets one more "Blighty" he'll stay there, he says. In spite of his name he speaks no French but many of his company are from Quebec and speak very little English.

There was a fair amount of shelling last evening; considerable patrolling activity on our side, and much sending up of flares by the Boche. In fact things are much the same as they used to be, except that we didn't sniff for mustard-gas then, and didn't walk about with "box-respirators in the alert position". I don't think I'm any worse than I was at Fricourt and Mametz. I would have enjoyed doing a patrol last night. But I feel a bit of a fool being up here with no responsibility for anything that happens, so it is rather a good test of one's nerves.

These trenches are narrow and not sandbagged. They will be very wet when it rains. At present they are as dry as dust. Very few rats. Company H.Q. is in a steel hut which would just stop a whizz-bang.

Duclos seems a fine chap. He was very friendly last night, and we sat and jawed about old battles and cursed the politicians and the people with cushy jobs—all the usual dug-out talk. And I went to sleep at stand-to (2.30) and woke with the usual trench mouth.

Odd that I should find myself back here, only a mile or two away from where I was wounded (and the Front Line a mile or two farther back after 14 months' fighting!).

I have returned into the past, but none of my old friends are here. I am looking across to the ridge where Ormand and Dunning and all those others were killed. Nothing can bring them back; and I come blundering into it all again to guffaw with a Canadian captain. The old crowd are gone; but young "Stiffy" and Howitt are just as good.

Expect I'll see more than enough of this sector, so I won't describe it in detail. The landscape is the deadly conventional Armageddon type. Low green-grey ridges fringed with a few isolated trees, half smashed; a broken wall here and there—straggling dull-grey silhouettes which were once French villages. Then there are open spaces broken only by ruined wire-tangles, old trenches, and the dismal remains of an occasional rest camp of huts. The June grass waves, poppies flame, shrapnel bursts in black puffs, an aeroplane drones, larks šing, and someone comes along the trench clinking a petrol tin (now used for water). And this is about all one sees as one stumps along the communication-trenches, dry and crumbling and chalky, with a dead mole lying about here and there.

* * *

Inside Company H.Q. I watch another conventional trench-warfare scene. Duclos snores on his wire-netting berth, while I sit at a table with one large yellow candle burning. On the table is a grease-spotted sheet of *The Sussex Express*. Heaven knows why it got here, but it enables me to read "Whist Drive at Heathfield" and "Weak Milk at Hellingly", and indulge in a few "free associations" about Sussex. At the other end of the tubular steel Nissen hut, daylight comes unnaturally through the door;

evening sunshine. The H.Q. runner, a boy of 19, leans against the door-post, steel hat tilted over his eyes and long eyelashes showing against the light. The signaller sits at a table with his back to me, making a gnat-like noise on his instrument. The servants are cooking, with sandbags soaked in candle-grease, and this typical smell completes the picture! From outside one hears dull bumpings of artillery and the leisurely trickle of shells passing overhead. Now and then the tap-tap of machine-gun fire. . . .

(*After midnight.*) Went out about 10 and dropped in for an unpleasant half-hour. The Germans put over a "box-barrage" including a lot of aerial torpedoes. No gas, however. The Battalion on our left were raided, and the uproar was hideous. When it was all over I came back here and read *Lamb's Letters*, which I'd brought with me as an antidote to such performances. I was much impressed by Duclos during the "strafe". He knows just how to walk along a trench when everything feels topsy-turvy and the semi-darkness is full of booms and flashes. He never hurries; quietly, with (one imagines) a wise, half-humorous look masking solid determination and mastery of the situation, he moves from sentry to sentry; now getting up on the fire-step to lean over beside some scared youngster who peers irresolutely into the drifting smoke which hides the wire where the Germans may be lying, ready to rush forward; now cracking a joke with some grim old soldier. "Everything Jake here?" he asks, going from post to post, always making for the place where the din seems loudest, and always leaving a sense of security in his wake. Men finger their bayonets and pull themselves together when his cigarette-end glows in the dusk, a little planet of unquenchable devotion to duty.

Sunday, June 9. I left the Front Line at 3 o'clock this afternoon. Two killed and eight wounded last night. Coming down the communication-trench I passed two men carrying a dead body slung on a pole. "What's the weight of *your* pig?" asked a man who met them, squeezing himself against the side of the trench to let them pass. Colonial realism!

After various delays I got back to Habarcq at 11 p.m. and here I am in my quiet room again, with the trees rustling outside and a very distinct series of War pictures in my head. The businesslike futility of it is amazing. But those Canadians were holding their sector magnificently, and gave me a fine object-lesson in trench-organization.

June 13. Too busy to write anything lately. I seem to be on my legs all the time. On Tuesday we did an attack with Tanks, Sitting on the back of a Tank, joy-riding across the wheat in afternoon sunshine, I felt as if it were all rather fun—like the chorus of haymakers in the opening scene of a melodrama! But when I see my 150 men on parade, with their brown healthy faces, and when I watch them doing their training exercises or marching sturdily along the roads, I sometimes think of what may be awaiting them. (Only a couple of weeks ago one of our best Service Battalions was practically wiped out in the fighting on the Aisne.) And so (to quote Duhamel again) I "realize the misery of the times and the magnitude of their sacrifice."

I have never seen such a well-behaved company. But when their day's work is over they have about four hours left, with nothing to do and nowhere to go except the estaminets. I calculate that about £500 a week is spent, by our Battalion alone, in the estaminets of this village, and every man goes to bed in varying degrees of intoxication! What else can they do, when there isn't so much as a Y.M.C.A. hut in the place? They aren't fond of reading, as I am!

Every night I come back to my big empty room, where the noise of bombardments miles away is like furniture being moved about overhead. And from 8.30 to 10.30 I read and do my day's thinking. Often I am too tired to think at all, and am pursued by worries about Lewis guns and small company details. And while I'm reading someone probably drops in for a talk and I must put down *Motley and Other Poems* and listen to somebody else's grumbles about the War (and Battalion arrangements).

Outside, the wind hushes the huge leafy trees; and I wake early and hear the chorus of birds through half-dissolved veils of sleep. But they only mean another day of harsh realities which wear me down.

It isn't easy to be a company commander with a suppressed "anti-war complex"! When I was out here as a platoon commander I was able to indulge in a fair amount of day-dreaming. But since I've been with this Battalion responsibility has been pushed on to me, and since we've been in France I haven't often allowed myself to relax my efforts to be efficient. Now that our intensive training is nearly finished I am easing off a bit and allowing myself to enjoy books. The result is that I immediately lose my grip on soldiering and begin to find everything intolerable except my interest in the welfare of the men. One cannot be a useful officer and a reader of imaginative literature at the same time. Efficiency depends on attention to a multitude of minor details. I shall find it easier when we get to the Line, where one alternates between intense concentration on real warfare and excusable recuperation afterwards. Here one is incessantly sniped at by the Orderly Room and everyone is being chivvied by the person above him. I have never been healthier in body than I am now. But under that mask of physical fitness the mind struggles and rebels against being denied its rights. The mechanical stupidity of infantry soldiering is the antithesis of intelligent thinking.

Sensitive and gifted people of all nations are enduring some such mental starvation in order to safeguard—whatever it is they are told that they are safeguarding. . . . And O, how I long for a good Symphony Concert! The mere thought of it is to get a glimpse of heaven.

June 14. At dinner this evening I was arguing with young "Stiffy", who has strong convictions of his own infallibility. But it was only about some detail of Lewis-gun training! Also he asserted that I'd got "a downer" on some N.C.O., which I stoutly denied. We got quite hot over it. Then the argument dissolved into jollity and fled from our minds for ever. After all, we'd had a good feed, and some red wine; to-morrow will be Saturday, an easy day's work; and the others had come in to the meal flushed and happy after a platoon football match. "Damn it, I'm fed up with all this training!" I exclaimed in a loud voice, scrooping back my chair on the brick floor and standing up. "I want to go up to the Line and really do something," added I—quite the dare-devil.

"Same here", agreed handsome boy Howitt in his soft voice. Howitt always agrees with me. He is gentle and unassuming and not easily roused, but he gets things done. "Stiffy" is thick-set and over-confident and inclined to contradict his elders, but good-natured.

I went out into the cool, grey, breezy evening. Miles away the guns muttered and rumbled as usual. "Come on, then; come on, you poor fool!" they seemed to be saying. I shivered, and came quickly up to the Château—to this quiet room where I spend my evenings ruminating and trying to tell myself the truth—this room where I become my real self, and feel omnipotent while reading Tolstoy and Walt Whitman (who had very little in common, I suppose, except their patriarchal beards). "I want to go up to the Line and really do something!" I had boasted thus in a moment of vin rouge elation, catching my mood from those lads who look to me as their leader. How should they know the shallowness of my words? They see me in the daylight of my activities, when I must acquiesce in the evil that is war. But in the darkness where I am alone my soul rebels against what we are doing. "Stiffy", grey-eyed and sensible and shrewd; Howitt, dark-eyed and loverlike and thoughtful; how long have you to live—you in the plenitude of youth, in your pride of being alive, your ignorance of life's narrowing and disillusioning road? It may be that I shall live to remember you as I remember all those others who were my companions for a while and whose names are no longer printed in the Army List. What can I do to defeat the injustice which claims you, perhaps, as victims, as it claimed those ghostly others? Sitting here with my one candle I know that I can do nothing. "Save his own soul he has no star."

PART FOUR: FINAL EXPERIENCES

I

I never went back to those trenches in front of Neuville-Vitasse.

The influenza epidemic defied all operation orders of the Divisional staff, and during the latter part of June more than half the men in our brigade were too ill to leave their billets. Owing to the fact that I began a new notebook after June 14th, and subsequently lost it, no contemporary record of my sensations and ideas is available; so I must now write the remainder of this story out of my head.

The first episode which memory recovers from this un-diaried period is a pleasant one. I acquired a second-in-command for my company.

Hitherto no such person had existed, and I was beginning to feel the strain. In that private life of mine which more or less emerges from my diary, solemn introspection was getting the better of my sense of humour.

But now a beneficent presence arrived in the shape of Velmore, and I very soon began to say to myself that I really didn't know what I'd have done without him. It was like having an extra head and a duplicate pair of eyes. Velmore was a tall, dark, young man who had been up at Oxford for an academic year when the outbreak of war interrupted his studies. More scholastic than soldier-like in appearance (mainly because he wore spectacles) he had the look of one who might some day occupy a professorial chair. His previous experience at the front gave him a solid basis of usefulness, and to this was added a temperament in which kindliness, humour, and intelligence divided the honours equally, with gentleness and modesty in readiness to assert themselves by the power of non-assertion.

With these valuable qualities he combined—to my

astonishment and delight—what in conventional military circles might have been described as "an almost rabid love of literature". To hear poetry talked about in our company mess was indeed a new experience for me. But Velmore, on his very first evening, calmly produced Flecker's poems from his pocket and asked young "Stiffy" if he had ever read *The Golden Journey to Samarkand*. When he volunteered to read some of it aloud the junior officers exchanged embarrassed glances and took an early opportunity to leave me alone with my second-in-command, who was soon enunciating, with ingratiating gusto:

> *Across the vast blue shadow-sweeping plain*
> *The gathered armies darken through the grain*
> *Swinging curved swords and dragon-sculptured spears,*
> *Footmen, and tiger-hearted cavaliers.*

A paraphrase of the last two lines became Velmore's stock joke when reporting that the company was on parade and it was a great consolation to me to hear that fine body of men described as "the footmen with their dragon-sculptured spears". But Velmore was never anything else but a consolation to me.

With an all-pervading sense of relief I used to smoke my pipe and watch him doing the office-work for me. Whenever an automatic annoyance arrived from Orderly Room I merely passed it on and he squared it up with facetious efficiency.

In the fourth year of the war the amount of general information which descended on us from higher quarters had become prodigious. But I no longer received it seriously now. Corps H.Q. could send along anything it chose and Orderly Room forward it on for my "necessary attention" but until Velmore decided that it was worth looking at, I allowed it to be superseded by the next consignment of "hot air" from those who were such experts at putting things on paper.

Toward the end of June we moved north. I can remember that Velmore, on a fat cob, ambled away in advance of us to act as brigade billeting officer. Our destination was

St. Hilaire, a village near Lillers, and I know that we were there on July 1st. This information is obtained from an army notebook which has accidentally survived destruction. My final entry in the company messing accounts reads as follows: "*St. Hilaire, July 1st. Rent of Mess. 24 francs. Sardines, etc. 41 francs.*" Not much to go on, is it? . . . Sardines, etc. . . . Those sardines never suspected that they would one day appear in print.

The influenza epidemic having blown over, we were now feeling fairly well tuned up for our first tour of trenches in France. As far as my own career was concerned it certainly seemed to be about time to be up and doing, for it was now fully seven months since my dim and distant medical board, and my offensiveness toward the enemy had so far been restricted to telling other people how to behave offensively when a future effort was required of them. On July 7th we were still awaiting the order to move up to the Line. It was a Sunday, and there was a church parade for the whole battalion. This was a special occasion, for we were addressed by a bishop in uniform, a fact which speaks for itself.

In a spare notebook I wrote down the main points of his sermon, so I am able to transcribe what might otherwise appear to be inaccurately remembered.

"The bishop began by saying how very proud and very pleased he was to have the privilege of welcoming us to the Western Front on behalf of his branch of the service. Every heart, he said, had thrilled with pride when the news came that our Division had captured Jerusalem. The armies in France had been enthusiastic about it. He then gave us the following information, speaking with stimulating heartiness, as one having authority from a Higher Quarter.

"(1) Owing to the Russian Revolution the Germans have got the initiative and are hammering us hard.

"(2) The troops are more enthusiastic about winning the War than they were last year. Our lads feel that they'd rather die than see their own land treated like Belgium.

"(3) It is religion which keeps the morale of the British Army so high.

"(4) (With extreme unction.) Thank God we hold the seas!

"(5) The Americans are coming across in large numbers.

"(6) A distinguished general told me last week that the Huns are getting weaker every week. Time is on our side!

"He then preached a bit about the spiritual aspects and implications of the labours, dangers, and sufferings of which we were about to partake.

"Great was the sacrifice, but it was supremely glorious. He compared us to the early Christians who were burnt alive and thrown to the lions. 'You must not forget' he added, 'that Christ is not the effete figure in stained-glass windows but the Warrior Son of God who moves among the troops and urges them to yet further efforts of sacrifice.'

"He concluded impressively by reciting, with lifted hand, two verses from the American hymn *God goes marching on*. Except, perhaps, for the early Christian comparison, the troops rather liked it."

Talking to Velmore (whose eye I had resolutely avoided during the oration) I remarked that it was the spiritual equivalent of Campbell's bayonet fighting lecture, and I still think that I was somewhere near the truth. It was the bishop's business to say that sort of thing to the troops, and no one was any the worse for it—least of all himself, for I never saw a man who looked more pink and well-nourished. Would he talk like that again, I wonder, if he got another chance?

Anyhow his optimism was confined to the immediate present and did not include the pluperfect future. What he should have said was, "We are going on with this War because we ruddy well don't intend to be beaten by the Germans. And I am here because I believe in keeping religion in touch with the iniquitous methods by which nations settle their disputes. And you are here to try and prevent it happening again." But when he told us that the Huns were getting weaker every week, not a man in the battalion believed him. They had heard that sort of thing too often before.

If he had told us that the War would end in four months' time we should have charitably assumed that he was suffering from martial religious mania. In July 1918 everyone took it for granted that we should hold on till the winter and then wait for the "1919 offensive" which staff-officers on the boat from Alexandria had discussed with such professional earnestness. It is worth remembering that the German collapse in the autumn came as a complete surprise to the armies in France. They knew nothing and had become extremely sceptical about everything they were told.

On that fine summer morning the bishop, like a one-armed sign-post pointing westward, directed us on the road to victory. But he did it without knowing that his optimism was to be justified by future events.

II

The village of St. Hilaire was at that time about nine miles from the line to which the British army had retreated during the German offensive in April. In the late afternoon of the following day I found myself riding up there on the company charger, a quadruped who has left me no describable memory, except that he suffered from string-halt and his hind-leg action was the only lively thing about him. Well primed with map-references and urgent instructions from Orderly Room, I was going up to obtain all possible information from the battalion we were to relieve next day. Jogging along the pavé road from Lillers to St. Venant I felt agreeably excited, though anxious lest I might fail to grasp (and jot down) the entire situation when I arrived there. As was usual in such emergencies, I assumed that everything would go wrong with the "relief" if I made the slightest mistake, and I felt no certainty that I could achieve what I had been told to do. It did not occur to my simple mind that by to-morrow afternoon our quarter-master would probably know quite as much about the essential facts as I should. Details of organization in the army always scared and over-impressed me. Such things seemed so much easier when one was actually doing them than when they were being conferred about and put on paper in the mysterious language of the military profession.

This anxious devotion to duty probably prevented me from acquiring a permanent mental picture of my surroundings while I was nearing the end of my ride. The fact remains that I can now only see myself as "a solitary horseman" crossing the La Bassée Canal in the dusk and then going on another two miles to battalion headquarters, which were in what appeared to be a fairly well-preserved farmhouse. There I was given food, drink, and technical enlightenment, and sent on to the Front Line.

Communication-trenches were non-existent. My guide led me along a footpath among damaged crops and looming willows, past the dug-outs of the support-company, until we arrived at an enormous shell-hole which contained a company headquarters. In a sort of rabbit-hole, with just enough room for three people in it, I was welcomed by two East Lancashire officers, and forthwith I scribbled five pages of rough notes in my Field Message Book. I could reproduce these notes in full, for the book is on my table now; but I will restrict myself to a single entry.

"Battalion code-word. ELU. No messages by buzzer except through an officer. Relief word. JAMA. (To be confirmed by runner.)" "To be confirmed by rumour" was what I actually thought as I wrote it down, but I kept the witticism to myself as the captain didn't look likely to be amused by it. He seemed a bit fussed, which caused me to feel rather confident and efficient in an unobtrusive way.

He was a decent little chap, and I got a laugh out of him by telling him that a bishop had told our battalion, only yesterday, that the Huns were getting weaker every week. Over a mug of tea he confided in me that his company would be doing a small raid, in about half an hour, and he was evidently worrying about it, though he didn't say so.

This, however, was more in my line than scribbling down what time water cart would be sent up to ration dump and how many food-containers and water tins would be taken over from out-going battalion, and it seemed much more to the point when I followed him up to the Front Line to get an idea of what the sector was like and see how the show went off. The front-line defences were still in their infancy compared with the Canadian trenches I'd visited a month before. A series of breast-high sentry-posts were connected by a shallow ditch, and no-man's-land was a cornfield which still seemed to be doing quite well. I was told that there was very little wire out in front. One felt that recent occupants of the sector had erred in the direction of a *laissez-faire* policy. It was a quiet moon-less night, and the raiding-party, about a dozen strong, were assembled, and appeared to be doing their best to let the Germans know that they intended to come over. Stage whispers in broad Lancashire accents were making the best of an unhopeful situation, and I suspected that a double rum ration had been prematurely issued. (Rum rations should not precede raids.)

Why weren't they slipping across from some place where the trench was shallow, I wondered—instead of clamber-ing clumsily over the parapet where it was highest? One by one they disappeared into the jungle of growing corn. The ensuing silence was accentuated by various sounds which clearly indicated human progress on all fours through a weak belt of barbed wire. Shortly afterwards the inevitable machine-gun demonstrated awareness of their where-abouts, flares went up from the other side, and there was a proper mix-up which ended when they blundered back, having achieved nothing but a few casualties less than half-way across. When the confusion had abated, I con-tinued my instructive investigations for an hour or two, but the next thing that I clearly remember is that I was riding home in the early morning.

Quite distinctly I can recover a certain moment when I was trotting past the shuttered houses of some unawakened village, with the sun just coming up beyond the roadside poplars. What I felt was a sort of personal manifesto of being intensely alive—a sense of physical adventure and improvident jubilation; and also, as I looked at the signs of military occupation around me, a feeling that I was in the

middle of some interesting historical tale. I was glad to be
there, it seemed; and perhaps my thoughts for a moment
revisited Slateford Hospital and were reminded of its unescapable atmosphere of humiliation. That was how active
service used to hoodwink us. Wonderful moments in the
War, we called them, and told people at home that after
all we wouldn't have missed it for worlds. But it was only
one's youngness, really, and the fact of being in a foreign
country with a fresh mind. Not because of the War, but in
spite of it, we felt such zest and fulfilment, and remembered
it later on with nostalgic regret, forgetting the miseries and
grumblings, and how we longed for it to come to an end.
Nevertheless, there I was, a living antithesis to the gloomier
entries in my diary, and a physical retraction of my last
year's protest against the "political errors and insincerities
for which the fighting men were being sacrificed".

But our inconsistencies are often what make us most
interesting, and it is possible that, in my zeal to construct
these memoirs carefully, I have eliminated too many of my
own self-contradictions. Anyhow, human nature being
what it is, I wasn't finding time to feel sorry for the raiding-party whose dud effort I'd recently witnessed. No; I
was callously resolving to make a far better job of it with
my own men, and wishing that I could consult the incom-
parable Captain Duclos. And I am afraid I was also cogitating about how I would demonstrate the superiority of
A Company over the other three. My Company's officers
were just up when I got back. I must have been tired out,
for my only recollection of returning to St. Hilaire is of
Velmore taking charge of my notebook and urging me to
stop talking and swallow my breakfast before having a
good sleep. Meanwhile he promised that he would faith-
fully expound to the Adjutant the details which I had
accumulated.

*   *   *

That evening we relieved the East Lancashires. Nothing
worth describing in that, I tell myself. But the remembering mind refuses to forget, and imbues the scene of past ex-

perience with significant finality. For when we marched away from the straggling village and out into the flat green fertile farmlands, the world did seem to be lit up as though for some momentous occasion. There had been thunder showers all the afternoon and the sunset flared with a sort of crude magnificence which dazzled us when our road took a sudden twist to the left. More memorable now, perhaps; but memorable even then, for me, whose senses were so teemingly alive as I gazed on that rich yet havoc-bordered landscape and thought of the darkness toward which we were going. The clouds flamed and the clover was crimson and the patches of tillage were vividly green as we splashed along between the poplars. And then, with dusk, the rain came down again as though to wash the picture out for ever.

We had five or six miles to go before we crossed the La Bassée Canal, and then it was another mile (with hundred yard intervals between platoons) to the rendezvous. Beyond the poplars was the ominous glare of the line, and the rattle of rifles and machine-guns competed with a local thunderstorm—"overhead artillery", one of the men called it. . . .

Here, at the cross roads, were the guides—quite a crowd of them, since we were the leading company. Two-minute intervals between platoons. Lead on Number One. I watched them file away into the gloom, while Velmore wiped his spectacles and conferred with the company sergeant-major in undertones. Lead on headquarters. And then a couple of miles easy walking brought us to the big shell-hole and its diminutive dug-outs. It was now one o'clock in the morning, and the relief was completed when I signed the list of trench-stores taken over. Referring to this document, I find that we "took over" 30,000 rounds of small arms ammunition, 12 gas gongs, 572 grenades, 120 shovels, 270 Véry lights, and 9 reaping hooks, besides other items too numerous to mention.

Howitt was the only platoon officer with the company. "Stiffy" had been made battalion Lewis-gun officer, and the other two were away on "courses". As I went up to

visit the trench-mortar battery on our left flank it struck
me that I was likely to have a fairly busy time while A
Company was being initiated into the mysteries of the
Western Front.

That didn't worry me, however, for I was, if anything, a
bit too much "on my toes", and the Great War had reduced itself to a little contest between my company and the
Central Powers, with Velmore standing by to send back
situation reports from our five hundred yard sector. Velmore, of course, was "on his toes" too, but in a more temperate style than mine. His methods were unobtrusive but
thorough. While on this subject I must mention Sergeant
Wickham, who was more "on his toes" than any of us, and
had no alternative relaxations, such as ruminating or reading Flecker's poems. Wickham had been through the Boer
War, and had already won a D.C.M. and a Military
Medal in this one. But he wasn't resting on his laurels, and
having recently returned from a month's "refresher course"
at the army school, he was a complete embodiment of the
offensive spirit. I think he was one of the most delightful
N.C.O.s I've ever known. Except for being a little over-
excitable, he had all the qualities of a fine soldier including
the "women and children first" kind of chivalry, which
made it easy for one to imagine him as the last to leave the
sinking troopship. Always smart and cheerful—was Sergeant Wickham—and if ever a man deserved to be shaken
hands with by his Sovereign, it was he. During our first
twenty-four hours in the line, however, his adventurous
spirit discovered nothing sensational except a long-dead
German up in an old knotted willow; and in the evening
Velmore sent him down to the support-line with a working
party, though he was obviously aching to go out on patrol.

At about eleven o'clock I went out myself with Howitt
and a couple of N.C.O.s, but it was only in order to get
them accustomed to being out there. Everything was very
quiet while we crawled along the company front in the wet
corn. The Germans had sent over a few admonitory 5.9's
just after "stand-down"; at long intervals they fired their
machine-guns just to show they were still there. The topo-

graphy of our bit of no-man's-land was mainly agricultural, so our patrolling was easy work. On the right, B Company were demonstrating their offensive spirit by using up a fair amount of ammunition, but I had given orders that not a shot was to be fired by our Company. An impressively menacing silence prevailed, which, I hoped, would impress the Germans. I felt almost supercilious as I stood in the trench watching some B Company enthusiast experiment-ing with the Véry light pistol.

That was one of my untroubled moments, when I could believe that I'd got a firm grip on what I was doing and could be oblivious to the whys and wherefores of the war. I was standing beside Corporal Griffiths, who had his Lewis gun between his elbows on the dew-soaked parapet. His face, visible in the sinking light of a flare, had the look of a man who was doing his simple duty without demand-ing explanations from the stars above him. Vigilant and serious he stared straight ahead of him, and a fine picture of fortitude he made. He was only a stolid young farmer from Montgomeryshire; only; but such men, I think were England, in those dreadful years of war.

Thus the strangeness of the night wore on—and stranger still it seems while I am revisiting it from to-day—and after I'd been along to all the sentry-posts a second time, I went back to the headquarter rabbit-hole to find Velmore doz-ing, with Flecker's poems fallen from his hand, and the sturdy little sergeant-major dozing likewise in his own little rabbit-hole near by, while the signaller brooded over the buzzer. Away from the shell-hole there was another dug-out—larger, but not very deep—where we slept and had our food. Everything seems to be going on quite well, I thought, groping my way in, to sit there, tired and wakeful, and soaked and muddy from my patrol, while one candle made unsteady brown shadows in the gloom, and young Howitt lay dead beat and asleep in an ungainly attitude, with that queer half-sullen look on his face.

The thought of that candle haunts me now; I don't know why, except that it seems to symbolize the weary end of a night at the War, and that unforgettable remoteness from the ordinary existences which we might have been leading; Howitt going to an office in the morning; and Velmore down from that idyllic pre-war Oxford with an honours degree; and all those men in the company still unmobilized from farms and factories and wherever else it was they had earned a living.

I seem to be in that stuffy dug-out now, with Howitt snoring, and my wakeful watch ticking on the wrist which supported my head, and the deathly map of France and Flanders all around me in huge darkness receding to the distant boom of a big gun. I seem to be back in my mind as it then was—a mind whose haggard vigilance had the power to deny its body rest, while with the clairvoyance of sleeplessness it strove to be detached from clogging discomfort and to achieve, in its individual isolation, some sort of mastery over the experience which it shared with those dead and sleeping multitudes, of whom young Howitt was the visible representation.

I wanted to know—to understand—before it was too late, whether there was any meaning in this human tragedy which sprawled across France, while those who planned yet further slaughter were like puppets directing operations on which the unknown gods had turned their backs in boredom with our blundering bombardments. I wanted to know the reason why Corporal Griffiths was being what he was in quiet fortitude.

And I felt a great longing to be liberated from these few hundred yards of ant-like activity—to travel all the way along the Western Front—to learn through my eyes and with my heart the organism of this monstrous drama which my mind had not the power to envision as a whole. But my mind could see no further than the walls of that dug-out with its one wobbling candle which now burnt low. Universalization of military experience fizzled out in my thinking that some day we should look back on these St. Floris trenches as a sort of Paradise compared with places in which we had afterwards found ourselves. Unlike those ditches and earthworks which had become fetid with recurrent human catastrophes—hummocks and slag-heaps and morasses whose names would live for ever in war histories —ours was an almost innocent sector, still recognizable as cultivated farmland. I could recognize that innocence when Bond had made me some tea, and I had emerged into the peace of daybreak. The pollard willows loomed somewhat strange and ominous against the sky, but before long I was looking out over the parapet at an immaculate morning, with St. Floris away on the left—a factory chimney rising from a huddle of mysterious roofs—mysterious only because they were on the edge of no-man's-land.

Aloof from our concerns, another day was beginning, and there seemed no special reason why the War should command us to keep our heads down. The country, as I said before, looked innocent; the morning air was like life's elixir, and hope went singing skyward with the lark.

*   *   *

Refreshed by a few hours' sleep, I was up in the Front Line an hour or two after midday, gazing at the incalculable country beyond the cornfield. My map told me that the town of Merville was about three miles away from me, but the level landscape prevented it from being visible. Our long-range gunners knew a lot about Merville, no doubt, but it was beyond my horizon, and I couldn't hear so much as a rumble of wheels coming from that direction. The outlook was sunlit and completely silent, for it was the quietest time of day.

I was half-way between two sentry-posts, on the extreme left of our sector, where no-man's-land was narrowest. The longer I stared at the cornfield the more I wanted to know what was on the other side, and this inquisitiveness gradually developed into a determination. Discarding all my obligations as Company Commander (my main obligation being to remain inside the trench and get it deepened by those 120 shovels, which we'd taken over) I took off all my equipment, strolled along to the nearest sentry, borrowed his bayonet, and told him that I was going out to have a look at the wire. Returning to my equipment, I added my tunic and steel helmet to the heap, took a deep breath, grasped the bayonet firmly in my right hand, and crawled out into the unknown. I wasn't doing this from a sense of duty. It would certainly be helpful if I could find out exactly what things were like on the other side, and whether, as was rumoured by staff experts, the Germans withdrew most of their trench garrison during the day. But my uppermost idea was, I must admit, that the first man of the 74th Division to arrive in the enemy trenches was going to be me. This was a silly idea and I deserved no credit at all for it. Relying on Velmore to hold the fort at company headquarters, I was lapsing into my rather feckless 1916 self. It was, in fact, what I called "playing my natural game". I can't believe that I really enjoyed it, but it was exciting to worm one's way across, trying not to rustle the corn stalks. After about 300 yards of this sort of thing I crept through a few strands of wire and came to the edge of the concealment zone. What on earth would Doctor Macamble say if he could see me, I wondered, trying to bluff myself into a belief that I wasn't the least bit nervous. He would probably have rebuked me for being "bloodthirsty"; but I didn't feel at all like that.

The shallow German trench was only a few yards away, and there was no one in it, which was a great relief to my mind. I got into it as quickly as I could and then sat down, feeling by no means at home. The bayonet in my hand didn't seem to give me any extra confidence, but there were some stick-bombs lying about, so I picked one up, thinking that it would be just as well to take something back as a surprise for old Velmore. I then proceeded along the trench, sedately but bent double. For the benefit of those who enjoy exact description I will add that I was going in the direction of the Germans who were opposite B Company, i.e. away from St. Floris. The trench was only waist-deep; almost at once I saw what I presumed to be a machine-gun team. There were four of them, and they were standing about thirty yards away, gazing in the other direction. They were wearing flat blue-grey caps and their demeanour suggested boredom and idleness. Anyhow I was at last more or less in contact with the enemies of

England. I had come from Edinburgh via Limerick and Jerusalem, drawing full pay for seven months, and I could now say that I had seen some of the people I was fighting against. And what I saw was four harmless young Germans who were staring up at a distant aeroplane.

Standing upright, I watched them with breathless interest until one of them turned and looked me straight in the face. He was a blond youth of Saxon type, and he registered complete astonishment. For several seconds we gaped at one another; then he turned to draw the attention of his companions to their unknown visitor, who immediately betook himself to the cover of the cornfield, to the best of his ability imitating a streak of light. I returned much quicker than I came, and while the Germans were talking it over at their leisure I resumed my tunic and tin hat and took the bayonet back to its owner who eyed the stick-bomb enquiringly. With a marked change of manner from my recent retreat on all fours, I laconically mentioned that I'd just slipped across and fetched it. I then returned in triumph to Velmore, who implored me not to do that sort of thing again without warning him.

We thereupon decided that, as the general had announced that he expected a prisoner as soon as possible, the obvious thing to do was to send Howitt across with a strong patrol some fine morning to bring back that machine-gun team and thus acquire a Military Cross. It had been great fun, I felt. And I regarded myself as having scored a point against the people who had asserted that I was suffering from shell-shock.

*　　　　*　　　　*

About ten o'clock that night I hunched my way into the rabbit-hole feeling somewhat the worse for wear. "Slight strafe on, it seems!" I remarked to Velmore, who was leaning his back against the far end where there was just room for the pair of us to sit side by side.

"We must try and stop the men moving about so much round headquarters by day," he suggested. I lit my pipe. There was no doubt they'd fairly put the wind up me a few minutes before when a batch of 5.9's had dropped all round me while I lay flat on the ground somewhere between number 8 and 9 sentry-posts. Velmore sympathized and commented on the accuracy of the Teutonic artillerymen. The Adjutant had been up that evening and had told him that a big shell had landed just outside Orderly Room window about breakfast time. Luckily it had fallen on the manure-heap. A thud and an earth-shaking explosion immediately behind our dug-out now caused me to propose that a spot of Flecker wouldn't do us any harm, and we had just begun to make the Golden Journey to Samarkand when another shell arrived plump on top of us. But there was no explosion. The smoke still curled up from Velmore's cigarette. "Our camels sniff the evening and are glad," quoted he. . . . A large fissure had appeared in the earth wall behind us; exactly between us the nose-cap of the shell protruded. Velmore, who had a talent for picturesque phrases, named the crack in the wall "the grin of death". I still consider it queer that only the dudness of that 5.9 preserved us from becoming the débris of a direct hit.

Consulting my watch, I found that it was time for me to be taking out my conducted tours in no-man's-land. (I took them out, two at a time, for twenty-minute crawls, and the "patrol proper" went out at 12.30.) "I think I'll come up with you," remarked Velmore. "It can't be more dangerous in the Front Line than it is here."

*   *   *

On the following night at much the same time we were squatting in exactly the same place, munching chocolate. We were agreeing that the company was getting through its first dose of the line extremely well. They were a fine steady lot, and had worked hard at strengthening the posts and deepening the shallow connecting trench. We had also improved the wire. Best of all, we should be relieved the next night. "And not a single casualty so far," said Velmore. I didn't touch wood, but as to-morrow was the thirteenth I produced my fire-opal and touched that. "Aren't opals supposed to be unlucky?" he enquired dubiously, shutting one eye while he admired the everlasting sunset glories of the jewel. "Mine isn't," I replied, adding that I intended to give it another test that night. "I'm going to do a really good patrol," I announced. Velmore looked worried and said he wished I wouldn't. He argued that there was no special reason for doing it. I reminded him that we must maintain our supremacy in no-man's-land. "Haven't you already shown your damned supremacy by going over and quelling the Fritzes with a look?" he protested. But I produced a plausible project. I was going to locate a machine-gun which had seemed to be firing from outside their trench with the intention of enfilading us, and anyhow it was all arranged, and I was going out with Corporal Davies at one o'clock, from No. 14 post (which was where our company front ended). Seeing that I was bent on going, Velmore became helpful, and the sergeant-major was told to send an urgent warning to B Company, as the objective I had in mind was on their front.

My real reason for seeking trouble like this was my need to escape from the worry and responsibility of being a Company Commander, plus annoyance with the idea of being blown to bits while sitting there watching Velmore inditing a nicely-worded situation report. I was tired and over-strained, and my old foolhardiness was taking control of me.

To be outside the trench with the possibility of bumping into an enemy patrol was at any rate an antidote to my suppressed weariness of the entire bloody business. I wanted to do something definite, and perhaps get free of the whole thing. It was the old story; I could only keep going by doing something spectacular.

So there was more bravado than bravery about it, and I should admire that vanished self of mine more if he had avoided taking needless risks. I blame him for doing his utmost to prevent my being here to write about him. But on the other hand I am grateful to him for giving me something to write about.

*   *   *

Leaving me in the rabbit-hole to ruminate and reserve my energies, Velmore toddled off to the Front Line, which was, to revert to golfing phraseology, only an easy iron-shot away. I cannot claim that I remember exactly what I ruminated about, but an intimate knowledge of my mental technique assures me that, with danger looming in the near future, my thoughts were soon far away from St. Floris. (Who was St. Floris, by the way?) Probably I scribbled half a page in that long lost notebook—not too self-consciously, I hope. And then my mind may have rambled off to see a few friends.

Having ceased to wonder when the War would be over, I couldn't imagine myself anywhere else but on active service, and I was no longer able to indulge in reveries about being at home. When I came out this last time I had turned my back on everything connected with peace-time enjoyment. I suppose this meant that I was making a forced effort to keep going till the end. Like many people, I had a feeling that ordinary human existence was being converted into a sort of nightmare. Things were being said and done which would have been considered madness before the War. The effects of the War had been the reverse of ennobling, it seemed. Social historians can decide whether I am wrong about it.

Anyhow, as I was saying, I probably thought vaguely about those kind hunting people at Limerick, and speculated on such problems as what The Mister did with himself during the summer months; it quite worried me when I thought of the old boy convivially consuming neat whisky in hot weather. But if I called to mind my more intimate friends, it was themselves that I saw and not the places where I had been happy with them.

And if my visual meditations included the face of Rivers I did not allow myself to consult him as to the advisability of avoiding needless risks. I knew that he would have dissuaded me from doing that patrol. And then, no doubt, I dozed off until Velmore came back to tell me that it was getting on for one o'clock and Corporal Davies all ready for me up at No. 14 post.

Corporal Davies was a trained scout, young, small and active. We had worked out our little scheme, such as it was, and he now informed me in a cheerful whisper that the machine-gun which was our objective had been firing now and again from its usual position, which was half-right, about four hundred yards away. (The German trench was about six hundred yards from ours at that point.) In my pocket I had my little automatic pistol to provide moral support, and we took three or four Mills' bombs apiece. Our intention was to get as near as we could and then put the wind up the machine-gunners with our bombs.

A sunken farm-road ran out from No. 14 post; along this we proceeded with intense caution. About a hundred yards out we forsook the road and bore right-handed. It was a warm still night and the moon was very properly elsewhere, but the clear summer sky diminished the darkness and one could see quite a lot after a bit. Under such conditions every clod of earth was liable to look like the head of a recumbent enemy and the rustle of a fieldmouse in the corn could cause a certain trepidation—intrepid trepidation, of course.

Obviously it takes a longish time to crawl three or four hundred yards with infinite caution, but as nothing occurred to hinder our progress there is nothing narratable about it. I hadn't the time on me; crawling on my stomach might have smashed my watch-glass if it had been in my pocket, and its luminosity would have been out of place on my wrist. But what a relief it was, to be away from time and its petty tyrannies, even when one's heart was in one's mouth.

Behind us loomed the sentry-posts and the impressive sweep of the line, where poor old Velmore was peering anxiously out while he awaited our return. It really felt as though Corporal Davies and I had got the best of it out there. We were beyond all interference by Brigadiers.

Just when I least expected it the German machine-gun fired a few rounds, for no apparent reason except to allow us to locate it. We were, as far as I could judge, less than fifty yards from it and it seemed uncomfortably near. I looked at Davies, whose countenance was only too visible, for the sky was growing pale and we must have been out there well over two hours. Davies needed no prompting. He had already pulled out the pin of a bomb. So, to cut a long story short, we crawled a bit nearer, loosed off the lot, and retreated with the rapidity of a pair of scared badgers. I don't for a moment suppose that we hit anybody, but the deed was done, and when we were more than half-way home I dropped into the sunken road, and only the fact that I was out on a patrol prevented me from slapping my leg with a loud guffaw.

*   *   *

Now that it was all over I was exuberantly excited. It had been tremendous fun, and that was all there was to say about it. Davies agreed, and his fresh young face seemed to be asserting not only our supremacy over no-man's-land, but the supreme satisfaction of being alive on a perfect summer's morning after what might be called a strenuous military escapade. Taking off my tin hat I allowed my head to feel glad to be relieved of the weight of the War, and there, for several minutes, we sat leaning against the bank and recovering our breath.

It seemed hardly worth while to continue our return journey on all fours, as we were well hidden from the German trenches; the embankment of No. 14 Post was just visible above the corn stalks and my conscience reminded me that Velmore's anxiety ought to be put an end to at once. With my tin hat in my hand I stood up and turned for a moment to look back at the German line.

A second later I was down again, half stunned by a terrific blow on the head. It seemed to me that there was a very large hole in the right side of my skull. I felt, and believed, that I was as good as dead. Had this been so I should have been unconscious of anything, but that idea didn't strike me.

Ideas were a thing of the past now. While the blood poured from my head, I was intensely aware of everything around me—the clear sky and the ripening corn and the early glow of sunrise on the horrified face of the little red-haired corporal who knelt beside me. I saw it all as though for the last time, and my whole body and being were possessed by a dreadful sense of unhappiness. Body and spirit were one, and both must perish. The world had been mine, and the fullness of life, and in a moment all had been changed and I was to lose it.

I had been young and exuberant, and now I was just a dying animal, on the verge of oblivion.

And then a queer thing happened. My sense of humour stirred in me, and—emerging from that limbo of desolate defeat—I thought "I suppose I ought to say something special—last words of dying soldier". . . . And do you know that I take great pride in that thought because I consider that it showed a certain invincibility of mind; for I really did believe that I was booked for the Roll of Honour. I need hardly say that I wasn't; after a bit the corporal investigated my head and became optimistic, and I plucked up courage and dared to wonder whether, perhaps, I was in such a bad way after all. And the end of it was that I felt very much better and got myself back to No. 14 Post without any assistance from Davies, who carried my tin hat for me.

Velmore's face was a study in mingled concern and relief, but the face of Sergeant Wickham was catastrophic.

For Wickham was there, and it was he who had shot me.

The fact was that his offensive spirit had led him astray. He had heard the banging of our bombs and had been so much on his toes that he'd forgotten to go and find out whether we had returned. Over-eager to accomplish something spectacular, he had waited and watched; and when he spotted someone approaching our trench had decided that the Germans were about to raid us. I was told afterwards that when he'd fired at me he rushed out shouting, "Surrender—you ——!" Which only shows what a gallant man he was—though everyone knew that already. It also showed that although he'd heard me lecturing to the company N.C.O.s on my "Four C's—i.e.—Confidence, Co-operation, Common sense, and Consolidation"—he had that morning been co-operating with nothing except his confident ambition to add a bar to his D.C.M. (which, I am glad to say, he ultimately did).

I suppose it was partly my fault. Both of us ought to have known better than to behave like that. The outcome was absurd, but logical. And to say that I was well out of it is an understatement of an extremely solemn fact.

III

Thus ended my last week at the War. And there, perhaps, my narrative also should end. For I seem to write these words of someone who never returned from France, someone whose effort to succeed in that final experience was finished when he lay down in the sunken road and wondered what he ought to say.

I state this quite seriously, though I am aware that it sounds somewhat nonsensical. But even now I wonder how it was that Wickham's bullet didn't go through my skull instead of only furrowing my scalp. For it had been a fixed idea of mine that something like that would happen. Amateur psychologists will say that I had a "death-wish", I suppose. But that seems to me to be much the same as wanting peace at any price, so we won't argue about it.

Anyhow I see a sort of intermediate version of myself, who afterwards developed into what I am now; I see him talking volubly to Velmore and Howitt on the way back to company H.Q.; and saying good-bye with a bandaged head and assuring them that he'd be back in a week or two, and then walking down to battalion H.Q., with his faithful batman Bond carrying his haversack and equipment; and then talking rather wildly to the Adjutant and Major Evans (who was now in command), and finally getting into the motor ambulance which took him to the casualty clearing station.

And two days later he is still talking rather wildly, but he is talking to himself now, and scribbling it down with a pencil as he lies in a bed at No. 8 Red Cross Hospital,

Boulogne. It is evidence of what I have just written, so I will reproduce it.

"I don't know how to begin this. It is meant to be a confession of my real feelings, or an attempt to find out what they really are. Time drifts between me and last week. Everything gets blurred. I know that I feel amputated from the battalion. It seemed all wrong to be leaving the Company behind and going away into safety. I told the company sergeant-major I should be back soon and then climbed out of the headquarters shell-hole. Down the path between wheat and oats and beans, and over the dangerous willow-bordered road until I came to the red-roofed farm. Five o'clock on a July morning. . . . I passed the little cluster of crosses, and blundered into the Aid Post to get my head seen to. Prolonged farewells to the C.O. and other H.Q. officers—sleepy men getting situation reports from the Front Line. 'You'll see me back in three weeks' I shouted, and turned the corner of the lane with a last confident gesture. And so from one dressing station to another, to spend a night at the big C.C.S. where I tried to persuade an R.A.M.C. Colonel to keep me there till my head was healed. Even now I hang on to my obsession about not going to Blighty. I write to people at home saying that I'm staying in France till I can go up to the line again. And I do it with an angry tortured feeling. 'I'll stay here just to spite those blighters who yell about our infamous enemies,' is what I think, and then I wonder what the hell I am to them. If I'd moved my head an inch I'd be dead now, and what would the patriots care? . . . Then I remember the kindly face of my servant, and see him putting my kit on to the ambulance. I smile at him and say 'Back soon,' and he promises to walk over to the C.C.S. next day with my letters and the latest news from the company. But I'd gone when he got there. . . . They'd sent me on to a place near St. Omer. If I'd kicked up a row and refused to go they'd have thought I was dotty, especially with a head wound. Who ever heard of anyone refusing to go down to the Base with a decent wound? Now I'm at Boulogne trying to be hearty and well. It's only a scalp-graze, I say; but I dare

not look the doctor in the face. It isn't all of me that wants
to stay in France now.

"Nurses make a fuss over me till I scarcely dare to behave like a healthy man.

"And still the memory of the Company haunts me and
wrings my heart and I hear them saying 'When's the Captain coming back?' It seems as if there's nothing to go back
to in England as long as the War goes on. Up in the line I
was at least doing something real, and I had lived myself
into a feeling of responsibility—inefficient and impulsive
though I was when in close contact with the Germans. All
that was decent in me disliked leaving Velmore and Howitt
and the troops. But now I begin to tell myself that perhaps
half of them will be casualties by the time I get back, and I
ask how many officers there are in the battalion who would
refuse to go to England if it were made easy for them.

"Not one, I believe; so why should I be the only one.
They'd only think me a fool, if they knew I'd gone back on
purpose to be with them.

"Yet it is the supreme thing that is asked of me, and
already I am shying at it. 'We'll be sending you across to
England in a few days,' murmurs the nurse while she is
dabbing my head. She says it quite naturally, as if it were
the only possible thing that could happen. I close my eyes,
and all I can see is the door into the garden at home and
Aunt Evelyn coming in with her basket of flowers. In a
final effort to quell those cravings for safety I try to see in
the dark the far-off vision of the line, with flares going up
and the whine and crash of shells scattered along the level
dusk. Men flitting across the gloom; low voices challenging
—'Halt; who are you?' Someone gasping by, carrying a
bag of rations—'Jesus, ain't we there yet?'—then he blunders into a shell-hole and crouches there while bullets hiss
overhead. I see the sentries in the forward posts, staring
patiently into the night—sombre shapes against a flickering sky. Oh yes, I see it all, from A to Z! Then I listen to
the chatter of the other wounded officers in this room,
talking about people being blown to bits. And I remember
a man at the C.C.S. with his jaw blown off by a bomb—

('a fine-looking chap, he was,' they said). He lay there with one hand groping at the bandages which covered his whole head and face, gurgling every time he breathed. His tongue was tied forward to prevent him swallowing it. The War had gagged him—smashed him—and other people looked at him and tried to forget what they'd seen. . . . All this I remember, while the desirable things of life, like living phantoms, steal quietly into my brain, look wistfully at me, and steal away again—beckoning, pointing—'to England in a few days'. . . . And though it's wrong I know I shall go there, because it is made so easy for me."

IV

On February 13th I had landed in France and again become part of the war machine which needed so much flesh and blood to keep it working. On July 20th the machine automatically returned me to London, and I was most carefully carried into a perfect hospital.

There, in a large ward whose windows overlooked Hyde Park, I lay and listened to the civilian rumour of London traffic which seemed to be specially subdued for the benefit of the patients. In this apotheosis (or nirvana) of physical comfort, I had no possible cause for complaint, and my only material adversity was the fact that while at Boulogne I had hung my opal talisman on the bedpost and someone had succumbed to the temptation. But the opal, as I reminded myself, had done its work, and I tried to regard its disappearance as symbolical. Sunday passed peacefully, graciously signalized by a visit from two members of the Royal Family, who did their duty with the maximum amount of niceness and genuine feeling. For the best part of a minute I was an object of sympathetic interest, and I really felt that having succeeded in becoming a casualty, I was doing the thing in the best possible style.

On the Monday I became comparatively active and instructed one of my friends to order a gramophone to be sent to A Company, plus a few "comforts" for the officers.

But Velmore and the others had vanished; their remoteness became more apparent every day, though I rejoiced when I received Velmore's letter announcing that Howitt had been across no-man's-land with ten men and had brought back five Germans and a machine-gun—these being the first prisoners captured by the 74th Division in France.

Outwardly I was being suavely compensated for whatever exactions the war machine had inflicted on me. I had nothing to do except lie there and wonder whether it was possible to be more comfortable, even though I'd got a half-healed hole in my head. But inwardly I was restless and overwrought. My war had stopped, but its after-effects were still with me. I couldn't sleep, so after a few days I was moved into a room where there was only one other bed, which was unoccupied. But in there my brain became busier than ever; the white-walled room seemed to imprison me, and my thoughts couldn't escape from themselves into that completed peace which was the only thing I wanted. I saw myself as one who had achieved nothing except an idiotic anti-climax, and my mind worked itself into a tantrum of self-disparagement. Why hadn't I stayed in France where I could at least escape from the War by being in it? Out there I had never despised my existence as I did now.

Life had seemed a glorious and desirable thing in those moments when I was believing that the bullet had finished me off, when it had seemed as if the living soul in me also was about to be extinguished. And now that angry feeling of wanting to be killed came over me—as though I were looking at my living self and longing to bash its silly face in. My little inferno was then interrupted by a nurse who brought me my tea. What the hell was wrong with me? I wondered, becoming less irrational and exasperated. And I told myself that if I wasn't careful I should go from bad to worse, realizing that the sun had been shining in at the window all the afternoon and I'd been lying there tearing myself to pieces and feeling miserable and frustrated. I suppose my nerves really are a bit rotten, I thought, lighting my pipe and trying to be sensible. But I was still worried by feeling so inglorious. I was nearly thirty-two and nothing that I'd done seemed to have been any good. There was some consolation in the feeling that one wasn't as old as one's age, but when I tried to think about the future I found that I couldn't see it. There was no future except "the rest of the War", and I didn't want that. My knight-errantry about the War had fizzled out in more ways than one, and I couldn't go back to being the same as I was before it started. The "good old days" had been pleasant enough in their way, but what could a repetition of them possibly lead to?

How could I begin my life all over again when I had no conviction about anything except that the War was a dirty trick which had been played on me and my generation? That, at any rate, was something to be angry and bitter about now that everything had fallen to pieces and one's mind was in a muddle and one's nerves were all on edge. . . .

Yes; my mind was in a muddle; and it seemed that I had learned but one thing from being a soldier—that if we continue to accept war as a social institution we must also recognize that the Prussian system is the best, and Prussian militarism must be taught to children in schools. They must be taught to offer their finest instincts for exploitation by the unpitying machinery of scientific warfare. And they must not be allowed to ask why they are doing it.

And then, unexpected and unannounced, Rivers came in and closed the door behind him. Quiet and alert, purposeful and unhesitating, he seemed to empty the room of everything that had needed exorcising.

My futile demons fled him—for his presence was a refutation of wrong-headedness. I knew then that I had been very lonely while I was at the War; I knew that I had a lot to learn, and that he was the only man who could help me.

Without a word he sat down by the bed; and his smile was benediction enough for all I'd been through. "Oh, Rivers, I've had such a funny time since I saw you last!" I exclaimed. And I understood that this was what I'd been waiting for.

He did not tell me that I had done my best to justify his belief in me. He merely made me feel that he took all that for granted, and now we must go on to something better still. And this was the beginning of the new life toward which he had shown me the way. . . .

It has been a long journey from that moment to this, when I write the last words of my book. And my last words shall be these—that it is only from the inmost silences of the heart that we know the world for what it is, and ourselves for what the world has made us.